Get the eBook FREE!
(PDF, ePub, Kindle, and liveBook all included)

We believe that once you buy a book from us, you should be able to read it in any format we have available. To get electronic versions of this book at no additional cost to you, purchase and then register this book at the Manning website.

Go to https://www.manning.com/freebook and follow the instructions to complete your pBook registration.

That's it!
Thanks from Manning!

Praise for the First Edition

"The clearest explanation of deep learning I have come across . . . it was a joy to read."
—Richard Tobias, Cephasonics

"Bridges the gap between the hype and a functioning deep-learning system."
—Peter Rabinovitch, Akamai

"All major topics and concepts of deep learning are covered and well-explained, using code examples and diagrams instead of mathematical formulas."
—Srdjan Santic, Springboard.com

Deep Learning with R

SECOND EDITION

FRANÇOIS CHOLLET
WITH TOMASZ KALINOWSKI
AND J.J. ALLAIRE

MANNING

SHELTER ISLAND

For online information and ordering of this and other Manning books, please visit
www.manning.com. The publisher offers discounts on this book when ordered in quantity.
For more information, please contact

    Special Sales Department
    Manning Publications Co.
    20 Baldwin Road
    PO Box 761
    Shelter Island, NY 11964
    Email: orders@manning.com

Manning Publications Co.
20 Baldwin Road
PO Box 761
Shelter Island, NY 11964

Development editor:	Jennifer Stout
Review editor:	Aleksandar Dragosavljević
Production editor:	Andy Marinkovich
Copy editor:	Pamela Hunt
Proofreader:	Keri Hales
Technical proofreader:	Ninoslav Cerkez
Typesetter:	Gordan Salinovic
Cover designer:	Marija Tudor

ISBN 9781633439849
Printed in the United States of America

contents

preface

If you've picked up this book, you're probably aware of the extraordinary progress that deep learning has represented for the field of artificial intelligence in the recent past. We went from near-unusable computer vision and natural language processing to highly performant systems deployed at scale in products you use every day. The consequences of this sudden progress extend to almost every industry. We're already applying deep learning to an amazing range of important problems across domains as different as medical imaging, agriculture, autonomous driving, education, disaster prevention, and manufacturing.

Yet, I believe deep learning is still in its early days. It has realized only a small fraction of its potential so far. Over time, it will make its way to every problem where it can help—a transformation that will take place over multiple decades.

To begin deploying deep learning technology to every problem that it could solve, we need to make it accessible to as many people as possible, including non-experts— people who aren't researchers or graduate students. For deep learning to reach its full potential, we need to radically democratize it. And today, I believe that we're at the cusp of a historical transition, where deep learning is moving out of academic labs and the R&D departments of large tech companies to become a ubiquitous part of the toolbox of every developer out there—not unlike the trajectory of web development in the late 1990s. Almost anyone can now build a website or web app for their business or community of a kind that would have required a small team of specialist engineers in 1998. In the not-so-distant future, anyone with an idea and basic coding skills will be able to build smart applications that learn from data.

When I released the first version of the Keras deep learning framework in March 2015, the democratization of AI wasn't what I had in mind. I had been doing research in machine learning for several years and had built Keras to help me with my own experiments. But since 2015, hundreds of thousands of newcomers have entered the field of deep learning; many of them picked up Keras as their tool of choice. As I watched scores of smart people use Keras in unexpected, powerful ways, I came to care deeply about the accessibility and democratization of AI. I realized that the further we spread these technologies, the more useful and valuable they become. Accessibility quickly became an explicit goal in the development of Keras, and over a few short years, the Keras developer community has made fantastic achievements on this front. We've put deep learning into the hands of hundreds of thousands of people, who in turn are using it to solve problems that were until recently thought to be unsolvable.

The book you're holding is another step on the way to making deep learning available to as many people as possible. Keras had always needed a companion course to simultaneously cover the fundamentals of deep learning, deep learning best practices, and Keras usage patterns. In 2016 and 2017, I did my best to produce such a course, which became the first edition of this book, released in December 2017. It quickly became a machine learning best seller that sold over 50,000 copies and was translated into 12 languages.

However, the field of deep learning advances fast. Since the release of the first edition, many important developments have taken place—the release of TensorFlow 2, the growing popularity of the Transformer architecture, and more. And so, in late 2019, I set out to update my book. I originally thought, quite naively, that it would feature about 50% new content and would end up being roughly the same length as the first edition. In practice, after two years of work, it turned out to be over a third longer, with about 75% novel content. More than a refresh, it is a whole new book.

I wrote it with a focus on making the concepts behind deep learning, and their implementation, as approachable as possible. Doing so didn't require me to dumb down anything—I strongly believe that there are no difficult ideas in deep learning. I hope you'll find this book valuable and that it will enable you to begin building intelligent applications and solve the problems that matter to you.

acknowledgments

First, I'd like to thank the Keras community for making this book possible. Over the past six years, Keras has grown to have hundreds of open source contributors and more than one million users. Your contributions and feedback have turned Keras into what it is today.

On a more personal note, I'd like to thank my wife for her endless support during the development of Keras and the writing of this book.

I'd also like to thank Google for backing the Keras project. It has been fantastic to see Keras adopted as TensorFlow's high-level API. A smooth integration between Keras and TensorFlow greatly benefits both TensorFlow users and Keras users and makes deep learning accessible to most.

I want to thank the people at Manning who made this book possible: publisher Marjan Bace and everyone on the editorial and production teams, including Michael Stephens, Jennifer Stout, Aleksandar Dragosavljević, Andy Marinkovich, Pamela Hunt, Susan Honeywell, Keri Hales, Paul Wells, and many others who worked behind the scenes.

Many thanks go to all the reviewers: Arnaldo Ayala Meyer, Davide Cremonesi, Dhinakaran Venkat, Edward Lee, Fernando García Sedano, Joel Kotarski, Marcio Nicolau, Michael Petrey, Peter Henstock, Shahnawaz Ali, Sourav Biswas, Thiago Britto Borges, Tony Dubitsky, Vlad Navitski, and all the other people who sent us feedback. Your suggestions helped make this a better book.

And on the technical side, special thanks go to Ninoslav Cerkez, who served as the book's technical proofreader.

about this book

This book was written for anyone who wishes to explore deep learning from scratch or broaden their understanding of deep learning. Whether you're a practicing machine learning engineer, a data scientist, or a college student, you'll find value in these pages.

You'll explore deep learning in an approachable way—starting simply, then working up to state-of-the-art techniques. You'll find that this book strikes a balance between intuition, theory, and hands-on practice. It avoids mathematical notation, preferring instead to explain the core ideas of machine learning and deep learning via detailed code snippets and intuitive mental models. You'll learn from abundant code examples that include extensive commentary, practical recommendations, and simple high-level explanations of everything you need to know to start using deep learning to solve concrete problems.

The code examples use the deep learning framework Keras, with TensorFlow 2 as its numerical engine. They demonstrate modern Keras and TensorFlow 2 best practices as of 2022.

After reading this book, you'll have a solid understand of what deep learning is, when it's applicable, and what its limitations are. You'll be familiar with the standard workflow for approaching and solving machine learning problems, and you'll know how to address commonly encountered issues. You'll be able to use Keras to tackle real-world problems ranging from computer vision to natural language processing: image classification, image segmentation, time-series forecasting, text classification, machine translation, text generation, and more.

Who should read this book?

This book is written for people with R programming experience who want to get started with machine learning and deep learning. But this book can also be valuable to many different types of readers:

- If you're a data scientist familiar with machine learning, this book will provide you with a solid, practical introduction to deep learning, the fastest growing and most significant subfield of machine learning.
- If you're a deep learning researcher or practitioner looking to get started with the Keras framework, you'll find this book to be the ideal Keras crash course.
- If you're a graduate student studying deep learning in a formal setting, you'll find this book to be a practical complement to your education, helping you build intuition around the behavior of deep neural networks and familiarizing you with key best practices.

Even technically-minded people who don't code regularly will find this book useful as an introduction to both basic and advanced deep learning concepts.

To understand the code examples, you'll need reasonable R proficiency. You don't need previous experience with machine learning or deep learning: this book covers, from scratch, all the necessary basics. You don't need an advanced mathematics background, either—high school–level mathematics should suffice to follow along.

About the code

This book contains many examples of source code both in numbered listings and in line with normal text. In both cases, source code is formatted in a `fixed-width font` `like this` to separate it from ordinary text. Output from running code is similarly formatted in fixed-width font, but is also adorned with a vertical gray bar on the left. Throughout the book you'll find code and code outputs interleaved like this:

```
print("R is awesome!")
```

```
[1] "R is awesome!"
```

In many cases, the original source code has been reformatted; we've added line breaks and reworked indentation to accommodate the available page space in the book. In rare cases, even this was not enough, and listings include line-continuation markers (➡). Additionally, comments in the source code have often been removed from the listings when the code is described in the text. Code annotations accompany many of the listings, highlighting important concepts.

You can get executable snippets of code from the liveBook (online) version of this book at https://livebook.manning.com/book/deep-learning-with-r-second-edition/, and as R scripts on GitHub at https://github.com/t-kalinowski/deep-learning-with-R-2nd-edition-code.

liveBook discussion forum

Purchase of *Deep Learning with R, Second Edition,* includes free access to liveBook, Manning's online reading platform. Using liveBook's exclusive discussion features, you can attach comments to the book globally or to specific sections or paragraphs. It's a snap to make notes for yourself, ask and answer technical questions, and receive help from the author and other users. To access the forum, go to at https://livebook.manning .com/book/deep-learning-with-r-second-edition/. You can also learn more about Manning's forums and the rules of conduct at https://livebook.manning.com/discussion.

Manning's commitment to our readers is to provide a venue where a meaningful dialogue between individual readers and between readers and the author can take place. It is not a commitment to any specific amount of participation on the part of the author, whose contribution to the forum remains voluntary (and unpaid). We suggest you try asking the author some challenging questions lest their interest stray! The forum and the archives of previous discussions will be accessible from the publisher's website as long as the book is in print.

About the cover illustration

The figure on the cover of *Deep Learning with R, Second Edition,* "Habit of a Chinese Lady in 1700," is taken from a book by Thomas Jefferys, published between 1757 and 1772.

In those days, it was easy to identify where people lived and what their trade or station in life was just by their dress. Manning celebrates the inventiveness and initiative of the computer business with book covers based on the rich diversity of regional culture centuries ago, brought back to life by pictures from collections such as this one.

about the authors

François Chollet is the creator of Keras, one of the most widely used deep learning frameworks. He is currently a software engineer at Google, where he leads the Keras team. In addition, he does research on abstraction, reasoning, and how to achieve greater generality in artificial intelligence.

Tomasz Kalinowski is a software engineer at RStudio, where he serves as maintainer of the TensorFlow and Keras R packages. In prior roles, he worked as a scientist and engineer, applying machine learning to a wide variety of datasets and domains.

J.J. Allaire is the founder of RStudio and the creator of the RStudio IDE. J.J. is the author of the R interfaces to TensorFlow and Keras.

What is deep learning? 1

This chapter covers

- High-level definitions of fundamental concepts
- Time line of the development of machine learning
- Key factors behind deep learning's rising popularity and future potential

In the past few years, artificial intelligence (AI) has been a subject of intense media hype. Machine learning, deep learning, and AI come up in countless articles, often outside of technology-minded publications. We're promised a future of intelligent chatbots, self-driving cars, and virtual assistants—a future sometimes painted in a grim light and other times as utopian, where human jobs will be scarce and most economic activity will be handled by robots or AI agents. For a future or current practitioner of machine learning, it's important to be able to recognize the signal amid the noise, so that you can tell world-changing developments from overhyped press releases. Our future is at stake, and it's a future in which you have an active role to play: after reading this book, you'll be one of those who develop those AI systems. So let's tackle these questions: What has deep learning achieved so far? How significant is it? Where are we headed next? Should you believe the hype?

This chapter provides essential context around artificial intelligence, machine learning, and deep learning.

1.1   *Artificial intelligence, machine learning, and deep learning*

First, we need to define clearly what we're talking about when we mention AI. What are artificial intelligence, machine learning, and deep learning (see figure 1.1)? How do they relate to each other?

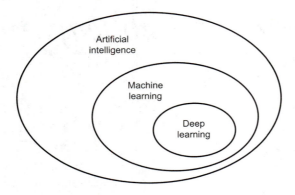

Figure 1.1   Artificial intelligence, machine learning, and deep learning

1.1.1   *Artificial intelligence*

Artificial intelligence was born in the 1950s, when a handful of pioneers from the nascent field of computer science started asking whether computers could be made to "think"—a question whose ramifications we're still exploring today.

Although many of the underlying ideas had been brewing in the years and even decades prior, "artificial intelligence" finally crystallized as a field of research in 1956, when John McCarthy, then a young assistant professor of mathematics at Dartmouth College, organized a summer workshop under the following proposal:

> *The study is to proceed on the basis of the conjecture that every aspect of learning or any other feature of intelligence can in principle be so precisely described that a machine can be made to simulate it. An attempt will be made to find how to make machines use language, form abstractions and concepts, solve kinds of problems now reserved for humans, and improve themselves. We think that a significant advance can be made in one or more of these problems if a carefully selected group of scientists work on it together for a summer.*

At the end of the summer, the workshop concluded without having fully solved the riddle it set out to investigate. Nevertheless, it was attended by many people who would move on to become pioneers in the field, and it set in motion an intellectual revolution that is still ongoing to this day.

Concisely, AI can be described as *the effort to automate intellectual tasks normally performed by humans.* As such, AI is a general field that encompasses machine learning and deep learning, but that also includes many more approaches that may not involve any learning. Consider that until the 1980s, most AI textbooks didn't mention "learning" at all! Early chess programs, for instance, involved only hardcoded rules crafted by programmers and didn't qualify as machine learning. In fact, for a fairly long time, most experts believed that human-level artificial intelligence could be achieved by having programmers handcraft a sufficiently large set of explicit rules for manipulating knowledge stored in explicit databases. This approach is known as *symbolic AI*. It was the dominant paradigm in AI from the 1950s to the late 1980s, and it reached its peak popularity during the *expert systems* boom of the 1980s.

Although symbolic AI proved suitable to solve well-defined, logical problems, such as playing chess, it turned out to be intractable to figure out explicit rules for solving more complex, fuzzy problems, such as image classification, speech recognition, or natural language translation. A new approach arose to take symbolic AI's place: *machine learning*.

1.1.2 Machine learning

In Victorian England, Lady Ada Lovelace was a friend and collaborator of Charles Babbage, the inventor of the *Analytical Engine*: the first-known general-purpose mechanical computer. Although visionary and far ahead of its time, the Analytical Engine wasn't meant as a general-purpose computer when it was designed in the 1830s and 1840s, because the concept of general-purpose computation had yet to be invented. It was merely meant as a way to use mechanical operations to automate certain computations from the field of mathematical analysis—hence the name Analytical Engine. As such, it was the intellectual descendant of earlier attempts at encoding mathematical operations in gear form, such as the Pascaline, or Leibniz's stepped reckoner, a refined version of the Pascaline. Designed by Blaise Pascal in 1642 (at age 19!), the Pascaline was the world's first mechanical calculator—it could add, subtract, multiply, or even divide digits.

In 1843, Ada Lovelace remarked on the invention of the Analytical Engine:

> *The Analytical Engine has no pretensions whatever to originate anything. It can do whatever we know how to order it to perform. . . . Its province is to assist us in making available what we're already acquainted with.*

Even with 179 years of historical perspective, Lady Lovelace's observation remains arresting. Could a general-purpose computer "originate" anything, or would it always be bound to dully execute processes we humans fully understand? Could it ever be capable of any original thought? Could it learn from experience? Could it show creativity?

Her remark was later quoted by AI pioneer Alan Turing as "Lady Lovelace's objection" in his landmark 1950 paper "Computing Machinery and Intelligence,"[1] which introduced the *Turing test* as well as key concepts that would come to shape AI.[2] Turing was of the opinion—highly provocative at the time—that computers could in principle be made to emulate all aspects of human intelligence.

---

[1] A.M. Turing, "Computing Machinery and Intelligence," *Mind* 59, no. 236 (1950): 433–460.

[2] Although the Turing test has sometimes been interpreted as a literal test—a goal the field of AI should set out to reach—Turing merely meant it as a conceptual device in a philosophical discussion about the nature of cognition.

The usual way to make a computer do useful work is to have a human programmer write down *rules*—a computer program—to be followed to turn input data into appropriate answers, just like Lady Lovelace writing down step-by-step instructions for the Analytical Engine to perform. Machine learning turns this around: the machine looks at the input data and the corresponding answers, and figures out what the rules should be (see figure 1.2). A

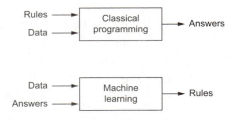

Figure 1.2   Machine learning: A new programming paradigm

machine learning system is *trained* rather than explicitly programmed. It's presented with many examples relevant to a task, and it finds statistical structure in these examples that eventually allows the system to come up with rules for automating the task. For instance, if you wished to automate the task of tagging your vacation pictures, you could present a machine learning system with many examples of pictures already tagged by humans, and the system would learn statistical rules for associating specific pictures to specific tags.

Although machine learning started to flourish only in the 1990s, it has quickly become the most popular and most successful subfield of AI, a trend driven by the availability of faster hardware and larger datasets. Machine learning is related to mathematical statistics, but it differs from statistics in several important ways, in the same sense that medicine is related to chemistry but cannot be reduced to chemistry, because medicine deals with its own distinct systems with their own distinct properties. Unlike statistics, machine learning tends to deal with large, complex datasets (such as a dataset of millions of images, each consisting of tens of thousands of pixels) for which classical statistical analysis such as Bayesian analysis would be impractical. As a result, machine learning, and especially deep learning, exhibits comparatively little mathematical theory—maybe too little—and is fundamentally an engineering discipline. Unlike theoretical physics or mathematics, machine learning is a very hands-on field driven by empirical findings and deeply reliant on advances in software and hardware.

1.1.3   Learning rules and representations from data

To define *deep learning* and understand the difference between deep learning and other machine learning approaches, first we need some idea of what machine learning algorithms do. We just stated that machine learning discovers rules for executing a data processing task, given examples of what's expected. So, to do machine learning, we need the following three things:

- *Input data points*—For instance, if the task is speech recognition, these data points could be sound files of people speaking. If the task is image tagging, they could be pictures.

- *Examples of the expected output*—In a speech-recognition task, these could be human-generated transcripts of sound files. In an image task, expected outputs could be tags such as "dog," "cat," and so on.
- *A way to measure whether the algorithm is doing a good job*—This is necessary to determine the distance between the algorithm's current output and its expected output. The measurement is used as a feedback signal to adjust the way the algorithm works. This adjustment step is what we call *learning*.

A machine learning model transforms its input data into meaningful outputs, a process that is "learned" from exposure to known examples of inputs and outputs. Therefore, the central problem in machine learning and deep learning is to *meaningfully transform data*: in other words, to learn useful *representations* of the input data at hand—representations that get us closer to the expected output.

Before we go any further: what's a representation? At its core, it's a different way to look at data—to represent or encode data. For instance, a color image can be encoded in the RGB format (red-green-blue) or in the HSV format (hue-saturation-value): these are two different representations of the same data. Some tasks that may be difficult with one representation can become easy with another. For example, the task "select all red pixels in the image" is simpler in the RGB format, whereas "make the image less saturated" is simpler in the HSV format. Machine learning models are all about finding appropriate representations for their input data—transformations of the data that make it more amenable to the task at hand.

Let's make this concrete. Consider an *x*-axis, a *y*-axis, and some points represented by their coordinates in the (x, y) system, as shown in figure 1.3.

As you can see, we have a few white points and a few black points. Let's say we want to develop an algorithm that can take the coordinates (x, y) of a point and output whether that point is likely to be black or white. In this case, we have the following data:

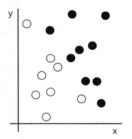

Figure 1.3   Some sample data

- The inputs are the coordinates of our points.
- The expected outputs are the colors of our points.
- A way to measure whether our algorithm is doing a good job could be, for instance, the percentage of points that are being correctly classified.

What we need here is a new representation of our data that cleanly separates the white points from the black points. One transformation we could use, among many other possibilities, would be a coordinate change, illustrated in figure 1.4.

In this new coordinate system, the coordinates of our points can be said to be a new representation of our data. And it's a good one! With this representation, the black/white classification problem can be expressed as a simple rule: "Black points are such that $x > 0$," or "White points are such that $x < 0$." This new representation, combined with this simple rule, neatly solves the classification problem.

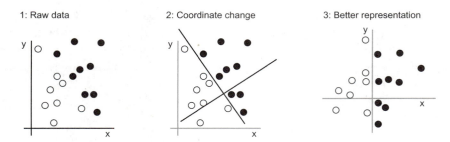

Figure 1.4   Coordinate change

In this case, we defined the coordinate change by hand: we used our human intelligence to come up with our own appropriate representation of the data. This is fine for such an extremely simple problem, but could you do the same if the task was to classify images of handwritten digits? Could you write down explicit, computer-executable image transformations that would illuminate the difference between a 6 and an 8, between a 1 and a 7, across all kinds of different handwriting?

This is possible to an extent. Rules based on representations of digits, such as "number of closed loops" or vertical and horizontal pixel histograms, can do a decent job of telling apart handwritten digits. But finding such useful representations by hand is hard work, and, as you can imagine, the resulting rule-based system is brittle—a nightmare to maintain. Every time you come across a new example of handwriting that breaks your carefully thought-out rules, you will have to add new data transformations and new rules, while taking into account their interaction with every previous rule.

You're probably thinking, if this process is so painful, could we automate it? What if we tried systematically searching for different sets of automatically generated representations of the data and rules based on them, identifying good ones by using as feedback the percentage of digits being correctly classified in some development dataset? We would then be doing machine learning. *Learning*, in the context of machine learning, describes an automatic search process for data transformations that produce useful representations of some data, guided by some feedback signal—representations that are amenable to simpler rules solving the task at hand.

These transformations can be coordinate changes (like in our 2-D coordinates classification example), or taking a histogram of pixels and counting loops (like in our digits classification example), but they could also be linear projections, translations, nonlinear operations (such as "select all points such that $x > 0$"), and so on. Machine learning algorithms aren't usually creative in finding these transformations; they're merely searching through a predefined set of operations, called a *hypothesis space*. For instance, the space of all possible coordinate changes would be our hypothesis space in the 2-D coordinates classification example.

So that's what machine learning is, concisely: searching for useful representations and rules over some input data, within a predefined space of possibilities, using guidance from a feedback signal. This simple idea allows for solving a remarkably broad range of intellectual tasks, from speech recognition to autonomous driving. Now that you understand what we mean by *learning*, let's take a look at what makes *deep learning* special.

1.1.4   The "deep" in "deep learning"

Deep learning is a specific subfield of machine learning: a new take on learning representations from data that emphasizes learning successive layers of increasingly meaningful representations. The "deep" in "deep learning" isn't a reference to any kind of deeper understanding achieved by the approach; rather, it stands for this idea of successive layers of representations. How many layers contribute to a model of the data is called the *depth* of the model. Other appropriate names for the field could have been *layered representations learning* or *hierarchical representations learning*. Modern deep learning often involves tens or even hundreds of successive layers of representations, and they're all learned automatically from exposure to training data. Meanwhile, other approaches to machine learning tend to focus on learning only one or two layers of representations of the data (say, taking a pixel histogram and then applying a classification rule); hence, they're sometimes called *shallow learning*.

In deep learning, these layered representations are learned via models called *neural networks*, structured in literal layers stacked on top of each other. The term "neural network" refers to neurobiology, but although some of the central concepts in deep learning were developed in part by drawing inspiration from our understanding of the brain (in particular, the visual cortex), deep learning models are not models of the brain. There's no evidence that the brain implements anything like the learning mechanisms used in modern deep learning models. You may come across pop-science articles proclaiming that deep learning works like the brain or was modeled after the brain, but that isn't the case. It would be confusing and counterproductive for newcomers to the field to think of deep learning as being in any way related to neurobiology; you don't need that shroud of "just like our minds" mystique and mystery, and you may as well forget anything you may have read about hypothetical links between deep learning and biology. For our purposes, deep learning is a mathematical framework for learning representations from data.

What do the representations learned by a deep learning algorithm look like? Let's examine how a network several layers deep (see figure 1.5) transforms an image of a digit to recognize what digit it is.

As you can see in figure 1.6, the network transforms the digit image into representations that are increasingly different from the original image and increasingly informative about the final result. You can think of a deep network as a multistage *information-distillation* process, where information goes through successive filters and comes out increasingly *purified* (that is, useful with regard to some task).

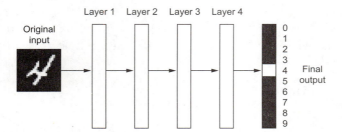

Figure 1.5   A deep neural network for digit classification

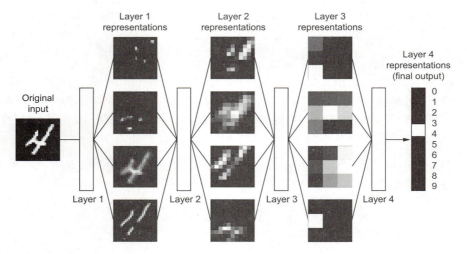

Figure 1.6   Data representations learned by a digit-classification model

So that's what deep learning is, technically: a multistage way to learn data representations. It's a simple idea—but, as it turns out, very simple mechanisms, sufficiently scaled, can end up looking like magic.

1.1.5   *Understanding how deep learning works, in three figures*

At this point, you know that machine learning is about mapping inputs (such as images) to targets (such as the label "cat"), which is done by observing many examples of input and targets. You also know that deep neural networks do this input-to-target mapping via a deep sequence of simple data transformations (layers) and that these data transformations are learned by exposure to examples. Now let's look at how this learning happens, concretely.

The specification of what a layer does to its input data is stored in the layer's *weights*, which in essence are a bunch of numbers. In technical terms, we'd say that the transformation implemented by a layer is *parameterized* by its weights (see figure 1.7). (Weights are also sometimes called the *parameters* of a layer.) In this context, *learning* means finding a set of values for the weights of all layers in a network, such that the

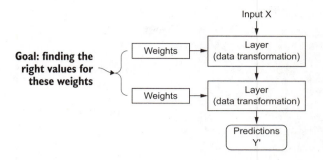

Figure 1.7 A neural network is parameterized by its weights.

network will correctly map example inputs to their associated targets. But here's the thing: a deep neural network can contain tens of millions of parameters. Finding the correct values for all of them may seem like a daunting task, especially given that modifying the value of one parameter will affect the behavior of all the others!

To control something, first you need to be able to observe it. To control the output of a neural network, you need to be able to measure how far this output is from what you expected. This is the job of the *loss function* of the network, also sometimes called the *objective function* or *cost function*. The loss function takes the predictions of the network and the true target (what you wanted the network to output) and computes a distance score, capturing how well the network has done on this specific example (see figure 1.8).

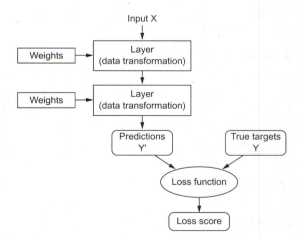

Figure 1.8 A loss function measures the quality of the network's output.

The fundamental trick in deep learning is to use this score as a feedback signal to adjust the value of the weights a little, in a direction that will lower the loss score for the current example (see figure 1.9). This adjustment is the job of the *optimizer*, which implements what's called the *backpropagation* algorithm: the central algorithm in deep learning. The next chapter explains in more detail how backpropagation works.

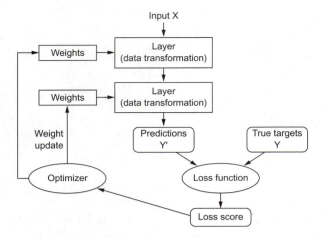

Figure 1.9   The loss score is used as a feedback signal to adjust the weights.

Initially, the weights of the network are assigned random values, so the network merely implements a series of random transformations. Naturally, its output is far from what it should ideally be, and the loss score is accordingly very high. But with every example the network processes, the weights are adjusted a little in the correct direction, and the loss score decreases. This is the *training loop*, which, repeated a sufficient number of times (typically tens of iterations over thousands of examples), yields weight values that minimize the loss function. A network with a minimal loss is one for which the outputs are as close as they can be to the targets: a trained network. Once again, it's a simple mechanism that, once scaled, ends up looking like magic.

1.1.6   *What deep learning has achieved so far*

Although deep learning is a fairly old subfield of machine learning, it rose to prominence only in the early 2010s. In the few years since, it has achieved nothing short of a revolution in the field, producing remarkable results on perceptual tasks and even natural language processing tasks—problems involving skills that seem natural and intuitive to humans but have long been elusive for machines. In particular, deep learning has enabled the following breakthroughs, all in historically difficult areas of machine learning:

- Near-human-level image classification
- Near-human-level speech transcription
- Near-human-level handwriting transcription
- Dramatically improved machine translation
- Dramatically improved text-to-speech conversion
- Digital assistants such as Google Assistant and Amazon Alexa
- Near-human-level autonomous driving
- Improved ad targeting, as used by Google, Baidu, or Bing
- Improved search results on the web

- Ability to answer natural language questions
- Superhuman Go playing

We're still exploring the full extent of what deep learning can do. We've started applying it with great success to a wide variety of problems that were thought to be impossible to solve just a few years ago—automatically transcribing the tens of thousands of ancient manuscripts held in the Vatican's Apostolic Archive, detecting and classifying plant diseases in fields using a simple smartphone, assisting oncologists or radiologists with interpreting medical imaging data, predicting natural disasters such as floods, hurricanes, or even earthquakes, and so on. With every milestone, we're getting closer to an age where deep learning assists us in every activity and every field of human endeavor—science, medicine, manufacturing, energy, transportation, software development, agriculture, and even artistic creation.

1.1.7 *Don't believe the short-term hype*

Although deep learning has led to remarkable achievements in recent years, expectations for what the field will be able to achieve in the next decade tend to run much higher than what will likely be possible. Although some world-changing applications, like autonomous cars, are already within reach, many more are likely to remain elusive for a long time, such as believable dialogue systems, human-level machine translation across arbitrary languages, and human-level natural language understanding. In particular, talk of human-level general intelligence shouldn't be taken too seriously. The risk with high expectations for the short term is that, as technology fails to deliver, research investment will dry up, slowing progress for a long time.

This has happened before. Twice in the past, AI went through a cycle of intense optimism followed by disappointment and skepticism, with a dearth of funding as a result. It started with symbolic AI in the 1960s. In those early days, projections about AI were flying high. One of the best-known pioneers and proponents of the symbolic AI approach was Marvin Minsky, who claimed in 1967, "Within a generation . . . the problem of creating 'artificial intelligence' will substantially be solved." Three years later, in 1970, he made a more precisely quantified prediction: "In from three to eight years we will have a machine with the general intelligence of an average human being." In 2022, such an achievement still appears to be far in the future—so far that we have no way to predict how long it will take—but in the 1960s and early 1970s, several experts believed it to be right around the corner (as do many people today). A few years later, as these high expectations failed to materialize, researchers and government funds turned away from the field, marking the start of the first *AI winter* (a reference to a nuclear winter, because this was shortly after the height of the Cold War).

It wouldn't be the last one. In the 1980s, a new take on symbolic AI, *expert systems*, started gathering steam among large companies. A few initial success stories triggered a wave of investment, with corporations around the world starting their own in-house AI departments to develop expert systems. Around 1985, companies were spending over $1 billion each year on the technology; but by the early 1990s, these systems had proven expensive to maintain, difficult to scale, and limited in scope, and interest died down. Thus began the second AI winter.

We may be currently witnessing the third cycle of AI hype and disappointment, and we're still in the phase of intense optimism. It's best to moderate our expectations for the short term and make sure people less familiar with the technical side of the field have a clear idea of what deep learning can and can't deliver.

1.1.8   *The promise of AI*

Although we may have unrealistic short-term expectations for AI, the long-term picture is looking bright. We're only getting started in applying deep learning to many important problems for which it could prove transformative, from medical diagnoses to digital assistants. AI research has been moving forward amazingly quickly in the past 10 years, in large part due to a level of funding never before seen in the short history of AI, but so far relatively little of this progress has made its way into the products and processes that form our world. Most of the research findings of deep learning aren't yet applied, or at least are not applied to the full range of problems they could solve across all industries. Your doctor doesn't yet use AI, and neither does your accountant. You probably don't use AI technologies very often in your day-to-day life. Of course, you can ask your smartphone simple questions and get reasonable answers, you can get fairly useful product recommendations on Amazon.com, and you can search for "birthday" on Google Photos and instantly find those pictures of your daughter's birthday party from last month. That's a far cry from where such technologies used to stand. But such tools are still only accessories to our daily lives. AI has yet to transition to being central to the way we work, think, and live.

Right now, it may seem hard to believe that AI could have a large impact on our world, because it isn't yet widely deployed—much as, back in 1995, it would have been difficult to believe in the future impact of the internet. Back then, most people didn't see how the internet was relevant to them and how it was going to change their lives. The same is true for deep learning and AI today. But make no mistake: AI is coming. In a not-so-distant future, AI will be your assistant, even your friend; it will answer your questions, help educate your kids, and watch over your health. It will deliver your groceries to your door and drive you from point A to point B. It will be your interface to an increasingly complex and information-intensive world. And, even more important, AI will help humanity as a whole move forward, by assisting human scientists in new breakthrough discoveries across all scientific fields, from genomics to mathematics.

On the way, we may face a few setbacks and maybe even a new AI winter—in much the same way the internet industry was overhyped in 1998–1999 and suffered from a crash that dried up investment throughout the early 2000s. But we'll get there eventually. AI will end up being applied to nearly every process that makes up our society and our daily lives, much like the internet is today.

Don't believe the short-term hype, but do believe in the long-term vision. It may take a while for AI to be deployed to its true potential—a potential the full extent of which no one has yet dared to dream—but AI is coming, and it will transform our world in a fantastic way.

1.2   Before deep learning: A brief history of machine learning

Deep learning has reached a level of public attention and industry investment never before seen in the history of AI, but it isn't the first successful form of machine learning. It's safe to say that most of the machine learning algorithms used in the industry today aren't deep learning algorithms. Deep learning isn't always the right tool for the job—sometimes there isn't enough data for deep learning to be applicable, and sometimes the problem is better solved by a different algorithm. If deep learning is your first contact with machine learning, you may find yourself in a situation where all you have is the deep learning hammer, and every machine learning problem starts to look like a nail. The only way not to fall into this trap is to be familiar with other approaches and practice them when appropriate.

A detailed discussion of classical machine learning approaches is outside of the scope of this book, but I'll briefly go over them and describe the historical context in which they were developed. This will allow us to place deep learning in the broader context of machine learning and better understand where deep learning comes from and why it matters.

1.2.1   Probabilistic modeling

Probabilistic modeling is the application of the principles of statistics to data analysis. It is one of the earliest forms of machine learning, and it's still widely used to this day. One of the best-known algorithms in this category is the naive Bayes algorithm.

Naive Bayes is a type of machine learning classifier based on applying Bayes' theorem while assuming that the features in the input data are all independent (a strong, or "naive" assumption, which is where the name comes from). This form of data analysis predates computers and was applied by hand decades before its first computer implementation (most likely dating back to the 1950s). Bayes' theorem and the foundations of statistics date back to the 18th century, and these are all you need to start using naive Bayes classifiers.

A closely related model is *logistic regression* (logreg for short), which is sometimes considered to be the "Hello World" of modern machine learning. Don't be misled by its name—logreg is a classification algorithm rather than a regression algorithm. Much like naive Bayes, logreg predates computing by a long time, yet it's still useful to this day, thanks to its simple and versatile nature. It's often the first thing a data scientist will try on a dataset to get a feel for the classification task at hand.

1.2.2   Early neural networks

Early iterations of neural networks have been completely supplanted by the modern variants covered in these pages, but it's helpful to be aware of how deep learning originated. Although the core ideas of neural networks were investigated in toy forms as early as the 1950s, the approach took decades to get started. For a long time, the missing piece was an efficient way to train large neural networks. This changed in the mid-1980s, when multiple people independently rediscovered the backpropagation algorithm—a way to train chains of parametric operations using gradient-descent optimization (we'll precisely define these concepts later in the book)—and started applying it to neural networks.

The first successful practical application of neural networks came in 1989 from Bell Labs, when Yann LeCun combined the earlier ideas of convolutional neural networks and backpropagation and applied them to the problem of classifying handwritten digits. The resulting network, dubbed *LeNet*, was used by the United States Postal Service in the 1990s to automate the reading of ZIP codes on mail envelopes.

1.2.3 *Kernel methods*

As neural networks started to gain some respect among researchers in the 1990s, thanks to this first success, a new approach to machine learning rose to fame and quickly sent neural networks back to oblivion: kernel methods. *Kernel methods* are a group of classification algorithms, the best known of which is the *Support Vector Machine* (SVM). The modern formulation of an SVM was developed by Vladimir Vapnik and Corinna Cortes in the early 1990s at Bell Labs and published in 1995,[3] although an older linear formulation was published by Vapnik and Alexey Chervonenkis as early as 1963.[4]

SVM is a classification algorithm that works by finding "decision boundaries" separating two classes (see figure 1.10). SVMs proceed to find these boundaries in the following two steps:

1 The data is mapped to a new high-dimensional representation where the decision boundary can be expressed as a hyperplane (if the data was two-dimensional, as in figure 1.10, a hyperplane would be a straight line).

2 A good decision boundary (a separation hyperplane) is computed by trying to maximize the distance between the hyperplane and the closest data points from each class, a step called *maximizing the margin*. This allows the boundary to generalize well to new samples outside of the training dataset.

Figure 1.10
A decision boundary

The technique of mapping data to a high-dimensional representation where a classification problem becomes simpler may look good on paper, but in practice, it's often computationally intractable. That's where the *kernel trick* comes in (the key idea that kernel methods are named after). Here's the gist of it: to find good decision hyperplanes in the new representation space, you don't

---

[3] Vladimir Vapnik and Corinna Cortes, "Support-Vector Networks," *Machine Learning* 20, no. 3 (1995): 273–297.
[4] Vladimir Vapnik and Alexey Chervonenkis, "A Note on One Class of Perceptrons," *Automation and Remote Control* 25 (1964).

have to explicitly compute the coordinates of your points in the new space; you just need to compute the distance between pairs of points in that space, which can be done efficiently using a kernel function. A *kernel function* is a computationally tractable operation that maps any two points in your initial space to the distance between these points in your target representation space, completely bypassing the explicit computation of the new representation. Kernel functions are typically crafted by hand rather than learned from data—in the case of an SVM, only the separation hyperplane is learned.

At the time they were developed, SVMs exhibited state-of-the-art performance on simple classification problems and were one of the few machine learning methods backed by extensive theory and amenable to serious mathematical analysis, making them well understood and easily interpretable. Because of these useful properties, SVMs became extremely popular in the field for a long time.

But SVMs proved hard to scale to large datasets and didn't provide good results for perceptual problems such as image classification. Because an SVM is a shallow method, applying an SVM to perceptual problems requires first extracting useful representations manually (a step called *feature engineering*), which is difficult and brittle. For instance, if you want to use an SVM to classify handwritten digits, you can't start from the raw pixels; you should first find by hand useful representations that make the problem more tractable, like the pixel histograms mentioned earlier.

1.2.4   *Decision trees, random forests, and gradient-boosting machines*

Decision trees are flowchart-like structures that let you classify input data points or predict output values given inputs (see figure 1.11). They're easy to visualize and interpret. Decision trees learned from data began to receive significant research interest in the 2000s, and by 2010, they were often preferred to kernel methods.

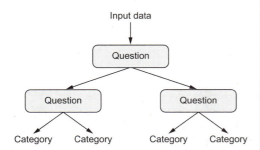

Figure 1.11   A decision tree: The parameters that are learned are the questions about the data. A question could be, for instance, "Is coefficient 2 in the data greater than 3.5?"

In particular, the *random forest* algorithm introduced a robust, practical take on decision tree learning that involves building a large number of specialized decision trees and then ensembling their outputs. Random forests are applicable to a wide range of problems—you could say that they're almost always the second-best algorithm for any shallow machine learning task. When the popular machine learning competition website Kaggle (http://kaggle.com) got started in 2010, random forests quickly became a favorite on the platform—until 2014, when *gradient-boosting machines* took over. A gradient-boosting machine, much like a random forest, is a machine learning technique based on ensembling weak prediction models, generally decision trees. It uses *gradient boosting*, a way to improve any machine learning model by iteratively training new models that specialize in addressing the weak points of the previous models. Applied to decision trees, the use of the gradient-boosting technique results in models that strictly outperform random forests most of the time, while having similar properties. It may be one of the best, if not *the* best, algorithm for dealing with nonperceptual data today. Alongside deep learning, it's one of the most commonly used techniques in Kaggle competitions.

1.2.5 Back to neural networks

Around 2010, although neural networks were almost completely shunned by the scientific community at large, a number of people still working on neural networks started to make important breakthroughs: the groups of Geoffrey Hinton at the University of Toronto, Yoshua Bengio at the University of Montreal, Yann LeCun at New York University, and IDSIA in Switzerland.

In 2011, Dan Cireşan from IDSIA began to win academic image-classification competitions with GPU-trained deep neural networks—the first practical success of modern deep learning. But the watershed moment came in 2012, with the entry of Hinton's group in the yearly large-scale image-classification challenge, ImageNet (ImageNet Large Scale Visual Recognition Challenge, or ILSVRC for short). The ImageNet challenge was notoriously difficult at the time, consisting of classifying high-resolution color images into 1,000 different categories after training on 1.4 million images. In 2011, the top-five accuracy of the winning model, based on classical approaches to computer vision, was only 74.3%.[5] Then, in 2012, a team led by Alex Krizhevsky and advised by Geoffrey Hinton was able to achieve a top-five accuracy of 83.6%—a significant breakthrough. The competition has been dominated by deep convolutional neural networks every year since. By 2015, the winner reached an accuracy of 96.4%, and the classification task on ImageNet was considered to be a completely solved problem.

Since 2012, deep convolutional neural networks (*convnets*) have become the go-to algorithm for all computer vision tasks; more generally, they work on all perceptual tasks. At any major computer vision conference after 2015, it was nearly impossible to find presentations that didn't involve convnets in some form. At the same time, deep learning has also found applications in many other types of problems, such as natural language processing. It has completely replaced SVMs and decision trees in a wide range of applications. For instance, for several years, the European Organization for Nuclear Research, CERN, used decision tree–based methods for analyzing particle data from the ATLAS detector at the Large Hadron Collider (LHC), but CERN even-

---

[5] "Top-five accuracy" measures how often the model selects the correct answer as part of its top five guesses (out of 1,000 possible answers, in the case of ImageNet).

tually switched to Keras-based deep neural networks due to their higher performance and ease of training on large datasets.

1.2.6 What makes deep learning different?

The primary reason deep learning took off so quickly is that it offered better performance for many problems. But that's not the only reason. Deep learning also makes problem-solving much easier, because it completely automates what used to be the most crucial step in a machine learning workflow: feature engineering.

Previous machine learning techniques—shallow learning—involved transforming the input data into only one or two successive representation spaces, usually via simple transformations such as high-dimensional nonlinear projections (SVMs) or decision trees. But the refined representations required by complex problems generally can't be attained by such techniques. As such, humans had to go to great lengths to make the initial input data more amenable to processing by these methods: they had to manually engineer good layers of representations for their data. This is called *feature engineering*. Deep learning, on the other hand, completely automates this step: with deep learning, you learn all features in one pass rather than having to engineer them yourself. This has greatly simplified machine learning workflows, often replacing sophisticated multistage pipelines with a single, simple, end-to-end deep learning model.

You may ask, if the crux of the issue is to have multiple successive layers of representations, could shallow methods be applied repeatedly to emulate the effects of deep learning? In practice, successive applications of shallow-learning methods produce fast-diminishing returns, because the optimal first representation layer in a three-layer model isn't the optimal first layer in a one-layer or two-layer model. What is transformative about deep learning is that it allows a model to learn all layers of representation *jointly*, at the same time, rather than in succession (*greedily*, as it's called). With joint feature learning, whenever the model adjusts one of its internal features, all other features that depend on it automatically adapt to the change, without requiring human intervention. Everything is supervised by a single feedback signal: every change in the model serves the end goal. This is much more powerful than greedily stacking shallow models, because it allows for complex, abstract representations to be learned by breaking them down into long series of intermediate spaces (layers); each space is only a simple transformation away from the previous one.

These are the two essential characteristics of how deep learning learns from data: the *incremental, layer-by-layer way in which increasingly complex representations are developed*, and the fact that *these intermediate incremental representations are learned jointly*, each layer being updated to follow both the representational needs of the layer above and the needs of the layer below. Together, these two properties have made deep learning vastly more successful than previous approaches to machine learning.

1.2.7 The modern machine learning landscape

A great way to get a sense of the current landscape of machine learning algorithms and tools is to look at machine learning competitions on Kaggle. Due to its highly competitive environment (some contests have thousands of entrants and million-dollar prizes) and to the wide variety of machine learning problems covered, Kaggle offers a realistic way to assess what works and what doesn't. So, what kind of algorithm is reliably winning competitions? What tools do top entrants use?

In early 2019, Kaggle ran a survey asking teams that ended in the top five of any competition since 2017 which primary software tool they had used in the competition (see figure 1.12). It turns out that top teams tend to use either deep learning methods (most often via the Keras library) or gradient-boosted trees (most often via the LightGBM or XGBoost libraries).

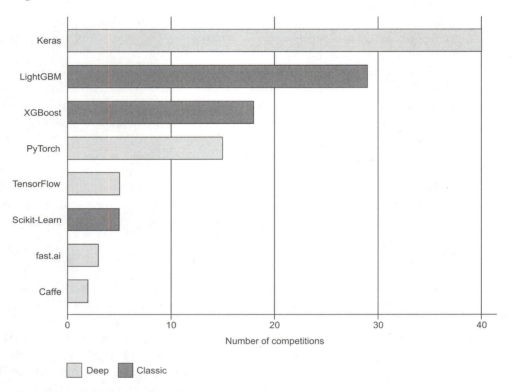

Figure 1.12   Machine learning tools used by top teams on Kaggle

It's not just competition champions, either. Kaggle also runs a yearly survey among machine learning and data science professionals worldwide. With tens of thousands of respondents, this survey is one of the most reliable sources about the state of the industry. Figure 1.13 shows the percentage of usage of different machine learning software frameworks.

From 2016 to 2020, the entire machine learning and data science industry has been dominated by these two approaches: deep learning and gradient-boosted trees. Specifically, gradient-boosted trees are used for problems where structured data is

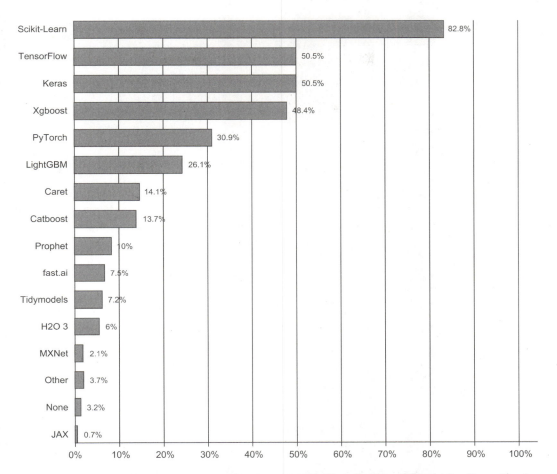

**Figure 1.13   Tool usage across the machine learning and data science industry (Source: http://www.kaggle
.com/kaggle-survey-2020)**

available, whereas deep learning is used for perceptual problems such as image
classification.

Users of gradient-boosted trees tend to use Scikit-Learn, XGBoost, or LightGBM.
Meanwhile, most practitioners of deep learning use Keras, often in combination with
its parent framework, TensorFlow. The common point of these tools is they're all available as R or Python libraries: R and Python are by far the most widely used language
for machine learning and data science.

You should be the most familiar with the following two techniques to be successful
in applied machine learning today: gradient-boosted trees, for shallow-learning problems; and deep learning, for perceptual problems. In technical terms, this means
you'll need to be familiar with XGBoost and Keras—the libraries that currently dominate Kaggle competitions. With this book in hand, you're already one big step closer.

1.3   Why deep learning? Why now?

The two key ideas of deep learning for computer vision—convolutional neural networks and backpropagation—were already well understood by 1990. The long short-term memory (LSTM) algorithm, which is fundamental to deep learning for time series, was developed in 1997 and has barely changed since. Why did deep learning take off only after 2012? What changed in these two decades? In general, the following three technical forces are driving advances in machine learning:

- Hardware
- Datasets and benchmarks
- Algorithmic advances

Because the field is guided by experimental findings rather than by theory, algorithmic advances become possible only when appropriate data and hardware are available to try new ideas (or to scale up old ideas, as is often the case). Machine learning isn't mathematics or physics, where major advances can be done with a pen and a piece of paper. It's an engineering science.

The real bottlenecks throughout the 1990s and 2000s were data and hardware. But here's what happened during that time: the internet took off and high-performance graphics chips were developed for the needs of the gaming market.

1.3.1   Hardware

Between 1990 and 2010, off-the-shelf CPUs became faster by a factor of approximately 5,000. As a result, nowadays it's possible to run small deep learning models on your laptop, whereas this would have been intractable 25 years ago.

But typical deep learning models used in computer vision or speech recognition require orders of magnitude more computational power than your laptop can deliver. Throughout the 2000s, companies like NVIDIA and AMD invested billions of dollars in developing fast, massively parallel chips (graphical processing units, or GPUs) to power the graphics of increasingly photorealistic video games—cheap, single-purpose supercomputers designed to render complex 3-D scenes on your screen in real time. This investment came to benefit the scientific community when, in 2007, NVIDIA launched CUDA (https://developer.nvidia.com/about-cuda), a programming interface for its line of GPUs. A small number of GPUs started replacing massive clusters of CPUs in various highly parallelizable applications, beginning with physics modeling. Deep neural networks, consisting mostly of many small matrix multiplications, are also highly parallelizable, and around 2011, some researchers began to write CUDA implementations of neural nets—Dan Cireşan[6] and Alex Krizhevsky[7] were among the first.

---

[6] See "Flexible, High Performance Convolutional Neural Networks for Image Classification," *Proceedings of the 22nd International Joint Conference on Artificial Intelligence* (2011), http://mng.bz/nN0K.

[7] See "ImageNet Classification with Deep Convolutional Neural Networks," *Advances in Neural Information Processing Systems* 25 (2012), http://mng.bz/2286.

What happened is that the gaming market subsidized supercomputing for the next generation of artificial intelligence applications. Sometimes, big things begin as games. The NVIDIA Titan RTX, a GPU that cost $2,500 at the end of 2019, can deliver a peak of 16 teraflops in single precision (16 trillion `float32` operations per second). That's about 500 times more computing power than the world's fastest supercomputer from 1990, the Intel Touchstone Delta. On a Titan RTX, it takes only a few hours to train an ImageNet model of the sort that would have won the ILSVRC competition around 2012 or 2013. Meanwhile, large companies train deep learning models on clusters of hundreds of GPUs.

What's more, the deep learning industry has been moving beyond GPUs and is investing in increasingly specialized, efficient chips for deep learning. In 2016, at its annual I/O convention, Google revealed its Tensor Processing Unit (TPU) project: a new chip design developed from the ground up to run deep neural networks significantly faster and far more energy efficiently than top-of-the-line GPUs. In 2020, the third iteration of the TPU card represents 420 teraflops of computing power. That's 10,000 times more than the Intel Touchstone Delta from 1990.

These TPU cards are designed to be assembled into large-scale configurations, called "pods." One pod (1024 TPU cards) peaks at 100 petaflops. For scale, that's about 10% of the peak computing power of the current largest supercomputer, the IBM Summit at Oak Ridge National Lab, which consists of 27,000 NVIDIA GPUs and peaks at around 1.1 exaflops.

1.3.2   Data

AI is sometimes heralded as the new industrial revolution. If deep learning is the steam engine of this revolution, then data is its coal: the raw material that powers our intelligent machines, without which nothing would be possible. When it comes to data, in addition to the exponential progress in storage hardware over the past 20 years (following Moore's law), the game changer has been the rise of the internet, making it feasible to collect and distribute very large datasets for machine learning. Today, large companies work with image datasets, video datasets, and natural language datasets that couldn't have been collected without the internet. User-generated image tags on Flickr, for instance, have been a treasure trove of data for computer vision. So are YouTube videos. And Wikipedia is a key dataset for natural language processing.

If there's one dataset that has been a catalyst for the rise of deep learning, it's the ImageNet dataset, consisting of 1.4 million images that have been hand annotated with 1,000 image categories (one category per image). But what makes ImageNet special isn't just its large size but also the yearly competition associated with it.[8]

As Kaggle has been demonstrating since 2010, public competitions are an excellent way to motivate researchers and engineers to push the envelope. Having common

---

[8] The ImageNet Large Scale Visual Recognition Challenge (ILSVRC), http://www.image-net.org/challenges/ LSVRC.

benchmarks that researchers compete to beat has greatly helped the rise of deep learning by highlighting its success against classical machine learning approaches.

1.3.3 Algorithms

In addition to hardware and data, until the late 2000s, we were missing a reliable way to train very deep neural networks. As a result, neural networks were still fairly shallow, using only one or two layers of representations; thus, they weren't able to shine against more-refined shallow methods such as SVMs and random forests. The key issue was that of *gradient propagation* through deep stacks of layers. The feedback signal used to train neural networks would fade away as the number of layers increased.

This changed around 2009–2010 with the advent of the following simple but important algorithmic improvements that allowed for better gradient propagation:

- Better *activation functions* for neural layers
- Better *weight-initialization schemes*, starting with layer-wise pretraining, which was then quickly abandoned
- Better *optimization schemes*, such as RMSprop and Adam

Only when these improvements began to allow for training models with 10 or more layers did deep learning start to shine. Finally, in 2014, 2015, and 2016, even more advanced ways to improve gradient propagation were discovered, such as batch normalization, residual connections, and depthwise separable convolutions.

Today, we can train models that are arbitrarily deep from scratch. This has unlocked the use of extremely large models, which hold considerable representational power—that is to say, which encode very rich hypothesis spaces. This extreme scalability is one of the defining characteristics of modern deep learning. Large-scale model architectures, which feature tens of layers and tens of millions of parameters, have brought about critical advances both in computer vision (for instance, architectures such as ResNet, Inception, or Xception) and natural language processing (for instance, large Transformer-based architectures such as BERT, GPT-3, or XLNet).

1.3.4 A new wave of investment

As deep learning became the new state of the art for computer vision in 2012–2013, and eventually for all perceptual tasks, industry leaders took note. What followed was a gradual wave of industry investment far beyond anything previously seen in the history of AI (see figure 1.14).

In 2011, right before deep learning took the spotlight, the total venture capital investment in AI worldwide was less than a billion dollars, which went almost entirely to practical applications of shallow machine learning approaches. In 2015, it had risen to over \$5 billion, and in 2017, to a staggering \$16 billion. Hundreds of startups launched in these few years, trying to capitalize on the deep learning hype. Meanwhile, large tech companies such as Google, Amazon, and Microsoft have invested in

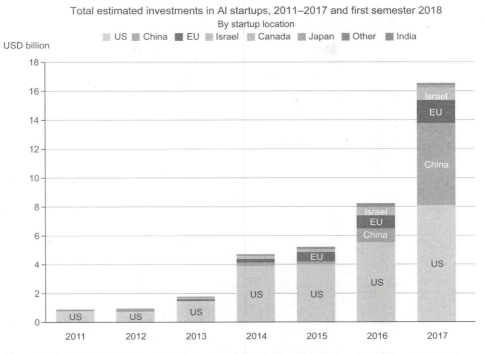

Figure 1.14   OECD estimate of total investments in AI startups (Source: http://mng.bz/zGN6)

internal research departments in amounts that would most likely dwarf the flow of venture-capital money.

Machine learning—in particular, deep learning—has become central to the product strategy of these tech giants. In late 2015, Google CEO Sundar Pichai stated, "Machine learning is a core, transformative way by which we're rethinking how we're doing everything. We're thoughtfully applying it across all our products, be it search, ads, YouTube, or Play. And we're in early days, but you'll see us—in a systematic way—apply machine learning in all these areas."[9]

As a result of this wave of investment, the number of people working on deep learning went from a few hundred to tens of thousands in less than 10 years, and research progress has reached a frenetic pace.

1.3.5   The democratization of deep learning

One of the key factors driving this inflow of new faces in deep learning has been the democratization of the toolsets used in the field. In the early days, doing deep learning required significant C++ and CUDA expertise, which few people possessed.

Nowadays, basic R or Python scripting skills suffice to do advanced deep learning research. This has been driven most notably by the development of the TensorFlow

---

[9] Sundar Pichai, Alphabet earnings call, Oct. 22, 2015.

library—a symbolic tensor-manipulation frameworks that supports autodifferentiation, greatly simplifying the implementation of new models—and by the rise of user-friendly libraries such as Keras, which makes deep learning as easy as manipulating LEGO bricks. After its release in early 2015, Keras quickly became the go-to deep learning solution for large numbers of new startups, graduate students, and researchers pivoting into the field.

1.3.6   *Will it last?*

Is there anything special about deep neural networks that makes them the "right" approach for companies to be investing in and for researchers to flock to? Or is deep learning just a fad that may not last? Will we still be using deep neural networks in 20 years?

Deep learning has several properties that justify its status as an AI revolution, and it's here to stay. We may not be using neural networks two decades from now, but whatever we use will directly inherit from modern deep learning and its core concepts. These important properties can be broadly sorted into the following three categories:

- *Simplicity*—Deep learning removes the need for feature engineering, replacing complex, brittle, engineering-heavy pipelines with simple, end-to-end trainable models that are typically built using only five or six different tensor operations.
- *Scalability*—Deep learning is highly amenable to parallelization on GPUs or TPUs, so it can take full advantage of Moore's law. In addition, deep learning models are trained by iterating over small batches of data, allowing them to be trained on datasets of arbitrary size. (The only bottleneck is the amount of parallel computational power available, which, thanks to Moore's law, is a fast-moving barrier.)
- *Versatility and reusability*—Unlike many prior machine learning approaches, deep learning models can be trained on additional data without restarting from scratch, making them viable for continuous online learning—an important property for very large production models. Furthermore, trained deep learning models are repurposable and thus reusable: for instance, it's possible to take a deep learning model trained for image classification and drop it into a video-processing pipeline. This allows us to reinvest previous work into increasingly complex and powerful models. This also makes deep learning applicable to fairly small datasets.

Deep learning has been in the spotlight for only a few years, and we may not yet have established the full scope of what it can do. With every passing year, we learn about new use cases and engineering improvements that lift previous limitations. Following a scientific revolution, progress generally follows a sigmoid curve: it starts with a period of fast progress, which gradually stabilizes as researchers hit hard limitations, and then further improvements become incremental.

When I was writing the first edition of this book, in 2016, I predicted that deep learning was still in the first half of that sigmoid, with much more transformative progress to come in the following few years. This has proven true in practice—2017 and 2018 have seen the rise of Transformer-based deep learning models for natural language processing, which have been a revolution in the field, while deep learning also kept delivering steady progress in computer vision and speech recognition. Today, in 2022, deep learning seems to have entered the second half of that sigmoid. We should still expect significant progress in the years to come, but we're probably out of the initial phase of explosive progress.

Today, I'm extremely excited about the deployment of deep learning technology to every problem it can solve—the list is endless. Deep learning is still a revolution in the making, and it will take many years to realize its full potential.

The mathematical building blocks of neural networks

This chapter covers

- A first example of a neural network
- Tensors and tensor operations
- How neural networks learn via backpropagation and gradient descent

Understanding deep learning requires familiarity with many simple mathematical concepts: *tensors, tensor operations, differentiation, gradient descent,* and so on. Our goal in this chapter will be to build up your intuition about these notions without getting overly technical. In particular, we'll steer away from mathematical notation, which can introduce unnecessary barriers for those without any mathematics background and isn't necessary to explain things well. The most precise, unambiguous description of a mathematical operation is its executable code.

To provide sufficient context for introducing tensors and gradient descent, we'll begin the chapter with a practical example of a neural network. Then we'll go over every new concept that's been introduced, point by point. Keep in mind that these concepts will be essential for you to understand the practical examples in the following chapters.

After reading this chapter, you'll have an intuitive understanding of the mathematical theory behind deep learning, and you'll be ready to start diving into Keras and TensorFlow in chapter 3.

2.1 A first look at a neural network

Let's look at a concrete example of a neural network that uses Keras to learn to classify handwritten digits. Unless you already have experience with Keras or similar libraries, you won't understand everything about this first example right away. That's fine. In the next chapter, we'll review each element in the example and explain them in detail. So don't worry if some steps seem arbitrary or look like magic to you—we've got to start somewhere.

The problem we're trying to solve here is to classify grayscale images of handwritten digits (28 × 28 pixels) into their 10 categories (0 through 9). We'll use the *MNIST dataset*, a classic in the machine learning community, which has been around almost as long as the field itself and has been intensively studied. It's a set of 60,000 training images, plus 10,000 test images, assembled by the National Institute of Standards and Technology (the NIST in MNIST) in the 1980s. You can think of "solving" MNIST as the "Hello World" of deep learning—it's what you do to verify that your algorithms are working as expected. As you become a machine learning practitioner, you'll see MNIST come up over and over again in scientific papers, blog posts, and so on. You can see some MNIST samples in figure 2.1.

Figure 2.1   MNIST sample digits

In machine learning, a *category* in a classification problem is called a *class*. Data points are called *samples*. The class associated with a specific sample is called a *label*.

You don't need to try to reproduce the example shown in the next code listing on your machine just now. If you wish to, you'll first need to set up a deep learning workspace, which is covered in chapter 3. The MNIST dataset comes preloaded in Keras, in the form of a set of four R arrays, organized into two lists named `train` and `test`.

Listing 2.1   Loading the MNIST dataset in Keras

```
library(tensorflow)
library(keras)
mnist <- dataset_mnist()
```

```
train_images <- mnist$train$x
train_labels <- mnist$train$y
test_images <- mnist$test$x
test_labels <- mnist$test$y
```

train_images and train_labels form the training set, the data that the model will learn from. The model will then be tested on the test set, test_images and test_labels. The images are encoded as R arrays, and the labels are an array of digits, ranging from 0 to 9. The images and labels have a one-to-one correspondence. Let's look at the training data, shown here:

```
str(train_images)
```

```
int [1:60000, 1:28, 1:28] 0 0 0 0 0 0 0 0 0 0 ...
```

```
str(train_labels)
```

```
int [1:60000(1d)] 5 0 4 1 9 2 1 3 1 4 ...
```

And here's the test data:

```
str(test_images)
```

```
int [1:10000, 1:28, 1:28] 0 0 0 0 0 0 0 0 0 0 ...
```

```
str(test_labels)
```

```
int [1:10000(1d)] 7 2 1 0 4 1 4 9 5 9 ...
```

The workflow will be as follows: first, we'll feed the neural network the training data, train_images and train_labels. Then the network will learn to associate images and labels. Finally, we'll ask the network to produce predictions for test_images, and we'll verify whether these predictions match the labels from test_labels.

Let's build the network, as shown in the next listing. Again, remember that you aren't expected to understand everything about this example yet.

Listing 2.2   The network architecture

```
model <- keras_model_sequential(list(
  layer_dense(units = 512, activation = "relu"),
  layer_dense(units = 10, activation = "softmax")
))
```

The core building block of neural networks is the *layer*. You can think of a layer as a filter for data: some data goes in, and it comes out in a more useful form. Specifically, layers extract *representations* out of the data fed into them—hopefully, representations that are more meaningful for the problem at hand. Most of deep learning consists of chaining together simple layers that will implement a form of progressive *data distillation*. A deep learning model is like a sieve for data processing, made of a succession of increasingly refined data filters—the layers.

Here, our model consists of a sequence of two Dense layers, which are densely connected (also called *fully connected*) neural layers. The second (and last) layer is a 10-way *softmax classification* layer, which means it will return an array of 10 probability scores (summing to 1). Each score will be the probability that the current digit image belongs to one of our 10 digit classes.

To make the model ready for training, we need to pick the following three things as part of the *compilation* step, shown in listing 2.3:

- *An optimizer*—The mechanism through which the model will update itself based on the training data it sees, so as to improve its performance.
- *A loss function*—How the model will be able to measure its performance on the training data, and thus how it will be able to steer itself in the right direction.
- *Metrics to monitor during training and testing*—Here, we care only about accuracy (the fraction of the images that were correctly classified).

The exact purpose of the loss function and the optimizer will be made clear throughout the next two chapters.

Listing 2.3   The compilation step

```
compile(model,
        optimizer = "rmsprop",
        loss = "sparse_categorical_crossentropy",
        metrics = "accuracy")
```

Note that we don't save the return value from compile() because the model is modified in place.

Before training, we'll preprocess the data by reshaping it into the shape the model expects and scaling it so that all values are in the [0, 1] interval, as shown next. Previously, our training images were stored in an array of shape (60000, 28, 28) of type integer with values in the [0, 255] interval. We'll transform it into a double array of shape (60000, 28 * 28) with values between 0 and 1.

Listing 2.4   Preparing the image data

```
train_images <- array_reshape(train_images, c(60000, 28 * 28))
train_images <- train_images / 255
test_images <- array_reshape(test_images, c(10000, 28 * 28))
test_images <- test_images / 255
```

Note that we use the array_reshape() function rather than the dim•() function to reshape the array. We'll explain why later, when we talk about tensor reshaping.

We're now ready to train the model, which in Keras is done via a call to the model's fit() method—we *fit* the model to its training data.

Listing 2.5   "Fitting" the model

```
fit(model, train_images, train_labels, epochs = 5, batch_size = 128)
```

```
Epoch 1/5
60000/60000 [==============================] - 5s - loss: 0.2524 - acc:
➡ 0.9273
Epoch 2/5
51328/60000 [======================>.....] - ETA: 1s - loss: 0.1035 -
➡ acc: 0.9692
```

Two quantities are displayed during training: the loss of the model over the training data, and the accuracy of the model over the training data. We quickly reach an accuracy of 0.989 (98.9%) on the training data.

Now that we have a trained model, we can use it to predict class probabilities for *new* digits—images that weren't part of the training data, like those from the test set.

Listing 2.6   Using the model to make predictions

```
test_digits <- test_images[1:10, ]
predictions <- predict(model, test_digits)
str(predictions)
```

```
num [1:10, 1:10] 3.10e-09 3.53e-11 2.55e-07 1.00 8.54e-07 ...
```

```
predictions[1, ]
```

```
[1] 3.103298e-09 1.175280e-10 1.060593e-06 4.761311e-05 4.189971e-12
[6] 4.062199e-08 5.244305e-16 9.999473e-01 2.753219e-07 3.826783e-06
```

Each number of index i in that array (`predictions[1, ]`) corresponds to the probability that digit image `test_digits[1, ]` belongs to class i. This first test digit has the highest probability score (0.9999473, almost 1) at index 8, so according to our model, it must be a 7 (because we start counting at 0):

```
which.max(predictions[1, ])
```

```
[1] 8
```

```
predictions[1, 8]
```

```
[1] 0.9999473
```

We can check that the test label agrees:

```
test_labels[1]
```

```
[1] 7
```

On average, how good is our model at classifying such never-before-seen digits? Let's check by computing average accuracy over the entire test set.

> **Listing 2.7   Evaluating the model on new data**

```
metrics <- evaluate(model, test_images, test_labels)
metrics["accuracy"]
```

```
accuracy
  0.9795
```

The test set accuracy turns out to be 97.9%—that's quite a bit lower than the training set accuracy (98.9%). This gap between training accuracy and test accuracy is an example of *overfitting*: the fact that machine learning models tend to perform worse on new data than on their training data. Overfitting is a central topic in chapter 3.

This concludes our first example. You just saw how you can build and train a neural network to classify handwritten digits in fewer than 15 lines of R code. In this chapter and the next, we'll go into detail about every moving piece we just previewed and clarify what's going on behind the scenes. You'll learn about tensors, the data-storing objects going into the model; tensor operations, which layers are made of; and gradient descent, which allows your model to learn from its training examples.

2.2 *Data representations for neural networks*

In the previous example, we started from data stored in multidimensional arrays, also called *tensors*. In general, all current machine learning systems use tensors as their basic data structure. Tensors are fundamental to the field—so fundamental that TensorFlow was named after them. So, what's a tensor?

At its core, a tensor is a container for data—usually numerical data—so, it's a container for numbers. You may be already familiar with matrices, which are rank 2 tensors: tensors are a generalization of matrices to an arbitrary number of *dimensions* (note that in the context of tensors, a dimension is often called an *axis*).

R provides an implementation of tensors: `array` objects (constructed via `base::array()`) are tensors. In this section we are focused on defining the concepts around tensors, so we will stick to using R arrays. Later in the book (chapter 3), we introduce another implementation of tensors (Tensorflow `Tensors`).

2.2.1 *Scalars (rank 0 tensors)*

A tensor that can contain only one number is called a *scalar* (or scalar tensor, or rank 0 tensor, or 0D tensor). R doesn't have a data type to represent scalars (all numeric objects are vectors), but an R vector of length 1 is conceptually similar to a scalar.

2.2.2 *Vectors (rank 1 tensors)*

An array of numbers is called a *vector*, or rank 1 tensor, or 1D tensor. A rank 1 tensor is said to have exactly one axis. The following is a tensor vector:

```
x <- as.array(c(12, 3, 6, 14, 7))
str(x)
```

```
num [1:5(1d)] 12 3 6 14 7
```

```
length(dim(x))
```

```
[1] 1
```

This vector has five entries and so is called a *five-dimensional vector*. Don't confuse a 5D vector with a 5D tensor! A 5D vector has only one axis and has five dimensions along its axis, whereas a 5D tensor has five axes (and may have any number of dimensions along each axis). *Dimensionality* can denote either the number of entries along a specific axis (as in the case of our 5D vector) or the number of axes in a tensor (such as a 5D tensor), which can be confusing at times. In the latter case, it's technically more correct to talk about a *tensor of rank 5* (the rank of a tensor being the number of axes), but the ambiguous notation *5D tensor* is common regardless.

2.2.3   *Matrices (rank 2 tensors)*

An array of vectors is a *matrix*, or rank 2 tensor, or 2D tensor. A matrix has two axes (often referred to as *rows* and *columns*). You can visually interpret a matrix as a rectangular grid of numbers:

```
x <- array(seq(3 * 5), dim = c(3, 5))
x
```

```
     [,1] [,2] [,3] [,4] [,5]
[1,]    1    4    7   10   13
[2,]    2    5    8   11   14
[3,]    3    6    9   12   15
```

```
dim(x)
```

```
[1] 3 5
```

The entries from the first axis are called the *rows*, and the entries from the second axis are called the *columns*. In the previous example, c(1, 4, 7, 10, 13) is the first row of x, and c(1, 2, 3) is the first column.

2.2.4   *Rank 3 and higher-rank tensors*

If you supply a length 3 vector to dim, you obtain a rank 3 tensor (or 3D tensor), which you can visually interpret as a cube of numbers or a stack of rank 2 tensors:

```
x <- array(seq(2 * 3 * 4), dim = c(2, 3, 4))
str(x)
```

```
int [1:2, 1:3, 1:4] 1 2 3 4 5 6 7 8 9 10 ...
```

```
length(dim(x))
```

```
[1] 3
```

By stacking rank 3 tensors, you can create a rank 4 tensor, and so on. In deep learning, you'll generally manipulate tensors with ranks 0 to 4, although you may go up to 5 if you process video data.

2.2.5   *Key attributes*

A tensor is defined by the following three key attributes:

- *Number of axes (rank)*—For instance, a rank 3 tensor has three axes, and a matrix has two axes. This is available from `length(dim(x))`.
- *Shape*—This is an integer vector that describes how many dimensions the tensor has along each axis. For instance, the previous matrix example has shape `(3, 5)`, and the rank 3 tensor example has shape `(2, 3, 4)`. A vector has a shape with a single element, such as `(5)`. R arrays don't distinguish between 1D vectors and scalar tensors, but conceptually, tensors can also be scalar with shape `()`.
- *Data type*—This is the type of the data contained in the tensor. R arrays have support for R's built-in data types like `double` and `integer`. Conceptually, however, tensors can support any type of homogeneous data type, and other tensor implementations also provide support for types like like `float16`, `float32`, `float64` (corresponding to R's `double`), `int32` (R's `integer` type), and so on. In TensorFlow, you are also likely to come across `string` tensors.

To make this more concrete, let's look back at the data we processed in the MNIST example. First, we load the MNIST dataset:

```
library(keras)
mnist <- dataset_mnist()
train_images <- mnist$train$x
train_labels <- mnist$train$y
test_images <- mnist$test$x
test_labels <- mnist$test$y
```

Next, we display the number of axes of the tensor `train_images`:

```
length(dim(train_images))
```

```
[1] 3
```

Here's its shape:

```
dim(train_images)
```

```
[1] 60000    28    28
```

And this is its R data type:

```
typeof(train_images)
```

```
[1] "integer"
```

So what we have here is a rank 3 tensor of integers. More precisely, it's a stack of 60,000 matrices of 28 × 28 integers. Each such matrix is a grayscale image, with coefficients between 0 and 255 of pixel intensity values.

Let's display the fifth digit in this rank 3 tensor (see figure 2.2).

Listing 2.8   Displaying the fifth digit

```
digit <- train_images[5, , ]
plot(as.raster(abs(255 - digit), max = 255))
```

Figure 2.2   The fifth sample in our dataset

Naturally, the corresponding label is the integer 9:

```
train_labels[5]
```

```
[1] 9
```

2.2.6   *Manipulating tensors in R*

In the previous example, we selected a specific digit alongside the first axis using the syntax `train_images[i, , ]`. Selecting specific elements in a tensor is called *tensor slicing*. Let's look at the tensor-slicing operations you can do on R arrays.

> **NOTE**   TensorFlow `Tensor`'s slicing is similar to R arrays but with some differences. In this section, we focus on R arrays and begin discussing TensorFlow Tensors in chapter 3.

The following example selects digits 10 to 99 and puts them in an array of shape (90, 28, 28):

```
my_slice <- train_images[10:99, , ]
dim(my_slice)
```

```
[1] 90 28 28
```

In general, you may select slices between any two indices along each tensor axis. For instance, to select 14 × 14 pixels in the bottom-right corner of all images, you would do this:

```
my_slice <- train_images[, 15:28, 15:28]
dim(my_slice)
```

```
[1] 60000    14    14
```

2.2.7   *The notion of data batches*

In general, the first axis in all data tensors you'll come across in deep learning will be the *samples axis* (sometimes called the *samples dimension*). In the MNIST example, "samples" are images of digits.

In addition, deep learning models don't process an entire dataset at once; rather, they break the data into small batches. Concretely, here's one batch of our MNIST digits, with a batch size of 128:

```
batch <- train_images[1:128, , ]
```

And here's the next batch:

```
batch <- train_images[129:256, , ]
```

And the *n*th batch:

```
n <- 3
batch <- train_images[seq(to = 128 * n, length.out = 128), , ]
```

When considering such a batch tensor, the first axis is called the *batch axis* or *batch dimension*. This is a term you'll frequently encounter when using Keras and other deep learning libraries.

2.2.8   *Real-world examples of data tensors*

Let's make data tensors more concrete with a few examples similar to what you'll encounter later. The data you'll manipulate will almost always fall into one of the following categories:

- *Vector data*—Rank 2 tensors of shape (samples, features), where each sample is a vector of numerical attributes ("features")
- *Times-series data or sequence data*—Rank 3 tensors of shape (samples, timesteps, features), where each sample is a sequence (of length timesteps) of feature vectors
- *Images*—Rank 4 tensors of shape (samples, height, width, channels), where each sample is a 2D grid of pixels, and each pixel is represented by a vector of values ("channels")
- *Video*—Rank 5 tensors of shape (samples, frames, height, width, channels), where each sample is a sequence (of length frames) of images

2.2.9   *Vector data*

This is one of the most common cases. In such a dataset, each single data point can be encoded as a vector, and thus a batch of data will be encoded as a rank 2 tensor (that is, a matrix), where the first axis is the *samples axis* and the second axis is the *features axis*.

Let's take a look at the next two examples:

- An actuarial dataset of people, where we consider each person's age, gender, and income. Each person can be characterized as a vector of 3 values, and thus an entire dataset of 100,000 people can be stored in a rank 2 tensor of shape `(100000, 3)`.

- A dataset of text documents, where we represent each document by the counts of how many times each word appears in it (out of a dictionary of 20,000 common words). Each document can be encoded as a vector of 20,000 values (one count per word in the dictionary), and thus an entire dataset of 500 documents can be stored in a tensor of shape `(500, 20000)`.

2.2.10 Time-series data or sequence data

Whenever time matters in your data (or the notion of sequence order), it makes sense to store it in a rank 3 tensor with an explicit time axis. Each sample can be encoded as a sequence of vectors (a rank 2 tensor), and thus a batch of data will be encoded as a rank 3 tensor (see figure 2.3).

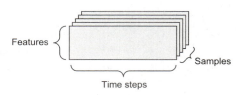

Figure 2.3   A rank 3 time-series data tensor

The time axis is always the second axis by convention. Let's look at a few examples:

- A dataset of stock prices. Every minute, we store the current price of the stock, the highest price in the past minute, and the lowest price in the past minute. Thus, every minute is encoded as a 3D vector, an entire day of trading is encoded as a matrix of shape `(390, 3)` (there are 390 minutes in a trading day), and 250 days' worth of data can be stored in a rank 3 tensor of shape `(250, 390, 3)`. Here, each sample would be one day's worth of data.

- A dataset of tweets, where we encode each tweet as a sequence of 280 characters out of an alphabet of 128 unique characters. In this setting, each character can be encoded as a binary vector of size 128 (an all-zeros vector except for a 1 entry at the index corresponding to the character). Then each tweet can be encoded as a rank 2 tensor of shape `(280, 128)`, and a dataset of one million tweets can be stored in a tensor of shape `(1000000, 280, 128)`.

2.2.11 Image data

Images typically have three dimensions: height, width, and color depth. Although grayscale images (like our MNIST digits) have only a single color channel and could thus be stored in rank 2 tensors, by convention, image tensors are always rank 3, with a one-dimensional color channel for grayscale images. A batch of 128 grayscale images of size 256 × 256 could thus be stored in a tensor of shape `(128, 256, 256, 1)`, and a batch of 128 color images could be stored in a tensor of shape `(128, 256, 256, 3)` (see figure 2.4).

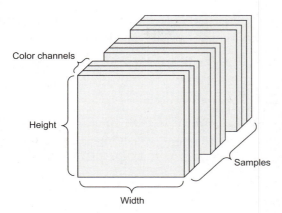

Figure 2.4   **A rank 4 image data tensor**

Two conventions for shapes of image tensors are the *channels-last* convention (which is standard in TensorFlow) and the *channels-first* convention (which is increasingly falling out of favor). The channels-last convention places the color-depth axis at the end: (samples, height, width, color_depth). Meanwhile, the channels-first convention places the color depth axis right after the batch axis: (samples, color_depth, height, width). With the channels-first convention, the previous examples would become (128, 1, 256, 256) and (128, 3, 256, 256). The Keras API provides support for both formats.

2.2.12 *Video data*

Video data is one of the few types of real-world data for which you'll need rank 5 tensors. A video can be understood as a sequence of frames, with each frame being a color image. Because each frame can be stored in a rank 3 tensor (height, width, color_depth), a sequence of frames can be stored in a rank 4 tensor (frames, height, width, color_depth), and thus a batch of different videos can be stored in a rank 5 tensor of shape (samples, frames, height, width, color_depth).

For instance, a 60-second, 144 × 256 YouTube video clip sampled at 4 frames per second would have 240 frames. A batch of four such video clips would be stored in a tensor of shape (4, 240, 144, 256, 3). That's a total of 106,168,320 values! If the data type of the tensor was R integers, each value would be stored in 32 bits, so the tensor would represent 405 MB. Heavy! Videos you encounter in real life are much lighter, because they aren't stored as R integers, and they're typically compressed by a large factor (such as in the MPEG format).

2.3   *The gears of neural networks: Tensor operations*

As much as any computer program can be ultimately reduced to a small set of binary operations on binary inputs (AND, OR, NOR, and so on), all transformations learned by deep neural networks can be reduced to a handful of *tensor operations* (or *tensor functions*) applied to tensors of numeric data. For instance, it's possible to add tensors, multiply tensors, and so on. In our initial example, we built our model by stacking Dense layers on top of each other. A Keras layer instance looks like this:

```
layer_dense(units = 512, activation = "relu")
```

```
<keras.layers.core.dense.Dense object at 0x7f7b0e8cf520>
```

This layer can be interpreted as a function, which takes as input a matrix and returns another matrix—a new representation for the input tensor. Specifically, the function is as follows (where W is a matrix and b is a vector, both properties of the layer):

```
output <- relu(dot(W, input) + b)
```

Let's unpack this. We have the following three tensor operations here:

- A dot product (dot) between the input tensor and a tensor named W
- An addition (+) between the resulting matrix and a vector b
- A relu operation: relu(x) is an element-wise max(x, 0); *relu* stands for rectified linear unit

Although this section deals entirely with linear algebra expressions, you won't find any mathematical notation here. I've found that mathematical concepts can be more readily mastered by programmers with no mathematical background if they're expressed as short code snippets instead of mathematical equations. So we'll use R and TensorFlow code throughout.

2.3.1   Element-wise operations

The relu operation and addition are element-wise operations: operations that are applied independently to each entry in the tensors being considered. This means these operations are highly amenable to massively parallel implementations (*vectorized implementations*, a term that comes from the *vector processor* supercomputer architecture from the 1970–1990 period). If you want to write a naive R implementation of an element-wise operation, you use a for loop, as in the following naive implementation of an element-wise relu operation:

```
naive_relu <- function(x) {
  stopifnot(length(dim(x)) == 2)     ◁— x is a rank 2
  for (i in 1:nrow(x))                    tensor (a matrix).
    for (j in 1:ncol(x))
      x[i, j] <- max(x[i, j], 0)
  x
}
```

You could do the same for addition:

```
naive_add <- function(x, y) {
  stopifnot(length(dim(x)) == 2, dim(x) == dim(y))   ◁— x and y are
  for (i in 1:nrow(x))                                    rank 2 tensors.
```

```
    for (j in 1:ncol(x))
      x[i, j]  <- x[i, j] + y[i, j]
  x
}
```

On the same principle, you can do element-wise multiplication, subtraction, and so on.

In practice, when dealing with R arrays, these operations are available as well-optimized built-in R functions, which themselves delegate the heavy lifting to a Basic Linear Algebra Subprograms (BLAS) implementation. BLAS are low-level, highly parallel, efficient tensor-manipulation routines that are typically implemented in Fortran or C. So, in R, you can do the following element-wise operation, and it will be blazing fast:

```
z <- x + y          ◁─────┐  Element-wise addition
z[z < 0] <- 0       ◁──────  Element-wise relu
```

Let's actually time the difference here:

```
random_array <- function(dim, min = 0, max = 1)
  array(runif(prod(dim), min, max),
        dim)

x <- random_array(c(20, 100))
y <- random_array(c(20, 100))

system.time({
  for (i in seq_len(1000)) {
    z <- x + y
    z[z < 0] <- 0
  }
})[["elapsed"]]
```

```
[1] 0.009
```

This takes 0.009 seconds. Meanwhile, the naive version takes a stunning 0.72 seconds:

```
system.time({
  for (i in seq_len(1000)) {
    z <- naive_add(x, y)
    z <- naive_relu(z)
  }
})[["elapsed"]]
```

```
[1] 0.724
```

Likewise, when running TensorFlow code on a GPU, element-wise operations are executed via fully vectorized CUDA implementations that can best utilize the highly parallel GPU chip architecture.

2.3.2 Broadcasting

Our earlier naive implementation of `naive_add` supports only the addition of rank 2 tensors with identical shapes. But in the `layer_dense()` introduced earlier, we added a rank 2 tensor with a vector. What happens with addition when the shapes of the two tensors being added differ?

What we'd like is for the smaller tensor to be *broadcast* to match the shape of the larger tensor. Broadcasting consists of the following two steps:

1 Axes (called *broadcast axes*) are added to the smaller tensor to match the `length(dim(x))` of the larger tensor.
2 The smaller tensor is repeated alongside these new axes to match the full shape of the larger tensor.

Note that Tensorflow `Tensors`, covered in chapter 3, have rich broadcasting functionality built in. Here, however, we are building up machine learning concepts from scratch using R arrays and are intentionally avoiding R's implicit recycling behavior when operating on two arrays of different dimensions. We can implement our own recycling approach by building up the smaller tensor to match the shape of the larger tensor, at which point we are again back to doing a standard element-wise operation.

Let's look at a concrete example. Consider `X` with shape `(32, 10)` and `y` with shape `(10)`:

```
X <- random_array(c(32, 10))      ◁——— X is a random matrix with shape (32, 10).
y <- random_array(c(10))          ◁——— y is a random vector with shape (10).
```

First, we add a size 1 first axis to `y`, whose shape becomes `(1, 10)`:

```
dim(y) <- c(1, 10)
str(y)              ◁——— The shape of y is now (1, 10).
```

```
num [1, 1:10] 0.885 0.429 0.737 0.553 0.426 ...
```

Then, we repeat `y` 32 times alongside this new axis, so that we end up with a tensor `Y` with shape `(32, 10)`, where `Y[i, ] == y` for i in `seq(32)`:

```
Y <- y[rep(1, 32), ]   ◁——┐ Repeat y 32 times along axis 1 to
str(Y)                     │ obtain Y, which has shape (32, 10).
```

```
num [1:32, 1:10] 0.885 0.885 0.885 0.885 0.885 ...
```

At this point, we can proceed to add `X` and `Y`, because they have the same shape.

In terms of implementation, ideally we want no new rank 2 tensor to be created, because that is terribly inefficient. In most tensor implementations, including R and TensorFlow, the repetition operation is entirely virtual: it happens at the algorithmic level rather than at the memory level. However, be aware that R's recycling and TensorFlow's (and NumPy's) broadcasting differ in their behavior (we go into details in chapter 3). Regardless, thinking of the vector being repeated 10 times alongside a new axis is a helpful mental model. Here's what a naive implementation would look like:

```
naive_add_matrix_and_vector <- function(x, y) {
  stopifnot(length(dim(x)) == 2,                    ◁──── x is a rank 2 tensor.
            length(dim(y)) == 1,   ◁─┐
            ncol(x) == dim(y))       │ y is a vector.
  for (i in seq(dim(x)[1]))
    for (j in seq(dim(x)[2]))
      x[i, j] <- x[i, j] + y[j]
  x
}
```

2.3.3 Tensor product

The *tensor product*, or *dot product* (not to be confused with an element-wise product, the * operator), is one of the most common, most useful tensor operations. In R, an element-wise product is done with the * operator, whereas dot products use the %*% operator:

```
x <- random_array(c(32))
y <- random_array(c(32))
z <- x %*% y
```

In mathematical notation, you'd note the operation with a dot (•):

```
z = x • y
```

Mathematically, what does the dot operation do? Let's start with the dot product of two vectors, x and y. It's computed as follows:

```
naive_vector_dot <- function(x, y) {
  stopifnot(length(dim(x)) == 1,        x and y are 1D vectors
            length(dim(y)) == 1,        of the same size.
            dim(x) == dim(y))
  z <- 0
  for (i in seq_along(x))
    z <- z + x[i] * y[i]
  z
}
```

You'll have noticed that the dot product between two vectors is a scalar and that only vectors with the same number of elements are compatible for a dot product.

You can also take the dot product between a matrix x and a vector y, which returns a vector where the coefficients are the dot products between y and the rows of x:

```
naive_matrix_vector_dot <- function(x, y) {      x is a 2D tensor (matrix).
  stopifnot(length(dim(x)) == 2,   ◁─────
            length(dim(y)) == 1,          ◁──── y is a 1D tensor (vector).
            nrow(x) == dim(y))   ◁─┐
                                   │ The first dimension of x must be the
                                   │ same as the first dimension of y!
```

```
z <- array(0, dim = dim(y))
for (i in 1:nrow(x))
  for (j in 1:ncol(x))
    z[i] <- z[i] + x[i, j] * y[j]
z
}
```

This operation returns a vector of zeros with the same shape as y.

You could also reuse the code we wrote previously, which highlights the relationship between a matrix-vector product and a vector product:

```
naive_matrix_vector_dot <- function(x, y) {
  z <- array(0, dim = c(nrow(x)))
  for (i in 1:nrow(x))
    z[i] <- naive_vector_dot(x[i, ], y)
  z
}
```

Note that as soon as one of the two tensors has a length(dim(x)) greater than 1, %*% is no longer *symmetric*, which is to say that x %*% y isn't the same as y %*% x.

Of course, a dot product generalizes to tensors with an arbitrary number of axes. The most common applications may be the dot product between two matrices. You can take the dot product of two matrices x and y (x %*% y) if and only if ncol(x) == nrow(y). The result is a matrix with shape (nrow(x), ncol(y)), where the coefficients are the vector products between the rows of x and the columns of y. The naive implementation is shown here:

x and y are 2D tensors (matrices).

The first dimension of x must be the same as the first dimension of y!

```
naive_matrix_dot <- function(x, y) {
  stopifnot(length(dim(x)) == 2,
            length(dim(y)) == 2,
            ncol(x) == nrow(y))
  z <- array(0, dim = c(nrow(x), ncol(y)))
  for (i in 1:nrow(x))
    for (j in 1:ncol(y)) {
      row_x <- x[i, ]
      column_y <- y[, j]
      z[i, j] <- naive_vector_dot(row_x, column_y)
    }
  z
}
```

This operation returns a matrix of zeros with a specific shape.

Iterate over the rows of x . . .

. . . and over the columns of y.

To understand dot-product shape compatibility, it helps to visualize the input and output tensors by aligning them as shown in figure 2.5.

In the figure, x, y, and z are pictured as rectangles (literal boxes of coefficients). Because the rows of x and the columns of y must have the same size, it follows that the width of x must match the height of y. If you go on to develop new machine learning algorithms, you'll likely be drawing such diagrams often.

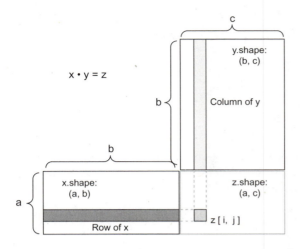

Figure 2.5   Matrix dot-product box diagram

More generally, you can take the dot product between higher-dimensional tensors, following the same rules for shape compatibility as outlined earlier for the 2D case:

```
(a, b, c, d) • (d) -> (a, b, c)
(a, b, c, d) • (d, e) -> (a, b, c, e)
```

And so on.

2.3.4   *Tensor reshaping*

A third type of tensor operation that's essential to understand is *tensor reshaping.* Although it wasn't used in the `layer_dense()` in our first neural network example, we used it when we preprocessed the digits data before feeding it into our model, as shown next:

```
train_images <- array_reshape(train_images, c(60000, 28 * 28))
```

Note that we use the `array_reshape()` function rather than the `` `dim<-`() `` function to reshape R arrays. This is so that the data is reinterpreted using row-major semantics (as opposed to R's default column-major semantics), which is in turn compatible with the way the numerical libraries called by Keras (NumPy, TensorFlow, and so on) interpret array dimensions. You should always use the `array_reshape()` function when reshaping R arrays that will be passed to Keras.

Reshaping a tensor means rearranging its rows and columns to match a target shape. Naturally, the reshaped tensor has the same total number of coefficients as the initial tensor. Reshaping is best understood via simple examples:

```
x <- array(1:6)
x
```

```
[1] 1 2 3 4 5 6
```

```
array_reshape(x, dim = c(3, 2))
```

```
      [,1] [,2]
[1,]    1    2
[2,]    3    4
[3,]    5    6
```

```
array_reshape(x, dim = c(2, 3))
```

```
      [,1] [,2] [,3]
[1,]    1    2    3
[2,]    4    5    6
```

A special case of reshaping that's commonly encountered is *transposition*. *Transposing* a matrix means exchanging its rows and its columns, so that `x[i, ]` becomes `x[, i]`. We can use the `t()` function to transpose a matrix:

```
x <- array(1:6, dim = c(3, 2))
x
```

```
      [,1] [,2]
[1,]    1    4
[2,]    2    5
[3,]    3    6
```

```
t(x)
```

```
      [,1] [,2] [,3]
[1,]    1    2    3
[2,]    4    5    6
```

2.3.5   *Geometric interpretation of tensor operations*

Because the contents of the tensors manipulated by tensor operations can be interpreted as coordinates of points in some geometric space, all tensor operations have a geometric interpretation. For instance, let's consider addition. We'll start with the following vector:

```
A = c(0.5, 1)
```

It's a point in a 2D space (see figure 2.6). It's common to picture a vector as an arrow linking the origin to the point, as shown in figure 2.7.

Let's consider a new point, `B = c(1, 0.25)`, which we'll add to the previous one. This is done geometrically by chaining together the vector arrows, with the resulting location

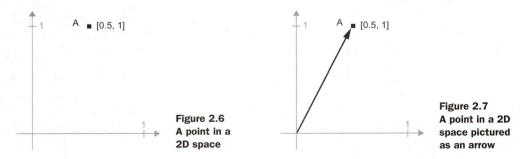

Figure 2.6
A point in a
2D space

Figure 2.7
A point in a 2D
space pictured
as an arrow

being the vector representing the sum of the previous two vectors (see figure 2.8). As you can see, adding a vector B to a vector A represents the action of copying point A in a new location, whose distance and direction from the original point A is determined by the vector B. If you apply the same vector addition to a group of points in the plane (an *object*), you would be creating a copy of the entire object in a new location (see figure 2.9). Tensor addition thus represents the action of *translating an object* (moving the object without distorting it) by a certain amount in a certain direction.

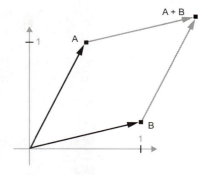

Figure 2.8   Geometric interpretation of the sum of two vectors

In general, elementary geometric operations such as translation, rotation, scaling, skewing, and so on can be expressed as tensor operations. Here are a few examples:

- *Translation*—As you just saw, adding a vector to a point will move the point by a fixed amount in a fixed direction. Applied to a set of points (such as a 2D object), this is called a "translation" (see figure 2.9).

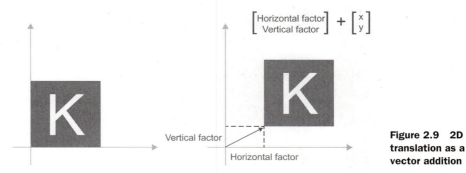

Figure 2.9   2D translation as a vector addition

- *Rotation*—A counterclockwise rotation of a 2D vector by an angle theta (see figure 2.10) can be achieved via a dot product with a 2 × 2 matrix R = rbind(c(cos(theta), -sin(theta)), c(sin(theta), cos(theta)).

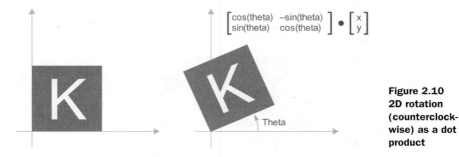

Figure 2.10 2D rotation (counterclockwise) as a dot product

- *Scaling*—A vertical and horizontal scaling of the image (see figure 2.11) can be achieved via a dot product with a 2 × 2 matrix S = rbind(c(horizontal_factor, 0), c(0, vertical_factor)) (note that such a matrix is called a *diagonal matrix*, because it has only non-zero coefficients in its "diagonal," going from the top left to the bottom right).

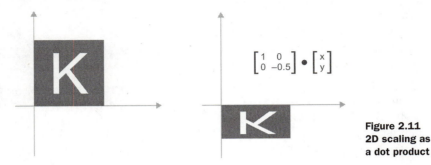

**Figure 2.11
2D scaling as
a dot product**

- *Linear transform*—A dot product with an arbitrary matrix implements a linear transform. Note that *scaling* and *rotation*, listed previously, are by definition linear transforms.
- *Affine transform*—An affine transform (see figure 2.12) is the combination of a linear transform (achieved via a dot product with some matrix) and a translation (achieved via a vector addition). As you have probably recognized, that's exactly the y = W • x + b computation implemented by layer_dense()! A Dense layer without an activation function is an affine layer.

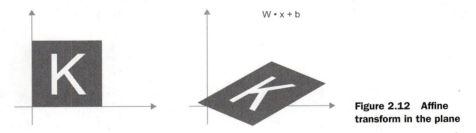

**Figure 2.12   Affine
transform in the plane**

- Dense *layer with* relu *activation*—An important observation about affine transforms is that if you apply many of them repeatedly, you still end up with an affine transform (so you could just have applied that one affine transform in the first place). Let's try it with two: affine2(affine1(x)) = W2 • (W1 • x + b1) + b2 = (W2 • W1) • x + (W2 • b1 + b2). That's an affine transform where the linear part is the matrix W2 • W1 and the translation part is the vector W2 • b1 + b2. As a consequence, a multilayer neural network made entirely of Dense layers without activations would be equivalent to a single Dense layer. This "deep" neural network would just be a linear model in disguise! This is why we need activation functions, like `relu` (seen in action in figure 2.13). Thanks to activation functions, a chain of `Dense` layers can be made to implement very complex, nonlinear geometric transformations, resulting in very rich hypothesis spaces for your deep neural networks. We'll cover this idea in more detail in the next chapter.

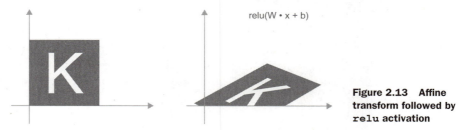

relu(W • x + b)

Figure 2.13   Affine transform followed by `relu` activation

2.3.6   A geometric interpretation of deep learning

You just learned that neural networks consist entirely of chains of tensor operations, and that these tensor operations are just simple geometric transformations of the input data. It follows that you can interpret a neural network as a very complex geometric transformation in a high-dimensional space, implemented via a series of simple steps.

In 3D, the following mental image may prove useful. Imagine two sheets of colored paper: one red and one blue. Put one on top of the other. Now crumple them together into a small ball. That crumpled paper ball is your input data, and each sheet of paper is a class of data in a classification problem. What a neural network is meant to do is figure out a transformation of the paper ball that would uncrumple it, so as to make the two classes cleanly separable again (see figure 2.14). With deep learning, this would be implemented as a series of simple transformations of the 3D space, such as those you could apply on the paper ball with your fingers, one movement at a time.

Figure 2.14   Uncrumpling a complicated manifold of data

Uncrumpling paper balls is what machine learning is about: finding neat representations for complex, highly folded data *manifolds* in high-dimensional spaces (a manifold is a continuous surface, like our crumpled sheet of paper). At this point, you should have a pretty good intuition as to why deep learning excels at this: it takes the approach of incrementally decomposing a complicated geometric transformation into a long chain of elementary ones, which is pretty much the strategy a human would follow to uncrumple a paper ball. Each layer in a deep network applies a transformation that disentangles the data a little, and a deep stack of layers makes tractable an extremely complicated disentanglement process.

2.4   *The engine of neural networks: Gradient-based optimization*

As you saw in the previous section, each neural layer from our first model example transforms its input data as follows:

```
output <- relu(dot(input, W) + b)
```

In this expression, `W` and `b` are tensors that are attributes of the layer. They're called the *weights* or *trainable parameters* of the layer (the `kernel` and `bias` attributes, respectively). These weights contain the information learned by the model from exposure to training data.

Initially, these weight matrices are filled with small random values (a step called *random initialization*). Of course, there's no reason to expect that `relu(dot(input, W) + b)`, when `W` and `b` are random, will yield any useful representations. The resulting representations are meaningless—but they're a starting point. What comes next is to gradually adjust these weights, based on a feedback signal. This gradual adjustment, also called *training*, is the learning that machine learning is all about. This happens within what's called a *training loop*, which works as follows. Repeat these steps in a loop, until the loss seems sufficiently low:

1   Draw a batch of training samples, x, and corresponding targets, y_true.
2   Run the model on x (a step called the *forward pass*) to obtain predictions, y_pred.
3   Compute the loss of the model on the batch, a measure of the mismatch between y_pred and y_true.
4   Update all weights of the model in a way that slightly reduces the loss on this batch.

You'll eventually end up with a model that has a very low loss on its training data: a low mismatch between predictions, y_pred, and expected targets, y_true. The model has "learned" to map its inputs to correct targets. From afar, it may look like magic, but when you reduce it to elementary steps, it turns out to be simple.

Step 1 sounds easy enough—just I/O code. Steps 2 and 3 are merely the application of a handful of tensor operations, so you could implement these steps purely from what you learned in the previous section. The difficult part is step 4: updating the model's weights. Given an individual weight coefficient in the model, how can you compute whether the coefficient should be increased or decreased, and by how much?

One naive solution would be to freeze all weights in the model except the one scalar coefficient being considered, and try different values for this coefficient. Let's say the initial value of the coefficient is 0.3. After the forward pass on a batch of data, the loss of the model on the batch is 0.5. If you change the coefficient's value to 0.35 and rerun the forward pass, the loss increases to 0.6. But if you lower the coefficient to 0.25, the loss falls to 0.4. In this case, it seems that updating the coefficient by –0.05 would contribute to minimizing the loss. This would have to be repeated for all coefficients in the model.

But such an approach would be horribly inefficient, because you'd need to compute two forward passes (which are expensive) for every individual coefficient (of which there are many—usually thousands and sometimes up to millions). Thankfully, there's a much better approach: *gradient descent*.

Gradient descent is the optimization technique that powers modern neural networks. Here's the gist of it: all of the functions used in our models (such as dot or +) transform their input in a smooth and continuous way. If you look at z = x + y, for instance, a small change in y results in only a small change in z, and if you know the direction of the change in y, you can infer the direction of the change in z. Mathematically, you'd say these functions are *differentiable*. If you chain together such functions, the bigger function you obtain is still differentiable. In particular, this applies to the function that maps the model's coefficients to the loss of the model on a batch of data: a small change in the model's coefficients results in a small, predictable change in the loss value. This enables you to use a mathematical operator called the *gradient* to describe how the loss varies as you move the model's coefficients in different directions. If you compute this gradient, you can use it to move the coefficients (all at once in a single update, rather than one at a time) in a direction that decreases the loss.

If you already know what *differentiable* means and what a *gradient* is, you can skip to section 2.4.3. Otherwise, the following two sections will help you understand these concepts.

2.4.1   What's a derivative?

Consider a continuous, smooth function f(x) = y, mapping a number, x, to a new number, y. We can use the function in figure 2.15 as an example.

Because the function is *continuous*, a small change in x can only result in a small change in y—that's the intuition behind *continuity*. Let's say you increase x by a small factor, epsilon_x: this results in a small epsilon_y change to y, as shown in figure 2.16.

In addition, because the function is *smooth* (its curve doesn't have any abrupt angles), when epsilon_x is small enough, around a certain point p, it's possible to approximate f as a linear function of slope a, so that epsilon_y becomes a * epsilon_x:

f(x + epsilon_x) = y + a * epsilon_x

Obviously, this linear approximation is valid only when x is close enough to p.

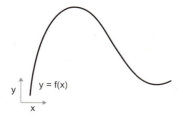

Figure 2.15   A continuous, smooth function

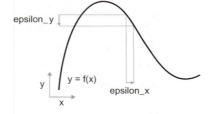

Figure 2.16   With a continuous function, a small change in x results in a small change in y.

The slope a is called the *derivative* of f in p. If a is negative, it means a small increase in x around p will result in a decrease of f(x) (as shown in figure 2.17), and if a is positive, a small increase in x will result in an increase of f(x). Further, the absolute value of a (the *magnitude* of the derivative) tells you how quickly this increase or decrease will happen.

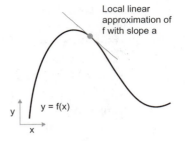

Figure 2.17   Derivative of f in p

For every differentiable function f(x) (*differentiable* means "can be differentiated to find the derivative": for example, smooth, continuous functions can be differentiated), there exists a derivative function f'(x) that maps values of x to the slope of the local linear approximation of f in those points. For instance, the derivative of cos(x) is -sin(x), the derivative of f(x) = a * x is f'(x) = a, and so on.

Being able to differentiate functions is a very powerful tool when it comes to *optimization*, the task of finding values of x that minimize the value of f(x). If you're trying to update x by a factor epsilon_x to minimize f(x), and you know the derivative of f, then your job is done: the derivative completely describes how f(x) evolves as you change x. If you want to reduce the value of f(x), you just need to move x a little in the opposite direction from the derivative.

2.4.2   *Derivative of a tensor operation: The gradient*

The function we were just looking at turned a scalar value x into another scalar value y: you could plot it as a curve in a 2D plane. Now imagine a function that turns a list of scalars (x, y) into a scalar value z: that would be a vector operation. You could plot it as a 2D *surface* in a 3D space (indexed by coordinates x, y, z). Likewise, you can imagine functions that take matrices as inputs, functions that take rank 3 tensors as inputs, and so on.

The concept of differentiation can be applied to any such function, as long as the surfaces they describe are continuous and smooth. The derivative of a tensor operation (or tensor function) is called a *gradient*. Gradients are just the generalization of the concept of derivatives to functions that take tensors as inputs. Remember how, for a scalar function, the derivative represents the *local slope* of the curve of the function? In the same way, the gradient of a tensor function represents the *curvature* of the multidimensional surface described by the function. It characterizes how the output of the function varies when its input parameters vary.

Let's look at an example grounded in machine learning. Consider the following:

- An input vector, x (a sample in a dataset)
- A matrix, W (the weights of a model)
- A target, y_true (what the model should learn to associate to x)
- A loss function, loss_fn() (meant to measure the gap between the model's current predictions and y_true)

You can use W to compute a target candidate y_pred, and then compute the loss, or mismatch, between the target candidate y_pred and the target y_true:

```
y_pred <- dot(W, x)
loss_value <- loss_fn(y_pred, y_true)
```
We use the model weights, W, to make a prediction for x.

We estimate how far off the prediction was.

Now we'd like to use gradients to figure out how to update `W` so as to make `loss_value` smaller. How do we do that? Given fixed inputs `x` and `y_true`, the preceding operations can be interpreted as a function mapping values of `W` (the model's weights) to loss values:

```
loss_value <- f(W)
```
f() describes the curve (or high-dimensional surface) formed by loss values when W varies.

Let's say the current value of `W` is `W0`. Then the derivative of `f()` at the point `W0` is a tensor `grad(loss_value, W0)`, with the same shape as `W`, where each coefficient `grad(loss_ value, W0)[i, j]` indicates the direction and magnitude of the change in `loss_value` you observe when modifying `W0[i, j]`. That tensor `grad(loss_value, W0)` is the gradient of the function `f(W) = loss_value` in `W0`, also called "gradient of `loss_value` with respect to `W` around `W0`."

Partial derivatives

The tensor operation `grad(f(W), W)` (which takes as input a matrix `W`) can be expressed as a combination of scalar functions, `grad_ij(f(W), w_ij)`, each of which would return the derivative of `loss_value = f(W)` with respect to the coefficient `W[i, j]` of `W`, assuming all other coefficients are constant. `grad_ij` is called the *partial derivative* of `f` with respect to `W[i, j]`.

Concretely, what does `grad(loss_value, W0)` represent? You saw earlier that the derivative of a function `f(x)` of a single coefficient can be interpreted as the slope of the curve of `f()`. Likewise, `grad(loss_value, W0)` can be interpreted as the tensor describing the *direction of steepest ascent* of `loss_value = f(W)` around `W0`, as well as the slope of this ascent. Each partial derivative describes the slope of `f()` in a specific direction.

For this reason, in much the same way that, for a function `f(x)`, you can reduce the value of `f(x)` by moving `x` a little in the opposite direction from the derivative, with a function `f(W)` of a tensor, you can reduce `loss_value = f(W)` by moving `W` in the opposite direction from the gradient: for example, `W1 = W0 - step * grad(f(W0), W0)` (where `step` is a small scaling factor). That means going against the direction of steepest ascent of `f`, which intuitively should put you lower on the curve. Note that the scaling factor `step` is needed because `grad(loss_value, W0)` approximates the curvature only when you're close to `W0`, so you don't want to get too far from `W0`.

2.4.3   *Stochastic gradient descent*

Given a differentiable function, it's theoretically possible to find its minimum analytically: it's known that a function's minimum is a point where the derivative is 0, so all you have to do is find all the points where the derivative goes to 0 and check for which of these points the function has the lowest value.

Applied to a neural network, that means finding analytically the combination of weight values that yields the smallest possible loss function. This can be done by solving the equation `grad(f(W), W) = 0` for `W`. This is a polynomial equation of `N` variables, where `N` is the number of coefficients in the model. Although it would be possible to solve such an equation for `N = 2` or `N = 3`, doing so is intractable for real neural networks, where the number of parameters is never less than a few thousand and can often be several tens of millions.

Instead, you can use the four-step algorithm outlined at the beginning of this section: modify the parameters little by little based on the current loss value for a random batch of data, as follows. Because you're dealing with a differentiable function, you can compute its gradient, which gives you an efficient way to implement step 4. If you update the weights in the opposite direction from the gradient, the loss will be a little less every time:

1 Draw a batch of training samples, `x`, and corresponding targets, `y_true`.
2 Run the model on `x` to obtain predictions, `y_pred` (this is called the *forward pass*).
3 Compute the loss of the model on the batch, a measure of the mismatch between `y_pred` and `y_true`.
4 Compute the gradient of the loss with regard to the model's parameters (this is called the *backward pass*).
5 Move the parameters a little in the opposite direction from the gradient—for example, `W = W - (learning_rate * gradient)`—thus reducing the loss on the batch a bit. The *learning rate* (`learning_rate` here) would be a scalar factor modulating the "speed" of the gradient descent process.

Easy enough! What we just described is called *mini-batch stochastic gradient descent* (mini-batch SGD). The term *stochastic* refers to the fact that each batch of data is drawn at random (*stochastic* is a scientific synonym of *random*). Figure 2.18 illustrates what happens in 1D, when the model has only one parameter and you have only one training sample.

As you can see, intuitively it's important to pick a reasonable value for the `learning_ rate` factor. If it's too small, the descent down the curve will take many iterations, and it could get stuck in a local minimum. If `learning_rate` is too large, your updates may end up taking you to completely random locations on the curve.

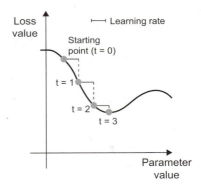

Figure 2.18   SGD down a 1D loss curve (one learnable parameter)

Note that a variant of the mini-batch SGD algorithm would be to draw a single sample and target at each iteration, rather than drawing a batch of data. This would be *true* SGD (as opposed to *mini-batch* SGD). Alternatively, going to the opposite extreme, you could run every step on *all* data available, which is called *batch gradient descent*. Each update would then be more accurate but far more expensive. The efficient compromise between these two extremes is to use mini-batches of reasonable size.

Although figure 2.18 illustrates gradient descent in a 1D parameter space, in practice you'll use gradient descent in highly dimensional spaces: every weight coefficient in a neural network is a free dimension in the space, and there may be tens of thousands or even millions of them. To help you build intuition about loss surfaces, you can also visualize gradient descent along a 2D loss surface, as shown in figure 2.19. But you can't possibly visualize what the actual process of training a neural network looks like—you can't represent a 1,000,000-dimensional space in a way that makes sense to humans. As such, it's good to keep in mind that the intuitions you develop through these low-dimensional representations may not always be accurate in practice. This has historically been a source of issues in the world of deep learning research.

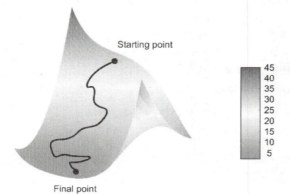

Figure 2.19   Gradient descent down a 2D loss surface (two learnable parameters)

Additionally, multiple variants of SGD exist that differ by taking into account previous weight updates when computing the next weight update, rather than just looking at the current value of the gradients. There is, for instance, SGD with momentum, as well as AdaGrad, RMSprop, and several others. Such variants are known as *optimization methods* or *optimizers*. In particular, the concept of *momentum*, which is used in many of these variants, deserves your attention. Momentum addresses two issues with SGD: convergence speed and local minima. Consider figure 2.20, which shows the curve of a loss as a function of a model parameter.

Figure 2.20   A local minimum and a global minimum

As you can see, around a certain parameter value, there is a *local minimum*: around that point, moving left would result in the loss increasing, but so would moving right. If the parameter under consideration were being optimized via SGD with a small learning rate, the optimization process could get stuck at the local minimum instead of making its way to the global minimum.

You can avoid such issues by using momentum, which draws inspiration from physics. A useful mental image here is to think of the optimization process as a small ball rolling down the loss curve. If it has enough momentum, the ball won't get stuck in a ravine and will end up at the global minimum. Momentum is implemented by moving the ball at each step based not only on the current slope value (current acceleration) but also on the current velocity (resulting from past acceleration). In practice, this means updating the parameter w based not only on the current gradient value but also on the previous parameter update, such as in this naive implementation:

```
past_velocity <- 0
momentum <- 0.1          Constant momentum factor
repeat {                 Optimization loop
  p <- get_current_parameters()
                         p contains: w, loss, gradient
  if (p$loss <= 0.01)
    break

  velocity <- past_velocity * momentum + learning_rate * p$gradient
  w <- p$w + momentum * velocity - learning_rate * p$gradient

  past_velocity <- velocity
  update_parameter(w)
}
```

2.4.4 *Chaining derivatives: The backpropagation algorithm*

In the preceding algorithm, we casually assumed that because a function is differentiable, we can easily compute its gradient. But is that true? How can we compute the gradient of complex expressions in practice? In the two-layer model we started the chapter with, how can we get the gradient of the loss with regard to the weights? That's where the *backpropagation algorithm* comes in.

THE CHAIN RULE

Backpropagation is a way to use the derivatives of simple operations (such as addition, relu, or tensor product) to easily compute the gradient of arbitrarily complex combinations of these atomic operations. Crucially, a neural network consists of many tensor operations chained together, each of which has a simple, known derivative. For instance, the model defined in listing 2.2 can be expressed as a function parameterized by the variables W1, b1, W2, and b2 (belonging to the first and second Dense layers, respectively), involving the atomic operations dot, relu, softmax, and +, as well as our loss function loss, which are all easily differentiable:

```
loss_value <- loss(y_true,
                   softmax(dot(relu(dot(inputs, W1) + b1), W2) + b2))
```

Calculus tells us that such a chain of functions can be derived using the following identity, called the *chain rule*.

Consider two functions f and g, as well as the composed function fg such that fg(x) == f(g(x)):

```
fg <- function(x) {
  x1 <- g(x)
  y <- f(x1)
  y
}
```

Then the chain rule states that grad(y, x) == grad(y, x1) * grad(x1, x). This enables you to compute the derivative of fg as long as you know the derivatives of f and g. The chain rule is named as it is because when you add more intermediate functions, it starts looking like a chain:

```
fghj <- function(x) {
    x1 <- j(x)
    x2 <- h(x1)
    x3 <- g(x2)
    y  <- f(x3)
    y
}
```

grad(y, x) == (grad(y, x3) * grad(x3, x2) *
➡ grad(x2, x1) * grad(x1, x))

Applying the chain rule to the computation of the gradient values of a neural network gives rise to an algorithm called *backpropagation*. Let's see how that works, concretely.

AUTOMATIC DIFFERENTIATION WITH COMPUTATION GRAPHS

A useful way to think about backpropagation is in terms of *computation graphs*. A computation graph is the data structure at the heart of TensorFlow and the deep learning revolution in general. It's a directed acyclic graph of operations—in our case, tensor operations. For instance, figure 2.21 shows the graph representation of our first model.

Computation graphs have been an extremely successful abstraction in computer science because they enable us to *treat computation as data*: a computable expression is encoded as a machine-readable data structure that can be used as the input or output of

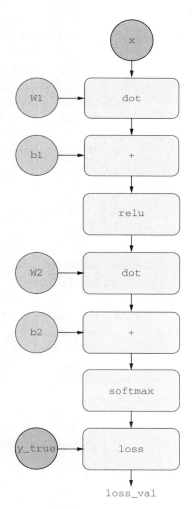

Figure 2.21 The computation graph representation of our two-layer model

another program. For instance, you could imagine a program that receives a computation graph and returns a new computation graph that implements a large-scale distributed version of the same computation. This would mean that you could distribute any computation without having to write the distribution logic yourself. Or imagine a program that receives a computation graph and can automatically generate the derivative of the expression it represents. It's much easier to do these things if your computation is expressed as an explicit graph data structure rather than, say, lines of ASCII characters in a .R file.

To explain backpropagation clearly, let's look at a really basic example of a computation graph (see figure 2.22). We'll consider a simplified version of figure 2.21, where we have only one linear layer and where all variables are scalar. We'll take two scalar variables `w` and `b`, a scalar input `x`, and apply some operations to them to combine them into an output `y`. Finally, we'll apply an absolute value error-loss function: `loss_val = abs(y_true - y)`. Because we want to update `w` and `b` in a way that will minimize `loss_val`, we are interested in computing `grad(loss_val, b)` and `grad(loss_val, w)`.

Let's set concrete values for the "input nodes" in the graph, that is to say, the input `x`, the target `y_true`, `w`, and `b`. We'll propagate these values to all nodes in the graph, from top to bottom, until we reach `loss_val`. This is the *forward pass* (see figure 2.23).

Now let's "reverse" the graph: for each edge in the graph going from `A` to `B`, we will create an opposite edge from `B` to `A`, and ask, how much does `B` vary when `A` varies? That is to say, what is `grad(B, A)`? We'll annotate each inverted edge with this value. This backward graph represents the *backward pass* (see figure 2.24).

We have the following:

- `grad(loss_val, x2) = 1`, because as x2 varies by an amount epsilon, `loss_val = abs (4 - x2)` varies by the same amount.
- `grad(x2, x1) = 1`, because as x1 varies by an amount epsilon, x2 = x1 + b = x1 + 1 varies by the same amount.

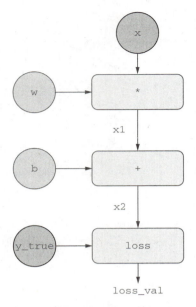

Figure 2.22   A basic example of a computation graph

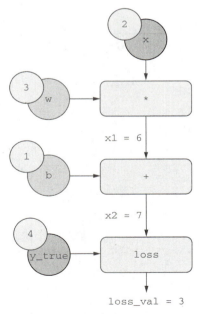

Figure 2.23   Running a forward pass

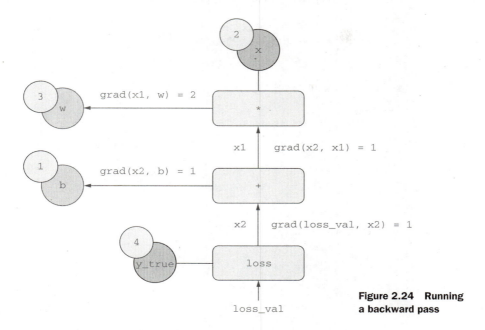

Figure 2.24 Running a backward pass

- `grad(x2, b) = 1`, because as `b` varies by an amount epsilon, `x2 = x1 + b = 6 + b` varies by the same amount.
- `grad(x1, w) = 2`, because as `w` varies by an amount epsilon, `x1 = x * w = 2 * w` varies by 2 * `epsilon`.

What the chain rule says about this backward graph is that you can obtain the derivative of a node with respect to another node by *multiplying the derivatives for each edge along the path linking the two nodes*, for instance, `grad(loss_val, w) = grad(loss_val, x2) * grad(x2, x1) * grad(x1, w)` (see figure 2.25).

By applying the chain rule to our graph, we obtain what we we're looking for:

- `grad(loss_val, w) = 1 * 1 * 2 = 2`
- `grad(loss_val, b) = 1 * 1 = 1`

If there are multiple paths linking the two nodes of interest, a and b, in the backward graph, we would obtain `grad(b, a)` by summing the contributions of all the paths.

And with that, you just saw backpropagation in action! Backpropagation is simply the application of the chain rule to a computation graph. There's nothing more to it. Backpropagation starts with the final loss value and works backward from the top layers to the bottom layers, computing the contribution that each parameter had in the loss value. That's where the name "backpropagation" comes from: we "back-propagate" the loss contributions of different nodes in a computation graph.

Nowadays people implement neural networks in modern frameworks that are capable of *automatic differentiation*, such as TensorFlow. Automatic differentiation is implemented with the kind of computation graph you've just seen. Automatic differentiation

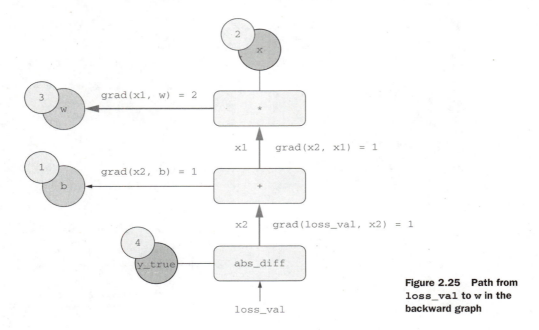

Figure 2.25   Path from `loss_val` to w in the backward graph

makes it possible to retrieve the gradients of arbitrary compositions of differentiable tensor operations without doing any extra work besides writing down the forward pass. When I (François) wrote my first neural networks in C in the 2000s, I had to write my gradients by hand. Now, thanks to modern automatic differentiation tools, you'll never have to implement backpropagation yourself. Consider yourself lucky!

THE GRADIENT TAPE IN TENSORFLOW

The API through which you can leverage TensorFlow's powerful automatic differentiation capabilities is the `GradientTape()`. It's a context manager that will "record" the tensor operations that run inside its scope, in the form of a computation graph (sometimes called a "tape"). This graph can then be used to retrieve the gradient of any output with respect to any variable or set of variables (instances of the TensorFlow `Variable` class). A `tf$Variable` is a specific kind of tensor meant to hold mutable state—for instance, the weights of a neural network are always TensorFlow `Variable` instances:

**Instantiate a scalar Variable
with an initial value of 0.**

Open a GradientTape scope.

```
library(tensorflow)
x <- tf$Variable(0)
with(tf$GradientTape() %as% tape, {
  y <- 2 * x + 3
})
grad_of_y_wrt_x <- tape$gradient(y, x)
```

**Inside the scope, apply some tensor
operations to our variable.**

Exit the scope.

**Use the tape to retrieve the gradient of the
output y with respect to our variable x.**

The GradientTape() works with tensor operations as follows:

**Instantiate a variable with shape (2, 2)
and an initial value of all zeros.**

```
x <- tf$Variable(array(0, dim = c(2, 2)))
with(tf$GradientTape() %as% tape, {
  y <- 2 * x + 3
})
grad_of_y_wrt_x <- as.array(tape$gradient(y, x))
```

**grad_of_y_wrt_x is a tensor of
shape (2, 2) (like x) describing the
curvature of y = 2 * a + 3 around
x = array(0, dim = c(2, 2)).**

Note that tape$gradient() returns a TensorFlow Tensor, which we convert to an R array with as.array(). GradientTape() also works with lists of variables:

```
W <- tf$Variable(random_array(c(2, 2)))
b <- tf$Variable(array(0, dim = c(2)))

x <- random_array(c(2, 2))
with(tf$GradientTape() %as% tape, {
    y <- tf$matmul(x, W) + b
})
grad_of_y_wrt_W_and_b <- tape$gradient(y, list(W, b))
str(grad_of_y_wrt_W_and_b)
```

**matmul is how you say "dot
product" in TensorFlow.**

**grad_of_y_wrt_W_and_b is
a list of two tensors with the
same shapes as W and b,
respectively.**

```
List of 2
 $ :<tf.Tensor: shape=(2, 2), dtype=float64, numpy=…>
 $ :<tf.Tensor: shape=(2), dtype=float64, numpy=array([2., 2.])>
```

You will learn more about the gradient tape in the next chapter.

2.5 Looking back at our first example

You're nearing the end of this chapter, and you should now have a general understanding of what's going on behind the scenes in a neural network. What was a magical black box at the start of the chapter has turned into a clearer picture, as illustrated in figure 2.26: the model, composed of layers that are chained together, maps the

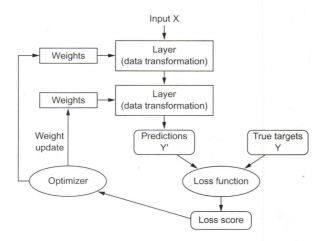

**Figure 2.26 Relationship between
the network, layers, loss function,
and optimizer**

input data to predictions. The loss function then compares these predictions to the targets, producing a loss value: a measure of how well the model's predictions match what was expected. The optimizer uses this loss value to update the model's weights.

Let's go back to the first example in this chapter and review each piece of it in the light of what you've learned since.

This was the input data:

```
library(keras)
mnist <- dataset_mnist()
train_images <- mnist$train$x
train_images <- array_reshape(train_images, c(60000, 28 * 28))
train_images <- train_images / 255

test_images <- mnist$test$x
test_images <- array_reshape(test_images, c(10000, 28 * 28))
test_images <- test_images / 255

train_labels <- mnist$train$y
test_labels <- mnist$test$y
```

Now you understand that the input images are stored in R arrays of shape (60000, 784) (training data) and (10000, 784) (test data) respectively.

This was our model:

```
model <- keras_model_sequential(list(
  layer_dense(units = 512, activation = "relu"),
  layer_dense(units = 10, activation = "softmax")
))
```

Now you understand that this model consists of a chain of two Dense layers, that each layer applies a few simple tensor operations to the input data, and that these operations involve weight tensors. Weight tensors, which are attributes of the layers, are where the *knowledge* of the model persists.

This was the model-compilation step:

```
compile(model,
        optimizer = "rmsprop",
        loss = "sparse_categorical_crossentropy",
        metrics = c("accuracy"))
```

Now you understand that sparse_categorical_crossentropy is the loss function that's used as a feedback signal for learning the weight tensors and which the training phase will attempt to minimize. You also know that this reduction of the loss happens via mini-batch stochastic gradient descent. The exact rules governing a specific use of gradient descent are defined by the rmsprop optimizer passed as the first argument.

Finally, this was the training loop:

```
fit(model, train_images, train_labels, epochs = 5, batch_size = 128)
```

Now you understand what happens when you call `fit`: the model will start to iterate on the training data in mini-batches of 128 samples, five times over (each iteration over all the training data is called an *epoch*). For each batch, the model will compute the gradient of the loss with regard to the weights (using the backpropagation algorithm, which derives from the chain rule in calculus) and move the weights in the direction that will reduce the value of the loss for this batch.

After these five epochs, the model will have performed 2,345 gradient updates (469 per epoch), and the loss of the model will be sufficiently low that the model will be capable of classifying handwritten digits with high accuracy.

At this point, you already know most of what there is to know about neural networks. Let's prove it by reimplementing a simplified version of that first example "from scratch" in TensorFlow, step by step.

2.5.1 *Reimplementing our first example from scratch in TensorFlow*

What better demonstrates full, unambiguous understanding than implementing everything from scratch? Of course, what "from scratch" means here is relative: we won't reimplement basic tensor operations, and we won't implement backpropagation. But we'll go to such a low level that we will barely use any Keras functionality at all.

Don't worry if you don't understand every little detail in this example just yet. The next chapter will dive in more detail into the TensorFlow API. For now, just try to follow the gist of what's going on—the intent of this example is to help crystallize your understanding of the mathematics of deep learning using a concrete implementation. Let's go!

A SIMPLE DENSE CLASS

You've learned earlier that the `Dense` layer implements the following input transformation, where `W` and `b` are model parameters, and `activation()` is an element-wise function (usually `relu()`, but it would be `softmax()` for the last layer):

```
output <- activation(dot(W, input) + b)
```

Let's implement a simple `Dense` layer as a plain R environment with a `class` attribute `NaiveDense`, two TensorFlow variables, `W` and `b`, and a `call()` method that applies the preceding transformation:

```
layer_naive_dense <- function(input_size, output_size, activation) {
  self <- new.env(parent = emptyenv())
  attr(self, "class") <- "NaiveDense"

  self$activation <- activation

  w_shape <- c(input_size, output_size)
  w_initial_value <- random_array(w_shape, min = 0, max = 1e-1)
  self$W <- tf$Variable(w_initial_value)       <-- Create a matrix, W, of shape (input_size,
                                                    output_size), initialized with random values.
  b_shape <- c(output_size)
```

```
    b_initial_value <- array(0, b_shape)
    self$b <- tf$Variable(b_initial_value)
```
◁── Create a vector, b, of shape (output_size), initialized with zeros.

```
    self$weights <- list(self$W, self$b)
```
◁── Convenience property for retrieving all the layer's weights

```
    self$call <- function(inputs) {
      self$activation(tf$matmul(inputs, self$W) + self$b)
    }

    self
}
```
◁── Apply the forward pass in a function named call.

We stick to TensorFlow operations in this function, so that GradientTape can track them. (We'll learn more about TensorFlow operations in chapter 3.)

A SIMPLE SEQUENTIAL CLASS

Now, let's create a `naive_model_sequential()` to chain these layers, as shown in the next code snippet. It wraps a list of layers and exposes a `call()` method that simply calls the underlying layers on the inputs, in order. It also features a `weights` property to easily keep track of the layers' parameters:

```
naive_model_sequential <- function(layers) {
  self <- new.env(parent = emptyenv())
  attr(self, "class") <- "NaiveSequential"

  self$layers <- layers

  weights <- lapply(layers, function(layer) layer$weights)
  self$weights <- do.call(c, weights)
```
◁── Flatten the nested list one level.

```
  self$call <- function(inputs) {
    x <- inputs
    for (layer in self$layers)
      x <- layer$call(x)
    x
  }

  self
}
```

Using this `NaiveDense` class and this `NaiveSequential` class, we can create a mock Keras model:

```
model <- naive_model_sequential(list(
  layer_naive_dense(input_size = 28 * 28, output_size = 512,
                    activation = tf$nn$relu),
  layer_naive_dense(input_size = 512, output_size = 10,
                    activation = tf$nn$softmax)
))
stopifnot(length(model$weights) == 4)
```

A BATCH GENERATOR

Next, we need a way to iterate over the MNIST data in mini-batches. This is easy:

```r
new_batch_generator <- function(images, labels, batch_size = 128) {
  self <- new.env(parent = emptyenv())
  attr(self, "class") <- "BatchGenerator"

  stopifnot(nrow(images) == nrow(labels))
  self$index <- 1
  self$images <- images
  self$labels <- labels
  self$batch_size <- batch_size
  self$num_batches <- ceiling(nrow(images) / batch_size)

  self$get_next_batch <- function() {
    start <- self$index
    if(start > nrow(images))
      return(NULL)                    ←——— Generator is finished.

    end <- start + self$batch_size - 1
    if(end > nrow(images))
      end <- nrow(images)             ←——— Last batch may be smaller.

    self$index <- end + 1
    indices <- start:end
    list(images = self$images[indices, ],
         labels = self$labels[indices])
  }

  self
}
```

2.5.2 Running one training step

The most difficult part of the process is the "training step": updating the weights of the model after running it on one batch of data. We need to do the following:

1. Compute the predictions of the model for the images in the batch.
2. Compute the loss value for these predictions, given the actual labels.
3. Compute the gradient of the loss with regard to the model's weights.
4. Move the weights by a small amount in the direction opposite to the gradient.

To compute the gradient, we will use the TensorFlow `GradientTape` object we introduced in section 2.4.4:

```r
one_training_step <- function(model, images_batch, labels_batch) {
  with(tf$GradientTape() %as% tape, {
    predictions <- model$call(images_batch)        ←
    per_sample_losses <-
      loss_sparse_categorical_crossentropy(labels_batch, predictions)
    average_loss <- mean(per_sample_losses)
  })
```

Run the forward pass (compute the model's predictions under a GradientTape scope).

```
    gradients <- tape$gradient(average_loss, model$weights)
    update_weights(gradients, model$weights)
    average_loss
}
```

Update the weights using the gradients (we will define this function shortly).

Compute the gradient of the loss with regard to the weights. The output gradients is a list where each entry corresponds to a weight from the model$weights list.

As you already know, the purpose of the "weight update" step (represented by the preceding `update_weights()` function) is to move the weights by "a bit" in a direction that will reduce the loss on this batch. The magnitude of the move is determined by the "learning rate," typically a small quantity. The simplest way to implement this `update_weights()` function is to subtract `gradient * learning_rate` from each weight:

```
learning_rate <- 1e-3

update_weights <- function(gradients, weights) {
  stopifnot(length(gradients) == length(weights))
  for (i in seq_along(weights))
    weights[[i]]$assign_sub(
      gradients[[i]] * learning_rate)
}
```

x$assign_sub(value) is the equivalent of x <- x - value for TensorFlow variables.

In practice, you would almost never implement a weight update step like this by hand. Instead, you would use an `Optimizer` instance from Keras:

```
optimizer <- optimizer_sgd(learning_rate = 1e-3)

update_weights <- function(gradients, weights)
    optimizer$apply_gradients(zip_lists(gradients, weights))
```

`zip_lists()` is a helper function that we use to turn the lists of gradients and weights into a list of (gradient, weight) pairs. We use it to pair gradients with weights for the optimizer. For example:

```
str(zip_lists(
  gradients = list("grad_for_wt_1", "grad_for_wt_2", "grad_for_wt_3"),
  weights = list("weight_1", "weight_2", "weight_3")))
```

```
List of 3
 $ :List of 2
  ..$ gradients: chr "grad_for_wt_1"
  ..$ weights  : chr "weight_1"
 $ :List of 2
  ..$ gradients: chr "grad_for_wt_2"
  ..$ weights  : chr "weight_2"
 $ :List of 2
  ..$ gradients: chr "grad_for_wt_3"
  ..$ weights  : chr "weight_3"
```

Now that our per-batch training step is ready, we can move on to implementing an entire epoch of training.

2.5.3 The full training loop

An epoch of training simply consists of repeating the training step for each batch in the training data, and the full training loop is simply the repetition of one epoch:

```
fit <- function(model, images, labels, epochs, batch_size = 128) {
  for (epoch_counter in seq_len(epochs)) {
    cat("Epoch ", epoch_counter, "\n")
    batch_generator <- new_batch_generator(images, labels)
    for (batch_counter in seq_len(batch_generator$num_batches)) {
      batch <- batch_generator$get_next_batch()
      loss <- one_training_step(model, batch$images, batch$labels)
      if (batch_counter %% 100 == 0)
        cat(sprintf("loss at batch %s: %.2f\n", batch_counter, loss))
    }
  }
}
```

Let's test-drive it:

```
mnist <- dataset_mnist()
train_images <- array_reshape(mnist$train$x, c(60000, 28 * 28)) / 255
test_images <- array_reshape(mnist$test$x, c(10000, 28 * 28)) / 255
test_labels <- mnist$test$y
train_labels <- mnist$train$y

fit(model, train_images, train_labels, epochs = 10, batch_size = 128)
```

```
Epoch  1
loss at batch 100: 2.37
loss at batch 200: 2.21
loss at batch 300: 2.15
loss at batch 400: 2.09
Epoch  2
loss at batch 100: 1.98
loss at batch 200: 1.83
loss at batch 300: 1.83
loss at batch 400: 1.75

...

Epoch  9
loss at batch 100: 0.85
loss at batch 200: 0.68
loss at batch 300: 0.83
loss at batch 400: 0.76
Epoch  10
loss at batch 100: 0.80
loss at batch 200: 0.63
loss at batch 300: 0.78
loss at batch 400: 0.72
```

2.5.4 Evaluating the model

We can evaluate the model by taking the `max.col()` of its predictions over the test images, and comparing it to the expected labels:

max.col(x) is a vectorized implementation of apply(x, 1, which.max)).

Convert the TensorFlow Tensor to an R array.

```
predictions <- model$call(test_images)
predictions <- as.array(predictions)       <-
predicted_labels <- max.col(predictions) - 1       <-
```

Subtract 1 because positions are offset from labels by 1, for example, the first position corresponds to digit 0.

```
matches <- predicted_labels == test_labels
cat(sprintf("accuracy: %.2f\n", mean(matches)))
```

```
accuracy: 0.82
```

All done! As you can see, it's quite a bit of work to do "by hand" what you can do in a few lines of Keras code. But because you've gone through these steps, you should now have a crystal-clear understanding of what goes on inside a neural network when you call `fit()`. Having this low-level mental model of what your code is doing behind the scenes will make you better able to leverage the high-level features of the Keras API.

Summary

- Tensors form the foundation of modern machine learning systems. They come in various flavors of type, rank, and shape.
- You can manipulate numerical tensors via tensor operations (such as addition, tensor product, or element-wise multiplication), which can be interpreted as encoding geometric transformations. In general, everything in deep learning is amenable to a geometric interpretation.
- Deep learning models consist of chains of simple tensor operations, parameterized by weights, which are themselves tensors. The weights of a model are where its "knowledge" is stored.
- Learning means finding a set of values for the model's weights that minimizes a loss function for a given set of training data samples and their corresponding targets.
- Learning happens by drawing random batches of data samples and their targets and computing the gradient of the model parameters with respect to the loss on the batch. The model parameters are then moved a bit (the magnitude of the move is defined by the learning rate) in the opposite direction from the gradient. This is called mini-batch stochastic gradient descent.
- The entire learning process is made possible by the fact that all tensor operations in neural networks are differentiable, and thus it's possible to apply the chain rule of derivation to find the gradient function mapping the current parameters and current batch of data to a gradient value. This is called backpropagation.

- Two key concepts you'll see frequently in future chapters are *loss* and *optimizer*. These are the two things you need to define before you begin feeding data into a model:
  - The *loss* is the quantity you'll attempt to minimize during training, so it should represent a measure of success for the task you're trying to solve.
  - The *optimizer* specifies the exact way in which the gradient of the loss will be used to update parameters: for instance, it could be the RMSprop optimizer, SGD with momentum, and so on.

Introduction to
Keras and TensorFlow

This chapter covers

- A closer look at TensorFlow, Keras, and their relationship
- Setting up a deep learning workspace
- An overview of how core deep learning concepts translate to Keras and TensorFlow

This chapter is meant to give you everything you need to start doing deep learning in practice. I'll give you a quick presentation of Keras (https://keras.rstudio.com) and TensorFlow (https://tensorflow.rstudio.com), the R-based deep learning tools that we'll use throughout the book. You'll find out how to set up a deep learning workspace with TensorFlow, Keras, and GPU support. Finally, building on top of the first contact you had with Keras and TensorFlow in chapter 2, we'll review the core components of neural networks and how they translate to the Keras and TensorFlow APIs.

By the end of this chapter, you'll be ready to move on to practical, real-world applications, which will start with chapter 4.

3.1 *What's TensorFlow?*

TensorFlow is a free, open source machine learning platform, developed primarily by Google. Much like R itself, the primary purpose of TensorFlow is to enable scientists, engineers, and researchers to manipulate mathematical expressions over numerical tensors. But TensorFlow brings to R the following new capabilities:

- It can automatically compute the gradient of any differentiable expression (as you saw in chapter 2), making it highly suitable for machine learning.
- It can run not only on CPUs but also on GPUs and TPUs, which are highly parallel hardware accelerators.
- Computation defined in TensorFlow can be easily distributed across many machines.
- TensorFlow programs can be exported to other runtimes, such as C++, Java-Script (for browser-based applications), or TensorFlow Lite (for applications running on mobile devices or embedded devices). This makes TensorFlow applications easy to deploy in practical settings.

It's important to keep in mind that TensorFlow is much more than a single library. It's really a platform, home to a vast ecosystem of components, some developed by Google and some developed by third parties. For instance, there's TF-Agents for reinforcement-learning research, TFX for industry-strength machine learning workflow management, TensorFlow Serving for production deployment, and the TensorFlow Hub repository of pretrained models. Together, these components cover a very wide range of use cases, from cutting-edge research to large-scale production applications.

TensorFlow scales fairly well: for instance, scientists from Oak Ridge National Lab have used it to train a 1.1 exaflops extreme weather forecasting model on the 27,000 GPUs of the IBM Summit supercomputer. Likewise, Google has used TensorFlow to develop very compute-intensive deep learning applications, such as the chess-playing and Go-playing agent AlphaZero. For your own models, if you have the budget, you can realistically hope to scale to around 10 petaflops on a small TPU pod or a large cluster of GPUs rented on Google Cloud or AWS. That would still be around 1% of the peak compute power of the top supercomputer in 2019!

3.2 *What's Keras?*

Keras is a deep learning API, built on top of TensorFlow, that provides a convenient way to define and train any kind of deep learning model. Keras was initially developed for research, with the aim of enabling fast deep learning experimentation.

Through TensorFlow, Keras can run on top of different types of hardware (see figure 3.1)—GPU, TPU, or plain CPU—and can be seamlessly scaled to thousands of machines.

Keras is known for prioritizing the developer experience. It's an API for human beings, not machines. It follows best practices for reducing cognitive load: it offers consistent and simple workflows, it minimizes the number of actions required for

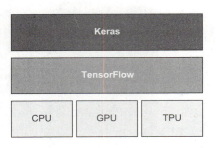

Deep learning development: layers, models, optimizers, losses, metrics...

Tensor manipulation infrastructure: tensors, variables, automatic differentiation, distribution...

Hardware: execution

Figure 3.1   Keras and TensorFlow: TensorFlow is a low-level tensor computing platform, and Keras is a high-level deep learning API.

common use cases, and it provides clear and actionable feedback upon user error. This makes Keras easy to learn for a beginner and highly productive to use for an expert.

Keras has well over a million users as of late 2021, ranging from academic researchers, engineers, and data scientists at both startups and large companies to graduate students and hobbyists. Keras is used at Google, Netflix, Uber, CERN, NASA, Yelp, Instacart, Square, and hundreds of startups working on a wide range of problems across every industry. Your YouTube recommendations originate from Keras models. The Waymo self-driving cars are developed with Keras models. Keras is also a popular framework on Kaggle, the machine learning competition website, where most deep learning competitions have been won using Keras.

Because Keras has a large and diverse user base, it doesn't force you to follow a single "true" way of building and training models. Rather, it enables a wide range of different workflows, from the very high level to the very low level, corresponding to different user profiles. For instance, you have a multitude of ways to build and train models, each representing a certain tradeoff between usability and flexibility. In chapter 5, we'll review in detail a good fraction of this spectrum of workflows. You could be using Keras like you would use most other high-level frameworks—just calling `fit()` and letting the framework do its thing—or you could be using it like you can base R, by taking full control of every little detail.

This means that everything you're learning now as you're getting started will still be relevant once you've become an expert. You can get started easily and then gradually dive into workflows where you're writing more and more logic from scratch. You won't have to switch to an entirely different framework as you go from student to researcher, or from data scientist to deep learning engineer.

This philosophy is not unlike that of R itself! Some languages only offer one way to write programs—for instance, object-oriented programming or functional programming. Meanwhile, R is a multiparadigm language: it offers an array of possible usage patterns that all work nicely together. This makes R suitable to a wide range of very different use cases: data science, machine learning engineering, web development . . . or just learning how to program. Likewise, you can think of Keras as the R of deep learning: a user-friendly deep learning language that offers a variety of workflows to different user profiles.

3.3 Keras and TensorFlow: A brief history

Keras predates TensorFlow by eight months. It was released in March 2015, and TensorFlow was released in November 2015. You may ask, if Keras is built on top of TensorFlow, how it could exist before TensorFlow was released? Keras was originally built on top of Theano, another tensor-manipulation library that provided automatic differentiation and GPU support—the earliest of its kind. Theano, developed at the Montréal Institute for Learning Algorithms (MILA) at the Université de Montréal, was in many ways a precursor of TensorFlow. It pioneered the idea of using static computation graphs for automatic differentiation and for compiling code to both CPU and GPU.

In late 2015, after the release of TensorFlow, Keras was refactored to a multiback-end architecture: it became possible to use Keras with either Theano or TensorFlow, and switching between the two was as easy as changing an environment variable. By September 2016, TensorFlow had reached a level of technical maturity where it became possible to make it the default backend option for Keras. In 2017, two new additional backend options were added to Keras: CNTK (developed by Microsoft) and MXNet (developed by Amazon). Nowadays, both Theano and CNTK are out of development, and MXNet is not widely used outside of Amazon. Keras is back to being a single-backend API—on top of TensorFlow.

Keras and TensorFlow have had a symbiotic relationship for many years. Through-out 2016 and 2017, Keras became well known as the user-friendly way to develop TensorFlow applications, funneling new users into the TensorFlow ecosystem. By late 2017, a majority of TensorFlow users were using it through Keras or in combination with Keras. In 2018, the TensorFlow leadership picked Keras as TensorFlow's official high-level API. As a result, the Keras API is front and center in TensorFlow 2.0, released in September 2019—an extensive redesign of TensorFlow and Keras that takes into account more than four years of user feedback and technical progress.

3.4 Python and R interfaces: A brief history

The R interfaces to TensorFlow and Keras were made available in late 2016 and early 2017, respectively. They are principally developed and maintained by RStudio.

The R interfaces to Keras and TensorFlow are built on top of the reticulate pack-age, which embeds a full Python process in R. For the majority of users, this is merely an implementation detail. However, as you progress on your journey, this setup will turn out to be a great boon, because it means that you have full access to everything available in *both* Python and R.

Throughout the book we use the R interface to Keras that works well with R idi-oms. However, in chapter 13, we show how you can directly use a Python library from R, even if no R interface is conveniently available for it.

By this point, you must be eager to start running Keras and TensorFlow code in practice. Let's get started!

3.5   *Setting up a deep learning workspace*

Before you can get started developing deep learning applications, you need to set up your development environment. It's highly recommended, although not strictly necessary, that you run deep learning code on a modern NVIDIA GPU rather than your computer's CPU. Some applications—in particular, image processing with convolutional networks—will be excruciatingly slow on CPU, even a fast multicore CPU. And even for applications that can realistically be run on CPU, you'll generally see the speed increase by a factor of 5 or 10 by using a recent GPU.

To do deep learning on a GPU, you have the following three options:

- Buy and install a physical NVIDIA GPU on your workstation.
- Use GPU instances on Google Cloud or Amazon EC2.
- Use the free GPU runtime from Kaggle, Colaboratory, or similar providers.

Free online providers like Colaboratory or Kaggle are the easiest way to get started, because they require no hardware purchase and no software installation—just open a tab in your browser and start coding. However, the free version of these services is suitable only for small workloads. If you want to scale up, you'll have to use the first or second option.

If you don't already have a GPU that you can use for deep learning (a recent, high-end NVIDIA GPU), then running deep learning experiments in the cloud is a simple, low-cost way for you to move to larger workloads without having to buy any additional hardware.

If you're a heavy user of deep learning, however, this setup isn't sustainable in the long term—or even for more than a few months. Cloud instances aren't cheap: you'd pay $2.48 per hour for a V100 GPU on Google Cloud in mid-2021. Meanwhile, a solid consumer-class GPU will cost you somewhere between $1,500 and $2,500—a price that has been fairly stable over time, even as the specs of these GPUs keep improving. If you're a heavy user of deep learning, consider setting up a local workstation with one or more GPUs.

Additionally, whether you're running locally or in the cloud, it's better to be using a Unix workstation. Although it's technically possible to run Keras on Windows directly, we don't recommend it. If you're a Windows user and you want to do deep learning on your own workstation, the simplest solution to get everything running is to set up an Ubuntu dual boot on your machine, or to leverage Windows Subsystem for Linux (WSL), a compatibility layer that enables you to run Linux applications from Windows. It may seem like a hassle, but it will save you a lot of time and trouble in the long run.

3.5.1 *Installing Keras and TensorFlow*

Installing Keras and TensorFlow on R on your local machine is straightforward:

1 Make sure you have R installed. The latest instructions for doing so are always available at https://cloud.r-project.org.
2 Install RStudio, available for download at http://mng.bz/v6JM. (You can safely skip this step if you prefer to use R from another environment.)
3 From the R console, run the following commands:

```
install.packages("keras")

library(reticulate)
virtualenv_create("r-reticulate", python = install_python())

library(keras)
install_keras(envname = "r-reticulate")
```

This also pulls in all R dependencies, like reticulate.

Set up R (reticulate) with a Python installation it can use.

Install TensorFlow and Keras (the Python modules).

And that's it! You now have a working Keras and TensorFlow installation.

INSTALLING CUDA

Note that if have a NVIDIA GPU on your machine and you want TensorFlow to use it, you will also need to download and install CUDA, cuDNN, and GPU drivers, all available for download from https://developer.nvidia.com/cuda-downloads and https://developer.nvidia.com/cudnn.

Each version of TensorFlow requires a specific version of CUDA and cuDNN, and it's rarely the case that the latest CUDA version works with the latest TensorFlow version. Typically, you will need to identify the specific CUDA version required by Tensor-Flow and then install it from the CUDA toolkit archive at https://developer.nvidia .com/cuda-toolkit-archive.

You can find the CUDA version required by the current TensorFlow release version by consulting http://mng.bz/44pV. If you are running an older version of TensorFlow, then you can consult the "Tested Build Configurations" table at https://www.tensorflow .org/install/source#gpu to find the entry corresponding to your TensorFlow version.

You can find out the TensorFlow version installed on your machine with:

```
tensorflow::tf_config()
```

```
TensorFlow v2.8.0
 (~/.virtualenvs/r-reticulate/lib/python3.9/site-packages/tensorflow)
Python v3.9 (~/.virtualenvs/r-reticulate/bin/python)
```

At this writing, the latest release of TensorFlow 2.8 requires CUDA 11.2 and cuDNN 8.1.

Note that the shelf life of specific incantations you can run at the terminal to install all the CUDA drivers is very short (not to mention specific to each OS). We don't include any such incantations in the book because they would likely be outdated before the book was even printed. Instead, you can always find the latest instructions at https://tensorflow.rstudio.com/installation/.

You now have a way to start running Keras code in practice. Next, let's see how the key ideas you learned about in chapter 2 translate to Keras and TensorFlow code.

3.6   *First steps with TensorFlow*

As you saw in the previous chapters, training a neural network revolves around the following concepts:

- First, low-level tensor manipulation—the infrastructure that underlies all modern machine learning. This translates to TensorFlow APIs:
  - *Tensors,* including special tensors that store the network's state (*variables*)
  - *Tensor operations* such as addition, `relu`, `matmul`
  - *Backpropagation,* a way to compute the gradient of mathematical expressions (handled in TensorFlow via the `GradientTape` object)
- Second, high-level deep learning concepts. This translates to Keras APIs:
  - *Layers,* which are combined into a *model*
  - A *loss function,* which defines the feedback signal used for learning
  - An *optimizer,* which determines how learning proceeds
  - *Metrics* to evaluate model performance, such as accuracy
  - A *training loop* that performs mini-batch stochastic gradient descent

In the previous chapter, you already had a quick look at some of the corresponding TensorFlow and Keras APIs. You've briefly used TensorFlow's `Variable` class, the `matmul` operation, and the `GradientTape`. You've instantiated Keras dense layers, packed them into a sequential model, and trained that model with the `fit()` method.

Now let's take a deeper dive into how all of these different concepts can be approached in practice using TensorFlow and Keras.

3.6.1   *TensorFlow tensors*

To do anything in TensorFlow, we're going to need some tensors. In the previous chapter, we introduced some tensor concepts and terminology, and used something you may already be familiar with, R arrays, as an example implementation. Here, we move beyond the concepts and introduce the specific implementation of tensors used by TensorFlow.

TensorFlow tensors are very much like R arrays; they are a container for data that also has some metadata, like shape and type. You can convert an R array to a TensorFlow tensor with `as_tensor()`:

```
r_array <- array(1:6, c(2, 3))
tf_tensor <- as_tensor(r_array)
tf_tensor
```

```
tf.Tensor(
[[1 3 5]
 [2 4 6]], shape=(2, 3), dtype=int32)
```

Like R arrays, tensors work with many of the same tensor operations you are already familiar with: functions like `dim()`, `length()`, built-in math generics like + and `log()`, and so on:

```
dim(tf_tensor)
```

```
[1] 2 3
```

```
tf_tensor + tf_tensor
```

```
tf.Tensor(
[[ 2  6 10]
 [ 4  8 12]], shape=(2, 3), dtype=int32)
```

The set of R generics that work with tensors is extensive:

```
methods(class = "tensorflow.tensor")
```

```
 [1] -           !           !=          [           [<-         *
 [7] /           &           %/%         %%          ^           +
[13] <           <=          ==          >           >=          |
[19] abs         acos        all         any         aperm       Arg
[25] asin        atan        cbind       ceiling     Conj        cos
[31] cospi       digamma     dim         exp         expm1       floor
[37] Im          is.finite   is.infinite is.nan      length      lgamma
[43] log         log10       log1p       log2        max         mean
[49] min         Mod         print       prod        range       rbind
[55] Re          rep         round       sign        sin         sinpi
[61] sort        sqrt        str         sum         t           tan
[67] tanpi
```

This means that you can often write the same code for TensorFlow tensors as you would for R arrays.

3.7 Tensor attributes

Unlike R arrays, tensors have some attributes you can access with $:

```
tf_tensor$ndim
```
⟵ **ndim returns a scalar integer, the rank of the tensor, equivalent to length(dim(x)).**

```
[1] 2
```

Length 1 R vectors are automatically converted to rank 0 tensors, whereas R vectors of length > 1 are converted to rank 1 tensors:

```
as_tensor(1)$ndim
```

```
[1] 0
```

```
as_tensor(1:2)$ndim
```

```
[1] 1
```

```
tf_tensor$shape
```

```
TensorShape([2, 3])
```

`tf_tensor$shape` returns a `tf.TensorShape` object. This a class object with support for undefined or unspecified dimensions, and a variety of methods and properties:

```
methods(class = class(shape())[1])
```

```
 [1] !=          [           [[          [[<-        [<-         ==
 [7] as_tensor   as.double   as.integer  as.list     as.numeric  c
[13] format      length      merge       print
```

For now, all you need to know is that you can convert a `TensorShape` to an integer vector with `as.integer()` (`dim(x)` is shorthand for `as.integer(x$shape)`), and you can construct a `TensorShape` object manually with the `shape()` function:

```
shape(2, 3)
```

```
TensorShape([2, 3])
```

```
tf_tensor$dtype
```

```
tf.int32
```

`tf_tensor$dtype` returns the data type of the array. TensorFlow provides support for many more data types than base R. For example, base R has one `integer` type, whereas TensorFlow provides support for 13! The R integer type corresponds to `int32`. Different data types make different tradeoffs between how much memory they can consume and the range of values they can represent. For example, a tensor with a `int8` dtype takes only one-quarter the space in memory as one with dtype `int32`, but it can only represent integers between –128 and 127, as opposed to –2147483648 to 2147483647.

We'll also be dealing with floating-point data throughout the book. In R, the default floating numeric datatype, `double`, is converted to `tf.float64`:

```
r_array <- array(1)
typeof(r_array)
```

```
[1] "double"
```

```
as_tensor(r_array)$dtype
```

```
tf.float64
```

For the majority of the book, we'll be using the smaller `float32` as the default floating point datatype, trading some accuracy for a smaller memory footprint and faster computation speed:

```
as_tensor(r_array, dtype = "float32")
```

```
tf.Tensor([1.], shape=(1), dtype=float32)
```

3.7.1   *Tensor shape and reshaping*

`as_tensor()` can also optionally take a `shape` argument, which you can use to expand a scalar or reshape a tensor. For example, to make an array of zeros, you could write:

```
as_tensor(0, shape = c(2, 3))
```

```
tf.Tensor(
[[0. 0. 0.]
 [0. 0. 0.]], shape=(2, 3), dtype=float32)
```

For R vectors that are not scalars (`length(x) > 1`), you can also reshape the tensor, so long as the overall size of the array stays the same:

```
as_tensor(1:6, shape = c(2, 3))
```

```
tf.Tensor(
[[1 2 3]
 [4 5 6]], shape=(2, 3), dtype=int32)
```

Note that the tensor was filled row-wise. This is different from R, which fills arrays column-wise:

```
array(1:6, dim = c(2, 3))
```

```
     [,1] [,2] [,3]
[1,]    1    3    5
[2,]    2    4    6
```

This difference between row-major and column-major ordering (also known as C and Fortran ordering, respectively) is one of the things to be on the lookout for when converting between R arrays and tensors. R arrays are always Fortran-ordered, and TensorFlow tensors are always C-ordered, and the distinction becomes important anytime you are reshaping an array.

When you are working with tensors, reshaping will use C-style ordering. Anytime you are handling R arrays, you can use `array_reshape()` if you want to be explicit about the reshaping behavior you want:

```
array_reshape(1:6, c(2, 3), order = "C")
```

```
     [,1] [,2] [,3]
[1,]    1    2    3
[2,]    4    5    6
```

```
array_reshape(1:6, c(2, 3), order = "F")
```

```
     [,1] [,2] [,3]
[1,]    1    3    5
[2,]    2    4    6
```

Finally, `array_reshape()` and `as_tensor()` allow you to leave the size of one of the axes unspecified, and it will be automatically inferred using the size of the array and the size of the remaining axes. You can pass -1 or NA for the axis you want inferred:

```
array_reshape(1:6, c(-1, 3))
```

```
     [,1] [,2] [,3]
[1,]    1    2    3
[2,]    4    5    6
```

```
as_tensor(1:6, shape = c(NA, 3))
```

```
tf.Tensor(
[[1 2 3]
 [4 5 6]], shape=(2, 3), dtype=int32)
```

3.7.2   *Tensor slicing*

Subsetting tensors is similar to subsetting R arrays, but not identical. Slicing tensors offers some conveniences that R arrays don't and vice versa.

Tensors allow you to slice with a missing value supplied to one end of a slice range, which implicitly means "the rest of the tensor in that direction" (R arrays don't offer this slicing convenience). For example, revisiting the example in chapter 2 where we want to slice out a crop of the MNIST images, we could have provided an NA to the slice instead:

```
train_images <- as_tensor(dataset_mnist()$train$x)
my_slice <- train_images[, 15:NA, 15:NA]
```

Be aware that the expression 15:NA will produce an R error in other contexts; it works only in the brackets of a tensor slicing operation.

It's also possible to use negative indices. Note that unlike R arrays, negative indices do not drop elements; instead, they indicate the index position relative to the end of the current axis. (Because this is a change from standard R subsetting behavior, a warning is issued the first time a negative slice index is encountered.) To crop the images to patches of 14×14 pixels centered in the middle, you could do this:

```
my_slice <- train_images[, 8:-8, 8:-8]
```

```
Warning:
Negative numbers are interpreted python-style
➥ when subsetting tensorflow tensors.
See ?`[.tensorflow.tensor` for details.
To turn off this warning,
➥ set `options(tensorflow.extract.warn_negatives_pythonic = FALSE)`
```

You can also use the special `all_dims()` object anytime you want to implicitly capture remaining dimensions, without supplying the exact number of commas (,) required in the call to [. For example, say you want to take the first 100 images only, you can write

```
my_slice <- train_images[1:100, all_dims()]
```

instead of

```
my_slice <- train_images[1:100, , ]
```

This comes in handy for writing code that can work with tensors of different ranks, for example, taking matching slices of model inputs and targets along the batch dimension.

3.7.3 Tensor broadcasting

We introduced broadcasting in chapter 2. *Broadcasting* is performed when we have an operation on two different-sized tensors, and we want the smaller tensor to be *broadcast* to match the shape of the larger tensor. Broadcasting consists of the following two steps:

1 Axes (called *broadcast axes*) are added to the smaller tensor to match the `ndim` of the larger tensor.
2 The smaller tensor is repeated alongside these new axes to match the full shape of the larger tensor.

With broadcasting, you can generally perform element-wise operations that take two input tensors if one tensor has shape (a, b, …n, n + 1, …m) and the other has shape (n, n + 1, …m). The broadcasting will then automatically happen for axes a through n - 1.

The following example applies the element-wise + operation to two tensors of different shapes via broadcasting:

```
x <- as_tensor(1, shape = c(64, 3, 32, 10))
y <- as_tensor(2, shape = c(32, 10))
z <- x + y                          ⟵──── The output z has shape (64, 3, 32, 10) like x.
```

Anytime you want to be explicit about broadcasting semantics, you can use a `tf$newaxis` to insert a size 1 dimension in a tensor:

```
z <- x + y[tf$newaxis, tf$newaxis, , ]
```

3.7.4   *The tf module*

Tensors need to be created with some initial value. You can generally stick to as_tensor() for creating tensors, but the tf module also contains many functions for creating tensors. For instance, you could create all-ones or all-zeros tensors, or tensors of values drawn from a random distribution.

```
library(tensorflow)
tf$ones(shape(1, 3))
```

```
tf.Tensor([[1. 1. 1.]], shape=(1, 3), dtype=float32)
```

Tensor of random values drawn from a normal distribution with mean 0 and standard deviation 1. Equivalent to array(rnorm(3 * 1, mean = 0, sd = 1), dim = c(1, 3).

```
tf$zeros(shape(1, 3))
```

```
tf.Tensor([[0. 0. 0.]], shape=(1, 3), dtype=float32)
```

```
tf$random$normal(shape(1, 3), mean = 0, stddev = 1)
```

```
tf.Tensor([[ 0.79165614
  -0.35886717   0.13686056]], shape=(1, 3), dtype=float32)
```

Tensor of random values drawn from a uniform distribution between 0 and 1. Equivalent to array(runif(3 * 1, min = 0, max = 1), dim = c(1, 3)).

```
tf$random$uniform(shape(1, 3))
```

```
tf.Tensor([[0.93715847 0.67879045 0.60081327]], shape=(1, 3), dtype=float32)
```

Note that the tf module exposes the full Python TensorFlow API. One thing to be aware of is that the Python API frequently expects integers, whereas a bare R numeric literal like 2 produces a double instead of an integer. In R, we can specify an integer literal by appending an L, as in 2L.

```
tf$ones(c(2, 1))
```
◁—— Providing R doubles here gives an error.

```
Error in py_call_impl(callable, dots$args, dots$keywords):
  TypeError: Cannot convert [2.0, 1.0] to EagerTensor of dtype int32
```

```
tf$ones(c(2L, 1L))
```
◁—— Provide integer literals to avoid the error.

```
tf.Tensor(
[[1.]
 [1.]], shape=(2, 1), dtype=float32)
```

When dealing with the tf module, we will often write literal integers with an L suffix where the Python API requires it.

Another thing to be aware of is that functions in the tf module use a 0-based index counting convention, that is, the first element of a list is element 0. For example, if you want to take the mean along the first axis of a 2D array (in other words, the column means of a matrix), you would do so like this:

```
m <- as_tensor(1:12, shape = c(3, 4))
tf$reduce_mean(m, axis = 0L, keepdims = TRUE)
```

```
tf.Tensor([[5 6 7 8]], shape=(1, 4), dtype=int32)
```

The corresponding R functions, however, use a 1-based counting convention:

```
mean(m, axis = 1, keepdims = TRUE)
```

```
tf.Tensor([[5 6 7 8]], shape=(1, 4), dtype=int32)
```

You can easily access the help for functions in the `tf` module, right from the RStudio IDE. Press F1 while your cursor is over a function in the `tf` module to open a webpage with the corresponding documentation at www.tensorflow.org.

3.7.5   *Constant tensors and variables*

A significant difference between R arrays and TensorFlow tensors is that TensorFlow tensors aren't modifiable: they're constant. For instance, in R, you can do the following.

Listing 3.1   R arrays are assignable

```
x <- array(1, dim = c(2, 2))
x[1, 1] <- 0
```

Try to do the same thing in TensorFlow, and you will get an error: "EagerTensor object does not support item assignment."

Listing 3.2   TensorFlow tensors are not assignable

```
x <- as_tensor(1, shape = c(2, 2))     This will fail, because a
x[1, 1] <- 0                  ◁─────    tensor isn't modifiable.
```

```
Error in `[<-.tensorflow.tensor`(`*tmp*`, 1, 1, value = 0):
  TypeError: 'tensorflow.python.framework.ops.EagerTensor'
              object does not support item assignment
```

To train a model, we'll need to update its state, which is a set of tensors. If tensors aren't modifiable, how do we do this? That's where *variables* come in. `tf$Variable` is the class meant to manage modifiable state in TensorFlow. You've already briefly seen it in action in the training loop implementation at the end of chapter 2.

To create a variable, you need to provide some initial value, such as a random tensor.

Listing 3.3   Creating a TensorFlow variable

```
v <- tf$Variable(initial_value = tf$random$normal(shape(3, 1)))
v
```

```
<tf.Variable 'Variable:0' shape=(3, 1) dtype=float32, numpy=
array([[-1.1629326 ],
       [ 0.53641343],
       [ 1.4736737 ]], dtype=float32)>
```

The state of a variable can be modified in place via its `assign` method, as follows.

Listing 3.4   Assigning a value to a TensorFlow variable

```
v$assign(tf$ones(shape(3, 1)))
```

```
<tf.Variable 'UnreadVariable' shape=(3, 1) dtype=float32, numpy=
array([[1.],
       [1.],
       [1.]], dtype=float32)>
```

It also works for a subset of the coefficients.

Listing 3.5   Assigning a value to a subset of a TensorFlow variable

```
v[1, 1]$assign(3)
```

```
<tf.Variable 'UnreadVariable' shape=(3, 1) dtype=float32, numpy=
array([[3.],
       [1.],
       [1.]], dtype=float32)>
```

Similarly, `assign_add()` and `assign_sub()` are efficient equivalents of x <- x + value and x <- x - value.

Listing 3.6   Using `assign_add()`

```
v$assign_add(tf$ones(shape(3, 1)))
```

```
<tf.Variable 'UnreadVariable' shape=(3, 1) dtype=float32, numpy=
array([[4.],
       [2.],
       [2.]], dtype=float32)>
```

3.7.6   *Tensor operations: Doing math in TensorFlow*

TensorFlow offers a large collection of tensor operations to express mathematical formulas. Here are a few examples.

Listing 3.7   A few basic math operations

```
Take the square.
   a <- tf$ones(c(2L, 2L))
┌> b <- tf$square(a)
│  c <- tf$sqrt(a)        ◁─────┐  Take the square root.
│  d <- b + c                   │
│                         ◁──── Add two tensors (element-wise).
```

```
e <- tf$matmul(a, b)
e <- e * d
```
Take the product of two tensors (as discussed in chapter 2).

Multiply two tensors (element-wise).

Note that some of these operations are invoked by their corresponding R generics. For example, calling `sqrt(x)` will call `tf$sqrt(x)` if x is a tensor.

Importantly, each of the preceding operations is executed on the fly: at any point, you can print the current result, just like regular R code. We call this *eager execution*.

3.7.7 A second look at the GradientTape API

So far, TensorFlow seems to look a lot like base R, just with different names for functions and some different tensor capabilities. But here's something R can't easily do: retrieve the gradient of any differentiable expression with respect to any of its inputs. Just open a `tf$GradientTape()` scope using `with()`, apply some computation to one or several input tensors, and retrieve the gradient of the result with respect to the inputs.

Listing 3.8 Using the `GradientTape`

```
input_var <- tf$Variable(initial_value = 3)
with(tf$GradientTape() %as% tape, {
  result <- tf$square(input_var)
})
gradient <- tape$gradient(result, input_var)
```

This is most commonly used to retrieve the gradients of the loss of a model with respect to its weights: `gradients <- tape$gradient(loss, weights)`. You saw this in action in chapter 2.

So far, you've only seen the case where the input tensors in `tape$gradient()` were TensorFlow variables. It's actually possible for these inputs to be any arbitrary tensor. However, only *trainable variables* are tracked by default. With a constant tensor, you'd have to manually mark it as being tracked by calling `tape$watch()` on it.

Listing 3.9 Using `GradientTape` with constant tensor inputs

```
input_const <- as_tensor(3)
with(tf$GradientTape() %as% tape, {
  tape$watch(input_const)
  result <- tf$square(input_const)
})
gradient <- tape$gradient(result, input_const)
```

Why is this necessary? Because it would be too expensive to preemptively store the information required to compute the gradient of anything with respect to anything. To avoid wasting resources, the tape needs to know what to watch. Trainable variables are watched by default because computing the gradient of a loss with regard to a list of trainable variables is the most common use of the gradient tape.

The gradient tape is a powerful utility, even capable of computing *second-order gradients*, that is to say, the gradient of a gradient. For instance, the gradient of the position of an object with regard to time is the speed of that object, and the second-order gradient is its acceleration.

If you measure the position of a falling apple along a vertical axis over time and find that it verifies `position(time) = 4.9 * time ^ 2`, what is its acceleration? Let's use two nested gradient tapes to find out.

Listing 3.10   Using nested gradient tapes to compute second-order gradients

```
time <- tf$Variable(0)
with(tf$GradientTape() %as% outer_tape, {        ◁──
  with(tf$GradientTape() %as% inner_tape, {
    position <- 4.9 * time ^ 2
  })
  speed <- inner_tape$gradient(position, time)
})
acceleration <- outer_tape$gradient(speed, time)
acceleration
```

> We use the outer tape to compute the gradient of the gradient from the inner tape. Naturally, the answer is 4.9 * 2 = 9.8.

```
tf.Tensor(9.8, shape=(), dtype=float32)
```

3.7.8   *An end-to-end example: A linear classifier in pure TensorFlow*

You know about tensors, variables, and tensor operations, and you know how to compute gradients. That's enough to build any machine learning model based on gradient descent. And you're only at chapter 3!

In a machine learning job interview, you may be asked to implement a linear classifier from scratch in TensorFlow: a very simple task that serves as a filter between candidates who have some minimal machine learning background and those who don't. Let's get you past that filter and use your newfound knowledge of TensorFlow to implement such a linear classifier.

First, let's come up with some nicely linearly separable synthetic data to work with: two classes of points in a 2D plane. We'll generate each class of points by drawing their coordinates from a random distribution with a specific covariance matrix and a specific mean. Intuitively, the covariance matrix describes the shape of the point cloud, and the mean describes its position in the plane. We'll reuse the same covariance matrix for both point clouds, but we'll use two different mean values—the point clouds will have the same shape, but different positions.

Listing 3.11   Generating two classes of random points in a 2D plane

```
num_samples_per_class <- 1000
Sigma <- rbind(c(1, 0.5),
               c(0.5, 1))
```

```
negative_samples <-
  MASS::mvrnorm(n = num_samples_per_class,
                mu = c(0, 3), Sigma = Sigma)
positive_samples <-
  MASS::mvrnorm(n = num_samples_per_class,
                mu = c(3, 0), Sigma = Sigma)
```

Generate the first class of points: 1,000 random 2D points. Sigma corresponds to an oval-like point cloud oriented from bottom left to top right.

Generate the other class of points with a different mean and the same covariance matrix.

In the preceding code, `negative_samples` and `positive_samples` are both arrays with shape `(1000, 2)`. Let's stack them into a single array with shape `(2000, 2)`.

Listing 3.12   Stacking the two classes into an array with shape (2000, 2)

```
inputs <- rbind(negative_samples, positive_samples)
```

Let's generate the corresponding target labels, an array of zeros and ones of shape `(2000, 1)`, where `targets[i, 1]` is 0 if `inputs[i]` belongs to class 1 (and inversely).

Listing 3.13   Generating the corresponding targets (0 and 1)

```
targets <- rbind(array(0, dim = c(num_samples_per_class, 1)),
                 array(1, dim = c(num_samples_per_class, 1)))
```

Next, let's plot our data.

Listing 3.14   Plotting the two point classes

```
plot(x = inputs[, 1], y = inputs[, 2],
     col = ifelse(targets[, 1] == 0, "purple", "green"))
```

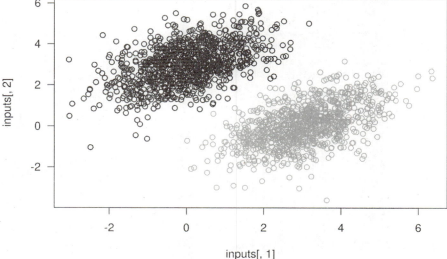

Now let's create a linear classifier that can learn to separate these two blobs. A linear classifier is an affine transformation (prediction = W • input + b) trained to minimize the square of the difference between predictions and the targets. As you'll see, it's actually a much simpler example than the end-to-end example of a toy two-layer neural network you saw at the end of chapter 2. However, this time you should be able to understand everything about the code, line by line.

Let's create our variables, W and b, initialized with random values and with zeros, respectively.

Listing 3.15   Creating the linear classifier variables

The inputs will be 2D points.

The output predictions will be a single score per sample (close to 0 if the sample is predicted to be in class 0, and close to 1 if the sample is predicted to be in class 1).

```
input_dim <- 2
output_dim <- 1
W <- tf$Variable(initial_value =
                     tf$random$uniform(shape(input_dim, output_dim)))
b <- tf$Variable(initial_value = tf$zeros(shape(output_dim)))
```

Here's our forward pass function.

Listing 3.16   The forward pass function

```
model <- function(inputs)
  tf$matmul(inputs, W) + b
```

Because our linear classifier operates on 2D inputs, W is really just two scalar coefficients, w1 and w2: W = [[w1], [w2]]. Meanwhile, b is a single scalar coefficient. As such, for a given input point [x, y], its prediction value is prediction = [[w1], [w2]] • [x, y] + b = w1 * x + w2 * y + b.

The following listing shows our loss function.

Listing 3.17   The mean squared error loss function

per_sample_losses will be a tensor with the same shape as targets and predictions, containing per-sample loss scores.

We need to average these per-sample loss scores into a single scalar loss value: this is what mean() does.

```
square_loss <- function(targets, predictions) {
  per_sample_losses <- (targets - predictions)^2
  mean(per_sample_losses)
}
```

Note that in square_loss(), both targets and predictions can be tensors, but they don't have to be. This is one of the niceties of the R interface—generics like mean(), ^, and - allow you to write the same code for tensors as you would for R arrays. When targets and predictions are tensors, the generics will dispatch to functions in the tf module. We can also write the equivalent square_loss using functions from the tf module directly:

```
square_loss <- function(targets, predictions) {
  per_sample_losses <- tf$square(tf$subtract(targets, predictions))
  tf$reduce_mean(per_sample_losses)
}
```

Next is the training step, which receives some training data and updates the weights `W` and `b` so as to minimize the loss on the data.

Listing 3.18   The training step function

```
learning_rate <- 0.1

training_step <- function(inputs, targets) {
  with(tf$GradientTape() %as% tape, {
    predictions <- model(inputs)
    loss <- square_loss(predictions, targets)
  })
  grad_loss_wrt <- tape$gradient(loss, list(W = W, b = b))
  W$assign_sub(grad_loss_wrt$W * learning_rate)
  b$assign_sub(grad_loss_wrt$b * learning_rate)
  loss
}
```

Forward pass, inside a gradient tape scope

Retrieve the gradient of the loss with regard to weights.

Update the weights.

For simplicity, we'll do *batch training* instead of *mini-batch training*: we'll run each training step (gradient computation and weight update) for all the data, rather than iterate over the data in small batches. On one hand, this means that each training step will take much longer to run, because we'll compute the forward pass and the gradients for 2,000 samples at once. On the other hand, each gradient update will be much more effective at reducing the loss on the training data, because it will encompass information from all training samples instead of, say, only 128 random samples. As a result, we will need many fewer steps of training, and we should use a larger learning rate than we would typically use for mini-batch training (we'll use `learning_rate =` `0.1`, defined in listing 3.18).

Listing 3.19   The batch training loop

```
inputs <- as_tensor(inputs, dtype = "float32")
for (step in seq(40)) {
  loss <- training_step(inputs, targets)
  cat(sprintf("Loss at step %s: %.4f\n", step, loss))
}
```

```
Loss at step 1: 0.7263
Loss at step 2: 0.0911

...

Loss at step 39: 0.0271
Loss at step 40: 0.0269
```

After 40 steps, the training loss seems to have stabilized around 0.025. Let's plot how our linear model classifies the training data points. Because our targets are zeros and ones, a given input point will be classified as 0 if its prediction value is below 0.5, and as 1 if it is above 0.5:

```
predictions <- model(inputs)

inputs <- as.array(inputs)                    Convert tensors to R
predictions <- as.array(predictions)          arrays for plotting.
plot(inputs[, 1], inputs[, 2],
     col = ifelse(predictions[, 1] <= 0.5, "purple", "green"))
```

Recall that the prediction value for a given point [x, y] is simply `prediction == [[w1], [w2]] • [x, y] + b == w1 * x + w2 * y + b`. Thus, class 1 is defined as `(w1 * x + w2 * y + b) < 0.5`, and class 2 is defined as `(w1 * x + w2 * y + b) > 0.5`. You'll notice that what you're looking at is really the equation of a line in the 2D plane: `w1 * x + w2 * y + b = 0.5`. Above the line is class 1, and below the line is class 0. You may be used to seeing line equations in the format `y = a * x + b`; in the same format, our line becomes `y = - w1 / w2 * x + (0.5 - b) / w2`.

Let's plot this line:

```
plot(x = inputs[, 1], y = inputs[, 2],                         Plot our model's
     col = ifelse(predictions[, 1] <= 0.5, "purple", "green"))  predictions.

slope <- -W[1, ] / W[2, ]              These are our line's
intercept <- (0.5 - b) / W[2, ]        equation values.
abline(as.array(intercept), as.array(slope), col = "red")      Plot our line.
```

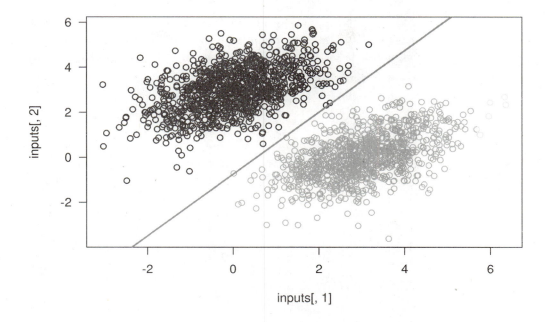

This is really what a linear classifier is all about: finding the parameters of a line (or, in higher-dimensional spaces, a hyperplane) neatly separating two classes of data.

3.8   Anatomy of a neural network: Understanding core Keras APIs

At this point, you know the basics of TensorFlow, and you can use it to implement a toy model from scratch, such as the batch linear classifier in the previous section, or the toy neural network at the end of chapter 2. That's a solid foundation to build upon. It's now time to move on to a more productive, more robust path to deep learning: the Keras API.

3.8.1   Layers: The building blocks of deep learning

The fundamental data structure in neural networks is the *layer*, to which you were introduced in chapter 2. A layer is a data-processing module that takes as input one or more tensors and that outputs one or more tensors. Some layers are stateless, but more frequently layers have a state: the layer's *weights*, one or several tensors learned with stochastic gradient descent, which together contain the network's *knowledge*.

Different types of layers are appropriate for different tensor formats and different types of data processing. For instance, simple vector data, stored in rank 2 tensors of shape (samples, features), is often processed by *densely connected* layers, also called *fully connected* or *dense* layers (built by the layer_dense() function in Keras). Sequence data, stored in rank 3 tensors of shape (samples, timesteps, features), is typically processed by *recurrent* layers, such as an LSTM layer (layer_lstm()), or 1D convolution layers (layer_conv_1d()). Image data, stored in rank 4 tensors, is usually processed by 2D convolution layers (layer_conv_2d()).

You can think of layers as the LEGO bricks of deep learning, a metaphor that is made explicit by Keras. Building deep learning models in Keras is done by clipping together compatible layers to form useful data-transformation pipelines.

THE LAYER CLASS IN KERAS

A simple API should have a single abstraction around which everything is centered. In Keras, that's the `Layer` class. Everything in Keras is either a `Layer` or something that closely interacts with a `Layer`.

A `Layer` is an object that encapsulates some state (weights) and some computation (a forward pass). The weights are typically defined in a `build()` method (although they could also be created in the `initialize()` method), and the computation is defined in the `call()` method.

In the previous chapter, we implemented a `layer_naive_dense()` that contained two weights, `W` and `b`, and applied the computation `output = activation(dot(input, W) + b)`. This is what the same layer would look like in Keras.

Listing 3.20 Implementing a dense layer as a Keras `Layer` class

```
layer_simple_dense <- new_layer_class(
  classname = "SimpleDense",

  initialize = function(units, activation = NULL) {
    super$initialize()
    self$units <- as.integer(units)
    self$activation <- activation
  },

  build = function(input_shape) {                ← Weight creation takes place in the build() method.
    input_dim <- input_shape[length(input_shape)]  ←—— Take the last dim.
    self$W <- self$add_weight(
      shape = c(input_dim, self$units),          ← add_weight() is a shortcut method for creating weights. It is also possible to create standalone variables and assign them as layer attributes, like this: self$W <- tf$Variable(tf$random$normal(w_shape)).
      initializer = "random_normal")
    self$b <- self$add_weight(
      shape = c(self$units),
      initializer = "zeros")
  },

  call = function(inputs) {                      ← We define the forward pass computation in the call() method.
    y <- tf$matmul(inputs, self$W) + self$b
    if (!is.null(self$activation))
      y <- self$activation(y)
    y
  }
)
```

This time, instead of building up an empty R environment, we use the `new_layer_class()` function provided by Keras. `new_layer_class()` returns a layer instance generator, just like `layer_naive_dense()` in chapter 2, but it also provides some additional convenient features for us (like composability with `%>%`, which we'll cover in a moment).

In the next section, we'll cover in detail the purpose of these `build()` and `call()` methods. Don't worry if you don't understand everything just yet!

Layers can be instantiated simply by calling a Keras function that starts with the `layer_` prefix. Then, once instantiated, a layer instance can be used just like a function, taking as input a TensorFlow tensor:

```
my_dense <- layer_simple_dense(units = 32,          Instantiate our layer,
                            activation = tf$nn$relu)  defined previously.
input_tensor <- as_tensor(1, shape = c(2, 784))
output_tensor <- my_dense(input_tensor)              Create some test inputs.
output_tensor$shape
                            Call the layer on the
                        inputs, just like a function.
TensorShape([2, 32])
```

You're probably wondering, why did we have to implement `call()` and `build()`, because we ended up using our layer by plainly calling it? It's because we want to be able to create the state just in time. Let's see how that works.

AUTOMATIC SHAPE INFERENCE: BUILDING LAYERS ON THE FLY

Just like with LEGO bricks, you can only "clip" together layers that are compatible. The notion of *layer compatibility* here refers specifically to the fact that every layer will accept only input tensors of a certain shape and will return output tensors of a certain shape. Consider the following example:

```
layer <- layer_dense(units = 32, activation = "relu")    A dense layer with
                                                          32 output units
```

This layer will return a tensor where the first dimension has been transformed to be 32. It can only be connected to a downstream layer that expects 32-dimensional vectors as its input.

When using Keras, you don't have to worry about size compatibility most of the time, because the layers you add to your models are dynamically built to match the shape of the incoming layer. For instance, suppose you write the following:

```
model <- keras_model_sequential(list(
    layer_dense(units = 32, activation = "relu"),
    layer_dense(units = 32)
))
```

The layers didn't receive any information about the shape of their inputs—instead, they automatically inferred their input shape as being the shape of the first inputs they see. In the toy version of the dense layer we implemented in chapter 2 (which we named `layer_naive_dense()`), we had to pass the layer's input size explicitly to the constructor to be able to create its weights. That's not ideal, because it would lead to models that look like the following code snippet, where each new layer needs to be made aware of the shape of the layer before it:

```
model <- model_naive_sequential(list(
  layer_naive_dense(input_size = 784, output_size = 32,
                    activation = "relu"),
  layer_naive_dense(input_size = 32, output_size = 64,
                    activation = "relu"),
  layer_naive_dense(input_size = 64, output_size = 32,
                    activation = "relu"),
  layer_naive_dense(input_size = 32, output_size = 10,
                    activation = "softmax")
))
```

It would be even worse if the rules used by a layer to produce its output shape are complex. For instance, what if our layer returned outputs of shape `if (input_size %% 2 == 0) c(batch, input_size * 2) else c(input_size * 3)`?

If we were to reimplement `layer_naive_dense()` as a Keras layer capable of automatic shape inference, it would look like the previous `layer_simple_dense()` layer (see listing 3.20), with its `build()` and `call()` methods.

In `layer_simple_dense()`, we no longer create weights in the constructor like in the `layer_naive_dense()` example; instead, we create them in a dedicated state-creation method, `build()`, which receives as an argument the first input shape seen by the layer. The `build()` method is called automatically the first time the layer is called. In fact, the function that's actually called when you call a layer is not `call()` directly but something that optionally first calls `build()` before calling `call()`.

The function that's called when you call a layer schematically looks like this:

```
layer <- function(inputs) {
  if(!self$built) {
    self$build(inputs$shape)
    self$built <- TRUE
  }
  self$call(inputs)
}
```

With automatic shape inference, our previous example becomes simple and neat:

```
model <- keras_model_sequential(list(
  layer_simple_dense(units = 32, activation = "relu"),
  layer_simple_dense(units = 64, activation = "relu"),
  layer_simple_dense(units = 32, activation = "relu"),
  layer_simple_dense(units = 10, activation = "softmax")
))
```

Note that automatic shape inference is not the only thing that the layer class handles. It takes care of many more things, in particular routing between *eager* and *graph* execution (a concept you'll learn about in chapter 7) and input masking (which we'll cover in chapter 11). For now, just remember: when implementing your own layers, put the forward pass in the `call()` method.

Composing layers with %>% (the pipe operator)

Although you can create layer instances directly and manipulate them, most often, all you will want to do is to compose the new layer instance with something, like a sequential model. For this reason, the first argument to all the `layer_` generator functions is `object`. If `object` is supplied, then a new layer instance is created and then immediately composed with `object`.

Previously we built the `keras_model_sequential()` by passing it a list of layers, but we can also build up a model by adding one layer at a time:

```
model <- keras_model_sequential()
layer_simple_dense(model, 32, activation = "relu")
layer_simple_dense(model, 64, activation = "relu")
layer_simple_dense(model, 32, activation = "relu")
layer_simple_dense(model, 10, activation = "softmax")
```

Here, because `model` is supplied as the first argument to `layer_simple_dense()`, the layer is constructed and then composed with the model (by calling `model$add(layer)`). Note that `model` is modified in place—we don't need to save the output of our calls to `layer_simple_dense()` when composing layers this way:

```
length(model$layers)
```

```
[1] 4
```

One subtlety is that when the layer constructor composes a layer with `object`, it returns the result of the composition, not the layer instance. Thus, if a `keras_model_sequential()` is supplied as the first argument, the same model is also returned, except now with one additional layer.

This means you can use the pipe (`%>%`) operator to add layers to a sequential model. This operator comes from the magrittr package; it's shorthand for passing the value on its left as the first argument to the function on its right.

You can use `%>%` with Keras like this:

```
model <- keras_model_sequential() %>%
  layer_simple_dense(32, activation = "relu") %>%
  layer_simple_dense(64, activation = "relu") %>%
  layer_simple_dense(32, activation = "relu") %>%
  layer_simple_dense(10, activation = "softmax")
```

What's the difference between this, and calling `keras_model_sequential()` with a list of layers? There is none—with both approaches you end up with the same model.

Using `%>%` results in code that's more readable and compact, so we'll use this form throughout the book. If you're using RStudio, you can insert `%>%` using the Ctrl-Shift-M keyboard shortcut. To learn more about the pipe operator, see http://r4ds.had.co .nz/pipes.html.

3.8.2   *From layers to models*

A deep learning model is a graph of layers. In Keras, that's the `Model` type. Until now, you've only seen sequential models, which are simple stacks of layers, mapping a single input to a single output. But as you move forward, you'll be exposed to a much broader variety of network topologies. These are some common ones:

- Two-branch networks
- Multihead networks
- Residual connections

Network topology can get quite involved. For instance, figure 3.2 shows the topology of the graph of layers of a Transformer, a common architecture designed to process text data.

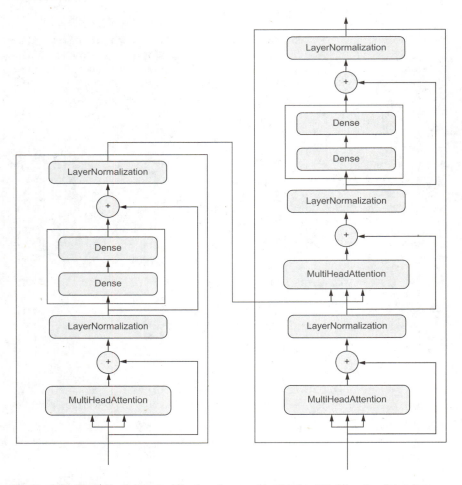

Figure 3.2   The Transformer architecture (covered in chapter 11). There's a lot going on here. Throughout the next few chapters, you'll climb your way up to understanding it.

There are generally two ways of building such models in Keras: you could directly define a `new_model_class()`, or you could use the Functional API, which lets you do more with less code. We'll cover both approaches in chapter 7.

The topology of a model defines a *hypothesis space.* You may remember that in chapter 1 we described machine learning as searching for useful representations of some input data, within a predefined *space of possibilities,* using guidance from a feedback signal. By choosing a network topology, you constrain your space of possibilities (hypothesis space) to a specific series of tensor operations, mapping input data to output data. What you'll then be searching for is a good set of values for the weight tensors involved in these tensor operations.

To learn from data, you have to make assumptions about it. These assumptions define what can be learned. As such, the structure of your hypothesis space—the architecture of your model—is extremely important. It encodes the assumptions you make about your problem—the prior knowledge that the model starts with. For instance, if you're working on a two-class classification problem with a model made of a single `layer_dense()` with no activation (a pure affine transformation), you are assuming that your two classes are linearly separable.

Picking the right network architecture is more an art than a science, and although you can rely on some best practices and principles, only practice can help you become a proper neural network architect. The next few chapters will both teach you explicit principles for building neural networks and help you develop intuition as to what works or doesn't work for specific problems. You'll build a solid intuition about what type of model architectures work for different kinds of problems, how to build these networks in practice, how to pick the right learning configuration, and how to tweak a model until it yields the results you want to see.

3.8.3 The "compile" step: Configuring the learning process

Once the model architecture is defined, you still have to choose three more things:

- *Loss function (objective function)*—The quantity that will be minimized during training. It represents a measure of success for the task at hand.
- *Optimizer*—Determines how the network will be updated based on the loss function. It implements a specific variant of stochastic gradient descent (SGD).
- *Metrics*—The measures of success you want to monitor during training and validation, such as classification accuracy. Unlike the loss, training will not optimize directly for these metrics. As such, metrics don't need to be differentiable.

Once you've picked your loss, optimizer, and metrics, you can use the `compile()` and `fit()` methods to start training your model. Alternatively, you could also write your own custom training loops—we'll cover how to do this in chapter 7. It's a lot more work! For now, let's take a look at `compile()` and `fit()`.

The `compile()` method configures the training process—you've already been introduced to it in your very first neural network example in chapter 2. It takes the arguments `optimizer`, `loss`, and `metrics`:

Define a linear classifier.

Specify the optimizer by name: RMSprop (case-insensitive).

```
model <- keras_model_sequential() %>% layer_dense(1)
model %>% compile(optimizer = "rmsprop",
                  loss = "mean_squared_error",
                  metrics = "accuracy")
```

Specify the loss by name: mean squared error.

Specify (potentially multiple) metrics: in this case, only accuracy.

In-place modification of models

We're using the `%>%` operator to call `compile()`. We could have written the network compilation step:

```
compile(model,
        optimizer = "rmsprop",
        loss = "mean_squared_error",
        metrics = "accuracy")
```

Using `%>%` for `compile` is less about compactness and more about providing a syntactic reminder of an important characteristic of Keras models: unlike most objects you work with in R, Keras models are modified in place. This is because Keras models are directed acyclic graphs of layers whose state is updated during training. You don't operate on network and then return a new network object. Rather, you do *something* to the network object. Placing the network to the left of `%>%` and not saving the results to a new variable signals to the reader that you're modifying in place.

In the preceding call to `compile()`, we passed the optimizer, loss, and metrics as strings (such as `"rmsprop"`). These strings are actually shortcuts that are converted to R objects. For instance, `"rmsprop"` becomes `optimizer_rmsprop()`. Importantly, it's also possible to specify these arguments as object instances:

```
model %>% compile(
  optimizer = optimizer_rmsprop(),
  loss = loss_mean_squared_error(),
  metrics = metric_binary_accuracy()
)
```

This is useful if you want to pass your own custom losses or metrics, or if you want to further configure the objects you're using—for instance, by passing a `learning_rate` argument to the optimizer:

```
model %>% compile(
  optimizer = optimizer_rmsprop(learning_rate = 1e-4),
  loss = my_custom_loss,
  metrics = c(my_custom_metric_1, my_custom_metric_2)
)
```

In chapter 7, we'll cover how to create custom losses and metrics. In general, you won't have to create your own losses, metrics, or optimizers from scratch, because Keras offers a wide range of built-in options that is likely to include what you need.

Optimizers:

```
ls(pattern = "^optimizer_", "package:keras")
```

```
[1] "optimizer_adadelta" "optimizer_adagrad"  "optimizer_adam"
[4] "optimizer_adamax"   "optimizer_nadam"    "optimizer_rmsprop"
[7] "optimizer_sgd"
```

Losses:

```
ls(pattern = "^loss_", "package:keras")
```

```
 [1] "loss_binary_crossentropy"
 [2] "loss_categorical_crossentropy"
 [3] "loss_categorical_hinge"
 [4] "loss_cosine_proximity"
 [5] "loss_cosine_similarity"
 [6] "loss_hinge"
 [7] "loss_huber"
 [8] "loss_kl_divergence"
 [9] "loss_kullback_leibler_divergence"
[10] "loss_logcosh"
[11] "loss_mean_absolute_error"
[12] "loss_mean_absolute_percentage_error"
[13] "loss_mean_squared_error"
[14] "loss_mean_squared_logarithmic_error"
[15] "loss_poisson"
[16] "loss_sparse_categorical_crossentropy"
[17] "loss_squared_hinge"
```

Metrics:

```
ls(pattern = "^metric_", "package:keras")
```

```
 [1] "metric_accuracy"
 [2] "metric_auc"
 [3] "metric_binary_accuracy"
 [4] "metric_binary_crossentropy"
 [5] "metric_categorical_accuracy"
 [6] "metric_categorical_crossentropy"
 [7] "metric_categorical_hinge"
 [8] "metric_cosine_proximity"
 [9] "metric_cosine_similarity"
[10] "metric_false_negatives"
[11] "metric_false_positives"
[12] "metric_hinge"
[13] "metric_kullback_leibler_divergence"
[14] "metric_logcosh_error"
[15] "metric_mean"
```

```
[16] "metric_mean_absolute_error"
[17] "metric_mean_absolute_percentage_error"
[18] "metric_mean_iou"
[19] "metric_mean_relative_error"
[20] "metric_mean_squared_error"
[21] "metric_mean_squared_logarithmic_error"
[22] "metric_mean_tensor"
[23] "metric_mean_wrapper"
[24] "metric_poisson"
[25] "metric_precision"
[26] "metric_precision_at_recall"
[27] "metric_recall"
[28] "metric_recall_at_precision"
[29] "metric_root_mean_squared_error"
[30] "metric_sensitivity_at_specificity"
[31] "metric_sparse_categorical_accuracy"
[32] "metric_sparse_categorical_crossentropy"
[33] "metric_sparse_top_k_categorical_accuracy"
[34] "metric_specificity_at_sensitivity"
[35] "metric_squared_hinge"
[36] "metric_sum"
[37] "metric_top_k_categorical_accuracy"
[38] "metric_true_negatives"
[39] "metric_true_positives"
```

Throughout this book, you'll see concrete applications of many of these options.

3.8.4   *Picking a loss function*

Choosing the right loss function for the right problem is extremely important: your network will take any shortcut it can to minimize the loss, so if the objective doesn't fully correlate with success for the task at hand, your network will end up doing things you may not have wanted. Imagine a stupid, omnipotent AI trained via SGD with this poorly chosen objective function: "maximizing the average well-being of all humans alive." To make its job easier, this AI might choose to kill all humans except a few and focus on the well-being of the remaining ones, because average well-being isn't affected by how many humans are left. That might not be what you intended! Just remember that all neural networks you build will be just as ruthless in lowering their loss function, so choose the objective wisely, or you'll have to face unintended side effects.

Fortunately, when it comes to common problems such as classification, regression, and sequence prediction, you can follow simple guidelines to choose the correct loss. For instance, you'll use binary cross-entropy for a two-class classification problem, categorical cross-entropy for a many-class classification problem, and so on. Only when you're working on truly new research problems will you have to develop your own loss functions. In the next few chapters, we'll detail explicitly which loss functions to choose for a wide range of common tasks.

3.8.5 Understanding the fit() method

After `compile()` comes `fit()`. The `fit()` method implements the training loop itself. These are its key arguments:

- The *data* (inputs and targets) to train on. It will typically be passed either in the form of R arrays, tensors, or a TensorFlow Dataset object. You'll learn more about the `tfdatasets` API in the next chapters.
- The number of *epochs* to train for: how many times the training loop should iterate over the data passed.
- The batch size to use within each epoch of mini-batch gradient descent: the number of training examples considered to compute the gradients for one weight update step.

Listing 3.21 Calling `fit()` with R arrays

The input examples, as an R array

The corresponding training targets, as an R array

```
history <- model %>%
  fit(inputs,
      targets,
      epochs = 5,
      batch_size = 128)
```

The training loop will iterate over the data five times.

The training loop will iterate over the data in batches of 128 examples.

The call to `fit()` returns a `history` object. This object contains a `metrics` property, which is a named list of their per-epoch values for `"loss"` and specific metric names:

```
str(history$metrics)
```

```
List of 2
 $ loss           : num [1:5] 14.2 13.6 13.1 12.6 12.1
 $ binary_accuracy: num [1:5] 0.55 0.552 0.554 0.557 0.559
```

3.8.6 Monitoring loss and metrics on validation data

The goal of machine learning is not to obtain models that perform well on the training data, which is easy—all you have to do is follow the gradient. The goal is to obtain models that perform well in general, and particularly on data points that the model has never encountered before. Just because a model performs well on its training data doesn't mean it will perform well on data it has never seen! For instance, it's possible that your model could end up merely *memorizing* a mapping between your training samples and their targets, which would be useless for the task of predicting targets for data the model has never seen before. We'll go over this point in much more detail in chapter 5.

To keep an eye on how the model does on new data, it's standard practice to reserve a subset of the training data as *validation data*: you won't be training the model on this data, but you will use it to compute a loss value and metrics value. You do this by using the `validation_data` argument in `fit()`. Like the training data, the validation data could be passed as R arrays or as a TensorFlow `Dataset` object.

Listing 3.22   Using the `validation_data` argument

```
model <- keras_model_sequential() %>%
  layer_dense(1)

model %>% compile(optimizer_rmsprop(learning_rate = 0.1),
                  loss = loss_mean_squared_error(),
                  metrics = metric_binary_accuracy())

n_cases <- dim(inputs)[1]
num_validation_samples <- round(0.3 * n_cases)
val_indices <-
  sample.int(n_cases, num_validation_samples)

val_inputs <- inputs[val_indices, ]
val_targets <- targets[val_indices, , drop = FALSE]
training_inputs <- inputs[-val_indices, ]
training_targets <-
  targets[-val_indices, , drop = FALSE]

model %>% fit(
  training_inputs,
  training_targets,
  epochs = 5,
  batch_size = 16,
  validation_data = list(val_inputs, val_targets)
)
```

Reserve 30% of the training inputs and targets for validation (we'll exclude these samples from training and reserve them to compute the validation loss and metrics).

Generate num_validation_samples random integers, in the range of [1, n_cases].

Pass drop = FALSE to prevent the R array [method from dropping the size-1 dimension, and instead return an array with shape (num_validation_samples, 1).

Training data, used to update the weights of the model

Validation data, used only to monitor the validation loss and metrics

The value of the loss on the validation data is called the *validation loss*, to distinguish it from the *training loss*. Note that it's essential to keep the training data and validation data strictly separate: the purpose of validation is to monitor whether what the model is learning is actually useful on new data. If any of the validation data has been seen by the model during training, your validation loss and metrics will be flawed.

Note that if you want to compute the validation loss and metrics after the training is complete, you can call the `evaluate()` method:

```
loss_and_metrics <- evaluate(model, val_inputs, val_targets,
                             batch_size = 128)
```

`evaluate()` will iterate in batches (of size `batch_size`) over the data passed and return numeric vector, where the first entry is the validation loss and the following entries are the validation metrics. If the model has no metrics, only the validation loss is returned (an R vector of length 1).

3.8.7 *Inference: Using a model after training*

Once you've trained your model, you're going to want to use it to make predictions on new data. This is called *inference*. To do this, a naive approach would simply be to call the model:

```
predictions <- model(new_inputs)
```
◁—┘ **Take an R array or TensorFlow tensor and returns a TensorFlow tensor.**

However, this will process all inputs in `new_inputs` at once, which may not be feasible if you're looking at a lot of data (in particular, it may require more memory than your GPU has).

A better way to do inference is to use the `predict()` method. It will iterate over the data in small batches and return an R array of predictions. And unlike calling the model, it can also process TensorFlow `Dataset` objects:

```
predictions <- model %>%
  predict(new_inputs, batch_size = 128)
```
◁—┘ **Take an R array or a TF Dataset and return an R array.**

For instance, if we use `predict()` on some of our validation data with the linear model we trained earlier, we get scalar scores that correspond to the model's prediction for each input sample:

```
predictions <- model %>%
  predict(val_inputs, batch_size = 128)
head(predictions, 10)
```

```
              [,1]
 [1,]  -0.11416233
 [2,]   0.43776459
 [3,]  -0.02436411
 [4,]  -0.19723934
 [5,]  -0.24584538
 [6,]  -0.18628466
 [7,]  -0.06967193
 [8,]   0.19761485
 [9,]  -0.28266442
[10,]   0.43299851
```

For now, this is all you need to know about Keras models. You are ready to move on to solving real-world machine learning problems with Keras in the next chapter.

Summary

- TensorFlow is an industry-strength numerical computing framework that can run on CPU, GPU, or TPU. It can automatically compute the gradient of any differentiable expression, it can be distributed to many devices, and it can export programs to various external runtimes—even JavaScript.
- Keras is the standard API for doing deep learning with TensorFlow. It's what we'll use throughout this book.

- Key TensorFlow objects include tensors, variables, tensor operations, and the gradient tape.
- The central type in Keras is the Layer. A *layer* encapsulates some weights and some computation. Layers are assembled into *models*.
- Before you start training a model, you need to pick an *optimizer*, a *loss*, and some *metrics*, which you specify via the model %>% compile() method.
- To train a model, you can use the fit() method, which runs mini-batch gradient descent for you. You can also use it to monitor your loss and metrics on *validation data*, a set of inputs that the model doesn't see during training.
- Once your model is trained, you use the model %>% predict() method to generate predictions on new inputs.

Getting started with neural networks: Classification and regression

This chapter is designed to get you started using neural networks to solve real problems. You'll consolidate the knowledge you gained from chapters 2 and 3, and you'll apply what you've learned to the following three new tasks covering the three most common use cases of neural networks:

- Classifying movie reviews as positive or negative (binary classification)
- Classifying news wires by topic (multiclass classification)
- Estimating the price of a house, given real estate data (scalar regression)

These examples will be your first contact with end-to-end machine learning workflows: you'll be introduced to data preprocessing, basic model architecture principles, and model evaluation.

Classification and regression glossary

Classification and regression involve many specialized terms. You've come across some of them in earlier examples, and you'll see more of them in future chapters. They have the following precise, machine learning–specific definitions, and you should be familiar with them:

- *Sample or input*—One data point that goes into your model.
- *Prediction or output*—What comes out of your model.
- *Target*—The truth. What your model should ideally have predicted, according to an external source of data.
- *Prediction error or loss value*—A measure of the distance between your model's prediction and the target.
- *Classes*—A set of possible labels to choose from in a classification problem. For example, when classifying cat and dog pictures, "dog" and "cat" are the two classes.
- *Label*—A specific instance of a class annotation in a classification problem. For instance, if picture #1234 is annotated as containing the class "dog," then "dog" is a label of picture #1234.
- *Ground-truth or annotations*—All targets for a dataset, typically collected by humans.
- *Binary classification*—A classification task where each input sample should be categorized into two exclusive categories.
- *Multiclass classification*—A classification task where each input sample should be categorized into more than two categories, for instance, classifying handwritten digits.
- *Multilabel classification*—A classification task where each input sample can be assigned multiple labels. For instance, a given image may contain both a cat and a dog and should be annotated with both the "cat" label and the "dog" label. The number of labels per image is usually variable.
- *Scalar regression*—A task where the target is a continuous scalar value. Predicting house prices is a good example: the different target prices form a continuous space.
- *Vector regression*—A task where the target is a set of continuous values, for example, a continuous vector. If you're doing regression against multiple values (such as the coordinates of a bounding box in an image), then you're doing vector regression.
- *Mini-batch or batch*—A small set of samples (typically between 8 and 128) that are processed simultaneously by the model. The number of samples is often a power of 2, to facilitate memory allocation on GPU. When training, a mini-batch is used to compute a single gradient descent update applied to the weights of the model.

By the end of this chapter, you'll be able to use neural networks to handle simple classification and regression tasks over vector data. You'll then be ready to start building a more principled, theory-driven understanding of machine learning in chapter 5.

4.1 Classifying movie reviews: A binary classification example

Two-class classification, or binary classification, is one of the most common kinds of machine learning problems. In this example, you'll learn to classify movie reviews as positive or negative, based on the text content of the reviews.

4.1.1 The IMDB dataset

You'll work with the *IMDB dataset*: a set of 50,000 highly polarized reviews from the Internet Movie Database. They're split into 25,000 reviews for training and 25,000 reviews for testing, each set consisting of 50% negative and 50% positive reviews.

Just like the MNIST dataset, the IMDB dataset comes packaged with Keras. It has already been preprocessed: the reviews (sequences of words) have been turned into sequences of integers, where each integer stands for a specific word in a dictionary. This enables us to focus on model building, training, and evaluation. In chapter 11, you'll learn how to process raw text input from scratch.

The following code will load the dataset (when you run it the first time, about 80 MB of data will be downloaded to your machine).

> **Listing 4.1   Loading the IMDB dataset**

```
library(keras)

imdb <- dataset_imdb(num_words = 10000)
c(c(train_data, train_labels), c(test_data, test_labels)) %<-% imdb
```

> **Using the multiassignment (%<-%) operator**
>
> The datasets built into Keras are all nested lists of training and test data. Here, we use the multiassignment operator (`%<-%`) from the zeallot package to unpack the list into a set of distinct variables. This could equally be written as follows:
>
> ```
> imdb <- dataset_imdb(num_words = 10000)
> train_data <- imdb$train$x
> train_labels <- imdb$train$y
> test_data <- imdb$test$x
> test_labels <- imdb$test$y
> ```
>
> The multiassignment version is preferable because it's more compact. The `%<-%` operator is automatically available whenever the R Keras package is attached.

The argument `num_words = 10000` means you'll keep only the top 10,000 most frequently occurring words in the training data. Rare words will be discarded. This allows us to work with vector data of manageable size. If we didn't set this limit, we'd be working with 88,585 unique words in the training data, which is unnecessarily large. Many of these words occur only in a single sample and thus can't be meaningfully used for classification.

The variables train_data and test_data are lists of reviews; each review is a list of word indices (encoding a sequence of words). train_labels and test_labels are lists of 0s and 1s, where 0 stands for *negative* and 1 stands for *positive*:

```
str(train_data)
```

```
List of 25000
 $ : int [1:218] 1 14 22 16 43 530 973 1622 1385 65 ...
 $ : int [1:189] 1 194 1153 194 8255 78 228 5 6 1463 ...
 $ : int [1:141] 1 14 47 8 30 31 7 4 249 108 ...
 $ : int [1:550] 1 4 2 2 33 2804 4 2040 432 111 ...
 $ : int [1:147] 1 249 1323 7 61 113 10 10 13 1637 ...
 $ : int [1:43] 1 778 128 74 12 630 163 15 4 1766 ...
 $ : int [1:123] 1 6740 365 1234 5 1156 354 11 14 5327 ...
 $ : int [1:562] 1 4 2 716 4 65 7 4 689 4367 ...
  [list output truncated]
```

```
str(train_labels)
```

```
int [1:25000] 1 0 0 1 0 0 1 0 1 0 ...
```

Because we're restricting ourselves to the top 10,000 most frequent words, no word index will exceed 10,000:

```
max(sapply(train_data, max))
```

```
[1] 9999
```

For kicks, here's how you can quickly decode one of these reviews back to English words.

Listing 4.2   Decoding reviews back to text

word_index is a named vector mapping words to an integer index.

Reverses it, mapping integer indices to words

Decodes the review. Note that the indices are offset by 3 because 0, 1, and 2 are reserved indices for "padding," "start of sequence," and "unknown."

```
word_index <- dataset_imdb_word_index()

reverse_word_index <- names(word_index)
names(reverse_word_index) <- as.character(word_index)

decoded_words <- train_data[[1]] %>%
  sapply(function(i) {
    if (i > 3) reverse_word_index[[as.character(i - 3)]]
    else "?"
    })
decoded_review <- paste0(decoded_words, collapse = " ")
cat(decoded_review, "\n")
```

```
? this film was just brilliant casting location scenery story direction
everyone's really suited the part they played and you could just imagine
being there robert ? is an amazing actor and now the same being director …
```

4.1.2   *Preparing the data*

You can't directly feed lists of integers into a neural network. They all have different lengths, but a neural network expects to process contiguous batches of data. You have to turn your lists into tensors. You can do that in the following two ways:

- Pad your lists so that they all have the same length, turn them into an integer tensor of shape `(samples, max_length)`, and start your model with a layer capable of handling such integer tensors (the `Embedding` layer, which we'll cover in detail later in the book).
- *Multi-hot encode* your lists to turn them into vectors of 0s and 1s. This would mean, for instance, turning the sequence `[8, 5]` into a 10,000-dimensional vector that would be all 0s except for indices 8 and 5, which would be 1s. Then you could use a `layer_dense()`, capable of handling floating-point vector data, as the first layer in your model.

Let's go with the latter solution to vectorize the data, which you'll do manually for maximum clarity.

> **Listing 4.3   Encoding the integer sequences via multi-hot encoding**

```
vectorize_sequences <- function(sequences, dimension = 10000) {
  results <- array(0, dim = c(length(sequences), dimension))
  for (i in seq_along(sequences)) {
    sequence <- sequences[[i]]
    for (j in sequence)
      results[i, j] <- 1
  }
  results
}
x_train <- vectorize_sequences(train_data)
x_test <- vectorize_sequences(test_data)
```

Create an all-zero matrix of shape (length(sequences), dimension).

Set specific indices of results to 1s.

Vectorize training data.

Vectorize test data.

Here's what the samples look like now:

```
str(x_train)
```

```
num [1:25000, 1:10000] 1 1 1 1 1 1 1 1 1 1 ...
```

You should also vectorize your labels, which is a straightforward cast of integers to floats:

```
y_train <- as.numeric(train_labels)
y_test <- as.numeric(test_labels)
```

Now the data is ready to be fed into a neural network.

4.1.3   Building your model

The input data is vectors, and the labels are scalars (1s and 0s): this is one of the simplest problem setups you'll ever encounter. A type of model that performs well on such a problem is a plain stack of densely connected layers (`layer_dense()`) with `relu` activations.

You need to make two key architecture decisions about such a stack of dense layers:

- How many layers to use
- How many units to choose for each layer

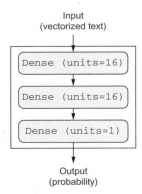

Figure 4.1   The three-layer model

In chapter 5, you'll learn formal principles to guide you in making these choices. For the time being, you'll have to trust me with the following architecture choices:

- Two intermediate layers with 16 units each
- A third layer that will output the scalar prediction regarding the sentiment of the current review

Figure 4.1 shows what the model looks like. And the following listing shows the Keras implementation, similar to the MNIST example you saw previously.

Listing 4.4   Model definition

```
model <- keras_model_sequential() %>%
  layer_dense(16, activation = "relu") %>%
  layer_dense(16, activation = "relu") %>%
  layer_dense(1, activation = "sigmoid")
```

The first argument being passed to each `layer_dense()` is the number of *units* in the layer: the dimensionality of representation space of the layer. Remember from chapters 2 and 3 that each such `layer_dense()` with a `relu` activation implements the following chain of tensor operations:

```
output <- relu(dot(input, W) + b)
```

Having 16 units means the weight matrix `W` will have shape `(input_dimension, 16)`: the dot product with `W` will project the input data onto a 16-dimensional representation space (and then you'll add the bias vector `b` and apply the `relu` operation). You can intuitively understand the dimensionality of your representation space as "how much freedom you're allowing the model to have when learning internal representations." Having more units (a higher-dimensional representation space) allows your model to learn more complex representations, but it makes the model more computationally expensive and may lead to learning unwanted patterns (patterns that will improve performance on the training data but not on the test data).

The intermediate layers use `relu` as their activation function, and the final layer uses a sigmoid activation so as to output a probability (a score between 0 and 1 indicating how likely the sample is to have the target "1": how likely the review is to be positive). A `relu` (rectified linear unit) is a function meant to zero out negative values (see figure 4.2), whereas a `sigmoid` "squashes" arbitrary values into the `[0, 1]` interval (see figure 4.3), outputting something that can be interpreted as a probability.

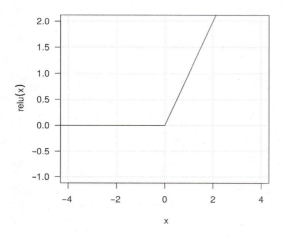

Figure 4.2   The `relu` function

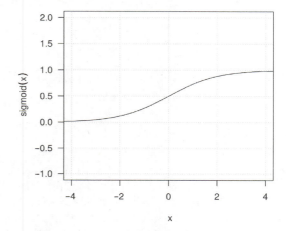

Figure 4.3   The `sigmoid` function

What are activation functions, and why are they necessary?

Without an activation function like `relu` (also called a *nonlinearity*), `layer_dense` would consist of two linear operations—a dot product and an addition:

```
output <- dot(input, W) + b
```

The layer could learn only *linear transformations* (affine transformations) of the input data: the *hypothesis space* of the layer would be the set of all possible linear transformations of the input data into a 16-dimensional space. Such a hypothesis space is too restricted and wouldn't benefit from multiple layers of representations, because a deep stack of linear layers would still implement a linear operation: adding more layers wouldn't extend the hypothesis space (as you saw in chapter 2).

To get access to a much richer hypothesis space that will benefit from deep representations, you need a nonlinearity, or activation function. `relu` is the most popular activation function in deep learning, but many other candidates exist, which all come with similarly strange names: `prelu`, `elu`, and so on.

Finally, you need to choose a loss function and an optimizer. Because you're facing a binary classification problem and the output of your model is a probability (you end your model with a single-unit layer with a sigmoid activation), it's best to use the `binary_crossentropy` loss. It isn't the only viable choice: for instance, you could use mean_squared_error. But cross-entropy is usually the best choice when you're dealing with models that output probabilities. *Cross-entropy* is a quantity from the field of information theory that measures the distance between probability distributions or, in this case, between the ground-truth distribution and your predictions. As for the choice of the optimizer, we'll go with rmsprop, which is a usually a good default choice for virtually any problem.

Here's the step where we configure the model with the rmsprop optimizer and the binary_crossentropy loss function. Note that we'll also monitor accuracy during training.

Listing 4.5   Compiling the model

```
model %>% compile(optimizer = "rmsprop",
                  loss = "binary_crossentropy",
                  metrics = "accuracy")
```

4.1.4   Validating your approach

As you learned in chapter 3, a deep learning model should never be evaluated on its training data—it's standard practice to use a validation set to monitor the accuracy of the model during training. Here, we'll create a validation set by setting apart 10,000 samples from the original training data.

Listing 4.6   Setting aside a validation set

```
x_val <- x_train[seq(10000), ]
partial_x_train <- x_train[-seq(10000), ]
y_val <- y_train[seq(10000)]
partial_y_train <- y_train[-seq(10000)]
```

We will now train the model for 20 epochs (20 iterations over all samples in the training data) in mini-batches of 512 samples. At the same time, we will monitor loss and accuracy on the 10,000 samples that we set apart. We do so by passing the validation data as the validation_data argument.

Listing 4.7   Training your model

```
history <- model %>% fit(
  partial_x_train,
  partial_y_train,
  epochs = 20,
  batch_size = 512,
  validation_data = list(x_val, y_val)
)
```

On a CPU, this will take less than 2 seconds per epoch—training is over in 20 seconds. At the end of every epoch is a slight pause as the model computes its loss and accuracy on the 10,000 samples of the validation data.

Note that the call to `model %>% fit()` returns a `history` object, as you saw in chapter 3. This object has a member `metrics`, which is a named list containing data about everything that happened during training. Let's look at it:

```
str(history$metrics)
```

```
List of 4
 $ loss        : num [1:20] 0.526 0.326 0.241 0.191 0.154 ...
 $ accuracy    : num [1:20] 0.799 0.899 0.921 0.937 0.951 ...
 $ val_loss    : num [1:20] 0.415 0.327 0.286 0.276 0.285 ...
 $ val_accuracy: num [1:20] 0.857 0.876 0.891 0.89 0.886 ...
```

The `metrics` list contains four entries: one per metric that was being monitored during training and during validation. We'll use the `plot()` method for the history object to plot the training and validation loss side by side, as well as the training and validation accuracy (see figure 4.4). Note that your own results may vary slightly due to a different random initialization of your model.

```
plot(history)
```

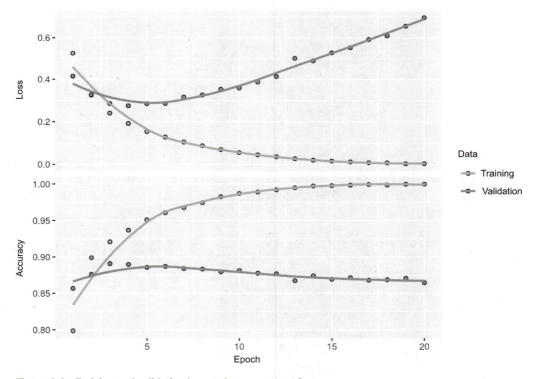

Figure 4.4 Training and validation loss and accuracy metrics

As you can see, the training loss decreases with every epoch, and the training accuracy increases with every epoch. That's what you would expect when running gradient descent optimization—the quantity you're trying to minimize should be less with every iteration. But that isn't the case for the validation loss and accuracy: they seem to peak at the fourth epoch. This is an example of what we warned against earlier: a model that performs better on the training data isn't necessarily a model that will do better on data it has never seen before. In precise terms, what you're seeing is *overfitting*: after the fourth epoch, you're overoptimizing on the training data, and you end up learning representations that are specific to the training data and don't generalize to data outside of the training set.

Training history plot() method

The `plot()` method for training history objects uses `ggplot2` for plotting if it's available (if it isn't, base graphics are used). The plot includes all specified metrics as well as the loss; it draws a smoothing line if there are 10 or more epochs. You can customize all of this behavior via various arguments to the `plot()` method. If you want to create a custom visualization, call the `as.data.frame()` method on `history` to obtain a data frame with factors for each metric as well as training versus validation:

```
history_df <- as.data.frame(history)
str(history_df)

'data.frame':   80 obs. of  4 variables:
 $ epoch : int  1 2 3 4 5 6 7 8 9 10 ...
 $ value : num  0.526 0.326 0.241 0.191 0.154 ...
 $ metric: Factor w/ 2 levels "loss","accuracy": 1 1 1 1 1 1 1 1 1 1 ...
 $ data  : Factor w/ 2 levels "training","validation": 1 1 1 1 1 1 1 ...
```

In this case, to prevent overfitting, you could stop training after four epochs. In general, you can use a range of techniques to mitigate overfitting, which we'll cover in chapter 5. Let's train a new model from scratch for four epochs and then evaluate it on the test data.

Listing 4.8   Retraining a model from scratch

```
model <- keras_model_sequential() %>%
  layer_dense(16, activation = "relu") %>%
  layer_dense(16, activation = "relu") %>%
  layer_dense(1, activation = "sigmoid")

model %>% compile(optimizer = "rmsprop",
                  loss = "binary_crossentropy",
                  metrics = "accuracy")

model %>% fit(x_train, y_train, epochs = 4, batch_size = 512)
results <- model %>% evaluate(x_test, y_test)
```

The final results are as follows:

```
results
```

```
      loss   accuracy
0.2999835 0.8819600
```

The first number, 0.29, is the test loss, and the second number, 0.88, is the test accuracy.

This fairly naive approach achieves an accuracy of 88%. With state-of-the-art approaches, you should be able to get close to 95%.

4.1.5 *Using a trained model to generate predictions on new data*

After having trained a model, you'll want to use it in a practical setting. You can generate the likelihood of reviews being positive by using the `predict()` method, as you learned in chapter 3:

```
model %>% predict(x_test)
```

```
           [,1]
[1,]  0.20960191
[2,]  0.99959260
[3,]  0.93098557
[4,]  0.83782458
[5,]  0.94010764
[6,]  0.79225385
[7,]  0.99964178
[8,]  0.01294626
 ...
```

As you can see, the model is confident for some samples (0.99 or more, or 0.01 or less) but less confident for others (0.6, 0.4).

4.1.6 *Further experiments*

The following experiments will help convince you that the architecture choices you've made are all fairly reasonable, although there's still room for improvement:

- You used two representation layers before the final classification layer. Try using one or three representation layers, and see how doing so affects validation and test accuracy.
- Try using layers with more units or fewer units: 32 units, 64 units, and so on.
- Try using the `mse` loss function instead of `binary_crossentropy`.
- Try using the `tanh` activation (an activation that was popular in the early days of neural networks) instead of `relu`.

4.1.7 *Wrapping up*

Here's what you should take away from this example:

- You usually need to do quite a bit of preprocessing on your raw data to be able to feed it—as tensors—into a neural network. Sequences of words can be encoded as binary vectors, but other encoding options are also available.

- Stacks of `layer_dense()` with `relu` activations can solve a wide range of problems (including sentiment classification), and you'll likely use them frequently.
- In a binary classification problem (two output classes), your model should end with a `layer_dense()` with one unit and a `sigmoid` activation: the output of your model should be a scalar between 0 and 1, encoding a probability.
- With such a scalar sigmoid output on a binary classification problem, the loss function you should use is `binary_crossentropy`.
- The `rmsprop` optimizer is generally a good enough choice, whatever your problem. That's one less thing for you to worry about.
- As they get better on their training data, neural networks eventually start overfitting and end up obtaining increasingly worse results on data they've never seen before. Be sure to always monitor performance on data that is outside of the training set.

4.2   *Classifying newswires: A multiclass classification example*

In the previous section, you saw how to classify vector inputs into two mutually exclusive classes using a densely connected neural network. But what happens when you have more than two classes?

In this section, we'll build a model to classify Reuters newswires into 46 mutually exclusive topics. Because we have many classes, this problem is an instance of *multiclass classification*, and because each data point should be classified into only one category, the problem is more specifically an instance of *single-label multiclass classification*. If each data point could belong to multiple categories (in this case, topics), we'd be facing a *multilabel multiclass classification* problem.

4.2.1   *The Reuters dataset*

You'll work with the *Reuters dataset*, a set of short newswires and their topics, published by Reuters in 1986. It's a simple, widely used toy dataset for text classification. The dataset contains 46 different topics; some topics are more represented than others, but each topic has at least 10 examples in the training set. Like IMDB and MNIST, the Reuters dataset comes packaged as part of Keras. Let's take a look.

> **Listing 4.9   Loading the Reuters dataset**

```
reuters <- dataset_reuters(num_words = 10000)
c(c(train_data, train_labels), c(test_data, test_labels)) %<-% reuters
```

As with the IMDB dataset, the argument `num_words = 10000` restricts the data to the 10,000 most frequently occurring words found in the data. You have 8,982 training examples and 2,246 test examples:

```
length(train_data)
```

```
[1] 8982
```

```
length(test_data)
```

```
[1] 2246
```

As with the IMDB reviews, each example is a list of integers (word indices):

```
str(train_data)
```

```
List of 8982
 $ : int [1:87] 1 2 2 8 43 10 447 5 25 207 ...
 $ : int [1:56] 1 3267 699 3434 2295 56 2 7511 9 56 ...
 $ : int [1:139] 1 53 12 284 15 14 272 26 53 959 ...
 $ : int [1:224] 1 4 686 867 558 4 37 38 309 2276 ...
 $ : int [1:101] 1 8295 111 8 25 166 40 638 10 436 ...
 $ : int [1:116] 1 4 37 38 309 213 349 1632 48 193 ...
 $ : int [1:100] 1 56 5539 925 149 8 16 23 931 3875 ...
 $ : int [1:100] 1 53 648 26 14 749 26 39 6207 5466 ...
 [list output truncated]
```

Here's how you can decode it back to words, in case you're curious.

Listing 4.10   Decoding newswires back to text

```
word_index <- dataset_reuters_word_index()

reverse_word_index <- names(word_index)
names(reverse_word_index) <- as.character(word_index)

decoded_words <- train_data[[1]] %>%                    Note that the indices
  sapply(function(i) {                                  are offset by 3 because
    if (i > 3) reverse_word_index[[as.character(i - 3)]]  ◁─  0, 1, and 2 are reserved
    else "?"                                            indices for "padding,"
    })                                                  "start of sequence,"
decoded_review <- paste0(decoded_words, collapse = " ")  and "unknown."
decoded_review
```

```
[1] "? ? ? said as a result of its december acquisition of space co it
➥ expects …"
```

The label associated with an example is an integer between 0 and 45—a topic index:

```
str(train_labels)
```

```
int [1:8982] 3 4 3 4 4 4 4 3 3 16 ...
```

4.2.2   *Preparing the data*

You can vectorize the data with the same approach as in the previous example.

Listing 4.11   Encoding the input data

```
vectorize_sequences <- function(sequences, dimension = 10000) {
  results <- matrix(0, nrow = length(sequences), ncol = dimension)
```

```
  for (i in seq_along(sequences))
    results[i, sequences[[i]]] <- 1
  results
}

x_train <- vectorize_sequences(train_data)   ⊲──┐  Vectorized training data
x_test <- vectorize_sequences(test_data)      ⊲──── Vectorized test data
```

To vectorize the labels, you have two possibilities: you can cast the label list as an integer tensor, or you can use *one-hot encoding*. One-hot encoding is a widely used format for categorical data, also called *categorical encoding*. In this case, one-hot encoding of the labels consists of embedding each label as an all-zero vector with a 1 in the place of the label index. The following listing shows an example.

> **Listing 4.12   Encoding the labels**

```
to_one_hot <- function(labels, dimension = 46) {
  results <- matrix(0, nrow = length(labels), ncol = dimension)
  labels <- labels + 1             ⊲──┐
  for(i in seq_along(labels)) {        │  Vectorized training labels
    j <- labels[[i]]
    results[i, j] <- 1
  }
  results
}
y_train <- to_one_hot(train_labels)   ⊲──┐  Vectorized test labels
y_test <- to_one_hot(test_labels)     ⊲──── Labels are 0-based
```

Note that there is a built-in way to do this in Keras:

```
y_train <- to_categorical(train_labels)
y_test <- to_categorical(test_labels)
```

4.2.3   *Building your model*

This topic-classification problem looks similar to the previous movie-review classification problem: in both cases, we're trying to classify short snippets of text. But there is a new constraint here: the number of output classes has gone from 2 to 46. The dimensionality of the output space is much larger.

In a stack of `layer_dense()`s like those we've been using, each layer can access only information present in the output of the previous layer. If one layer drops some information relevant to the classification problem, this information can never be recovered by later layers: each layer can potentially become an information bottleneck. In the previous example, we used 16-dimensional intermediate layers, but a 16-dimensional space may be too limited to learn to separate 46 different classes: such small layers may act as information bottlenecks, permanently dropping relevant information. For this reason we'll use larger layers. Let's go with 64 units.

Listing 4.13   Model definition

```
model <- keras_model_sequential() %>%
  layer_dense(64, activation = "relu") %>%
  layer_dense(64, activation = "relu") %>%
  layer_dense(46, activation = "softmax")
```

You should note two other things about this architecture. First, we end the model with a layer_dense() of size 46. This means for each input sample, the network will output a 46-dimensional vector. Each entry in this vector (each dimension) will encode a different output class.

Second, the last layer uses a softmax activation. You saw this pattern in the MNIST example. It means the model will output a *probability distribution* over the 46 different output classes—for every input sample, the model will produce a 46-dimensional output vector, where output[i] is the probability that the sample belongs to class i. The 46 scores will sum to 1.

The best loss function to use in this case is categorical_crossentropy. It measures the distance between two probability distributions: here, between the probability distribution output by the model and the true distribution of the labels. By minimizing the distance between these two distributions, you train the model to output something as close as possible to the true labels.

Listing 4.14   Compiling the model

```
model %>% compile(optimizer = "rmsprop",
                  loss = "categorical_crossentropy",
                  metrics = "accuracy")
```

4.2.4   Validating your approach

Let's set apart 1,000 samples in the training data to use as a validation set.

Listing 4.15   Setting aside a validation set

```
val_indices <- 1:1000

x_val <- x_train[val_indices, ]
partial_x_train <- x_train[-val_indices, ]

y_val <- y_train[val_indices, ]
partial_y_train <- y_train[-val_indices, ]
```

Now let's train the model for 20 epochs.

Listing 4.16   Training the model

```
history <- model %>% fit(
  partial_x_train,
```

```
    partial_y_train,
    epochs = 20,
    batch_size = 512,
    validation_data = list(x_val, y_val)
)
```

And finally, let's display its loss and accuracy curves (see figure 4.5).

Listing 4.17   Plotting the training and validation loss and accuracy

```
plot(history)
```

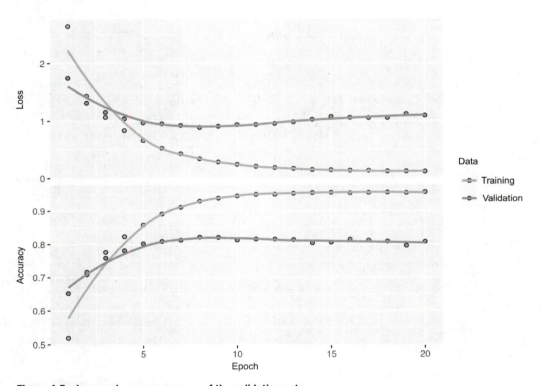

Figure 4.5   Loss and accuracy curves of the validation set

The model begins to overfit after nine epochs. Let's train a new model from scratch for nine epochs and then evaluate it on the test set.

Listing 4.18   Retraining a model from scratch

```
model <- keras_model_sequential() %>%
  layer_dense(64, activation = "relu") %>%
  layer_dense(64, activation = "relu") %>%
  layer_dense(46, activation = "softmax")
```

```
model %>% compile(optimizer = "rmsprop",
                  loss = "categorical_crossentropy",
                  metrics = "accuracy")

model %>% fit(x_train, y_train, epochs = 9, batch_size = 512)

results <- model %>% evaluate(x_test, y_test)
```

Here are the final results:

```
results
```

```
    loss  accuracy
0.9562974 0.7898486
```

This approach reaches an accuracy of ~80%. With a balanced binary classification problem, the accuracy reached by a purely random classifier would be 50%. But in this case, we have 46 classes, and they may not be equally represented. What would be the accuracy of a random baseline? We could try quickly checking this empirically:

```
mean(test_labels == sample(test_labels))
```

```
[1] 0.190561
```

As you can see, a random classifier would score around 19% classification accuracy, so the results of our model seem pretty good in that light.

4.2.5   Generating predictions on new data

Calling the model's predict() method on new samples returns a class probability distribution over all 46 topics for each sample. Let's generate topic predictions for all of the test data:

```
predictions <- model %>% predict(x_test)
```

Each entry (row) in "predictions" is a vector of length 46:

```
str(predictions)
```

```
num [1:2246, 1:46] 0.0000873 0.0013171 0.0094679 0.0001123 0.0001032 ...
```

The coefficients in this vector sum to 1, because they form a probability distribution:

```
sum(predictions[1, ])
```

```
[1] 1
```

The largest entry is the predicted class—the class with the highest probability:

```
which.max(predictions[1, ])
```

```
[1] 5
```

4.2.6   *A different way to handle the labels and the loss*

We mentioned earlier that another way to encode the labels would be to preserve their integer values, like this:

```
y_train <- train_labels
y_test <- test_labels
```

The only thing this approach would change is the choice of the loss function. The loss function used in listing 4.18, `categorical_crossentropy`, expects the labels to follow a categorical encoding. With integer labels, you should use `sparse_categorical_crossentropy`:

```
model %>% compile(
  optimizer = "rmsprop",
  loss = "sparse_categorical_crossentropy",
  metrics = "accuracy")
```

This new loss function is still mathematically the same as `categorical_crossentropy`; it just has a different interface.

4.2.7   *The importance of having sufficiently large intermediate layers*

We mentioned earlier that because the final outputs are 46-dimensional, you should avoid intermediate layers with many fewer than 46 units. Now let's see what happens when we introduce an information bottleneck by having intermediate layers that are significantly less than 46-dimensional: for example, 4-dimensional.

> **Listing 4.19   A model with an information bottleneck**

```
model <- keras_model_sequential() %>%
  layer_dense(64, activation = "relu") %>%
  layer_dense(4, activation = "relu") %>%
  layer_dense(46, activation = "softmax")

model %>% compile(optimizer = "rmsprop",
                  loss = "categorical_crossentropy",
                  metrics = "accuracy")

model %>% fit(
  partial_x_train,
  partial_y_train,
  epochs = 20,
```

```
    batch_size = 128,
    validation_data = list(x_val, y_val)
)
```

The model now peaks at ~71% validation accuracy, an 8% absolute drop. This drop is mostly because we're trying to compress a lot of information (enough information to recover the separation hyperplanes of 46 classes) into an intermediate space that is too low-dimensional. The model is able to cram *most* of the necessary information into these 4-dimensional representations, but not all of it.

4.2.8 Further experiments

Like in the previous example, I encourage you to try out the following experiments to train your intuition about the kind of configuration decisions you have to make with such models:

- Try using larger or smaller layers: 32 units, 128 units, and so on.
- You used two intermediate layers before the final softmax classification layer. Now try using a single intermediate layer, or three intermediate layers.

4.2.9 Wrapping up

Here's what you should take away from this example: if you're trying to classify data points among *N* classes, your model should end with a `layer_dense()` of size *N*.

In a single-label, multiclass classification problem, your model should end with a `softmax` activation so that it will output a probability distribution over the *N* output classes.

`categorical_crossentropy` is almost always the loss function you should use for such problems. It minimizes the distance between the probability distributions output by the model and the true distribution of the targets.

You can handle labels in multiclass classification in the following two ways:

- Encode the labels via categorical encoding (also known as one-hot encoding) and use `categorical_crossentropy` as a loss function.
- Encode the labels as integers and use the `sparse_categorical_crossentropy` loss function.

If you need to classify data into a large number of categories, you should avoid creating information bottlenecks in your model due to intermediate layers that are too small.

4.3 Predicting house prices: A regression example

The two previous examples were considered classification problems, where the goal was to predict a single discrete label of an input data point. Another common type of machine learning problem is *regression*, which consists of predicting a continuous value instead of a discrete label, for instance, predicting the temperature tomorrow, given meteorological data, or predicting the time that a software project will take to complete, given its specifications.

Don't confuse *regression* with the *logistic regression* algorithm. Confusingly, logistic regression isn't a regression algorithm—it's a classification algorithm.

4.3.1 *The Boston housing price dataset*

In this section, we'll attempt to predict the median price of homes in a given Boston suburb in the mid-1970s, given data points about the suburb at the time, such as the crime rate, the local property tax rate, and so on. The dataset we'll use has an interesting difference from the two previous examples. It has relatively few data points: only 506, split between 404 training samples and 102 test samples. And each *feature* in the input data (e.g., the crime rate) has a different scale. For instance, some values are proportions, which take values between 0 and 1, others take values between 1 and 12, others between 0 and 100, and so on.

Listing 4.20   Loading the Boston housing dataset

```
boston <- dataset_boston_housing()
c(c(train_data, train_targets), c(test_data, test_targets)) %<-% boston
```

Let's look at the data:

```
str(train_data)
```

```
num [1:404, 1:13] 1.2325 0.0218 4.8982 0.0396 3.6931 ...
```

```
str(test_data)
```

```
num [1:102, 1:13] 18.0846 0.1233 0.055 1.2735 0.0715 ...
```

As you can see, we have 404 training samples and 102 test samples, each with 13 numerical features, such as per capita crime rate, average number of rooms per dwelling, accessibility to highways, and so on. The targets are the median values of owner-occupied homes, in thousands of dollars:

```
str(train_targets)
```

```
num [1:404(1d)] 15.2 42.3 50 21.1 17.7 18.5 11.3 15.6 15.6 14.4 ...
```

The prices are typically between $10,000 and $50,000. If that sounds cheap, remember that this was the mid-1970s, and these prices aren't adjusted for inflation.

4.3.2 *Preparing the data*

It would be problematic to feed into a neural network values that all take wildly different ranges. The model might be able to automatically adapt to such heterogeneous data, but it would definitely make learning more difficult. A widespread best practice for dealing with such data is to do feature-wise normalization: for each feature in the input data (a column in the input data matrix), we subtract the mean of the feature and divide by the standard deviation, so that the feature is centered around 0 and has a unit standard deviation. This is easily done in R using the `scale()` function.

Listing 4.21 Normalizing the data

```
mean <- apply(train_data, 2, mean)
sd <- apply(train_data, 2, sd)
train_data <- scale(train_data, center = mean, scale = sd)
test_data <- scale(test_data, center = mean, scale = sd)
```

Note that the quantities used for normalizing the test data are computed using the training data. You should never use any quantity computed on the test data in your workflow, even for something as simple as data normalization.

4.3.3 Building your model

Because so few samples are available, we'll use a very small model with two intermediate layers, each with 64 units. In general, the less training data you have, the worse overfitting will be, and using a small model is one way to mitigate overfitting.

Listing 4.22 Model definition

```
build_model <- function() {          ◁─────┐   Because we need to instantiate the same model
                                            │   multiple times, we use a function to construct it.
  model <- keras_model_sequential() %>%
    layer_dense(64, activation = "relu") %>%
    layer_dense(64, activation = "relu") %>%
    layer_dense(1)

  model %>% compile(optimizer = "rmsprop",
                    loss = "mse",
                    metrics = "mae")
  model
}
```

The model ends with a single unit and no activation (it will be a linear layer). This is a typical setup for scalar regression (a regression where you're trying to predict a single continuous value). Applying an activation function would constrain the range the output can take: for instance, if you applied a `sigmoid` activation function to the last layer, the model could learn to predict values only between 0 and 1. Here, because the last layer is purely linear, the model is free to learn to predict values in any range.

Note that we compile the model with the `mse` loss function—*mean squared error* (MSE), the square of the difference between the predictions and the targets. This is a widely used loss function for regression problems.

We're also monitoring a new metric during training: *mean absolute error* (MAE). It's the absolute value of the difference between the predictions and the targets. For instance, an MAE of 0.5 on this problem would mean your predictions are off by $500 on average.

4.3.4   Validating your approach using K-fold validation

To evaluate our model while we keep adjusting its parameters (such as the number of epochs used for training), we could split the data into a training set and a validation set, as we did in the previous examples. But because we have so few data points, the validation set would end up being very small (e.g., about 100 examples). As a consequence, the validation scores might change a lot depending on which data points we chose for validation and which we chose for training: the validation scores might have a high *variance* with regard to the validation split. This would prevent us from reliably evaluating our model.

The best practice in such situations is to use *K*-fold cross-validation (see figure 4.6).

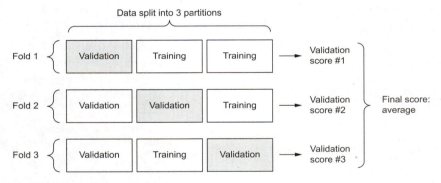

Figure 4.6   *K*-fold cross-validation with K = 3

It consists of splitting the available data into *K* partitions (typically *K* = 4 or 5), instantiating *K* identical models, and training each one on *K*– 1 partitions while evaluating on the remaining partition. The validation score for the model used is then the average of the *K* validation scores obtained. In terms of code, this is straightforward.

Listing 4.23   *K*-fold validation

```
k <- 4
fold_id <- sample(rep(1:k, length.out = nrow(train_data)))
num_epochs <- 100
all_scores <- numeric()

for (i in 1:k) {
  cat("Processing fold #", i, "\n")
```

```
  val_indices <- which(fold_id == i)
```
**Prepare the validation data:
data from partition #k.**
```
  val_data <- train_data[val_indices, ]
  val_targets <- train_targets[val_indices]

  partial_train_data <- train_data[-val_indices, ]
  partial_train_targets <- train_targets[-val_indices]
```
**Prepare the training
data: data from all
other partitions.**
```
  model <- build_model()
```
**Build the Keras model
(already compiled).**
```
  model %>% fit(
    partial_train_data,
    partial_train_targets,
    epochs = num_epochs,
    batch_size = 16,
    verbose = 0
  )
```
**Train the model (in silent
mode, verbose = 0).**
```
  results <- model %>%
    evaluate(val_data, val_targets, verbose = 0)
  all_scores[[i]] <- results[['mae']]
}
```
**Evaluate the model on
the validation data.**

```
Processing fold # 1
Processing fold # 2
Processing fold # 3
Processing fold # 4
```

Running this with num_epochs = 100 yields the following results:

```
all_scores
```

```
[1] 2.435980 2.165334 2.252230 2.362636
```

```
mean(all_scores)
```

```
[1] 2.304045
```

The different runs do indeed show rather different validation scores, from 2.1 to 2.4. The average (2.3) is a much more reliable metric than any single score—that's the entire point of *K*-fold cross-validation. In this case, we're off by $2,300 on average, which is significant considering that the prices range from $10,000 to $50,000.

Let's try training the model a bit longer: 500 epochs. To keep a record of how well the model does at each epoch, we'll modify the training loop to save the per-epoch validation score log for each fold.

Listing 4.24   Saving the validation logs at each fold

```
num_epochs <- 500
all_mae_histories <- list()
for (i in 1:k) {
  cat("Processing fold #", i, "\n")
```

```
val_indices <- which(fold_id == i)
val_data <- train_data[val_indices, ]
val_targets <- train_targets[val_indices]
```
Prepare the validation data: data from partition #k.

```
partial_train_data <- train_data[-val_indices, ]
partial_train_targets <- train_targets[-val_indices]
```
Prepare the training data: data from all other partitions.

Build the Keras model (already compiled).
```
model <- build_model()
history <- model %>% fit(
    partial_train_data, partial_train_targets,
    validation_data = list(val_data, val_targets),
    epochs = num_epochs, batch_size = 16, verbose = 0
)
mae_history <- history$metrics$val_mae
all_mae_histories[[i]] <- mae_history
}
```
Train the model (in silent mode, verbose = 0).

```
Processing fold # 1
Processing fold # 2
Processing fold # 3
Processing fold # 4

all_mae_histories <- do.call(cbind, all_mae_histories)
```

We can then compute the average of the per-epoch MAE scores for all folds.

Listing 4.25   Building the history of successive mean *K*-fold validation scores

```
average_mae_history <- rowMeans(all_mae_histories)
```

Let's plot this; see figure 4.7.

Listing 4.26   Plotting validation scores

```
plot(average_mae_history, xlab = "epoch", type = 'l')
```

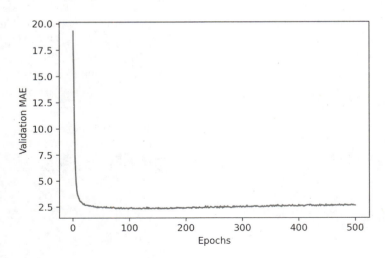

Figure 4.7   Validation MAE by epoch

It may be a little difficult to read the plot, due to a scaling issue: the validation MAE for the first few epochs is dramatically higher than the values that follow. Let's omit the first 10 data points, which are on a different scale than the rest of the curve.

Listing 4.27   Plotting validation scores, excluding the first 10 data points

```
truncated_mae_history <- average_mae_history[-(1:10)]
plot(average_mae_history, xlab = "epoch", type = 'l',
     ylim = range(truncated_mae_history))
```

As you can see in figure 4.8, validation MAE stops improving significantly after 100–140 epochs (this number includes the 10 epochs we omitted). Past that point, we start overfitting.

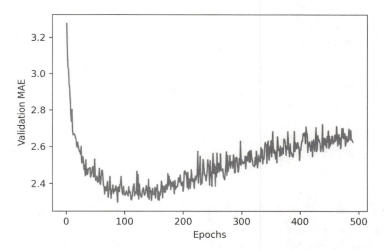

Figure 4.8
Validation MAE by epoch, excluding the first 10 data points

Once you're finished tuning other parameters of the model (in addition to the number of epochs, you could also adjust the size of the intermediate layers), you can train a final production model on all of the training data, with the best parameters, and then look at its performance on the test data.

Listing 4.28   Training the final model

Get a fresh, compiled model.
```
model <- build_model()
model %>% fit(train_data, train_targets,
              epochs = 120, batch_size = 16, verbose = 0)
result <- model %>% evaluate(test_data, test_targets)
```
Train it on the entirety of the data.

Here's the final result:

```
result["mae"]
```

```
     mae
2.476283
```

We're still off by a bit under $2,500. It's an improvement! Just like with the two previous tasks, you can try varying the number of layers in the model, or the number of units per layer, to see if you can squeeze out a lower test error.

4.3.5 *Generating predictions on new data*

When calling `predict()` on our binary classification model, we retrieved a scalar score between 0 and 1 for each input sample. With our multiclass classification model, we retrieved a probability distribution over all classes for each sample. Now, with this scalar regression model, `predict()` returns the model's guess for the sample's price in thousands of dollars:

```
predictions <- model %>% predict(test_data)
predictions[1, ]
```

```
[1] 10.27619
```

The first house in the test set is predicted to have a price of about $10,000.

4.3.6 *Wrapping up*

Here's what you should take away from this scalar regression example:

- Regression is done using different loss functions than we used for classification. Mean squared error (MSE) is a loss function commonly used for regression.
- Similarly, evaluation metrics to be used for regression differ from those used for classification; naturally, the concept of accuracy doesn't apply for regression. A common regression metric is mean absolute error (MAE).
- When features in the input data have values in different ranges, you should scale each feature independently as a preprocessing step.
- When there is little data available, using *K*-fold validation is a great way to reliably evaluate a model.
- When little training data is available, it's preferable to use a small model with few intermediate layers (typically only one or two), in order to avoid severe overfitting.

Summary

- The three most common kinds of machine learning tasks on vector data are binary classification, multiclass classification, and scalar regression.
  - The "Wrapping up" sections earlier in the chapter summarize the important points you've learned regarding each task.
  - Regression uses different loss functions and different evaluation metrics than classification.
- You'll usually need to preprocess raw data before feeding it into a neural network.
- When your data has features with different ranges, scale each feature independently as part of preprocessing.
- As training progresses, neural networks eventually begin to overfit and obtain worse results on never-before-seen data.
- If you don't have much training data, use a small model with only one or two intermediate layers, to avoid severe overfitting.
- If your data is divided into many categories, you may cause information bottlenecks if you make the intermediate layers too small.
- When you're working with little data, *K*-fold validation can help reliably evaluate your model.

Fundamentals of
machine learning

After the three practical examples in chapter 4, you should be starting to feel familiar with how to approach classification and regression problems using neural networks, and you've witnessed the central problem of machine learning: overfitting. This chapter will formalize some of your new intuition about machine learning into a solid conceptual framework, highlighting the importance of accurate model evaluation and the balance between training and generalization.

5.1 Generalization: The goal of machine learning

In the three examples presented in chapter 4—predicting movie reviews, topic classification, and house-price regression—we split the data into a training set, a validation set, and a test set. The reason not to evaluate the models on the same data they were trained on quickly became evident: after just a few epochs, performance on never-before-seen data started diverging from performance on the training data, which always improves as training progresses. The models started to *overfit*. Overfitting happens in every machine learning problem.

The fundamental issue in machine learning is the tension between optimization and generalization. *Optimization* refers to the process of adjusting a model to get the best performance possible on the training data (the *learning* in *machine learning*), whereas *generalization* refers to how well the trained model performs on data it has never seen before. The goal of the game is to get good generalization, of course, but you don't control generalization; you can only fit the model to its training data. If you do that *too well*, overfitting kicks in and generalization suffers.

But what causes overfitting? How can we achieve good generalization?

5.1.1 *Underfitting and overfitting*

For the models you saw in the previous chapter, performance on the held-out validation data started improving as training went on and then inevitably peaked after a while. This pattern (illustrated in figure 5.1) is universal. You'll see it with any model type and any dataset.

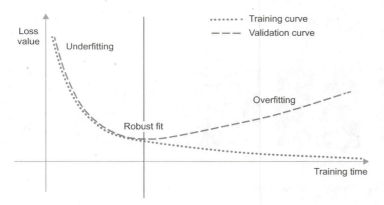

Figure 5.1 Canonical overfitting behavior

At the beginning of training, optimization and generalization are correlated: the lower the loss on training data, the lower the loss on test data. While this is happening, your model is said to be *underfit*: there is still progress to be made; the network hasn't yet modeled all relevant patterns in the training data. But after a certain number of iterations on the training data, generalization stops improving, validation metrics stall, and then begin to degrade: the model is starting to overfit. That is, it's beginning to learn patterns that are specific to the training data but that are misleading or irrelevant when it comes to new data.

Overfitting is particularly likely to occur when your data is noisy, if it involves uncertainty, or if it includes rare features. Let's look at some concrete examples.

NOISY TRAINING DATA

In real-world datasets, it's fairly common for some inputs to be invalid. Perhaps a MNIST digit could be an all-black image, for instance, or something like figure 5.2.

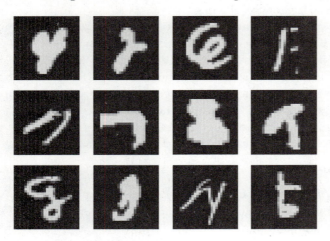

Figure 5.2   **Some pretty weird MNIST training samples**

What are these? I don't know, either. But they're all part of the MNIST training set. What's even worse, however, is having perfectly valid inputs that end up mislabeled, like those in figure 5.3.

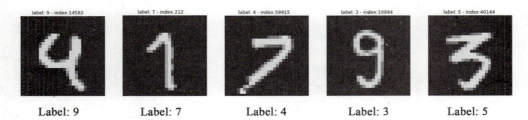

| label: 9 - index:14582 | label: 7 - index:212 | label: 4 - index:59915 | label: 3 - index:10994 | label: 5 - index:40144 |

| Label: 9 | Label: 7 | Label: 4 | Label: 3 | Label: 5 |

Figure 5.3   Mislabeled MNIST training samples

If a model goes out of its way to incorporate such outliers, its generalization performance will degrade, as shown in figure 5.4. For instance, a 4 that looks very close to the mislabeled 4 in figure 5.3 may end up getting classified as a 9.

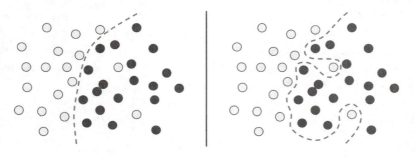

Figure 5.4 Dealing with outliers: Robust fit vs. overfitting

AMBIGUOUS FEATURES

Not all data noise comes from inaccuracies—even perfectly clean and neatly labeled data can be noisy when the problem involves uncertainty and ambiguity. In classification tasks, it is often the case that some regions of the input feature space are associated with multiple classes at the same time. Let's say you're developing a model that takes an image of a banana and predicts whether the banana is unripe, ripe, or rotten. These categories have no objective boundaries, so the same picture might be classified as either unripe or ripe by different human labelers. Similarly, many problems involve randomness. You could use atmospheric pressure data to predict whether it will rain tomorrow, but the exact same measurements may be followed sometimes by rain and sometimes by a clear sky, with some probability.

A model could overfit to such probabilistic data by being too confident about ambiguous regions of the feature space, like in figure 5.5. A more robust fit would ignore individual data points and look at the bigger picture.

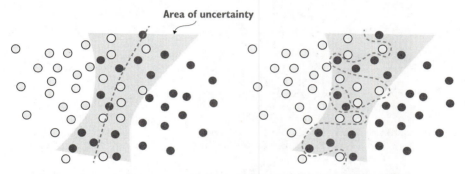

Figure 5.5   Robust fit vs. overfitting given an ambiguous area of the feature space

RARE FEATURES AND SPURIOUS CORRELATIONS

If you've only ever seen two orange tabby cats in your life, and they both happened to be terribly antisocial, you might infer that orange tabby cats are generally likely to be antisocial. That's overfitting: if you had been exposed to a wider variety of cats, including more orange ones, you'd have learned that cat color is not well correlated with character.

Likewise, machine learning models trained on datasets that include rare feature values are highly susceptible to overfitting. In a sentiment classification task, if the word *cherimoya* (a fruit native to the Andes) appears in only one text in the training data, and this text happens to be negative in sentiment, a poorly regularized model might put a very high weight on this word and always classify new texts that mention cherimoyas as negative, whereas, objectively, there's nothing negative about the cherimoya.[1]

Importantly, a feature value doesn't need to occur only a couple of times to lead to spurious correlations. Consider a word that occurs in 100 samples in your training

---

[1] Mark Twain even called it "the most delicious fruit known to men."

data that's associated with a positive sentiment 54% of the time and with a negative sentiment 46% of the time. That difference may well be a complete statistical fluke, yet your model is likely to learn to leverage that feature for its classification task. This is one of the most common sources of overfitting.

Here's a striking example. Using MNIST, create a new training set by concatenating 784 white noise dimensions to the existing 784 dimensions of the data, so half of the data is now noise. For comparison, also create an equivalent dataset by concatenating 784 all-zeros dimensions. Our concatenation of meaningless features does not at all affect the information content of the data: we're only adding something. Human classification accuracy wouldn't be affected by these transformations at all.

Listing 5.1   Adding white noise channels or all-zeros channels to MNIST

```
library(keras)

mnist <- dataset_mnist()
train_labels <- mnist$train$y
train_images <- array_reshape(mnist$train$x / 255,
                              c(60000, 28 * 28))

random_array <- function(dim) array(runif(prod(dim)), dim)

noise_channels <- random_array(dim(train_images))
train_images_with_noise_channels <- cbind(train_images, noise_channels)

zeros_channels <- array(0, dim(train_images))
train_images_with_zeros_channels <- cbind(train_images, zeros_channels)
```

Now let's train the model from chapter 2 on both of these training sets.

Listing 5.2   Training the same model with noise channels or all-zeros channels

```
get_model <- function() {
  model <- keras_model_sequential() %>%
    layer_dense(512, activation = "relu") %>%
    layer_dense(10, activation = "softmax")

  model %>% compile(
    optimizer = "rmsprop",
    loss = "sparse_categorical_crossentropy",
    metrics = "accuracy")

  model
}

model <- get_model()
history_noise <- model %>% fit(
  train_images_with_noise_channels, train_labels,
  epochs = 10,
  batch_size = 128,
```

```
  validation_split = 0.2)

model <- get_model()
history_zeros <- model %>% fit(
  train_images_with_zeros_channels, train_labels,
  epochs = 10,
  batch_size = 128,
  validation_split = 0.2)
```

Let's compare how the validation accuracy of each model evolves over time. The result is shown in figure 5.6.

Listing 5.3 Plotting a validation accuracy comparison

```
plot(NULL,
     main = "Effect of Noise Channels on Validation Accuracy",
     xlab = "Epochs", xlim = c(1, history_noise$params$epochs),
     ylab = "Validation Accuracy", ylim = c(0.9, 1), las = 1)
lines(history_zeros$metrics$val_accuracy, lty = 1, type = "o")
lines(history_noise$metrics$val_accuracy, lty = 2, type = "o")
legend("bottomright", lty = 1:2,
       legend = c("Validation accuracy with zeros channels",
                  "Validation accuracy with noise channels"))
```

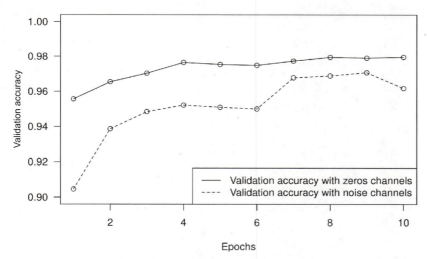

Figure 5.6   Effect of noise channels on validation accuracy

Despite the data holding the same information in both cases, the validation accuracy of the model trained with noise channels ends up about one percentage point lower—purely through the influence of spurious correlations. The more noise channels you add, the further accuracy will degrade.

Noisy features inevitably lead to overfitting. As such, in cases where you aren't sure whether the features you have are informative or distracting, it's common to do *feature selection* before training. Restricting the IMDB data to the top 10,000 most common words was a crude form of feature selection, for instance. The typical way to do feature selection is to compute some usefulness score for each feature available—a measure of how informative the feature is with respect to the task, such as the mutual information between the feature and the labels—and keep only features that are above some threshold. Doing this would filter out the white noise channels in the preceding example.

5.1.2   *The nature of generalization in deep learning*

A remarkable fact about deep learning models is that they can be trained to fit anything, as long as they have enough representational power.

Don't believe me? Try shuffling the MNIST labels and train a model on that. Even though there is no relationship whatsoever between the inputs and the shuffled labels, the training loss goes down just fine, even with a relatively small model. Naturally, the validation loss does not improve at all over time, because there is no possibility of generalization in this setting (see the following graph).

Listing 5.4   Fitting an MNIST model with randomly shuffled labels

```
c(c(train_images, train_labels), .) %<-% dataset_mnist()

train_images <- array_reshape(train_images / 255,
                              c(60000, 28 * 28))

random_train_labels <- sample(train_labels)

model <- keras_model_sequential() %>%
  layer_dense(512, activation = "relu") %>%
  layer_dense(10, activation = "softmax")

model %>% compile(optimizer = "rmsprop",
                  loss = "sparse_categorical_crossentropy",
                  metrics = "accuracy")

history <- model %>% fit(train_images, random_train_labels,
                         epochs = 100,
                         batch_size = 128,
                         validation_split = 0.2)
```

Use . in a %<-% multi-assign call to ignore some elements. Here, we're ignoring the test portion of MNIST.

```
plot(history)
```

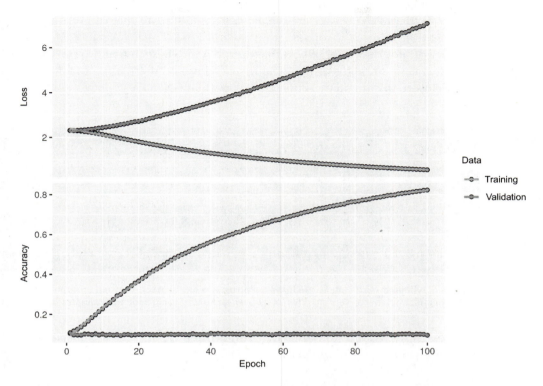

In fact, you don't even need to do this with MNIST data—you could just generate white noise inputs and random labels. You could fit a model on that, too, as long as it has enough parameters. It would just end up memorizing specific inputs, much like a hash table.

If this is the case, then how come deep learning models generalize at all? Shouldn't they just learn an ad hoc mapping between training inputs and targets, like a fancy hash table? What expectation can we have that this mapping will work for new inputs?

As it turns out, the nature of generalization in deep learning has rather little to do with deep learning models themselves and much to do with the structure of information in the real world. Let's take a look at what's really going on here.

THE MANIFOLD HYPOTHESIS

The input to an MNIST classifier (before preprocessing) is a 28 × 28 array of integers between 0 and 255. The total number of possible input values is thus 256 to the power of 784—much greater than the number of atoms in the universe. However, very few of these inputs would look like valid MNIST samples: actual handwritten digits occupy only a tiny *subspace* of the parent space of all possible 28 × 28 integer arrays. What's more, this subspace isn't just a set of points sprinkled at random in the parent space: it is highly structured.

First, the subspace of valid handwritten digits is *continuous*: if you take a sample and modify it a little, it will still be recognizable as the same handwritten digit. Further, all samples in the valid subspace are *connected* by smooth paths that run through the subspace. This means that if you take two random MNIST digits A and B, there exists a sequence of "intermediate" images that morph A into B, such that two consecutive digits are very close to each other (see figure 5.7). Perhaps there will be a few ambiguous shapes close to the boundary between two classes, but even these shapes would still look very digit-like.

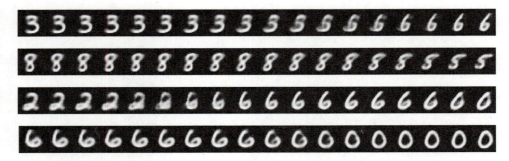

Figure 5.7   Different MNIST digits gradually morphing into one another, showing that the space of handwritten digits forms a manifold. This image was generated using code from chapter 12.

In technical terms, you would say that handwritten digits form a *manifold* within the space of possible 28 × 28 integer arrays. That's a big word, but the concept is pretty intuitive. A manifold is a lower-dimensional subspace of some parent space that is locally similar to a linear (Euclidian) space. For instance, a smooth curve in the plane is a 1D manifold within a 2D space, because for every point on the curve, you can draw a tangent (the curve can be approximated by a line at every point). A smooth surface within a 3D space is a 2D manifold. And so on.

More generally, the *manifold hypothesis* posits that all natural data lies on a low-dimensional manifold within the high-dimensional space where it is encoded. That's a pretty strong statement about the structure of information in the universe. As far as we know, it's accurate, and it's the reason deep learning works. It's true for MNIST digits, but also for human faces, tree morphology, the sounds of the human voice, and even natural language.

The manifold hypothesis implies that

- Machine learning models only have to fit relatively simple, low-dimensional, highly-structured subspaces within their potential input space (latent manifolds).
- Within one of these manifolds, it's always possible to *interpolate* between two inputs, that is to say, morph one into another via a continuous path along which all points fall on the manifold.

The ability to interpolate between samples is the key to understanding generalization in deep learning.

INTERPOLATION AS A SOURCE OF GENERALIZATION

If you work with data points that can be interpolated, you can start making sense of points you've never seen before by relating them to other points that lie close on the manifold. In other words, you can make sense of the *totality* of the space using only a *sample* of the space. You can use interpolation to fill in the blanks.

Note that interpolation on the latent manifold is different from linear interpolation in the parent space, as illustrated in figure 5.8. For instance, the average of pixels between two MNIST digits is usually not a valid digit.

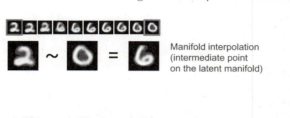

Manifold interpolation
(intermediate point
on the latent manifold)

Linear interpolation
(average in the encoding space)

Figure 5.8   The difference between linear interpolation and interpolation on the latent manifold. Every point on the latent manifold of digits is a valid digit, but the average of two digits usually isn't.

Crucially, although deep learning achieves generalization via interpolation on a learned approximation of the data manifold, it would be a mistake to assume that interpolation is *all* there is to generalization. It's the tip of the iceberg. Interpolation can only help you make sense of things that are very close to what you've seen before: it enables *local generalization*. But remarkably, humans deal with extreme novelty all the time, and we do just fine. You don't need to be trained in advance on countless examples of every situation you'll ever have to encounter. Every single one of your days is different from any day you've experienced before, and different from any day experienced by anyone since the dawn of humanity. You can switch between spending a week in New York City, a week in Shanghai, and a week in Bangalore without requiring thousands of lifetimes of learning and rehearsal for each city.

Humans are capable of *extreme generalization*, which is enabled by cognitive mechanisms other than interpolation: abstraction, symbolic models of the world, reasoning, logic, common sense, innate priors about the world—what we generally call *reason*, as opposed to intuition and pattern recognition. The latter are largely interpolative in nature, but the former isn't. Both are essential to intelligence. We'll talk more about this in chapter 14.

WHY DEEP LEARNING WORKS

Remember the crumpled paper ball metaphor from chapter 2? A sheet of paper represents a 2D manifold within 3D space (see figure 5.9). A deep learning model is a tool for uncrumpling paper balls, that is, for disentangling latent manifolds.

A deep learning model is basically a very high-dimensional curve—a curve that is smooth and continuous (with additional constraints on its structure, originating from model architecture priors), because it needs to be differentiable. And that curve is

Figure 5.9   Uncrumpling a complicated manifold of data

fitted to data points via gradient descent, smoothly and incrementally. By its very nature, deep learning is about taking a big, complex curve—a manifold—and incrementally adjusting its parameters until it fits some training data points.

The curve involves enough parameters that it could fit anything—indeed, if you let your model train for long enough, it will effectively end up purely memorizing its training data and won't generalize at all. However, the data you're fitting to isn't made of isolated points sparsely distributed across the underlying space. Your data forms a highly structured, low-dimensional manifold within the input space—that's the manifold hypothesis. And because fitting your model curve to this data happens gradually and smoothly over time as gradient descent progresses, there will be an intermediate point during training at which the model roughly approximates the natural manifold of the data, as you can see in figure 5.10.

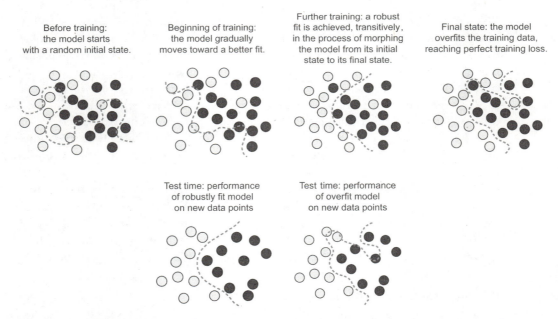

Figure 5.10   Going from a random model to an overfit model and achieving a robust fit as an intermediate state

Moving along the curve learned by the model at that point will come close to moving along the actual latent manifold of the data. As such, the model will be capable of making sense of never-before-seen inputs via interpolation between training inputs.

Besides the trivial fact that they have sufficient representational power, deep learning models have the following properties that make them particularly well-suited to learning latent manifolds:

- Deep learning models implement a smooth, continuous mapping from their inputs to their outputs. It has to be smooth and continuous because it must be differentiable, by necessity (you couldn't do gradient descent otherwise). This smoothness helps approximate latent manifolds, which follow the same properties.
- Deep learning models tend to be structured in a way that mirrors the "shape" of the information in their training data (via architecture priors). This is particularly the case for image-processing models (discussed in chapters 8 and 9) and sequence-processing models (chapter 10). More generally, deep neural networks structure their learned representations in a hierarchical and modular way, which echoes the way natural data is organized.

TRAINING DATA IS PARAMOUNT

Although deep learning is indeed well suited to manifold learning, the power to generalize is more a consequence of the natural structure of your data than a consequence of any property of your model. You'll be able to generalize only if your data forms a manifold where points can be interpolated. The more informative and the less noisy your features are, the better you will be able to generalize, because your input space will be simpler and better structured. Data curation and feature engineering are essential to generalization.

Further, because deep learning is curve fitting, for a model to perform well, *it needs to be trained on a dense sampling of its input space.* A dense sampling in this context means that the training data should densely cover the entirety of the input data manifold (see figure 5.11). This is especially true near decision boundaries. With a sufficiently dense

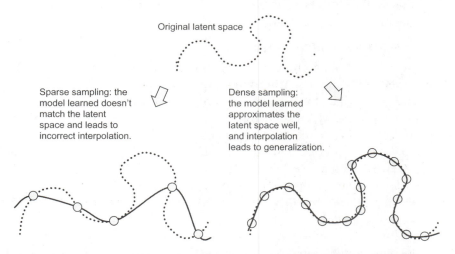

Figure 5.11   A dense sampling of the input space is necessary to learn a model capable of accurate generalization.

sampling, it becomes possible to make sense of new inputs by interpolating between past training inputs without having to use common sense, abstract reasoning, or external knowledge about the world—all things that machine learning models have no access to. As such, you should always keep in mind that the best way to improve a deep learning model is to train it on more data or better data (of course, adding overly noisy or inaccurate data will harm generalization). A denser coverage of the input data manifold will yield a model that generalizes better. You should never expect a deep learning model to perform anything more than crude interpolation between its training samples, and thus you should do everything you can to make interpolation as easy as possible. The only thing you will find in a deep learning model is what you put into it: the priors encoded in its architecture and the data it was trained on.

When getting more data isn't possible, the next best solution is to modulate the quantity of information that your model is allowed to store or to add constraints on the smoothness of the model curve. If a network can afford to memorize only a small number of patterns, or very regular patterns, the optimization process will force it to focus on the most prominent patterns, which have a better chance of generalizing well. The process of fighting overfitting this way is called *regularization*. We'll review regularization techniques in depth in section 5.4.4.

Before you can start tweaking your model to help it generalize better, you'll need a way to assess how your model is currently doing. In the following section, you'll learn how you can monitor generalization during model development: model evaluation.

5.2   *Evaluating machine learning models*

You can control only what you can observe. Because your goal is to develop models that can successfully generalize to new data, it's essential to be able to reliably measure the generalization power of your model. In this section, I'll formally introduce the different ways you can evaluate machine learning models. You've already seen most of them in action in the previous chapter.

5.2.1   *Training, validation, and test sets*

Evaluating a model always boils down to splitting the available data into three sets: training, validation, and test. You train on the training data and evaluate your model on the validation data. Once your model is ready for prime time, you test it one final time on the test data, which is meant to be as similar as possible to production data. Then you can deploy the model in production.

You may ask, why not have two sets: a training set and a test set? You'd train on the training data and evaluate on the test data. Much simpler!

The reason is that developing a model always involves tuning its configuration, for example, choosing the number of layers or the size of the layers (called the *hyperparameters* of the model, to distinguish them from the *parameters*, which are the network's weights). You do this tuning by using, as a feedback signal, the performance of the model on the validation data. In essence, this tuning is a form of *learning*: a search for a good configuration in some parameter space. As a result, tuning the configuration of the model based on its performance on the validation set can quickly result in *over-fitting to the validation set*, even though your model is never directly trained on it.

Central to this phenomenon is the notion of *information leaks*. Every time you tune a hyperparameter of your model based on the model's performance on the validation set, some information about the validation data leaks into the model. If you do this only once, for one parameter, then very few bits of information will leak, and your validation set will remain reliable for evaluating the model. But if you repeat this many times—running one experiment, evaluating on the validation set, and modifying your model as a result—then you'll leak an increasingly significant amount of information about the validation set into the model.

At the end of the day, you'll end up with a model that performs artificially well on the validation data, because that's what you optimized it for. You care about performance on completely new data, not on the validation data, so you need to use a completely different, never-before-seen dataset to evaluate the model: the test dataset. Your model shouldn't have had access to *any* information about the test set, even indirectly. If anything about the model has been tuned based on test set performance, then your measure of generalization will be flawed.

Splitting your data into training, validation, and test sets may seem straightforward, but we have a few advanced ways to do it that can come in handy when little data is available. Let's review three classic evaluation recipes: simple holdout validation, *K*-fold validation, and iterated *K*-fold validation with shuffling. We'll also talk about the use of common-sense baselines to check that your training is going somewhere.

SIMPLE HOLDOUT VALIDATION

Set apart some fraction of your data as your test set. Train on the remaining data, and evaluate on the test set. As you saw in the previous sections, to prevent information leaks, you shouldn't tune your model based on the test set, and, therefore, you should *also* reserve a validation set.

Schematically, holdout validation looks like figure 5.12. Listing 5.5 shows a simple implementation.

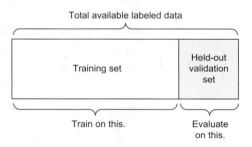

Figure 5.12   Simple holdout validation split

Listing 5.5   Holdout validation (note that labels are omitted for simplicity)

Assembling the validation set from a random sampling of the data is usually appropriate.

```
num_validation_samples <- 10000
val_indices <- sample.int(num_validation_samples, nrow(data))
validation_data <- data[val_indices, ]
training_data <- data[-val_indices, ]
model <- get_model()
fit(model, training_data, ...)
```

Define the validation set.

Define the training set.

Train a model on the training data, and evaluate it on the validation data.

```
validation_score <- evaluate(model, validation_data, ...)
...
```
> At this point you can tune your model, retrain it, evaluate it, tune it again.

```
model <- get_model()
fit(model, data, ...)
test_score <- evaluate(model, test_data, ...)
```
> Once you've tuned your hyperparameters, it's common to train your final model from scratch on all non-test data available (the training_data and validation_data combined).

> **NOTE** In these examples, we assume data is a rank 2 tensor. Add commas to the [call as needed for higher rank data. For example, data[idx, ,] if data is rank 3, data[idx, , ,] for rank 4, and so on.

This is the simplest evaluation protocol, and it suffers from one flaw: if little data is available, then your validation and test sets may contain too few samples to be statistically representative of the data at hand. This is easy to recognize: if different random shuffling rounds of the data before splitting end up yielding very different measures of model performance, then you're having this issue. *K*-fold validation and iterated *K*-fold validation are two ways to address this, as discussed next.

K-FOLD VALIDATION

With this approach, you split your data into K partitions of equal size. For each partition i, train a model on the remaining K - 1 partitions, and evaluate it on partition i. Your final score is then the averages of the *K* scores obtained. This method is helpful when the performance of your model shows significant variance based on your train-test split. Like holdout validation, this method doesn't exempt you from using a distinct validation set for model calibration.

Schematically, *K*-fold cross-validation looks like figure 5.13. Listing 5.6 shows a simple implementation.

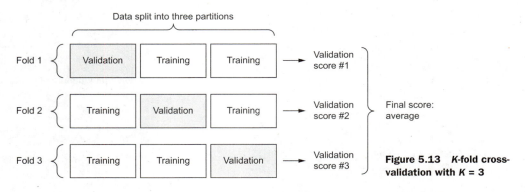

Figure 5.13   *K*-fold cross-validation with *K* = 3

> **Listing 5.6   *K*-fold cross-validation (note that labels are omitted for simplicity)**

```
k <- 3
fold_id <- sample(rep(1:k, length.out = nrow(data)))
validation_scores <- numeric()
```

```
for (fold in seq_len(k)) {
  validation_idx <- which(fold_id == fold)
```
Select the validation-data partition.

```
  validation_data <- data[validation_idx, ]
  training_data <- data[-validation_idx, ]
```
Use the remainder of the data as training data.

```
  model <- get_model()
```
Create a brand-new instance of the model (untrained).

```
  fit(model, training_data, ...)
  validation_score <- evaluate(model, validation_data, ...)
  validation_scores[[fold]] <- validation_score
}
```

```
validation_score <- mean(validation_scores)
```
Validation score: average of the validation scores of the K-folds

```
model <- get_model()
fit(model, data, ...)
test_score <- evaluate(model, test_data, ...)
```
Train the final model on all non-test data available.

ITERATED K-FOLD VALIDATION WITH SHUFFLING

This one is for situations in which you have relatively little data available and you need to evaluate your model as precisely as possible. I've found it to be extremely helpful in Kaggle competitions. It consists of applying *K*-fold validation multiple times, shuffling the data every time before splitting it K ways. The final score is the average of the scores obtained at each run of *K*-fold validation. Note that you end up training and evaluating P * K models (where P is the number of iterations you use), which can be very expensive.

5.2.2 Beating a common-sense baseline

Besides the different evaluation protocols you have available, one last thing you should know about is the use of common-sense baselines.

Training a deep learning model is a bit like pressing a button that launches a rocket in a parallel world. You can't hear it or see it. You can't observe the manifold learning process—it's happening in a space with thousands of dimensions, and even if you projected it to 3D, you couldn't interpret it. The only feedback you have is your validation metrics—like an altitude meter on your invisible rocket.

It's particularly important to be able to tell whether you're getting off the ground at all. What was the altitude you started at? Your model seems to have an accuracy of 15%—is that any good? Before you start working with a dataset, you should always pick a trivial baseline that you'll try to beat. If you cross that threshold, you'll know you're doing something right: your model is actually using the information in the input data to make predictions that generalize, and you can keep going. This baseline could be the performance of a random classifier or the performance of the simplest non–machine learning technique you can imagine.

For instance, in the MNIST digit-classification example, a simple baseline would be a validation accuracy greater than 0.1 (random classifier); in the IMDB example, it would be a validation accuracy greater than 0.5. In the Reuters example, it would be around 0.18–0.19, due to class imbalance. If you have a binary classification problem where 90% of samples belong to class A and 10% belong to class B, then a classifier that always predicts A already achieves 0.9 in validation accuracy, and you'll need to do better than that.

Having a common-sense baseline you can refer to is essential when you're getting started on a problem no one has solved before. If you can't beat a trivial solution, your model is worthless—perhaps you're using the wrong model, or perhaps the problem you're tackling can't even be approached with machine learning in the first place. Time to go back to the drawing board.

5.2.3   Things to keep in mind about model evaluation

Keep an eye out for the following when you're choosing an evaluation protocol:

- *Data representativeness*—You want both your training set and test set to be representative of the data at hand. For instance, if you're trying to classify images of digits, and you're starting from an array of samples where the samples are ordered by their class, taking the first 80% of the array as your training set and the remaining 20% as your test set will result in your training set containing only classes 0–7, whereas your test set will contain only classes 8–9. This seems like a ridiculous mistake, but it's surprisingly common. For this reason, you usually should *randomly shuffle* your data before splitting it into training and test sets.
- *The arrow of time*—If you're trying to predict the future given the past (e.g., tomorrow's weather, stock movements, and so on), you should not randomly shuffle your data before splitting it, because doing so will create a *temporal leak*: your model will effectively be trained on data from the future. In such situations, you should always make sure all data in your test set is *posterior* to the data in the training set.
- *Redundancy in your data*—If some data points in your data appear twice (fairly common with real-world data), then shuffling the data and splitting it into a training set and a validation set will result in redundancy between the training and validation sets. In effect, you'll be testing on part of your training data, which is the worst thing you can do! Make sure your training set and validation set are disjoint.

Having a reliable way to evaluate the performance of your model is how you'll be able to monitor the tension at the heart of machine learning—between optimization and generalization, underfitting and overfitting.

5.3   Improving model fit

To achieve the perfect fit, you must first overfit. Because you don't know in advance where the boundary lies, you must cross it to find it. Thus, your initial goal as you start working on a problem is to achieve a model that shows some generalization power and that is able to overfit. Once you have such a model, you'll focus on refining generalization by fighting overfitting.

There are three common problems you'll encounter at this stage:

- Training doesn't get started: your training loss doesn't go down over time.
- Training gets started just fine, but your model doesn't meaningfully generalize: you can't beat the common-sense baseline you set.
- Training and validation loss both go down over time, and you can beat your baseline, but you don't seem to be able to overfit, which indicates you're still underfitting.

Let's see how you can address these issues to achieve the first big milestone of a machine learning project: getting a model that has some generalization power (it can beat a trivial baseline) and that is able to overfit.

5.3.1 *Tuning key gradient descent parameters*

Sometimes training doesn't get started, or it stalls too early. Your loss is stuck. This is *always* something you can overcome: remember that you can fit a model to random data. Even if nothing about your problem makes sense, you should *still* be able to train something, if only by memorizing the training data.

When this happens, it's always a problem with the configuration of the gradient descent process: your choice of optimizer, the distribution of initial values in the weights of your model, your learning rate, or your batch size. All these parameters are interdependent, and as such, it is usually sufficient to tune the learning rate and the batch size while keeping the rest of the parameters constant.

Let's look at a concrete example: let's train the MNIST model from chapter 2 with an inappropriately large learning rate of value 1.

Listing 5.7   Training an MNIST model with an incorrectly high learning rate

```
c(c(train_images, train_labels), .) %<-% dataset_mnist()
train_images <- array_reshape(train_images / 255,
                              c(60000, 28 * 28))

model <- keras_model_sequential() %>%
  layer_dense(units = 512, activation = "relu") %>%
  layer_dense(units = 10, activation = "softmax")

model %>% compile(optimizer = optimizer_rmsprop(1),
                  loss = "sparse_categorical_crossentropy",
                  metrics = "accuracy")

history <- model %>% fit(train_images, train_labels,
                         epochs = 10, batch_size = 128,
                         validation_split = 0.2)
```

```
plot(history)
```

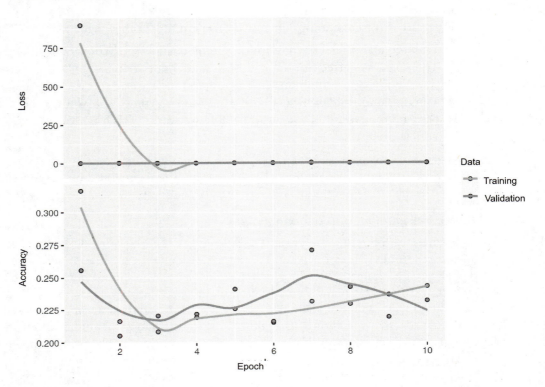

The model quickly reaches a training and validation accuracy in the 20%–30% range, but cannot get past that. Let's try to lower the learning rate to a more reasonable value of 1e-2.

Listing 5.8   The same model with a more appropriate learning rate

```
model <- keras_model_sequential() %>%
  layer_dense(units = 512, activation = "relu") %>%
  layer_dense(units = 10, activation = "softmax")

model %>% compile(optimizer = optimizer_rmsprop(1e-2),
                  loss = "sparse_categorical_crossentropy",
                  metrics = "accuracy")

model %>%
  fit(train_images, train_labels,
      epochs = 10, batch_size = 128,
      validation_split = 0.2) ->
  history
```

`plot(history)`

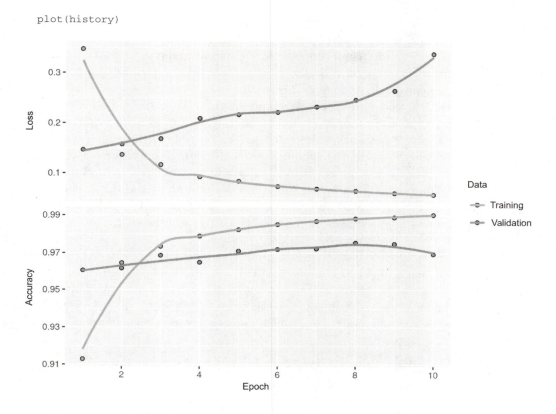

The model is now able to train.

If you find yourself in a similar situation, try the following:

- *Lowering or increasing the learning rate*—A learning rate that is too high may lead to updates that vastly overshoot a proper fit, like in the preceding example, and a learning rate that is too low may make training so slow that it appears to stall.

- *Increasing the batch size*—A batch with more samples will lead to gradients that are more informative and less noisy (lower variance).

You will, eventually, find a configuration that gets training started.

5.3.2 *Leveraging better architecture priors*

You have a model that fits, but for some reason your validation metrics aren't improving at all. They remain no better than what a random classifier would achieve: your model trains but doesn't generalize. What's going on?

This is perhaps the worst machine learning situation you can find yourself in. It indicates that *something is fundamentally wrong with your approach*, and it may not be easy to tell what. Here are some tips.

First, it may be that the input data you're using simply doesn't contain sufficient information to predict your targets: the problem as formulated is not solvable. This is what happened earlier when we tried to fit an MNIST model where the labels were shuffled: the model would train just fine, but validation accuracy would stay stuck at 10%, because it was plainly impossible to generalize with such a dataset.

It may also be that the kind of model you're using is not suited for the problem at hand. For instance, in chapter 10, you'll see an example of a time-series prediction problem where a densely connected architecture isn't able to beat a trivial baseline, whereas a more appropriate recurrent architecture does manage to generalize well. Using a model that makes the right assumptions about the problem is essential to achieve generalization: you should leverage the right architecture priors.

In the following chapters, you'll learn about the best architectures to use for a variety of data modalities—images, text, time series, and so on. In general, you should always make sure to read up on architecture best practices for the kind of task you're attacking—chances are you're not the first person to attempt it.

5.3.3   Increasing model capacity

If you manage to get to a model that fits, where validation metrics are going down, and that seems to achieve at least some level of generalization power, congratulations: you're almost there. Next, you need to get your model to start overfitting. Consider the following small model—a simple logistic regression—trained on MNIST pixels.

> **Listing 5.9   A simple logistic regression on MNIST**

```
model <- keras_model_sequential() %>%
  layer_dense(10, activation = "softmax")

model %>% compile(optimizer = "rmsprop",
                  loss = "sparse_categorical_crossentropy",
                  metrics = "accuracy")

history_small_model <- model %>%
  fit(train_images, train_labels,
      epochs = 20,
      batch_size = 128,
      validation_split = 0.2)

plot(history_small_model$metrics$val_loss, type = 'o',
     main = "Effect of Insufficient Model Capacity on Validation Loss",
     xlab = "Epochs", ylab = "Validation Loss")
```

You get loss curves that look like figure 5.14.

Validation metrics seem to stall, or to improve very slowly, instead of peaking and reversing course. The validation loss goes to 0.26 and just stays there. You can fit, but you can't clearly overfit, even after many iterations over the training data. You're likely to encounter similar curves often in your career.

Remember that it should always be possible to overfit. Much like the problem where the training loss doesn't go down, this is an issue that can always be solved. If

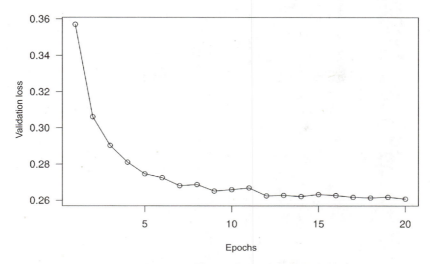

Figure 5.14   Effect of insufficient model capacity on validation loss

you can't seem to be able to overfit, it's likely a problem with the *representational power* of your model: you're going to need a bigger model, one with more *capacity*, that is, one able to store more information. You can increase representational power by adding more layers, using bigger layers (layers with more parameters), or using kinds of layers that are more appropriate for the problem at hand (better architecture priors).

Let's try training a bigger model, one with two intermediate layers with 96 units each:

```
model <- keras_model_sequential() %>%
    layer_dense(96, activation = "relu") %>%
    layer_dense(96, activation = "relu") %>%
    layer_dense(10, activation = "softmax")

model %>% compile(optimizer = "rmsprop",
                  loss = "sparse_categorical_crossentropy",
                  metrics = "accuracy")

history_large_model <- model %>%
  fit(train_images, train_labels,
      epochs = 20,
      batch_size = 128,
      validation_split = 0.2)
```

The validation curve now looks exactly like it should: the model fits fast and starts overfitting after eight epochs (see figure 5.15):

```
plot(history_large_model$metrics$val_loss, type = 'o',
    main = "Validation Loss for a Model with Appropriate Capacity",
    xlab = "Epochs", ylab = "Validation Loss")
```

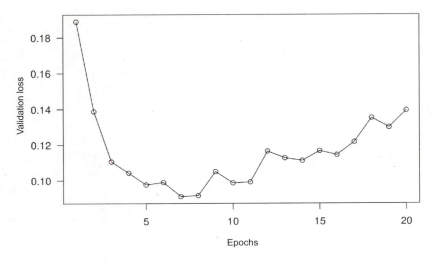

Figure 5.15   Validation loss for a model with appropriate capacity

5.4   *Improving generalization*

Once your model has shown itself to have some generalization power and to be able to overfit, it's time to switch your focus to maximizing generalization.

5.4.1   *Dataset curation*

You've already learned that generalization in deep learning originates from the latent structure of your data. If your data makes it possible to smoothly interpolate between samples, you will be able to train a deep learning model that generalizes. If your problem is overly noisy or fundamentally discrete, like, say, list sorting, deep learning will not help you. Deep learning is curve fitting, not magic.

As such, it is essential that you make sure that you're working with an appropriate dataset. Spending more effort and money on data collection almost always yields a much greater return on investment than spending the same on developing a better model.

- Make sure you have enough data. Remember that you need a *dense sampling* of the input-cross-output space. More data will yield a better model. Sometimes, problems that seem impossible at first become solvable with a larger dataset.
- Minimize labeling errors—visualize your inputs to check for anomalies, and proofread your labels.
- Clean your data and deal with missing values (we'll cover this in the next chapter).
- If you have many features and you aren't sure which ones are actually useful, do feature selection.

A particularly important way to improve the generalization potential of your data is feature engineering. For most machine learning problems, feature engineering is a key ingredient for success. Let's take a look.

5.4.2   Feature engineering

Feature engineering is the process of using your own knowledge about the data and about the machine learning algorithm at hand (in this case, a neural network) to make the algorithm work better by applying hardcoded (nonlearned) transformations to the data before it goes into the model. In many cases, it isn't reasonable to expect a machine learning model to be able to learn from completely arbitrary data. The data needs to be presented to the model in a way that will make the model's job easier.

Let's look at an intuitive example. Suppose you're trying to develop a model that can take as input an image of a clock and can output the time of day (see figure 5.16).

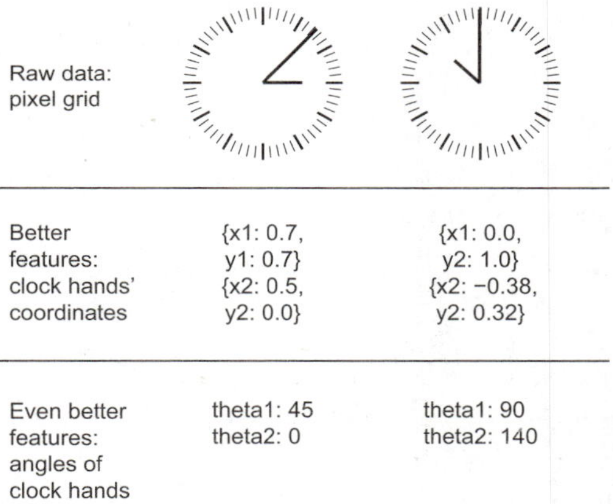

Raw data: pixel grid		
Better features: clock hands' coordinates	{x1: 0.7, y1: 0.7} {x2: 0.5, y2: 0.0}	{x1: 0.0, y2: 1.0} {x2: −0.38, y2: 0.32}
Even better features: angles of clock hands	theta1: 45 theta2: 0	theta1: 90 theta2: 140

Figure 5.16   Feature engineering for reading the time on a clock

If you choose to use the raw pixels of the image as input data, you have a difficult machine learning problem on your hands. You'll need a convolutional neural network to solve it, and you'll have to expend quite a bit of computational resources to train the network.

But if you already understand the problem at a high level (you understand how humans read time on a clock face), you can come up with much better input features for a machine learning algorithm: for instance, it's easy to write a five-line R script to follow the black pixels of the clock hands and output the (x, y) coordinates of the tip of each hand. Then a simple machine learning algorithm can learn to associate these coordinates with the appropriate time of day.

You can go even further: do a coordinate change and express the (x, y) coordinates as polar coordinates with regard to the center of the image. Your input will become the angle theta of each clock hand. At this point, your features are making the problem so easy that no machine learning is required; a simple rounding operation and dictionary lookup are enough to recover the approximate time of day.

That's the essence of feature engineering: making a problem easier by expressing it in a simpler way. Make the latent manifold smoother, simpler, and better organized. Doing so usually requires understanding the problem in depth.

Before deep learning, feature engineering used to be the most important part of the machine learning workflow, because classical shallow algorithms didn't have hypothesis spaces rich enough to learn useful features by themselves. The way you presented the data to the algorithm was absolutely critical to its success. For instance, before convolutional neural networks became successful on the MNIST digit-classification problem, solutions were typically based on hardcoded features such as the number of loops in a digit image, the height of each digit in an image, a histogram of pixel values, and so on.

Fortunately, modern deep learning removes the need for most feature engineering, because neural networks are capable of automatically extracting useful features from raw data. Does this mean you don't have to worry about feature engineering as long as you're using deep neural networks? No, for the following two reasons:

- Good features still allow you to solve problems more elegantly while using fewer resources. For instance, it would be ridiculous to solve the problem of reading a clock face using a convolutional neural network.
- Good features let you solve a problem with far less data. The ability of deep learning models to learn features on their own relies on having lots of training data available; if you have only a few samples, the information value in their features becomes critical.

5.4.3 *Using early stopping*

In deep learning, we always use models that are vastly overparameterized: they have way more degrees of freedom than the minimum necessary to fit to the latent manifold of the data. This overparameterization is not an issue, because *you never fully fit a deep learning model*. Such a fit wouldn't generalize at all. You will always interrupt training long before you've reached the minimum possible training loss.

Finding the exact point during training where you've reached the most generalizable fit—the exact boundary between an underfit curve and an overfit curve—is one of the most effective things you can do to improve generalization.

In the examples in the previous chapter, we would start by training our models for longer than needed to figure out the number of epochs that yielded the best validation metrics, and then we would retrain a new model for exactly that number of epochs. This is pretty standard, but it requires you to do redundant work, which can sometimes be expensive. Naturally, you could just save your model at the end of each epoch, and once you've found the best epoch, reuse the closest saved model you have. In Keras, it's typical to do this with `callback_early_stopping`, which will interrupt training as soon as validation metrics have stopped improving, while remembering the best known model state. You'll learn to use callbacks in chapter 7.

5.4.4 Regularizing your model

Regularization techniques are a set of best practices that actively impede the model's ability to fit perfectly to the training data, with the goal of making the model perform better during validation. This is called *regularizing* the model, because it tends to make the model simpler, more "regular," and its curve smoother, more "generic"; thus it is less specific to the training set and better able to generalize by more closely approximating the latent manifold of the data.

Keep in mind that regularizing a model is a process that should always be guided by an accurate evaluation procedure. You will achieve generalization only if you can measure it.

Let's review some of the most common regularization techniques and apply them in practice to improve the movie-classification model from chapter 4.

REDUCING THE NETWORK'S SIZE

You've already learned that a model that is too small will not overfit. The simplest way to mitigate overfitting is to reduce the size of the model (the number of learnable parameters in the model, determined by the number of layers and the number of units per layer). If the model has limited memorization resources, it won't be able to simply memorize its training data; thus, to minimize its loss, it will have to resort to learning compressed representations that have predictive power regarding the targets—precisely the type of representations we're interested in. At the same time, keep in mind that you should use models that have enough parameters that they don't underfit: your model shouldn't be starved for memorization resources. There is a compromise to be found between *too much capacity* and *not enough capacity*.

Unfortunately, there is no magical formula to determine the right number of layers or the right size for each layer. You must evaluate an array of different architectures (on your validation set, not on your test set, of course) to find the correct model size for your data. The general workflow for finding an appropriate model size is to start with relatively few layers and parameters and increase the size of the layers or add new layers until you see diminishing returns with regard to validation loss.

Let's try this on the movie-review classification model. The following listing shows our original model.

Listing 5.10 Original model

```
c(c(train_data, train_labels), .) %<-% dataset_imdb(num_words = 10000)

vectorize_sequences <- function(sequences, dimension = 10000) {
    results <- matrix(0, nrow = length(sequences), ncol = dimension)
    for(i in seq_along(sequences))
        results[i, sequences[[i]]] <- 1
    results
}

train_data <- vectorize_sequences(train_data)
```

```
model <- keras_model_sequential() %>%
    layer_dense(16, activation = "relu") %>%
    layer_dense(16, activation = "relu") %>%
    layer_dense(1, activation = "sigmoid")

model %>% compile(optimizer = "rmsprop",
                  loss = "binary_crossentropy",
                  metrics = "accuracy")

history_original <- model %>%
  fit(train_data, train_labels,
      epochs = 20, batch_size = 512, validation_split = 0.4)
```

Now let's try to replace it with this smaller model.

Listing 5.11   Version of the model with lower capacity

```
model <- keras_model_sequential() %>%
  layer_dense(4, activation = "relu") %>%
  layer_dense(4, activation = "relu") %>%
  layer_dense(1, activation = "sigmoid")

model %>% compile(optimizer = "rmsprop",
                  loss = "binary_crossentropy",
                  metrics = "accuracy")

history_smaller_model <- model %>%
  fit(train_data, train_labels,
      epochs = 20, batch_size = 512, validation_split = 0.4)
```

Let's generate a plot (figure 5.17) to compare the validation losses of the original model and the smaller model:

```
plot(
  NULL,                                         NULL tells plot() to set up the plot
  main = "Original Model vs. Smaller Model on IMDB Review Classification",
  xlab = "Epochs",                              region but not draw any data yet.
  xlim = c(1, history_original$params$epochs),
  ylab = "Validation Loss",
  ylim = extendrange(history_original$metrics$val_loss),    Draw grid
  panel.first = abline(v = 1:history_original$params$epochs,  lines.
                       lty = "dotted", col = "lightgrey")
)

lines(history_original      $metrics$val_loss, lty = 2)
lines(history_smaller_model$metrics$val_loss, lty = 1)
legend("topleft", lty = 2:1,
       legend = c("Validation loss of original model",
                  "Validation loss of smaller model"))
```

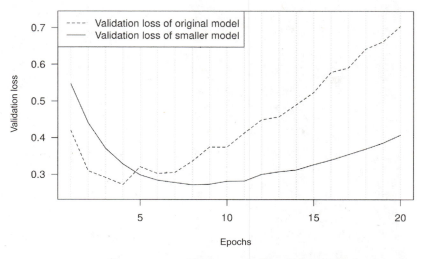

Figure 5.17   Original model vs. smaller model on IMDB review classification

As you can see, the smaller model starts overfitting later than the reference model (after six epochs rather than four), and its performance degrades more slowly once it starts overfitting.

Now let's add to our benchmark a model that has much more capacity—far more than the problem warrants. Although it is standard to work with models that are significantly overparameterized for what they're trying to learn, there can definitely be such a thing as *too much* memorization capacity. You'll know your model is too large if it starts overfitting right away and if its validation loss curve looks choppy with high variance (although choppy validation metrics could also be a symptom of using an unreliable validation process, such as a validation split that's too small).

Listing 5.12   Version of the model with higher capacity

```
model <- keras_model_sequential() %>%
    layer_dense(512, activation = "relu") %>%
    layer_dense(512, activation = "relu") %>%
    layer_dense(1, activation = "sigmoid")

model %>% compile(optimizer = "rmsprop",
                  loss = "binary_crossentropy",
                  metrics = "accuracy")

history_larger_model <- model %>%
  fit(train_data, train_labels,
      epochs = 20, batch_size = 512, validation_split = 0.4)
```

```
plot(
  NULL,
  main =
    "Original Model vs. Much Larger Model on IMDB Review Classification",
  xlab = "Epochs", xlim = c(1, history_original$params$epochs),
  ylab = "Validation Loss",
  ylim = range(c(history_original$metrics$val_loss,
                 history_larger_model$metrics$val_loss)),
  panel.first = abline(v = 1:history_original$params$epochs,
                       lty = "dotted", col = "lightgrey")
)
lines(history_original    $metrics$val_loss, lty = 2)
lines(history_larger_model$metrics$val_loss, lty = 1)
legend("topleft", lty = 2:1,
       legend = c("Validation loss of original model",
                  "Validation loss of larger model"))
```

Figure 5.18 shows how the bigger model fares compared with the reference model.

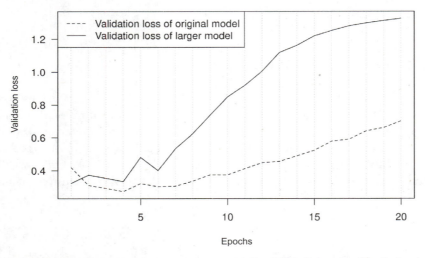

Figure 5.18   Original model vs. much larger model on IMDB review classification

The bigger model starts overfitting almost immediately, after just one epoch, and it overfits much more severely. Its validation loss is also noisier. It gets training loss near zero very quickly. The more capacity the model has, the more quickly it can model the training data (resulting in a low training loss), but the more susceptible it is to overfitting (resulting in a large difference between the training and validation loss).

ADDING WEIGHT REGULARIZATION

You may be familiar with the principle of *Occam's razor*: given two explanations for something, the explanation most likely to be correct is the simplest one—the one that makes fewer assumptions. This idea also applies to the models learned by neural networks: given some training data and a network architecture, multiple sets of weight values (multiple *models*) could explain the data. Simpler models are less likely to overfit than complex ones.

A *simple model* in this context is a model where the distribution of parameter values has less entropy (or a model with fewer parameters, as you saw in the previous section). Thus, a common way to mitigate overfitting is to put constraints on the complexity of a model by forcing its weights to take only small values, which makes the distribution of weight values more *regular*. This is called *weight regularization*, and it's done by adding to the loss function of the model a cost associated with having large weights. This cost comes in two flavors:

- *L1 regularization*—The cost added is proportional to the *absolute value of the weight coefficients* (the *L1 norm* of the weights).
- *L2 regularization*—The cost added is proportional to the *square of the value of the weight coefficients* (the *L2 norm* of the weights). L2 regularization is also called *weight decay* in the context of neural networks. Don't let the different name confuse you: weight decay is mathematically the same as L2 regularization.

In Keras, weight regularization is added by passing *weight regularizer instances* to layers as keyword arguments. Let's add L2 weight regularization to our initial movie-review classification model.

Listing 5.13 Adding L2 weight regularization to the model

```
model <- keras_model_sequential() %>%
  layer_dense(16, activation = "relu",
              kernel_regularizer = regularizer_l2(0.002)) %>%
  layer_dense(16, activation = "relu",
              kernel_regularizer = regularizer_l2(0.002)) %>%
  layer_dense(1, activation = "sigmoid")

model %>% compile(optimizer = "rmsprop",
                  loss = "binary_crossentropy",
                  metrics = "accuracy")

history_l2_reg <- model %>% fit(
  train_data, train_labels,
  epochs = 20, batch_size = 512, validation_split = 0.4)
```

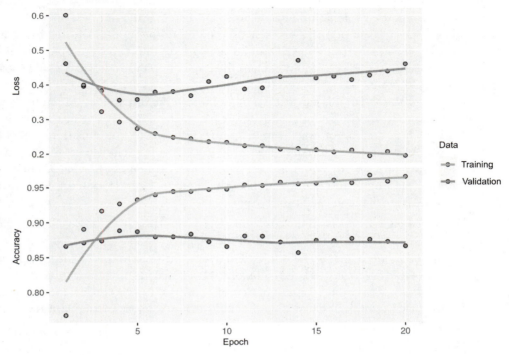

In the preceding listing, `regularizer_l2(0.002)` means every coefficient in the weight matrix of the layer will add `0.002 * weight_coefficient_value ^ 2` to the total loss of the model. Note that because this penalty is *added only at training time*, the loss for this model will be much higher at training than at test time.

Figure 5.19 shows the impact of the L2 regularization penalty. As you can see, the model with L2 regularization has become much more resistant to overfitting than the reference model, even though both models have the same number of parameters.

Listing 5.14   Generating a plot to demonstrate the effect of L2 weight regularization

```
plot(NULL,
     main = "Effect of L2 Weight Regularization on Validation Loss",
     xlab = "Epochs", xlim = c(1, history_original$params$epochs),
     ylab = "Validation Loss",
     ylim = range(c(history_original$metrics$val_loss,
                    history_l2_reg  $metrics$val_loss)),
     panel.first = abline(v = 1:history_original$params$epochs,
                          lty = "dotted", col = "lightgrey"))
lines(history_original$metrics$val_loss, lty = 2)
lines(history_l2_reg  $metrics$val_loss, lty = 1)
legend("topleft", lty = 2:1,
       legend = c("Validation loss of original model",
                  "Validation loss of L2-regularized model"))
```

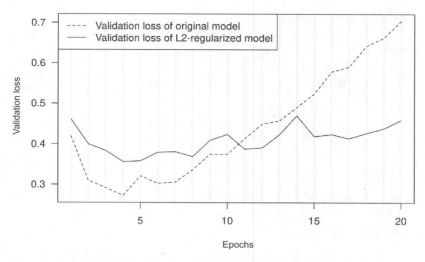

Figure 5.19 **Effect of L2 weight regularization on validation loss**

As an alternative to L2 regularization, you can use one of the following Keras weight regularizers.

Listing 5.15 Different weight regularizers available in Keras

```
regularizer_l1(0.001)                        ◁——— L1 regularization
regularizer_l1_l2(l1 = 0.001, l2 = 0.001)    ◁——
                                                    Simultaneous L1 and
<keras.regularizers.L1 object at 0x7f81cc3df340>    L2 regularization
<keras.regularizers.L1L2 object at 0x7f81cc651c40>
```

Note that weight regularization is more typically used for smaller deep learning models. Large deep learning models tend to be so overparameterized that imposing constraints on weight values doesn't have much impact on model capacity and generalization. In these cases, a different regularization technique is preferred: dropout.

ADDING DROPOUT

Dropout is one of the most effective and most commonly used regularization techniques for neural networks; it was developed by Geoff Hinton and his students at the University of Toronto. Dropout, applied to a layer, consists of randomly *dropping out* (setting to zero) a number of output features of the layer during training. Let's say a given layer would normally return a vector c(0.2, 0.5, 1.3, 0.8, 1.1) for a given input sample during training. After applying dropout, this vector will have a few zero entries distributed at random: for example, c(0, 0.5, 1.3, 0, 1.1). The *dropout rate* is the fraction of the features that are zeroed out; it's usually set between 0.2 and 0.5. At test time, no units are dropped out; instead, the layer's output values are scaled down by a factor equal to the dropout rate, to balance for the fact that more units are active than at training time.

Consider a matrix containing the output of a layer, `layer_output`, of shape (batch_size, features). At training time, we zero out at random a fraction of the values in the matrix:

```
zero_out <- random_array(dim(layer_output)) < .5
layer_output[zero_out] <- 0
```
At training time, drops out 50% of the units in the output

At test time, we scale down the output by the dropout rate. Here, we scale by 0.5 (because we previously dropped half the units):

```
layer_output <- layer_output * .5        At test time
```

Note that this process can be implemented by doing both operations at training time and leaving the output unchanged at test time, which is often the way it's implemented in practice (see figure 5.20):

At training time. Note that we're scaling up rather than scaling down in this case.

```
layer_output[random_array(dim(layer_output)) < dropout_rate] <- 0
layer_output <- layer_output / .5
```

0.3	0.2	1.5	0.0
0.6	0.1	0.0	0.3
0.2	1.9	0.3	1.2
0.7	0.5	1.0	0.0

50% dropout →

0.0	0.2	1.5	0.0
0.6	0.1	0.0	0.3
0.0	1.9	0.3	0.0
0.7	0.0	0.0	0.0

* 2

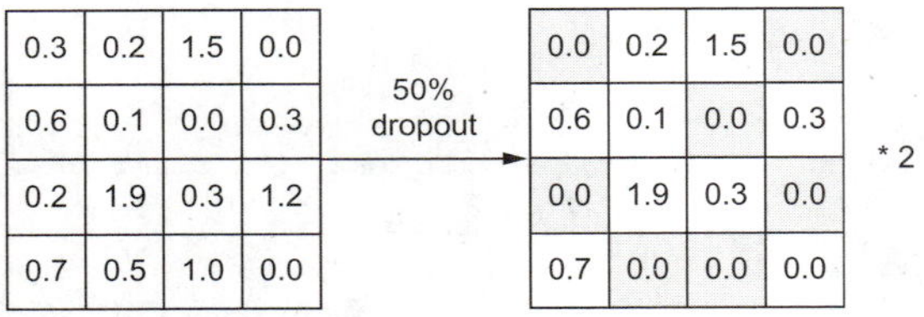

Figure 5.20   Dropout applied to an activation matrix at training time, with rescaling happening during training. At test time, the activation matrix is unchanged.

This technique may seem strange and arbitrary. Why would this help reduce overfitting? Hinton says he was inspired by, among other things, a fraud-prevention mechanism used by banks. In his own words, "I went to my bank. The tellers kept changing, and I asked one of them why. He said he didn't know, but they got moved around a lot. I figured it must be because it would require cooperation between employees to successfully defraud the bank. This made me realize that randomly removing a different subset of neurons on each example would prevent conspiracies and thus reduce overfitting." The core idea is that introducing noise in the output values of a layer can break up happenstance patterns that aren't significant (what Hinton refers to as *conspiracies*), which the model will start memorizing if no noise is present.

In Keras, you can introduce dropout in a model via `layer_dropout`, which applies dropout to the output of the layer right before it. Let's add two `layer_dropouts` to the IMDB model to see how well they do at reducing overfitting.

Listing 5.16   Adding dropout to the IMDB model

```
model <- keras_model_sequential() %>%
  layer_dense(16, activation = "relu") %>%
  layer_dropout(0.5) %>%
```

```
  layer_dense(16, activation = "relu") %>%
  layer_dropout(0.5) %>%
  layer_dense(1, activation = "sigmoid")

model %>% compile(optimizer = "rmsprop",
                  loss = "binary_crossentropy",
                  metrics = "accuracy")

history_dropout <- model %>% fit(
  train_data, train_labels,
  epochs = 20, batch_size = 512,
  validation_split = 0.4
)

plot(history_dropout)
```

Figure 5.21 shows a plot of the results. This is a clear improvement over the reference model—it also seems to be working much better than L2 regularization, because the lowest validation loss reached has improved.

Listing 5.17   Generating a plot to demonstrate the effect of dropout on validation loss

```
plot(NULL,
     main = "Effect of Dropout on Validation Loss",
     xlab = "Epochs", xlim = c(1, history_original$params$epochs),
```

```
        ylab = "Validation Loss",
        ylim = range(c(history_original$metrics$val_loss,
                     history_dropout $metrics$val_loss)),
        panel.first = abline(v = 1:history_original$params$epochs,
                           lty = "dotted", col = "lightgrey"))
lines(history_original$metrics$val_loss, lty = 2)
lines(history_dropout $metrics$val_loss, lty = 1)
legend("topleft", lty = 1:2,
        legend = c("Validation loss of dropout-regularized model",
                   "Validation loss of original model"))
```

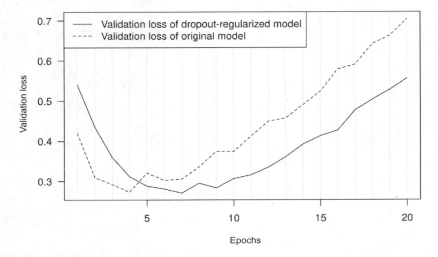

Figure 5.21   Effect of dropout on validation loss

To recap, these are the most common ways to maximize generalization and prevent overfitting in neural networks:

- Get more training data, or better training data.
- Develop better features.
- Reduce the capacity of the model.
- Add weight regularization (for smaller models).
- Add dropout.

Summary

- The purpose of a machine learning model is to *generalize*: to perform accurately on never-before-seen inputs. It's harder than it seems.
- A deep neural network achieves generalization by learning a parametric model that can successfully *interpolate* between training samples—such a model can be said to have learned the "latent manifold" of the training data. This is why deep learning models can make sense of only inputs that are very close to what they've seen during training.

- The fundamental problem in machine learning is *the tension between optimization and generalization*: to attain generalization, you must first achieve a good fit to the training data, but improving your model's fit to the training data will inevitably start hurting generalization after a while. Every single deep learning best practice deals with managing this tension.

- The ability of deep learning models to generalize comes from the fact that they manage to learn to approximate the *latent manifold* of their data and can thus make sense of new inputs via interpolation.

- It's essential to be able to accurately evaluate the generalization power of your model while you're developing it. You have at your disposal an array of evaluation methods, from simple holdout validation to *K*-fold cross-validation and iterated *K*-fold cross-validation with shuffling. Remember to always keep a completely separate test set for final model evaluation, because information leaks from your validation data to your model may have occurred.

- When you start working on a model, your goal is first to achieve a model that has some generalization power and that can overfit. Best practices for doing this include tuning your learning rate and batch size, leveraging better architecture priors, increasing model capacity, or simply training longer.

- As your model starts overfitting, your goal switches to improving generalization through *model regularization*. You can reduce your model's capacity, add dropout or weight regularization, and use early stopping. And naturally, a larger or better dataset is always the number one way to help a model generalize.

The universal workflow
of machine learning

Our previous examples have assumed that we already had a labeled dataset to start from, and that we could immediately start training a model. In the real world, this is often not the case. You don't start from a dataset; you start from a problem.

Imagine that you're starting your own machine learning consulting shop. You incorporate, you put up a fancy website, you notify your network. The following projects start rolling in:

- A personalized photo search engine for a picture-sharing social network— type in "wedding" and retrieve all the pictures you took at weddings, without any manual tagging needed.
- Flagging spam and offensive text content among the posts of a budding chat app.

- Building a music recommendation system for users of an online radio station.
- Detecting credit card fraud for an e-commerce website.
- Predicting display ad click-through rates to decide which ad to serve to a given user at a given time.
- Flagging anomalous cookies on the conveyor belt of a cookie-manufacturing line.
- Using satellite images to predict the location of as-yet-unknown archeological sites.

> ### Note on ethics
>
> You may sometimes be offered ethically dubious projects, such as "building an AI that rates the trustworthiness of someone from a picture of their face." First of all, the validity of the project is in doubt: it isn't clear why trustworthiness would be reflected on someone's face. Second, such a task opens the door to all kinds of ethical problems. Collecting a dataset for this task would amount to recording the biases and prejudices of the people who label the pictures. The models you would train on such data would merely encode these same biases into a black-box algorithm that would give them a thin veneer of legitimacy. In a largely tech-illiterate society like ours, "the AI algorithm said this person cannot be trusted" strangely appears to carry more weight and objectivity than "John Smith said this person cannot be trusted," despite the former being a learned approximation of the latter. Your model would be laundering and operationalizing at scale the worst aspects of human judgment, with negative effects on the lives of real people.
>
> Technology is never neutral. If your work has any impact on the world, this impact has a moral direction: technical choices are also ethical choices. Always be deliberate about the values you want your work to support.

It would be very convenient if you could access the correct dataset with `keras::dataset_mydataset()` and start fitting some deep learning models. Unfortunately, in the real world, you'll have to start from scratch.

In this chapter, you'll learn about a universal step-by-step blueprint that you can use to approach and solve any machine learning problem, like those in the previous list. This template will bring together and consolidate everything you've learned in chapters 4 and 5 and will give you the wider context that should anchor what you'll learn in the next chapters.

The universal workflow of machine learning is broadly structured in three parts:

1 *Define the task*—Understand the problem domain and the business logic underlying what the customer asked for. Collect a dataset, understand what the data represents, and choose how you will measure success on the task.

2 *Develop a model*—Prepare your data so that it can be processed by a machine learning model, select a model-evaluation protocol and a simple baseline to beat, train a first model that has generalization power and that can overfit, and then regularize and tune your model until you achieve the best possible generalization performance.

3   *Deploy the model*—Present your work to stakeholders; ship the model to a web server, a mobile app, a web page, or an embedded device; monitor the model's performance in the wild; and start collecting the data you'll need to build the next-generation model.

Let's dive in.

6.1   Define the task

You can't do good work without a deep understanding of the context of what you're doing. Why is your customer trying to solve this particular problem? What value will they derive from the solution—how will your model be used, and how will it fit into your customer's business processes? What kind of data is available or could be collected? What kind of machine learning task can be mapped to the business problem?

6.1.1   Frame the problem

Framing a machine learning problem usually involves many detailed discussions with stakeholders. Here are the questions that should be on the top of your mind:

What will your input data be? What are you trying to predict? You can learn to predict something only if you have training data available: for example, you can learn to classify the sentiment of movie reviews only if you have both movie reviews and sentiment annotations available. As such, data availability is usually the limiting factor at this stage. In many cases, you will have to resort to collecting and annotating new datasets yourself (which we'll cover in the next section).

What type of machine learning task are you facing? Is it binary classification? Multiclass classification? Scalar regression? Vector regression? Multiclass, multilabel classification? Image segmentation? Ranking? Something else, like clustering, generation, or reinforcement learning? In some cases, it may be that machine learning isn't even the best way to make sense of the data, and you should use something else, such as plain old-school statistical analysis:

- The photo search engine project is a multiclass, multilabel classification task.
- The spam detection project is a binary classification task. If you set "offensive content" as a separate class, it's a three-way classification task.
- The music recommendation engine turns out to be better handled not via deep learning but via matrix factorization (collaborative filtering).
- The credit card fraud-detection project is a binary classification task.
- The click-through rate prediction project is a scalar regression task.
- Anomalous cookie detection is a binary classification task, but it will also require an object detection model as a first stage to correctly crop out the cookies in raw images. Note that the set of machine learning techniques known as "anomaly detection" would not be a good fit in this setting!
- The project for finding new archeological sites from satellite images is an image-similarity ranking task: you need to retrieve new images that look the most like known archeological sites.

What do existing solutions look like? Perhaps your customer already has a hand-crafted algorithm that handles spam filtering or credit card fraud detection, with lots of nested `if` statements. Perhaps a human is currently in charge of manually handling the process under consideration—monitoring the conveyor belt at the cookie plant and manually removing the bad cookies, or crafting playlists of song recommendations to be sent out to users who liked a specific artist. You should make sure you understand what systems are already in place and how they work.

Are there particular constraints you will need to deal with? For example, you could find out that the app for which you're building a spam-detection system is strictly end-to-end encrypted, so that the spam-detection model will have to live on the end user's phone and must be trained on an external dataset. Perhaps the cookie-filtering model has such latency constraints that it will need to run on an embedded device at the factory rather than on a remote server. You should understand the full context in which your work will fit.

Once you've done your research, you should know what your inputs will be, what your targets will be, and what broad type of machine learning task the problem maps to. Be aware of the hypotheses you're making at this stage:

- You hypothesize that your targets can be predicted given your inputs.
- You hypothesize that the data that's available (or that you will soon collect) is sufficiently informative to learn the relationship between inputs and targets.

Until you have a working model, these are merely hypotheses, waiting to be validated or invalidated. Not all problems can be solved with machine learning; just because you've assembled examples of inputs X and targets Y doesn't mean X contains enough information to predict Y. For instance, if you're trying to predict the movements of a stock on the stock market given its recent price history, you're unlikely to succeed, because price history doesn't contain much predictive information.

6.1.2 Collect a dataset

Once you understand the nature of the task and you know what your inputs and targets are going to be, it's time for data collection—the most arduous, time-consuming, and costly part of most machine learning projects:

- The photo search engine project requires you to first select the set of labels you want to classify—you settle on 10,000 common image categories. Then you need to manually tag hundreds of thousands of your past user-uploaded images with labels from this set.
- For the chat app's spam-detection project, because user chats are end-to-end encrypted, you cannot use their contents for training a model. You need to gain access to a separate dataset of tens of thousands of unfiltered social media posts and manually tag them as spam, offensive, or acceptable.

- For the music recommendation engine, you can just use the "likes" of your users. No new data needs to be collected. Likewise for the click-through rate prediction project: you have an extensive record of click-through rates for your past ads, going back years.
- For the cookie-flagging model, you will need to install cameras above the conveyor belts to collect tens of thousands of images, and then someone will need to manually label these images. The people who know how to do this currently work at the cookie factory, but it doesn't seem too difficult. You should be able to train people to do it.
- The satellite imagery project will require a team of archeologists to collect a database of existing sites of interest, and for each site you will need to find existing satellite images taken in different weather conditions. To get a good model, you're going to need thousands of different sites.

You learned in chapter 5 that a model's ability to generalize comes almost entirely from the properties of the data it is trained on: the number of data points you have, the reliability of your labels, the quality of your features. A good dataset is an asset worthy of care and investment. If you get an extra 50 hours to spend on a project, chances are that the most effective way to allocate them is to collect more data rather than search for incremental modeling improvements.

The point that data matters more than algorithms was most famously made in a 2009 paper by Google researchers titled, "The Unreasonable Effectiveness of Data" (the title is a riff on the well-known 1960 article "The Unreasonable Effectiveness of Mathematics in the Natural Sciences" by Eugene Wigner). This was before deep learning was popular, but, remarkably, the rise of deep learning has only made the importance of data greater.

If you're doing supervised learning, then once you've collected inputs (such as images) you're going to need *annotations* for them (such as tags for those images)—the targets you will train your model to predict. Sometimes, annotations can be retrieved automatically, such as those for the music recommendation task or the click-through rate prediction task. But often you have to annotate your data by hand. This is a labor-heavy process.

INVESTING IN DATA ANNOTATION INFRASTRUCTURE

Your data annotation process will determine the quality of your targets, which in turn determine the quality of your model. Carefully consider the options you have available:

- Should you annotate the data yourself?
- Should you use a crowdsourcing platform like Mechanical Turk to collect labels?
- Should you use the services of a specialized data-labeling company?

Outsourcing can potentially save you time and money, but it takes away control. Using something like Mechanical Turk is likely to be inexpensive and scale well, but your annotations may end up being quite noisy.

To pick the best option, consider the constraints you're working with:

- Do the data labelers need to be subject matter experts, or could anyone annotate the data? The labels for a cat-versus-dog image-classification problem can be selected by anyone, but those for a dog breed classification task require specialized knowledge. Meanwhile, annotating CT scans of bone fractures pretty much requires a medical degree.
- If annotating the data requires specialized knowledge, can you train people to do it? If not, how can you get access to relevant experts?
- Do you, yourself, understand the way experts come up with the annotations? If you don't, you will have to treat your dataset as a black box, and you won't be able to perform manual feature engineering—this isn't critical, but it can be limiting.

If you decide to label your data in-house, ask yourself what software you will use to record annotations. You may well need to develop that software yourself. Productive data annotation software will save you a lot of time, so it's worth investing in it early in a project.

Beware of nonrepresentative data

Machine learning models can only make sense of inputs that are similar to what they've seen before. As such, it's critical that the data used for training should be *representative* of the production data. This concern should be the foundation of all your data-collection work.

Suppose you're developing an app where users can take pictures of a plate of food to find out the name of the dish. You train a model using pictures from an image-sharing social network that's popular with foodies. Come deployment time, feedback from angry users starts rolling in: your app gets the answer wrong 8 times out of 10 times. What's going on? Your accuracy on the test set was well over 90%! A quick look at user-uploaded data reveals that mobile picture uploads of random dishes from random restaurants taken with random smartphones look nothing like the professional-quality, well-lit, appetizing pictures you trained the model on: *your training data wasn't representative of the production data*. That's a cardinal sin—welcome to machine learning hell.

If possible, collect data directly from the environment where your model will be used. A movie-review sentiment-classification model should be used on new IMDB reviews, not on Yelp restaurant reviews or on Twitter status updates. If you want to rate the sentiment of a tweet, start by collecting and annotating actual tweets from a similar set of users as those you're expecting in production. If it's not possible to train on production data, then make sure you fully understand how your training and production data differ and that you are actively correcting for these differences.

A related phenomenon you should be aware of is *concept drift*. You'll encounter concept drift in almost all real-world problems, especially those that deal with user-generated data. Concept drift occurs when the properties of the production data change over time, causing model accuracy to gradually decay. A music-recommendation engine trained in the year 2013 may not be very effective today. Likewise, the IMDB dataset you worked with was collected in 2011, and a model trained on it would likely not perform as well on reviews from 2020 compared to reviews from 2012, because vocabulary, expressions, and movie genres evolve over time. Concept drift is particularly acute in adversarial contexts like credit card fraud detection, where fraud patterns change practically every day. Dealing with fast concept drift requires constant data collection, annotation, and model retraining.

Keep in mind that machine learning can only be used to memorize patterns that are present in your training data. You can only recognize what you've seen before. Using machine learning trained on past data to predict the future is making the assumption that the future will behave like the past. That often isn't the case.

The problem of sampling bias

A particularly insidious and common case of nonrepresentative data is *sampling bias*. Sampling bias occurs when your data-collection process interacts with what you are trying to predict, resulting in biased measurements. A famous historical example occurred in the 1948 US presidential election. On election night, the *Chicago Tribune* printed the headline "DEWEY DEFEATS TRUMAN." The next morning, Truman emerged as the winner. The editor of the *Tribune* had trusted the results of a phone survey—but phone users in 1948 were not a random, representative sample of the voting population. They were more likely to be richer and conservative and to have voted for Dewey, the Republican candidate.

"DEWEY DEFEATS TRUMAN": A famous example of sampling bias

Nowadays, every phone survey takes sampling bias into account. That doesn't mean that sampling bias is a thing of the past in political polling—far from it. But unlike in 1948, pollsters are aware of it and take steps to correct it.

6.1.3 Understand your data

It's pretty bad practice to treat a dataset as a black box. Before you start training models, you should explore and visualize your data to gain insights about what makes it predictive, which will inform feature engineering and screen for potential issues:

- If your data includes images or natural language text, take a look at a few samples (and their labels) directly.
- If your data contains numerical features, it's a good idea to plot the histogram of feature values to get a feel for the range of values taken and the frequency of different values.
- If your data includes location information, plot it on a map. Do any clear patterns emerge?
- Are some samples missing values for some features? If so, you'll need to deal with this when you prepare the data (we'll cover how to do this in the next section).
- If your task is a classification problem, print the number of instances of each class in your data. Are the classes roughly equally represented? If not, you will need to account for this imbalance.
- Check for *target leaking*: the presence of features in your data that provide information about the targets and which may not be available in production. If you're training a model on medical records to predict whether someone will be treated for cancer in the future, and the records include the feature "this person has been diagnosed with cancer," then your targets are being artificially leaked into your data. Always ask yourself, is every feature in your data something that will be available in the same form in production?

6.1.4 Choose a measure of success

To control something, you need to be able to observe it. To achieve success on a project, you must first define what you mean by success. Accuracy? Precision and recall? Customer retention rate? Your metric for success will guide all of the technical choices you make throughout the project. It should directly align with your higher-level goals, such as the business success of your customer.

For balanced classification problems, where every class is equally likely, accuracy and the area under a *receiver operating characteristic* (ROC) curve, abbreviated as ROC AUC, are common metrics. For class-imbalanced problems, ranking problems, or multilabel classification, you can use precision and recall, as well as a weighted form of accuracy or ROC AUC. It isn't uncommon to have to define your own custom metric by which to measure success. To get a sense of the diversity of machine learning success metrics and how they relate to different problem domains, it's helpful to browse the data science competitions on Kaggle (https://kaggle.com); they showcase a wide range of problems and evaluation metrics.

6.2 Develop a model

Once you know how you will measure your progress, you can get started with model development. Most tutorials and research projects assume that this is the only step—skipping problem definition and dataset collection, which are assumed already done, and skipping model deployment and maintenance, which are assumed to be handled by someone else. In fact, model development is only one step in the machine learning workflow, and if you ask me, it's not the most difficult one. The hardest things in machine learning are framing problems and collecting, annotating, and cleaning data. So cheer up—what comes next will be easy in comparison!

6.2.1 Prepare the data

As you've learned earlier, deep learning models typically don't ingest raw data. Data preprocessing aims at making the raw data at hand more amenable to neural networks. This includes vectorization, normalization, or handling missing values. Many preprocessing techniques are domain-specific (e.g., specific to text data or image data); we'll cover those in the following chapters as we encounter them in practical examples. For now, we'll review the basics that are common to all data domains.

VECTORIZATION

All inputs and targets in a neural network must typically be tensors of floating-point data (or, in specific cases, tensors of integers or strings). Whatever data you need to process—sound, images, or text—you must first turn it into tensors, a step called *data vectorization*. For instance, in the two text-classification examples in chapter 4, we started with text represented as lists of integers (standing for sequences of words), and we used one-hot encoding to turn them into a tensor of `float32` data. In the examples of classifying digits and predicting house prices, the data came in vectorized form, so we were able to skip this step.

VALUE NORMALIZATION

In the MNIST digit-classification example from chapter 2, we started with image data encoded as integers in the 0–255 range, encoding grayscale values. Before we fed this data into our network, we divide by 255 so we'd end up with floating-point values in the 0–1 range. Similarly, when predicting house prices, we started with features that took a variety of ranges—some features had small floating-point values, and others had fairly large integer values. Before we fed this data into our network, we had to normalize each feature independently so that it had a standard deviation of 1 and a mean of 0.

In general, it isn't safe to feed into a neural network data that takes relatively large values (e.g., multidigit integers that are much larger than the initial values taken by the weights of a network) or data that is heterogeneous (e.g., data where one feature is in the range 0–1 and another is in the range 100–200). Doing so can trigger large gradient updates that will prevent the network from converging. To make learning easier for your network, your data should have the following characteristics:

- *Take small values*—Typically, most values should be in the 0–1 range.
- *Be homogenous*—All features should take values in roughly the same range.

Additionally, the following stricter normalization practice is common and can help, although it isn't always necessary (e.g., we didn't do this in the digit-classification example):

- Normalize each feature independently to have a mean of 0.
- Normalize each feature independently to have a standard deviation of 1.

This is easy to do using the `scale()` function:

```
x <- scale(x)   ⊲─── Assuming x is a 2D data matrix of shape (samples, features)
```

HANDLING MISSING VALUES

You may sometimes have missing values in your data. For instance, in the house-price example, the first feature was the per capita crime rate. What if this feature wasn't available for all samples? You'd then have missing values in the training or test data. You could just discard the feature entirely, but you don't necessarily have to do so:

- If the feature is categorical, it's safe to create a new category that means "the value is missing." The model will automatically learn what this implies with respect to the targets.
- If the feature is numerical, avoid inputting an arbitrary value like 0, because it may create a discontinuity in the latent space formed by your features, making it harder for a model trained on it to generalize. Instead, consider replacing the missing value with the average or median value for the feature in the dataset. You could also train a model to predict the feature value given the values of other features.

Note that if you're expecting missing categorical features in the test data, but the network was trained on data without any missing values, the network won't have learned to ignore missing values! In this situation, you should artificially generate training samples with missing entries: copy some training samples several times, and drop some of the categorical features that you expect are likely to be missing in the test data.

6.2.2 Choose an evaluation protocol

As you learned in the previous chapter, the purpose of a model is to achieve generalization, and every modeling decision you will make throughout the model-development process will be guided by *validation metrics* that seek to measure generalization performance. The goal of your validation protocol is to accurately estimate what your success metric of choice (such as accuracy) will be on actual production data. The reliability of that process is critical to building a useful model. In chapter 5, we reviewed three common evaluation protocols:

- *Maintaining a holdout validation set*—This is the way to go when you have plenty of data.
- *Doing K-fold cross-validation*—This is the right choice when you have too few samples for holdout validation to be reliable.
- *Doing iterated K-fold validation*—This is for performing highly accurate model evaluation when little data is available.

Pick one of these. In most cases, the first will work well enough. As you learned, though, always be mindful of the *representativity* of your validation set, and be careful not to have redundant samples between your training set and your validation set.

6.2.3   *Beat a baseline*

As you start working on the model itself, your initial goal is to achieve *statistical power*, as you saw in chapter 5: that is, to develop a small model that is capable of beating a simple baseline. At this stage, these are the three most important things you should focus on:

- *Feature engineering*—Filter out uninformative features (feature selection), and use your knowledge of the problem to develop new features that are likely to be useful.
- *Selecting the correct architecture priors*—What type of model architecture will you use? A densely connected network, a convnet, a recurrent neural network, a transformer? Is deep learning even a good approach for the task, or should you use something else?
- *Selecting a good-enough training configuration*—What loss function should you use? What batch size and learning rate?

For most problems, you can start from existing templates. You're not the first person to try to build a spam detector, a music recommendation engine, or an image classifier. Make sure you research prior art to identify the feature-engineering techniques and model architectures that are most likely to perform well on your task.

Note that it's not always possible to achieve statistical power. If you can't beat a simple baseline after trying multiple reasonable architectures, it may be that the answer to the question you're asking isn't present in the input data. Remember that you're making two hypotheses:

- You hypothesize that your outputs can be predicted given your inputs.
- You hypothesize that the available data is sufficiently informative to learn the relationship between inputs and outputs.

It may well be that these hypotheses are false, in which case you must go back to the drawing board.

Picking the right loss function

It's often not possible to directly optimize for the metric that measures success on a problem. Sometimes there is no easy way to turn a metric into a loss function; loss functions, after all, need to be computable given only a mini-batch of data (ideally, a loss function should be computable for as little as a single data point) and must be differentiable (otherwise, you can't use backpropagation to train your network). For instance, the widely used classification metric ROC AUC can't be directly optimized. Hence, in classification tasks, it's common to optimize for a proxy metric of ROC AUC, such as cross-entropy. In general, you can hope that the lower the cross-entropy gets, the higher the ROC AUC will be.

The following table can help you choose a last-layer activation and a loss function for a few common problem types.

Choosing the right last-layer activation and loss function

Problem type	Last-layer activation	Loss function
Binary classification	sigmoid	binary_crossentropy
Multiclass, single-label classification	softmax	categorical_crossentropy
Multiclass, multilabel classification	sigmoid	binary_crossentropy

6.2.4 Scale up: Develop a model that overfits

Once you've obtained a model that has statistical power, the question becomes, is your model sufficiently powerful? Does it have enough layers and parameters to properly model the problem at hand? For instance, a logistic regression model has statistical power on MNIST but wouldn't be sufficient to solve the problem well. Remember that the universal tension in machine learning is between optimization and generalization. The ideal model is one that stands right at the border between underfitting and overfitting, between undercapacity and overcapacity. To figure out where this border lies, first you must cross it.

To figure out how big a model you'll need, you must develop a model that overfits. This is fairly easy, as you learned in chapter 5:

1 Add layers.
2 Make the layers bigger.
3 Train for more epochs.

Always monitor the training loss and validation loss, as well as the training and validation values for any metrics you care about. When you see that the model's performance on the validation data begins to degrade, you've achieved overfitting.

6.2.5   *Regularize and tune your model*

Once you've achieved statistical power and you're able to overfit, you know you're on the right path. At this point, your goal becomes to maximize generalization performance.

This phase will take the most time: you'll repeatedly modify your model, train it, evaluate on your validation data (not the test data at this point), modify it again, and repeat, until the model is as good as it can get. Here are some things you should try:

- Try different architectures; add or remove layers.
- Add dropout.
- If your model is small, add L1 or L2 regularization.
- Try different hyperparameters (such as the number of units per layer or the learning rate of the optimizer) to find the optimal configuration.
- Optionally, iterate on data curation or feature engineering: collect and annotate more data, develop better features, or remove features that don't seem to be informative.

It's possible to automate a large chunk of this work by using *automated hyperparameter tuning software*, such as KerasTuner. We'll cover this in chapter 13.

Be mindful of the following: Every time you use feedback from your validation process to tune your model, you leak information about the validation process into the model. Repeated just a few times, this is innocuous; done systematically over many iterations, it will eventually cause your model to overfit to the validation process (even though no model is directly trained on any of the validation data). This makes the evaluation process less reliable.

Once you've developed a satisfactory model configuration, you can train your final production model on all the available data (training and validation) and evaluate it one last time on the test set. If it turns out that performance on the test set is significantly worse than the performance measured on the validation data, this may mean either that your validation procedure wasn't reliable after all, or that you began overfitting to the validation data while tuning the parameters of the model. In this case, you may want to switch to a more reliable evaluation protocol (such as iterated *K*-fold validation).

6.3   *Deploy the model*

Your model has successfully cleared its final evaluation on the test set—it's ready to be deployed and to begin its productive life.

6.3.1   *Explain your work to stakeholders and set expectations*

Success and customer trust are about consistently meeting or exceeding people's expectations. The actual system you deliver is only half of that picture; the other half is setting appropriate expectations before launch.

The expectations of nonspecialists toward AI systems are often unrealistic. For example, they might expect that the system "understands" its task and is capable of exercising human-like common sense in the context of the task. To address this, you should consider showing some examples of the *failure modes* of your model (e.g., show what incorrectly classified samples look like, especially those for which the misclassification seems surprising).

They might also expect human-level performance, especially for processes that were previously handled by people. Most machine learning models, because they are (imperfectly) trained to approximate human-generated labels, do not nearly get there. You should clearly convey model performance expectations. Avoid using abstract statements like "The model has 98% accuracy" (which most people mentally round up to 100%), and prefer talking, for instance, about false negative rates and false positive rates. You could say, "With these settings, the fraud detection model would have a 5% false negative rate and a 2.5% false positive rate. Every day, an average of 200 valid transactions would be flagged as fraudulent and sent for manual review, and an average of 14 fraudulent transactions would be missed. An average of 266 fraudulent transactions would be correctly caught." Clearly relate the model's performance metrics to business goals.

You should also make sure to discuss with stakeholders the choice of key launch parameters—for instance, the probability threshold at which a transaction should be flagged (different thresholds will produce different false negative and false positive rates). Such decisions involve tradeoffs that can be handled only with a deep understanding of the business context.

6.3.2 *Ship an inference model*

A machine learning project doesn't end when you arrive at a script that can save a trained model. You rarely put in production the exact same model object that you manipulated during training. First, you may want to export your model to something other than R:

- Your production environment may not support R at all—for instance, if it's a mobile app or an embedded system.
- If the rest of the app isn't in R (it could be in JavaScript, C++, etc.), the use of R to serve a model may induce significant overhead.

Second, because your production model will be used only to output predictions (a phase called *inference*), rather than for training, you have room to perform various optimizations that can make the model faster and reduce its memory footprint. Let's take a quick look at the different model deployment options you have available.

DEPLOYING A MODEL AS A REST API

This is perhaps the common way to turn a model into a product: install TensorFlow on a server or cloud instance, and query the model's predictions via a REST API. You could build your own serving app using something like Shiny (or any other R web development library), or the tfdeploy R package, which uses TensorFlow's own library for shipping models as APIs, called *TensorFlow Serving* (http://www.tensorflow.org/tfx/guide/serving). With `tfdeploy` and TensorFlow Serving, you can deploy a Keras model in minutes.

You should use this deployment setup when:

- The application that will consume the model's prediction will have reliable access to the internet (obviously). For instance, if your application is a mobile app, serving predictions from a remote API means that the application won't be usable in airplane mode or in a low-connectivity environment.
- The application does not have strict latency requirements: the request, inference, and answer round trip will typically take around 500 ms.
- The input data sent for inference is not highly sensitive: the data will need to be available on the server in a decrypted form, because it will need to be seen by the model (but note that you should use SSL encryption for the HTTP request and answer).

For instance, the image search engine project, the music recommendation system, the credit card fraud detection project, and the satellite imagery project are all good fits for serving via a REST API.

An important question when deploying a model as a REST API is whether you want to host the code on your own, or whether you want to use a fully managed third-party cloud service. For instance, Cloud AI Platform, a Google product, lets you simply upload your TensorFlow model to Google Cloud Storage (GCS), and it gives you an API endpoint to query it. It takes care of many practical details such as batching predictions, load balancing, and scaling.

DEPLOYING A MODEL ON A DEVICE

Sometimes, you may need your model to live on the same device that runs the application that uses it—maybe a smartphone, an embedded ARM CPU on a robot, or a microcontroller on a tiny device. You may have seen a camera capable of automatically detecting people and faces in the scenes you pointed it at: that was probably a small deep learning model running directly on the camera.

You should use this setup when:

- Your model has strict latency constraints or needs to run in a low-connectivity environment. If you're building an immersive augmented reality application, querying a remote server is not a viable option.
- Your model can be made sufficiently small that it can run under the memory and power constraints of the target device. You can use the TensorFlow Model Optimization Toolkit to help with this (http://www.tensorflow.org/model_optimization).
- Getting the highest possible accuracy isn't mission critical for your task. There is always a tradeoff between runtime efficiency and accuracy, so memory and power constraints often require you to ship a model that isn't quite as good as the best model you could run on a large GPU.

- The input data is strictly sensitive and thus shouldn't be decryptable on a remote server.

Our spam detection model will need to run on the end user's smartphone as part of the chat app, because messages are end-to-end encrypted and thus cannot be read by a remotely hosted model. Likewise, the bad-cookie detection model has strict latency constraints and will need to run at the factory. Thankfully, in this case, we don't have any power or space constraints, so we can actually run the model on a GPU.

To deploy a Keras model on a smartphone or embedded device, your go-to solution is TensorFlow Lite (http://www.tensorflow.org/lite). It's a framework for efficient on-device deep learning inference that runs on Android and iOS smartphones, as well as ARM64-based computers, Raspberry Pi, or certain microcontrollers. It includes a converter that can straightforwardly turn your Keras model into the TensorFlow Lite format.

DEPLOYING A MODEL IN THE BROWSER

Deep learning is often used in browser-based or desktop-based JavaScript applications. Although it is usually possible to have the application query a remote model via a REST API, there can be key advantages in having the model run directly in the browser, on the user's computer (utilizing GPU resources if they're available).

Use this setup when:

- You want to offload compute to the end user, which can dramatically reduce server costs.
- The input data needs to stay on the end user's computer or phone. For instance, in our spam detection project, the web version and the desktop version of the chat app (implemented as a cross-platform app written in JavaScript) should use a locally run model.
- Your application has strict latency constraints. Although a model running on the end user's laptop or smartphone is likely to be slower than one running on a large GPU on your own server, you don't have the extra 100 ms of network round trip.
- You need your app to keep working without connectivity, after the model has been downloaded and cached.

You should go with this option only if your model is small enough that it won't hog the CPU, GPU, or RAM of your user's laptop or smartphone. In addition, because the entire model will be downloaded to the user's device, you should make sure that nothing about the model needs to stay confidential. Be mindful of the fact that, given a trained deep learning model, it is usually possible to recover some information about the training data: better not to make your trained model public if it was trained on sensitive data.

To deploy a model in JavaScript, the TensorFlow ecosystem includes TensorFlow.js (http://www.tensorflow.org/js), a JavaScript library for deep learning that implements almost all of the Keras API (originally developed under the working name WebKeras) as well as many lower-level TensorFlow APIs. You can easily import a saved Keras model into TensorFlow.js to query it as part of your browser-based JavaScript app or your desktop Electron app.

INFERENCE MODEL OPTIMIZATION

Optimizing your model for inference is especially important when deploying in an environment with strict constraints on available power and memory (smartphones and embedded devices) or for applications with low latency requirements. You should always seek to optimize your model before importing into TensorFlow.js or exporting it to TensorFlow Lite.

You can apply two popular optimization techniques:

- *Weight pruning*—Not every coefficient in a weight tensor contributes equally to the predictions. It's possible to considerably lower the number of parameters in the layers of your model by keeping only the most significant ones. This reduces the memory and compute footprint of your model, at a small cost in performance metrics. By deciding how much pruning you want to apply, you are in control of the tradeoff between size and accuracy.
- *Weight quantization*—Deep learning models are trained with single-precision floating-point (float32) weights. However, it's possible to *quantize* weights to 8-bit signed integers (int8) to get an inference-only model that's a quarter the size but remains near the accuracy of the original model.

The TensorFlow ecosystem includes a weight pruning and quantization toolkit (http://www.tensorflow.org/model_optimization) that is deeply integrated with the Keras API.

6.3.3 *Monitor your model in the wild*

You've exported an inference model, you've integrated it into your application, and you've done a dry run on production data—the model behaved exactly as you expected. You've written unit tests as well as logging and status-monitoring code—perfect. Now it's time to press the big red button and deploy to production.

Even this is not the end. Once you've deployed a model, you need to keep monitoring its behavior, its performance on new data, its interaction with the rest of the application, and its eventual impact on business metrics:

- Is user engagement in your online radio station up or down after deploying the new music recommendation system? Has the average ad click-through rate increased after switching to the new click-through-rate-prediction model? Consider using *randomized A/B testing* to isolate the impact of the model itself from other changes: a subset of cases should go through the new model, whereas another control subset should stick to the old process. Once sufficiently many cases have been processed, the difference in outcomes between the two is likely attributable to the model.

- If possible, do a regular manual audit of the model's predictions on production data. It's generally possible to reuse the same infrastructure as for data annotation: send some fraction of the production data to be manually annotated, and compare the model's predictions to the new annotations. For instance, you should definitely do this for the image search engine and the bad-cookie flagging system.
- When manual audits are impossible, consider alternative evaluation avenues such as user surveys (e.g., in the case of the spam and offensive-content flagging system).

6.3.4 *Maintain your model*

Finally, no model lasts forever. You've already learned about *concept drift*: over time, the characteristics of your production data will change, gradually degrading the performance and relevance of your model. The life span of your music recommendation system will be counted in weeks. For the credit card fraud detection system, it will be days; a couple of years is the best case for the image search engine.

As soon as your model has launched, you should be getting ready to train the next generation that will replace it. As such:

- Watch out for changes in the production data. Are new features becoming available? Should you expand or otherwise edit the label set?
- Keep collecting and annotating data, and keep improving your annotation pipeline over time. In particular, you should pay special attention to collecting samples that seem to be difficult for your current model to classify—such samples are the most likely to help improve performance.

This concludes the universal workflow of machine learning—that's a lot of things to keep in mind. It takes time and experience to become an expert, but don't worry: you're already a lot wiser than you were a few chapters ago. You are now familiar with the big picture—the entire spectrum of what machine learning projects entail. Although most of this book will focus on model development, you're now aware that it's only one part of the entire workflow. Always keep in mind the big picture!

Summary

- When you take on a new machine learning project, first define the problem at hand:
  - Understand the broader context of what you're setting out to do—what's the end goal and what are the constraints?
  - Collect and annotate a dataset; make sure you understand your data in depth.
  - Choose how you'll measure success for your problem—what metrics will you monitor on your validation data?

- Once you understand the problem and you have an appropriate dataset, develop a model:
  - Prepare your data.
  - Pick your evaluation protocol: holdout validation? *K*-fold validation? Which portion of the data should you use for validation?
  - Achieve statistical power: beat a simple baseline.
  - Scale up: develop a model that can overfit.
  - Regularize your model and tune its hyperparameters, based on performance on the validation data. A lot of machine learning research tends to focus only on this step, but keep the big picture in mind.
- When your model is ready and yields good performance on the test data, it's time for deployment:
  - First, make sure you set appropriate expectations with stakeholders.
  - Optimize a final model for inference, and ship a model to the deployment environment of choice—web server, mobile, browser, embedded device, and so on.
  - Monitor your model's performance in production, and keep collecting data so you can develop the next generation of the model.

Working with Keras: A deep dive

This chapter covers

- Creating Keras models with `keras_model_sequential()`, the Functional API, and model subclassing
- Using built-in Keras training and evaluation loops
- Using Keras callbacks to customize training
- Using TensorBoard to monitor training and evaluation metrics
- Writing training and evaluation loops from scratch

You've now got some experience with Keras—you're familiar with the Sequential model, dense layers, and built-in APIs for training, evaluation, and inference—`compile()`, `fit()`, `evaluate()`, and `predict()`. You even learned in chapter 3 how to use `new_layer_class()` to create custom layers, and how to use the TensorFlow `GradientTape()` to implement a step-by-step training loop.

In the coming chapters, we'll dig into computer vision, time-series forecasting, natural language processing, and generative deep learning. These complex applications will require much more than a `keras_model_sequential()` architecture and the default `fit()` loop. So, let's first turn you into a Keras expert! In this chapter, you'll get a complete overview of the key ways to work with Keras APIs: everything you're going to need to handle the advanced deep learning use cases you'll encounter next.

7.1   A spectrum of workflows

The design of the Keras API is guided by the principle of *progressive disclosure of complexity*: make it easy to get started, yet make it possible to handle high-complexity use cases, requiring only incremental learning at each step. Simple use cases should be easy and approachable, and arbitrarily advanced workflows should be *possible*: no matter how niche and complex the thing you want to do, there should be a clear path to it—a path that builds upon the various things you've learned from simpler workflows. This means that you can grow from beginner to expert and still use the same tools, only in different ways.

As such, there's not a single "true" way of using Keras. Rather, Keras offers a *spectrum of workflows*, from the very simple to the very flexible. There are different ways to build Keras models, and different ways to train them, answering different needs. Because all these workflows are based on shared APIs, such as `Layer` and `Model`, components from any workflow can be used in any other workflow—they can all talk to each other.

7.2   Different ways to build Keras models

Three APIs exist for building models in Keras (see figure 7.1):

- The *Sequential model*, the most approachable API—it's basically a list. As such, it's limited to simple stacks of layers.
- The *Functional API*, which focuses on graph-like model architectures. It represents a nice midpoint between usability and flexibility, and as such, it's the most commonly used model-building API.
- *Model subclassing*, a low-level option where you write everything yourself from scratch. This is ideal if you want full control over every little thing. However, you won't get access to many built-in Keras features, and you will be more at risk of making mistakes.

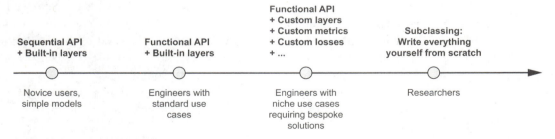

Figure 7.1   Progressive disclosure of complexity for model building

7.2.1 The Sequential model

The simplest way to build a Keras model is to use `keras_model_sequential()`, which you already know about.

Listing 7.1 `keras_model_sequential()`

```
library(keras)

model <- keras_model_sequential() %>%
  layer_dense(64, activation = "relu") %>%
  layer_dense(10, activation = "softmax")
```

Note that it's possible to build the same model incrementally with `%>%`.

Listing 7.2 Incrementally building a Sequential model

```
model <- keras_model_sequential()
model %>% layer_dense(64, activation = "relu")
model %>% layer_dense(10, activation = "softmax")
```

You saw in chapter 4 that layers get built (which is to say, create their weights) only when they are called for the first time. That's because the shape of the layers' weights depends on the shape of their input: until the input shape is known, they can't be created.

As such, the preceding Sequential model does not have any weights (listing 7.3) until you actually call it on some data, or call its `build()` method with an input shape (listing 7.4).

Listing 7.3 Models that aren't yet built have no weights

```
model$weights        ⊲——— At that point, the model isn't built yet.
```

```
Error in py_get_attr_impl(x, name, silent):
ValueError: Weights for model sequential_1 have not yet been created. Weights
are created when the Model is first called on inputs or `build()` is called
with an `input_shape`.
```

Listing 7.4 Calling a model for the first time to build it

**Build the model—now the model will expect samples of shape (3). The
NA in the input shape signals that the batch size could be anything.**

```
  ⌐▷ model$build(input_shape = shape(NA, 3))
     str(model$weights)            ⊲——— Now you can retrieve the model's weights.
```

```
List of 4
 $ :<tf.Variable 'dense_2/kernel:0' shape=(3, 64) dtype=float32, numpy=…>
 $ :<tf.Variable 'dense_2/bias:0' shape=(64) dtype=float32, numpy=…>
 $ :<tf.Variable 'dense_3/kernel:0' shape=(64, 10) dtype=float32, numpy=…>
 $ :<tf.Variable 'dense_3/bias:0' shape=(10) dtype=float32, numpy=…>
```

After the model is built, you can display its contents via the `print()` method, which comes in handy for debugging.

Listing 7.5   The `print()` method

```
model

Model: "sequential_1"

_____
 Layer (type)                    Output Shape                  Param #
======================================================================
 dense_2 (Dense)                 (None, 64)                    256
 dense_3 (Dense)                 (None, 10)                    650
======================================================================
Total params: 906
Trainable params: 906
Non-trainable params: 0
_____
```

As you can see, this model happens to be named "sequential_1." You can give names to everything in Keras—every model, every layer.

Listing 7.6   Naming models and layers with the `name` argument

```
model <- keras_model_sequential(name = "my_example_model")
model %>% layer_dense(64, activation = "relu", name = "my_first_layer")
model %>% layer_dense(10, activation = "softmax", name = "my_last_layer")
model$build(shape(NA, 3))
model

Model: "my_example_model"

_____
 Layer (type)                    Output Shape                  Param #
======================================================================
 my_first_layer (Dense)          (None, 64)                    256
 my_last_layer (Dense)           (None, 10)                    650
======================================================================
Total params: 906
Trainable params: 906
Non-trainable params: 0
_____
```

When building a Sequential model incrementally, it's useful to be able to print a summary of what the current model looks like after you add each layer. But you can't print a summary until the model is built! There's actually a way to have your `Sequential` model built on the fly: just declare the shape of the model's inputs in advance. You can do this by passing `input_shape` to `keras_model_sequential()`.

Listing 7.7 Specifying the input shape of your model in advance

```
model <-
  keras_model_sequential(input_shape = c(3)) %>%
  layer_dense(64, activation = "relu")
```

> **Supply input_shape to declare the shape of the inputs. Note that the shape argument must be the shape of each sample, not the shape of one batch.**

Now you can use `print()` to follow how the output shape of your model changes as you add more layers:

```
model
```

```
Model: "sequential_2"

_____
 Layer (type)                    Output Shape                    Param #
========================================================================
 dense_4 (Dense)                 (None, 64)                      256
========================================================================
Total params: 256
Trainable params: 256
Non-trainable params: 0
_____
```

```
model %>% layer_dense(10, activation = "softmax")
model
```

```
Model: "sequential_2"

_____
 Layer (type)                    Output Shape                    Param #
========================================================================
 dense_4 (Dense)                 (None, 64)                      256
 dense_5 (Dense)                 (None, 10)                      650
========================================================================
Total params: 906
Trainable params: 906
Non-trainable params: 0
_____
```

This is a pretty common debugging workflow when dealing with layers that transform their inputs in complex ways, such as the convolutional layers you'll learn about in chapter 8.

7.2.2 The Functional API

The Sequential model is easy to use, but its applicability is extremely limited: it can only express models with a single input and a single output, applying one layer after the other in a sequential fashion. In practice, it's pretty common to encounter models with multiple inputs (say, an image and its metadata), multiple outputs (different things you want to predict about the data), or a nonlinear topology.

In such cases, you'd build your model using the Functional API. This is what most Keras models you'll encounter in the wild use. It's fun and powerful—it feels like playing with LEGO bricks.

A SIMPLE EXAMPLE

Let's start with something simple: the stack of two layers we used in the previous section. Its Functional API version looks like the following listing.

> **Listing 7.8   A simple Functional model with two Dense layers**

```
inputs <- layer_input(shape = c(3), name = "my_input")
features <- inputs %>% layer_dense(64, activation = "relu")
outputs <- features %>% layer_dense(10, activation = "softmax")
model <- keras_model(inputs = inputs, outputs = outputs)
```

Let's go over this step by step. We started by declaring a `layer_input()` (note that you can also give names to these input objects, like everything else):

```
inputs <- layer_input(shape = c(3), name = "my_input")
```

This `inputs` object holds information about the shape and dtype of the data that the model will process:

```
inputs$shape
```
◁—— **The model will process batches where each sample has shape (3). The number of samples per batch is variable (indicated by the None batch size).**

```
TensorShape([None, 3])
```

```
inputs$dtype
```
◁—— **These batches will have dtype float32.**

```
tf.float32
```

We call such an object a *symbolic tensor*. It doesn't contain any actual data, but it encodes the specifications of the actual tensors of data that the model will see when you use it. It *stands for* future tensors of data.

Next, we create a layer and compose with the input:

```
features <- inputs %>% layer_dense(64, activation = "relu")
```

In the Functional API, piping a symbolic tensor into a layer constructor invokes the layer's `call()` method. In essence, this is what is happening:

```
layer_instance <- layer_dense(units = 64, activation = "relu")
features <- layer_instance(inputs)
```

This is different from the Sequential API, where composing a layer with a model (`model %>% layer_dense()`) means this:

```
layer_instance <- layer_dense(units = 64, activation = "relu")
model$add(layer_instance)
```

All Keras layers can be called both on real tensors of data and on these symbolic tensors. In the latter case, they return a new symbolic tensor, with updated shape and dtype information:

```
features$shape
```

```
TensorShape([None, 64])
```

Note that symbolic tensors work with almost all the same R generic methods as eager tensors. This means that you can also do something like this to get the shape as an R integer vector:

```
dim(features)
```

```
[1] NA 64
```

After obtaining the final outputs, we instantiated the model by specifying its inputs and outputs in the `keras_model()` constructor:

```
outputs <- layer_dense(features, 10, activation = "softmax")
model <- keras_model(inputs = inputs, outputs = outputs)
```

Here's the summary of our model:

```
model
```

```
Model: "model_1"
```

Layer (type)	Output Shape	Param #
my_input (InputLayer)	[(None, 3)]	0
dense_8 (Dense)	(None, 64)	256
dense_9 (Dense)	(None, 10)	650

```
Total params: 906
Trainable params: 906
Non-trainable params: 0
```

MULTI-INPUT, MULTI-OUTPUT MODELS

Unlike this toy model, most deep learning models don't look like lists—they look like graphs. They may, for instance, have multiple inputs or multiple outputs. It's for this kind of model that the Functional API really shines.

Let's say you're building a system to rank customer support tickets by priority and route them to the appropriate department. Your model has three inputs:

- The title of the ticket (text input)
- The text body of the ticket (text input)
- Any tags added by the user (categorical input, assumed here to be one-hot encoded)

We can encode the text inputs as arrays of ones and zeros of size `vocabulary_size` (see chapter 11 for detailed information about text encoding techniques). Your model also has two outputs:

- The priority score of the ticket, a scalar between 0 and 1 (sigmoid output)
- The department that should handle the ticket (a softmax over the set of departments)

You can build this model in a few lines with the Functional API.

Listing 7.9   A multi-input, multi-output Functional model

Define the model inputs.

```
vocabulary_size <- 10000
num_tags <- 100
num_departments <- 4

title     <- layer_input(shape = c(vocabulary_size), name = "title")
text_body <- layer_input(shape = c(vocabulary_size), name = "text_body")
tags      <- layer_input(shape = c(num_tags),        name = "tags")

features <-
  layer_concatenate(list(title, text_body, tags)) %>%
  layer_dense(64, activation = "relu")

priority <- features %>%
  layer_dense(1, activation = "sigmoid", name = "priority")

department <- features %>%
  layer_dense(num_departments, activation = "softmax", name = "department")

model <- keras_model(
  inputs = list(title, text_body, tags),
  outputs = list(priority, department)
)
```

Combine the input features into a single tensor by concatenating them.

Apply an intermediate layer to recombine input features into richer representations.

Define the model outputs.

Create the model by specifying its inputs and outputs.

The Functional API is a simple, LEGO-like, yet very flexible way to define arbitrary graphs of layers like these.

TRAINING A MULTI-INPUT, MULTI-OUTPUT MODEL

You can train your model in much the same way as you would train a Sequential model, by calling `fit()` with lists of input and output data. These lists of data should be in the same order as the inputs you passed to the `keras_model()` constructor.

Listing 7.10   Training a model by providing lists of input and target arrays

```
num_samples <- 1280

random_uniform_array <- function(dim)
  array(runif(prod(dim)), dim)

random_vectorized_array <- function(dim)
  array(sample(0:1, prod(dim), replace = TRUE), dim)
```

Dummy input data

```
title_data       <- random_vectorized_array(c(num_samples, vocabulary_size))
text_body_data <- random_vectorized_array(c(num_samples, vocabulary_size))
tags_data        <- random_vectorized_array(c(num_samples, num_tags))
```

Dummy target data

```
priority_data      <- random_vectorized_array(c(num_samples, 1))
department_data <- random_vectorized_array(c(num_samples, num_departments))

model %>% compile(
  optimizer = "rmsprop",
  loss = c("mean_squared_error", "categorical_crossentropy"),
  metrics = c("mean_absolute_error", "accuracy")
)

model %>% fit(
  x = list(title_data, text_body_data, tags_data),
  y = list(priority_data, department_data),
  epochs = 1
)
model %>% evaluate(x = list(title_data, text_body_data, tags_data),
                   y = list(priority_data, department_data))
```

```
                     loss                  priority_loss
              39.8363457                      0.5007812
         department_loss    priority_mean_absolute_error
              39.3355637                      0.5007812
        priority_accuracy department_mean_absolute_error
               0.4992188                      0.5046247
      department_accuracy
               0.2351563

c(priority_preds, department_preds) %<-% {
   model %>% predict(list(title_data, text_body_data, tags_data))
}
```

To use %<-% and %>% in the same expression, you need to wrap the pipe sequence with {} or () to override the default operator precedence.

If you don't want to rely on input order (for instance, because you have many inputs or outputs), you can also leverage the names you gave to the input_shape and the output layers, and pass data via a named list.

IMPORTANT   When using named lists, the order of the list is not guaranteed to be preserved. Be sure to keep track of items *either* by position *or* by name, but not a combination of both.

Listing 7.11   Training a model by providing named lists of input and target arrays

```
model %>%
  compile(optimizer = "rmsprop",
          loss = c(priority = "mean_squared_error",
                   department = "categorical_crossentropy"),
          metrics = c(priority = "mean_absolute_error",
                      department = "accuracy"))
```

```
model %>%
  fit(list(title = title_data,
           text_body = text_body_data,
           tags = tags_data),
      list(priority = priority_data,
           department = department_data), epochs = 1)

model %>%
  evaluate(list(title = title_data,
                text_body = text_body_data,
                tags = tags_data),
           list(priority = priority_data,
                department = department_data))
```

```
loss                priority_loss
          35.7301750                          0.5007812
        department_loss priority_mean_absolute_error
          35.2293930                          0.5007812
      department_accuracy
          0.1320312
```

```
c(priority_preds, department_preds) %<-%
  predict(model, list(title = title_data,
                      text_body = text_body_data,
                      tags = tags_data))
```

THE POWER OF THE FUNCTIONAL API: ACCESS TO LAYER CONNECTIVITY

A Functional model is an explicit graph data structure. This makes it possible to inspect how layers are connected and reuse previous graph nodes (which are layer outputs) as part of new models. It also nicely fits the "mental model" that most researchers use when thinking about a deep neural network: a graph of layers. This enables two important use cases: model visualization and feature extraction.

Let's visualize the connectivity of the model we just defined (the *topology* of the model). You can plot a Functional model as a graph with the plot() method (see figure 7.2):

```
plot(model)
```

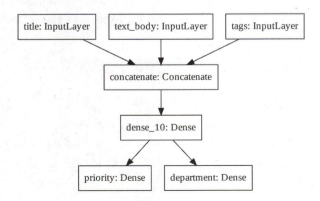

Figure 7.2   Plot generated by plot(model) on our ticket classifier model

You can add to this plot the input and output shapes of each layer in the model, which can be helpful during debugging (see figure 7.3):

```
plot(model, show_shapes = TRUE)
```

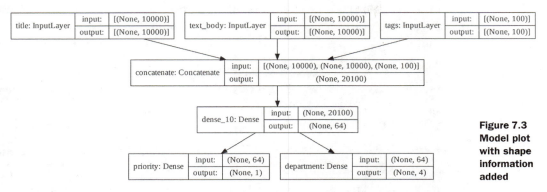

**Figure 7.3
Model plot
with shape
information
added**

The "None" in the tensor shapes represents the batch size: this model allows batches of any size.

Access to layer connectivity also means that you can inspect and reuse individual nodes (layer calls) in the graph. The model$layers model property provides the list of layers that make up the model, and for each layer you can query layer$input and layer$output.

Listing 7.12   Retrieving the inputs or outputs of a layer in a Functional model

```
str(model$layers)
```

```
List of 7
 $ :<keras.engine.input_layer.InputLayer object at 0x7fc962da63a0>
 $ :<keras.engine.input_layer.InputLayer object at 0x7fc962da6430>
 $ :<keras.engine.input_layer.InputLayer object at 0x7fc962da68e0>
 $ :<keras.layers.merge.Concatenate object at 0x7fc962d2e130>
 $ :<keras.layers.core.dense.Dense object at 0x7fc962da6c40>
 $ :<keras.layers.core.dense.Dense object at 0x7fc962da6340>
 $ :<keras.layers.core.dense.Dense object at 0x7fc962d331f0>
```

```
str(model$layers[[4]]$input)
```

```
List of 3
 $ :<KerasTensor: shape=(None, 10000) dtype=float32 (created by layer
➥ 'title')>
 $ :<KerasTensor: shape=(None, 10000) dtype=float32 (created by layer
➥ 'text_body')>
 $ :<KerasTensor: shape=(None, 100) dtype=float32 (created by layer 'tags')>
```

```
str(model$layers[[4]]$output)
```

```
<KerasTensor: shape=(None, 20100) dtype=float32 (created by layer
➥ 'concatenate')>
```

This enables you to do *feature extraction*, creating models that reuse intermediate features from another model.

Let's say you want to add another output to the previous model—you want to estimate how long a given issue ticket will take to resolve, a kind of difficulty rating. You could do this via a classification layer over three categories: "quick," "medium," and "difficult." You don't need to recreate and retrain a model from scratch. You can start from the intermediate features of your previous model, because you have access to them, like this.

Listing 7.13   Creating a new model by reusing intermediate layer outputs

```
features <- model$layers[[5]]$output            ◄──        layer[[5]] is our
difficulty <- features %>%                                 intermediate dense
  layer_dense(3, activation = "softmax", name = "difficulty")   layer. You can also
                                                           retrieve a layer
new_model <- keras_model(                                  by name with
  inputs = list(title, text_body, tags),                  get_layer().
  outputs = list(priority, department, difficulty)
)
```

Let's plot our new model (see figure 7.4):

```
plot(new_model, show_shapes = TRUE)
```

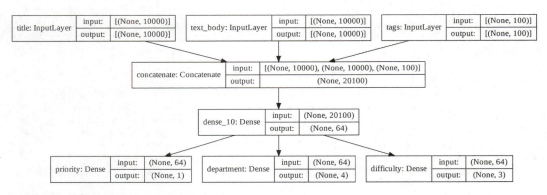

Figure 7.4   Plot of our new model: Updated ticket classifier

7.2.3   *Subclassing the Model class*

The last model-building pattern you should know about is the most advanced one: Model subclassing. You learned in chapter 3 how to use new_layer_class() to subclass the Layer class and create custom layers. Using new_model_class() to subclass Model class is pretty similar:

- In the `initialize()` method, define the layers the model will use.
- In the `call()` method, define the forward pass of the model, reusing the layers previously created.
- Instantiate your subclass, and call it on data to create its weights.

REWRITING OUR PREVIOUS EXAMPLE AS A SUBCLASSED MODEL

Let's take a look at a simple example: we will reimplement the customer support ticket management model using `new_model_class()` to define a `Model` subclass.

Listing 7.14 A simple subclassed model

```
CustomerTicketModel <- new_model_class(
  classname = "CustomerTicketModel",

  initialize = function(num_departments) {          Don't forget to call
    super$initialize()                              the super$initialize()!
    self$concat_layer <- layer_concatenate()
    self$mixing_layer <-                            Define the sublayers in the
      layer_dense(units = 64, activation = "relu")  constructor. Note that we're
    self$priority_scorer <-                         specifying the units argument
      layer_dense(units = 1, activation = "sigmoid") name here, so that we get
    self$department_classifier <-                   back a layer instance.
      layer_dense(units = num_departments,  activation = "softmax")
  },

  call = function(inputs) {          Define the forward pass
    title <- inputs$title           in the call() method.
    text_body <- inputs$text_body
    tags <- inputs$tags             For inputs, we'll provide the
                                    model with a named list.
    features <- list(title, text_body, tags) %>%
      self$concat_layer() %>%
      self$mixing_layer()
    priority <- self$priority_scorer(features)
    department <- self$department_classifier(features)
    list(priority, department)
  }
)
```

We implemented a bare-bones version of `Model` in chapter 3. The key thing to be aware of is that we're defining a custom class, our model, that subclasses `Model`. `Model` provides many methods and capabilities that you can opt-in to, as you'll see in the coming sections.

Once you've defined the model, you can instantiate it. Note that it will create its weights only the first time you call it on some data, much like `Layer` subclasses:

```
model <- CustomerTicketModel(num_departments = 4)

c(priority, department) %<-% model(list(title = title_data,
                                        text_body = text_body_data,
                                        tags = tags_data))
```

Models are, fundamentally, a type of Layer. That means you can easily add the ability for a model to compose nicely with %>% by using create_layer_wrapper(), like this:

```
inputs <- list(title = title_data,
               text_body = text_body_data,
               tags = tags_data)

layer_customer_ticket_model <- create_layer_wrapper(CustomerTicketModel)

outputs <- inputs %>%
  layer_customer_ticket_model(num_departments = 4)
c(priority, department) %<-% outputs
```

So far, everything looks very similar to Layer subclassing, a workflow you encountered in chapter 3. What, then, is the difference between a Layer subclass and a Model subclass? It's simple: a "layer" is a building block you use to create models, and a "model" is the top-level object that you will actually train, export for inference, and so on. In short, a Model has fit(), evaluate(), and predict() methods. Layers don't. Other than that, the two classes are virtually identical. (Another difference is that you can *save* a model to a file on disk, which we will cover in a few sections.) You can compile and train a Model subclass just like a Sequential or Functional model:

```
model %>%
  compile(optimizer = "rmsprop",
          loss = c("mean_squared_error",           ◁─── The structure of what you pass as
                   "categorical_crossentropy"),          the loss and metrics arguments must
          metrics = c("mean_absolute_error", "accuracy"))    match exactly what gets returned by
                                                              call()—here, a lists of two elements.
x <- list(title = title_data,          ◁───  The structure of the input data must match
          text_body = text_body_data,        exactly what is expected by the call() method—
          tags = tags_data)                  here, a named list with entries title, text_body,
y <- list(priority_data, department_data) ◁┐ and tags. (Remember, list order is ignored when
                                             matching by names!)
model %>% fit(x, y, epochs = 1)
model %>% evaluate(x, y)               The structure of the target data must match exactly
                                       what is returned by the call() method—here, a list
                                       of two elements.
```

```
                  loss             output_1_loss
            24.02798843               0.50078124
        output_2_loss output_1_mean_absolute_error
            23.52721024               0.50078124
        output_1_accuracy output_2_mean_absolute_error
             0.49921876               0.50347400
        output_2_accuracy
             0.06328125
```

```
c(priority_preds, department_preds) %<-% {
  model %>% predict(x)
}
```

The Model subclassing workflow is the most flexible way to build a model. It enables you to build models that cannot be expressed as directed acyclic graphs of layers—

imagine, for instance, a model where the `call()` method uses layers inside a `for` loop, or even calls them recursively. Anything is possible—you're in charge.

BEWARE: WHAT SUBCLASSED MODELS DON'T SUPPORT

This freedom comes at a cost: with subclassed models, you are responsible for more of the model logic, which means your potential error surface is much larger. As a result, you will have more debugging work to do. You are developing a new class object, not just snapping together LEGO bricks.

Functional and subclassed models are also substantially different in nature. A Functional model is an explicit data structure—a graph of layers, which you can view, inspect, and modify. A subclassed model is a collection of R code—a class with a `call()` method that is an R function. This is the source of the subclassing workflow's flexibility—you can code up whatever functionality you like—but it introduces new limitations.

For instance, because the way layers are connected to each other is hidden inside the body of the `call()` method, you cannot access that information. Calling `summary()` will not display layer connectivity, and you cannot plot the model topology via `plot()`. Likewise, if you have a subclassed model, you cannot access the nodes of the graph of layers to do feature extraction because there is simply no graph. Once the model is instantiated, its forward pass becomes a complete black box.

7.2.4 *Mixing and matching different components*

Crucially, choosing one of these patterns—the Sequential model, the Functional API, or `Model` subclassing—does not lock you out of the others. All models in the Keras API can smoothly interoperate with each other, whether they're Sequential models, Functional models, or subclassed models written from scratch. They're all part of the same spectrum of workflows. For instance, you can use a subclassed layer or model in a Functional model.

Listing 7.15 Creating a Functional model that includes a subclassed model

```
ClassifierModel <- new_model_class(
  classname = "Classifier",
  initialize = function(num_classes = 2) {
    super$initialize()
    if (num_classes == 2) {
      num_units <- 1
      activation <- "sigmoid"
    } else {
      num_units <- num_classes
      activation <- "softmax"
    }
    self$dense <- layer_dense(units = num_units, activation = activation)
  },

  call = function(inputs)
    self$dense(inputs)
)
```

```r
inputs  <- layer_input(shape = c(3))
classifier <- ClassifierModel(num_classes = 10)

outputs <- inputs %>%
  layer_dense(64, activation = "relu") %>%
  classifier()

model <- keras_model(inputs = inputs, outputs = outputs)
```

Inversely, you can use a Functional model as part of a subclassed layer or model.

Listing 7.16   Creating a subclassed model that includes a Functional model

```r
inputs <- layer_input(shape = c(64))
outputs <- inputs %>% layer_dense(1, activation = "sigmoid")
binary_classifier <- keras_model(inputs = inputs, outputs = outputs)

MyModel <- new_model_class(
  classname = "MyModel",
  initialize = function(num_classes = 2) {
    super$initialize()
    self$dense <- layer_dense(units = 64, activation = "relu")
    self$classifier <- binary_classifier
  },

  call = function(inputs) {
    inputs %>%
      self$dense() %>%
      self$classifier()
  }
)

model <- MyModel()
```

7.2.5   *Remember: Use the right tool for the job*

You've learned about the spectrum of workflows for building Keras models, from the simplest workflow, the Sequential model, to the most advanced one, model subclassing. When should you use one over the other? Each one has its pros and cons—pick the one most suitable for the job at hand.

In general, the Functional API provides you with a pretty good tradeoff between ease of use and flexibility. It also gives you direct access to layer connectivity, which is very powerful for use cases such as model plotting or feature extraction. If you *can* use the Functional API—that is, if your model can be expressed as a directed acyclic graph of layers—I recommend using it over model subclassing.

Going forward, all examples in this book will use the Functional API, simply because all the models we will work with are expressible as graphs of layers. We will, however, make frequent use of subclassed layers (using `new_layer_class()`). In general, using Functional models that include subclassed layers provides the best of both worlds: high development flexibility while retaining the advantages of the Functional API.

7.3   Using built-in training and evaluation loops

The principle of progressive disclosure of complexity—access to a spectrum of workflows that go from dead easy to arbitrarily flexible, one step at a time—also applies to model training. Keras provides you with different workflows for training models. They can be as simple as calling `fit()` on your data or as advanced as writing a new training algorithm from scratch.

You are already familiar with the `compile()`, `fit()`, `evaluate()`, `predict()` workflow. As a reminder, take a look at the following listing.

Listing 7.17   The standard workflow: `compile()`, `fit()`, `evaluate()`, `predict()`

```
get_mnist_model <- function() {                    Create a model (we factor this into a
  inputs <- layer_input(shape = c(28 * 28))        separate function so as to reuse it later).
  outputs <- inputs %>%
    layer_dense(512, activation = "relu") %>%
    layer_dropout(0.5) %>%
    layer_dense(10, activation = "softmax")

  keras_model(inputs, outputs)
}                                                   Load your data,
                                                    reserving some
c(c(images, labels), c(test_images, test_labels)) %<-%    for validation.
  dataset_mnist()

images <- array_reshape(images, c(-1, 28 * 28)) / 255
test_images <- array_reshape(test_images, c(-1, 28 * 28)) / 255

val_idx <- seq(10000)
val_images <- images[val_idx, ]                     Compile the model by specifying its
val_labels <- labels[val_idx]                       optimizer, the loss function to minimize,
train_images <- images[-val_idx, ]                  and the metrics to monitor.
train_labels <- labels[-val_idx]
                                                    Use fit() to train the
model <- get_mnist_model()                          model, optionally pro-
model %>% compile(optimizer = "rmsprop",            viding validation data
            loss = "sparse_categorical_crossentropy",   to monitor performance
            metrics = "accuracy")                   on unseen data.
model %>% fit(train_images, train_labels,
          epochs = 3,                               Use evaluate() to
          validation_data = list(val_images, val_labels))   compute the loss and
test_metrics <-  model %>% evaluate(test_images,    metrics on new data.
                              test_labels)
predictions <- model %>% predict(test_images)       Use predict() to compute classification
                                                    probabilities on new data.
```

There are a couple of ways you can customize this simple workflow:

- Provide your own custom metrics.
- Pass *callbacks* to the `fit()` method to schedule actions to be taken at specific points during training.

Let's take a look at these.

7.3.1   *Writing your own metrics*

Metrics are key to measuring the performance of your model, in particular, to measuring the difference between its performance on the training data and its performance on the test data. Commonly used metrics for classification and regression are already part of the keras package, all starting with the prefix metric_, and most of the time that's what you will use. But if you're doing anything out of the ordinary, you will need to be able to write your own metrics. It's simple!

A Keras metric is a subclass of the Keras Metric class. Like layers, a metric has an internal state stored in TensorFlow variables. Unlike layers, these variables aren't updated via backpropagation, so you have to write the state-update logic yourself, which happens in the update_state() method. For example, here's a simple custom metric that measures the root mean squared error (RMSE).

Listing 7.18   Implementing a custom metric by subclassing the Metric class

```
library(tensorflow)          ◁──┐ We will be using tf
                                 │ module functions here.
metric_root_mean_squared_error <- new_metric_class(   ◁──┘
  classname = "RootMeanSquaredError",

  initialize = function(name = "rmse", ...) {   ◁─────
    super$initialize(name = name, ...)
    self$mse_sum <- self$add_weight(name = "mse_sum",
                                    initializer = "zeros",
                                    dtype = "float32")
    self$total_samples <- self$add_weight(name = "total_samples",
                                          initializer = "zeros",
                                          dtype = "int32")
  },

  update_state = function(y_true, y_pred, sample_weight = NULL) {
    num_samples <- tf$shape(y_pred)[1]
    num_features <- tf$shape(y_pred)[2]

    y_true <- tf$one_hot(y_true, depth = num_features)   ◁──────

    mse <- sum((y_true - y_pred) ^ 2)          ◁───
    self$mse_sum$assign_add(mse)
    self$total_samples$assign_add(num_samples)
  },
```

Define a new class that subclasses the Metric base class.

Define the state variables in the constructor. Like for layers, you have access to the add_weight() method.

To match our MNIST model, we expect categorical predictions and integer labels.

Remember, tf module functions use 0-based counting conventions. A value of 0 in y_true places the 1 in the first position of the one-hot vector.

We could also write this as tf$reduce_sum (tf$square(tf$subtract(y_true, y_pred))).

Implement the state update logic in update_state(). The y_true argument is the targets (or labels) for one batch, and y_pred represents the corresponding predictions from the model. You can ignore the sample_weight argument—we won't use it here.

```
  result = function() {
    sqrt(self$mse_sum /
         tf$cast(self$total_samples, "float32"))     ◁────  Cast total_samples to match
  },                                                         the dtype of mse_sum.

  reset_state = function() {
    self$mse_sum$assign(0)
    self$total_samples$assign(0L)
  }
}
)
```

Note that in `update_state()` we use `tf$shape(y_pred)` instead of `y_pred$shape`. `tf$shape()` returns the shape as a `tf.Tensor`, instead of a `tf.TensorShape` like `y_pred$shape` would. `tf$shape()` allows `tf_function()` to compile a function that can operate on tensors with undefined shapes, like our inputs here which have a undefined batch dimension. We learn more about `tf_function()` soon.

You use the `result()` method to return the current value of the metric:

```
result = function()
    sqrt(self$mse_sum /
         tf$cast(self$total_samples, "float32"))
```

Meanwhile, you also need to expose a way to reset the metric state without having to reinstantiate it—this enables the same metric objects to be used across different epochs of training or across both training and evaluation. You do this with the `reset_state()` method:

```
reset_state = function() {
    self$mse_sum$assign(0)
    self$total_samples$assign(0L)     ◁────  Note that we pass an integer because
  }                                           total_samples has an integer dtype.
```

Custom metrics can be used just like built-in ones. Let's test-drive our own metric:

```
model <- get_mnist_model()
model %>%
  compile(optimizer = "rmsprop",
          loss = "sparse_categorical_crossentropy",
          metrics = list("accuracy", metric_root_mean_squared_error()))
model %>%
  fit(train_images, train_labels,
      epochs = 3,
      validation_data = list(val_images, val_labels))
test_metrics <- model %>% evaluate(test_images, test_labels)
```

You can now see the `fit()` progress bar displaying the RMSE of your model.

7.3.2 Using callbacks

Launching a training run on a large dataset for tens of epochs using the model `fit()` method can be a bit like launching a paper airplane: past the initial impulse, you don't have any control over its trajectory or its landing spot. If you want to avoid bad outcomes (and thus wasted paper airplanes), it's smarter to use not a paper plane but a drone that can sense its environment, send data back to its operator, and automatically make steering decisions based on its current state. The Keras *callbacks* API will help you transform your call to `fit(model)` from a paper airplane into a smart, autonomous drone that can self-introspect and dynamically take action.

A callback is an object (a class instance implementing specific methods) that is passed to the model in the call to `fit()` and that is called by the model at various points during training. It has access to all the available data about the state of the model and its performance, and it can take action: interrupt training, save a model, load a different weight set, or otherwise alter the state of the model. Here are some examples of ways you can use callbacks:

- *Model checkpointing*—Saving the current state of the model at different points during training.
- *Early stopping*—Interrupting training when the validation loss is no longer improving (and, of course, saving the best model obtained during training).
- *Dynamically adjusting the value of certain parameters during training*—Such as the learning rate of the optimizer.
- *Logging training and validation metrics during training, or visualizing the representations learned by the model as they're updated*—The `fit()` progress bar that you're familiar with is in fact a callback!

The keras package includes a number of built-in callbacks (this is not an exhaustive list):

```
callback_model_checkpoint()
callback_early_stopping()
callback_learning_rate_scheduler()
callback_reduce_lr_on_plateau()
callback_csv_logger()
...
```

Let's review two of them to give you an idea of how to use them: `callback_early_stopping()` and `callback_model_checkpoint()`.

THE EARLY STOPPING AND MODEL CHECKPOINT CALLBACKS

When you're training a model, there are many things you can't predict from the start. In particular, you can't tell how many epochs will be needed to get to an optimal validation loss. Our examples so far have adopted the strategy of training for enough epochs that you begin overfitting, using the first run to figure out the proper number of epochs to train for, and then finally launching a new training run from scratch using this optimal number. Of course, this approach is wasteful. A much better way to handle this is to stop training when you measure that the validation loss is no longer improving. This can be achieved using `callback_early_stopping()`.

The early stopping callback interrupts training once a target metric being monitored has stopped improving for a fixed number of epochs. For instance, this callback allows you to interrupt training as soon as you start overfitting, thus avoiding having to retrain your model for a smaller number of epochs. This callback is typically used in combination with `callback_model_checkpoint()`, which lets you continually save the model during training (and, optionally, save only the current best model so far: the version of the model that achieved the best performance at the end of an epoch).

Listing 7.19   Using the `callbacks` argument in the `fit()` method

Path to the destination model file

Interrupt training when validation accuracy has stopped improving for two epochs.

```
callbacks_list <- list(
  callback_early_stopping(
    monitor = "val_accuracy", patience = 2),
  callback_model_checkpoint(
    filepath = "checkpoint_path.keras",
    monitor = "val_loss", save_best_only = TRUE)
)

model <- get_mnist_model()
model %>% compile(
  optimizer = "rmsprop",
  loss = "sparse_categorical_crossentropy",
  metrics = "accuracy")
model %>% fit(
  train_images, train_labels,
  epochs = 10,
  callbacks = callbacks_list,
  validation_data = list(val_images, val_labels))
```

Save the current weights after every epoch.

These two arguments mean you won't overwrite the model file unless val_loss has improved, which allows you to keep the best model seen during training.

You monitor accuracy, so it should be part of the model's metrics.

Note that because the callback will monitor validation loss and validation accuracy, you need to pass validation_data to the call to fit().

Callbacks are passed to the model via the callbacks argument in fit(), which takes a list of callbacks. You can pass any number of callbacks.

Note that you can always save models manually after training as well—just call `save_model_tf(model, 'my_checkpoint_path')`. To reload the model you've saved, just use the following:

```
model <- load_model_tf("checkpoint_path.keras")
```

7.3.3   *Writing your own callbacks*

If you need to take a specific action during training that isn't covered by one of the built-in callbacks, you can write your own callback. Callbacks are implemented by subclassing the Keras `Callback` class with `new_callback_class()`. You can then implement any number of the following transparently named methods, which are called at various points during training:

Called at the start of every epoch

Called at the end of every epoch

Called right before processing each batch

Called right after processing each batch

Called at the start of training

Called at the end of training

```
on_epoch_begin(epoch, logs)
on_epoch_end(epoch, logs)
on_batch_begin(batch, logs)
on_batch_end(batch, logs)
on_train_begin(logs)
on_train_end(logs)
```

These methods are all called with a `logs` argument, which is a named list containing information about the previous batch, epoch, or training run—training and validation metrics, and so on. The `on_epoch_*` and `on_batch_*` methods also take the epoch or batch index as their first argument (an integer).

Here's a simple example that saves a list of per-batch loss values during training and saves a graph of these values at the end of each epoch.

Listing 7.20   Creating a custom callback by subclassing the `Callback` class

```r
callback_plot_per_batch_loss_history <- new_callback_class(
  classname = "PlotPerBatchLossHistory",

  initialize = function(file = "training_loss.pdf") {
    private$outfile <- file
  },

  on_train_begin = function(logs = NULL) {
    private$plots_dir <- tempfile()
    dir.create(private$plots_dir)
    private$per_batch_losses <-
      fastmap::faststack(init = self$params$steps)
  },

  on_epoch_begin = function(epoch, logs = NULL) {
    private$per_batch_losses$reset()
  },

  on_batch_end = function(batch, logs = NULL) {
    private$per_batch_losses$push(logs$loss)
  },

  on_epoch_end = function(epoch, logs = NULL) {
    losses <- as.numeric(private$per_batch_losses$as_list())

    filename <- sprintf("epoch_%04i.pdf", epoch)
    filepath <- file.path(private$plots_dir, filename)

    pdf(filepath, width = 7, height = 5)
    on.exit(dev.off())

    plot(losses, type = "o",
```

```
        ylim = c(0, max(losses)),
        panel.first = grid(),
        main = sprintf("Training Loss for Each Batch\n(Epoch %i)", epoch),
        xlab = "Batch", ylab = "Loss")
    },

    on_train_end = function(logs) {
      private$per_batch_losses <- NULL
      plots <- sort(list.files(private$plots_dir, full.names = TRUE))
      qpdf::pdf_combine(plots, private$outfile)
      unlink(private$plots_dir, recursive = TRUE)
    }
)
```

Growing R objects with `fastmap::faststack()`

Growing R vectors with `c()` or `[[<-` is typically slow and best avoided. In this example, we're using `fastmap::faststack()` instead to collect the per-batch losses more efficiently.

`private` and `self` in custom class methods

In all the previous examples, we've used `self` to keep track of instance properties, but in this callback example we used `private`. What's the difference? Any property like `self$foo` is also accessible directly from the class instance at `instance$foo`. Properties of `private`, however, are accessible only from inside class methods.

Another important difference is that Keras automatically converts everything assigned to `self` to a Keras native format. This helps Keras automatically find, for example, all the `tf.Variable`s associated with a custom Layer. This automatic conversion, however, can sometimes have a performance impact, or even fail for certain types of R objects (like `faststack()`). `private`, on the other hand, is a plain R environment that is left untouched by Keras. Only the class methods you write will directly interact with `private` properties.

```
model <- get_mnist_model()
model %>% compile(optimizer = "rmsprop",
                  loss = "sparse_categorical_crossentropy",
                  metrics = "accuracy")
model %>% fit(train_images, train_labels,
              epochs = 10,
              callbacks = list(callback_plot_per_batch_loss_history()),
              validation_data = list(val_images, val_labels))
```

We get plots that look like figure 7.5.

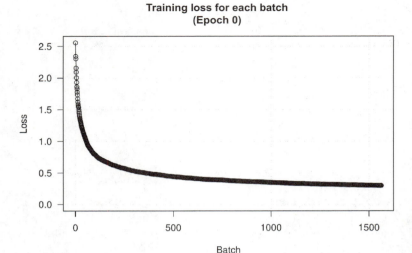

Figure 7.5
The output of our custom history plotting callback

7.3.4   *Monitoring and visualization with TensorBoard*

To do good research or develop good models, you need rich, frequent feedback about what's going on inside your models during your experiments. That's the point of running experiments: to get information about how well a model performs—as much information as possible. Making progress is an iterative process, a loop: you start with an idea and express it as an experiment, attempting to validate or invalidate your idea. You run this experiment and process the information it generates. This inspires your next idea. The more iterations of this loop you're able to run, the more refined and powerful your ideas become. Keras helps you go from idea to experiment in the least possible time, and fast GPUs can help you get from experiment to result as quickly as possible. But what about processing the experiment's results? That's where TensorBoard comes in (see figure 7.6).

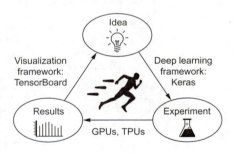

Figure 7.6   **The loop of progress**

TensorBoard (http://www.tensorflow.org/tensorboard) is a browser-based application that you can run locally. It's the best way to monitor everything that goes on inside your model during training. With TensorBoard, you can

- Visually monitor metrics during training
- Visualize your model architecture
- Visualize histograms of activations and gradients
- Explore embeddings in 3D

If you're monitoring more information than just the model's final loss, you can develop a clearer vision of what the model does and doesn't do, and you can make progress more quickly. The easiest way to use TensorBoard with a Keras model and the `fit()` method is to use `callback_tensorboard()`. In the simplest case, just specify where you want the callback to write logs, and you're good to go:

```
model <- get_mnist_model()
model %>% compile(optimizer = "rmsprop",
                  loss = "sparse_categorical_crossentropy",
                  metrics = "accuracy")

model %>% fit(train_images, train_labels,
              epochs = 10,
              validation_data = list(val_images, val_labels),
              callbacks = callback_tensorboard(log_dir = "logs/"))   <─┐ Path to
                                                                       │ your log
                                                                       │ dir
```

Once the model starts running, it will write logs at the target location. You can then view the logs by calling `tensorboard()`; this will launch a browser with tensorboard running:

```
tensorboard(log_dir = "logs/")   <──── Launches a browser with TensorBoard
```

In the TensorBoard interface, you will be able to monitor live graphs of your training and evaluation metrics (see figure 7.7).

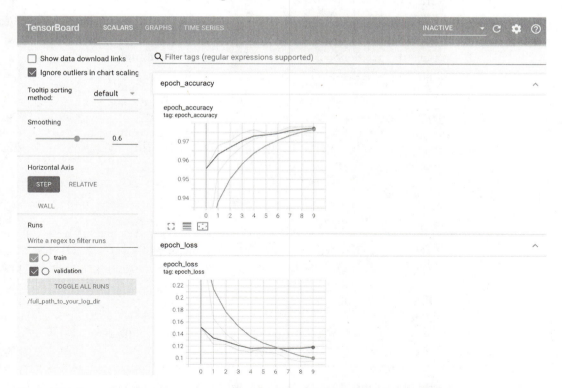

Figure 7.7   TensorBoard can be used for easy monitoring of training and evaluation metrics.

7.4   *Writing your own training and evaluation loops*

The `fit()` workflow strikes a nice balance between ease of use and flexibility. It's what you will use most of the time. However, it isn't meant to support everything a deep learning researcher may want to do, even with custom metrics, custom losses, and custom callbacks.

After all, the built-in `fit()` workflow is solely focused on *supervised learning*: a setup where there are known *targets* (also called *labels* or *annotations*) associated with your input data, and where you compute your loss as a function of these targets and the model's predictions. However, not every form of machine learning falls into this category. There are other setups where no explicit targets are present, such as *generative learning* (which we will discuss in chapter 12), *self-supervised learning* (where targets are obtained from the inputs), and *reinforcement learning* (where learning is driven by occasional "rewards," much like training a dog). Even if you're doing regular supervised learning, as a researcher, you may want to add some novel bells and whistles that require low-level flexibility.

Whenever you find yourself in a situation where the built-in `fit()` is not enough, you will need to write your own custom training logic. You already saw simple examples of low-level training loops in chapters 2 and 3. As a reminder, the contents of a typical training loop look like this:

1   Run the forward pass (compute the model's output) inside a gradient tape to obtain a loss value for the current batch of data.
2   Retrieve the gradients of the loss with regard to the model's weights.
3   Update the model's weights so as to lower the loss value on the current batch of data.

These steps are repeated for as many batches as necessary. This is essentially what `fit()` does under the hood. In this section, you will learn to reimplement `fit()` from scratch, which will give you all the knowledge you need to write any training algorithm you may come up with. Let's go over the details.

7.4.1   *Training vs. inference*

In the low-level training loop examples you've seen so far, step 1 (the forward pass) was done via `predictions <- model(inputs)`, and step 2 (retrieving the gradients computed by the gradient tape) was done via `gradients <- tape$gradient(loss, model$weights)`. In the general case, there are actually two subtleties you need to take into account.

Some Keras layers, such as `layer_dropout()`, have different behaviors during *training* and during *inference* (when you use them to generate predictions). Such layers expose a `training` Boolean argument in their `call()` method. Calling `dropout (inputs, training = TRUE)` will drop some activation entries, whereas calling `dropout (inputs, training = FALSE)` does nothing. By extension, Functional and Sequential models also expose this `training` argument in their `call()` methods. Remember to pass `training = TRUE` when you call a Keras model during the forward pass! Our forward pass thus becomes `predictions <- model(inputs, training = TRUE)`.

In addition, note that when you retrieve the gradients of the weights of your model, you should not use `tape$gradients(loss, model$weights)`, but rather `tape$gradients(loss, model$trainable_weights)`. Indeed, layers and models own two kinds of weights:

- *Trainable weights*—These are meant to be updated via backpropagation to minimize the loss of the model, such as the kernel and bias of a `Dense` layer.
- *Nontrainable weights*—These are meant to be updated during the forward pass by the layers that own them. For instance, if you wanted a custom layer to keep a counter of how many batches it has processed so far, that information would be stored in a nontrainable weight, and at each batch, your layer would increment the counter by one.

Among Keras built-in layers, the only layer that features nontrainable weights is `layer_batch_normalization()`, which we will discuss in chapter 9. The batch normalization layer needs nontrainable weights to track information about the mean and standard deviation of the data that passes through it, so as to perform an online approximation of *feature normalization* (a concept you learned about in chapter 6). Taking into account these two details, a supervised-learning training step ends up looking like this:

```
library(tensorflow)

train_step <- function(inputs, targets) {
  with(tf$GradientTape() %as% tape, {
    predictions <- model(inputs, training = TRUE)
    loss <- loss_fn(targets, predictions)
  })

  gradients <- tape$gradients(loss, model$trainable_weights)
  optimizer$apply_gradients(zip_lists(gradients, model$trainable_weights))
}
```

> We introduced
> zip_lists() in chapter 2.

7.4.2   *Low-level usage of metrics*

In a low-level training loop, you will probably want to leverage Keras metrics (whether custom ones or the built-in ones). You've already learned about the metrics API: simply call `update_state(y_true, y_pred)` for each batch of targets and predictions, and then use `result()` to query the current metric value:

```
metric <- metric_sparse_categorical_accuracy()
targets <- c(0, 1, 2)
predictions <- rbind(c(1, 0, 0),
                     c(0, 1, 0),
                     c(0, 0, 1))
metric$update_state(targets, predictions)
current_result <- metric$result()
sprintf("result: %.2f", as.array(current_result))
```

> **as.array() to convert
> Tensor to R value**

```
[1] "result: 1.00"
```

You may also need to track the average of a scalar value, such as the model's loss. You can do this via `metric_mean()`:

```
values <- c(0, 1, 2, 3, 4)
mean_tracker <- metric_mean()
for (value in values)
    mean_tracker$update_state(value)
sprintf("Mean of values: %.2f", as.array(mean_tracker$result()))
```

```
[1] "Mean of values: 2.00"
```

Remember to use `metric$reset_state()` when you want to reset the current results (at the start of a training epoch or at the start of evaluation).

7.4.3   *A complete training and evaluation loop*

Let's combine the forward pass, backward pass, and metrics tracking into a `fit()`-like training step function that takes a batch of data and targets and returns the logs that would get displayed by the `fit()` progress bar.

Listing 7.21   Writing a step-by-step training loop: The training step function

```
model <- get_mnist_model()                                      ← Prepare the loss function.

loss_fn <- loss_sparse_categorical_crossentropy()   ←           Prepare the optimizer.
optimizer <- optimizer_rmsprop()                    ←
metrics <- list(metric_sparse_categorical_accuracy())  ←        Prepare the list of
loss_tracking_metric <- metric_mean()   ←                       metrics to monitor.

train_step <- function(inputs, targets) {                       Prepare a metric_mean() tracker
                                                                to keep track of the loss average.

  with(tf$GradientTape() %as% tape, {                           Run the forward pass. Note
    predictions <- model(inputs, training = TRUE)  ←            that we pass training = TRUE.
    loss <- loss_fn(targets, predictions)
  })                                                            Run the backward
  gradients <- tape$gradient(loss,                              pass. Note that we use
                             model$trainable_weights)           model$trainable_weights.
  optimizer$apply_gradients(zip_lists(gradients,
                                      model$trainable_weights))

  logs <- list()
  for (metric in metrics) {                          ←——— Keep track of metrics.
    metric$update_state(targets, predictions)
    logs[[metric$name]] <- metric$result()
  }

  loss_tracking_metric$update_state(loss)   ←——— Keep track of the loss average.
  logs$loss <- loss_tracking_metric$result()
  logs         ←
}                       Return the current values of the metrics and the loss.
```

We will need to reset the state of our metrics at the start of each epoch and before running evaluation. Here's a utility function to do it.

Listing 7.22 Writing a step-by-step training loop: Resetting the metrics

```
reset_metrics <- function() {
  for (metric in metrics)
    metric$reset_state()
  loss_tracking_metric$reset_state()
}
```

We can now lay out our complete training loop. Note that we use a TensorFlow Dataset object from the tfdatasets package to turn our R array data into an iterator that iterates over the data in batches of size 32. The mechanics are identical to the dataset iterator we implemented in chapter 2, just the names are different now. We build the TensorFlow Dataset instance from our R arrays with `tensor_slices_dataset()`, convert it to an iterator with `as_iterator()`, and then repeatedly call `iter_next()` on the iterator to get the next batch. One difference between what we saw in chapter 2 and now is that `iter_next()` returns `Tensor` objects, not R arrays. We cover much more about tfdatasets in chapter 8.

Listing 7.23 Writing a step-by-step training loop: The loop itself

```
library(tfdatasets)
training_dataset <-
  list(inputs = train_images, targets = train_labels) %>%
  tensor_slices_dataset() %>%
  dataset_batch(32)

epochs <- 3
for (epoch in seq(epochs)) {
  reset_metrics()
  training_dataset_iterator <- as_iterator(training_dataset)
  repeat {
    batch <- iter_next(training_dataset_iterator)
    if (is.null(batch))                         ⟵———————————— iterator exhausted
      break
    logs <- train_step(batch$inputs, batch$targets)
  }

  writeLines(c(
    sprintf("Results at the end of epoch %s", epoch),
    sprintf("...%s: %.4f", names(logs), sapply(logs, as.numeric))
  ))
}
```

```
Results at the end of epoch 1
...sparse_categorical_accuracy: 0.9156
...loss: 0.2687
Results at the end of epoch 2
...sparse_categorical_accuracy: 0.9539
...loss: 0.1659
Results at the end of epoch 3
...sparse_categorical_accuracy: 0.9630
...loss: 0.1371
```

And here's the evaluation loop: a simple `for` loop that repeatedly calls a `test_step()` function, which processes a single batch of data. The `test_step()` function is just a subset of the logic of `train_step()`. It omits the code that deals with updating the weights of the model—that is to say, everything involving the `GradientTape()` and the optimizer.

Listing 7.24   Writing a step-by-step evaluation loop

```
test_step <- function(inputs, targets) {
  predictions <- model(inputs, training = FALSE)        ◁──┐  Note that we pass
  loss <- loss_fn(targets, predictions)                     │  training = FALSE.

  logs <- list()
  for (metric in metrics) {
    metric$update_state(targets, predictions)
    logs[[paste0("val_", metric$name)]] <- metric$result()
  }

  loss_tracking_metric$update_state(loss)
  logs[["val_loss"]] <- loss_tracking_metric$result()
  logs
}

val_dataset <- list(val_images, val_labels) %>%
  tensor_slices_dataset() %>%
  dataset_batch(32)

reset_metrics()

val_dataset_iterator <- as_iterator(val_dataset)
repeat {                                               ┌─ iter_next() returns NULL
  batch <- iter_next(val_dataset_iterator)             │  once the dataset batch
  if(is.null(batch)) break          ◁─────────────────┘  iterator is exhausted.
  c(inputs_batch, targets_batch) %<-% batch
  logs <- test_step(inputs_batch, targets_batch)
}

writeLines(c(
  "Evaluation results:",
  sprintf("...%s: %.4f", names(logs), sapply(logs, as.numeric))
))
```

```
Evaluation results:
...val_sparse_categorical_accuracy: 0.9461
...val_loss: 0.1871
```

Congrats—you've just reimplemented `fit()` and `evaluate()`! Or almost: `fit()` and `evaluate()` support many more features, including large-scale distributed computation, which requires a bit more work. It also includes several key performance optimizations. Let's take a look at one of these optimizations: TensorFlow function compilation.

7.4.4 **Make it fast with tf_function()**

You may have noticed that your custom loops are running significantly slower than the built-in `fit()` and `evaluate()`, despite implementing essentially the same logic. That's because, by default, TensorFlow code is executed line by line, *eagerly*, much like regular R code using R arrays. Eager execution makes it easier to debug your code, but it is far from optimal from a performance standpoint.

It's more performant to *compile* your TensorFlow code into a *computation graph* that can be globally optimized in a way that code interpreted line by line cannot. The syntax to do this is very simple: just call `tf_function()` on any function you want to compile before executing, as shown in the following listing.

Listing 7.25   Using `tf_function()` with our evaluation-step function

Pass the test_step we defined previously to tf_function().

Reuse the same TF Dataset defined in the previous example, but make a new iterator.

```
tf_test_step <- tf_function(test_step)

val_dataset_iterator <- as_iterator(val_dataset)
reset_metrics()

while(!is.null(iter_next(val_dataset_iterator) -> batch)) {
  c(inputs_batch, targets_batch) %<-% batch
  logs <- tf_test_step(inputs_batch, targets_batch)
}
```

Use the compiled test step function this time.

```
writeLines(c(
  "Evaluation results:",
  sprintf("...%s: %.4f", names(logs), sapply(logs, as.numeric))
))
```

```
Evaluation results:
...val_sparse_categorical_accuracy: 0.5190
...val_loss: 1.6764
```

On my machine we go from taking 2.4 seconds to run the evaluation loop to only 0.6 seconds. Much faster!

The speedup is even greater when the TF Dataset iteration loop is also compiled as a graph operation. You can use `tf_function()` to compile the full evaluation loop like this:

```
my_evaluate <- tf_function(function(model, dataset) {
  reset_metrics()

  for (batch in dataset) {
    c(inputs_batch, targets_batch) %<-% batch
    logs <- test_step(inputs_batch, targets_batch)
  }
  logs
})
```

```
system.time(my_evaluate(model, val_dataset))["elapsed"]
```

```
elapsed
  0.283
```

This cuts the evaluation time by more than half again!

Remember, while you are debugging your code, prefer running it eagerly, without any calls to tf_function(). It's easier to track bugs this way. Once your code is working and you want to make it fast, add a tf_function() decorator to your training step and your evaluation step or any other performance-critical function.

7.4.5 *Leveraging fit() with a custom training loop*

In the previous sections, we were writing our own training loop entirely from scratch. Doing so provides you with the most flexibility, but you end up writing a lot of code while simultaneously missing out on many convenient features of fit(), such as callbacks or built-in support for distributed training.

What if you need a custom training algorithm, but you still want to leverage the power of the built-in Keras training logic? There's actually a middle ground between fit() and a training loop written from scratch: you can provide a custom training step function and let the framework do the rest.

You can do this by overriding the train_step() method of the Model class. This is the function that is called by fit() for every batch of data. You will then be able to call fit() as usual, and it will be running your own learning algorithm under the hood. Here's a simple example:

- We create a new class that subclasses Model by calling new_model_class().
- We override the method train_step(data). Its contents are nearly identical to what we used in the previous section. It returns a named list mapping metric names (including the loss) to their current values.
- We implement a metrics active property that tracks the model's Metric instances. This enables the model to automatically call reset_state() on the model's metrics at the start of each epoch and at the start of a call to evaluate(), so you don't have to do it by hand:

```
loss_fn <- loss_sparse_categorical_crossentropy()      ◁─────  This metric object will be used to
loss_tracker <- metric_mean(name = "loss")     ◁─────         track the average of per-batch losses
                                                              during training and evaluation.

CustomModel <- new_model_class(
  classname = "CustomModel",

  train_step = function(data) {    ◁───┐ We override the          We use self(inputs, training =
    c(inputs, targets) %<-% data        │ train_step method.     TRUE) instead of model(inputs,
    with(tf$GradientTape() %as% tape, {                          training = TRUE), because our
      predictions <- self(inputs, training = TRUE)   ◁───┘      model is the class itself.
      loss <- loss_fn(targets, predictions)
    })
    gradients <- tape$gradient(loss, model$trainable_weights)
```

```
    optimizer$apply_gradients(zip_lists(gradients, model$trainable_weights))

    loss_tracker$update_state(loss)
    list(loss = loss_tracker$result())
  },
```

We update the loss tracker metric that tracks the average of the loss.

```
  metrics = mark_active(function() list(loss_tracker))
)
```

Any metric you would like to reset across epochs should be listed here.

We return the average loss so far by querying the loss tracker metric.

We can now instantiate our custom model, compile it (we pass only the optimizer, because the loss is already defined outside of the model), and train it using fit() as usual:

```
inputs <- layer_input(shape = c(28 * 28))
features <- inputs %>%
  layer_dense(512, activation = "relu") %>%
  layer_dropout(0.5)
outputs <- features %>%
  layer_dense(10, activation = "softmax")

model <- CustomModel(inputs = inputs, outputs = outputs)
```

Because we didn't provide an initialize() method, the same signature as keras_model() is used: inputs, outputs, and optionally name.

```
model %>% compile(optimizer = optimizer_rmsprop())
model %>% fit(train_images, train_labels, epochs = 3)
```

There are a couple of points to note:

- This pattern does not prevent you from building models with the Functional API. You can do this whether you're building Sequential models, Functional API models, or subclassed models.
- You don't need to call tf_function() when you override train_step—the framework does it for you.

Now, what about metrics, and what about configuring the loss via compile()? After you've called compile(), you get access to the following:

- self$compiled_loss—The loss function you passed to compile().
- self$compiled_metrics—A wrapper for the list of metrics you passed, which allows you to call self$compiled_metrics$update_state() to update all of your metrics at once.
- self$metrics—The actual list of metrics you passed to compile(). Note that it also includes a metric that tracks the loss, similar to what we did manually with our loss_tracking_metric earlier.

We can thus write:

```
CustomModel <- new_model_class(

  classname = "CustomModel",

  train_step = function(data) {
    c(inputs, targets) %<-% data
    with(tf$GradientTape() %as% tape, {
      predictions <- self(inputs, training = TRUE)
      loss <- self$compiled_loss(targets, predictions)
    })
    gradients <- tape$gradient(loss, model$trainable_weights)
    optimizer$apply_gradients(zip_lists(gradients, model$trainable_weights))
    self$compiled_metrics$update_state(
      targets, predictions)

    results <- list()
    for(metric in self$metrics)
      results[[metric$name]] <- metric$result()
    results
  }
)
```

Compute the loss via self$compiled_loss.

Update the model's metrics via self$compiled_metrics.

Return a named list mapping metric names to their current value.

Let's try it:

```
inputs <- layer_input(shape = c(28 * 28))
features <- inputs %>%
  layer_dense(512, activation = "relu") %>%
  layer_dropout(0.5)

outputs <- features %>% layer_dense(10, activation = "softmax")
model <- CustomModel(inputs = inputs, outputs = outputs)

model %>% compile(optimizer = optimizer_rmsprop(),
                  loss = loss_sparse_categorical_crossentropy(),
                  metrics = metric_sparse_categorical_accuracy())
model %>% fit(train_images, train_labels, epochs = 3)
```

That was a lot of information, but you now know enough to use Keras to do almost anything.

Summary

- Keras offers a spectrum of different workflows, based on the principle of *progressive disclosure of complexity*. They all smoothly operate together.
- You can build models via the Sequential API with `keras_model_sequential()`, via the Functional API with `keras_model()`, or by subclassing the `Model` class with `new_model_class()`. Most of the time, you'll be using the Functional API.
- The simplest way to train and evaluate a model is via the default `fit()` and `evaluate()` methods.

- Keras callbacks provide a simple way to monitor models during your call to `fit()` and automatically take action based on the state of the model.
- You can also fully take control of what `fit()` does by overriding the `train_step()` method.
- Beyond `fit()`, you can also write your own training loops entirely from scratch. This is useful for researchers implementing brand-new training algorithms.

Introduction to deep learning for computer vision

Computer vision is the earliest and biggest success story of deep learning. Every day, you're interacting with deep vision models—via Google Photos, Google image search, YouTube, video filters in camera apps, OCR software, and many more. These models are also at the heart of cutting-edge research in autonomous driving, robotics, AI-assisted medical diagnosis, autonomous retail checkout systems, and even autonomous farming.

Computer vision is the problem domain that led to the initial rise of deep learning between 2011 and 2015. A type of deep learning model called *convolutional neural networks* started getting remarkably good results on image-classification competitions around that time, first with Dan Ciresan winning two niche competitions (the ICDAR 2011 Chinese character recognition competition and the IJCNN 2011 German traffic signs recognition competition), and then more notably in fall 2012 with Hinton's group winning the high-profile ImageNet large-scale visual recognition challenge. Many more promising results quickly started bubbling up in other computer vision tasks.

Interestingly, these early successes weren't quite enough to make deep learning mainstream at the time—it took a few years. The computer vision research community had spent many years investing in methods other than neural networks, and it wasn't quite ready to give up on them just because there was a new kid on the block. In 2013 and 2014, deep learning still faced intense skepticism from many senior computer vision researchers. It was only in 2016 that it finally became dominant. I (François) remember exhorting an ex-professor of mine, in February 2014, to pivot to deep learning. "It's the next big thing!" I would say. "Well, maybe it's just a fad," he replied. By 2016, his entire lab was doing deep learning. There's no stopping an idea whose time has come.

This chapter introduces convolutional neural networks, also known as *convnet*, the type of deep learning model that is now used almost universally in computer vision applications. You'll learn to apply convnets to image-classification problems—in particular those involving small training datasets, which are the most common use case if you aren't a large tech company.

8.1 Introduction to convnets

We're about to dive into the theory of what convnets are and why they have been so successful at computer vision tasks. But first, let's take a practical look at a simple convnet example that classifies MNIST digits, a task we performed in chapter 2 using a densely connected network (our test accuracy then was 97.8%). Even though the convnet will be basic, its accuracy will blow our densely connected model from chapter 2 out of the water.

The following listing shows what a basic convnet looks like. It's a stack of `layer_conv_2d()` and `layer_max_pooling_2d()` layers. You'll see in a minute exactly what they do. We'll build the model using the Functional API, which we introduced in the previous chapter.

Listing 8.1 Instantiating a small convnet

```
inputs <- layer_input(shape = c(28, 28, 1))

outputs <- inputs %>%
  layer_conv_2d(filters = 32, kernel_size = 3, activation = "relu") %>%
  layer_max_pooling_2d(pool_size = 2) %>%
  layer_conv_2d(filters = 64, kernel_size = 3, activation = "relu") %>%
```

```
    layer_max_pooling_2d(pool_size = 2) %>%
    layer_conv_2d(filters = 128, kernel_size = 3, activation = "relu") %>%
    layer_flatten() %>%
    layer_dense(10, activation = "softmax")

model <- keras_model(inputs, outputs)
```

Importantly, a convnet takes as input tensors of shape `(image_height, image_width, image_channels)`, not including the batch dimension. In this case, we'll configure the convnet to process inputs of size `(28, 28, 1)`, which is the format of MNIST images.

Let's display the architecture of our convnet.

Listing 8.2   Displaying the model's summary

```
model
```

```
Model: "model"
_____
 Layer (type)                      Output Shape              Param #
===========================================================================
 input_1 (InputLayer)              [(None, 28, 28, 1)]       0
 conv2d_2 (Conv2D)                 (None, 26, 26, 32)        320
 max_pooling2d_1 (MaxPooling2D)    (None, 13, 13, 32)        0
 conv2d_1 (Conv2D)                 (None, 11, 11, 64)        18496
 max_pooling2d (MaxPooling2D)      (None, 5, 5, 64)          0
 conv2d (Conv2D)                   (None, 3, 3, 128)         73856
 flatten (Flatten)                 (None, 1152)              0
 dense (Dense)                     (None, 10)                11530
===========================================================================
Total params: 104,202
Trainable params: 104,202
Non-trainable params: 0
_____
```

You can see that the output of every `Conv2D` and `MaxPooling2D` layer is a rank 3 tensor of shape `(height, width, channels)`. The width and height dimensions tend to shrink as you go deeper in the model. The number of channels is controlled by the first argument passed to the `layer_conv_2d()` layers (32, 64, or 128).

After the last `Conv2D` layer, we end up with an output of shape `(3, 3, 128)`—a 3 × 3 feature map of 128 channels. The next step is to feed this output into a densely connected classifier like those you're already familiar with: a stack of `Dense` layers. These classifiers process vectors, which are 1D, whereas the current output is a rank 3 tensor. To bridge the gap, we flatten the 3D outputs to 1D with a `Flatten` layer before adding the `Dense` layers. Finally, we do 10-way classification, so our last layer has 10 outputs and a softmax activation.

Now, let's train the convnet on the MNIST digits. We'll reuse a lot of the code from the MNIST example in chapter 2. Because we're doing 10-way classification with a softmax output, we'll use the categorical cross-entropy loss, and because our labels are integers, we'll use the sparse version, `sparse_categorical_crossentropy`.

Listing 8.3 Training the convnet on MNIST images

```
c(c(train_images, train_labels), c(test_images, test_labels)) %<-%
  dataset_mnist()
train_images <- array_reshape(train_images, c(60000, 28, 28, 1)) / 255
test_images <- array_reshape(test_images, c(10000, 28, 28, 1)) / 255

model %>% compile(optimizer = "rmsprop",
                  loss = "sparse_categorical_crossentropy",
                  metrics = c("accuracy"))
model %>% fit(train_images, train_labels, epochs = 5, batch_size = 64)
```

Let's evaluate the model on the test data.

Listing 8.4 Evaluating the convnet

```
result <- evaluate(model, test_images, test_labels)
cat("Test accuracy:", result['accuracy'], "\n")
```

```
Test accuracy: 0.9915
```

Whereas the densely connected model from chapter 2 had a test accuracy of 97.8%, the basic convnet has a test accuracy of 99.1%: we decreased the error rate by about 60% (relative). Not bad!

Why does this simple convnet work so well, compared to a densely connected model? To answer this, let's dive into what the `Conv2D` and `MaxPooling2D` layers do.

8.1.1 *The convolution operation*

The fundamental difference between a densely connected layer and a convolution layer is this: `Dense` layers learn global patterns in their input feature space (e.g., for a MNIST digit, patterns involving all pixels), whereas convolution layers learn local patterns—in the case of images, patterns found in small 2D windows of the inputs (see figure 8.1). In the previous example, these windows were all 3×3.

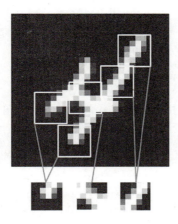

Figure 8.1 Images can be broken into local patterns such as edges, textures, and so on.

This key characteristic gives convnets two interesting properties:

- *The patterns they learn are translation-invariant*—After learning a certain pattern in the lower-right corner of a picture, a convnet can recognize it anywhere—for example, in the upper-left corner. A densely connected model would have to learn the pattern anew if it appeared at a new location. This makes convnets data-efficient when processing images (because the *visual world is fundamentally translation invariant*): they need fewer training samples to learn representations that have generalization power.
- *They can learn spatial hierarchies of patterns*—A first convolution layer will learn small local patterns such as edges, a second convolution layer will learn larger patterns made of the features of the first layers, and so on (see figure 8.2). This allows convnets to efficiently learn increasingly complex and abstract visual concepts, because *the visual world is fundamentally spatially hierarchical.*

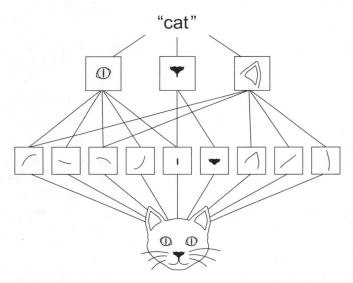

Figure 8.2   The visual world forms a spatial hierarchy of visual modules: elementary lines or textures combine into simple objects such as eyes or ears, which combine into high-level concepts such as "cat."

Convolutions operate over rank 3 tensors called *feature maps*, with two spatial axes (*height* and *width*) as well as a *depth* axis (also called the *channels* axis). For an RGB image, the dimension of the depth axis is 3, because the image has three color channels: red, green, and blue. For a black-and-white picture, like the MNIST digits, the depth is 1 (levels of gray). The convolution operation extracts patches from its input feature map and applies the same transformation to all of these patches, producing an *output feature map*. This output feature map is still a rank 3 tensor: it has a width and a height. Its depth can be arbitrary, because the output depth is a parameter of the layer, and the different channels in that depth axis no longer stand for specific colors as in RGB input; rather, they stand for *filters*. Filters encode specific aspects of the input data: at a high level, a single filter could encode the concept "presence of a face in the input," for instance.

In the MNIST example, the first convolution layer takes a feature map of size (28, 28, 1) and outputs a feature map of size (26, 26, 32): it computes 32 filters over its input. Each of these 32 output channels contains a 26 × 26 grid of values, which is a *response map* of the filter over the input, indicating the response of that filter pattern at different locations in the input (see figure 8.3).

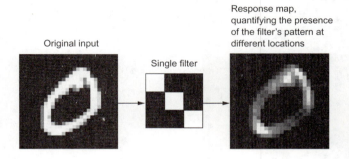

Figure 8.3   The concept of a response map: A 2D map of the presence of a pattern at different locations in an input

That is what the term *feature map* means: every dimension in the depth axis is a *feature* (or filter), and the rank 2 tensor output[, , n] is the 2D spatial *map* of the response of this filter over the input.

Convolutions are defined by two key parameters:

- *Size of the patches extracted from the inputs*—These are typically 3 × 3 or 5 × 5. In the example, they were 3 × 3, which is a common choice.
- *Depth of the output feature map*—This is the number of filters computed by the convolution. The example started with a depth of 32 and ended with a depth of 64.

In layer_conv_2d(), these parameters are the first arguments passed to the layer (after the inputs to compose with): inputs %>% layer_conv_2d(output_depth, c(window_height, window_width)).

A convolution works by *sliding* these windows of size 3 × 3 or 5 × 5 over the 3D input feature map, stopping at every possible location, and extracting the 3D patch of surrounding features (shape (window_height, window_width, input_depth)). Each such 3D patch is then transformed into a 1D vector of shape (output_depth), which is done via a tensor product with a learned weight matrix, called the *convolution kernel*—the same kernel is reused across every patch. All of these vectors (one per patch) are then spatially reassembled into a 3D output map of shape (height, width, output_ depth). Every spatial location in the output feature map corresponds to the same location in the input feature map (e.g., the lower-right corner of the output contains information about the lower-right corner of the input). For instance, with 3 × 3 windows, the vector output[i, j,] comes from the 3D patch input[(i-1):(i+1), (j-1):(j+1),]. The full process is detailed in figure 8.4.

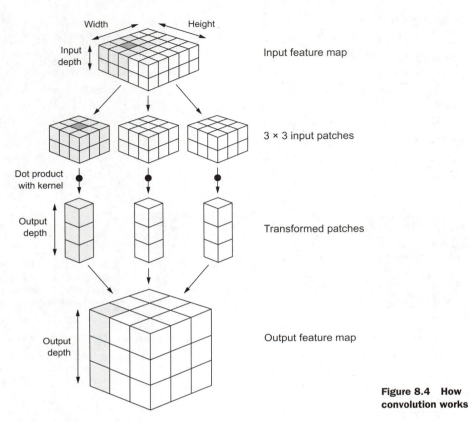

Figure 8.4 How convolution works

Note that the output width and height may differ from the input width and height for two reasons:

- Border effects, which can be countered by padding the input feature map
- The use of *strides*, which I'll define in a second

Let's take a deeper look at these notions.

UNDERSTANDING BORDER EFFECTS AND PADDING

Consider a 5 × 5 feature map (25 tiles total). There are only 9 tiles around which you can center a 3 × 3 window, forming a 3 × 3 grid (see figure 8.5). Hence, the output feature map will be 3 × 3. It shrinks a little: by exactly two tiles alongside each dimension, in this case. You can see this border effect in action in the earlier example: you start with 28 × 28 inputs, which become 26 × 26 after the first convolution layer.

If you want to get an output feature map with the same spatial dimensions as the input, you can use *padding*. Padding consists of adding an appropriate number of rows and columns on each side of the input feature map so as to make it possible to fit center convolution windows around every input tile. For a 3 × 3 window, you add one column on the right, one column on the left, one row at the top, and one row at the bottom. For a 5 × 5 window, you add two rows (see figure 8.6).

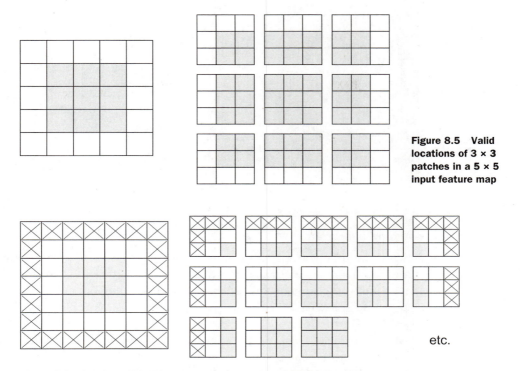

Figure 8.5   Valid locations of 3 × 3 patches in a 5 × 5 input feature map

etc.

Figure 8.6   Padding a 5 × 5 input to be able to extract 25 3 × 3 patches

In `layer_conv_2d()`, padding is configurable via the `padding` argument, which takes two values: `"valid"`, which means no padding (only valid window locations will be used), and `"same"`, which means "pad in such a way as to have an output with the same width and height as the input." The `padding` argument defaults to `"valid"`.

UNDERSTANDING CONVOLUTION STRIDES

The other factor that can influence output size is the notion of *strides*. Our description of convolution so far has assumed that the center tiles of the convolution windows are all contiguous. But the distance between two successive windows is a parameter of the convolution, called its *stride*, which defaults to 1. It's possible to have *strided convolutions*: convolutions with a stride higher than 1. In figure 8.7, you can see the patches extracted by a 3 × 3 convolution with stride 2 over a 5 × 5 input (without padding).

Using stride 2 means the width and height of the feature map are downsampled by a factor of 2 (in addition to any changes induced by border effects). Strided convolutions are rarely used in classification models, but they come in handy for some types of models, as you will see in the next chapter.

In classification models, instead of strides, we tend to use the *max-pooling* operation to downsample feature maps, which you saw in action in our first convnet example. Let's look at it in more depth.

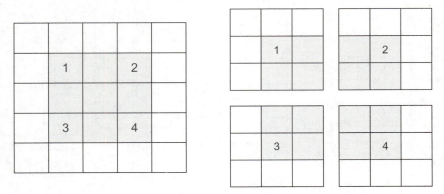

Figure 8.7   3 × 3 convolution patches with 2 × 2 strides

8.1.2   *The max-pooling operation*

In the convnet example, you may have noticed that the size of the feature maps is halved after every `layer_max_pooling_2d()`. For instance, before the first `layer_max_pooling_2d()`, the feature map is 26 × 26, but the max-pooling operation halves it to 13 × 13. That's the role of max pooling: to aggressively downsample feature maps, much like strided convolutions.

Max pooling consists of extracting windows from the input feature maps and outputting the max value of each channel. It's conceptually similar to convolution, except that instead of transforming local patches via a learned linear transformation (the convolution kernel), they're transformed via a hardcoded `max` tensor operation. A big difference from convolution is that max pooling is usually done with 2 × 2 windows and stride 2, to downsample the feature maps by a factor of 2. On the other hand, convolution is typically done with 3 × 3 windows and no stride (stride 1).

Why downsample feature maps this way? Why not remove the max-pooling layers and keep fairly large feature maps all the way up? Let's look at this option. Our model would then look like the following listing.

Listing 8.5   An incorrectly structured convnet missing its max-pooling layers

```
inputs <- layer_input(shape = c(28, 28, 1))
outputs <- inputs %>%
  layer_conv_2d(filters = 32, kernel_size = 3, activation = "relu") %>%
  layer_conv_2d(filters = 64, kernel_size = 3, activation = "relu") %>%
  layer_conv_2d(filters = 128, kernel_size = 3, activation = "relu") %>%
  layer_flatten() %>%
  layer_dense(10, activation = "softmax")
model_no_max_pool <- keras_model(inputs = inputs, outputs = outputs)
```

Here's a summary of the model:

```
model_no_max_pool
```

```
Model: "model_1"
```

Layer (type)	Output Shape	Param #
input_2 (InputLayer)	[(None, 28, 28, 1)]	0
conv2d_5 (Conv2D)	(None, 26, 26, 32)	320
conv2d_4 (Conv2D)	(None, 24, 24, 64)	18496
conv2d_3 (Conv2D)	(None, 22, 22, 128)	73856
flatten_1 (Flatten)	(None, 61952)	0
dense_1 (Dense)	(None, 10)	619530

```
Total params: 712,202
Trainable params: 712,202
Non-trainable params: 0
```

What's wrong with this setup? Two things:

- It isn't conducive to learning a spatial hierarchy of features. The 3×3 windows in the third layer will contain information coming from only 7×7 windows in the initial input. The high-level patterns learned by the convnet will still be very small with regard to the initial input, which may not be enough to learn to classify digits (try recognizing a digit by looking at it through windows that are only 7×7 pixels!). We need the features from the previous convolution layer to contain information about the totality of the input.

- The final feature map has $22 \times 22 \times 128 = 61,952$ total coefficients per sample. This is huge. When you flatten it to stick a `layer_dense` of size 10 on top, that layer would have over half a million parameters. This is far too large for such a small model and would result in intense overfitting.

In short, the reason to use downsampling is to reduce the number of feature-map coefficients to process, as well as to induce spatial-filter hierarchies by making successive convolution layers look at increasingly large windows (in terms of the fraction of the original input they cover).

Note that max pooling isn't the only way you can achieve such downsampling. As you already know, you can also use strides in the prior convolution layer. And you can use average pooling instead of max pooling, where each local input patch is transformed by taking the average value of each channel over the patch, rather than the max. But max pooling tends to work better than these alternative solutions. The reason is that features tend to encode the spatial presence of some pattern or concept over the different tiles of the feature map (hence the term *feature map*), and it's more informative to look at the *maximal presence* of different features than at their *average presence*. The most reasonable subsampling strategy is to first produce dense maps of features (via unstrided convolutions) and then look at the maximal activation of the features over small patches, rather than looking at sparser windows of the inputs (via strided convolutions) or averaging input patches, which could cause you to miss or dilute feature-presence information.

At this point, you should understand the basics of convnets—feature maps, convolution, and max pooling—and you should know how to build a small convnet to solve a toy problem such as MNIST digits classification. Now let's move on to more useful, practical applications.

8.2   Training a convnet from scratch on a small dataset

Having to train an image-classification model using very little data is a common situation, which you'll likely encounter in practice if you ever do computer vision in a professional context. A "few" samples can mean anywhere from a few hundred to a few tens of thousands of images. As a practical example, we'll focus on classifying images as dogs or cats in a dataset containing 5,000 pictures of cats and dogs (2,500 cats, 2,500 dogs). We'll use 2,000 pictures for training, 1,000 for validation, and 2,000 for testing.

In this section, we'll review one basic strategy to tackle this problem: training a new model from scratch using what little data you have. We'll start by naively training a small convnet on the 2,000 training samples, without any regularization, to set a baseline for what can be achieved. This will get us to a classification accuracy of about 70%. At that point, the main issue will be overfitting. Then we'll introduce *data augmentation*, a powerful technique for mitigating overfitting in computer vision. By using data augmentation, we'll improve the model to reach an accuracy of 80–85%.

In the next section, we'll review two more essential techniques for applying deep learning to small datasets: *feature extraction with a pretrained model* (which will get us to an accuracy of 97.5%) and *fine-tuning a pretrained model* (which will get us to a final accuracy of 98.5%). Together, these three strategies—training a small model from scratch, doing feature extraction using a pretrained model, and fine-tuning a pretrained model—will constitute your future toolbox for tackling the problem of performing image classification with small datasets.

8.2.1   The relevance of deep learning for small data problems

What qualifies as "enough samples" to train a model is relative—relative to the size and depth of the model you're trying to train, for starters. It isn't possible to train a convnet to solve a complex problem with just a few tens of samples, but a few hundred can potentially suffice if the model is small and well regularized and the task is simple. Because convnets learn local, translation-invariant features, they're highly data efficient on perceptual problems. Training a convnet from scratch on a very small image dataset will yield reasonable results despite a relative lack of data, without the need for any custom feature engineering. You'll see this in action in this section.

What's more, deep learning models are by nature highly repurposable: you can take, say, an image-classification or speech-to-text model trained on a large-scale dataset and reuse it on a significantly different problem with only minor changes. Specifically, in the case of computer vision, many pretrained models (usually trained on the

ImageNet dataset) are now publicly available for download and can be used to bootstrap powerful vision models out of very little data. This is one of the greatest strengths of deep learning: feature reuse. You'll explore this in the next section. Let's start by getting our hands on the data.

8.2.2   Downloading the data

The Dogs vs. Cats dataset that we will use isn't packaged with Keras. It was made available by Kaggle as part of a computer vision competition in late 2013, back when convnets weren't mainstream. You can download the original dataset from http://www.kaggle.com/c/dogs-vs-cats/data (you'll need to create a Kaggle account if you don't already have one—don't worry, the process is painless). You can also use the Kaggle command line API to download the dataset.

> ### Downloading a Kaggle dataset
>
> Kaggle makes available an easy-to-use API to programmatically download Kaggle-hosted datasets. You can use it to download the Dogs vs. Cats dataset to your local computer, for instance. Downloading this dataset is as easy as running a single command in R.
>
> However, access to the API is restricted to Kaggle users, so to run the preceding command, you first need to authenticate yourself. The kaggle package will look for your login credentials in a JSON file located at ~/.kaggle/kaggle.json. Let's create this file.
>
> First, you need to create a Kaggle API key and download it to your local machine. Just navigate to the Kaggle website in a web browser, log in, and go to the My Account page. In your account settings, you'll find an API section. Clicking the Create New API Token button will generate a kaggle.json key file and will download it to your machine.
>
> Finally, create a ~/.kaggle folder. As a security best practice, you should also make sure that the file is readable only by the current user, yourself. (This applies only if you're on Mac or Linux, not Windows.)
>
> Because we'll be doing a nontrivial amount of filesystem operations in the coming chapters, we'll use the fs R package, which is a little nicer to work with than base R filesystem functions. (You can install it from CRAN with `install.packages("fs")`.)
>
> Prepare the Kaggle API key:
>
> ```
> library(fs)
> dir_create("~/.kaggle")
> file_move("~/Downloads/kaggle.json", "~/.kaggle/")
> file_chmod("~/.kaggle/kaggle.json", "0600")
> ```
>
> Mark the file readable only by yourself.
>
> Install the `kaggle` package via `pip`:
>
> ```
> reticulate::py_install("kaggle", pip = TRUE)
> ```
>
> You can now download the data we're about to use:
>
> ```
> system('kaggle competitions download -c dogs-vs-cats')
> ```

(continued)

The first time you try to download the data, you may get a "403 Forbidden" error. That's because you need to accept the terms associated with the dataset before you download it—you'll have to go to http://www.kaggle.com/c/dogs-vs-cats/rules (while logged in to your Kaggle account) and click the I Understand and Accept button. You need to do this only once.

Finally, the data is downloaded as a compressed zip file, dogs-vs-cats.zip. That zip file itself contains another compressed zip file, train.zip, which is the training data we'll use. We uncompress train.zip into a new directory, dogs-vs-cats, using the zip R package (installable from CRAN with `install.packages("zip")`:

```
zip::unzip('dogs-vs-cats.zip', exdir = "dogs-vs-cats", files = "train.zip")
zip::unzip("dogs-vs-cats/train.zip", exdir = "dogs-vs-cats")
```

The pictures in our dataset are medium-resolution color JPEGs. Figure 8.8 shows some examples.

Figure 8.8   Samples from the Dogs vs. Cats dataset. Sizes weren't modified: The samples come in different sizes, colors, backgrounds, and so on.

Unsurprisingly, the original dogs-versus-cats Kaggle competition, all the way back in 2013, was won by entrants who used convnets. The best entries achieved up to 95% accuracy. In this example, we will get fairly close to this accuracy (in the next section), even though we will train our models on less than 10% of the data that was available to the competitors.

This dataset contains 25,000 images of dogs and cats (12,500 from each class) and is 543 MB (compressed). After downloading and uncompressing the data, we'll create a new dataset containing three subsets: a training set with 1,000 samples of each class, a validation set with 500 samples of each class, and a test set with 1,000 samples of each class. Why do this? Because many of the image datasets you'll encounter in your career contain only a few thousand samples, not tens of thousands. Having more data available would make the problem easier, so it's good practice to learn with a small dataset.

The subsampled dataset we will work with will have the following directory structure:

```
cats_vs_dogs_small/
...train/
......cat/          ◁——————| Contains 1,000 cat images
......dog/          ◁—————— Contains 1,000 dog images
...validation/
......cat/          ◁—————— Contains 500 cat images
......dog/          ◁
...test/                   Contains 500 dog images
......cat/          ◁
......dog/          ◁——————| Contains 1,000 cat images

                           Contains 1,000 dog images
```

Let's make it happen with a couple calls to {fs} functions.

Listing 8.6   Copying images to training, validation, and test directories

Path to the directory where the
original dataset was uncompressed

Directory where
we will store our
smaller dataset

Utility function that copies cat
and dog images between indexes
start_index and end_index to the
subdirectory new_base_dir/
{subset_name}/cat (and /dog).
The "subset_name" will be either
"train", "validation", or "test".

```r
library(fs)
original_dir <- path("dogs-vs-cats/train")
new_base_dir <- path("cats_vs_dogs_small")

make_subset <- function(subset_name,
                        start_index, end_index) {
  for (category in c("dog", "cat")) {
    file_name <- glue::glue("{category}.{ start_index:end_index }.jpg")
    dir_create(new_base_dir / subset_name / category)
    file_copy(original_dir / file_name,
              new_base_dir / subset_name / category / file_name)
  }
}

make_subset("train", start_index = 1, end_index = 1000)
make_subset("validation", start_index = 1001, end_index = 1500)
make_subset("test", start_index = 1501, end_index = 2500)
```

Create the training subset
with the first 1,000 images
of each category.

Create the validation
subset with the next
500 images of each
category.

Create the test subset with the next
1,000 images of each category.

We now have 2,000 training images, 1,000 validation images, and 2,000 test images. Each split contains the same number of samples from each class: this is a balanced binary-classification problem, which means classification accuracy will be an appropriate measure of success.

8.2.3 Building the model

We will reuse the same general model structure you saw in the first example: the convnet will be a stack of alternated `layer_conv_2d()` (with `relu` activation) and `layer_max_pooling_2d()` layers.

But because we're dealing with bigger images and a more complex problem, we'll make our model larger, accordingly: it will have two more `layer_conv_2d()` and `layer_max_pooling_2d()` stages. This serves both to augment the capacity of the model and to further reduce the size of the feature maps so they aren't overly large when we reach the `layer_flatten()`. Here, because we start from inputs of size 180 pixels × 180 pixels (a somewhat arbitrary choice), we end up with feature maps of size 7 × 7 just before the `layer_flatten()`.

The depth of the feature maps progressively increases in the model (from 32 to 256), whereas the size of the feature maps decreases (from 180 × 180 to 7 × 7). This is a pattern you'll see in almost all convnets.

Because we're looking at a binary-classification problem, we'll end the model with a single unit (a `layer_dense()` of size 1) and a `sigmoid` activation. This unit will encode the probability that the model is looking at one class or the other.

One last small difference: we will start the model with a `layer_rescaling()`, which will rescale image inputs (whose values are originally in the [0, 255] range) to the [0, 1] range.

Listing 8.7 Instantiating a small convnet for dogs vs. cats classification

The model expects RGB images of size 180 × 180.

Rescale inputs to the [0, 1] range by dividing them by 255.

```
inputs <- layer_input(shape = c(180, 180, 3))
outputs <- inputs %>%
  layer_rescaling(1 / 255) %>%
  layer_conv_2d(filters = 32, kernel_size = 3, activation = "relu") %>%
  layer_max_pooling_2d(pool_size = 2) %>%
  layer_conv_2d(filters = 64, kernel_size = 3, activation = "relu") %>%
  layer_max_pooling_2d(pool_size = 2) %>%
  layer_conv_2d(filters = 128, kernel_size = 3, activation = "relu") %>%
  layer_max_pooling_2d(pool_size = 2) %>%
  layer_conv_2d(filters = 256, kernel_size = 3, activation = "relu") %>%
  layer_max_pooling_2d(pool_size = 2) %>%
  layer_conv_2d(filters = 256, kernel_size = 3, activation = "relu") %>%
  layer_flatten() %>%
  layer_dense(1, activation = "sigmoid")
model <- keras_model(inputs, outputs)
```

Let's look at how the dimensions of the feature maps change with every successive layer:

```
model
```

```
Model: "model_2"
_____
 Layer (type)                    Output Shape              Param #
=================================================================
 input_3 (InputLayer)            [(None, 180, 180, 3)]     0
 rescaling (Rescaling)           (None, 180, 180, 3)       0
 conv2d_10 (Conv2D)              (None, 178, 178, 32)      896
 max_pooling2d_5 (MaxPooling2D)  (None, 89, 89, 32)        0
 conv2d_9 (Conv2D)               (None, 87, 87, 64)        18496
 max_pooling2d_4 (MaxPooling2D)  (None, 43, 43, 64)        0
 conv2d_8 (Conv2D)               (None, 41, 41, 128)       73856
 max_pooling2d_3 (MaxPooling2D)  (None, 20, 20, 128)       0
 conv2d_7 (Conv2D)               (None, 18, 18, 256)       295168
 max_pooling2d_2 (MaxPooling2D)  (None, 9, 9, 256)         0
 conv2d_6 (Conv2D)               (None, 7, 7, 256)         590080
 flatten_2 (Flatten)             (None, 12544)             0
 dense_2 (Dense)                 (None, 1)                 12545
=================================================================
Total params: 991,041
Trainable params: 991,041
Non-trainable params: 0
_____
```

For the compilation step, we'll go with the RMSprop optimizer, as usual. Because we ended the model with a single sigmoid unit, we'll use binary cross-entropy as the loss (as a reminder, check out table 6.1 in chapter 6 for a cheat sheet on which loss function to use in various situations).

Listing 8.8 Configuring the model for training

```
model %>% compile(loss = "binary_crossentropy",
                  optimizer = "rmsprop",
                  metrics = "accuracy")
```

8.2.4 Data preprocessing

As you know by now, data should be formatted into appropriately preprocessed floating-point tensors before being fed into the model. Currently, the data sits on a drive as JPEG files, so the steps for getting it into the model are roughly as follows:

1 Read the picture files.
2 Decode the JPEG content to RGB grids of pixels.
3 Convert these into floating-point tensors.
4 Resize them to a shared size (we'll use 180 × 180).
5 Pack them into batches (we'll use batches of 32 images).

It may seem a bit daunting, but fortunately Keras has utilities to take care of these steps automatically. In particular, Keras features the utility function `image_dataset_` `from_directory()`, which lets you quickly set up a data pipeline that can automatically turn image files on disk into batches of preprocessed tensors. This is what we'll use here.

Calling `image_dataset_from_directory(directory)` will first list the subdirectories of `directory` and assume each one contains images from one of our classes. It will then index the image files in each subdirectory. Finally, it will create and return a TF Dataset object configured to read these files, shuffle them, decode them to tensors, resize them to a shared size, and pack them into batches.

Listing 8.9   Using `image_dataset_from_directory` to read images

```
train_dataset <-
  image_dataset_from_directory(new_base_dir / "train",
                               image_size = c(180, 180),
                               batch_size = 32)
validation_dataset <-
  image_dataset_from_directory(new_base_dir / "validation",
                               image_size = c(180, 180),
                               batch_size = 32)
test_dataset <-
  image_dataset_from_directory(new_base_dir / "test",
                               image_size = c(180, 180),
                               batch_size = 32)
```

Understanding tfdatasets

The tfdatasets package can be used to create efficient input pipelines for machine learning models. Its core object type is the TF Dataset.

A TF Dataset object is an iterable: you can call `as_iterator()` on it to produce an iterator, and then repeatedly call `iter_next()` on the iterator to generate sequences of data. You will typically use TF Dataset objects to produce batches of input data and labels. You can pass a TF Dataset object directly to the `fit()` method of a Keras model.

The TF Dataset object handles many key features that would otherwise be cumbersome to implement yourself—in particular, asynchronous data prefetching (preprocessing the next batch of data while the previous one is being handled by the model, which keeps execution flowing without interruptions).

The tfdatasets package provides a functional-style API for modifying Datasets. Here's a quick example: let's create a TF Dataset instance from a R array of an integer sequence. We'll consider 100 samples, where each sample is a vector of size 6 (in other words, our starting R array is a matrix with shape `(100, 6)`):

```
library(tfdatasets)
example_array <- array(seq(100*6), c(100, 6))
head(example_array)
```

```
        [,1] [,2] [,3] [,4] [,5] [,6]
[1,]       1  101  201  301  401  501
[2,]       2  102  202  302  402  502
[3,]       3  103  203  303  403  503
[4,]       4  104  204  304  404  504
[5,]       5  105  205  305  405  505
[6,]       6  106  206  306  406  506

dataset <- tensor_slices_dataset(example_array)
```

The tensor_slices_dataset() function can be used to create a TF Dataset from an R array, or a list (optionally named) of R arrays.

At first, our dataset just yields single samples:

```
dataset_iterator <- as_iterator(dataset)
for(i in 1:3) {
  element <- iter_next(dataset_iterator)
  print(element)
}
```

```
tf.Tensor([  1 101 201 301 401 501], shape=(6), dtype=int32)
tf.Tensor([  2 102 202 302 402 502], shape=(6), dtype=int32)
tf.Tensor([  3 103 203 303 403 503], shape=(6), dtype=int32)
```

Note that the TF Dataset iterator yields Tensorflow `Tensor`s by default. This is typically what you want, and the most appropriate type for methods like `fit()`. In some situations, however, you may prefer if the iterator yields batches of R arrays instead; in that situation, you can call `as_array_iterator()` instead of `as_iterator()`:

```
dataset_array_iterator <- as_array_iterator(dataset)
for(i in 1:3) {
  element <- iter_next(dataset_array_iterator)
  str(element)
}
```

```
 int [1:6(1d)] 1 101 201 301 401 501
 int [1:6(1d)] 2 102 202 302 402 502
 int [1:6(1d)] 3 103 203 303 403 503
```

We can use the `dataset_batch()` to batch the data:

```
batched_dataset <- dataset %>%
  dataset_batch(3)
batched_dataset_iterator <- as_iterator(batched_dataset)
for(i in 1:3) {
  element <- iter_next(batched_dataset_iterator)
  print(element)
}
```

(continued)

```
tf.Tensor(
[[   1 101 201 301 401 501]
 [   2 102 202 302 402 502]
 [   3 103 203 303 403 503]], shape=(3, 6), dtype=int32)
tf.Tensor(
[[   4 104 204 304 404 504]
 [   5 105 205 305 405 505]
 [   6 106 206 306 406 506]], shape=(3, 6), dtype=int32)
tf.Tensor(
[[   7 107 207 307 407 507]
 [   8 108 208 308 408 508]
 [   9 109 209 309 409 509]], shape=(3, 6), dtype=int32)
```

More broadly, we have access to a range of useful dataset methods, such as

- `dataset_shuffle(buffer_size)`—Shuffles elements within a buffer
- `dataset_prefetch(buffer_size)`—Prefetches a buffer of elements in GPU memory to achieve better device utilization
- `dataset_map(fn)`—Applies an arbitrary transformation to each element of the dataset (the function `fn`, which expects to take as input a single element yielded by the dataset)

The `dataset_map()` method, in particular, is one that you will use often. Here's an example. We'll use it to reshape the elements in our toy dataset from shape `(6)` to shape `(2, 3)`:

```
reshaped_dataset <- dataset %>%
  dataset_map(function(element) tf$reshape(element, shape(2, 3)))

reshaped_dataset_iterator <- as_iterator(reshaped_dataset)
for(i in 1:3) {
  element <- iter_next(reshaped_dataset_iterator)      Note that tf$reshape()
  print(element)                                        reshapes using C style
}                                                       (row-major) semantics.
```

```
tf.Tensor(
[[   1 101 201]
 [301 401 501]], shape=(2, 3), dtype=int32)
tf.Tensor(
[[   2 102 202]
 [302 402 502]], shape=(2, 3), dtype=int32)
tf.Tensor(
[[   3 103 203]
 [303 403 503]], shape=(2, 3), dtype=int32)
```

You're about to see more `dataset_map()` action in this chapter.

Let's look at the output of one of these Dataset objects: it yields batches of 180×180 RGB images (shape (32, 180, 180, 3)) and integer labels (shape (32)). There are 32 samples in each batch (the batch size).

> **Listing 8.10   Displaying the shapes of the data and labels yielded by the `Dataset`**

```
c(data_batch, labels_batch) %<-% iter_next(as_iterator(train_dataset))
data_batch$shape
```

```
TensorShape([32, 180, 180, 3])
```

```
labels_batch$shape
```

```
TensorShape([32])
```

Let's fit the model on our dataset. We'll use the validation_data argument in fit() to monitor validation metrics on a separate TF Dataset object.

Note that we'll also use a callback_model_checkpoint() to save the model after each epoch. We'll configure it with the path specifying where to save the file, as well as the arguments save_best_only = TRUE and monitor = "val_loss": they tell the callback to only save a new file (overwriting any previous one) when the current value of the val_loss metric is lower than at any previous time during training. This guarantees that your saved file will always contain the state of the model corresponding to its best-performing training epoch, in terms of its performance on the validation data. As a result, we won't have to retrain a new model for a lower number of epochs if we start overfitting: we can just reload our saved file.

> **Listing 8.11   Fitting the model using a TensorFlow Dataset**

```
callbacks <- list(
  callback_model_checkpoint(
    filepath = "convnet_from_scratch.keras",
    save_best_only = TRUE,
    monitor = "val_loss"
  )
)

history <- model %>%
  fit(
    train_dataset,
    epochs = 30,
    validation_data = validation_dataset,
    callbacks = callbacks
  )
```

Let's plot the loss and accuracy of the model over the training and validation data during training (see figure 8.9).

> **Listing 8.12   Displaying curves of loss and accuracy during training**

```
plot(history)
```

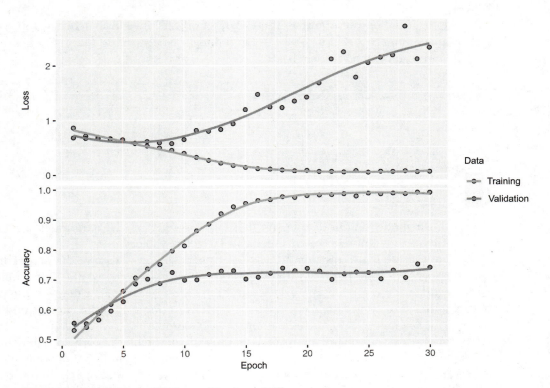

Figure 8.9   Training and validation metrics for a simple convnet

These plots are characteristic of overfitting. The training accuracy increases linearly over time, until it reaches nearly 100%, whereas the validation accuracy peaks at 75%. The validation loss reaches its minimum after only 10 epochs and then increases, whereas the training loss keeps decreasing linearly as training proceeds.

Let's check the test accuracy. We'll reload the model from its saved file to evaluate it as it was before it started overfitting.

Listing 8.13   Evaluating the model on the test set

```
test_model <- load_model_tf("convnet_from_scratch.keras")
result <- evaluate(test_model, test_dataset)
cat(sprintf("Test accuracy: %.3f\n", result["accuracy"]))
```

```
Test accuracy: 0.740
```

We get a test accuracy of 74%. (Due to the randomness of neural network initializations, you may get slightly different numbers.)

Because we have relatively few training samples (2,000), overfitting will be our number one concern. You already know about a number of techniques that can help mitigate overfitting, such as dropout and weight decay (L2 regularization). We're now going to work with a new one, specific to computer vision and used almost universally when processing images with deep learning models: *data augmentation.*

8.2.5 Using data augmentation

Overfitting is caused by having too few samples to learn from, rendering you unable to train a model that can generalize to new data. Given infinite data, your model would be exposed to every possible aspect of the data distribution at hand: you would never overfit. Data augmentation takes the approach of generating more training data from existing training samples by *augmenting* the samples via a number of random transformations that yield believable-looking images. The goal is that, at training time, your model will never see the exact same picture twice. This helps expose the model to more aspects of the data so it can generalize better.

In Keras, this can be done by adding a number of *data augmentation layers* at the start of your model. Let's get started with an example: the following `keras_model_sequential()` chains several random image transformations. In our model, we'd include it right before the `layer_rescaling()`.

Listing 8.14 Defining a data augmentation stage to add to an image model

```
data_augmentation <- keras_model_sequential() %>%
  layer_random_flip("horizontal") %>%
  layer_random_rotation(0.1) %>%
  layer_random_zoom(0.2)
```

These are just a few of the layers available (for more, see the Keras documentation). Let's quickly go over this code:

- `layer_random_flip("horizontal")`—Applies horizontal flipping to a random 50% of the images that go through it
- `layer_random_rotation(0.1)`—Rotates the input images by a random value in the range `[-10%, +10%]` (these are fractions of a full circle—in degrees, the range would be `[-36 degrees, +36 degrees]`)
- `layer_random_zoom(0.2)`—Zooms in or out of the image by a random factor in the range `[-20%, +20%]`

Let's look at the augmented images (see figure 8.10).

Listing 8.15 Displaying some randomly augmented training images

```
library(tfdatasets)
batch <- train_dataset %>%
  as_iterator() %>%
  iter_next()

c(images, labels) %<-% batch

par(mfrow = c(3, 3), mar = rep(.5, 4))   ◄─┐  Prepare the graphics
                                             device for nine images.
```

```
image <- images[1, , , ]
plot(as.raster(as.array(image), max = 255))

for (i in 2:9) {
  augmented_images <- data_augmentation(images)
  augmented_image <- augmented_images[1, , , ]
  plot(as.raster(as.array(augmented_image), max = 255))
}
```

Plot the first image of the batch, without augmentation.

Apply the augmentation stage to the batch of images.

Display the first image in the output batch. For each of the eight iterations, this is a different augmentation of the same image.

Figure 8.10 Generating variations of a very good boy via random data augmentation

If we train a new model using this data-augmentation configuration, the model will never see the same input twice. But the inputs it sees are still heavily intercorrelated because they come from a small number of original images—we can't produce new information; we can only remix existing information. As such, this may not be enough to completely get rid of overfitting. To further fight overfitting, we'll also add a `layer_dropout()` to our model right before the densely connected classifier.

One last thing you should know about random image augmentation layers: just like `layer_dropout()`, they're inactive during inference (when we call `predict()` or `evaluate()`). During evaluation, our model will behave just the same as when it did not include data augmentation and dropout.

Listing 8.16   Defining a new convnet that includes image augmentation and dropout

```
inputs <- layer_input(shape = c(180, 180, 3))
outputs <- inputs %>%
  data_augmentation() %>%
  layer_rescaling(1 / 255) %>%
  layer_conv_2d(filters = 32, kernel_size = 3, activation = "relu") %>%
  layer_max_pooling_2d(pool_size = 2) %>%
  layer_conv_2d(filters = 64, kernel_size = 3, activation = "relu") %>%
  layer_max_pooling_2d(pool_size = 2) %>%
  layer_conv_2d(filters = 128, kernel_size = 3, activation = "relu") %>%
  layer_max_pooling_2d(pool_size = 2) %>%
  layer_conv_2d(filters = 256, kernel_size = 3, activation = "relu") %>%
  layer_max_pooling_2d(pool_size = 2) %>%
  layer_conv_2d(filters = 256, kernel_size = 3, activation = "relu") %>%
  layer_flatten() %>%
  layer_dropout(0.5) %>%
  layer_dense(1, activation = "sigmoid")

model <- keras_model(inputs, outputs)

model %>% compile(loss = "binary_crossentropy",
                  optimizer = "rmsprop",
                  metrics = "accuracy")
```

Let's train the model using data augmentation and dropout. Because we expect overfitting to occur much later during training, we will train for three times as many epochs—one hundred.

Listing 8.17   Training the regularized convnet

```
callbacks <- list(
  callback_model_checkpoint(
    filepath = "convnet_from_scratch_with_augmentation.keras",
    save_best_only = TRUE,
    monitor = "val_loss"
  )
)
```

```
history <- model %>% fit(
  train_dataset,
  epochs = 100,
  validation_data = validation_dataset,
  callbacks = callbacks
)
```

Let's plot the results again: see figure 8.11. Thanks to data augmentation and drop-out, we start overfitting much later, around epochs 60–70 (compared to epoch 10 for the original model). The validation accuracy ends up consistently in the 80–85% range—a big improvement over our first try:

```
plot(history)
```

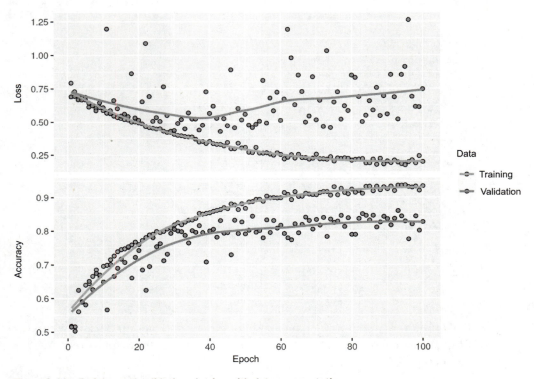

Figure 8.11   Training and validation metrics with data augmentation

Let's check the test accuracy.

Listing 8.18   Evaluating the model on the test set

```
test_model <- load_model_tf("convnet_from_scratch_with_augmentation.keras")
result <- evaluate(test_model, test_dataset)
cat(sprintf("Test accuracy: %.3f\n", result["accuracy"]))
```

```
Test accuracy: 0.814
```

We get a test accuracy of 81.4%. It's starting to look good! If you're running the code, make sure to keep the saved file (convnet_from_scratch_with_augmentation.keras), because we will use it for some experiments in the next chapter.

By further tuning the model's configuration (such as the number of filters per convolution layer, or the number of layers in the model), we might be able to get an even better accuracy, likely up to 90%. But it would prove difficult to go any higher just by training our own convnet from scratch, because we have so little data to work with. As a next step to improve our accuracy on this problem, we'll have to use a pretrained model, which is the focus of the next two sections.

8.3   Leveraging a pretrained model

A common and highly effective approach to deep learning on small image datasets is to use a pretrained model. A *pretrained model* is a model that was previously trained on a large dataset, typically on a large-scale image-classification task. If this original dataset is large enough and general enough, the spatial hierarchy of features learned by the pretrained model can effectively act as a generic model of the visual world, and hence, its features can prove useful for many different computer vision problems, even though these new problems may involve completely different classes than those of the original task. For instance, you might train a model on ImageNet (where classes are mostly animals and everyday objects) and then repurpose this trained model for something as remote as identifying furniture items in images. Such portability of learned features across different problems is a key advantage of deep learning compared to many older, shallow learning approaches, and it makes deep learning very effective for small-data problems.

In this case, let's consider a large convnet trained on the ImageNet dataset (1.4 million labeled images and 1,000 different classes). ImageNet contains many animal classes, including different species of cats and dogs, and you can thus expect it to perform well on the dogs-versus-cats classification problem.

We'll use the VGG16 architecture, developed by Karen Simonyan and Andrew Zisserman in 2014.[1] Although it's an older model, far from the current state of the art and somewhat heavier than many other recent models, I chose it because its architecture is similar to what you're already familiar with, and it's easy to understand without introducing any new concepts. This may be your first encounter with one of these cutesy model names—VGG, ResNet, Inception, Xception, and so on; you'll get used to them because they will come up frequently if you keep doing deep learning for computer vision.

There are two ways to use a pretrained model: *feature extraction* and *fine-tuning*. We'll cover both of them. Let's start with feature extraction.

---

[1] Karen Simonyan and Andrew Zisserman, "Very Deep Convolutional Networks for Large-Scale Image Recognition," arXiv (2014), https://arxiv.org/abs/1409.1556.

8.3.1 *Feature extraction with a pretrained model*

Feature extraction consists of using the representations learned by a previously trained model to extract interesting features from new samples. These features are then run through a new classifier, which is trained from scratch.

As you saw previously, convnets used for image classification comprise two parts: they start with a series of pooling and convolution layers, and they end with a densely connected classifier. The first part is called the *convolutional base* of the model. In the case of convnets, feature extraction consists of taking the convolutional base of a previously trained network, running the new data through it, and training a new classifier on top of the output (see figure 8.12).

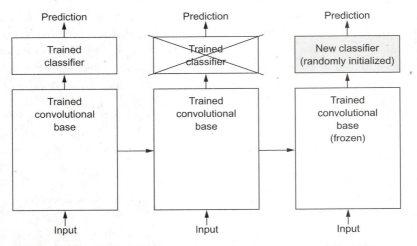

Figure 8.12   Swapping classifiers while keeping the same convolutional base

Why reuse only the convolutional base? Could we reuse the densely connected classifier as well? In general, doing so should be avoided. The reason is that the representations learned by the convolutional base are likely to be more generic and, therefore, more reusable: the feature maps of a convnet are presence maps of generic concepts over a picture, which are likely to be useful regardless of the computer vision problem at hand. But the representations learned by the classifier will necessarily be specific to the set of classes on which the model was trained—they will contain only information about the presence probability of this or that class in the entire picture. Additionally, representations found in densely connected layers no longer contain any information about where objects are located in the input image; these layers get rid of the notion of space, whereas the object location is still described by convolutional feature maps. For problems where object location matters, densely connected features are largely useless.

Note that the level of generality (and, therefore, reusability) of the representations extracted by specific convolution layers depends on the depth of the layer in the model. Layers that come earlier in the model extract local, highly generic feature maps (such as visual edges, colors, and textures), whereas layers that are higher up extract more-abstract concepts (such as "cat ear" or "dog eye"). So if your new dataset differs a lot from the dataset on which the original model was trained, you may be better off using only the first few layers of the model to do feature extraction, rather than the entire convolutional base.

In this case, because the ImageNet class set contains multiple dog and cat classes, it's likely to be beneficial to reuse the information contained in the densely connected layers of the original model. But we'll choose not to, to cover the more general case where the class set of the new problem doesn't overlap the class set of the original model. Let's put this into practice by using the convolutional base of the VGG16 network, trained on ImageNet, to extract interesting features from cat and dog images and then train a dogs-versus-cats classifier on top of these features.

The VGG16 model, among others, comes prepackaged with Keras. They all are exported as functions with the prefix `application_`. Many other image-classification models (all pretrained on the ImageNet dataset) are available as part of the Keras applications:

- Xception
- MobileNet
- DenseNet
- ResNet
- EfficientNet
- And so on

Let's instantiate the VGG16 model.

> **Listing 8.19 Instantiating the VGG16 convolutional base**

```
conv_base <- application_vgg16(
  weights = "imagenet",
  include_top = FALSE,
  input_shape = c(180, 180, 3)
)
```

We pass three arguments to the application function:

- `weights` specifies the weight checkpoint from which to initialize the model.
- `include_top` refers to including (or not) the densely connected classifier on top of the network. By default, this densely connected classifier corresponds to the 1,000 classes from ImageNet. Because we intend to use our own densely connected classifier (with only two classes: `cat` and `dog`), we don't need to include it.
- `input_shape` is the shape of the image tensors that we'll feed to the network. This argument is purely optional: if we don't pass it, the network will be able to process inputs of any size. Here we pass it so that we can visualize (in the following summary) how the size of the feature maps shrinks with each new convolution and pooling layer.

Here's the detail of the architecture of the VGG16 convolutional base. It's similar to the simple convnets you're already familiar with:

```
conv_base

Model: "vgg16"
_____
Layer (type)                 Output Shape              Param #
=================================================================
input_5 (InputLayer)         [(None, 180, 180, 3)]     0
block1_conv1 (Conv2D)        (None, 180, 180, 64)      1792
block1_conv2 (Conv2D)        (None, 180, 180, 64)      36928
block1_pool (MaxPooling2D)   (None, 90, 90, 64)        0
block2_conv1 (Conv2D)        (None, 90, 90, 128)       73856
block2_conv2 (Conv2D)        (None, 90, 90, 128)       147584
block2_pool (MaxPooling2D)   (None, 45, 45, 128)       0
block3_conv1 (Conv2D)        (None, 45, 45, 256)       295168
block3_conv2 (Conv2D)        (None, 45, 45, 256)       590080
block3_conv3 (Conv2D)        (None, 45, 45, 256)       590080
block3_pool (MaxPooling2D)   (None, 22, 22, 256)       0
block4_conv1 (Conv2D)        (None, 22, 22, 512)       1180160
block4_conv2 (Conv2D)        (None, 22, 22, 512)       2359808
block4_conv3 (Conv2D)        (None, 22, 22, 512)       2359808
block4_pool (MaxPooling2D)   (None, 11, 11, 512)       0
block5_conv1 (Conv2D)        (None, 11, 11, 512)       2359808
block5_conv2 (Conv2D)        (None, 11, 11, 512)       2359808
block5_conv3 (Conv2D)        (None, 11, 11, 512)       2359808
block5_pool (MaxPooling2D)   (None, 5, 5, 512)         0
=================================================================
Total params: 14,714,688
Trainable params: 14,714,688
Non-trainable params: 0
_____
```

The final feature map has shape (5, 5, 512). That's the feature map on top of which we'll stick a densely connected classifier.

At this point, we could proceed in two ways:

- Run the convolutional base over our dataset, record its output (arrays) to a file array on disk, and then use this data as input to a standalone, densely connected classifier similar to those you saw in chapter 4 of this book. This solution is fast and cheap to run, because it requires running the convolutional base only once for every input image, and the convolutional base is by far the most expensive part of the pipeline. But for the same reason, this technique won't allow us to use data augmentation.

- Extend the model we have (conv_base) by adding Dense layers on top, and run the whole thing from end to end on the input data. This will allow us to use data augmentation, because every input image goes through the convolutional base every time it's seen by the model. But for the same reason, this technique is far more expensive than the first.

We'll cover both techniques. Let's walk through the code required to set up the first one: recording the output of conv_base on our data and using these outputs as inputs to a new model.

FAST FEATURE EXTRACTION WITHOUT DATA AUGMENTATION

We'll start by extracting features as R arrays by calling the `predict()` method of the `conv_base` model on our training, validation, and testing datasets.

Let's iterate over our datasets to extract the VGG16 features.

Listing 8.20 Extracting the VGG16 features and corresponding labels

```r
get_features_and_labels <- function(dataset) {
  n_batches <- length(dataset)
  all_features <- vector("list", n_batches)
  all_labels <- vector("list", n_batches)
  iterator <- as_array_iterator(dataset)
  for (i in 1:n_batches) {
    c(images, labels) %<-% iter_next(iterator)
    preprocessed_images <- imagenet_preprocess_input(images)
    features <- conv_base %>% predict(preprocessed_images)

    all_labels[[i]] <- labels
    all_features[[i]] <- features
  }

  all_features <- listarrays::bind_on_rows(all_features)
  all_labels <- listarrays::bind_on_rows(all_labels)

  list(all_features, all_labels)
}

c(train_features, train_labels) %<-% get_features_and_labels(train_dataset)
c(val_features, val_labels) %<-% get_features_and_labels(validation_dataset)
c(test_features, test_labels) %<-% get_features_and_labels(test_dataset)
```

> **Combine a list of R arrays along the first axis, the batch dimension.**

Importantly, `predict()` expects only images, not labels, but our current dataset yields batches that contain both images and their labels. Moreover, the VGG16 model expects inputs that are preprocessed with the function `imagenet_preprocess_input()`, which scales pixel values to an appropriate range. The extracted features are currently of shape (samples, 5, 5, 512):

```r
dim(train_features)
```

```
[1] 2000    5    5  512
```

At this point, we can define our densely connected classifier (note the use of dropout for regularization) and train it on the data and labels that we just recorded.

Listing 8.21 Defining and training the densely connected classifier

```r
inputs <- layer_input(shape = c(5, 5, 512))
outputs <- inputs %>%
  layer_flatten() %>%
  layer_dense(256) %>%
  layer_dropout(.5) %>%
  layer_dense(1, activation = "sigmoid")
model <- keras_model(inputs, outputs)
```

> **Note the use of the layer_flatten() before passing the features to a layer_dense().**

```
model %>% compile(loss = "binary_crossentropy",
                  optimizer = "rmsprop",
                  metrics = "accuracy")

callbacks <- list(
  callback_model_checkpoint(
    filepath = "feature_extraction.keras",
    save_best_only = TRUE,
    monitor = "val_loss"
  )
)

history <- model %>% fit(
  train_features, train_labels,
  epochs = 20,
  validation_data = list(val_features, val_labels),
  callbacks = callbacks
)
```

Training is very fast because we have to deal with only two dense layers—an epoch takes less than one second, even on a CPU.

Let's look at the loss and accuracy curves during training (see figure 8.13).

Listing 8.22   Plotting the results

```
plot(history)
```

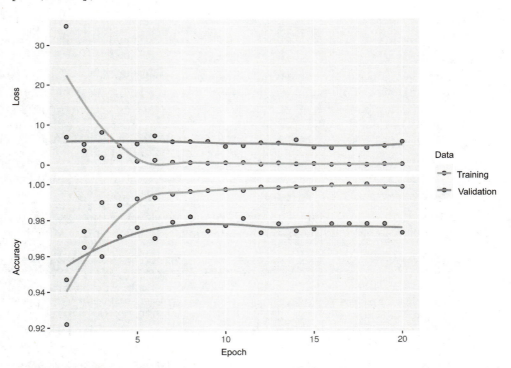

Figure 8.13   Training and validation metrics for plain feature extraction

We reach a validation accuracy of about 97%—much better than we achieved in the previous section with the small model trained from scratch. This is a bit of an unfair comparison, however, because ImageNet contains many dog and cat instances, which means that our pretrained model already has the exact knowledge required for the task at hand. This won't always be the case when you use pretrained features.

However, the plots also indicate that we're overfitting almost from the start, despite using dropout with a fairly large rate. That's because this technique doesn't use data augmentation, which is essential for preventing overfitting with small image datasets.

FEATURE EXTRACTION TOGETHER WITH DATA AUGMENTATION

Now let's review the second technique I mentioned for doing feature extraction, which is much slower and more expensive, but which allows us to use data augmentation during training: creating a model that chains the conv_base with a new dense classifier, and training it end to end on the inputs.

To do this, we will first *freeze the convolutional base*. *Freezing* a layer or set of layers means preventing their weights from being updated during training. If we don't do this, the representations that were previously learned by the convolutional base will be modified during training. Because the dense layers on top are randomly initialized, very large weight updates would be propagated through the network, effectively destroying the representations previously learned. In Keras, we freeze a layer or model by calling freeze_weights().

Listing 8.23   Instantiating and freezing the VGG16 convolutional base

```
conv_base <- application_vgg16(
    weights = "imagenet",
    include_top = FALSE)
freeze_weights(conv_base)
```

Calling freeze_weights() empties the list of trainable weights of the layer or model.

Listing 8.24   Printing the list of trainable weights before and after freezing

```
unfreeze_weights(conv_base)
cat("This is the number of trainable weights",
    "before freezing the conv base:",
    length(conv_base$trainable_weights), "\n")
```

This is the number of trainable weights before freezing the conv base: 26

```
freeze_weights(conv_base)
cat("This is the number of trainable weights",
    "after freezing the conv base:",
    length(conv_base$trainable_weights), "\n")
```

This is the number of trainable weights after freezing the conv base: 0

Now we can create a new model that chains together

1 A data augmentation stage
2 Our frozen convolutional base
3 A dense classifier

```
data_augmentation <- keras_model_sequential() %>%
  layer_random_flip("horizontal") %>%
  layer_random_rotation(0.1) %>%
  layer_random_zoom(0.2)

inputs <- layer_input(shape = c(180, 180, 3))
outputs <- inputs %>%
  data_augmentation() %>%                         <--------  Apply data augmentation.
  imagenet_preprocess_input() %>%      <--
  conv_base() %>%                                           Apply input value scaling.
  layer_flatten() %>%
  layer_dense(256) %>%
  layer_dropout(0.5) %>%
  layer_dense(1, activation = "sigmoid")
model <- keras_model(inputs, outputs)
model %>% compile(loss = "binary_crossentropy",
                  optimizer = "rmsprop",
                  metrics = "accuracy")
```

With this setup, only the weights from the two dense layers that we added will be trained. That's a total of four weight tensors: two per layer (the main weight matrix and the bias vector). Note that for these changes to take effect, you must first compile the model. If you ever modify weight trainability after compilation, you should then recompile the model, or these changes will be ignored.

Let's train our model. Thanks to data augmentation, it will take much longer for the model to start overfitting, so we can train for more epochs—let's do 50.

This technique is expensive enough that you should attempt it only if you have access to a GPU—it's intractable on CPU. If you can't run your code on GPU, then the previous technique is the way to go:

```
callbacks <- list(
  callback_model_checkpoint(
    filepath = "feature_extraction_with_data_augmentation.keras",
    save_best_only = TRUE,
    monitor = "val_loss"
  )
)

history <- model %>% fit(
  train_dataset,
  epochs = 50,
  validation_data = validation_dataset,
  callbacks = callbacks
)
```

Let's plot the results again (see figure 8.14). As you can see, we reach a validation accuracy of over 98%. This is a strong improvement over the previous model.

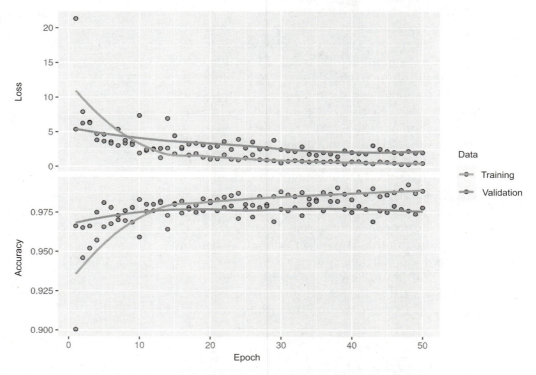

Figure 8.14 Training and validation metrics for feature extraction with data augmentation

Let's check the test accuracy.

Listing 8.25 Evaluating the model on the test set

```
test_model <- load_model_tf(
  "feature_extraction_with_data_augmentation.keras")
result <- evaluate(test_model, test_dataset)
cat(sprintf("Test accuracy: %.3f\n", result["accuracy"]))
```

```
Test accuracy: 0.977
```

We get a test accuracy of 97.7%. This is only a modest improvement compared to the previous test accuracy, which is a bit disappointing, given the strong results on the validation data. A model's accuracy always depends on the set of samples you evaluate it on. Some sample sets may be more difficult than others, and strong results on one set won't necessarily fully translate to all other sets.

8.3.2   *Fine-tuning a pretrained model*

Another widely used technique for model reuse, complementary to feature extraction, is *fine-tuning* (see figure 8.15). Fine-tuning consists of unfreezing a few of the top layers of a frozen model base used for feature extraction and jointly training both the newly added part of the model (in this case, the fully connected classifier) and these top layers. This is called *fine-tuning* because it slightly adjusts the more abstract representations of the model being reused to make them more relevant for the problem at hand.

I stated earlier that it's necessary to freeze the convolution base of VGG16 to be able to train a randomly initialized classifier on top. For the same reason, it's possible to fine-tune the top layers of the convolutional base only once the classifier on top has already been trained. If the classifier isn't already trained, the error signal propagating through the network during training will be too large, and the representations previously learned by the layers being fine-tuned will be destroyed. Thus the steps for fine-tuning a network are as follows:

1 Add our custom network on top of an already-trained base network.
2 Freeze the base network.
3 Train the part we added.
4 Unfreeze some layers in the base network. (Note that you should not unfreeze "batch normalization" layers, which are not relevant here because there are no such layers in VGG16. Batch normalization and its impact on fine-tuning is explained in the next chapter.)
5 Jointly train both these layers and the part we added.

You already completed the first three steps when doing feature extraction. Let's proceed with step 4: we'll unfreeze our conv_base and then freeze individual layers inside it.

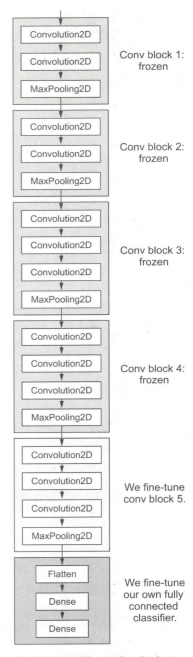

Figure 8.15 Fine-tuning the last convolutional block of the VGG16 network

As a reminder, this is what our convolutional base looks like:

```
conv_base
```

```
Model: "vgg16"
```

Layer (type)	Output Shape	Param #	Trainable
input_7 (InputLayer)	[(None, None, None, 3)]	0	N
block1_conv1 (Conv2D)	(None, None, None, 64)	1792	N
block1_conv2 (Conv2D)	(None, None, None, 64)	36928	N
block1_pool (MaxPooling2D)	(None, None, None, 64)	0	N
block2_conv1 (Conv2D)	(None, None, None, 128)	73856	N
block2_conv2 (Conv2D)	(None, None, None, 128)	147584	N
block2_pool (MaxPooling2D)	(None, None, None, 128)	0	N
block3_conv1 (Conv2D)	(None, None, None, 256)	295168	N
block3_conv2 (Conv2D)	(None, None, None, 256)	590080	N
block3_conv3 (Conv2D)	(None, None, None, 256)	590080	N
block3_pool (MaxPooling2D)	(None, None, None, 256)	0	N
block4_conv1 (Conv2D)	(None, None, None, 512)	1180160	N
block4_conv2 (Conv2D)	(None, None, None, 512)	2359808	N
block4_conv3 (Conv2D)	(None, None, None, 512)	2359808	N
block4_pool (MaxPooling2D)	(None, None, None, 512)	0	N
block5_conv1 (Conv2D)	(None, None, None, 512)	2359808	N
block5_conv2 (Conv2D)	(None, None, None, 512)	2359808	N
block5_conv3 (Conv2D)	(None, None, None, 512)	2359808	N
block5_pool (MaxPooling2D)	(None, None, None, 512)	0	N

```
Total params: 14,714,688
Trainable params: 0
Non-trainable params: 14,714,688
```

We'll fine-tune the last three convolutional layers, which means all layers up to `block4_pool` should be frozen, and the layers `block5_conv1`, `block5_conv2`, and `block5_conv3` should be trainable.

Why not fine-tune more layers? Why not fine-tune the entire convolutional base? You could. But you need to consider the following:

- Earlier layers in the convolutional base encode more generic, reusable features, whereas layers higher up encode more specialized features. It's more useful to fine-tune the more specialized features, because these are the ones that need to be repurposed on your new problem. There would be fast-decreasing returns in fine-tuning lower layers.
- The more parameters you're training, the more you're at risk of overfitting. The convolutional base has 15 million parameters, so it would be risky to attempt to train it on your small dataset.

Thus, in this situation, it's a good strategy to fine-tune only the top two or three layers in the convolutional base. Let's set this up, starting from where we left off in the previous example.

Listing 8.26   Freezing all layers until the fourth from the last

```
unfreeze_weights(conv_base, from = -4)
conv_base
```
from = -4 is shorthand for
length(conv_base$layers) + 1 - 4

```
Model: "vgg16"
```

Layer (type)	Output Shape	Param #	Trainable
input_1 (InputLayer)	[(None, None, None, 3)]	0	N
block1_conv1 (Conv2D)	(None, None, None, 64)	1792	N
block1_conv2 (Conv2D)	(None, None, None, 64)	36928	N
block1_pool (MaxPooling2D)	(None, None, None, 64)	0	N
block2_conv1 (Conv2D)	(None, None, None, 128)	73856	N
block2_conv2 (Conv2D)	(None, None, None, 128)	147584	N
block2_pool (MaxPooling2D)	(None, None, None, 128)	0	N
block3_conv1 (Conv2D)	(None, None, None, 256)	295168	N
block3_conv2 (Conv2D)	(None, None, None, 256)	590080	N
block3_conv3 (Conv2D)	(None, None, None, 256)	590080	N
block3_pool (MaxPooling2D)	(None, None, None, 256)	0	N
block4_conv1 (Conv2D)	(None, None, None, 512)	1180160	N
block4_conv2 (Conv2D)	(None, None, None, 512)	2359808	N
block4_conv3 (Conv2D)	(None, None, None, 512)	2359808	N
block4_pool (MaxPooling2D)	(None, None, None, 512)	0	N
block5_conv1 (Conv2D)	(None, None, None, 512)	2359808	Y
block5_conv2 (Conv2D)	(None, None, None, 512)	2359808	Y
block5_conv3 (Conv2D)	(None, None, None, 512)	2359808	Y
block5_pool (MaxPooling2D)	(None, None, None, 512)	0	Y

```
Total params: 14,714,688
Trainable params: 7,079,424
Non-trainable params: 7,635,264
```

Now we can begin fine-tuning the model. We'll do this with the RMSprop optimizer, using a very low learning rate. The reason for using a low learning rate is that we want to limit the magnitude of the modifications we make to the representations of the three layers we're fine-tuning. Updates that are too large may harm these representations.

Listing 8.27   Fine-tuning the model

```
model %>% compile(
  loss = "binary_crossentropy",
  optimizer = optimizer_rmsprop(learning_rate = 1e-5),
  metrics = "accuracy"
)

callbacks <- list(
  callback_model_checkpoint(
    filepath = "fine_tuning.keras",
    save_best_only = TRUE,
    monitor = "val_loss"
)
```

```
)

history <- model %>% fit(
  train_dataset,
  epochs = 30,
  validation_data = validation_dataset,
  callbacks = callbacks
)
```

We can finally evaluate this model on the test data:

```
model <- load_model_tf("fine_tuning.keras")
result <-  evaluate(model, test_dataset)
cat(sprintf("Test accuracy: %.3f\n", result["accuracy"]))
```

```
Test accuracy: 0.985
```

Here, we get a test accuracy of 98.5% (again, your own results may be within one percentage point). In the original Kaggle competition around this dataset, this would have been one of the top results. It's not quite a fair comparison, however, because we used pretrained features that already contained prior knowledge about cats and dogs, which competitors couldn't use at the time.

On the positive side, by leveraging modern deep learning techniques, we managed to reach this result using only a small fraction of the training data that was available for the competition (about 10%). There is a huge difference between being able to train on 20,000 samples compared to 2,000 samples!

Now you have a solid set of tools for dealing with image-classification problems—in particular, with small datasets.

Summary

- Convnets are the best type of machine learning models for computer vision tasks. It's possible to train one from scratch, even on a very small dataset, with decent results.
- Convnets work by learning a hierarchy of modular patterns and concepts to represent the visual world.
- On a small dataset, overfitting will be the main issue. Data augmentation is a powerful way to fight overfitting when you're working with image data.
- It's easy to reuse an existing convnet on a new dataset via feature extraction. This is a valuable technique for working with small image datasets.
- As a complement to feature extraction, you can use fine-tuning, which adapts to a new problem some of the representations previously learned by an existing model. This pushes performance a bit further.

Advanced deep learning
for computer vision

This chapter covers

- The different branches of computer vision: image classification, image segmentation, and object detection
- Modern convnet architecture patterns: residual connections, batch normalization, and depthwise separable convolutions
- Techniques for visualizing and interpreting what convnets learn

The previous chapter gave you a first introduction to deep learning for computer vision via simple models (stacks of `layer_conv_2d()` and `layer_max_pooling_2d()` layers) and a simple use case (binary image classification). But there's more to computer vision than image classification! This chapter dives deeper into more diverse applications and advanced best practices.

9.1 *Three essential computer vision tasks*

So far, we've focused on image classification models: an image goes in, a label comes out: "This image likely contains a cat; this other one likely contains a dog." But image classification is only one of several possible applications of deep learning in computer vision. In general, there are three essential computer vision tasks you need to know about:

- *Image classification*—Where the goal is to assign one or more labels to an image. It may be either single-label classification (an image can only be in one category, excluding the others), or multilabel classification (tagging all categories that an image belongs to, as seen in figure 9.1). For example, when you search for a keyword on the Google Photos app, behind the scenes you're querying a very large multilabel classification model—one with over 20,000 different classes, trained on millions of images.

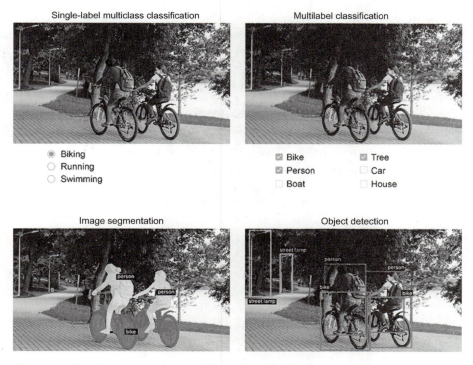

Figure 9.1   The three main computer vision tasks: Classification, segmentation, detection

- *Image segmentation*—Where the goal is to "segment" or "partition" an image into different areas, with each area usually representing a category (as seen in figure 9.1). For instance, when Zoom or Google Meet diplays a custom background behind you in a video call, it's using an image segmentation model to tell your face apart from what's behind it, at pixel precision.

■ *Object detection*—Where the goal is to draw rectangles (called *bounding boxes*) around objects of interest in an image and associate each rectangle with a class. A self-driving car could use an object-detection model to monitor cars, pedestrians, and signs in view of its cameras, for instance.

Deep learning for computer vision also encompasses a number of somewhat more niche tasks besides these three, such as image similarity scoring (estimating how visually similar two images are), keypoint detection (pinpointing attributes of interest in an image, such as facial features), pose estimation, 3D mesh estimation, and so on. But to start with, image classification, image segmentation, and object detection form the foundation that every machine learning engineer should be familiar with. Most computer vision applications boil down to one of these three.

You've seen image classification in action in the previous chapter. Next, let's dive into image segmentation. It's a very useful and versatile technique, and you can straightforwardly approach it with what you've already learned so far.

Note that we won't cover object detection, because it would be too specialized and too complicated for an introductory book. However, you can check out the RetinaNet example on keras.rstudio.com/examples, which shows how to build and train an object detection model from scratch in R using Keras.

9.2   *An image segmentation example*

Image segmentation with deep learning is about using a model to assign a class to each pixel in an image, thus *segmenting* the image into different zones (such as "background" and "foreground," or "road," "car," and "sidewalk"). This general category of techniques can be used to power a considerable variety of valuable applications in image and video editing, autonomous driving, robotics, medical imaging, and so on. There are two different flavors of image segmentation that you should know about:

■ *Semantic segmentation*, where each pixel is independently classified into a semantic category, like "cat." If there are two cats in the image, the corresponding pixels are all mapped to the same generic "cat" category (see figure 9.2).

■ *Instance segmentation*, which seeks not only to classify image pixels by category but also to parse out individual object instances. In an image with two cats in it, instance segmentation would treat "cat 1" and "cat 2" as two separate classes of pixels (see figure 9.2).

In this example, we'll focus on semantic segmentation: we'll be looking once again at images of cats and dogs, and this time we'll learn how to tell apart the main subject and its background.

We'll work with the Oxford-IIIT Pets dataset (http://www.robots.ox.ac.uk/~vgg/data/pets/), which contains 7,390 pictures of various breeds of cats and dogs, together with foreground-background segmentation masks for each picture. A *segmentation mask* is the image-segmentation equivalent of a label: it's an image the same size

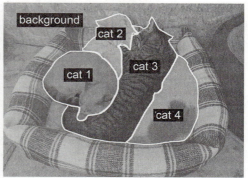

Figure 9.2 Semantic segmentation vs. instance segmentation

as the input image, with a single color channel where each integer value corresponds to the class of the corresponding pixel in the input image. In our case, the pixels of our segmentation masks can take one of three integer values:

- 1 (foreground)
- 2 (background)
- 3 (contour)

Let's start by downloading and uncompressing our dataset, using the the `download.file()` and `untar()` utilities provided by R. Just like in chapter 8, we'll use the fs package for filesystem operations:

```
library(fs)
data_dir <- path("pets_dataset")
dir_create(data_dir)

data_url <- path("http://www.robots.ox.ac.uk/~vgg/data/pets/data")
for (filename in c("images.tar.gz", "annotations.tar.gz")) {
  download.file(url = data_url / filename,
                destfile = data_dir / filename)
  untar(data_dir / filename, exdir = data_dir)
}
```

The input pictures are stored as JPG files in the images/ folder (such as images/Abyssinian_1.jpg), and the corresponding segmentation mask is stored as a PNG file with the same name in the annotations/trimaps/ folder (such as annotations/trimaps/Abyssinian_1.png).

Let's prepare a `data.frame` (technically, a `tibble`) with columns for our input file paths, as well as the list of the corresponding mask file paths:

```
input_dir <- data_dir / "images"
target_dir <- data_dir / "annotations/trimaps/"

image_paths <- tibble::tibble(
  input = sort(dir_ls(input_dir, glob = "*.jpg")),
  target = sort(dir_ls(target_dir, glob = "*.png")))
```

To make sure we match up the image with the correct target, we sort the two lists. The path vectors sort the same because targets and image paths share the same base file-name. Then, to help us keep track of the paths and make sure that our input and target vectors stay in sync, we combine them into a two-column data frame (we use `tibble()` to make the data.frame):

```
tibble::glimpse(image_paths)
```

```
Rows: 7,390
Columns: 2
$ input  <fs::path> "pets_dataset/images/Abyssinian_1.jpg", "pets_dataset/…
$ target <fs::path> "pets_dataset/annotations/trimaps/Abyssinian_1.png", "…
```

What does one of these inputs and its mask look like? Let's take a quick look. We'll use TensorFlow utilities for reading the image, so we can get familiar with the API. First, we define a helper function that will plot a TensorFlow Tensor containing an image using R's `plot()` function:

Default to no margins when plotting images.

```
display_image_tensor <- function(x, ..., max = 255,
                                 plot_margins = c(0, 0, 0, 0)) {
  if(!is.null(plot_margins))
    par(mar = plot_margins)

  x %>%
  as.array() %>%
  drop() %>%
  as.raster(max = max) %>%
  plot(..., interpolate = FALSE)
}
```

Convert the Tensor to an R array.

drop() removes axes that are size 1. For example, if x is a grayscale image with one color channel, it would squeeze the Tensor shape from (height, width, 1) to (height, width).

Convert the R array to a 'raster' object.

interpolate = FALSE tells the R graphics device to draw pixels with sharp edges, with no blending or interpolation of colors between pixels.

In the `as.raster()` call we set `max = 255` because, just like with MNIST, the images are encoded as `uint8`. Unsigned 8-bit integers can encode values only in the range of [0, 255]. By setting `max = 255`, we tell the R graphics device to plot pixel values of 255 as white and 0 as black and interpolate linearly for values in between to different shades of grey.

Now we can read an image into a Tensor, and view it using our helper `display_image_tensor()` (see figure 9.3):

```
library(tensorflow)
image_tensor <- image_paths$input[10] %>%
  tf$io$read_file() %>%
  tf$io$decode_jpeg()

str(image_tensor)
```

```
<tf.Tensor: shape=(448, 500, 3), dtype=uint8, numpy=…>

display_image_tensor(image_tensor)
```

Display input image Abyssinian_107.jpg.

Figure 9.3   An example image

We'll also define a helper to display a target image. The target image is also read in as a `uint8`, but this time only values of (1, 2, 3) are found in the target image tensor. To plot it, we subtract 1 so that the labels range from 0 to 2, and then set `max = 2` so that the labels become 0 (black), 1 (gray), and 2 (white).

And here is its corresponding target (see figure 9.4):

```
display_target_tensor <- function(target)
  display_image_tensor(target - 1, max = 2)

target <- image_paths$target[10] %>%
  tf$io$read_file() %>%
  tf$io$decode_png()

str(target)
```

```
<tf.Tensor: shape=(448, 500, 1), dtype=uint8, numpy=…>
```

```
display_target_tensor(target)
```

Figure 9.4   The corresponding target mask

Next, let's load our inputs and targets into two TF Datasets, and let's split the files into training and validation sets. Because the dataset is very small, we can just load everything into memory:

```r
library(tfdatasets)
```

Here we define a helper to read in and resize the image using TensorFlow operations.

```r
tf_read_image <-
  function(path, format = "image", resize = NULL, ...) {

    img <- path %>%
      tf$io$read_file() %>%
      tf$io[[paste0("decode_", format)]](...)

    if (!is.null(resize))
      img <- img %>%
        tf$image$resize(as.integer(resize))

    img
  }

img_size <- c(200, 200)

tf_read_image_and_resize <- function(..., resize = img_size)
  tf_read_image(..., resize = resize)
```

Look up decode_image(), decode_jpeg(), or decode_png() from the tf$io submodule.

We make sure to call the tf module function with integers using as.integer().

We resize everything to 200 × 200.

The R function passed to dataset_map() is called with symbolic tensors and must return symbolic tensors. dataset_map() receives a single argument here, a named list of two scalar string tensors, containing file paths to the input and target images.

```r
make_dataset <- function(paths_df) {
  tensor_slices_dataset(paths_df) %>%
    dataset_map(function(path) {
      image <- path$input %>%
        tf_read_image_and_resize("jpeg", channels = 3L)
      target <- path$target %>%
        tf_read_image_and_resize("png", channels = 1L)
      target <- target - 1
      list(image, target)
    }) %>%
    dataset_cache() %>%
    dataset_shuffle(buffer_size = nrow(paths_df)) %>%
    dataset_batch(32)
}

num_val_samples <- 1000
val_idx <- sample.int(nrow(image_paths), num_val_samples)

val_paths <- image_paths[val_idx, ]
train_paths <- image_paths[-val_idx, ]

validation_dataset <- make_dataset(val_paths)
train_dataset <- make_dataset(train_paths)
```

Each input image has three channels: RGB values.

Each target image has a single channel: integer labels for each pixel.

Subtract 1 so that our labels become 0, 1, and 2.

Caching the dataset will store the full dataset in memory after the first run. If your computer doesn't have enough RAM, remove this call, and the image files will be loaded dynamically as needed throughout training.

Shuffle the images, using the total number of samples in the data as a buffer_size. We make sure to call shuffle after cache.

Reserve 1,000 samples for validation.

Split the data into training and validation sets.

Now it's time to define our model:

```
get_model <- function(img_size, num_classes) {
```

> **Define local functions conv() and conv_transpose(), so we can avoid passing the same arguments to each call: padding = "same", activation = "relu".**

```
  conv <- function(..., padding = "same", activation = "relu")
    layer_conv_2d(..., padding = padding, activation = activation)

  conv_transpose <- function(..., padding = "same", activation = "relu")
    layer_conv_2d_transpose(..., padding = padding, activation = activation)
```

We use padding = "same" everywhere to avoid the influence of border padding on feature map size.

```
  input <- layer_input(shape = c(img_size, 3))
  output <- input %>%
    layer_rescaling(scale = 1/255) %>%
    conv(64, 3, strides = 2) %>%
    conv(64, 3) %>%
    conv(128, 3, strides = 2) %>%
    conv(128, 3) %>%
    conv(256, 3, strides = 2) %>%
    conv(256, 3) %>%
    conv_transpose(256, 3) %>%
    conv_transpose(256, 3, strides = 2) %>%
    conv_transpose(128, 3) %>%
    conv_transpose(128, 3, strides = 2) %>%
    conv_transpose(64, 3) %>%
    conv_transpose(64, 3, strides = 2) %>%
    conv(num_classes, 3, activation = "softmax")

  keras_model(input, output)
}

model <- get_model(img_size = img_size, num_classes = 3)
```

> **Don't forget to rescale input images to the [0–1] range.**

> **We end the model with a per-pixel three-way softmax to classify each output pixel into one of our three categories.**

Here is the model summary:

```
model
```

```
Model: "model"
```

Layer (type)	Output Shape	Param #
input_1 (InputLayer)	[(None, 200, 200, 3)]	0
rescaling (Rescaling)	(None, 200, 200, 3)	0
conv2d_6 (Conv2D)	(None, 100, 100, 64)	1792
conv2d_5 (Conv2D)	(None, 100, 100, 64)	36928
conv2d_4 (Conv2D)	(None, 50, 50, 128)	73856
conv2d_3 (Conv2D)	(None, 50, 50, 128)	147584
conv2d_2 (Conv2D)	(None, 25, 25, 256)	295168
conv2d_1 (Conv2D)	(None, 25, 25, 256)	590080
conv2d_transpose_5 (Conv2DTranspose)	(None, 25, 25, 256)	590080
conv2d_transpose_4 (Conv2DTranspose)	(None, 50, 50, 256)	590080
conv2d_transpose_3 (Conv2DTranspose)	(None, 50, 50, 128)	295040
conv2d_transpose_2 (Conv2DTranspose)	(None, 100, 100, 128)	147584
conv2d_transpose_1 (Conv2DTranspose)	(None, 100, 100, 64)	73792

```
conv2d_transpose (Conv2DTranspose)    (None, 200, 200, 64)        36928
conv2d (Conv2D)                       (None, 200, 200, 3)          1731
=================================================================
Total params: 2,880,643
Trainable params: 2,880,643
Non-trainable params: 0
```

The first half of the model closely resembles the kind of convnet you'd use for image classification: a stack of `Conv2D` layers, with gradually increasing filter sizes. We downsample our images three times by a factor of two each, ending up with activations of size `(25, 25, 256)`. The purpose of this first half is to encode the images into smaller feature maps, where each spatial location (or pixel) contains information about a large spatial chunk of the original image. You can understand it as a kind of compression.

One important difference between the first half of this model and the classification models you've seen before is the way we do downsampling: in the classification convnets from the last chapter, we used `MaxPooling2D` layers to downsample feature maps. Here, we downsample by adding strides to every other convolution layer (if you don't remember the details of how convolution strides work, see "Understanding convolution strides" in section 8.1.1). We do this because, in the case of image segmentation, we care a lot about the *spatial location* of information in the image, because we need to produce per-pixel target masks as output of the model. When you do 2 × 2 max pooling, you are completely destroying location information within each pooling window: you return one scalar value per window, with zero knowledge of which of the four locations in the windows the value came from. So although max pooling layers perform well for classification tasks, they would hurt us quite a bit for a segmentation task. Meanwhile, strided convolutions do a better job at downsampling feature maps while retaining location information. Throughout this book, you'll notice that we tend to use strides instead of max pooling in any model that cares about feature location, such as the generative models in chapter 12.

The second half of the model is a stack of `Conv2DTranspose` layers. What are those? Well, the output of the first half of the model is a feature map of shape `(25, 25, 256)`, but we want our final output to have the same shape as the target masks, `(200, 200, 3)`. Therefore, we need to apply a kind of *inverse* of the transformations we've applied so far—something that will *upsample* the feature maps instead of downsampling them. That's the purpose of the `Conv2DTranspose` layer: you can think of it as a kind of convolution layer that *learns to upsample*. If you have an input of shape `(100, 100, 64)`, and you run it through a layer `layer_conv_2d(128, 3, strides = 2, padding = "same")`, you get an output of shape `(50, 50, 128)`. If you run this output through a layer `layer_conv_2d_transpose(64, 3, strides = 2, padding = "same")`, you get back an output of shape `(100, 100, 64)`, the same as the original. So after compressing our inputs into feature maps of shape `(25, 25, 256)` via a stack of `Conv2D` layers, we can simply apply the corresponding sequence of `Conv2DTranspose` layers to get back to images of shape `(200, 200, 3)`.

We can now compile and fit our model:

```
model %>%
  compile(optimizer = "rmsprop",
          loss = "sparse_categorical_crossentropy")

callbacks <- list(
  callback_model_checkpoint("oxford_segmentation.keras",
                            save_best_only = TRUE))

history <- model %>% fit(
  train_dataset,
  epochs = 50,
  callbacks = callbacks,
  validation_data = validation_dataset
)
```

NOTE During training, you may see a warning like `Corrupt JPEG data: pre-mature end of data segment`. The image dataset is not perfect, but the `tf$io` module functions can recover gracefully.

Let's display our training and validation loss (see figure 9.5):

```
plot(history)
```

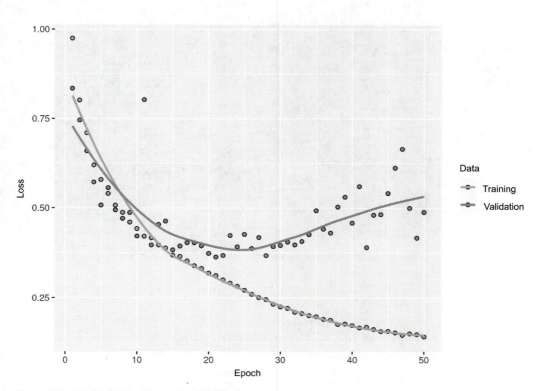

Figure 9.5 Displaying training and validation loss curves

You can see that we start overfitting midway, around epoch 25. Let's reload our best-performing model according to the validation loss and demonstrate how to use it to predict a segmentation mask (see figure 9.6):

```
model <- load_model_tf("oxford_segmentation.keras")

test_image <- val_paths$input[309] %>%
  tf_read_image_and_resize("jpeg", channels = 3L)

predicted_mask_probs <-
  model(test_image[tf$newaxis, , , ])

predicted_mask <-
  tf$argmax(predicted_mask_probs, axis = -1L)

predicted_target <- predicted_mask + 1

par(mfrow = c(1, 2))
display_image_tensor(test_image)
display_target_tensor(predicted_target)
```

tf$newaxis adds a batch dimension, because our model expects batches of images. model() returns a Tensor with shape=(1, 200, 200, 3), dtype=float32.

tf$argmax() is similar to which.max() in R. A key difference is that tf$argmax() returns 0-based values. The base R equivalent of tf$argmax(x, axis = -1L) is apply(x, c(1, 2, 3), which.max) - 1L.

predicted_mask is a Tensor with shape=(1, 200, 200), dtype=int64.

Figure 9.6 A test image and its predicted segmentation mask

There are a couple of small artifacts in our predicted mask. Nevertheless, our model appears to work nicely.

By this point, throughout chapter 8 and the beginning of chapter 9, you've learned the basics of how to perform image classification and image segmentation: you can already accomplish a lot with what you know. However, the convnets that experienced engineers develop to solve real-world problems aren't quite as simple as those we've been using in our demonstrations so far. You're still lacking the essential mental models and thought processes that enable experts to make quick and accurate decisions about how to put together state-of-the-art models. To bridge that gap, you need to learn about *architecture patterns*. Let's dive in.

9.3   *Modern convnet architecture patterns*

A model's "architecture" is the sum of the choices that went into creating it: which layers to use, how to configure them, and in what arrangement to connect them. These choices define the *hypothesis space* of your model: the space of possible functions that gradient descent can search over, parameterized by the model's weights. Like feature engineering, a good hypothesis space encodes *prior knowledge* that you have about the problem at hand and its solution. For instance, using convolution layers means that you know in advance that the relevant patterns present in your input images are translation invariant. To effectively learn from data, you need to make assumptions about what you're looking for.

Model architecture is often the difference between success and failure. If you make inappropriate architecture choices, your model may be stuck with suboptimal metrics, and no amount of training data will save it. Inversely, a good model architecture will accelerate learning and will enable your model to make efficient use of the training data available, reducing the need for large datasets. A good model architecture is one that *reduces the size of the search space* or otherwise *makes it easier to converge to a good point of the search space.* Just like feature engineering and data curation, model architecture is all about *making the problem simpler* for gradient descent to solve. And remember that gradient descent is a pretty stupid search process, so it needs all the help it can get.

Model architecture is more an art than a science. Experienced machine learning engineers are able to intuitively cobble together high-performing models on their first try, while beginners often struggle to create a model that trains at all. The keyword here is *intuitively*: no one can give you a clear explanation of what works and what doesn't. Experts rely on pattern-matching, an ability that they acquire through extensive practical experience. You'll develop your own intuition throughout this book. However, it's not *all* about intuition, either—there isn't much in the way of actual science, but as in any engineering discipline, there are best practices.

In the following sections, we'll review a few essential convnet architecture best practices: in particular, *residual connections*, *batch normalization*, and *separable convolutions.* Once you master how to use them, you will be able to build highly effective image models. We will apply them to our cat vs. dog classification problem.

Let's start from the bird's-eye view: the modularity-hierarchy-reuse (MHR) formula for system architecture.

9.3.1   *Modularity, hierarchy, and reuse*

If you want to make a complex system simpler, you can apply a universal recipe: just structure your amorphous soup of complexity into *modules*, organize the modules into a *hierarchy*, and start *reusing* the same modules in multiple places as appropriate ("reuse" is another word for *abstraction* in this context). That's the MHR formula (modularity-hierarchy-reuse), and it underlies system architecture across pretty much every domain where the term "architecture" is used. It's at the heart of the organization of any system of meaningful complexity, whether it's a cathedral, your own body, the US Navy, or the Keras codebase (see figure 9.7).

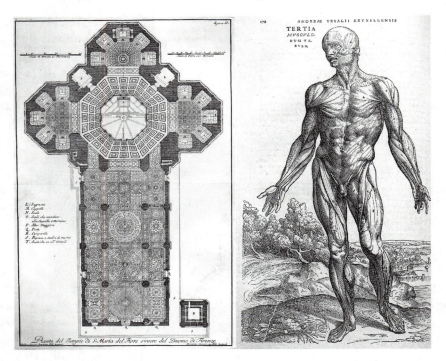

Figure 9.7 Complex systems follow a hierarchical structure and are organized into distinct modules, which are reused multiple times (such as your four limbs, which are all variants of the same blueprint, or your 20 "fingers").

If you're a software engineer, you're already keenly familiar with these principles: an effective codebase is one that is modular and hierarchical and where you don't reimplement the same thing twice, but instead rely on reusable classes and functions. If you factor your code by following these principles, you could say you're doing "software architecture."

Deep learning itself is simply the application of this recipe to continuous optimization via gradient descent: you take a classic optimization technique (gradient descent over a continuous function space), and you structure the search space into modules (layers), organized into a deep hierarchy (often just a stack, the simplest kind of hierarchy), where you reuse whatever you can (e.g., convolutions are all about reusing the same information in different spatial locations).

Likewise, deep learning model architecture is primarily about making clever use of modularity, hierarchy, and reuse. You'll notice that all popular convnet architectures are not only structured into layers, they're structured into repeated groups of layers (called "blocks" or "modules"). For instance, the popular VGG16 architecture we used in the previous chapter is structured into repeated "conv, conv, max pooling" blocks (see figure 9.8).

Further, most convnets often feature pyramid-like structures (*feature hierarchies*). Recall, for example, the progression in the number of convolution filters we used in the first convnet we built in the previous chapter: 32, 64, 128. The number of filters grows with layer depth, whereas the size of the feature maps shrinks accordingly. You'll notice the same pattern in the blocks of the VGG16 model (see figure 9.8).

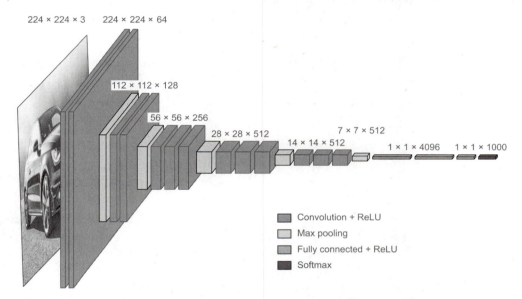

Figure 9.8   The VGG16 architecture: Note the repeated layer blocks and the pyramid-like structure of the feature maps.

Deeper hierarchies are intrinsically good because they encourage feature reuse and, therefore, abstraction. In general, a deep stack of narrow layers performs better than a shallow stack of large layers. However, there's a limit to how deep you can stack layers, due to the problem of *vanishing gradients*. This leads us to our first essential model architecture pattern: residual connections.

On the importance of ablation studies in deep learning research

Deep learning architectures are often more *evolved* than designed—they were developed by repeatedly trying things and selecting what seemed to work. Much like in biological systems, if you take any complicated experimental deep learning setup, chances are you can remove a few modules (or replace some trained features with random ones) with no loss of performance.

(continued)

This is made worse by the incentives that deep learning researchers face: by making a system more complex than necessary, they can make it appear more interesting or more novel and thus increase their chances of getting a paper through the peer-review process. If you read lots of deep learning papers, you will notice that they're often optimized for peer review in both style and content in ways that actively hurt clarity of explanation and reliability of results. For instance, mathematics in deep learning papers is rarely used for clearly formalizing concepts or deriving non-obvious results—rather, it gets leveraged as a *signal of seriousness*, like an expensive suit on a salesman.

The goal of research shouldn't be merely to publish but to generate reliable knowledge. Crucially, understanding *causality* in your system is the most straightforward way to generate reliable knowledge. And there's a very low-effort way to look into causality: *ablation studies*. Ablation studies consist of systematically trying to remove parts of a system—making it simpler—to identify where its performance actually comes from. If you find that X + Y + Z gives you good results, also try X, Y, Z, X + Y, X + Z, and Y + Z, and see what happens.

If you become a deep learning researcher, cut through the noise in the research process: do ablation studies for your models. Always ask, "Could there be a simpler explanation? Is this added complexity really necessary? Why?"

9.3.2 *Residual connections*

You probably know about the game of Telephone, also called Chinese Whispers in the UK and *téléphone arabe* in France, where an initial message is whispered in the ear of a player, who then whispers it in the ear of the next player, and so on. The final message ends up bearing little resemblance to its original version. It's a fun metaphor for the cumulative errors that occur in sequential transmission over a noisy channel.

As it happens, backpropagation in a sequential deep learning model is pretty similar to the game of Telephone. You've got a chain of functions, like this one:

```
y = f4(f3(f2(f1(x))))
```

The name of the game is to adjust the parameters of each function in the chain based on the error recorded on the output of f4 (the loss of the model). To adjust f1, you'll need to percolate error information through f2, f3, and f4. However, each successive function in the chain introduces some amount of noise. If your function chain is too deep, this noise starts overwhelming gradient information, and backpropagation stops working. Your model won't train at all. This is the *vanishing gradients* problem.

The fix is simple: just force each function in the chain to be nondestructive—to retain a noiseless version of the information contained in the previous input. The easiest way to implement this is to use a *residual connection*.

It's dead easy: just add the input of a layer or block of layers back to its output (see figure 9.9). The residual connection acts as an *information shortcut* around destructive or noisy blocks (such as blocks that contain `relu` activations or dropout layers), enabling error gradient information from early layers to propagate noiselessly through a deep network. This technique was introduced in 2015 with the ResNet family of models (developed by He et al. at Microsoft).[1]

In practice, you'd implement a residual connection as follows.

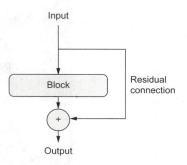

Figure 9.9 A residual connection around a processing block

Listing 9.1 A residual connection in pseudocode

```
x <- ...          ◁─── Some input tensor
residual <- x
x <- block(x)              ◁───
x <- layer_add(c(x, residual))    ◁───
```

Save a pointer to the original input. This is called the residual.

This computation block can potentially be destructive or noisy, and that's fine.

Add the original input to the layer's output: the final output will thus always preserve full information about the original input.

Note that adding the input back to the output of a block implies that the output should have the same shape as the input. However, this is not the case if your block includes convolutional layers with an increased number of filters or a max-pooling layer. In such cases, use a 1 × 1 `layer_conv_2d()` with no activation to linearly project the residual to the desired output shape (see listing 9.2). You'd typically use `padding = "same"` in the convolution layers in your target block so as to avoid spatial downsampling due to padding, and you'd use strides in the residual projection to match any downsampling caused by a max pooling layer (see listing 9.3).

Listing 9.2 Residual block where the number of filters changes

This is the layer around which we create a residual connection: it increases the number of output filers from 32 to 64. Note that we use padding = "same" to avoid downsampling due to padding.

Set aside the residual.

```
inputs <- layer_input(shape = c(32, 32, 3))
x <- inputs %>% layer_conv_2d(32, 3, activation = "relu")
residual <- x
x <- x %>% layer_conv_2d(64, 3, activation = "relu", padding = "same")   ◁───
residual <- residual %>% layer_conv_2d(64, 1)      ◁───
x <- layer_add(c(x, residual))
```

Now the block output and the residual have the same shape and can be added.

The residual had only 32 filters, so we use a 1 × 1 layer_conv_2d to project it to the correct shape.

---

[1] Kaiming He et al., "Deep Residual Learning for Image Recognition," Conference on Computer Vision and Pattern Recognition (2015), https://arxiv.org/abs/1512.03385.

Listing 9.3   Case where the target block includes a max-pooling layer

This is the block of two layers around which we create a residual connection: it includes a 2 × 2 max pooling layer. Note that we use padding = "same" in both the convolution layer and the max-pooling layer to avoid downsampling due to padding.

Set aside the residual.

```
inputs <- layer_input(shape = c(32, 32, 3))
x <- inputs %>% layer_conv_2d(32, 3, activation = "relu")
residual <- x
x <- x %>%
   layer_ccnv_2d(64, 3, activation = "relu", padding = "same") %>%
   layer_max_pooling_2d(2, padding = "same")
residual <- residual %>%
   layer_conv_2d(64, 1, strides = 2)
x <- layer_add(list(x, residual))
```

We use strides = 2 in the residual projection to match the downsampling created by the max-pooling layer.

Now the block output and the residual have the same shape and can be added.

To make these ideas more concrete, here's an example of a simple convnet structured into a series of blocks, each made of two convolution layers and one optional max-pooling layer, with a residual connection around each block:

```
inputs <- layer_input(shape = c(32, 32, 3))
x <- layer_rescaling(inputs, scale = 1/255)

residual_block <- function(x, filters,
                           pooling = FALSE) {
  residual <- x
  x <- x %>%
    layer_conv_2d(filters, 3, activation = "relu", padding = "same") %>%
    layer_conv_2d(filters, 3, activation = "relu", padding = "same")

  if (pooling) {
    x <- x %>% layer_max_pooling_2d(pool_size = 2, padding = "same")
    residual <- residual %>% layer_conv_2d(filters, 1, strides = 2)
  } else if (filters != dim(residual)[4]) {
    residual <- residual %>% layer_conv_2d(filters, 1)
  }

  layer_add(list(x, residual))
}

outputs <- x %>%
  residual_block(filters = 32, pooling = TRUE) %>%
  residual_block(filters = 64, pooling = TRUE) %>%
  residual_block(filters = 128, pooling = FALSE) %>%
  layer_global_average_pooling_2d() %>%
  layer_dense(units = 1, activation = "sigmoid")

model <- keras_model(inputs = inputs, outputs = outputs)
```

Utility function to apply a convolutional block with a residual connection, with an option to add max pooling

If we use max pooling, we add a strided convolution to project the residual to the expected shape.

If we don't use max pooling, we project the residual only if the number of channels has changed.

Second block; note the increasing filter count in each block.

First block

The last block doesn't need a max-pooling layer, because we will apply global average pooling right after it.

This is the model summary we get:

```
model
```

```
Model: "model_1"
```

Layer (type)	Output Shape	Param #	Connected to
input_2 (InputLayer)	[(None, 32, 32, 3)]	0	[]
rescaling_1 (Rescaling)	(None, 32, 32, 3)	0	['input_2[0][0]']
conv2d_8 (Conv2D)	(None, 32, 32, 32)	896	['rescaling_1[0][0]']
conv2d_7 (Conv2D)	(None, 32, 32, 32)	9248	['conv2d_8[0][0]']
max_pooling2d (MaxPooling2D)	(None, 16, 16, 32)	0	['conv2d_7[0][0]']
conv2d_9 (Conv2D)	(None, 16, 16, 32)	128	['rescaling_1[0][0]']
add (Add)	(None, 16, 16, 32)	0	['max_pooling2d[0][0]', 'conv2d_9[0][0]']
conv2d_11 (Conv2D)	(None, 16, 16, 64)	18496	['add[0][0]']
conv2d_10 (Conv2D)	(None, 16, 16, 64)	36928	['conv2d_11[0][0]']
max_pooling2d_1 (MaxPooling2D)	(None, 8, 8, 64)	0	['conv2d_10[0][0]']
conv2d_12 (Conv2D)	(None, 8, 8, 64)	2112	['add[0][0]']
add_1 (Add)	(None, 8, 8, 64)	0	['max_pooling2d_1[0][0]', 'conv2d_12[0][0]']
conv2d_14 (Conv2D)	(None, 8, 8, 128)	73856	['add_1[0][0]']
conv2d_13 (Conv2D)	(None, 8, 8, 128)	147584	['conv2d_14[0][0]']
conv2d_15 (Conv2D)	(None, 8, 8, 128)	8320	['add_1[0][0]']
add_2 (Add)	(None, 8, 8, 128)	0	['conv2d_13[0][0]', 'conv2d_15[0][0]']
global_average_pooling2d (GlobalAveragePooling2D)	(None, 128)	0	['add_2[0][0]']
dense (Dense)	(None, 1)	129	['global_average_pooling2d[0][0]']

```
Total params: 297,697
Trainable params: 297,697
Non-trainable params: 0
```

With residual connections, you can build networks of arbitrary depth, without having to worry about vanishing gradients.

Now let's move on to the next essential convnet architecture pattern: *batch normalization*.

9.3.3   *Batch normalization*

Normalization is a broad category of methods that seek to make different samples seen by a machine learning model more similar to each other, which helps the model learn and generalize well to new data. The most common form of data normalization is one you've already seen several times in this book: centering the data on zero by subtracting the mean from the data and giving the data a unit standard deviation by dividing the data by its standard deviation. In effect, this makes the assumption that the data follows a normal (or Gaussian) distribution and makes sure this distribution is centered and scaled to unit variance:

```
normalize_data <- apply(data, <axis>, function(x) (x - mean(x)) / sd(x))
```

Previous examples in this book normalized data before feeding it into models. But data normalization may be of interest after every transformation operated by the network: even if the data entering a `Dense` or `Conv2D` network has a 0 mean and unit variance, there's no reason to expect a priori that this will be the case for the data coming out. Could normalizing intermediate activations help?

Batch normalization does just that. It's a type of layer (`layer_batch_normalization()` in Keras) introduced in 2015 by Ioffe and Szegedy[2]; it can adaptively normalize data even as the mean and variance change over time during training. During training, it uses the mean and variance of the current batch of data to normalize samples, and during inference (when a big enough batch of representative data may not be available), it uses an exponential moving average of the batchwise mean and variance of the data seen during training.

Although the original paper stated that batch normalization operates by "reducing internal covariate shift," no one really knows for sure why batch normalization helps. Various hypotheses exist, but no certitudes. You'll find that this is true of many things in deep learning—it is not an exact science but a set of ever-changing, empirically derived engineering best practices, woven together by unreliable narratives. You will sometimes feel like the book you have in hand tells you *how* to do something but doesn't quite satisfactorily say *why* it works: that's because we know the how but we don't know the why. Whenever a reliable explanation is available, I make sure to mention it. Batch normalization isn't one of those cases.

In practice, the main effect of batch normalization appears to be that it helps with gradient propagation—much like residual connections—and thus allows for deeper networks. Some very deep networks can be trained only if they include multiple `BatchNormalization` layers. For instance, batch normalization is used liberally in many of the advanced convnet architectures that come packaged with Keras, such as ResNet50, EfficientNet, and Xception.

`layer_batch_normalization()` can be used after any layer—`layer_dense()`, `layer_conv_2d()`, and so on:

```
x <- ...                    For example, a layer_input(),
                            keras_model_sequential(), or    Because the output of
x <- x %>%                  output from another layer       the layer_conv_2d() is
  layer_conv_2d(32, 3, use_bias = FALSE) %>%                normalized, the layer doesn't
  layer_batch_normalization()                               need its own bias vector.
```

---

[2] Sergey Ioffe and Christian Szegedy, "Batch Normalization: Accelerating Deep Network Training by Reducing Internal Covariate Shift," *Proceedings of the 32nd International Conference on Machine Learning* (2015), https://arxiv.org/abs/1502.03167.

Both `layer_dense()` and `layer_conv_2d()` involve a *bias vector*, a learned variable whose purpose is to make the layer *affine* rather than purely linear. For instance, `layer_conv_2d()` returns, schematically, `y = conv(x, kernel) + bias`, and `layer_dense()` returns `y = dot(x, kernel) + bias`. Because the normalization step will take care of centering the layer's output on zero, the bias vector is no longer needed when using `layer_batch_normalization()`, and the layer can be created without it via the option `use_bias = FALSE`. This makes the layer slightly leaner.

Importantly, I would generally recommend placing the previous layer's activation *after* the batch normalization layer (although this is still a subject of debate). So instead of doing what is shown in listing 9.4, you would do what's shown in listing 9.5.

Listing 9.4 How not to use batch normalization

```
x %>%
  layer_conv_2d(32, 3, activation = "relu") %>%
  layer_batch_normalization()
```

Listing 9.5 How to use batch normalization: The activation comes last

```
x %>%
  layer_conv_2d(32, 3, use_bias = FALSE) %>%    <——— Note the lack of activation here.
  layer_batch_normalization() %>%
  layer_activation("relu")          <——  We place the activation after
                                          layer_batch_normalization().
```

The intuitive reason for this approach is that batch normalization will center your inputs on zero, whereas your `relu` activation uses zero as a pivot for keeping or dropping activated channels: doing normalization before the activation maximizes the utilization of the `relu`. That said, this ordering best practice is not exactly critical, so if you do convolution, then activation, and then batch normalization, your model will still train, and you won't necessarily see worse results.

On batch normalization and fine-tuning

Batch normalization has many quirks. One of the main ones relates to fine-tuning: when fine-tuning a model that includes `BatchNormalization` layers, I recommend leaving these layers frozen (call `freeze_weights()` to set their `trainable` attribute to `FALSE`). Otherwise, they will keep updating their internal mean and variance, which can interfere with the very small updates applied to the surrounding `Conv2D` layers:

```
batch_norm_layer_s3_classname <- class(layer_batch_normalization())[1]
batch_norm_layer_s3_classname
```

```
[1] "keras.layers.normalization.batch_normalization.BatchNormalization"
```

```
is_batch_norm_layer <- function(x)
  inherits(x, batch_norm_layer_s3_classname)

model <- application_efficientnet_b0()
for(layer in model$layers)
  if(is_batch_norm_layer(layer))
    layer$trainable <- FALSE          <——
```

Example of how to set trainable <- FALSE to freeze only BatchNormalization layers. Note: you can also call freeze_weights(model, which = is_batch_norm_layer) to achieve the same outcome.

Now let's take a look at the last architecture pattern in our series: depthwise separable convolutions.

9.3.4   *Depthwise separable convolutions*

What if I told you that there's a layer you can use as a drop-in replacement for `layer_conv_2d()` that will make your model smaller (fewer trainable weight parameters) and leaner (fewer floating-point operations) and cause it to perform a few percentage points better on its task? That is precisely what the *depthwise separable convolution* layer does (`layer_separable_conv_2d()` in Keras). This layer performs a spatial convolution on each channel of its input, independently, before mixing output channels via a pointwise convolution (a 1 × 1 convolution), as shown in figure 9.10.

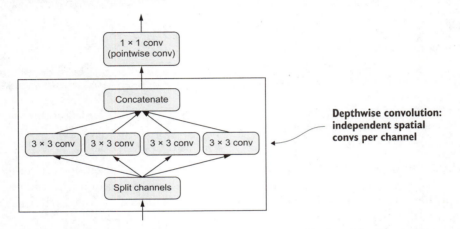

Figure 9.10   Depthwise separable convolution: A depthwise convolution followed by a pointwise convolution

This is equivalent to separating the learning of spatial features and the learning of channel-wise features. In much the same way that convolution relies on the assumption that the patterns in images are not tied to specific locations, depthwise separable convolution relies on the assumption that *spatial locations* in intermediate activations are *highly correlated*, but *different channels* are *highly independent* . Because this assumption is generally true for the image representations learned by deep neural networks, it serves as a useful prior that helps the model make more efficient use of its training data. A model with stronger priors about the structure of the information it will have to process is a better model—as long as the priors are accurate.

Depthwise separable convolution requires significantly fewer parameters and involves fewer computations compared to regular convolution, while having comparable representational power. It results in smaller models that converge faster and are less prone to overfitting. These advantages become especially important when you're training small models from scratch on limited data.

When it comes to larger-scale models, depthwise separable convolutions are the basis of the Xception architecture, a high-performing convnet that comes packaged with Keras. You can read more about the theoretical grounding for depthwise separable convolutions and Xception in the paper "Xception: Deep Learning with Depthwise Separable Convolutions."[3]

The co-evolution of hardware, software, and algorithms

Consider a regular convolution operation with a 3 × 3 window, 64 input channels, and 64 output channels. It uses 3 * 3 * 64 * 64 = 36,864 trainable parameters, and when you apply it to an image, it runs a number of floating-point operations that is proportional to this parameter count. Meanwhile, consider an equivalent depthwise separable convolution: it involves only 3 * 3 * 64 + 64 * 64 = 4,672 trainable parameters and proportionally fewer floating-point operations. This efficiency improvement only increases as the number of filters or the size of the convolution windows gets larger.

As a result, you would expect depthwise separable convolutions to be dramatically faster, right? Hold on. This would be true if you were writing simple CUDA or C implementations of these algorithms—in fact, you do see a meaningful speedup when running on CPU, where the underlying implementation is parallelized C. But in practice, you're probably using a GPU, and what you're executing on it is far from a "simple" CUDA implementation: it's a *cuDNN kernel*, a piece of code that has been extraordinarily optimized, down to each machine instruction. It certainly makes sense to spend a lot of effort optimizing this code, since cuDNN convolutions on NVIDIA hardware are responsible for many exaFLOPS of computation every day. But a side effect of this extreme micro-optimization is that alternative approaches have little chance to compete on performance—even approaches that have significant intrinsic advantages, like depthwise separable convolutions.

Despite repeated requests to NVIDIA, depthwise separable convolutions have not benefited from nearly the same level of software and hardware optimization as regular convolutions, and as a result they remain only about as fast as regular convolutions, even though they're using quadratically fewer parameters and floating-point operations. Note, though, that using depthwise separable convolutions remains a good idea even if it does not result in a speedup: their lower parameter count means that you are less at risk of overfitting, and their assumption that channels should be uncorrelated leads to faster model convergence and more robust representations.

What is a slight inconvenience in this case can become an impassable wall in other situations: because the entire hardware and software ecosystem of deep learning has been micro-optimized for a very specific set of algorithms (in particular, convnets trained via backpropagation), there's an extremely high cost to steering away from the beaten path.

---

[3] François Chollet, "Xception: Deep Learning with Depthwise Separable Convolutions," Conference on Computer Vision and Pattern Recognition (2017), https://arxiv.org/abs/1610.02357.

(continued)

If you were to experiment with alternative algorithms, such as gradient-free optimization or spiking neural networks, the first few parallel C++ or CUDA implementations you'd come up with would be orders of magnitude slower than a good old convnet, no matter how clever and efficient your ideas were. Convincing other researchers to adopt your method would be a tough sell, even if it were just plain better.

You could say that modern deep learning is the product of a co-evolution process between hardware, software, and algorithms: the availability of NVIDIA GPUs and CUDA led to the early success of backpropagation-trained convnets, which led NVIDIA to optimize its hardware and software for these algorithms, which in turn led to consolidation of the research community behind these methods. At this point, figuring out a different path would require a multiyear re-engineering of the entire ecosystem.

9.3.5 *Putting it together: A mini Xception-like model*

As a reminder, here are the convnet architecture principles you've learned so far:

- Your model should be organized into repeated *blocks* of layers, usually made of multiple convolution layers and a max-pooling layer.
- The number of filters in your layers should increase as the size of the spatial feature maps decreases.
- Deep and narrow is better than broad and shallow.
- Introducing residual connections around blocks of layers helps you train deeper networks.
- It can be beneficial to introduce batch normalization layers after your convolution layers.
- It can be beneficial to replace `layer_conv_2d()` with `layer_separable_conv_2d()`, which are more parameter efficient.

Let's bring these ideas together into a single model. Its architecture will resemble a smaller version of Xception, and we'll apply it to the dogs vs. cats task from the previous chapter. For data loading and model training, we'll simply reuse the setup we used in section 8.2.5, but we'll replace the model definition with the following convnet:

```
data_augmentation <- keras_model_sequential() %>%        We use the same
  layer_random_flip("horizontal") %>%                    data augmentation
  layer_random_rotation(0.1) %>%                          configuration as before.
  layer_random_zoom(0.2)

inputs <- layer_input(shape = c(180, 180, 3))            Don't forget input rescaling!

x <- inputs %>%
  data_augmentation() %>%
  layer_rescaling(scale = 1 / 255)

x <- x %>%
  layer_conv_2d(32, 5, use_bias = FALSE)
```

Don't forget input rescaling!

Note that the assumption that underlies separable convolution, "feature channels are largely independent," does not hold for RGB images! Red, green, and blue color channels are actually highly correlated in natural images. As such, the first layer in our model is a regular `layer_conv_2d()` layer. We'll start using `layer_separable_conv_2d()` afterward.

```
for (size in c(32, 64, 128, 256, 512)) {
  residual <- x

  x <- x %>%
    layer_batch_normalization() %>%
    layer_activation("relu") %>%

    layer_separable_conv_2d(size, 3, padding = "same", use_bias = FALSE) %>%
    layer_batch_normalization() %>%
    layer_activation("relu") %>%

    layer_separable_conv_2d(size, 3, padding = "same", use_bias = FALSE) %>%
    layer_max_pooling_2d(pool_size = 3, strides = 2, padding = "same")

  residual <- residual %>%
    layer_conv_2d(size, 1, strides = 2, padding = "same", use_bias = FALSE)

  x <- layer_add(list(x, residual))
}

outputs <- x %>%
  layer_global_average_pooling_2d() %>%
  layer_dropout(0.5) %>%
  layer_dense(1, activation = "sigmoid")

model <- keras_model(inputs, outputs)

train_dataset <- image_dataset_from_directory(
  "cats_vs_dogs_small/train",
  image_size = c(180, 180),
  batch_size = 32
)

validation_dataset <- image_dataset_from_directory(
  "cats_vs_dogs_small/validation",
  image_size = c(180, 180),
  batch_size = 32
)

model %>%
  compile(
    loss = "binary_crossentropy",
    optimizer = "rmsprop",
    metrics = "accuracy"
  )

history <- model %>%
  fit(
    train_dataset,
    epochs = 100,
    validation_data = validation_dataset)
```

> **We apply a series of convolutional blocks with increasing feature depth. Each block consists of two batch-normalized depthwise separable convolution layers and a max-pooling layer, with a residual connection around the entire block.**

> **In the original model, we used a layer_flatten() before the layer_dense(). Here, we go with a layer_global_average_pooling_2d().**

> **Like in the original model, we add a dropout layer for regularization.**

This convnet has a total parameter count of 721,857, slightly lower than the 991,041 parameters of the original model we defined in chapter 8 (Listing 8.7), but still in the same ballpark. Figure 9.11 shows its training and validation curves.

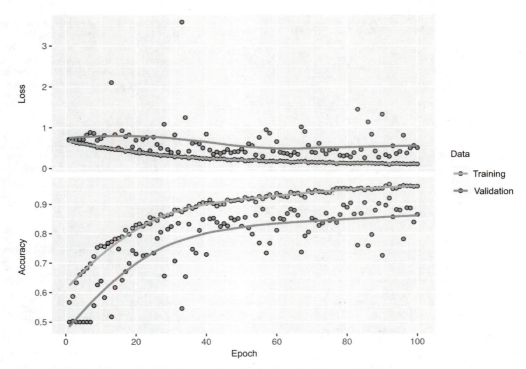

Figure 9.11   Training and validation metrics with an Xception-like architecture

You'll find that our new model achieves a test accuracy of 90.8%, compared to 81.4% for the naive model in the previous chapter. As you can see, following architecture best practices does have an immediate, sizable impact on model performance!

At this point, if you want to further improve performance, you should start systematically tuning the hyperparameters of your architecture—a topic we'll cover in detail in chapter 13. We haven't gone through this step here, so the configuration of the preceding model is purely based on the best practices we discussed, plus, when it comes to gauging model size, a small amount of intuition.

Note that these architecture best practices are relevant to computer vision in general, not just image classification. For example, Xception is used as the standard convolutional base in DeepLabV3, a popular state-of-the-art image segmentation solution.[4]

This concludes our introduction to essential convnet architecture best practices. With these principles in hand, you'll be able to develop higher-performing models across a wide range of computer vision tasks. You're now well on your way to becoming a proficient computer vision practitioner. To further deepen your expertise, there's one last important topic we need to cover: interpreting how a model arrives at its predictions.

---

[4] Liang-Chieh Chen et al., "Encoder-Decoder with Atrous Separable Convolution for Semantic Image Segmentation," ECCV (2018), https://arxiv.org/abs/1802.02611.

9.4   *Interpreting what convnets learn*

A fundamental problem when building a computer vision application is that of *interpretability*: *why* did your classifier think a particular image contained a fridge, when all you can see is a truck? This is especially relevant to use cases where deep learning is used to complement human expertise, such as in medical imaging use cases. We will end this chapter by getting you familiar with a range of different techniques for visualizing what convnets learn and understanding the decisions they make.

It's often said that deep learning models are "black boxes": they learn representations that are difficult to extract and present in a human-readable form. Although this is partially true for certain types of deep learning models, it's definitely not true for convnets. The representations learned by convnets are highly amenable to visualization, in large part because they're *representations of visual concepts*. Since 2013, a wide array of techniques has been developed for visualizing and interpreting these representations. We won't survey all of them, but we'll cover three of the most accessible and useful ones:

- *Visualizing intermediate convnet outputs (intermediate activations)*—Useful for understanding how successive convnet layers transform their input, and for getting a first idea of the meaning of individual convnet filters
- *Visualizing convnet filters*—Useful for understanding precisely what visual pattern or concept each filter in a convnet is receptive to
- *Visualizing heatmaps of class activation in an image*—Useful for understanding which parts of an image were identified as belonging to a given class, thus allowing you to localize objects in images

For the first method—activation visualization—we'll use the small convnet that we trained from scratch on the dogs-versus-cats classification problem in section 8.2. For the next two methods, we'll use a pretrained Xception model.

9.4.1   *Visualizing intermediate activations*

Visualizing intermediate activations consists of displaying the values returned by various convolution and pooling layers in a model, given a certain input (the output of a layer is often called its *activation*, the output of the activation function). This gives a view into how an input is decomposed into the different filters learned by the network. We want to visualize feature maps with three dimensions: width, height, and depth (channels). Each channel encodes relatively independent features, so the proper way to visualize these feature maps is by independently plotting the contents of every channel as a 2D image. Let's start by loading the model that you saved in section 8.2:

```
model <- load_model_tf("convnet_from_scratch_with_augmentation.keras")
model
```

```
Model: "model_3"
```

Layer (type)	Output Shape	Param #
input_4 (InputLayer)	[(None, 180, 180, 3)]	0
sequential (Sequential)	(None, 180, 180, 3)	0
rescaling_1 (Rescaling)	(None, 180, 180, 3)	0
conv2d_15 (Conv2D)	(None, 178, 178, 32)	896
max_pooling2d_9 (MaxPooling2D)	(None, 89, 89, 32)	0
conv2d_14 (Conv2D)	(None, 87, 87, 64)	18496
max_pooling2d_8 (MaxPooling2D)	(None, 43, 43, 64)	0
conv2d_13 (Conv2D)	(None, 41, 41, 128)	73856
max_pooling2d_7 (MaxPooling2D)	(None, 20, 20, 128)	0
conv2d_12 (Conv2D)	(None, 18, 18, 256)	295168
max_pooling2d_6 (MaxPooling2D)	(None, 9, 9, 256)	0
conv2d_11 (Conv2D)	(None, 7, 7, 256)	590080
flatten_3 (Flatten)	(None, 12544)	0
dropout (Dropout)	(None, 12544)	0
dense_3 (Dense)	(None, 1)	12545

```
Total params: 991,041
Trainable params: 991,041
Non-trainable params: 0
```

Next, we'll get an input image—a picture of a cat, not part of the images the network was trained on.

Listing 9.6   Preprocessing a single image

```
img_path <- get_file(        <——— Download a test image.
  fname = "cat.jpg",
  origin = "https://img-datasets.s3.amazonaws.com/cat.jpg")

img_tensor <- img_path %>%           <——| Read and resize the image to a float32
  tf_read_image(resize = c(180, 180))     Tensor of shape (180, 180, 3).
```

Let's display the picture (see figure 9.12).

Listing 9.7   Displaying the test picture

```
display_image_tensor(img_tensor)
```

Figure 9.12 The test cat picture

To extract the feature maps we want to look at, we'll create a Keras model that takes batches of images as input and that outputs the activations of all convolution and pooling layers.

Listing 9.8 Instantiating a model that returns layer activations

```
conv_layer_s3_classname <-
  class(layer_conv_2d(NULL, 1, 1))[1]
pooling_layer_s3_classname <-
  class(layer_max_pooling_2d(NULL))[1]

is_conv_layer <- function(x) inherits(x, conv_layer_s3_classname)
is_pooling_layer <- function(x) inherits(x, pooling_layer_s3_classname)

layer_outputs <- list()
for (layer in model$layers)
  if (is_conv_layer(layer) || is_pooling_layer(layer))
    layer_outputs[[layer$name]] <- layer$output

activation_model <- keras_model(inputs = model$input,
                                outputs = layer_outputs)
```

> Make dummy conv and pooling layers to determine what the S3 classname is. This is generally a long string like "keras.layers.convolutional.Conv2D", but because it can change between Tensorflow versions, it's better to not hardcode it.

> Extract the outputs of all Conv2D and MaxPooling2D layers and put them in a named list.

> Create a model that will return these outputs, given the model input.

When fed an image input, this model returns the values of the layer activations in the original model, as a list. This is the first time you've encountered a multi-output model in this book in practice since you learned about them in chapter 7; until now, the models you've seen have had exactly one input and one output. This one has one input and nine outputs: one output per layer activation.

Listing 9.9   Using the model to compute layer activations

predict() returns a list of nine R arrays: one array per layer activation.

Call [tf$newaxis, , ,] to change img_tensor shape from (180, 180, 3) to (1, 180, 180, 3). In other words, adds a batch dimension, because the model expects input to be a batch of images, not a single image.

```
activations <- activation_model %>%
  predict(img_tensor[tf$newaxis, , , ])
```

Because we passed a named list for outputs when we built the model, we get back a named list of R arrays when we call predict() on the model:

```
str(activations)
```

```
List of 9
 $ conv2d_15     : num [1, 1:178, 1:178, 1:32] 0.00418 0.0016 0.00453 0 ...
 $ max_pooling2d_9: num [1, 1:89, 1:89, 1:32] 0.01217 0.00453 0.00742 0.00514
 $ conv2d_14     : num [1, 1:87, 1:87, 1:64] 0 0 0 0 0.00531 ...
 $ max_pooling2d_8: num [1, 1:43, 1:43, 1:64] 0 0 0.00531 0 0 ...
 $ conv2d_13     : num [1, 1:41, 1:41, 1:128] 0 0 0.0288 0 0.0342 ...
 $ max_pooling2d_7: num [1, 1:20, 1:20, 1:128] 0.0313 0.0288 0.0342 0.4004 0.
 $ conv2d_12     : num [1, 1:18, 1:18, 1:256] 0 0 0 0 0 0 0 0 ...
 $ max_pooling2d_6: num [1, 1:9, 1:9, 1:256] 0 0 0 0 0 0 0 0 0 ...
  [list output truncated]
```

Lets take a closer look at the first layer activations:

```
first_layer_activation <- activations[[ names(layer_outputs)[1] ]]
dim(first_layer_activation)
```

```
[1]   1 178 178   32
```

It's a 178 × 178 feature map with 32 channels. Let's try plotting the fifth channel of the activation of the first layer of the original model (see figure 9.13).

Listing 9.10   Visualizing the fifth channel

```
plot_activations <- function(x, ...) {

  x <- as.array(x)          Convert Tensors
                            to arrays.
  if(sum(x) == 0)
    return(plot(as.raster("gray")))

  rotate <- function(x) t(apply(x, 2, rev))
  image(rotate(x), asp = 1, axes = FALSE, useRaster = TRUE,
        col = terrain.colors(256), ...)
}

plot_activations(first_layer_activation[, , , 5])
```

All-zero channels (i.e., no activations) are plotted as a gray rectangle, so they're easy to distinguish.

Rotate the image clockwise for easier viewing.

Figure 9.13   Fifth channel of the activation of the first layer on the test cat picture

This channel appears to encode a diagonal edge detector—but note that your own channels may vary, because the specific filters learned by convolution layers aren't deterministic.

Now let's plot a complete visualization of all the activations in the network (see figure 9.14). We'll extract and plot every channel in each of the layer activations, and we'll stack the results in one big grid, with channels stacked side by side.

Listing 9.11   Visualizing every channel in every intermediate activation

Iterate over the activations (and the names of the corresponding layers).

```
for (layer_name in names(layer_outputs)) {
    layer_output <- activations[[layer_name]]

    n_features <- dim(layer_output) %>% tail(1)
    par(mfrow = n2mfrow(n_features, asp = 1.75),
        mar = rep(.1, 4), oma = c(0, 0, 1.5, 0))
    for (j in 1:n_features)
      plot_activations(layer_output[, , , j])
    title(main = layer_name, outer = TRUE)
}
```

The layer activation has shape (1, height, width, n_features).

Prepare to display all the channels in this activation in one plot.

This is a single channel (or feature).

There are a few things to note here:

- The first layer acts as a collection of various edge detectors. At that stage, the activations retain almost all of the information present in the initial picture.
- As you go deeper, the activations become increasingly abstract and less visually interpretable. They begin to encode higher-level concepts such as "cat ear" and "cat eye." Deeper presentations carry increasingly less information about the visual contents of the image and increasingly more information related to the class of the image.

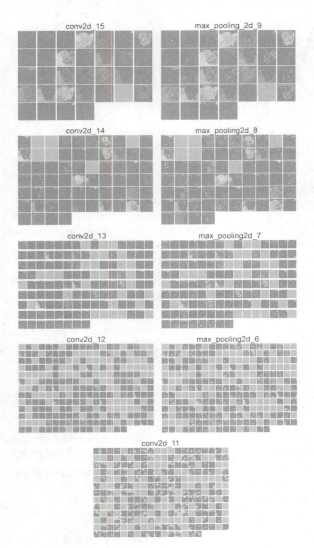

Figure 9.14   Every channel of every layer activation on the test cat picture

- The sparsity of the activations increases with the depth of the layer: in the first layer, almost all filters are activated by the input image, but in the following layers, more and more filters are blank. This means the pattern encoded by the filter isn't found in the input image.

We have just evidenced an important universal characteristic of the representations learned by deep neural networks: the features extracted by a layer become increasingly abstract with the depth of the layer. The activations of higher layers carry less and less information about the specific input being seen and more and more information about the target (in this case, the class of the image: cat or dog). A deep neural network effectively acts as an *information distillation pipeline*, with raw data going in (in this case, RGB pictures) and being repeatedly transformed so that irrelevant information is filtered out (e.g., the specific visual appearance of the image) and useful information is magnified and refined (e.g., the class of the image).

This is analogous to the way humans and animals perceive the world: after observing a scene for a few seconds, a human can remember which abstract objects were present in it (bicycle, tree) but can't remember the specific appearance of these objects. In fact, if you tried to draw a generic bicycle from memory, chances are you couldn't get it even remotely right, even though you've seen thousands of bicycles in your lifetime (see, for example, figure 9.15). Try it right now: this effect is absolutely real. Your brain has learned to completely abstract its visual input—to transform it into high-level visual concepts while filtering out irrelevant visual details—making it tremendously difficult to remember how things around you look.

Figure 9.15 Left: Attempts to draw a bicycle from memory; right: What a schematic bicycle should look like

9.4.2 *Visualizing convnet filters*

Another easy way to inspect the filters learned by convnets is to display the visual pattern that each filter is meant to respond to. This can be done with *gradient ascent in input space*: applying *gradient descent* to the value of the input image of a convnet so as to *maximize* the response of a specific filter, starting from a blank input image. The resulting input image will be one that the chosen filter is maximally responsive to.

Let's try this with the filters of the Xception model, pretrained on ImageNet. The process is simple: we'll build a loss function that maximizes the value of a given filter in a given convolution layer, and then we'll use stochastic gradient descent to adjust the values of the input image so as to maximize this activation value. This will be our second example of a low-level gradient descent loop leveraging the `GradientTape()` object (the first one was in chapter 2). First, let's instantiate the Xception model, loaded with weights pretrained on the ImageNet dataset.

Listing 9.12 **Instantiating the Xception convolutional base**

```
model <- application_xception(
  weights = "imagenet",
  include_top = FALSE
)
```

The classification layers are irrelevant for this use case, so we don't include the top stage of the model.

We're interested in the convolutional layers of the model—the Conv2D and Separa-bleConv2D layers. We'll need to know their names so we can retrieve their outputs. Let's print their names, in order of depth.

Listing 9.13   Printing the names of all convolutional layers in Xception

```
for (layer in model$layers)
  if(any(grepl("Conv2D", class(layer))))
    print(layer$name)

[1] "block1_conv1"
[1] "block1_conv2"
[1] "block2_sepconv1"
[1] "block2_sepconv2"
[1] "conv2d_29"

...

[1] "block14_sepconv1"
[1] "block14_sepconv2"
```

You'll notice that the separable conv 2D layers here are all named something like block6_sepconv1, block7_sepconv2, and so forth. Xception is structured into blocks, each containing several convolutional layers.

Now let's create a second model that returns the output of a specific layer—a *feature extractor* model. Because our model is a Functional API model, it is inspectable: we can query the output of one of its layers and reuse it in a new model. No need to copy the entire Xception code.

Listing 9.14   Creating a feature extractor model

You could replace this with the name of any layer in the Xception convolutional base.

This is the layer object we're interested in.

We use model$input and layer$output to create a model that, given an input image, returns the output of our target layer.

```
layer_name <- "block3_sepconv1"
layer <- model %>% get_layer(name = layer_name)
feature_extractor <- keras_model(inputs = model$input,
                                 outputs = layer$output)
```

To use this model, simply call it on some input data (note that Xception requires inputs to be preprocessed via the xception_preprocess_input() function).

Listing 9.15   Using the feature extractor

```
activation <- img_tensor %>%
  .[tf$newaxis, , , ] %>%
  xception_preprocess_input() %>%
  feature_extractor()
```

Note that this time we're calling the model directly, instead of using predict(), and that activation is a tf.Tensor, not an R array. (More on this soon.)

```
str(activation)

<tf.Tensor: shape=(1, 44, 44, 256), dtype=float32, numpy=…>
```

Let's use our feature extractor model to define a function that returns a scalar value quantifying how much a given input image "activates" a given filter in the layer. This is the "loss function" that we'll maximize during the gradient ascent process:

The loss function takes an image tensor and the index of the filter we are considering (an integer).

We cast filter_index to an tensor integer here to make sure we have consistent behavior when we're running this function eagerly (i.e., not through tf_function()).

```
compute_loss <- function(image, filter_index) {
  activation <- feature_extractor(image)

  filter_index <- as_tensor(filter_index, "int32")
  filter_activation <-
    activation[, , , filter_index, style = "python"]

  mean(filter_activation[, 3:-3, 3:-3])

}
```

Tell [that filter_index is zero-based with style="python".

Note that we avoid border artifacts by only involving nonborder pixels in the loss; we discard the first two pixels along the sides of the activation.

Return the mean of the activation values for the filter.

> **NOTE** We'll be tracing `compute_loss()` with `tf_function()` later, with `filter_index` as a tracing tensors. Python style (0-based) indexing is currently the only supported style when the index is itself a tensor (this may change in the future). We inform [that filter_index is zero-based with `style = "python"`.

The difference between `predict(model, x)` and `model(x)`

In the previous chapter, we used `predict(x)` for feature extraction. Here, we're using `model(x)`. What gives?

Both `y <- predict(model, x)` and `y <- model(x)` (where x is an array of input data) mean "run the model on x and retrieve the output y." Yet they aren't exactly the same thing.

`predict()` loops over the data in batches (in fact, you can specify the batch size via `predict(x, batch_size = 64)`), and it extracts the R array value of the outputs. It's schematically equivalent to this:

```
predict <- function(model, x) {
  y <- list()
  for(x_batch in split_into_batches(x)) {
    y_batch <- as.array(model(x_batch))
    y[[length(y)+1]] <- y_batch
  }
  unsplit_batches(y)
}
```

This means that `predict()` calls can scale to very large arrays. Meanwhile, `model(x)` happens in-memory and doesn't scale. On the other hand, `predict()` is not differentiable: you cannot retrieve its gradient if you call it in a `GradientTape()` scope.

You should use `model(x)` when you need to retrieve the gradients of the model call, and you should use `predict()` if you just need the output value. In other words, always use `predict()` unless you're in the middle of writing a low-level gradient descent loop (as we are now).

Let's set up the gradient ascent step function, using the `GradientTape()`. A nonobvious trick to help the gradient descent process go smoothly is to normalize the gradient tensor by dividing it by its L2 norm (the square root of the average of the square of the values in the tensor). This ensures that the magnitude of the updates done to the input image is always within the same range.

Listing 9.16   Loss maximization via stochastic gradient ascent

```
gradient_ascent_step <-
  function(image, filter_index, learning_rate) {
    with(tf$GradientTape() %as% tape, {
      tape$watch(image)
      loss <- compute_loss(image, filter_index)
    })
    grads <- tape$gradient(loss, image)
    grads <- tf$math$l2_normalize(grads)
    image + (learning_rate * grads)
  }
```

Explicitly watch the image tensor, because it isn't a TensorFlow Variable (only Variables are automatically watched in a gradient tape).

Compute the loss scalar, indicating how much the current image activates the filter.

Compute the gradients of the loss with respect to the image.

Apply the "gradient normalization trick."

Move the image a little bit in a direction that activates our target filter more strongly. Return the updated image so we can run the step function in a loop.

Now we have all the pieces. Let's put them together into an R function that takes as input a layer name and a filter index and returns a tensor representing the pattern that maximizes the activation of the specified filter. Note that we'll use `tf_function()` to speed it up.

Listing 9.17   Function to generate filter visualizations

Initialize an image tensor with random values. (The Xception model expects input values in the [0, I] range, so here we pick a range centered on 0.5.)

```
c(img_width, img_height) %<-% c(200, 200)

generate_filter_pattern <- tf_function(function(filter_index) {
  iterations <- 30
  learning_rate <- 10
  image <- tf$random$uniform(
    minval = 0.4, maxval = 0.6,
    shape = shape(1, img_width, img_height, 3)
  )
  for (i in seq(iterations))
    image <- gradient_ascent_step(image, filter_index, learning_rate)

  image[1, , , ]
})
```

Number of gradient ascent steps to apply

Amplitude of a single step

Repeatedly update the values of the image tensor so as to maximize our loss function.

Drop the batch dim and return the image.

The resulting image tensor is a floating-point array of shape (200, 200, 3), with values that may not be integers within [0, 255]. Hence, we need to postprocess this tensor to turn it into a displayable image. We do so with the following straightforward utility function. We'll do this with tensor operations and wrap in a `tf_function()` to speed it up as well.

Listing 9.18   Utility function to convert a tensor into a valid image

```
deprocess_image <- tf_function(function(image, crop = TRUE) {
  image <- image - mean(image)
  image <- image / tf$math$reduce_std(image)
  image <- (image * 64) + 128
  image <- tf$clip_by_value(image, 0, 255)
  if(crop)
    image <- image[26:-26, 26:-26, ]
  image
})
```

Normalize image values within the [0, 255] range.

mean() invokes tf$math$reduce_mean().

Center-crop to avoid border artifacts.

Let's try it (see figure 9.16):

```
generate_filter_pattern(filter_index = as_tensor(2L)) %>%
  deprocess_image() %>%
  display_image_tensor()
```

Figure 9.16   Pattern that the second channel in layer block3_sepconv1 responds to maximally

Note that we cast `filter_index` with `as_tensor()` here. We do this because a `tf_function()` compiles a separate optimized function for each unique way it's called, and a different constant literal counts as a unique call signature. If we didn't call `as_tensor()` here, then in the coming loop where we plot the first 64 activations, `tf_function()` would trace and compile `generate_filter_pattern()` 64 times! Calling the `tf_function()` decorated function with a tensor, however, even a constant tensor, doesn't count as a unique function signature for `tf_function()`, and `generate_filter_pattern()` is traced only once.

It seems that the third filter in layer `block3_sepconv1` is responsive to a horizontal lines pattern, somewhat water-like or fur-like.

Now the fun part: you can start visualizing every filter in the layer, and even every filter in every layer in the model

Listing 9.19　Generating a grid of all filter response patterns in a layer

```
par(mfrow = c(8, 8))
for (i in seq(0, 63)) {          ⟵——  Generate and plot visualizations
  generate_filter_pattern(filter_index = as_tensor(i)) %>%    for the first 64 filters in the layer.
    deprocess_image() %>%
    display_image_tensor(plot_margins = rep(.1, 4))
}
```

These filter visualizations (see figure 9.17) tell you a lot about how convnet layers see the world: each layer in a convnet learns a collection of filters such that their inputs can

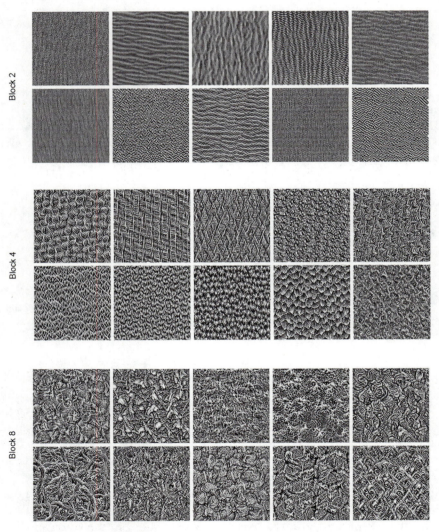

Figure 9.17　Some filter patterns for layers `block2_sepconv1`, `block4_sepconv1`, and `block8_sepconv1`

be expressed as a combination of the filters. This is similar to how the Fourier transform decomposes signals onto a bank of cosine functions. The filters in these convnet filter banks get increasingly complex and refined as you go deeper in the model:

- The filters from the first layers in the model encode simple directional edges and colors (or colored edges, in some cases).
- The filters from layers a bit further up the stack, such as `block4_sepconv1`, encode simple textures made from combinations of edges and colors.
- The filters in higher layers begin to resemble textures found in natural images: feathers, eyes, leaves, and so on.

9.4.3 Visualizing heatmaps of class activation

We'll introduce one last visualization technique—one that is useful for understanding which parts of a given image led a convnet to its final classification decision. This is helpful for "debugging" the decision process of a convnet, particularly in the case of a classification mistake (a problem domain called *model interpretability*). It can also allow you to locate specific objects in an image.

This general category of techniques is called *class activation map* (CAM) visualization, and it consists of producing heatmaps of class activation over input images. A class activation heatmap is a 2D grid of scores associated with a specific output class, computed for every location in any input image, indicating how important each location is with respect to the class under consideration. For instance, given an image fed into a dogs-versus-cats convnet, CAM visualization would allow you to generate a heatmap for the class "cat," indicating how catlike different parts of the image are, and also a heatmap for the class "dog," indicating how doglike parts of the image are.

The specific implementation we'll use is the one described in an article titled, "Grad-CAM: Visual Explanations from Deep Networks via Gradient-based Localization."[5]

Grad-CAM consists of taking the output feature map of a convolution layer, given an input image, and weighing every channel in that feature map by the gradient of the class with respect to the channel. Intuitively, one way to understand this trick is to imagine that you're weighting a spatial map of "how intensely the input image activates different channels" by "how important each channel is with regard to the class," resulting in a spatial map of "how intensely the input image activates the class." Let's demonstrate this technique using the pretrained Xception model.

Listing 9.20 Loading the Xception network with pretrained weights

```
model <- application_xception(weights = "imagenet")
```
Note that we include the densely connected classifier on top; in all previous cases, we discarded it.

Consider the image of two African elephants shown in figure 9.18, possibly a mother and her calf, strolling on the savanna. Let's convert this image into something the Xception

---

[5] Ramprasaath R. Selvaraju et al., arXiv (2017), https://arxiv.org/abs/1610.02391.

Figure 9.18   Test picture of African elephants

model can read: the model was trained on images of size 299 × 299, preprocessed according to a few rules that are packaged in the `xception_preprocess_input()` utility function.

So we need to load the image, resize it to 299 × 299, convert it to a `float32` tensor, and apply these preprocessing rules.

Listing 9.21   Preprocessing an input image for Xception

Download the image and store it
locally under the path img_path.

```
img_path <- get_file(
    fname = "elephant.jpg",
    origin = "https://img-datasets.s3.amazonaws.com/elephant.jpg")
```

```
img_tensor <- tf_read_image(img_path, resize = c(299, 299))
preprocessed_img <- img_tensor[tf$newaxis, , , ] %>%
  xception_preprocess_input()
```

Read the image as a tensor and resize it to 299 × 299. img_tensor is float32 with shape (299, 299, 3).

Add a dimension to transform the array into a batch of size (1, 299, 299, 3).

Preprocess the batch (this does channel-wise color normalization).

You can now run the pretrained network on the image and decode its prediction vector back to a human-readable format:

```
preds <- predict(model, preprocessed_img)
str(preds)
```

```
num [1, 1:1000] 0.00000551 0.00002746 0.00001734 0.00001188 0.00001152 ...
```

```
imagenet_decode_predictions(preds, top=3)[[1]]
```

```
  class_name class_description      score
1  n02504458   African_elephant 0.90519804
2  n01871265             tusker 0.05259838
3  n02504013    Indian_elephant 0.01615972
```

The top three classes predicted for this image are as follows:

- African elephant (with 90% probability)
- Tusker (with 5% probability)
- Indian elephant (with 2% probability)

The network has recognized the image as containing an undetermined quantity of African elephants. The entry in the prediction vector that was maximally activated is the one corresponding to the "African elephant" class, at index 387:

```
which.max(preds[1, ])
```

```
[1] 387
```

To visualize which parts of the image are the most African-elephant-like, let's set up the Grad-CAM process. First, we create a model that maps the input image to the activations of the last convolutional layer.

Listing 9.22   Setting up a model that returns the last convolutional output

```
last_conv_layer_name <- "block14_sepconv2_act"
classifier_layer_names <- c("avg_pool", "predictions")
last_conv_layer <- model %>% get_layer(last_conv_layer_name)
last_conv_layer_model <- keras_model(model$inputs,
                                     last_conv_layer$output)
```

Names of last two layers in the Xception model

Second, we create a model that maps the activations of the last convolutional layer to the final class predictions.

Listing 9.23   Reapplying the classifier on top of the last convolutional output

```
classifier_input <- layer_input(batch_shape = last_conv_layer$output$shape)

x <- classifier_input
for (layer_name in classifier_layer_names)
  x <- get_layer(model, layer_name)(x)

classifier_model <- keras_model(classifier_input, x)
```

Then we compute the gradient of the top predicted class for our input image with respect to the activations of the last convolution layer.

Listing 9.24   Retrieving the gradients of the top predicted class

Compute activations of the last conv layer and make the tape watch it.

Retrieve the activation channel corresponding to the top predicted class.

```
with (tf$GradientTape() %as% tape, {
  last_conv_layer_output <- last_conv_layer_model(preprocessed_img)
  tape$watch(last_conv_layer_output)
  preds <- classifier_model(last_conv_layer_output)
  top_pred_index <- tf$argmax(preds[1, ])
  top_class_channel <- preds[, top_pred_index, style = "python"]
})

grads <- tape$gradient(top_class_channel, last_conv_layer_output)
```

This is the gradient of the top predicted class with regard to the output feature map of the last convolutional layer.

Now we apply pooling and importance weighting to the gradient tensor to obtain our heatmap of class activation.

Listing 9.25   Gradient pooling and channel-importance weighting

We take advantage of Tensor broadcasting rules here to avoid writing a for loop. The size-1 axes of pooled_grads are automatically broadcast to match the corresponding axes of last_conv_layer_output.

pooled_grads is a vector where each entry is the mean intensity of the gradient for a given channel. It quantifies the importance of each channel with regard to the top predicted class.

```
pooled_grads <- mean(grads, axis = c(1, 2, 3), keepdims = TRUE)

heatmap <-
  (last_conv_layer_output * pooled_grads) %>%
  mean(axis = -1) %>%
  .[1, , ]
```

pooled_grads has shape (1, 1, 1, 2048).

grads and last_conv_layer_output have the same shape, (1, 10, 10, 2048).

Shape: (1, 10, 10, 2048)

Shape: (1, 10, 10)

The channel-wise mean of the resulting feature map is our heatmap of class activation.

Drop batch dim; output shape: (10, 10).

Multiply each channel in the output of the last convolutional layer by "how important this channel is."

The result is shown in figure 9.19.

Listing 9.26   Heatmap postprocessing

```
par(mar = c(0, 0, 0, 0))
plot_activations(heatmap)
```

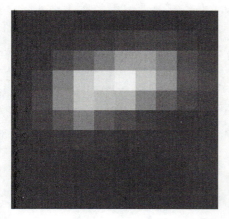

Figure 9.19   Standalone class activation heatmap

Finally, let's superimpose the activations heatmap over the original image. We cut() the heatmap values to a sequential color palette, and then convert to an R raster object. Note we make sure to pass alpha = .4 to the palette, so that we can still see the original image when we superimpose the heatmap over it. (See figure 9.20.)

Listing 9.27   Superimposing the heatmap on the original picture

```
pal <- hcl.colors(256, palette = "Spectral", alpha = .4, rev = TRUE)
heatmap <- as.array(heatmap)
heatmap[] <- pal[cut(heatmap, 256)]
heatmap <- as.raster(heatmap)

img <- tf_read_image(img_path, resize = NULL)       Load the original image,
display_image_tensor(img)                            without resizing this time.
rasterImage(heatmap, 0, 0, ncol(img), nrow(img), interpolate = FALSE)
```

Superimpose the heatmap over the original image, with the heatmap at 40% opacity. We pass ncol(img) and nrow(img) so that the heatmap, which has fewer pixels, is drawn to match the size of the original image. We pass interpolate = FALSE so we can clearly see where the activation map pixel boundaries are.

This visualization technique answers two important questions:

- Why did the network think this image contained an African elephant?
- Where is the African elephant located in the picture?

In particular, it's interesting to note that the ears of the elephant calf are strongly activated: this is probably how the network can tell the difference between African and Indian elephants.

Figure 9.20   African elephant class activation heatmap over the test picture

Summary

- You can do three essential computer vision tasks with deep learning: image classification, image segmentation, and object detection.
- Following modern convnet architecture best practices will help you get the most out of your models. Some of these best practices include using residual connections, batch normalization, and depthwise separable convolutions.
- The representations that convnets learn are easy to inspect—convnets are the opposite of black boxes!
- You can generate visualizations of the filters learned by your convnets, as well as heatmaps of class activity.

Deep learning for time series

This chapter covers

- Examples of machine learning tasks that involve time-series data
- Understanding recurrent neural networks (RNNs)
- Applying RNNs to a temperature-forecasting example
- Advanced RNN usage patterns

10.1 Different kinds of time-series tasks

A *time series* can be any data obtained via measurements at regular intervals, like the daily price of a stock, the hourly electricity consumption of a city, or the weekly sales of a store. Time series are everywhere, whether we're looking at natural phenomena (like seismic activity, the evolution of fish populations in a river, or the weather at a location) or human activity patterns (like visitors to a website, a country's GDP, or credit card transactions). Unlike the types of data you've encountered so far, working with time series involves understanding the *dynamics* of a system—its periodic cycles, how it trends over time, its regular regime, and its sudden spikes.

By far, the most common time-series-related task is *forecasting*: predicting what will happen next in a series; forecasting electricity consumption a few hours in advance so you can anticipate demand; forecasting revenue a few months in advance so you can plan your budget; forecasting the weather a few days in advance so you can plan your schedule. Forecasting is what this chapter focuses on. But there's actually a wide range of other things you can do with time series:

- *Classification*—Assign one or more categorical labels to a time series. For instance, given the time series of the activity of a visitor on a website, classify whether the visitor is a bot or a human.
- *Event detection*—Identify the occurrence of a specific expected event within a continuous data stream. A particularly useful application is "hotword detection," where a model monitors an audio stream and detects utterances like "OK, Google" or "Hey, Alexa."
- *Anomaly detection*—Detect anything unusual happening within a continuous datastream. Unusual activity on your corporate network? Might be an attacker. Unusual readings on a manufacturing line? Time for a human to go take a look. Anomaly detection is typically done via unsupervised learning, because you often don't know what kind of anomaly you're looking for, so you can't train on specific anomaly examples.

When working with time series, you'll encounter a wide range of domain-specific data-representation techniques. For instance, you have likely already heard about the *Fourier transform*, which consists of expressing a series of values in terms of a superposition of waves of different frequencies. The Fourier transform can be highly valuable when preprocessing any data that is primarily characterized by its cycles and oscillations (like sound, the vibrations of the frame of a skyscraper, or your brain waves). In the context of deep learning, Fourier analysis (or the related Mel-frequency analysis) and other domain-specific representations can be useful as a form of feature engineering, a way to prepare data before training a model on it, to make the job of the model easier. However, we won't cover these techniques in these pages; we will instead focus on the modeling part.

In this chapter, you'll learn about recurrent neural networks (RNNs) and how to apply them to time-series forecasting.

10.2 *A temperature-forecasting example*

Throughout this chapter, all of our code examples will target a single problem: predicting the temperature 24 hours in the future, given a time series of hourly measurements of quantities such as atmospheric pressure and humidity, recorded over the recent past by a set of sensors on the roof of a building. As you will see, it's a fairly challenging problem!

We'll use this temperature-forecasting task to highlight what makes time-series data fundamentally different from the kinds of datasets you've encountered so far.

You'll see that densely connected networks and convolutional networks aren't well-equipped to deal with this kind of dataset, whereas a different kind of machine learning technique—recurrent neural networks (RNNs)—really shines on this type of problem.

We'll work with a weather time-series dataset recorded at the weather station at the Max Planck Institute for Biogeochemistry in Jena, Germany.[1] In this dataset, 14 different quantities (such as temperature, pressure, humidity, and wind direction) were recorded every 10 minutes over several years. The original data goes back to 2003, but the subset of the data we'll download is limited to 2009–2016. Let's start by downloading and uncompressing the data:

```
url <-
  "https://s3.amazonaws.com/keras-datasets/jena_climate_2009_2016.csv.zip"
download.file(url, destfile = basename(url))
zip::unzip(zipfile = "jena_climate_2009_2016.csv.zip",
           files = "jena_climate_2009_2016.csv")
```

Now let's look at the data. We'll use `readr::read_csv()` to read in the data.

Listing 10.1   Inspecting the data of the Jena weather dataset

```
full_df <- readr::read_csv("jena_climate_2009_2016.csv")
```

Note that you can also skip the zip::unzip() call above and pass the zip filepath directly to read_csv().

This outputs a data.frame with 420,451 rows and 15 columns. Each row is a time step: a record of a date and 14 weather-related values.

```
full_df
```

```
# A tibble: 420,451 × 15
    `Date Time`       `p (mbar)` `T (degC)` `Tpot (K)` `Tdew (degC)` `rh (%)`
    <chr>                  <dbl>      <dbl>      <dbl>         <dbl>    <dbl>
 1 01.01.2009 00:10…       997.      -8.02       265.          -8.9     93.3
 2 01.01.2009 00:20…       997.      -8.41       265.         -9.28     93.4
 3 01.01.2009 00:30…       997.      -8.51       265.         -9.31     93.9
 4 01.01.2009 00:40…       997.      -8.31       265.         -9.07     94.2
 5 01.01.2009 00:50…       997.      -8.27       265.         -9.04     94.1
 6 01.01.2009 01:00…       996.      -8.05       265.         -8.78     94.4
 7 01.01.2009 01:10…       996.      -7.62       266.          -8.3     94.8
 8 01.01.2009 01:20…       996.      -7.62       266.         -8.36     94.4
 9 01.01.2009 01:30…       996.      -7.91       266.         -8.73     93.8
10 01.01.2009 01:40…       997.      -8.43       265.         -9.34     93.1
# … with 420,441 more rows, and 9 more variables: `VPmax (mbar)` <dbl>,
#   `VPact (mbar)` <dbl>, `VPdef (mbar)` <dbl>, `sh (g/kg)` <dbl>,
#   `H2OC (mmol/mol)` <dbl>, `rho (g/m**3)` <dbl>, `wv (m/s)` <dbl>,
#   `max. wv (m/s)` <dbl>, `wd (deg)` <dbl>
```

---

[1] Adam Erickson and Olaf Kolle, http://www.bgc-jena.mpg.de/wetter.

read_csv() parsed all the columns correctly as numeric vectors, except for the "Date Time" column, which it parsed as a character vector instead of as a date-time vector. We won't be training on the Date Time column, so this is not an issue, but just for completeness, we can convert the character column to an R POSIXct format. Note that we pass tz = "Etc/GMT+1" instead of tz = "Europe/Berlin", because the time-stamps in the dataset do not adjust for Central European Summer Time (also known as Daylight Saving Time), but are instead always at Central European Time:

```
full_df$`Date Time` %<>%
  as.POSIXct(tz = "Etc/GMT+1", format = "%d.%m.%Y %H:%M:%S")
```

The %<>% assignment pipe

In the previous example, we use the assignment pipe for the first time. x %<>% fn() is shorthand for x <- x %>% fn(). It is useful because it allows you to write more read-able code and avoid repeating the same variable name multiple times. We could also have written this to achieve the same outcome:

```
full_df$`Date Time` <- full_df$`Date Time` %>%
  as.POSIXct(tz = "Etc/GMT+1", format = "%d.%m.%Y %H:%M:%S")
```

The assignment pipe is made available by calling library(keras).

Figure 10.1 shows the plot of temperature (in degrees Celsius) over time. On this plot, you can clearly see the yearly periodicity of temperature—the data spans 8 years.

Listing 10.2 | Plotting the temperature time series

```
plot(`T (degC)` ~ `Date Time`, data = full_df, pch = 20, cex = .3)
```

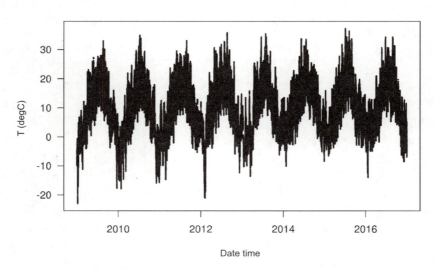

Figure 10.1   Temperature over the full temporal range of the dataset (°C)

Figure 10.2 shows a more narrow plot of the first 10 days of temperature data. Because the data is recorded every 10 minutes, you get 24 × 6 = 144 data points per day.

Listing 10.3 Plotting the first 10 days of the temperature time series

```
plot(`T (degC)` ~ `Date Time`, data = full_df[1:1440, ])
```

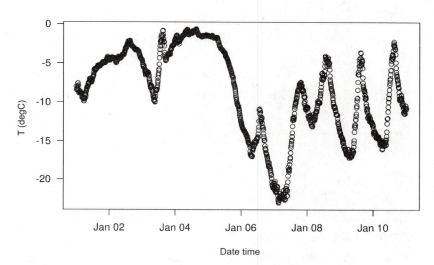

Figure 10.2 Temperature over the first 10 days of the dataset (°C)

On this plot, you can see daily periodicity, especially for the last four days. Also note that this 10-day period is coming from a fairly cold winter month.

Always look for periodicity in your data

Periodicity over multiple time scales is an important and very common property of time-series data. Whether you're looking at the weather, mall parking occupancy, traffic to a website, sales of a grocery store, or steps logged in a fitness tracker, you'll see daily cycles and yearly cycles (human-generated data also tends to feature weekly cycles). When exploring your data, make sure to look for these patterns.

With our dataset, if you were trying to predict average temperature for the next month given a few months of past data, the problem would be easy, due to the reliable year-scale periodicity of the data. But looking at the data over a scale of days, the temperature looks a lot more chaotic. Is this time series predictable at a daily scale? Let's find out.

In all our experiments, we'll use the first 50% of the data for training, the following 25% for validation, and the last 25% for testing. When working with time-series data, it's important to use validation and test data that is more recent than the training data, because you're trying to predict the future given the past, not the reverse, and your validation/test splits should reflect that. Some problems happen to be considerably simpler if you reverse the time axis!

```
num_train_samples <- round(nrow(full_df) * .5)
num_val_samples <- round(nrow(full_df) * 0.25)
num_test_samples <- nrow(full_df) - num_train_samples - num_val_samples

train_df <- full_df[seq(num_train_samples), ]          First 50% of rows, 1:210226

val_df <- full_df[seq(from = nrow(train_df) + 1,       Next 25% of rows, 210227:315339
                      length.out = num_val_samples), ]

test_df <- full_df[seq(to = nrow(full_df),             Last 25% of rows, 315340:420451
                      length.out = num_test_samples), ]

cat("num_train_samples:", nrow(train_df), "\n")
cat("num_val_samples:", nrow(val_df), "\n")
cat("num_test_samples:", nrow(test_df), "\n")
```

```
num_train_samples: 210226
num_val_samples: 105113
num_test_samples: 105112
```

10.2.1 Preparing the data

The exact formulation of the problem will be as follows: given data covering the previous five days and sampled once per hour, can we predict the temperature in 24 hours?

First, let's preprocess the data to a format a neural network can ingest. This is easy: the data is already numerical, so you don't need to do any vectorization. But each time series in the data is on a different scale (e.g., atmospheric pressure, measured in mbar, is around 1,000, whereas H2OC, measured in millimoles per mole, is around 3). We'll normalize each time series (column) independently so that they all take small values on a similar scale. We're going to use the first 210,226 time steps as training data, so we'll compute the mean and standard deviation only on this fraction of the data.

```
input_data_colnames <- names(full_df) %>%         Our model input will be all the columns
  setdiff(c("Date Time"))                         except for the Date Time column.

normalization_values <-                                    We compute the
  zip_lists(mean = lapply(train_df[input_data_colnames], mean),   normalization
            sd   = lapply(train_df[input_data_colnames], sd))     values using
                                                           only the
str(normalization_values)                                  training data.
```

```
List of 14
 $ p (mbar)       :List of 2
  ..$ mean: num 989
  ..$ sd  : num 8.51
 $ T (degC)       :List of 2
```

```
  ..$ mean: num 8.83
  ..$ sd   : num 8.77
$ Tpot (K)         :List of 2
  ..$ mean: num 283
  ..$ sd   : num 8.87
$ Tdew (degC)      :List of 2
  ..$ mean: num 4.31
  ..$ sd   : num 7.08
$ rh (%)           :List of 2
  ..$ mean: num 75.9
  ..$ sd   : num 16.6
$ VPmax (mbar)     :List of 2
  ..$ mean: num 13.1
  ..$ sd   : num 7.6
$ VPact (mbar)     :List of 2
  ..$ mean: num 9.19
  ..$ sd   : num 4.15
$ VPdef (mbar)     :List of 2
  ..$ mean: num 3.95
  ..$ sd   : num 4.77
  [list output truncated]
```

```
normalize_input_data <- function(df) {
  normalize <- function(x, center, scale)        ◁——┐
      (x - center) / scale

  for(col_nm in input_data_colnames) {
    col_nv <- normalization_values[[col_nm]]
    df[[col_nm]] %<>% normalize(., col_nv$mean, col_nv$sd)
  }

  df
}
```

> **You can also call scale(col, center = train_col_mean, scale = train_col_sd) instead, but for maximum clarity we define a local function: normalize().**

Next, let's create a TF Dataset object that yields batches of data from the past five days along with a target temperature 24 hours in the future. Because the samples in the dataset are highly redundant (sample *N* and sample *N* + 1 will have most of their time steps in common), it would be wasteful to explicitly allocate memory for every sample. Instead, we'll generate the samples on the fly while only keeping in memory the original data arrays, and nothing more.

We could easily write an R function to do this, but there's a built-in dataset utility in Keras that does just that—(`timeseries_dataset_from_array()`)—so we can save ourselves some work by using it. You can generally use it for any kind of time-series forecasting task.

Understanding `timeseries_dataset_from_array()`

To understand what `timeseries_dataset_from_array()` does, let's look at a simple example. The general idea is that you provide an array of time-series data (the `data` argument), and `timeseries_dataset_from_array()` gives you windows extracted from the original time series (we'll call them "sequences").

(continued)

For example, if you use `data = [0 1 2 3 4 5 6]` and `sequence_length = 3`, then `timeseries_dataset_from_array()` will generate the following samples: `[0 1 2]`, `[1 2 3]`, `[2 3 4]`, `[3 4 5]`, `[4 5 6]`.

You can also pass a `targets` argument (an array) to `timeseries_dataset_from_array()`. The first entry of the `targets` array should match the desired target for the first sequence that will be generated from the `data` array. So, if you're doing time-series forecasting, `targets` should be the same array as `data`, offset by some amount.

For instance, with `data = [0 1 2 3 4 5 6 …]` and `sequence_length = 3`, you could create a dataset to predict the next step in the series by passing `targets = [3 4 5 6 …]`. Let's try it:

```r
library(keras)
int_sequence <- seq(10)                          # Generate an array of sorted integers from 1 to 10.
dummy_dataset <- timeseries_dataset_from_array(
  data = head(int_sequence, -3),                 # The sequences we generate will be sampled from [1 2 3 4 5 6 7] (drop last 3).
  targets = tail(int_sequence, -3),              # The target for the sequence that starts at data[N] will be data[N + 4] (tail drops first 3).
  sequence_length = 3,                           # The sequences will be three steps long.
  batch_size = 2                                 # The sequences will be batched in batches of size 2.
)

library(tfdatasets)
dummy_dataset_iterator <- as_array_iterator(dummy_dataset)

repeat {
  batch <- iter_next(dummy_dataset_iterator)
  if (is.null(batch))                            # The iterator is exhausted.
    break
  c(inputs, targets) %<-% batch
  for (r in 1:nrow(inputs))
    cat(sprintf("input: [ %s ]  target: %s\n",
                paste(inputs[r, ], collapse = " "), targets[r]))
  cat(strrep("-", 27), "\n")                     # Demark batches.
}
```

This bit of code prints the following results:

```
input: [ 1 2 3 ]  target: 4
input: [ 2 3 4 ]  target: 5
---------------------------
input: [ 3 4 5 ]  target: 6
input: [ 4 5 6 ]  target: 7
---------------------------
input: [ 5 6 7 ]  target: 8
---------------------------
```

We'll use `timeseries_dataset_from_array()` to instantiate three datasets: one for training, one for validation, and one for testing. We'll use the following parameter values:

- `sampling_rate = 6`—Observations will be sampled at one data point per hour: we will keep only one data point out of 6.
- `sequence_length = 120`—Observations will go back five days (120 hours).
- `delay = sampling_rate * (sequence_length + 24 - 1)`—The target for a sequence will be the temperature 24 hours after the end of the sequence.

Listing 10.6   Instantiating datasets for training, validation, and testing

```
sampling_rate <- 6
sequence_length <- 120
delay <- sampling_rate * (sequence_length + 24 - 1)
batch_size <- 256

df_to_inputs_and_targets <- function(df) {
  inputs <- df[input_data_colnames] %>%          Convert data.frame
    normalize_input_data() %>%                    to a numeric array.
    as.matrix()              <-

  targets <- as.array(df$`T (degC)`)   <---- We don't normalize the targets.

  list(                              Drop the last delay samples.
    head(inputs, -delay),    <-
    tail(targets, -delay)    <-
  )                                  Drop the first delay samples.
}

make_dataset <- function(df) {
  c(inputs, targets) %<-% df_to_inputs_and_targets(df)
  timeseries_dataset_from_array(
    inputs, targets,
    sampling_rate = sampling_rate,
    sequence_length = sequence_length,
    shuffle = TRUE,
    batch_size = batch_size
  )
}

train_dataset <- make_dataset(train_df)
val_dataset <- make_dataset(val_df)
test_dataset <- make_dataset(test_df)
```

Each dataset yields batches as a pair of `(samples, targets)`, where `samples` is a batch of 256 samples, each containing 120 consecutive hours of input data, and `targets` is the corresponding array of 256 target temperatures. Note that the samples are randomly shuffled, so two consecutive sequences in a batch (like `samples[1, ]` and `samples[2, ])` aren't necessarily temporally close.

Listing 10.7   Inspecting the output of one of our datasets

```
c(samples, targets) %<-% iter_next(as_iterator(train_dataset))
cat("samples shape: ", format(samples$shape), "\n",
    "targets shape: ", format(targets$shape), "\n", sep = "")
```

```
samples shape: (256, 120, 14)
targets shape: (256)
```

10.2.2   *A common-sense, non–machine learning baseline*

Before we start using black-box deep learning models to solve the temperature-prediction problem, let's try a simple, common-sense approach. It will serve as a sanity check, and it will establish a baseline that we'll have to beat to demonstrate the usefulness of more-advanced machine learning models. Such common-sense baselines can be useful when you're approaching a new problem for which there is no known solution (yet). A classic example is that of unbalanced classification tasks, where some classes are much more common than others. If your dataset contains 90% instances of class A and 10% instances of class B, then a common-sense approach to the classification task is to always predict "A" when presented with a new sample. Such a classifier is 90% accurate overall, and any learning-based approach should therefore beat this 90% score to demonstrate usefulness. Sometimes, such elementary baselines can prove surprisingly hard to beat.

In this case, the temperature time series can safely be assumed to be continuous (the temperatures tomorrow are likely to be close to the temperatures today) as well as periodical with a daily period. Thus a common-sense approach is to always predict that the temperature 24 hours from now will be equal to the temperature right now. Let's evaluate this approach, using the mean absolute error (MAE) metric, defined as follows:

```
mean(abs(preds - targets))
```

Here's the evaluation code. Rather than evaluating it all eagerly in R using `for`, `as_array_iterator()`, and `iter_next()`, we can just as easily do it with TF Dataset transformations. First we call `dataset_unbatch()` so that each dataset element becomes a single case of `(samples, target)`. Next we use `dataset_map()` to calculate the absolute error for each pair of `(samples, target)`, and then `dataset_reduce()` to accumulate the total error and total samples seen.

Recall that functions passed to `dataset_map()` and `dataset_reduce()` will be called with symbolic tensors. Slicing a tensor with a negative number like `samples[-1, ]` selects the last slice along that axis, as if we had written `samples[nrow(samples), ]`.

Listing 10.8   Computing the common-sense baseline MAE

```
evaluate_naive_method <- function(dataset) {

  unnormalize_temperature <- function(x) {
```

```
  nv <- normalization_values$`T (degC)`
  (x * nv$sd) + nv$mean
}

temp_col_idx <- match("T (degC)", input_data_colnames)
```

2, the second column

```
reduction <- dataset %>%
  dataset_unbatch() %>%
  dataset_map(function(samples, target) {
    last_temp_in_input <- samples[-1, temp_col_idx]
    pred <- unnormalize_temperature(last_temp_in_input)
    abs(pred - target)
  }) %>%
  dataset_reduce(
    initial_state = list(total_samples_seen = 0L,
                          total_abs_error = 0),
    reduce_func = function(state, element) {
      state$total_samples_seen %<>% `+`(1L)
      state$total_abs_error %<>% `+`(element)
      state
    }
  ) %>%
  lapply(as.numeric)
```

Slice out the last temperature measurement in the input sequence.

Recall that we normalized our features, so to retrieve a temperature in degrees Celsius, we need to unnormalize it by multiplying it by the standard deviation and adding back the mean.

Convert Tensors to R numerics.

```
  mae <- with(reduction,
              total_abs_error / total_samples_seen)
  mae
}

sprintf("Validation MAE: %.2f", evaluate_naive_method(val_dataset))
sprintf("Test MAE: %.2f", evaluate_naive_method(test_dataset))
```

reduction is a named list of two R scalar numbers.

```
[1] "Validation MAE: 2.43"
[1] "Test MAE: 2.62"
```

This common-sense baseline achieves a validation MAE of 2.44 degrees Celsius and a test MAE of 2.62 degrees Celsius. So if you always assume that the temperature 24 hours in the future will be the same as it is now, you will be off by two and a half degrees on average. It's not too bad, but you probably won't launch a weather forecasting service based on this heuristic. Now the game is to use your knowledge of deep learning to do better.

10.2.3   Let's try a basic machine learning model

In the same way that it's useful to establish a common-sense baseline before trying machine learning approaches, it's useful to try simple, cheap machine learning models (such as small, densely connected networks) before looking into complicated and computationally expensive models such as RNNs. This is the best way to make sure any further complexity you throw at the problem is legitimate and delivers real benefits.

Listing 10.9 shows a fully connected model that starts by flattening the data and then runs it through two `layer_dense()`s. Note the lack of an activation function on the last `layer_dense()`, which is typical for a regression problem. We use mean squared error (MSE) as the loss, rather than MAE, because unlike MAE, it's smooth around zero, which is a useful property for gradient descent. We will monitor MAE by adding it as a metric in `compile()`.

Listing 10.9   Training and evaluating a densely connected model

```
ncol_input_data <- length(input_data_colnames)

inputs <- layer_input(shape = c(sequence_length, ncol_input_data))
outputs <- inputs %>%
  layer_flatten() %>%
  layer_dense(16, activation = "relu") %>%
  layer_dense(1)
model <- keras_model(inputs, outputs)

callbacks = list(
    callback_model_checkpoint("jena_dense.keras",      ◁──┐  We use a callback to save
                              save_best_only = TRUE)         the best-performing model.
)

model %>%
  compile(optimizer = "rmsprop",
          loss = "mse",
          metrics = "mae")

history <- model %>%
  fit(train_dataset,
      epochs = 10,
      validation_data = val_dataset,
      callbacks = callbacks)
                                                    Reload the best model, and
                                                    evaluate it on the test data.
model <- load_model_tf("jena_dense.keras")    ◁──
sprintf("Test MAE: %.2f", evaluate(model, test_dataset)["mae"])
```

```
[1] "Test MAE: 2.71"
```

Let's display the loss curves for validation and training (see figure 10.3).

Listing 10.10   Plotting results

```
plot(history, metrics = "mae")
```

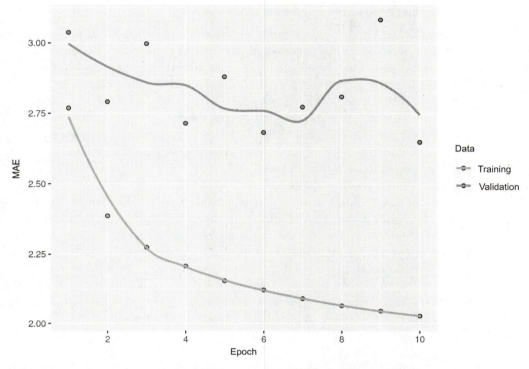

Figure 10.3   Training and validation MAE on the Jena temperature-forecasting task with a simple, densely connected network

Some of the validation losses are close to the no-learning baseline, but not reliably. This goes to show the merit of having this baseline in the first place: it turns out to be not easy to outperform. Your common sense contains a lot of valuable information to which a machine learning model doesn't have access.

You may wonder, if a simple, well-performing model exists to go from the data to the targets (the common-sense baseline), why doesn't the model you're training find it and improve on it? Well, the space of models in which you're searching for a solution—that is, your hypothesis space—is the space of all possible two-layer networks with the configuration you defined. The common-sense heuristic is just one model among millions that can be represented in this space. It's like looking for a needle in a haystack. Just because a good solution technically exists in your hypothesis space doesn't mean you'll be able to find it via gradient descent.

That's a pretty significant limitation of machine learning in general: unless the learning algorithm is hardcoded to look for a specific kind of simple model, it can sometimes fail to find a simple solution to a simple problem. That's why leveraging good feature engineering and relevant architecture priors is essential: you need to precisely tell your model what it should be looking for.

10.2.4 *Let's try a 1D convolutional model*

Speaking of leveraging the right architecture priors, because our input sequences feature daily cycles, perhaps a convolutional model could work. A temporal convnet could reuse the same representations across different days, much like a spatial convnet can reuse the same representations across different locations in an image.

You already know about `layer_conv_2d()` and `layer_separable_conv_2d()`, which see their inputs through small windows that swipe across 2D grids. There are also 1D and even 3D versions of these layers: `layer_conv_1d()`, `layer_separable_conv_1d()`, and `layer_conv_3d()`.[2] The `layer_conv_1d()` layer relies on 1D windows that slide across input sequences, and the `layer_conv_3d()` layer relies on cubic windows that slide across input volumes.

You can thus build 1D convnets, strictly analogous to 2D convnets. They're a great fit for any sequence data that follows the translation invariance assumption (meaning that if you slide a window over the sequence, the content of the window should follow the same properties independently of the location of the window).

Let's try one on our temperature-forecasting problem. We'll pick an initial window length of 24, so that we look at 24 hours of data at a time (one cycle). As we downsample the sequences (via `layer_max_pooling_1d()` layers), we'll reduce the window size accordingly:

```
inputs <- layer_input(shape = c(sequence_length, ncol_input_data))
outputs <- inputs %>%
  layer_conv_1d(8, 24, activation = "relu") %>%
  layer_max_pooling_1d(2) %>%
  layer_conv_1d(8, 12, activation = "relu") %>%
  layer_max_pooling_1d(2) %>%
  layer_conv_1d(8, 6, activation = "relu") %>%
  layer_global_average_pooling_1d() %>%
  layer_dense(1)
model <- keras_model(inputs, outputs)

callbacks <- list(callback_model_checkpoint("jena_conv.keras",
                                            save_best_only = TRUE))

model %>% compile(optimizer = "rmsprop",
                  loss = "mse",
                  metrics = "mae")

history <- model %>% fit(
  train_dataset,
  epochs = 10,
  validation_data = val_dataset,
  callbacks = callbacks
)
```

---

[2] Note that there isn't a `layer_separable_conv_3d()`, not for any theoretical reason, but simply because I haven't implemented it.

```
model <- load_model_tf("jena_conv.keras")
sprintf("Test MAE: %.2f", evaluate(model, test_dataset)["mae"])
```

```
[1] "Test MAE: 3.20"
```

We get the training and validation curves shown in figure 10.4.

```
plot(history)
```

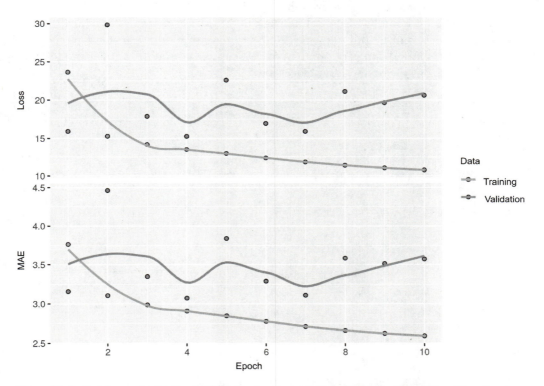

Figure 10.4   Training and validation MAE on the Jena temperature-forecasting task with a 1D convnet

As it turns out, this model performs even worse than the densely connected one, only achieving a test MAE of 3.2 degrees, far from the common-sense baseline. What went wrong here? Two things:

- First, weather data doesn't quite respect the translation invariance assumption. Although the data does feature daily cycles, data from a morning follows different properties than data from an evening or from the middle of the night. Weather data is translation invariant for only a very specific timescale.
- Second, order in our data matters—a lot. The recent past is far more informative for predicting the next day's temperature than data from five days ago. A 1D convnet is not able to leverage this fact. In particular, our max-pooling and global average pooling layers are largely destroying order information.

10.2.5 *A first recurrent baseline*

Neither the fully connected approach nor the convolutional approach did well, but that doesn't mean machine learning isn't applicable to this problem. The densely connected approach first flattened the time series, which removed the notion of time from the input data. The convolutional approach treated every segment of the data in the same way, even applying pooling, which destroyed order information. Let's instead look at the data as what it is: a sequence, where causality and order matter.

There's a family of neural network architectures designed specifically for this use case: recurrent neural networks. Among them, the long short-term memory (LSTM) layer has long been very popular. We'll see in a minute how these models work, but let's start by giving the LSTM layer a try.

> **Listing 10.11   A simple LSTM-based model**

```
inputs <- layer_input(shape = c(sequence_length, ncol_input_data))
outputs <- inputs %>%
  layer_lstm(16) %>%
  layer_dense(1)
model <- keras_model(inputs, outputs)

callbacks <- list(callback_model_checkpoint("jena_lstm.keras",
                                            save_best_only = TRUE))

model %>% compile(optimizer = "rmsprop",
                  loss = "mse",
                  metrics = "mae")

history <- model %>% fit(
  train_dataset,
  epochs = 10,
  validation_data = val_dataset,
  callbacks = callbacks
)

model <- load_model_tf("jena_lstm.keras")
sprintf("Test MAE: %.2f", evaluate(model, test_dataset)["mae"])
```

```
[1] "Test MAE: 2.52"
```

Figure 10.5 shows the results. Much better! We achieve a test MAE of 2.52 degrees. The LSTM-based model can finally beat the common-sense baseline (albeit just by a bit, for now), demonstrating the value of machine learning on this task.

But why did the LSTM model perform markedly better than the densely connected one or the convnet? And how can we further refine the model? To answer this, let's take a closer look at recurrent neural networks.

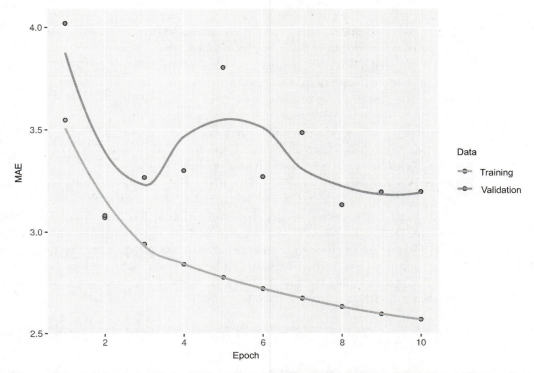

Figure 10.5 Training and validation MAE on the Jena temperature-forecasting task with an LSTM-based model (note that we omit epoch 1 on this graph, because the high training MAE at the first epoch would distort the scale)

10.3 *Understanding recurrent neural networks*

A major characteristic of all neural networks you've seen so far, such as densely connected networks and convnets, is that they have no memory. Each input shown to them is processed independently, with no state kept between inputs. With such networks, to process a sequence or a temporal series of data points, you have to show the entire sequence to the network at once: turn it into a single data point. For instance, this is what we did in the densely connected network example: we flattened our five days of data into a single large vector and processed it in one go. Such networks are called *feed-forward networks*.

In contrast, as you're reading the present sentence, you're processing it word by word—or rather, eye saccade by eye saccade—while keeping memories of what came before; this gives you a fluid representation of the meaning conveyed by this sentence. Biological intelligence processes information incrementally while maintaining an internal model of what it's processing, built from past information and constantly updated as new information comes in.

A *recurrent neural network* (RNN) adopts the same principle, albeit in an extremely simplified version: it processes sequences by iterating through the sequence elements and maintaining a *state* that contains information relative to what it has seen so far. In effect, an RNN is a type of neural network that has an internal *loop* (see figure 10.6).

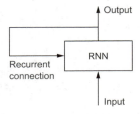

The state of the RNN is reset between processing two different, independent sequences (such as two samples in a batch), so you still consider one sequence to be a single data point: a single input to the network. What changes is that this data point is no longer processed in a single step; rather, the network internally loops over sequence elements.

Figure 10.6   A recurrent network: A network with a loop

To make these notions of *loop* and *state* clear, let's implement the forward pass of a toy RNN. This RNN takes as input a sequence of vectors, which we'll encode as a rank 2 tensor of size (timesteps, input_features). It loops over time steps, and at each time step, it considers its current state at t and the input at t (of shape (input_features)), and combines them to obtain the output at t. We'll then set the state for the next step to be this previous output. For the first time step, the previous output isn't defined; hence, there is no current state. So we'll initialize the state as an all-zero vector called the *initial* state of the network. In pseudocode, the following listing shows the RNN.

Listing 10.12   Pseudocode RNN

```
state_t <- 0                          The state at t
for (input_t in input_sequence) {
  output_t <- f(input_t, state_t)     Iterate over sequence elements.
  state_t <- output_t
}                                      The previous output becomes
                                       the state for the next iteration.
```

You can even flesh out the function f: the transformation of the input and state into an output will be parameterized by two matrices, W and U, and a bias vector. It's similar to the transformation operated by a densely connected layer in a feed-forward network.

Listing 10.13   More-detailed pseudocode for the RNN

```
state_t <- 0
for (input_t in input_sequence) {
  output_t <- activation(dot(W, input_t) + dot(U, state_t) + b)
  state_t <- output_t
}
```

To make these notions absolutely unambiguous, let's write a naive R implementation of the forward pass of the simple RNN.

Listing 10.14   Base R implementation of a simple RNN

```
random_array <- function(dim) array(runif(prod(dim)), dim)

timesteps <- 100                  ◁──────┐  Number of time steps in the input sequence
input_features <- 32              ◁──── Dimensionality of the input feature space
output_features <- 64             ◁────┐
                                       Dimensionality of the output feature space

inputs <- random_array(c(timesteps, input_features)) ◁──┐  Input data: random noise
state_t <- array(0, dim = output_features)                 for the sake of the example

W <- random_array(c(output_features, input_features))      ┐ Create random
U <- random_array(c(output_features, output_features))     │ weight matrices.
b <- random_array(c(output_features, 1))                   ┘
successive_outputs <- array(0, dim = c(timesteps, output_features))

for(ts in 1:timesteps) {               input_t is a vector of
  input_t <- inputs[ts, ]   ◁────      shape (input_features).
  output_t <- tanh((W %*% input_t) + (U %*% state_t) + b)   ◁──

  successive_outputs[ts, ] <- output_t   ◁──── Store this output.
  state_t <- output_t   ◁────  Update the state of the network
}                                for the next time step.
final_output_sequence <- successive_outputs   ◁────
```

Initial state: an all-zero vector

Combine the input with the current state (the previous output) to obtain the current output. We use tanh to add nonlinearity (we could use any other activation function).

W %*% input_t, U %*% input_t, and b all have the same shape: (output_features, 1).

The final output is a rank 2 tensor of shape (timesteps, output_features).

That's easy enough. In summary, an RNN is a `for` loop that reuses quantities computed during the previous iteration of the loop, nothing more. Of course, you could build many different RNNs that fit this definition—this example is one of the simplest RNN formulations. RNNs are characterized by their step function, such as the following function in this case (see figure 10.7).

```
output_t <- tanh((W %*% input_t) + (U %*% state_t) + b)
```

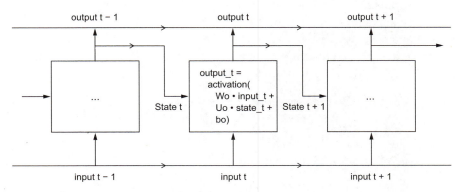

Figure 10.7   A simple RNN, unrolled over time

In this example, the final output is a rank 2 tensor of shape `(timesteps, output_features)`, where each time step is the output of the loop at time t. Each time step t in the output tensor contains information about time steps 1 to t in the input sequence—about the entire past. For this reason, in many cases, you don't need this full sequence of outputs; you just need the last output (`output_t` at the end of the loop), because it already contains information about the entire sequence.

10.3.1 *A recurrent layer in Keras*

The process we just naively implemented in R corresponds to an actual Keras layer—the `layer_simple_rnn()`. There is one minor difference: `layer_simple_rnn()` processes batches of sequences, like all other Keras layers, not a single sequence as in the R example. This means it takes inputs of shape `(batch_size, timesteps, input_features)`, rather than `(timesteps, input_features)`. When specifying the `shape` argument of the initial input, note that you can set the `timesteps` entry to `NA`, which enables your network to process sequences of arbitrary length.

> **Listing 10.15   An RNN layer that can process sequences of any length**

```
num_features <- 14
inputs <- layer_input(shape = c(NA, num_features))
outputs <- inputs %>% layer_simple_rnn(16)
```

This is especially useful if your model is meant to process sequences of variable length. However, if all of your sequences have the same length, I recommend specifying a complete input shape, because it enables the model `print()` method to display output length information, which is always nice, and it can unlock some performance optimizations (see the sidebar box in section 10.4.1, "RNN runtime performance").

All recurrent layers in Keras (`layer_simple_rnn()`, `layer_lstm()`, and `layer_gru()`) can be run in two different modes: they can return either full sequences of successive outputs for each time step (a rank 3 tensor of shape `(batch_size, timesteps, output_features)`) or return only the last output for each input sequence (a rank 2 tensor of shape `(batch_size, output_features)`). These two modes are controlled by the `return_sequences` argument. Let's look at an example that uses `layer_simple_rnn()` and returns only the output at the last time step.

> **Listing 10.16   An RNN layer that returns only its last output step**

```
num_features <- 14
steps <- 120
inputs <- layer_input(shape = c(steps, num_features))
outputs <- inputs %>%
  layer_simple_rnn(16, return_sequences = FALSE)    ◁——— Note that return_sequences = FALSE is the default.
outputs$shape
```

```
TensorShape([None, 16])
```

The following example returns the full state sequence.

```
num_features <- 14
steps <- 120
inputs <- layer_input(shape = c(steps, num_features))
outputs <- inputs %>% layer_simple_rnn(16, return_sequences = TRUE)
outputs$shape
```

```
TensorShape([None, 120, 16])
```

It's sometimes useful to stack several recurrent layers one after the other to increase the representational power of a network. In such a setup, you have to get all of the intermediate layers to return a full sequence of outputs.

```
inputs <- layer_input(shape = c(steps, num_features))
outputs <- inputs %>%
  layer_simple_rnn(16, return_sequences = TRUE) %>%
  layer_simple_rnn(16, return_sequences = TRUE) %>%
  layer_simple_rnn(16)
```

In practice, you'll rarely work with `layer_simple_rnn()`. It's generally too simplistic to be of real use. In particular, `layer_simple_rnn()` has a major issue: although it should theoretically be able to retain at time `t` information about inputs seen many time steps before, such long-term dependencies prove impossible to learn in practice. This is due to the *vanishing-gradient problem,* an effect that is similar to what is observed with nonrecurrent networks (feed-forward networks) that are many layers deep: as you keep adding layers to a network, the network eventually becomes untrainable. The theoretical reasons for this effect were studied by Hochreiter, Schmidhuber, and Bengio in the early 1990s.[3]

Thankfully, `layer_simple_rnn()` isn't the only recurrent layer available in Keras. There are two others, `layer_lstm()` and `layer_gru()`, which were designed to address these issues.

Let's consider `layer_lstm()`. The underlying long short-term memory (LSTM) algorithm was developed by Hochreiter and Schmidhuber in 1997[4]; it was the culmination of their research on the vanishing-gradient problem.

This layer is a variant of the `layer_simple_rnn()` you already know about; it adds a way to carry information across many time steps. Imagine a conveyor belt running parallel to the sequence you're processing. Information from the sequence can jump onto the conveyor belt at any point, be transported to a later time step, and jump off,

---

[3] See, for example, Yoshua Bengio, Patrice Simard, and Paolo Frasconi, "Learning Long-Term Dependencies with Gradient Descent Is Difficult," *IEEE Transactions on Neural Networks* 5, no. 2 (1994).

[4] Sepp Hochreiter and Jürgen Schmidhuber, "Long Short-Term Memory," *Neural Computation* 9, no. 8 (1997).

intact, when you need it. This is essentially what LSTM does: it saves information for later, thus preventing older signals from gradually vanishing during processing. This should remind you of *residual connections*, which you learned about in chapter 9: it's pretty much the same idea.

To understand this process in detail, let's start from the `layer_simple_rnn()` cell (see figure 10.8). Because you'll have a lot of weight matrices, index the W and U matrices in the cell, with the letter o (Wo and Uo) for *output*.

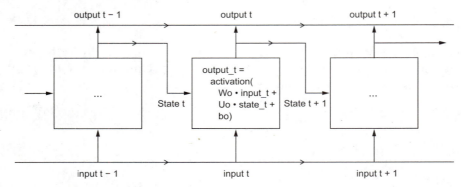

Figure 10.8   The starting point of an LSTM layer: a SimpleRNN

Let's add to this picture an additional data flow that carries information across time steps. Call its values at different time steps c_t, where c stands for *carry*. This information will have the following impact on the cell: it will be combined with the input connection and the recurrent connection (via a dense transformation: a dot product with a weight matrix followed by a bias add and the application of an activation function), and it will affect the state being sent to the next time step (via an activation function and a multiplication operation). Conceptually, the carry dataflow is a way to modulate the next output and the next state (see figure 10.9). Simple so far.

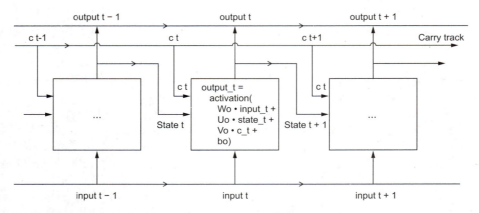

Figure 10.9   Going from a SimpleRNN to an LSTM: Adding a carry track

Now the subtlety—the way the next value of the carry dataflow is computed. It involves three distinct transformations. All three have the form of a `SimpleRNN` cell:

```
y <- activation((state_t %*% U) + (input_t %*% W) + b)
```

But all three transformations have their own weight matrices, which we'll index with the letters i, f, and k. Here's what we have so far (it may seem a bit arbitrary, but bear with me).

Listing 10.19   Pseudocode details of the LSTM architecture (1/2)

```
output_t <-
        activation((state_t %*% Uo) + (input_t %*% Wo) + (c_t %*% Vo) + bo)
i_t <- activation((state_t %*% Ui) + (input_t %*% Wi) + bi)
f_t <- activation((state_t %*% Uf) + (input_t %*% Wf) + bf)
k_t <- activation((state_t %*% Uk) + (input_t %*% Wk) + bk)
```

We obtain the new carry state (the next c_t) by combining i_t, f_t, and k_t.

Listing 10.20   Pseudocode details of the LSTM architecture (2/2)

```
c_t+1 = i_t * k_t + c_t * f_t
```

Add this as shown in figure 10.10, and that's it. Not so complicated—merely a tad complex.

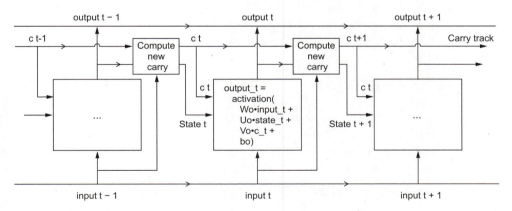

Figure 10.10   Anatomy of an LSTM

If you want to get philosophical, you can interpret what each of these operations is meant to do. For instance, you can say that multiplying c_t and f_t is a way to deliberately forget irrelevant information in the carry dataflow. Meanwhile, i_t and k_t provide information about the present, updating the carry track with new information. But at the end of the day, these interpretations don't mean much, because what these operations *actually* do is determined by the contents of the weights parameterizing them; and the weights are learned in an end-to-end fashion, starting over with each training round, making it impossible to credit this or that operation with a specific purpose. The specification of an RNN cell (as just described) determines your hypothesis space—the space in which you'll search for a good model configuration during training—but it doesn't determine what the cell does; that is up to the cell weights. The same cell with different weights can be doing very different things. So the combination of operations making up an RNN cell is better interpreted as a set of *constraints* on your search, not as a *design* in an engineering sense.

Arguably, the choice of such constraints—the question of how to implement RNN cells—is better left to optimization algorithms (like genetic algorithms or reinforcement-learning processes) than to human engineers. In the future, that's how we'll build our models. In summary: you don't need to understand anything about the specific architecture of an LSTM cell; as a human, it shouldn't be your job to understand it. Just keep in mind what the LSTM cell is meant to do: allow past information to be reinjected at a later time, thus fighting the vanishing-gradient problem.

10.4   Advanced use of recurrent neural networks

So far you've learned

- What RNNs are and how they work
- What LSTM is, and why it works better on long sequences than a naive RNN
- How to use Keras RNN layers to process sequence data

Next, we'll review a number of more advanced features of RNNs, which can help you get the most out of your deep learning sequence models. By the end of the section, you'll know most of what there is to know about using recurrent networks with Keras. We'll cover the following:

- *Recurrent dropout*—This is a variant of dropout, used to fight overfitting in recurrent layers.
- *Stacking recurrent layers*—This increases the representational power of the model (at the cost of higher computational loads).
- *Bidirectional recurrent layers*—These present the same information to a recurrent network in different ways, increasing accuracy and mitigating forgetting issues.

We'll use these techniques to refine our temperature-forecasting RNN.

10.4.1   Using recurrent dropout to fight overfitting

Let's go back to the LSTM-based model we used in section 10.2.5—our first model able to beat the common-sense baseline. If you look at the training and validation curves (figure 10.5), it's evident that the model is quickly overfitting, despite having only very few units: the training and validation losses start to diverge considerably after a few epochs. You're already familiar with a classic technique for fighting this phenomenon: dropout, which randomly zeros out input units of a layer to break happenstance correlations in the training data that the layer is exposed to. But how to correctly apply dropout in recurrent networks isn't a trivial question.

It has long been known that applying dropout before a recurrent layer hinders learning rather than helping with regularization. In 2016, Yarin Gal, as part of his PhD thesis on Bayesian deep learning,[5] determined the proper way to use dropout with a recurrent network: the same dropout mask (the same pattern of dropped units) should be applied at every time step, instead of using a dropout mask that varies randomly from time step to time step. What's more, to regularize the representations formed by the recurrent gates of layers such as `layer_gru()` and `layer_lstm()`, a temporally constant dropout mask should be applied to the inner recurrent activations of the layer (a recurrent dropout mask). Using the same dropout mask at every time step allows the network to properly propagate its learning error through time; a temporally random dropout mask would disrupt this error signal and be harmful to the learning process.

Yarin Gal did his research using Keras and helped build this mechanism directly into Keras recurrent layers. Every recurrent layer in Keras has two dropout-related arguments: `dropout`, a float specifying the dropout rate for input units of the layer, and `recurrent_dropout`, specifying the dropout rate of the recurrent units. Let's add recurrent dropout to the `layer_lstm()` of our first LSTM example and see how doing so impacts overfitting.

Thanks to dropout, we won't need to rely as much on network size for regularization, so we'll use an LSTM layer with twice as many units, which should, hopefully, be more expressive (without dropout, this network would have started overfitting right away—try it). Because networks being regularized with dropout always take much longer to fully converge, we'll train the model for five times as many epochs.

Listing 10.21 Training and evaluating a dropout-regularized LSTM

```
inputs <- layer_input(shape = c(sequence_length, ncol_input_data))
outputs <- inputs %>%
  layer_lstm(32, recurrent_dropout = 0.25) %>%
  layer_dropout(0.5) %>%                        ◁── To regularize the dense layer, we also
  layer_dense(1)                                      add a dropout layer after the LSTM.
model <- keras_model(inputs, outputs)

callbacks <- list(callback_model_checkpoint("jena_lstm_dropout.keras",
                                            save_best_only = TRUE))

model %>% compile(optimizer = "rmsprop",
                  loss = "mse",
                  metrics = "mae")

history <- model %>% fit(
  train_dataset,
  epochs = 50,
  validation_data = val_dataset,
  callbacks = callbacks
)
```

---

[5] See Yarin Gal, "Uncertainty in Deep Learning," PhD thesis (2016), http://mng.bz/WBq1.

Figure 10.11 shows the results. Success! We're no longer overfitting during the first 15 epochs. We achieve a validation MAE as low as 2.37 degrees (2.5% improvement over the no-learning baseline) and a test MAE of 2.45 degrees (6.5% improvement over the baseline). Not too bad.

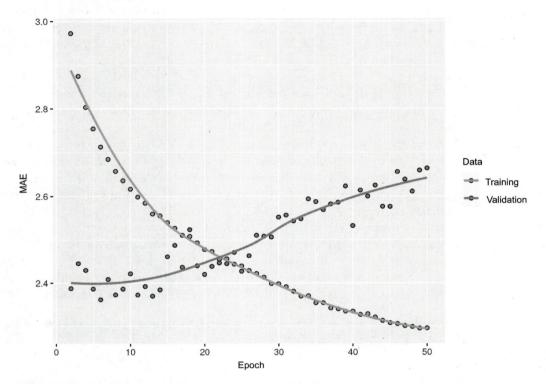

Figure 10.11   Training and validation loss on the Jena temperature-forecasting task with a dropout-regularized LSTM

RNN runtime performance

Recurrent models with very few parameters, like the ones in this chapter, tend to be significantly faster on a multicore CPU than on GPU, because they involve only small matrix multiplications, and the chain of multiplications is not well parallelizable due to the presence of a `for` loop. But larger RNNs can greatly benefit from a GPU runtime.

When using a Keras `LSTM` or `GRU` layer on GPU with default arguments, your layer will be leveraging a cuDNN kernel, a highly optimized, low-level, NVIDIA-provided implementation of the underlying algorithm (I mentioned these in the previous chapter).

As usual, cuDNN kernels are a mixed blessing: they're fast, but inflexible—if you try to do anything not supported by the default kernel, you will suffer a dramatic slow-down, which more or less forces you to stick to what NVIDIA happens to provide.

For instance, recurrent dropout isn't supported by the LSTM and GRU cuDNN kernels, so adding it to your layers forces the runtime to fall back to the regular TensorFlow implementation, which is generally two to five times slower on GPU (even though its computational cost is the same).

As a way to speed up your RNN layer when you can't use cuDNN, you can try *unrolling* it. Unrolling a `for` loop consists of removing the loop and simply inlining its content *N* times. In the case of the `for` loop of an RNN, unrolling can help TensorFlow optimize the underlying computation graph. However, it will also considerably increase the memory consumption of your RNN. As such, it's viable for only relatively small sequences (around 100 steps or fewer). Also, note that you can do this only if the number of time steps in the data is known in advance by the model (that is to say, if you pass a `shape` without any `NA` entries to your initial `layer_input()`). It works like this:

sequence_length cannot be NA.

```
inputs <- layer_input(shape = c(sequence_length, num_features))
x <- inputs %>%
    layer_lstm(32, recurrent_dropout = 0.2, unroll = TRUE)
```

Pass unroll = TRUE to enable unrolling.

10.4.2 Stacking recurrent layers

Because you're no longer overfitting but seem to have hit a performance bottleneck, you should consider increasing the capacity and expressive power of the network. Recall the description of the universal machine learning workflow: it's generally a good idea to increase the capacity of your model until overfitting becomes the primary obstacle (assuming you're already taking basic steps to mitigate overfitting, such as using dropout). As long as you aren't overfitting too badly, you're likely under capacity.

Increasing network capacity is typically done by increasing the number of units in the layers or adding more layers. Recurrent layer stacking is a classic way to build more powerful recurrent networks: for instance, not too long ago the Google Translate algorithm was powered by a stack of seven large LSTM layers—that's huge.

To stack recurrent layers on top of each other in Keras, all intermediate layers should return their full sequence of outputs (a rank 3 tensor) rather than their output at the last time step. As you've already learned, this is done by specifying `return_sequences = TRUE`.

In the following example, we'll try a stack of two dropout-regularized recurrent layers. For a change, we'll use Gated Recurrent Unit (GRU) layers instead of LSTM. GRU is very similar to LSTM—you can think of it as a slightly simpler, streamlined version of the LSTM architecture. It was introduced in 2014 by Cho et al. when recurrent networks were just starting to gain interest anew in the then-tiny research community.[6]

Listing 10.22 Training and evaluating a dropout-regularized, stacked GRU model

```
inputs <- layer_input(shape = c(sequence_length, ncol_input_data))
outputs <- inputs %>%
  layer_gru(32, recurrent_dropout = 0.5, return_sequences = TRUE) %>%
  layer_gru(32, recurrent_dropout = 0.5) %>%
  layer_dropout(0.5) %>%
  layer_dense(1)
model <- keras_model(inputs, outputs)

callbacks <- list(
  callback_model_checkpoint("jena_stacked_gru_dropout.keras",
                            save_best_only = TRUE)
)

model %>% compile(optimizer = "rmsprop",
                  loss = "mse",
                  metrics = "mae")

history <- model %>% fit(
  train_dataset,
  epochs = 50,
  validation_data = val_dataset,
  callbacks = callbacks
)


model <- load_model_tf("jena_stacked_gru_dropout.keras")
sprintf("Test MAE: %.2f", evaluate(model, test_dataset)["mae"])

[1] "Test MAE: 2.42"
```

Figure 10.12 shows the results. We achieve a test MAE of 2.42 degrees (a 7.6% improvement over the baseline). You can see that the added layer does improve the results a bit, though not dramatically. You may be seeing diminishing returns from increasing network capacity at this point.

---

[6] See Cho et al., "On the Properties of Neural Machine Translation: Encoder-Decoder Approaches" (2014), https://arxiv.org/abs/1409.1259.

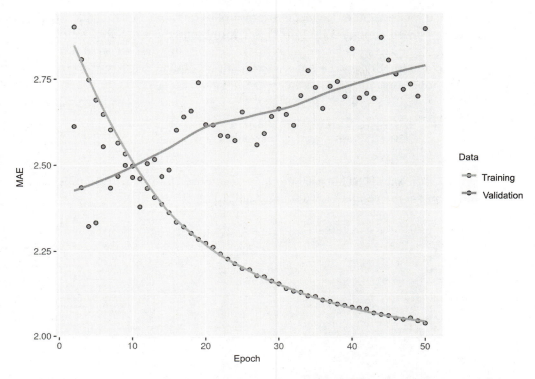

Figure 10.12   Training and validation loss on the Jena temperature-forecasting task with a stacked GRU network

10.4.3 *Using bidirectional RNNs*

The last technique we'll look at in this section is the *bidirectional RNN*. A bidirectional RNN is a common RNN variant that can offer greater performance than a regular RNN on certain tasks. It's frequently used in natural language processing—you could call it the Swiss Army knife of deep learning for natural language processing.

RNNs are notably order dependent: they process the time steps of their input sequences in order, and shuffling or reversing the time steps can completely change the representations the RNN extracts from the sequence. This is precisely the reason they perform well on problems where order is meaningful, such as the temperature-forecasting problem. A bidirectional RNN exploits the order sensitivity of RNNs: it uses two regular RNNs, such as the GRU and LSTM layers you're already familiar with, each of which processes the input sequence in one direction (chronologically and antichronologically), and then merges their representations. By processing a sequence both ways, a bidirectional RNN can catch patterns that may be overlooked by a unidirectional RNN.

Remarkably, the fact that the RNN layers in this section have processed sequences in chronological order (with older time steps first) may have been an arbitrary decision.

At least it's a decision we've made no attempt to question so far. Could the RNNs have performed well enough if they processed input sequences in antichronological order, for instance (with newer time steps first)? Let's try this and see what happens. All you need to do is modify the TF Dataset so the input sequences are reverted along the time dimension. Just transform the dataset with `dataset_map()` like this:

```
ds %>%
  dataset_map(function(samples, targets) {
    list(samples[, NA:NA:-1, ], targets)
  })
```

Training the same LSTM-based model that you used in the first experiment in this section, you get the results shown in figure 10.13.

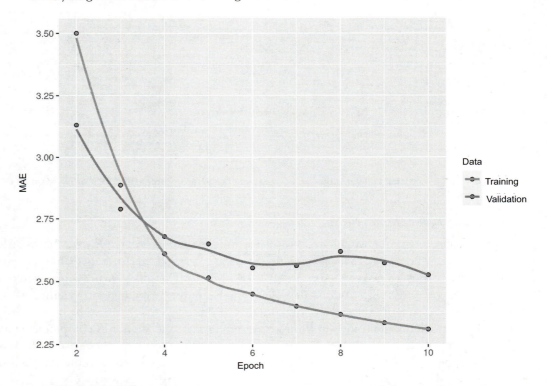

Figure 10.13   Training and validation loss on the Jena temperature-forecasting task with an LSTM trained on reversed sequences

The reversed-order LSTM strongly underperforms even the common-sense baseline, indicating that in this case, chronological processing is important to the success of the approach. This makes perfect sense: the underlying LSTM layer will typically be better at remembering the recent past than the distant past, and naturally the more recent weather data points are more predictive than older data points for the problem (that's what makes the common-sense baseline fairly strong). Thus the chronological version of the layer is bound to outperform the reversed-order version.

However, this isn't true for many other problems, including natural language: intuitively, the importance of a word in understanding a sentence isn't usually dependent on its position in the sentence. On text data, reversed-order processing works just as well as chronological processing—you can read text backward just fine (try it!). Although word order does matter in understanding language, *which order* you use isn't crucial. Importantly, an RNN trained on reversed sequences will learn different representations than one trained on the original sequences, much as you would have different mental models if time flowed backward in the real world—if you lived a life where you died on your first day and were born on your last day. In machine learning, representations that are *different* yet *useful* are always worth exploiting, and the more they differ, the better: they offer a new angle from which to look at your data, capturing aspects of the data that were missed by other approaches, and thus they can help boost performance on a task. This is the intuition behind *ensembling*, a concept we'll explore in chapter 13.

A bidirectional RNN exploits this idea to improve on the performance of chronological-order RNNs. It looks at its input sequence both ways (see figure 10.14), obtaining potentially richer representations and capturing patterns that may have been missed by the chronological-order version alone.

To instantiate a bidirectional RNN in Keras, you use the `bidirectional()` layer, which takes as its first argument a recurrent layer instance. `bidirectional()` creates a second, separate instance of this recurrent layer and uses one instance for processing the input sequences in chronological order and the other instance for processing the input sequences in reversed order. You can try it on our temperature-forecasting task.

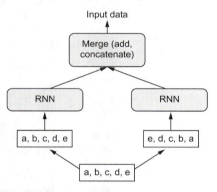

Figure 10.14   How a bidirectional RNN layer works

```
inputs <- layer_input(shape = c(sequence_length, ncol_input_data))
outputs <- inputs %>%
  bidirectional(layer_lstm(units = 16)) %>%
  layer_dense(1)

model <- keras_model(inputs, outputs)

model %>% compile(optimizer = "rmsprop",
                  loss = "mse",
                  metrics = "mae")
```

Note that layer_lstm() is not composed with inputs directly.

```
history <- model %>%
  fit(train_dataset,
      epochs = 10,
      validation_data = val_dataset)
```

You'll find that it doesn't perform as well as the plain `layer_lstm()`. It's easy to understand why: all the predictive capacity must come from the chronological half of the network, because the antichronological half is known to be severely underperforming on this task (again, because the recent past matters much more than the distant past, in this case). At the same time, the presence of the antichronological half doubles the network's capacity and causes it to start overfitting much earlier.

However, bidirectional RNNs are a great fit for text data, or any other kind of data where order matters, yet where *which order* you use doesn't matter. In fact, for a while in 2016, bidirectional LSTMs were considered the state of the art on many natural language processing tasks (before the rise of the Transformer architecture, which you will learn about in the next chapter).

10.4.4 *Going even further*

There are many other things you could try in order to improve performance on the temperature-forecasting problem:

- Adjust the number of units in each recurrent layer in the stacked setup, as well as the amount of dropout. The current choices are largely arbitrary and thus probably suboptimal.
- Adjust the learning rate used by the RMSprop optimizer, or try a different optimizer.
- Try using a stack of `layer_dense()` as the regressor on top of the recurrent layer, instead of a single `layer_dense()`.
- Improve the input to the model: try using longer or shorter sequences or a different sampling rate, or start doing feature engineering.

As always, deep learning is more an art than a science. We can provide guidelines that suggest what is likely to work or not work on a given problem, but, ultimately, every dataset is unique; you'll have to evaluate different strategies empirically. There is currently no theory that will tell you in advance precisely what you should do to optimally solve a problem. You must iterate.

In my experience, improving on the no-learning baseline by about 10% is likely the best you can do with this dataset. This isn't so great, but these results make sense: while near-future weather is highly predictable if you have access to data from a wide grid of different locations, it's not very predictable if you have measurements only from a single location. The evolution of the weather where you are depends on current weather patterns in surrounding locations.

Markets and machine learning

Some readers are bound to want to take the techniques I've introduced here and try them on the problem of forecasting the future price of securities on the stock market (or currency exchange rates, and so on). However, markets have very different statistical characteristics than natural phenomena such as weather patterns. When it comes to markets, past performance is *not* a good predictor of future returns—looking in the rear-view mirror is a bad way to drive. Machine learning, on the other hand, is applicable to datasets where the past *is* a good predictor of the future, like weather, electricity consumption, or foot traffic at a store.

Always remember that all trading is fundamentally *information arbitrage*: gaining an advantage by leveraging data or insights that other market participants are missing. Trying to use well-known machine learning techniques and publicly available data to beat the markets is effectively a dead end, because you won't have any information advantage compared to everyone else. You're likely to waste your time and resources with nothing to show for it.

Summary

- As you first learned in chapter 5, when approaching a new problem, it's good to first establish common-sense baselines for your metric of choice. If you don't have a baseline to beat, you can't tell whether you're making real progress.
- Try simple models before expensive ones, to make sure the additional expense is justified. Sometimes a simple model will turn out to be your best option.
- When you have data where ordering matters, and in particular for time-series data, *recurrent networks* are a great fit and easily outperform models that first flatten the temporal data. The two essential RNN layers available in Keras are the LSTM layer and the GRU layer.
- To use dropout with recurrent networks, you should use a time-constant dropout mask and recurrent dropout mask. These are built into Keras recurrent layers, so all you have to do is use the recurrent_dropout arguments of recurrent layers.
- Stacked RNNs provide more representational power than a single RNN layer. They're also much more expensive and thus not always worth it. Although they offer clear gains on complex problems (such as machine translation), they may not always be relevant to smaller, simpler problems.

Deep learning for text

11.1 Natural language processing: The bird's-eye view

In computer science, we refer to human languages, like English or Mandarin, as "natural" languages, to distinguish them from languages that were designed for machines, like Assembly, LISP, or XML. Every machine language was *designed*: its starting point was a human engineer writing down a set of formal rules to describe what statements you could make in that language and what they meant. Rules came first, and people started using the language only once the rule set was complete. With human language, it's the reverse: usage comes first, and rules arise later. Natural language was shaped by an evolution process, much like biological organisms— that's what makes it "natural." Its "rules," like the grammar of English, were formalized after the fact and are often ignored or broken by its users. As a result, although machine-readable language is highly structured and rigorous, using precise syntactic rules to weave together exactly defined concepts from a fixed vocabulary, natural language is messy—ambiguous, chaotic, sprawling, and constantly in flux.

Creating algorithms that can make sense of natural language is a big deal: language—and in particular, text—underpins most of our communications and our cultural production. The internet is mostly text. Language is how we store almost all of our knowledge. Our very thoughts are largely built upon language. However, the ability to understand natural language has long eluded machines. Some people once naively thought that you could simply write down the "rule set of English," much like one can write down the rule set of LISP. Early attempts to build natural language processing (NLP) systems were thus made through the lens of "applied linguistics." Engineers and linguists would handcraft complex sets of rules to perform basic machine translation or create simple chatbots, like the famous ELIZA program from the 1960s, which used pattern matching to sustain very basic conversation. But language is a rebellious thing: it's not easily pliable to formalization. After several decades of effort, the capabilities of these systems remained disappointing.

Handcrafted rules held out as the dominant approach well into the 1990s. But starting in the late 1980s, faster computers and greater data availability started making a better alternative viable. When you find yourself building systems that are big piles of ad hoc rules, as a clever engineer, you're likely to start asking: "Could I use a corpus of data to automate the process of finding these rules? Could I search for the rules within some kind of rule space, instead of having to come up with them myself?" And just like that, you've graduated to doing machine learning. And so, in the late 1980s, we started seeing machine learning approaches to natural language processing. The earliest ones were based on decision trees—the intent was literally to automate the development of the kind of if/then/else rules of previous systems. Then statistical approaches started gaining speed, starting with logistic regression. Over time, learned parametric models fully took over, and linguistics came to be seen as more of a hindrance than a useful tool. Frederick Jelinek, an early speech recognition researcher, joked in the 1990s: "Every time I fire a linguist, the performance of the speech recognizer goes up."

That's what modern NLP is about: using machine learning and large datasets to give computers the ability not to *understand* language, which is a more lofty goal, but to ingest a piece of language as input and return something useful, like predicting the following:

- "What's the topic of this text?" (text classification)
- "Does this text contain abuse?" (content filtering)
- "Does this text sound positive or negative?" (sentiment analysis)
- "What should be the next word in this incomplete sentence?" (language modeling)
- "How would you say this in German?" (translation)
- "How would you summarize this article in one paragraph?" (summarization)
- And so on.

Of course, keep in mind throughout this chapter that the text-processing models you will train won't possess a human-like understanding of language; rather, they simply look for statistical regularities in their input data, which turns out to be sufficient to perform well on many simple tasks. In much the same way that computer vision is pattern recognition applied to pixels, NLP is pattern recognition applied to words, sentences, and paragraphs.

The toolset of NLP—decision trees and logistic regression—saw only slow evolution from the 1990s to the early 2010s. Most of the research focus was on feature engineering. When I (François) won my first NLP competition on Kaggle in 2013, my model was, you guessed it, based on decision trees and logistic regression. However, around 2014–2015, things started changing at last. Multiple researchers began to investigate the language-understanding capabilities of recurrent neural networks, in particular LSTM—a sequence-processing algorithm from the late 1990s that had stayed under the radar until then.

In early 2015, Keras made available the first open source, easy-to-use implementation of LSTM, just at the start of a massive wave of renewed interest in recurrent neural networks. Until then, there had only been "research code" that couldn't be readily reused. Then from 2015 to 2017, recurrent neural networks dominated the booming NLP scene. Bidirectional LSTM models, in particular, set the state of the art on many important tasks, from summarization to question-answering to machine translation.

Finally, around 2017–2018, a new architecture rose to replace RNNs: the Transformer, which you will learn about in the second half of this chapter. Transformers unlocked considerable progress across the field in a short period of time, and today most NLP systems are based on them.

Let's dive into the details. This chapter will take you from the very basics to doing machine translation with a Transformer.

11.2 Preparing text data

Deep learning models, being differentiable functions, can process only numeric tensors: they can't take raw text as input. *Vectorizing* text is the process of transforming text into numeric tensors. Text vectorization processes come in many shapes and forms, but they all follow the same template (see figure 11.1):

- First, you *standardize* the text to make it easier to process, such as by converting it to lowercase or removing punctuation.
- You split the text into units (called *tokens*), such as characters, words, or groups of words. This is called *tokenization*.
- You convert each such token into a numerical vector. This will usually involve first *indexing* all tokens present in the data.

Let's review each of these steps.

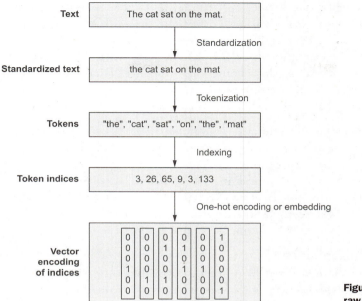

Figure 11.1   From raw text to vectors

11.2.1 Text standardization

Consider these two sentences:

- "sunset came. i was staring at the Mexico sky. Isnt nature splendid??"
- "Sunset came; I stared at the México sky. Isn't nature splendid?"

They're very similar—in fact, they're almost identical. Yet, if you were to convert them to byte strings, they would end up with very different representations, because "i" and "I" are two different characters, "Mexico" and "México" are two different words, "isnt" isn't "isn't," and so on. A machine learning model doesn't know a priori that "i" and "I" are the same letter, that "é" is an "e" with an accent, or that "staring" and "stared" are two forms of the same verb.

   Text standardization is a basic form of feature engineering that aims to erase encoding differences that you don't want your model to have to deal with. It's not exclusive to machine learning, either—you'd have to do the same thing if you were building a search engine.

   One of the simplest and most widespread standardization schemes is "convert to lowercase and remove punctuation characters." Our two sentences would become

- "sunset came i was staring at the mexico sky isnt nature splendid"
- "sunset came i stared at the méxico sky isnt nature splendid"

Much closer already. Another common transformation is to convert special characters to a standard form, such as replacing "é" with "e," "æ" with "ae," and so on. Our token "méxico" would then become "mexico".

Lastly, a much more advanced standardization pattern that is more rarely used in a machine learning context is *stemming*: converting variations of a term (such as different conjugated forms of a verb) into a single shared representation, like turning "caught" and "been catching" into "[catch]" or "cats" into "[cat]". With stemming, "was staring" and "stared" would become something like "[stare]", and our two similar sentences would finally end up with an identical encoding:

- "sunset came i [stare] at the mexico sky isnt nature splendid"

With these standardization techniques, your model will require less training data and will generalize better—it won't need abundant examples of both "Sunset" and "sunset" to learn that they mean the same thing, and it will be able to make sense of "México", even if it has only seen "mexico" in its training set. Of course, standardization may also erase some amount of information, so always keep the context in mind: for instance, if you're writing a model that extracts questions from interview articles, it should definitely treat "?" as a separate token instead of dropping it, because it's a useful signal for this specific task.

11.2.2 Text splitting (tokenization)

Once your text is standardized, you need to break it up into units to be vectorized (tokens), a step called *tokenization*. You could do this in three different ways:

- *Word-level tokenization*—Where tokens are space-separated (or punctuation-separated) substrings. A variant of this is to further split words into subwords when applicable, for instance, treating "staring" as "star+ing" or "called" as "call+ed."
- *N-gram tokenization*—Where tokens are groups of *N* consecutive words. For instance, "the cat" or "he was" would be 2-gram tokens (also called bigrams).
- *Character-level tokenization*—Where each character is its own token. In practice, this scheme is rarely used, and you only really see it in specialized contexts, like text generation or speech recognition.

In general, you'll always use either word-level or *N*-gram tokenization. There are two kinds of text-processing models: those that care about word order, called *sequence models*, and those that treat input words as a set, discarding their original order, called *bag-of-words models*. If you're building a sequence model, you'll use word-level tokenization, and if you're building a bag-of-words model, you'll use *N*-gram tokenization. *N*-grams are a way to artificially inject a small amount of local word-order information into the model. Throughout this chapter, you'll learn more about each type of model and when to use them.

> ### Understanding *N*-grams and bag-of-words
>
> Word *N*-grams are groups of *N* (or fewer) consecutive words that you can extract from a sentence. The same concept may also be applied to characters instead of words.
>
> Here's a simple example. Consider the sentence "the cat sat on the mat." It may be decomposed into the following set of 2-grams:
>
> ```
> c("the", "the cat", "cat", "cat sat", "sat",
>  "sat on", "on", "on the", "the mat", "mat")
> ```

It may also be decomposed into the following set of 3-grams:

```
c("the", "the cat", "cat", "cat sat", "the cat sat",
  "sat", "sat on", "on", "cat sat on", "on the",
  "sat on the", "the mat", "mat", "on the mat")
```

Such a set is called a *bag-of-2-grams or bag-of-3-grams*, respectively. The term "bag" here refers to the fact that you're dealing with a set of tokens rather than a list or sequence: the tokens have no specific order. This family of tokenization methods is called *bag-of-words* (or *bag-of-N-grams*).

Because bag-of-words isn't an order-preserving tokenization method (the tokens generated are understood as a set, not a sequence, and the general structure of the sentences is lost), it tends to be used in shallow language-processing models rather than in deep learning models. Extracting *N*-grams is a form of feature engineering, and deep learning sequence models do away with this manual approach, replacing it with hierarchical feature learning. One-dimensional convnets, recurrent neural networks, and Transformers are capable of learning representations for groups of words and characters without being explicitly told about the existence of such groups, by looking at continuous word or character sequences.

11.2.3 *Vocabulary indexing*

Once your text is split into tokens, you need to encode each token into a numerical representation. You could potentially do this in a stateless way, such as by hashing each token into a fixed binary vector, but in practice, the way you'd go about it is to build an index of all terms found in the training data (the "vocabulary"), and assign a unique integer to each entry in the vocabulary, something like this:

```
vocabulary <- character()
for (string in text_dataset) {
  tokens <- string %>%
    standardize() %>%
    tokenize()
  vocabulary <- unique(c(vocabulary, tokens))
}
```

You can then convert the integer index position into a vector encoding that can be processed by a neural network, like a one-hot vector:

```
one_hot_encode_token <- function(token) {
  vector <- array(0, dim = length(vocabulary))
  token_index <- match(token, vocabulary)
  vector[token_index] <- 1
  vector
}
```

Note that at this step it's common to restrict the vocabulary to only the top 20,000 or 30,000 most common words found in the training data. Any text dataset tends to feature an extremely large number of unique terms, most of which show up only once or twice. Indexing those rare terms would result in an excessively large feature space, where most features would have almost no information content.

Remember when you were training your first deep learning models on the IMDB dataset in chapters 4 and 5? The data you were using from `dataset_imdb()` was already preprocessed into sequences of integers, where each integer stood for a given word. Back then, we used the setting `num_words = 10000`, to restrict our vocabulary to the top 10,000 most common words found in the training data.

Now, there's an important detail here that we shouldn't overlook: when we look up a new token in our vocabulary index, it may not necessarily exist. Your training data may not have contained any instance of the word "cherimoya" (or maybe you excluded it from your index because it was too rare), so doing `token_index = match("cherimoya", vocabulary)` may return `NA`. To handle this, you should use an "out of vocabulary" index (abbreviated as *OOV index*)—a catch-all for any token that wasn't in the index. It's usually index 1: you're actually doing `token_index = match("cherimoya", vocabulary, nomatch = 1)`. When decoding a sequence of integers back into words, you'll replace 1 with something like "[UNK]" (which you'd call an "OOV token").

"Why use 1 and not 0?" you may ask. That's because 0 is already taken. There are two special tokens that you will commonly use: the OOV token (index 1), and the *mask token* (index 0). Although the OOV token means "here was a word we did not recognize," the mask token tells us "ignore me, I'm not a word." You'd use it in particular to pad sequence data: because data batches need to be contiguous, all sequences in a batch of sequence data must have the same length, so shorter sequences should be padded to the length of the longest sequence. If you want to make a batch of data with the sequences `c(5, 7, 124, 4, 89)` and `c(8, 34, 21)`, it would have to look like this:

```
rbind(c(5,  7, 124, 4, 89),
      c(8, 34,  21, 0,  0))
```

The batches of integer sequences for the IMDB dataset that you worked with in chapters 4 and 5 were padded with zeros in this way.

11.2.4   *Using layer_text_vectorization*

Every step I've introduced so far would be very easy to implement in pure R. Maybe you could write something like this:

```
new_vectorizer <- function() {
  self <- new.env(parent = emptyenv())
  attr(self, "class") <- "Vectorizer"

  self$vocabulary <- c("[UNK]")
```

```
  self$standardize <- function(text) {
    text <- tolower(text)
    gsub("[[:punct:]]", "", text)    <———— Remove punctuation.
  }

  self$tokenize <- function(text) {                        Split on whitespace and return
    unlist(strsplit(text, "[[:space:]]+"))    <——          a flattened character vector.
  }
                                                           text_dataset will be a vector of
  self$make_vocabulary <- function(text_dataset) {  <——    strings, that is, an R character
    tokens <- text_dataset %>%                             vector.
      self$standardize() %>%
      self$tokenize()
    self$vocabulary <- unique(c(self$vocabulary, tokens))
  }

  self$encode <- function(text) {
    tokens <- text %>%
      self$standardize() %>%
      self$tokenize()                                      nomatch matches
    match(tokens, table = self$vocabulary, nomatch = 1)  <—— to "[UNK]".
  }

  self$decode <- function(int_sequence) {        The mask token is typically
    vocab_w_mask_token <- c("", self$vocabulary)  encoded as a 0 integer, and
    vocab_w_mask_token[int_sequence + 1]    <——   decoded as an empty string: "".
  }

  self
}


vectorizer <- new_vectorizer()

dataset <- c("I write, erase, rewrite",    <———— Haiku by poet Hokushi
             "Erase again, and then",
             "A poppy blooms.")

vectorizer$make_vocabulary(dataset)
```

It does the job:

```
test_sentence <- "I write, rewrite, and still rewrite again"
encoded_sentence <- vectorizer$encode(test_sentence)
print(encoded_sentence)
```

```
[1] 2 3 5 7 1 5 6
```

```
decoded_sentence <- vectorizer$decode(encoded_sentence)
print(decoded_sentence)
```

```
[1] "i"       "write"   "rewrite" "and"     "[UNK]"   "rewrite" "again"
```

However, using something like this wouldn't be very performant. In practice, you'll work with the Keras `layer_text_vectorization()`, which is fast and efficient and can be dropped directly into a TF Dataset pipeline or a Keras model. This is what `layer_text_vectorization()` looks like:

```
text_vectorization <-
  layer_text_vectorization(output_mode = "int")
```

Configure the layer to return sequences of words encoded as integer indices. There are several other output modes available, which you will see in action in a bit.

By default, `layer_text_vectorization()` will use the setting "convert to lowercase and remove punctuation" for text standardization, and "split on whitespace" for tokenization. But importantly, you can provide custom functions for standardization and tokenization, which means the layer is flexible enough to handle any use case. Note that such custom functions should operate on `tf.string` dtype tensors, not regular R character vectors! For instance, the default layer behavior is equivalent to the following:

```
library(tensorflow)
custom_standardization_fn <- function(string_tensor) {
  string_tensor %>%
    tf$strings$lower() %>%
    tf$strings$regex_replace("[[:punct:]]", "")
}

custom_split_fn <- function(string_tensor) {
  tf$strings$split(string_tensor)
}

text_vectorization <- layer_text_vectorization(
  output_mode = "int",
  standardize = custom_standardization_fn,
  split = custom_split_fn
)
```

Convert strings to lowercase.

Replace punctuation characters with the empty string.

Split strings on whitespace.

To index the vocabulary of a text corpus, just call the `adapt()` method of the layer with a TF Dataset object that yields strings, or just with an R character vector:

```
dataset <- c("I write, erase, rewrite",
             "Erase again, and then",
             "A poppy blooms.")
adapt(text_vectorization, dataset)
```

Note that you can retrieve the computed vocabulary via `get_vocabulary()`. This can be useful if you need to convert text encoded as integer sequences back into words. The first two entries in the vocabulary are the mask token (index 0) and the OOV token (index 1). Entries in the vocabulary list are sorted by frequency, so with a real-world dataset, very common words like "the" or "a" would come first.

Listing 11.1 Displaying the vocabulary

```
get_vocabulary(text_vectorization)
```

```
[1] ""          "[UNK]"  "erase"  "write"  "then"    "rewrite" "poppy"
[8] "i"          "blooms" "and"    "again"  "a"
```

For a demonstration, let's try to encode and then decode an example sentence:

```
vocabulary <- text_vectorization %>% get_vocabulary()
test_sentence <- "I write, rewrite, and still rewrite again"
encoded_sentence <- text_vectorization(test_sentence)
decoded_sentence <- paste(vocabulary[as.integer(encoded_sentence) + 1],
                          collapse = " ")

encoded_sentence
```

```
tf.Tensor([ 7  3  5  9  1  5 10], shape=(7), dtype=int64)
```

```
decoded_sentence
```

```
[1] "i write rewrite and [UNK] rewrite again"
```

Using `layer_text_vectorization()` in a TF Dataset pipeline or as part of a model

Because `layer_text_vectorization()` is mostly a dictionary lookup operation that converts tokens to integers, it can't be executed on a GPU (or TPU)—only on a CPU. So, if you're training your model on a GPU, your `layer_text_vectorization()` will run on the CPU before sending its output to the GPU. This has important performance implications.

There are two ways we could use our `layer_text_vectorization()`. The first option is to put it in the TF Dataset pipeline, like this:

```
int_sequence_dataset <- string_dataset %>%     ◁── string_dataset would be a TF
  dataset_map(text_vectorization,                  Dataset that yields string tensors.
              num_parallel_calls = 4)     ◁──  The num_parallel_calls argument is
                                                used to parallelize the dataset_map()
                                                call across multiple CPU cores.
```

The second option is to make it part of the model (after all, it's a Keras layer), like this (in pseudocode):

```
                                         Create a symbolic input that expects strings.
text_input <- layer_input(shape = shape(), dtype = "string")  ◁──
vectorized_text <- text_vectorization(text_input)  ◁──
embedded_input <- vectorized_text %>% layer_embedding(...)      Apply the text
output <- embedded_input %>% ...   ◁──                          vectorization
model <- keras_model(text_input, output)                       layer to it.
```

You can keep chaining new layers on top—
just your regular Functional API model.

(continued)

There's an important difference between the two: if the vectorization step is part of the model, it will happen synchronously with the rest of the model. This means that at each training step, the rest of the model (placed on the GPU) will have to wait for the output of the `layer_text_vectorization()` (placed on the CPU) to be ready before it can get to work. Meanwhile, putting the layer in the TF Dataset pipeline enables you to do asynchronous preprocessing of your data on CPU: while the GPU runs the model on one batch of vectorized data, the CPU stays busy by vectorizing the next batch of raw strings.

If you're training the model on GPU or TPU, you'll probably want to go with the first option to get the best performance. This is what we will do in all practical examples throughout this chapter. When training on a CPU, though, synchronous processing is fine: you will get 100% utilization of your cores, regardless of which option you go with.

Now, if you were to export our model to a production environment, you would want to ship a model that accepts raw strings as input, like in the code snippet for the second option above; otherwise, you would have to reimplement text standardization and tokenization in your production environment (maybe in JavaScript?), and you would face the risk of introducing small preprocessing discrepancies that would hurt the model's accuracy. Thankfully, the `layer_text_vectorization()` enables you to include text preprocessing right into your model, making it easier to deploy, even if you were originally using the layer as part of a TF Dataset pipeline. In the sidebar box later in the chapter, "Exporting a model that processes raw strings," you'll learn how to export an inference-only trained model that incorporates text preprocessing.

You've now learned everything you need to know about text preprocessing. Let's move on to the modeling stage.

11.3 Two approaches for representing groups of words: Sets and sequences

How a machine learning model should represent *individual words* is a relatively uncontroversial question: they're categorical features (values from a predefined set), and we know how to handle those. They should be encoded as dimensions in a feature space, or as category vectors (word vectors in this case). A much more problematic question, however, is how to encode *the way words are woven into sentences*: word order.

The problem of order in natural language is an interesting one: unlike the steps of a time series, words in a sentence don't have a natural, canonical order. Different languages order similar words in very different ways. For instance, the sentence structure of English is quite different from that of Japanese. Even within a given language, you can typically say the same thing in different ways by reshuffling the words a bit. Even further, if you fully randomize the words in a short sentence, you can still largely figure out what it was saying, though in many cases, significant ambiguity seems to arise. Order is clearly important, but its relationship to meaning isn't straightforward.

How to represent word order is the pivotal question from which different kinds of NLP architectures spring. The simplest thing you could do is just discard order and treat text as an unordered set of words—this gives you bag-of-words models. You could also decide that words should be processed strictly in the order in which they appear, one at a time, like steps in a time series—you could then leverage the recurrent models from the last chapter. Finally, a hybrid approach is also possible: the Transformer architecture is technically order agnostic, yet it injects word-position information into the representations it processes, which enables it to simultaneously look at different parts of a sentence (unlike RNNs) while still being order aware. Because they take into account word order, both RNNs and Transformers are called *sequence models*.

Historically, most early applications of machine learning to NLP just involved bag-of-words models. Interest in sequence models started rising only in 2015, with the rebirth of recurrent neural networks. Today, both approaches remain relevant. Let's see how they work and when to leverage which.

We'll demonstrate each approach on a well-known text classification benchmark: the IMDB movie review sentiment-classification dataset. In chapters 4 and 5, you worked with a prevectorized version of the IMDB dataset; now let's process the raw IMDB text data, just like you would do when approaching a new text-classification problem in the real world.

11.3.1   *Preparing the IMDB movie reviews data*

Let's start by downloading the dataset from the Stanford page of Andrew Maas and uncompressing it:

```
url <- "https://ai.stanford.edu/~amaas/data/sentiment/aclImdb_v1.tar.gz"
filename <- basename(url)
options(timeout = 60 * 10)          ◁——— 10-minute timeout
download.file(url, destfile = filename)
untar(filename)
```

You're left with a directory named aclImdb, with the following structure:

```
fs::dir_tree("aclImdb", recurse = 1, type = "directory")
```

```
aclImdb
├── test
│   ├── neg
│   └── pos
└── train
    ├── neg
    └── pos
```

For instance, the train/pos/ directory contains a set of 12,500 text files, each of which contains the text body of a positive-sentiment movie review to be used as training data. The negative-sentiment reviews live in the "neg" directories. In total, there are 25,000 text files for training and another 25,000 for testing.

There's also a train/unsup subdirectory in there, which we don't need. Let's delete it:

```
fs::dir_delete("aclImdb/train/unsup/")
```

Take a look at the content of a few of these text files. Whether you're working with text data or image data, remember to always inspect what your data looks like before you dive into modeling it. It will ground your intuition about what your model is actually doing:

```
writeLines(readLines("aclImdb/train/pos/4077_10.txt", warn = FALSE))
```

```
I first saw this back in the early 90s on UK TV, i did like it then but i
missed the chance to tape it, many years passed but the film always stuck
with me and i lost hope of seeing it TV again, the main thing that stuck
with me was the end, the hole castle part really touched me, its easy to
watch, has a great story, great music, the list goes on and on, its OK me
saying how good it is but everyone will take there own best bits away with
them once they have seen it, yes the animation is top notch and beautiful
to watch, it does show its age in a very few parts but that has now become
part of it beauty, i am so glad it has came out on DVD as it is one of my
top 10 films of all time. Buy it or rent it just see it, best viewing is
at night alone with drink and food in reach so you don't have to stop the
film.<br /><br />Enjoy
```

Next, let's prepare a validation set by setting apart 20% of the training text files in a new directory, aclImdb/val. As before, we'll use the fs R package:

```
library(fs)
set.seed(1337)          ◁    Set a seed, to ensure we get
base_dir <- path("aclImdb")      the same validation set from
                                  the sample() call every time
                                  we run the code.

for (category in c("neg", "pos")) {
  filepaths <- dir_ls(base_dir / "train" / category)
  num_val_samples <- round(0.2 * length(filepaths))   ◁  Take 20% of the training
  val_files <- sample(filepaths, num_val_samples)        files to use for validation.

  dir_create(base_dir / "val" / category)      Move the files to aclImdb/val/neg
  file_move(val_files,              ◁          and aclImdb/val/pos.
            base_dir / "val" / category)
}
```

Remember how, in chapter 8, we used the `image_dataset_from_directory()` utility to create a batched TF Dataset of images and their labels for a directory structure? You can do the exact same thing for text files using the `text_dataset_from_directory()` utility. Let's create three TF Dataset objects for training, validation, and testing:

```
library(keras)          Running this line should output "Found 20000 files belonging to 2
library(tfdatasets)     classes"; if you see "Found 70000 files belonging to 3 classes," it
                        means you forgot to delete the aclImdb/train/unsup directory.

train_ds <- text_dataset_from_directory("aclImdb/train")    ◁
val_ds <- text_dataset_from_directory("aclImdb/val")
test_ds <- text_dataset_from_directory("aclImdb/test")      ◁
```

The default batch_size is 32. If you encounter out-of-memory errors when
training models on your machine, you can try a smaller batch_size:
text_dataset_from_directory("aclImdb/train", batch_size = 8).

These datasets yield inputs that are TensorFlow `tf.string` tensors and targets that are `int32` tensors encoding the value "0" or "1."

Listing 11.2   Displaying the shapes and dtypes of the first batch

```
c(inputs, targets) %<-% iter_next(as_iterator(train_ds))
str(inputs)
```

```
  <tf.Tensor: shape=(32), dtype=string, numpy=…>
```

```
str(targets)
```

```
  <tf.Tensor: shape=(32), dtype=int32, numpy=…>
```

```
inputs[1]
```

```
tf.Tensor(b'Let me start by saying that I\'d read a number of reviews before
renting this film and kind of knew what to expect. Still, I was surprised by
just how bad it was. <br /><br />I am a big werewolf fan, and have grown
...
Otherwise, give this one a miss.', shape=(), dtype=string)
```

```
targets[1]
```

```
tf.Tensor(0, shape=(), dtype=int32)
```

All set. Now let's try learning something from this data.

11.3.2   Processing words as a set: The bag-of-words approach

The simplest way to encode a piece of text for processing by a machine learning model is to discard order and treat it as a set (a "bag") of tokens. You could either look at individual words (unigrams) or try to recover some local order information by looking at groups of consecutive tokens (*N*-grams).

SINGLE WORDS (UNIGRAMS) WITH BINARY ENCODING

If you use a bag of single words, the sentence "the cat sat on the mat" becomes a character vector where we ignore order:

```
c("cat", "mat", "on", "sat", "the")
```

The main advantage of this encoding is that you can represent an entire text as a single vector, where each entry is a presence indicator for a given word. For instance, using binary encoding (multi-hot), you'd encode a text as a vector with as many dimensions as there are words in your vocabulary, with 0s almost everywhere and some 1s for dimensions that encode words present in the text. This is what we did when we worked with text data in chapters 4 and 5. Let's try this on our task.

First, let's process our raw text datasets with a `layer_text_vectorization()` layer so that they yield multi-hot-encoded binary word vectors. Our layer will look only at single words (that is to say, *unigrams*).

Listing 11.3   Preprocessing our datasets with `layer_text_vectorization()`

Limit the vocabulary to the 20,000 most frequent words. Otherwise we'd be indexing every word in the training data—potentially tens of thousands of terms that occur only once or twice and thus aren't informative. In general, 20,000 is the right vocabulary size for text classification.

```
text_vectorization <-
    layer_text_vectorization(max_tokens = 20000,
                             output_mode = "multi_hot")
```

Encode the output tokens as multi-hot binary vectors.

```
text_only_train_ds <- train_ds %>%
    dataset_map(function(x, y) x)

adapt(text_vectorization, text_only_train_ds)
```

Prepare a dataset that yields only raw text inputs (no labels).

Use that dataset to index the dataset vocabulary via the adapt() method.

```
binary_1gram_train_ds <- train_ds %>%
    dataset_map( ~ list(text_vectorization(.x), .y),
                num_parallel_calls = 4)
binary_1gram_val_ds <- val_ds %>%
    dataset_map( ~ list(text_vectorization(.x), .y),
                num_parallel_calls = 4)
binary_1gram_test_ds <- test_ds %>%
    dataset_map( ~ list(text_vectorization(.x), .y),
                num_parallel_calls = 4)
```

Prepare processed versions of our training, validation, and test dataset. Make sure to specify num_parallel_calls to leverage multiple CPU cores.

~ formula function definition

For the `map_func` argument to `dataset_map()`, we passed a formula defined with `~`, not a function. If the `map_func` argument is a formula, e.g. `~ .x + 2`, it is converted to a function. There are three ways to refer to the arguments:

- For a single argument function, use `.x`.
- For a two argument function, use `.x` and `.y`.
- For more arguments, use `..1`, `..2`, `..3` and so on.

This syntax allows you to create very compact anonymous functions. For more details and examples, see the `?purrr::map()` help page in R.

You can try to inspect the output of one of these datasets.

Listing 11.4   Inspecting the output of our binary unigram dataset

```
c(inputs, targets) %<-% iter_next(as_iterator(binary_1gram_train_ds))
str(inputs)
```
```
<tf.Tensor: shape=(32, 20000), dtype=float32, numpy=…>
```
```
str(targets)
```
```
<tf.Tensor: shape=(32), dtype=int32, numpy=…>
```
```
inputs[1, ]
```

Inputs are batches of 20,000-dimensional vectors. These vectors consist entirely of ones and zeros.

```
tf.Tensor([1. 1. 1. ... 0. 0. 0.], shape=(20000), dtype=float32)

targets[1]
```

```
tf.Tensor(1, shape=(), dtype=int32)
```

Next, let's write a reusable model-building function that we'll use in all of our experiments in this section.

```
get_model <- function(max_tokens = 20000, hidden_dim = 16) {
  inputs <- layer_input(shape = c(max_tokens))
  outputs <- inputs %>%
    layer_dense(hidden_dim, activation = "relu") %>%
    layer_dropout(0.5) %>%
    layer_dense(1, activation = "sigmoid")
  model <- keras_model(inputs, outputs)
  model %>% compile(optimizer = "rmsprop",
                    loss = "binary_crossentropy",
                    metrics = "accuracy")
  model
}
```

Finally, let's train and test our model.

```
model <- get_model()
model
```

```
Model: "model"

_____
 Layer (type)                Output Shape              Param #
========================================================================
 input_1 (InputLayer)        [(None, 20000)]           0
 dense_1 (Dense)             (None, 16)                320016
 dropout (Dropout)           (None, 16)                0
 dense (Dense)               (None, 1)                 17
========================================================================
Total params: 320,033
Trainable params: 320,033
Non-trainable params: 0
_____
```

```
callbacks <- list(
  callback_model_checkpoint("binary_1gram.keras", save_best_only = TRUE)
)

model %>% fit(
  dataset_cache(binary_1gram_train_ds),
```

```
      validation_data = dataset_cache(binary_1gram_val_ds),
      epochs = 10,
      callbacks = callbacks
  )

model <- load_model_tf("binary_1gram.keras")
cat(sprintf(
  "Test acc: %.3f\n", evaluate(model, binary_1gram_test_ds)["accuracy"]))
```

Test acc: 0.887

We call dataset_cache() on the datasets to cache them in memory: this way, we will do the preprocessing only once, during the first epoch, and we'll reuse the preprocessed texts for the following epochs. This can only be done if the data is small enough to fit in memory.

This gets us to a test accuracy of 88.7%: not bad! Note that in this case, because the dataset is a balanced two-class classification dataset (there are as many positive samples as negative samples), the "naive baseline" we could reach without training an actual model would only be 50%. Meanwhile, the best score that can be achieved on this dataset without leveraging external data is around 95% test accuracy.

BIGRAMS WITH BINARY ENCODING

Of course, discarding word order is very reductive, because even atomic concepts can be expressed via multiple words: the term "United States" conveys a concept that is quite distinct from the meaning of the words "states" and "united" taken separately. For this reason, you will usually end up re-injecting local order information into your bag-of-words representation by looking at *N*-grams rather than single words (most commonly, bigrams).

With bigrams, our sentence becomes:

```
c("the", "the cat", "cat", "cat sat", "sat",
  "sat on", "on", "on the", "the mat", "mat")
```

The `layer_text_vectorization()` layer can be configured to return arbitrary *N*-grams: bigrams, trigrams, and so on. Just pass an `ngrams = N` argument as in the following listing.

> **Listing 11.7 Configuring `layer_text_vectorization()` to return bigrams**

```
text_vectorization <-
  layer_text_vectorization(ngrams = 2,
                           max_tokens = 20000,
                           output_mode = "multi_hot")
```

Let's test how our model performs when trained on such binary-encoded bags of bigrams (listing 11.8).

Listing 11.8   Training and testing the binary bigram model

```
adapt(text_vectorization, text_only_train_ds)

dataset_vectorize <- function(dataset) {
  dataset %>%
    dataset_map(~ list(text_vectorization(.x), .y),
                num_parallel_calls = 4)
}

binary_2gram_train_ds <- train_ds %>% dataset_vectorize()
binary_2gram_val_ds <- val_ds %>% dataset_vectorize()
binary_2gram_test_ds <- test_ds %>% dataset_vectorize()

model <- get_model()
model
```

◁ ── **Define a helper function for applying the text_vectorization layer to a text TF Dataset because we'll be doing this multiple times (with different text_vectorization layers) throughout the chapter.**

```
Model: "model_1"
_____
 Layer (type)                  Output Shape                  Param #
========================================================================
 input_2 (InputLayer)          [(None, 20000)]               0
 dense_3 (Dense)               (None, 16)                    320016
 dropout_1 (Dropout)           (None, 16)                    0
 dense_2 (Dense)               (None, 1)                     17
========================================================================
Total params: 320,033
Trainable params: 320,033
Non-trainable params: 0
_____
```

```
callbacks <- list(callback_model_checkpoint("binary_2gram.keras",
                                             save_best_only = TRUE))

model %>% fit(
  dataset_cache(binary_2gram_train_ds),
  validation_data = dataset_cache(binary_2gram_val_ds),
  epochs = 10,
  callbacks = callbacks
)

model <- load_model_tf("binary_2gram.keras")
evaluate(model, binary_2gram_test_ds)["accuracy"] %>%
  sprintf("Test acc: %.3f\n", .) %>% cat()
```

```
Test acc: 0.895
```

We're now getting 89.5% test accuracy, a marked improvement! Turns out local order is pretty important.

BIGRAMS WITH TF-IDF ENCODING

You can also add a bit more information to this representation by counting how many times each word or *N*-gram occurs, that is to say, by taking the histogram of the words over the text:

```
c("the" = 2, "the cat" = 1, "cat" = 1, "cat sat" = 1, "sat" = 1,
  "sat on" = 1, "on" = 1, "on the" = 1, "the mat" = 1, "mat" = 1)
```

If you're doing text classification, knowing how many times a word occurs in a sample is critical: any sufficiently long movie review may contain the word "terrible" regardless of sentiment, but a review that contains many instances of the word "terrible" is likely a negative one. Here's how you'd count bigram occurrences with `layer_text_vectorization()`:

Listing 11.9 Configuring `layer_text_vectorization()` to return token counts

```
text_vectorization <-
  layer_text_vectorization(ngrams = 2,
                           max_tokens = 20000,
                           output_mode = "count")
```

Now, of course, some words are bound to occur more often than others no matter what the text is about. The words "the," "a," "is," and "are" will always dominate your word count histograms, drowning out other words, despite being pretty much useless features in a classification context. How could we address this?

You already guessed it: via normalization. We could just normalize word counts by subtracting the mean and dividing by the variance (computed across the entire training dataset). That would make sense. Except most vectorized sentences consist almost entirely of zeros (our previous example features 12 nonzero entries and 19,988 zero entries), a property called "sparsity." That's a great property to have, because it dramatically reduces compute load and reduces the risk of overfitting. If we subtracted the mean from each feature, we'd wreck sparsity. Thus, whatever normalization scheme we use should be divide-only. What, then, should we use as the denominator? The best practice is to go with something called *TF-IDF normalization*—TF-IDF stands for "term frequency, inverse document frequency."

Understanding TF-IDF normalization

The more a given term appears in a document, the more important that term is for understanding what the document is about. At the same time, the frequency at which the term appears across all documents in your dataset matters, too: terms that appear in almost every document (like "the" or "a") aren't particularly informative, while terms that appear only in a small subset of all texts (like "Herzog") are very distinctive and, thus, important. TF-IDF is a metric that fuses these two ideas. It weights a given term by taking "term frequency," how many times the term appears in the current document, and dividing it by a measure of "document frequency," which estimates how often the term comes up across the dataset. You'd compute it as follows:

(continued)
```r
tf_idf <- function(term, document, dataset) {
  term_freq <- sum(document == term)
  doc_freqs <- sapply(dataset, function(doc) sum(doc == term))
  doc_freq <- log(1 + sum(doc_freqs))
  term_freq / doc_freq
}
```

Count the number times 'term' appears in the document.

Count the number times 'term' appears across the full dataset.

TF-IDF is so common that it's built into `layer_text_vectorization()`. All you need to do to start using it is to switch the `output_mode` argument to `"tf_idf"`.

Listing 11.10 Configuring `layer_text_vectorization` to return TF-IDF outputs

```r
text_vectorization <-
  layer_text_vectorization(ngrams = 2,
                           max_tokens = 20000,
                           output_mode = "tf_idf")
```

Let's train a new model with this scheme.

Listing 11.11 Training and testing the TF-IDF bigram model

The adapt() call will learn the TF-IDF weights in addition to the vocabulary.

We pin this operation to a CPU only, because it uses operations that a GPU device doesn't support yet.

```r
with(tf$device("CPU"), {
  adapt(text_vectorization, text_only_train_ds)
})

tfidf_2gram_train_ds <- train_ds %>% dataset_vectorize()
tfidf_2gram_val_ds <- val_ds %>% dataset_vectorize()
tfidf_2gram_test_ds <- test_ds %>% dataset_vectorize()

model <- get_model()
model
```

```
Model: "model_2"
_____
 Layer (type)                  Output Shape                Param #
========================================================================
 input_3 (InputLayer)          [(None, 20000)]             0
 dense_5 (Dense)               (None, 16)                  320016
 dropout_2 (Dropout)           (None, 16)                  0
 dense_4 (Dense)               (None, 1)                   17
========================================================================
Total params: 320,033
Trainable params: 320,033
Non-trainable params: 0
_____
```

```r
callbacks <- list(callback_model_checkpoint("tfidf_2gram.keras",
                                            save_best_only = TRUE))
```

```
model %>% fit(
  dataset_cache(tfidf_2gram_train_ds),
  validation_data = dataset_cache(tfidf_2gram_val_ds),
  epochs = 10,
  callbacks = callbacks
)

model <- load_model_tf("tfidf_2gram.keras")
evaluate(model, tfidf_2gram_test_ds)["accuracy"] %>%
  sprintf("Test acc: %.3f", .) %>% cat("\n")
```

```
Test acc: 0.896
```

This gets us an 89.6% test accuracy on the IMDB classification task: it doesn't seem to be particularly helpful in this case. However, for many text-classification datasets, it would be typical to see a one-percentage-point increase when using TF-IDF compared to plain binary encoding.

Exporting a model that processes raw strings

In the preceding examples, we did our text standardization, splitting, and indexing as part of the TF Dataset pipeline. But if we want to export a standalone model independent of this pipeline, we should make sure that it incorporates its own text preprocessing (otherwise, you'd have to reimplement in the production environment, which can be challenging or can lead to subtle discrepancies between the training data and the production data). Thankfully, this is easy.

Just create a new model that reuses your `text_vectorization` layer and adds to it the model you just trained:

```
inputs <- layer_input(shape = c(1), dtype = "string")    ◁——  One input sample
outputs <- inputs %>%                                          would be one string.
  text_vectorization() %>%    ◁——  Apply text preprocessing.
  model()                     ◁————  Apply the previously trained model.
inference_model <- keras_model(inputs, outputs)    ◁——
                                                   Instantiate the
                                                   end-to-end model.
```

The resulting model can process batches of raw strings:

```
raw_text_data <- "That was an excellent movie, I loved it." %>%
  as_tensor(shape = c(-1, 1))                    ◁——————
predictions <- inference_model(raw_text_data)
str(predictions)
```

```
<tf.Tensor: shape=(1, 1), dtype=float32, numpy=array([[0.93249124]],
  dtype=float32)>
```
The model expects inputs to be a batch of samples, that is, a one-column matrix.

```
cat(sprintf("%.2f percent positive\n",
            as.numeric(predictions) * 100))
```

```
93.25 percent positive
```

11.3.3 *Processing words as a sequence: The sequence model approach*

These past few examples clearly show that word order matters: manual engineering of order-based features, such as bigrams, yields a nice accuracy boost. Now remember: the history of deep learning is that of a move away from manual feature engineering, toward letting models learn their own features from exposure to data alone. What if, instead of manually crafting order-based features, we exposed the model to raw word sequences and let it figure out such features on its own? This is what *sequence models* are about.

To implement a sequence model, you'd start by representing your input samples as sequences of integer indices (one integer standing for one word). Then, you'd map each integer to a vector to obtain vector sequences. Finally, you'd feed these sequences of vectors into a stack of layers that could cross-correlate features from adjacent vectors, such as a 1D convnet, an RNN, or a Transformer.

For some time, around 2016–2017, bidirectional RNNs (in particular, bidirectional LSTMs) were considered to be the state of the art for sequence modeling. Because you're already familiar with this architecture, this is what we'll use in our first sequence model examples. However, nowadays sequence modeling is almost universally done with Transformers, which we will cover shortly. Oddly, one-dimensional convnets were never very popular in NLP, even though, in my own experience, a residual stack of depthwise-separable 1D convolutions can often achieve comparable performance to a bidirectional LSTM, at a greatly reduced computational cost.

A FIRST PRACTICAL EXAMPLE

Let's try out a first sequence model in practice. First, let's prepare datasets that return integer sequences.

Listing 11.12 Preparing integer sequence datasets

```
max_length <- 600
max_tokens <- 20000

text_vectorization <- layer_text_vectorization(
  max_tokens = max_tokens,
  output_mode = "int",
  output_sequence_length = max_length
)

adapt(text_vectorization, text_only_train_ds)

int_train_ds <- train_ds %>% dataset_vectorize()
int_val_ds <- val_ds %>% dataset_vectorize()
int_test_ds <- test_ds %>% dataset_vectorize()
```

> **To keep a manageable input size, we'll truncate the inputs after the first 600 words. This is a reasonable choice, because the average review length is 233 words, and only 5% of reviews are longer than 600 words.**

Next, let's make a model. The simplest way to convert our integer sequences to vector sequences is to one-hot-encode the integers (each dimension would represent one possible term in the vocabulary). On top of these one-hot vectors, we'll add a simple bidirectional LSTM.

Listing 11.13   A sequence model built on one-hot-encoded vector sequences

One input is a sequence of integers.

```
inputs <- layer_input(shape(NULL), dtype = "int64")
embedded <- inputs %>%
  tf$one_hot(depth = as.integer(max_tokens))
outputs <- embedded %>%
  bidirectional(layer_lstm(units = 32)) %>%
  layer_dropout(.5) %>%
  layer_dense(1, activation = "sigmoid")

model <- keras_model(inputs, outputs)
model %>% compile(optimizer = "rmsprop",
                  loss = "binary_crossentropy",
                  metrics = "accuracy")
model
```

Encode the integers into binary 20,000-dimensional vectors.

Add a bidirectional LSTM.

Finally, add a classification layer.

```
Model: "model_4"
_____
 Layer (type)                Output Shape              Param #
================================================================
 input_5 (InputLayer)        [(None, None)]            0
 tf.one_hot (TFOpLambda)     (None, None, 20000)       0
 bidirectional (Bidirectional) (None, 64)              5128448
 dropout_3 (Dropout)         (None, 64)                0
 dense_6 (Dense)             (None, 1)                 65
================================================================
Total params: 5,128,513
Trainable params: 5,128,513
Non-trainable params: 0
```

Now, let's train our model.

Listing 11.14   Training a first basic sequence model

```
callbacks <- list(
  callback_model_checkpoint("one_hot_bidir_lstm.keras",
                            save_best_only = TRUE))
```

A first observation: this model trains very slowly, especially compared to the light-weight model of the previous section. This is because our inputs are quite large: each input sample is encoded as a matrix of size `(600, 20000)` (600 words per sample, 20,000 possible words). That's 12,000,000 floats for a single movie review. Our bidirectional LSTM has a lot of work to do. Second, the model gets only to 87% test accuracy—it doesn't perform nearly as well as our (very fast) binary unigram model.

Clearly, using one-hot encoding to turn words into vectors, which was the simplest thing we could do, wasn't a great idea. There's a better way: *word embeddings*.

Reduce `batch_size` to avoid out-of-memory errors

Depending on your machine and the available RAM your GPU has, you may encounter out-of-memory errors trying to train this larger, bidirectional model. If that happens, try training with a smaller batch size. You can pass a smaller `batch_size` argument to `text_dataset_from_directory(batch_size = )`, or you can rebatch an existing TF Dataset like this:

```
int_train_ds_smaller <- int_train_ds %>%
  dataset_unbatch() %>%
  dataset_batch(16)


model %>% fit(int_train_ds_smaller, validation_data = int_val_ds,
              epochs = 10, callbacks = callbacks)


model <- load_model_tf("one_hot_bidir_lstm.keras")
sprintf("Test acc: %.3f", evaluate(model, int_test_ds)["accuracy"])
```

```
[1] "Test acc: 0.873"
```

UNDERSTANDING WORD EMBEDDINGS

Crucially, when you encode something via one-hot encoding, you're making a feature-engineering decision. You're injecting into your model a fundamental assumption about the structure of your feature space. That assumption is that *the different tokens you're encoding are all independent from each other*: indeed, one-hot vectors are all orthogonal to one another. And in the case of words, that assumption is clearly wrong. Words form a structured space: they share information with each other. The words "movie" and "film" are interchangeable in most sentences, so the vector that represents "movie" should not be orthogonal to the vector that represents "film"—they should be the same vector, or close enough.

To get a bit more abstract, the *geometric relationship* between two word vectors should reflect the *semantic relationship* between these words. For instance, in a reasonable word vector space, you would expect synonyms to be embedded into similar word vectors, and in general, you would expect the geometric distance (such as the cosine distance or L2 distance) between any two word vectors to relate to the "semantic distance" between the associated words. Words that mean different things should lie far away from each other, whereas related words should be closer.

Word embeddings are vector representations of words that achieve exactly this: they map human language into a structured geometric space. Whereas the vectors obtained through one-hot encoding are binary, sparse (mostly made of zeros), and very high-dimensional (the same dimensionality as the number of words in the vocabulary), word embeddings are low-dimensional floating-point vectors (i.e., dense vectors, as opposed to sparse vectors); see figure 11.2. It's common to see word embeddings that are 256-dimensional, 512-dimensional, or 1,024-dimensional when dealing with very large vocabularies. On the other hand, one-hot-encoding words generally leads to vectors that are 20,000-dimensional or greater (capturing a vocabulary of 20,000 tokens, in this case). So, word embeddings pack more information into far fewer dimensions.

One-hot word vectors:
- Sparse
- High-dimensional
- Hardcoded

Word embeddings:
- Dense
- Lower-dimensional
- Learned from data

Figure 11.2   Word representations obtained from one-hot encoding or hashing are sparse, high-dimensional, and hardcoded. Word embeddings are dense, relatively low-dimensional, and learned from data.

Besides being *dense* representations, word embeddings are also *structured* representations, and their structure is learned from data. Similar words are embedded in close locations, and further, specific *directions* in the embedding space are meaningful. To make this clearer, let's look at a concrete example.

In figure 11.3, four words are embedded on a 2D plane: *cat, dog, wolf,* and *tiger.* With the vector representations we chose here, some semantic relationships between these words can be encoded as geometric transformations. For instance, the same vector allows us to go from *cat* to *tiger* and from *dog* to *wolf*: this vector could be interpreted as the "from pet to wild animal" vector. Similarly, another vector lets us go from *dog* to *cat* and from *wolf* to *tiger,* which could be interpreted as a "from canine to feline" vector.

In real-world word-embedding spaces, common examples of meaningful geometric transformations are "gender" vectors and "plural" vectors. For instance, by adding a "female" vector to the vector "king," we obtain the vector "queen." By adding a "plural" vector, we obtain "kings." Word-embedding spaces typically feature thousands of such interpretable and potentially useful vectors.

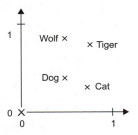

Figure 11.3   A toy example of a word-embedding space

Let's look at how to use such an embedding space in practice. There are two ways to obtain word embeddings:

- Learn word embeddings jointly with the main task you care about (such as document classification or sentiment prediction). In this setup, you start with random word vectors and then learn word vectors in the same way you learn the weights of a neural network.
- Load into your model word embeddings that were precomputed using a different machine learning task than the one you're trying to solve. These are called *pretrained word embeddings*.

Let's review each of these approaches.

LEARNING WORD EMBEDDINGS WITH THE EMBEDDING LAYER

Is there some ideal word-embedding space that would perfectly map human language and could be used for any natural language processing task? Possibly, but we have yet to compute anything of the sort. Also, there is no such a thing as *human language*—there are many different languages, and they aren't isomorphic to one another, because a language is the reflection of a specific culture and a specific context. But more pragmatically, what makes a good word-embedding space depends heavily on your task: the perfect word-embedding space for an English-language movie-review sentiment-analysis model may look different from the perfect embedding space for an English-language legal-document classification model, because the importance of certain semantic relationships varies from task to task.

It's thus reasonable to *learn* a new embedding space with every new task. Fortunately, backpropagation makes this easy, and Keras makes it even easier. It's about learning the weights of a layer: `layer_embedding()`.

Listing 11.15 Instantiating a `layer_embedding`

```
embedding_layer <- layer_embedding(input_dim = max_tokens,
                                   output_dim = 256)
```

`layer_embedding()` takes at least two arguments: the number of possible tokens and the dimensionality of the embeddings (here, 256).

`layer_embedding()` is best understood as a dictionary that maps integer indices (which stand for specific words) to dense vectors. It takes integers as input, looks up these integers in an internal dictionary, and returns the associated vectors. It's effectively a dictionary lookup (see figure 11.4).

Word index ⟶ Embedding layer ⟶ Corresponding word vector

Figure 11.4 The Embedding layer

The embedding layer takes as input a rank 2 tensor of integers, of shape (`batch_size`, `sequence_length`), where each entry is a sequence of integers. The layer then returns a 3D floating-point tensor of shape (batch_size, sequence_length, embedding_dimensionality).

When you instantiate a layer_embedding(), its weights (its internal dictionary of token vectors) are initially random, just as with any other layer. During training, these word vectors are gradually adjusted via backpropagation, structuring the space into something the downstream model can exploit. Once fully trained, the embedding space will show a lot of structure—a kind of structure specialized for the specific problem for which you're training your model.

Let's build a model that includes a layer_embedding() and benchmark it on our task.

Listing 11.16   Model that uses a layer_embedding trained from scratch

```
inputs <- layer_input(shape(NA), dtype = "int64")
embedded <- inputs %>%
  layer_embedding(input_dim = max_tokens, output_dim = 256)
outputs <- embedded %>%
  bidirectional(layer_lstm(units = 32)) %>%
  layer_dropout(0.5) %>%
  layer_dense(1, activation = "sigmoid")
model <- keras_model(inputs, outputs)
model %>%
  compile(optimizer = "rmsprop",
          loss = "binary_crossentropy",
          metrics = "accuracy")
model
```

```
Model: "model_5"
```

Layer (type)	Output Shape	Param #
input_6 (InputLayer)	[(None, None)]	0
embedding_1 (Embedding)	(None, None, 256)	5120000
bidirectional_1 (Bidirectional)	(None, 64)	73984
dropout_4 (Dropout)	(None, 64)	0
dense_7 (Dense)	(None, 1)	65

```
Total params: 5,194,049
Trainable params: 5,194,049
Non-trainable params: 0
```

```
callbacks <- list(callback_model_checkpoint("embeddings_bidir_lstm.keras",
                                             save_best_only = TRUE))

model %>%
  fit(int_train_ds,
      validation_data = int_val_ds,
      epochs = 10,
      callbacks = callbacks)

model <- load_model_tf("embeddings_bidir_lstm.keras")
evaluate(model, int_test_ds)["accuracy"] %>%
  sprintf("Test acc: %.3f\n", .) %>% cat()
```

```
Test acc: 0.842
```

It trains much faster than the one-hot model (because the LSTM has to process only 256-dimensional vectors instead of 20,000-dimensional ones), and its test accuracy is comparable (84%). However, we're still some way off from the results of our basic bigram model. Part of the reason is simply that the model is looking at slightly less data: the bigram model processed full reviews, whereas our sequence model truncates sequences after 600 words.

UNDERSTANDING PADDING AND MASKING

One thing that's slightly hurting model performance here is that our input sequences are full of zeros. This comes from our use of the `output_sequence_length = max_length` option in `layer_text_vectorization()` (with `max_length` equal to 600): sentences longer than 600 tokens are truncated to a length of 600 tokens, and sentences shorter than 600 tokens are padded with zeros at the end so that they can be concatenated with other sequences to form contiguous batches.

We're using a bidirectional RNN: two RNN layers running in parallel, with one processing the tokens in their natural order, and the other processing the same tokens in reverse. The RNN that looks at the tokens in their natural order will spend its last iterations seeing only vectors that encode padding—possibly for several hundreds of iterations if the original sentence was short. The information stored in the internal state of the RNN will gradually fade out as it is exposed to these meaningless inputs.

We need some way to tell the RNN that it should skip these iterations. There's an API for that: *masking*. `layer_embedding()` is capable of generating a "mask" that corresponds to its input data. This mask is a tensor of ones and zeros (or TRUE/FALSE Booleans), of shape `(batch_size, sequence_length)`, where the entry `mask[i, t]` indicates whether time step `t` of sample `i` should be skipped or not (the time step will be skipped if `mask[i, t]` is 0 or FALSE, and processed otherwise).

By default, this option isn't active—you can turn it on by passing `mask_zero = TRUE` to your `layer_embedding()`. You can retrieve the mask with the `compute_mask()` method:

```
embedding_layer <- layer_embedding(input_dim = 10, output_dim = 256,
                                   mask_zero = TRUE)
some_input <- rbind(c(4, 3, 2, 1, 0, 0, 0),
                    c(5, 4, 3, 2, 1, 0, 0),
                    c(2, 1, 0, 0, 0, 0, 0))
mask <- embedding_layer$compute_mask(some_input)
mask
```

```
tf.Tensor(
[[ True  True  True  True False False False]
 [ True  True  True  True  True False False]
 [ True  True False False False False False]], shape=(3, 7), dtype=bool)
```

In practice, you will almost never have to manage masks by hand. Instead, Keras will automatically pass on the mask to every layer that is able to process it (as a piece of metadata attached to the sequence it represents). This mask will be used by RNN layers to skip masked steps. If your model returns an entire sequence, the mask will also be used by the loss function to skip masked steps in the output sequence. Let's try retraining our model with masking enabled.

Listing 11.17 Using an embedding layer with masking enabled

```
inputs <- layer_input(c(NA), dtype = "int64")
embedded <- inputs %>%
  layer_embedding(input_dim = max_tokens,
                  output_dim = 256,
                  mask_zero = TRUE)

outputs <- embedded %>%
  bidirectional(layer_lstm(units = 32)) %>%
  layer_dropout(0.5) %>%
  layer_dense(1, activation = "sigmoid")

model <- keras_model(inputs, outputs)
model %>% compile(optimizer = "rmsprop",
                  loss = "binary_crossentropy",
                  metrics = "accuracy")
model
```

```
Model: "model_6"

_____
 Layer (type)                  Output Shape              Param #
========================================================================
 input_7 (InputLayer)          [(None, None)]            0
 embedding_3 (Embedding)       (None, None, 256)         5120000
 bidirectional_2 (Bidirectional) (None, 64)              73984
 dropout_5 (Dropout)           (None, 64)                0
 dense_8 (Dense)               (None, 1)                 65
========================================================================
Total params: 5,194,049
Trainable params: 5,194,049
Non-trainable params: 0
_____
```

```
callbacks <- list(
  callback_model_checkpoint("embeddings_bidir_lstm_with_masking.keras",
                            save_best_only = TRUE)
)

model %>% fit(
  int_train_ds,
  validation_data = int_val_ds,
  epochs = 10,
  callbacks = callbacks
)

model <- load_model_tf("embeddings_bidir_lstm_with_masking.keras")
cat(sprintf("Test acc: %.3f\n",
            evaluate(model, int_test_ds)["accuracy"]))
```

```
Test acc: 0.880
```

This time we get to 88% test accuracy—a small but noticeable improvement.

USING PRETRAINED WORD EMBEDDINGS

Sometimes you have so little training data available that you can't use your data alone to learn an appropriate task-specific embedding of your vocabulary. In such cases, instead of learning word embeddings jointly with the problem you want to solve, you can load embedding vectors from a precomputed embedding space that you know is highly structured and exhibits useful properties—one that captures generic aspects of language structure. The rationale behind using pretrained word embeddings in natural language processing is much the same as for using pretrained convnets in image classification: you don't have enough data available to learn truly powerful features on your own, but you expect that the features you need are fairly generic—that is, common visual features or semantic features. In this case, it makes sense to reuse features learned on a different problem.

Such word embeddings are generally computed using word-occurrence statistics (observations about what words co-occur in sentences or documents), using a variety of techniques, some involving neural networks, others not. The idea of a dense, low-dimensional embedding space for words, computed in an unsupervised way, was initially explored by Bengio et al. in the early 2000s,[1] but it started to take off in research and industry applications only after the release of one of the most famous and successful word-embedding schemes: the Word2Vec algorithm (https://code.google.com/archive/p/word2vec), developed by Tomas Mikolov at Google in 2013. Word2Vec dimensions capture specific semantic properties, such as gender.

You can download various precomputed databases of word embeddings and use them in a Keras `layer_embedding()`. Word2Vec is one of them. Another popular one is called Global Vectors for Word Representation (GloVe, https://nlp.stanford.edu/projects/glove), which was developed by Stanford researchers in 2014. This embedding technique is based on factorizing a matrix of word co-occurrence statistics. Its developers have made available precomputed embeddings for millions of English tokens, obtained from Wikipedia and Common Crawl data.

Let's look at how you can get started using GloVe embeddings in a Keras model. The same method is valid for Word2Vec embeddings or any other word-embedding database. We'll start by downloading the GloVe files and parsing them. We'll then load the word vectors into a Keras `layer_embedding()` layer, which we'll use to build a new model.

First, let's download the GloVe word embeddings precomputed on the 2014 English Wikipedia dataset. It's an 822 MB zip file containing 100-dimensional embedding vectors for 400,000 words (or nonword tokens):

```
download.file("http://nlp.stanford.edu/data/glove.6B.zip",
              destfile = "glove.6B.zip")
zip::unzip("glove.6B.zip")
```

[1] Yoshua Bengio et al., "A Neural Probabilistic Language Model," *Journal of Machine Learning Research* (2003).

Let's parse the unzipped file (a .txt file) to build an index that maps words (as strings) to their vector representation. Because the file structure is essentially a numeric matrix with row names, that's what we'll make in R.

Listing 11.18 Parsing the GloVe word-embeddings file

read_table() returns a data.frame. col_names = FALSE tells read_table() the text file does not have a header line, and the data itself starts at the first line.

Passing col_types is not necessary, but is a best practice and a good guard against surprises (e.g., if you're reading a corrupted file, or the wrong file!). Here we tell read_table() the first column is of type 'character', and then the next 100 are of type 'numeric'.

```r
path_to_glove_file <- "glove.6B.100d.txt"
embedding_dim <- 100

df <- readr::read_table(
  path_to_glove_file,
  col_names = FALSE,
  col_types = paste0("c", strrep("n", 100))
)
embeddings_index <- as.matrix(df[, -1])
rownames(embeddings_index) <- df[[1]]
colnames(embeddings_index) <- NULL
rm(df)
```

The first column is the word, and the remaining 100 columns are the numeric embeddings.

Discard the column names that read_table() automatically created (R data.frames must have column names).

Clear the temporary data.frame from memory.

Here is what embedding_matrix looks like:

```r
str(embeddings_index)
```

```
num [1:400000, 1:100] -0.0382 -0.1077 -0.3398 -0.1529 -0.1897 ...
 - attr(*, "dimnames")=List of 2
  ..$ : chr [1:400000] "the" "," "." "of" ...
  ..$ : NULL
```

Next, let's build an embedding matrix that you can load into a layer_embedding(), It must be a matrix of shape (max_words, embedding_dim), where each entry *i* contains the embedding_dim-dimensional vector for the word of index *i* in the reference word index (built during tokenization).

Listing 11.19 Preparing the GloVe word-embeddings matrix

```r
vocabulary <- text_vectorization %>% get_vocabulary()
str(vocabulary)
```

Retrieve the vocabulary indexed by our previous text_vectorization layer.

```
chr [1:20000] "" "[UNK]" "the" "a" "and" "of" "to" "is" "in" "it" "i" ...
```

```r
tokens <- head(vocabulary[-1], max_tokens)

i <- match(vocabulary, rownames(embeddings_index),
           nomatch = 0)
```

i is an integer vector of the row-number in embeddings_index that matched to each corresponding word in vocabulary, and 0 if there was no matching word.

[-1] to remove the mask token "" in the first position. head(, max_tokens) is just a sanity check—we passed the same max_tokens to text_vectorization earlier.

```
embedding_matrix <- array(0, dim = c(max_tokens, embedding_dim))
embedding_matrix[i != 0, ] <- embeddings_index[i, ]

str(embedding_matrix)

num [1:20000, 1:100] 0 0 -0.0382 -0.2709 -0.072 ...
```

0s in indexes passed to [for R arrays are ignored. For example: (1:10)[c(1,0,2,0,3)] returns c(1, 2, 3).

Prepare a matrix of all zeros that we'll fill with the GloVe vectors.

Fill entries in the matrix with the corresponding word vector. Row numbers of rows embedding_matrix corresponds to index positions of words in vocabulary. Words not found in the embedding index will be all zeros.

Finally, we use a `initializer_constant()` to load the pretrained embeddings in a `layer_embedding()`. So as not to disrupt the pretrained representations during training, we freeze the layer via `trainable = FALSE`:

```
embedding_layer <- layer_embedding(
  input_dim = max_tokens,
  output_dim = embedding_dim,
  embeddings_initializer = initializer_constant(embedding_matrix),
  trainable = FALSE,
  mask_zero = TRUE
)
```

We're now ready to train a new model—identical to our previous model, but leveraging the 100-dimensional pretrained GloVe embeddings instead of 128-dimensional learned embeddings.

Listing 11.20   Model that uses a pretrained embedding layer

```
inputs <- layer_input(shape(NA), dtype = "int64")
embedded <- embedding_layer(inputs)
outputs <- embedded %>%
  bidirectional(layer_lstm(units = 32)) %>%
  layer_dropout(0.5) %>%
  layer_dense(1, activation = "sigmoid")
model <- keras_model(inputs, outputs)

model %>% compile(optimizer = "rmsprop",
                  loss = "binary_crossentropy",
                  metrics = "accuracy")
model
```

```
Model: "model_7"
```

Layer (type)	Output Shape	Param #	Trainable
input_8 (InputLayer)	[(None, None)]	0	Y
embedding_4 (Embedding)	(None, None, 100)	2000000	N
bidirectional_3 (Bidirectional)	(None, 64)	34048	Y
dropout_6 (Dropout)	(None, 64)	0	Y
dense_9 (Dense)	(None, 1)	65	Y

```
=============================================================================
Total params: 2,034,113
Trainable params: 34,113
Non-trainable params: 2,000,000
```

```
callbacks <- list(
  callback_model_checkpoint("glove_embeddings_sequence_model.keras",
                            save_best_only = TRUE)
)
model %>%
  fit(int_train_ds, validation_data = int_val_ds,
      epochs = 10, callbacks = callbacks)

model <- load_model_tf("glove_embeddings_sequence_model.keras")
cat(sprintf(
  "Test acc: %.3f\n", evaluate(model, int_test_ds)["accuracy"]))
```

```
Test acc: 0.877
```

You'll find that on this particular task, pretrained embeddings aren't very helpful, because the dataset contains enough samples that it is possible to learn a specialized enough embedding space from scratch. However, leveraging pretrained embeddings can be very helpful when you're working with a smaller dataset.

11.4   *The Transformer architecture*

Starting in 2017, a new model architecture started overtaking recurrent neural networks across most natural language processing tasks: the Transformer. Transformers were introduced in the seminal paper "Attention Is All You Need" by Vaswani et al.[2] The gist of the paper is right there in the title: as it turned out, a simple mechanism called "neural attention" could be used to build powerful sequence models that didn't feature any recurrent layers or convolution layers.

This finding unleashed nothing short of a revolution in natural language processing and beyond. Neural attention has fast become one of the most influential ideas in deep learning. In this section, you'll get an in-depth explanation of how it works and why it has proven so effective for sequence data. We'll then leverage self-attention to create a Transformer encoder, one of the basic components of the Transformer architecture, and we'll apply it to the IMDB movie review classification task.

11.4.1   *Understanding self-attention*

As you're going through this book, you may be skimming some parts and attentively reading others, depending on what your goals or interests are. What if your models did the same? It's a simple yet powerful idea: not all input information seen by a model is equally important to the task at hand, so models should "pay more attention"

---

[2] Ashish Vaswani et al., "Attention Is All You Need" (2017), https://arxiv.org/abs/1706.03762.

to some features and "pay less attention" to other features. Does that sound familiar? You've already encountered a similar concept twice in this book:

- Max pooling in convnets looks at a pool of features in a spatial region and selects just one feature to keep. That's an "all or nothing" form of attention: keep the most important feature and discard the rest.
- TF-IDF normalization assigns importance scores to tokens based on how much information different tokens are likely to carry. Important tokens are boosted while irrelevant tokens are faded out. That's a continuous form of attention.

There are many different forms of attention you could imagine, but they all start by computing importance scores for a set of features, with higher scores for more relevant features and lower scores for less relevant ones (see figure 11.5). How these scores should be computed, and what you should do with them, will vary from approach to approach.

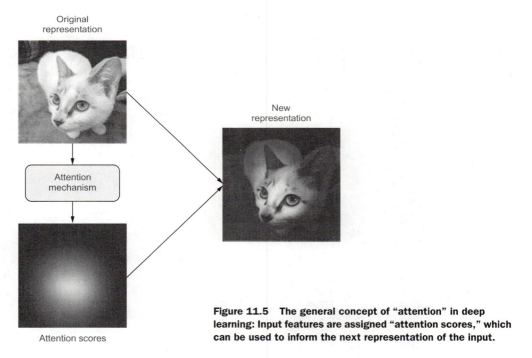

Figure 11.5   The general concept of "attention" in deep learning: Input features are assigned "attention scores," which can be used to inform the next representation of the input.

Crucially, this kind of attention mechanism can be used for more than just highlighting or erasing certain features. It can be used to make features *context aware*. You've just learned about word embeddings: vector spaces that capture the "shape" of the semantic relationships between different words. In an embedding space, a single word has a fixed position—a fixed set of relationships with every other word in the space. But that's not quite how language works: the meaning of a word is usually context specific. When you mark the date, you're not talking about the same "date" as when you go on a date, nor is it the kind of date you'd buy at the market. When you say, "I'll see you soon," the meaning of the word "see" is subtly different from the "see" in "I'll see this project to its end" or "I see what you mean." And, of course, the meaning of pronouns like "he," "it," "you," and so on is entirely sentence specific and can even change multiple times within a single sentence.

Clearly, a smart embedding space would provide a different vector representation for a word depending on the other words surrounding it. That's where *self-attention* comes in. The purpose of self-attention is to modulate the representation of a token by using the representations of related tokens in the sequence. This produces context-aware token representations. Consider an example sentence: "The train left the station on time." Now, consider one word in the sentence: station. What kind of station are we talking about? Could it be a radio station? Maybe the International Space Station? Let's figure it out algorithmically via self-attention (see figure 11.6).

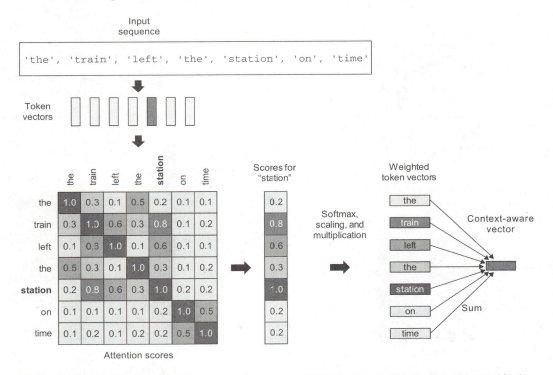

Figure 11.6   Self-attention: Attention scores are computed between "station" and every other word in the sequence, and they are then used to weight a sum of word vectors that becomes the new "station" vector.

Step 1 is to compute relevancy scores between the vector for "station" and every other word in the sentence. These are our "attention scores." We're simply going to use the dot product between two word vectors as a measure of the strength of their relationship. It's a very computationally efficient distance function, and it was already the standard way to relate two word embeddings to each other long before Transformers. In practice, these scores will also go through a scaling function and a softmax, but for now, that's just an implementation detail.

Step 2 is to compute the sum of all word vectors in the sentence, weighted by our relevancy scores. Words closely related to "station" will contribute more to the sum (including the word "station" itself), whereas irrelevant words will contribute almost nothing. The resulting vector is our new representation for "station": a representation that incorporates the surrounding context. In particular, it includes part of the "train" vector, clarifying that it is, in fact, a "train station."

You'd repeat this process for every word in the sentence, producing a new sequence of vectors encoding the sentence. Let's see it in R-like pseudocode:

```
self_attention <- function(input_sequence) {
  c(sequence_len, embedding_size) %<-% dim(input_sequence)

  output <- array(0, dim(input_sequence))

  for (i in 1:sequence_len) {          # Iterate over each token
                                        # in the input sequence.

    pivot_vector <- input_sequence[i, ]

    scores <- sapply(1:sequence_len, function(j)    # Compute the dot product
      pivot_vector %*% input_sequence[j, ])         # (attention score) between the
                                                    # token and every other token.

    scores <- softmax(scores / sqrt(embedding_size))    # %*% with two 1D vectors
                                                         # returns a scalar, the dot
    broadcast_scores <-                                  # product. scores has
      as.matrix(scores)[, rep(1, embedding_size)]        # shape (sequence_len).

    new_pivot_representation <-
      colSums(input_sequence * broadcast_scores)    # Scale by a
                                                     # normalization factor,
                                                     # and apply a softmax.
    output[i, ] <- new_pivot_representation
  }
  output                    # Sum the score-adjusted input
}                           # sequences to make a new
                            # embedding vector.

softmax <- function(x) {
  e <- exp(x - max(x))
  e / sum(e)
}
```

Broadcast the scores vector (shape: (sequence_len)) into a matrix of shape (sequence_len, embedding_size), the shape of input_sequence.

Of course, in practice you'd use a vectorized implementation. Keras has a built-in layer to handle it: `layer_multi_head_attention()`. Here's how you would use it:

```
num_heads <- 4
embed_dim <- 256
```

```
mha_layer <- layer_multi_head_attention(num_heads = num_heads,
                                         key_dim = embed_dim)
outputs <- mha_layer(inputs, inputs, inputs)
```

inputs has shape (batch_size, sequence_length, embed_dim).

Reading this, you're probably wondering:

- Why are we passing the inputs to the layer *three* times? That seems redundant.
- What are these "multiple heads" we're referring to? That sounds intimidating—do they also grow back if you cut them?

Both of these questions have simple answers. Let's take a look.

GENERALIZED SELF-ATTENTION: THE QUERY-KEY-VALUE MODEL

So far, we have considered only one input sequence. However, the Transformer architecture was originally developed for machine translation, where you have to deal with two input sequences: the source sequence you're currently translating (such as "How's the weather today?"), and the target sequence you're converting it to (such as "¿Qué tiempo hace hoy?"). A Transformer is a *sequence-to-sequence* model: it was designed to convert one sequence into another. You'll learn about sequence-to-sequence models in depth later in this chapter.

Now let's take a step back. The self-attention mechanism as we've introduced it performs the following, schematically:

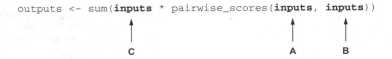

```
outputs <- sum(inputs * pairwise_scores(inputs, inputs))
                  C                         A        B
```

This means "for each token in `inputs` (A), compute how much the token is related to every token in `inputs` (B), and use these scores to weight a sum of tokens from `inputs` (C)." Crucially, there's nothing that requires A, B, and C to refer to the same input sequence. In the general case, you could be doing this with three different sequences. We'll call them "query," "keys," and "values." The operation becomes "for each element in the query, compute how much the element is related to every key, and use these scores to weight a sum of values":

```
outputs <- sum(values * pairwise_scores(query, keys))
```

This terminology comes from search engines and recommender systems (see figure 11.7). Imagine that you're typing up a query to retrieve a photo from your collection, "dogs on the beach." Internally, each of your pictures in the database is described by a set of keywords—"cat," "dog," "party," and so forth. We'll call those "keys." The search engine will start by comparing your query to the keys in the database. "Dog" yields a match of 1, and "cat" yields a match of 0. It will then rank those keys by strength of match—relevance—and it will return the pictures associated with the top *N* matches, in order of relevance.

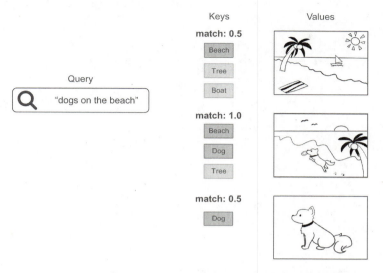

Figure 11.7   Retrieving images from a database: The "query" is compared to a set of "keys," and the match scores are used to rank "values" (images).

Conceptually, this is what Transformer-style attention is doing. You've got a reference sequence that describes something you're looking for: the query. You've got a body of knowledge that you're trying to extract information from: the values. Each value is assigned a key that describes the value in a format that can be readily compared to a query. You simply match the query to the keys. Then you return a weighted sum of values.

In practice, the keys and the values are often the same sequence. In machine translation, for instance, the query would be the target sequence, and the source sequence would play the roles of both keys and values: for each element of the target (like "tiempo"), you want to go back to the source ("How's the weather today?") and identify the different bits that are related to it ("tiempo" and "weather" should have a strong match). And naturally, if you're just doing sequence classification, then query, keys, and values are all the same: you're comparing a sequence to itself, to enrich each token with context from the whole sequence.

That explains why we needed to pass `inputs` three times to our `layer_multi_head_attention()` layer. But why "multi-head" attention?

11.4.2 *Multi-head attention*

"Multi-head attention" is an extra tweak to the self-attention mechanism, introduced in "Attention Is All You Need." The "multi-head" moniker refers to the fact that the output space of the self-attention layer is factored into a set of independent subspaces, learned separately: the initial query, key, and value are sent through three independent sets of dense projections, resulting in three separate vectors. Each vector is processed via neural attention, and the three outputs are concatenated back into a single output sequence. Each such subspace is called a "head." The full picture is shown in figure 11.8.

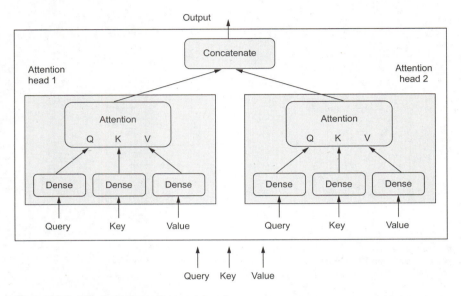

Figure 11.8   The `MultiHeadAttention` layer

The presence of the learnable dense projections enables the layer to actually learn something, as opposed to being a purely stateless transformation that would require additional layers before or after it to be useful. In addition, having independent heads helps the layer learn different groups of features for each token, where features within one group are correlated with each other but are mostly independent from features in a different group.

This is similar in principle to what makes depthwise-separable convolutions work: in a depthwise-separable convolution, the output space of the convolution is factored into many subspaces (one per input channel) that are learned independently. The "Attention Is All You Need" paper was written at a time when the idea of factoring feature spaces into independent subspaces had been shown to provide great benefits for computer vision models, both in the case of depthwise-separable convolutions and in the case of a closely related approach, *grouped convolutions*. Multi-head attention is simply the application of the same idea to self-attention.

11.4.3 *The Transformer encoder*

If adding extra dense projections is so useful, why don't we also apply one or two to the output of the attention mechanism? Actually, that's a great idea—let's do that. And our model is starting to do a lot, so we might want to add residual connections to make sure we don't destroy any valuable information along the way; you learned in chapter 9 that they're a must for any sufficiently deep architecture. And there's another thing you learned in chapter 9: normalization layers are supposed to help gradients flow better during backpropagation. Let's add those, too.

That's roughly the thought process that I imagine unfolded in the minds of the inventors of the Transformer architecture at the time. Factoring outputs into multiple independent spaces, adding residual connections, adding normalization layers—all of these are standard architecture patterns that one would be wise to leverage in any complex model. Together, these bells and whistles form the Transformer encoder—one of two critical parts that make up the Transformer architecture (see figure 11.9).

The original Transformer architecture consists of two parts: a *Transformer encoder* that processes the source sequence, and a *Transformer decoder* that uses the source sequence to generate a translated version. You'll learn about the decoder part in a minute.

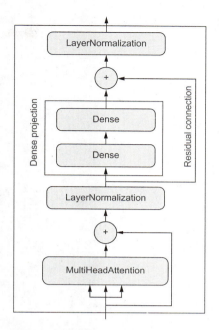

Figure 11.9 **The Transformer-Encoder chains a `layer_multi_head_attention()` with a dense projection and adds normalization as well as residual connections.**

Crucially, the encoder part can be used for text classification. It's a very generic module that ingests a sequence and learns to turn it into a more useful representation. Let's implement a Transformer encoder and try it on the movie review sentiment classification task.

Listing 11.21   Transformer encoder implemented as a subclassed `Layer`

```
layer_transformer_encoder <- new_layer_class(
  classname = "TransformerEncoder",
  initialize = function(embed_dim, dense_dim, num_heads, ...) {
    super$initialize(...)
    self$embed_dim <- embed_dim          Size of the input token vectors
    self$dense_dim <- dense_dim          Size of the inner dense layer
    self$num_heads <- num_heads
    self$attention <-                    Number of attention heads
      layer_multi_head_attention(num_heads = num_heads,
                                 key_dim = embed_dim)

    self$dense_proj <- keras_model_sequential() %>%
      layer_dense(dense_dim, activation = "relu") %>%
      layer_dense(embed_dim)

    self$layernorm_1 <- layer_layer_normalization()
```

```
    self$layernorm_2 <- layer_layer_normalization()
},

call = function(inputs, mask = NULL) {          ◄───| Computation goes in call()
  if (!is.null(mask))
      mask <- mask[, tf$newaxis, ]              ├─ The mask that will be generated by the embedding
                                                   layer will be 2D, but the attention layer expects it
                                                   to be 3D or 4D, so we expand its rank.

  inputs %>%
    { self$attention(., ., attention_mask = mask) + . } %>%  ◄─┐   Add residual
      self$layernorm_1() %>%                                      connection
    { self$dense_proj(.) + . } %>%  ◄─── Add residual connection to        to output of
      self$layernorm_2()                 output of the dense_proj() layer.  attention
},                                                                          layer.

get_config = function() {          ◄───| Implement serialization so
  config <- super$get_config()           we can save the model.
  for(name in c("embed_dim", "num_heads", "dense_dim"))
    config[[name]] <- self[[name]]
  config
}
)
```

%>% and { }

In the above example, we pipe with `%>%` into an expression that is wrapped with `{ }`. This is an advanced feature of `%>%`, which allows you to pipe into complex or compound expressions. `%>%` will place in the piped argument to each location we request with the `.` symbol. For example:

```
x %>% { fn(., .) + . }
```

is equivalent to:

```
fn(x, x) + x
```

If we were to write the `call()` method of `layer_transformer_encoder()` without `%>%`, it would look like this:

```
call = function(inputs, mask = NULL) {
  if (!is.null(mask))
    mask <- mask[, tf$newaxis, ]
  attention_output <- self$attention(inputs, inputs,
                                      attention_mask = mask)
  proj_input <- self$layernorm_1(inputs + attention_output)
  proj_output <- self$dense_proj(proj_input)
  self$layernorm_2(proj_input + proj_output)
}
```

Saving custom layers

When you write custom layers, make sure to implement the `get_config()` method: this enables the layer to be reinstantiated from its config, which is useful during model saving and loading. The method should return a named R list that contains the values of the constructor arguments used to create the layer.

All Keras layers can be serialized and deserialized as follows:

```
config <- layer$get_config()
new_layer <- do.call(layer_<type>, config)
```

where `layer_<type>` is the original layer constructor. For example:

> **The config does not contain weight values, so all weights in the layer are initialized from scratch.**

> **config is a regular named R list. You can safely save it to disk as an rds, then load it in a new R session.**

```
layer <- layer_dense(units = 10)
config <- layer$get_config()
new_layer <- do.call(layer_dense, config)
```

You can also access the unwrapped original layer constructor from any existing layer directly via the special symbol __class__ (though you rarely need to do so):

```
layer$`__class__`
```

```
<class 'keras.layers.core.dense.Dense'>
```

```
new_layer <- layer$`__class__`$from_config(config)
```

Defining the `get_config()` method in custom layer classes enables the same work-flow. For instance:

```
layer <- layer_transformer_encoder(embed_dim = 256, dense_dim = 32,
                                   num_heads = 2)
config <- layer$get_config()
new_layer <- do.call(layer_transformer_encoder, config)
# -- or --
new_layer <- layer$`__class__`$from_config(config)
```

When saving a model that contains custom layers, the saved file will contain these configs. When loading the model from the file, you should provide the custom layer classes to the loading process, so that it can make sense of the config objects:

```
model <- save_model_tf(model, filename)
model <- load_model_tf(filename,
                       custom_objects = list(layer_transformer_encoder))
```

Note that if the list supplied to `custom_objects` is named, then names are matched to the `classname` argument that was provided when the custom object was constructed:

```
model <- load_model_tf(
  filename,
  custom_objects = list(TransformerEncoder = layer_transformer_encoder))
```

You'll note that the normalization layers we're using here aren't `layer_batch_normalization()` like those we've used before in image models. That's because `layer_batch_normalization()` doesn't work well for sequence data. Instead, we're using the `layer_layer_normalization()`, which normalizes each sequence independently from other sequences in the batch. Like this, in R pseudocode:

```
layer_normalization <- function(batch_of_sequences) {
  c(batch_size, sequence_length, embedding_dim) %<-%
    dim(batch_of_sequences)                          ◁────  Input shape: (batch_size,
  means <- variances <-                                     sequence_length, embedding_dim)
    array(0, dim = dim(batch_of_sequences))
  for (b in seq(batch_size))
    for (s in seq(sequence_length)) {
      embedding <- batch_of_sequences[b, s, ]        ◁────┐  To compute mean and variance, we
      means[b, s, ] <- mean(embedding)                    │  pool data only over the last axis
      variances[b, s, ] <- var(embedding)                 │  (axis -1, the embedding axis).
    }
  (batch_of_sequences - means) / variances
}
```

Compare to `layer_batch_normalization()` (during training):

```
batch_normalization <- function(batch_of_images) {
  c(batch_size, height, width, channels) %<-%
    dim(batch_of_images)                             ◁────  Input shape: (batch_size,
  means <- variances <-                                     height, width, channels)
    array(0, dim = dim(batch_of_images))
  for (ch in seq(channels)) {
    channel <- batch_of_images[, , , ch]             ◁────┐  Pool the data over the batch axis (the
    means[, , , ch] <- mean(channel)                      │  first axis), which creates interactions
    variances[, , , ch] <- var(channel)                   │  between samples in a batch.
  }
  (batch_of_images - means) / variances
}
```

Although `batch_normalization()` collects information from many samples to obtain accurate statistics for the feature means and variances, `layer_normalization()` pools data within each sequence separately, which is more appropriate for sequence data.

Now that we've implemented our `TransformerEncoder`, we can use it to assemble a text-classification model similar to the LSTM-based one you've seen previously.

Listing 11.22   Using the Transformer Encoder for text classification

```
vocab_size <- 20000
embed_dim <- 256
num_heads <- 2
dense_dim <- 32

inputs <- layer_input(shape(NA), dtype = "int64")
outputs <- inputs %>%
  layer_embedding(vocab_size, embed_dim) %>%
```

```
  layer_transformer_encoder(embed_dim, dense_dim, num_heads) %>%
  layer_global_average_pooling_1d() %>%   ◄
  layer_dropout(0.5) %>%
  layer_dense(1, activation = "sigmoid")
model <-  keras_model(inputs, outputs)
model %>% compile(optimizer = "rmsprop",
                  loss = "binary_crossentropy",
                  metrics = "accuracy")
model
```

> Because TransformerEncoder returns full sequences, we need to reduce each sequence to a single vector for classification via a global pooling layer.

```
Model: "model_8"
_____
 Layer (type)                      Output Shape            Param #
========================================================================
 input_10 (InputLayer)             [(None, None)]          0
 embedding_5 (Embedding)           (None, None, 256)       5120000
 transformer_encoder_1 (Transform  (None, None, 256)       543776
 erEncoder)
 global_average_pooling1d (Global  (None, 256)             0
 AveragePooling1D)
 dropout_7 (Dropout)               (None, 256)             0
 dense_17 (Dense)                  (None, 1)               257
========================================================================
Total params: 5,664,033
Trainable params: 5,664,033
Non-trainable params: 0
_____
```

Let's train it. It gets to 88.5% test accuracy.

Listing 11.23 Training and evaluating the Transformer encoder–based model

```
callbacks = list(callback_model_checkpoint("transformer_encoder.keras",
                                           save_best_only = TRUE))

model %>% fit(
  int_train_ds,
  validation_data = int_val_ds,
  epochs = 20,
  callbacks = callbacks
)

model <- load_model_tf(
  "transformer_encoder.keras",
  custom_objects = layer_transformer_encoder)   ◄

sprintf("Test acc: %.3f", evaluate(model, int_test_ds)["accuracy"])
```

> Provide the custom TransformerEncoder class to the model-loading process.

```
[1] "Test acc: 0.885"
```

At this point, you should start to feel a bit uneasy. Something's off here. Can you tell what it is?

This section is ostensibly about "sequence models." I started off by highlighting the importance of word order. I said that Transformer was a sequence-processing architecture, originally developed for machine translation. And yet . . . the Transformer encoder you just saw in action wasn't a sequence model at all. Did you notice? It's composed of dense layers that process sequence tokens independently from each other, and an attention layer that looks at the tokens *as a set.* You could change the order of the tokens in a sequence, and you'd get the exact same pairwise attention scores and the exact same context-aware representations. If you were to completely scramble the words in every movie review, the model wouldn't notice, and you'd still get the exact same accuracy. Self-attention is a set-processing mechanism, focused on the relationships between pairs of sequence elements (see figure 11.10)—it's blind to whether these elements occur at the beginning, at the end, or in the middle of a sequence. So why do we say that Transformer is a sequence model? And how could it possibly be good for machine translation if it doesn't look at word order?

I hinted at the solution earlier in the chapter: I mentioned in passing that Transformer was a hybrid approach that is technically order agnostic but that manually injects order information in the representations it processes. This is the missing ingredient! It's called *positional encoding.* Let's take a look.

	Word order awareness	Context awareness (cross-words interactions)
Bag-of-unigrams	No	No
Bag-of-bigrams	Very limited	No
RNN	Yes	No
Self-attention	No	Yes
Transformer	Yes	Yes

Figure 11.10   Features of different types of NLP models

USING POSITIONAL ENCODING TO REINJECT ORDER INFORMATION

The idea behind positional encoding is very simple: to give the model access to word-order information, we're going to add the word's position in the sentence to each word embedding. Our input word embeddings will have two components: the usual word vector, which represents the word independently of any specific context, and a position vector, which represents the position of the word in the current sentence. Hopefully, the model will then figure out how to best leverage this additional information.

The simplest scheme you could come up with would be to concatenate the word's position to its embedding vector. You'd add a "position" axis to the vector and fill it with 0 for the first word in the sequence, 1 for the second, and so on. That may not be ideal, however, because the positions can potentially be very large integers, which will disrupt the range of values in the embedding vector. As you know, neural networks don't like very large input values, or discrete input distributions.

The original "Attention Is All You Need" paper used an interesting trick to encode word positions: it added to the word embeddings a vector containing values in the range [-1, 1] that varied cyclically depending on the position (it used cosine functions to achieve this). This trick offers a way to uniquely characterize any integer in a large range via a vector of small values. It's clever, but it's not what we're going to use in our case. We'll do something simpler and more effective: we'll learn position-embedding vectors the same way we learn to embed word indices. We'll then proceed to add our position embeddings to the corresponding word embeddings, to obtain a position-aware word embedding. This technique is called "positional embedding." Let's implement it.

Listing 11.24   Implementing positional embedding as a subclassed layer

```
layer_positional_embedding <- new_layer_class(
  classname = "PositionalEmbedding",

  initialize = function(sequence_length,
                        input_dim, output_dim, ...) {
    super$initialize(...)
    self$token_embeddings <-
      layer_embedding(input_dim = input_dim,
                      output_dim = output_dim)
    self$position_embeddings <-
      layer_embedding(input_dim = sequence_length,
                      output_dim = output_dim)
    self$sequence_length <- sequence_length
    self$input_dim <- input_dim
    self$output_dim <- output_dim
  },

  call = function(inputs) {
    len <- tf$shape(inputs)[-1]
    positions <-
      tf$range(start = 0L, limit = len, delta = 1L)
    embedded_tokens <- self$token_embeddings(inputs)
    embedded_positions <- self$position_embeddings(positions)
    embedded_tokens + embedded_positions
  },

  compute_mask = function(inputs, mask = NULL) {
    inputs != 0
  },

  get_config = function() {
    config <- super$get_config()
    for(name in c("output_dim", "sequence_length", "input_dim"))
      config[[name]] <- self[[name]]
    config
  }
)
```

A downside of position embeddings is that the sequence length needs to be known in advance.

Prepare a layer_embedding() for the token indices.

Prepare another one for the token positions.

tf$shape(inputs)[-1] slices out the last element of the shape, the size of the embedding dimension. (tf$shape() returns the shape as a tensor.)

tf$range() is similar to seq() in R, makes a integer sequence: [0, 1, 2, ..., limit - 1].

Add both embedding vectors together.

Like layer_embedding(), this layer should be able to generate a mask so we can ignore padding 0s in the inputs. The compute_mask() method will called automatically by the framework, and the mask will be propagated to the next layer.

Implement serialization so we can save the model.

You would use this `layer_positional_embedding()` just like a regular `layer_embedding()`. Let's see it in action!

PUTTING IT ALL TOGETHER: A TEXT-CLASSIFICATION TRANSFORMER

All you have to do to start taking word order into account is swap the old `layer_embedding()` with our position-aware version.

Listing 11.25   Combining the Transformer encoder with positional embedding

```r
vocab_size <- 20000
sequence_length <- 600
embed_dim <- 256
num_heads <- 2
dense_dim <- 32

inputs <- layer_input(shape(NULL), dtype = "int64")

outputs <- inputs %>%
  layer_positional_embedding(sequence_length, vocab_size, embed_dim) %>%
  layer_transformer_encoder(embed_dim, dense_dim, num_heads) %>%
  layer_global_average_pooling_1d() %>%
  layer_dropout(0.5) %>%
  layer_dense(1, activation = "sigmoid")

model <-
  keras_mcdel(inputs, outputs) %>%
  compile(optimizer = "rmsprop",
          loss = "binary_crossentropy',
          metrics = "accuracy")

model
```

```
Model: "mcdel_9"
_____
 Layer (type)                     Output Shape              Param #
========================================================================
 input_11 (InputLayer)            [(None, None)]            0
 positional_embedding (Positional (None, None, 256)         5273600
 Embedding)
 transformer_encoder_2 (Transform (None, None, 256)         543776
 erEncoder)
 global_average_pooling1d_1 (Glob (None, 256)               0
 alAveragePooling1D)
 dropout_8 (Dropout)              (None, 256)               0
 dense_22 (Dense)                 (None, 1)                 257
========================================================================
Total params: 5,817,633
Trainable params: 5,817,633
Non-trainable params: 0
```

```r
callbacks <- list(
  callback_model_checkpoint("full_transformer_encoder.keras",
                            save_best_only = TRUE)
)

model %>% fit(
  int_train_ds,
  validation_data = int_val_ds,
  epochs = 20,
  callbacks = callbacks
)
```

```
model <- load_model_tf(
  "full_transformer_encoder.keras",
  custom_objects = list(layer_transformer_encoder,
                        layer_positional_embedding))

cat(sprintf(
  "Test acc: %.3f\n", evaluate(model, int_test_ds)["accuracy"]))
```

Test acc: 0.886

Look here! We get to 88.6% test accuracy—an improvement that demonstrates the value of word-order information for text classification. This is our best sequence model so far! However, it's still one notch below the bag-of-words approach.

11.4.4 When to use sequence models over bag-of-words models

You may sometimes hear that bag-of-words methods are outdated and that Transformer-based sequence models are the way to go, no matter what task or dataset you're looking at. This is definitely not the case: a small stack of dense layers on top of a bag-of-bigrams remains a perfectly valid and relevant approach in many cases. In fact, among the various techniques that we've tried on the IMDB dataset throughout this chapter, the best performing so far was the bag-of-bigrams! So, when should you prefer one approach over the other?

In 2017, my team and I ran a systematic analysis of the performance of various text-classification techniques across many different types of text datasets, and we discovered a remarkable and surprising rule of thumb for deciding whether to go with a bag-of-words model or a sequence model (http://mng.bz/AOzK)—a golden constant of sorts. It turns out that when approaching a new text-classification task, you should pay close attention to the ratio between the number of samples in your training data and the mean number of words per sample (see figure 11.11). If that ratio is small—less than 1,500—then the bag-of-bigrams model will perform better (and as a bonus, it will be much faster to train and to iterate on, too). If that ratio is higher than 1,500, then you should go with a sequence model. In other words, sequence models work best when lots of training data is available and when each sample is relatively short.

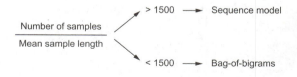

Figure 11.11 A simple heuristic for selecting a text-classification model: The ratio between the number of training samples and the mean number of words per sample

So, if you're classifying 1,000-word long documents, and you have 100,000 of them (a ratio of 100), you should go with a bigram model. If you're classifying tweets that are 40 words long on average, and you have 50,000 of them (a ratio of 1,250), you should also go with a bigram model. But if you increase your dataset size to 500,000 tweets (a ratio of 12,500), go with a Transformer encoder. What about the IMDB movie-review classification task? We had 20,000 training samples and an average word count of 233, so our rule of thumb points toward a bigram model, which confirms what we found in practice.

This intuitively makes sense: the input of a sequence model represents a richer and more complex space, and thus it takes more data to map out that space; meanwhile, a plain set of terms is a space so simple that you can train a logistic regression on top using just a few hundreds or thousands of samples. In addition, the shorter a sample is, the less the model can afford to discard any of the information it contains—in particular, word order becomes more important, and discarding it can create ambiguity. The sentences "this movie is the bomb" and "this movie was a bomb" have very close unigram representations, which could confuse a bag-of-words model, but a sequence model could tell which one is negative and which one is positive. With a longer sample, word statistics would become more reliable and the topic or sentiment would be more apparent from the word histogram alone.

Now, keep in mind that this heuristic rule was developed specifically for text classification. It may not necessarily hold for other NLP tasks—when it comes to machine translation, for instance, Transformer shines especially for very long sequences, compared to RNNs. Our heuristic is also just a rule of thumb, rather than a scientific law, so expect it to work most of the time, but not necessarily every time.

11.5   *Beyond text classification: Sequence-to-sequence learning*

You now possess all of the tools you will need to tackle most natural language processing tasks. However, you've seen these tools in action on only a single problem: text classification. This is an extremely popular use case, but there's a lot more to NLP than classification. In this section, you'll deepen your expertise by learning about *sequence-to-sequence models*.

A sequence-to-sequence model takes a sequence as input (often a sentence or paragraph) and translates it into a different sequence. This is the task at the heart of many of the most successful applications of NLP:

- *Machine translation*—Convert a paragraph in a source language to its equivalent in a target language.
- *Text summarization*—Convert a long document to a shorter version that retains the most important information.
- *Question answering*—Convert an input question into its answer.
- *Chatbots*—Convert a dialogue prompt into a reply to this prompt, or convert the history of a conversation into the next reply in the conversation.
- *Text generation*—Convert a text prompt into a paragraph that completes the prompt.
- And so forth.

The general template behind sequence-to-sequence models is described in figure 11.12. During training:

- An *encoder* model turns the source sequence into an intermediate representation.
- A *decoder* is trained to predict the next token `i` in the target sequence by looking at both previous tokens (`1` to `i - 1`) and the encoded source sequence.

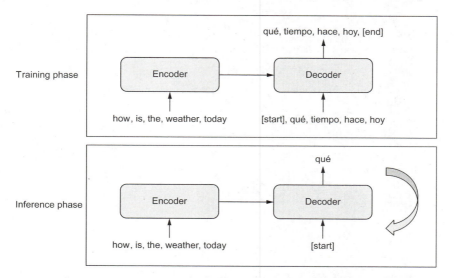

Figure 11.12 Sequence-to-sequence learning: The source sequence is processed by the encoder and is then sent to the decoder. The decoder looks at the target sequence so far and predicts the target sequence offset by one step in the future. During inference, we generate one target token at a time and feed it back into the decoder.

During inference, we don't have access to the target sequence—we're trying to predict it from scratch. We'll have to generate it one token at a time:

1. We obtain the encoded source sequence from the encoder.
2. The decoder starts by looking at the encoded source sequence as well as an initial "seed" token (such as the string `"[start]"`), and uses that to predict the first real token in the sequence.
3. The predicted sequence so far is fed back into the decoder, which generates the next token, and so on, until it generates a stop token (such as the string `"[end]"`).

Everything you've learned so far can be repurposed to build this new kind of model. Let's dive in.

11.5.1 A machine translation example

We'll demonstrate sequence-to-sequence modeling on a machine translation task. Machine translation is precisely what Transformer was developed for! We'll start with a recurrent sequence model, and we'll follow up with the full Transformer architecture.

We'll be working with an English-to-Spanish translation dataset available at http://www.manythings.org/anki/. Let's download it:

```
download.file(
  "http://storage.googleapis.com/download.tensorflow.org/data/spa-eng.zip",
  destfile = "spa-eng.zip")
zip::unzip("spa-eng.zip")
```

The text file contains one example per line: an English sentence, followed by a tab character, followed by the corresponding Spanish sentence. Let's use `readr::read_tsv()` since we have tab-separated values:

Each line contains an English phrase and its Spanish translation, tab separated.

Read the file using read_tsv() (tab-separated values).

Two-character columns

We prepend "[start]" and append "[end]" to the spanish sentence, to match the template from figure 11.12.

```
text_file <- "spa-eng/spa.txt"
text_pairs <- text_file %>%
  readr::read_tsv(col_names = c("english", "spanish"),
                  col_types = c("cc")) %>%
  within(spanish %<>% paste("[start]", ., "[end]"))
```

Our `text_pairs` look like this:

```
str(text_pairs[sample(nrow(text_pairs), 1), ])
```

```
tibble [1 × 2] (S3: tbl_df/tbl/data.frame)
 $ english: chr "I'm staying in Italy."
 $ spanish: chr "[start] Me estoy quedando en Italia. [end]"
```

Let's shuffle them and split them into the usual training, validation, and test sets:

```
num_test_samples <- num_val_samples <-
  round(0.15 * nrow(text_pairs))
num_train_samples <- nrow(text_pairs) - num_val_samples - num_test_samples

pair_group <- sample(c(
  rep("train", num_train_samples),
  rep("test", num_test_samples),
  rep("val", num_val_samples)
))

train_pairs <- text_pairs[pair_group == "train", ]
test_pairs <- text_pairs[pair_group == "test", ]
val_pairs <- text_pairs[pair_group == "val", ]
```

Next, let's prepare two separate `TextVectorization` layers: one for English and one for Spanish. We're going to need to customize the way strings are preprocessed:

- We need to preserve the `"[start]"` and `"[end]"` tokens that we've inserted. By default, the characters `[` and `]` would be stripped, but we want to keep them so we can tell apart the word "start" and the start token `"[start]"`.

- Punctuation is different from language to language! In the Spanish `Text-Vectorization` layer, if we're going to strip punctuation characters, we need to also strip the character ¿.

Note that for a non-toy translation model, we would treat punctuation characters as separate tokens rather than stripping them, because we would want to be able to generate correctly punctuated sentences. In our case, for simplicity, we'll get rid of all punctuation.

We prepare a custom string standardization function for the Spanish `TextVectorization` layer: it preserves [and] but strips ¿, ¡, and all other characters from the [:punct:] class. (The double negation of the [:punct:] class cancels out, as if it was not negated at all. However, having the outer negated regex grouping lets us specifically exclude [and] from the [:punct:] regex class. We use | to add other special characters that are not in the [:punct:] character class, like ¡ and ¿.)

Listing 11.26 Vectorizing the English and Spanish text pairs

```
punctuation_regex <- "[^[:^punct:][\\]]|[¡¿]"        ⊲── Essentially, [[:punct:]], except it omits
                                                          "[" and "]" and adds "¿" and "¡".
library(tensorflow)
custom_standardization <- function(input_string) {  ⊲── Note: this time we're using
  input_string %>%                                      tensor operations. This allows
    tf$strings$lower() %>%                               the function to be traced into
    tf$strings$regex_replace(punctuation_regex, "")      a TensorFlow graph.
}

input_string <- as_tensor("[start] ¡corre! [end]")       Preserved the [] of
custom_standardization(input_string)                     [start] and [end],
                                                         and stripped out ¡
tf.Tensor(b'[start] corre [end]', shape=(), dtype=string)  ⊲── and !.
```

> **WARNING** The TensorFlow regex has minor differences from the R regex engine. Consult the source documentation if you need advanced regular expressions: https://github.com/google/re2/wiki/Syntax.

```
vocab_size <- 15000        ⊲── To keep things simple, we'll look at only the top 15,000 words
sequence_length <- 20          in each language, and we'll restrict sentences to 20 words.

source_vectorization <- layer_text_vectorization(  ⊲──┐
  max_tokens = vocab_size,                             The English layer
  output_mode = "int",
  output_sequence_length = sequence_length
)

target_vectorization <- layer_text_vectorization(   ⊲──── The Spanish layer
  max_tokens = vocab_size,
  output_mode = "int",
  output_sequence_length = sequence_length + 1,  ⊲──┐ Generate Spanish sentences that
  standardize = custom_standardization               have one extra token, because
)                                                     we'll need to offset the sentence
                                                      by one step during training.
```

```
adapt(source_vectorization, train_pairs$english)        Learn the vocabulary
adapt(target_vectorization, train_pairs$spanish)        of each language.
```

Finally, we can turn our data into a TF Dataset pipeline. We want it to return a pair (inputs, target) where inputs is a named list with two entries, the english sentence (the encoder input), and the spanish sentence (the decoder input), and target is the Spanish sentence offset by one step ahead.

Listing 11.27   Preparing datasets for the translation task

```
format_pair <- function(pair) {                 The vectorization layer can be called
  eng <- source_vectorization(pair$english)     with either batched or unbatched data.
  spa <- target_vectorization(pair$spanish)     Here, we apply the vectorization before
                                                batching the data.

  inputs <- list(english = eng,                 Omit the last token from the Spanish sentence,
                 spanish = spa[NA:-2])           so inputs and targets are the same length.
  targets <- spa[2:NA]                           [NA:-2] drops the last element of a tensor.
  list(inputs, targets)
}                                                [2:NA] drops the first
                                                 element of a tensor.
batch_size <- 64
                                                 The target Spanish sentence is
library(tfdatasets)                              one step ahead. Both are still the
make_dataset <- function(pairs) {                same length (20 words).
  tensor_slices_dataset(pairs) %>%
    dataset_map(format_pair, num_parallel_calls = 4) %>%
    dataset_cache() %>%
    dataset_shuffle(2048) %>%          Use in-memory caching to
    dataset_batch(batch_size) %>%      speed up preprocessing.
    dataset_prefetch(16)
}
train_ds <- make_dataset(train_pairs)
val_ds <- make_dataset(val_pairs)
```

Here's what our dataset outputs look like:

```
c(inputs, targets) %<-% iter_next(as_iterator(train_ds))
str(inputs)
```

```
List of 2
 $ english:<tf.Tensor: shape=(64, 20), dtype=int64, numpy=...>
 $ spanish:<tf.Tensor: shape=(64, 20), dtype=int64, numpy=...>
```

```
str(targets)
```

```
<tf.Tensor: shape=(64, 20), dtype=int64, numpy=...>
```

The data is now ready—time to build some models. We'll start with a recurrent sequence-to-sequence model before moving on to a Transformer.

11.5.2 *Sequence-to-sequence learning with RNNs*

Recurrent neural networks dominated sequence-to-sequence learning from 2015–2017 before being overtaken by Transformer. They were the basis for many real-world machine translation systems, as mentioned in chapter 10. Google Translate circa 2017 was powered by a stack of seven large LSTM layers. It's still worth learning about this approach today, because it provides an easy entry point to understanding sequence-to-sequence models.

The simplest, naive way to use RNNs to turn a sequence into another sequence is to keep the output of the RNN at each time step. In Keras, it would look like this:

```
inputs <- layer_input(shape = c(sequence_length), dtype = "int64")
outputs <- inputs %>%
  layer_embedding(input_dim = vocab_size, output_dim = 128) %>%
  layer_lstm(32, return_sequences = TRUE) %>%
  layer_dense(vocab_size, activation = "softmax")
model <- keras_model(inputs, outputs)
```

However, this approach has two major issues:

- The target sequence must always be the same length as the source sequence. In practice, this is rarely the case. Technically, this isn't critical, because you could always pad either the source sequence or the target sequence to make their lengths match.
- Due to the step-by-step nature of RNNs, the model will be looking only at tokens $1…N$ in the source sequence to predict token N in the target sequence. This constraint makes this setup unsuitable for most tasks, particularly translation. Consider translating "The weather is nice today" to French—that would be "Il fait beau aujourd'hui." You'd need to be able to predict "Il" from just "The," "Il fait" from just "The weather," and so on, which is simply impossible.

If you're a human translator, you'd start by reading the entire source sentence before starting to translate it. This is especially important if you're dealing with languages that have wildly different word ordering, like English and Japanese. And that's exactly what standard sequence-to-sequence models do.

In a proper sequence-to-sequence setup (see figure 11.13), you would first use an RNN (the encoder) to turn the entire source sequence into a single vector (or set of vectors). This could be the last output of the RNN, or alternatively, its final internal state vectors. Then you would use this vector (or vectors) as the *initial state* of another RNN (the decoder), which would look at elements $1…N$ in the target sequence, and try to predict step $N+1$ in the target sequence.

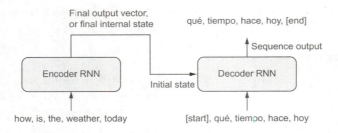

Figure 11.13 A sequence-to-sequence RNN: an RNN encoder is used to produce a vector that encodes the entire source sequence, which is used as the initial state for an RNN decoder.

Let's implement this in Keras with GRU-based encoders and decoders. The choice of GRU rather than LSTM makes things a bit simpler, because GRU has only a single state vector, whereas LSTM has multiple. Let's start with the encoder.

Listing 11.28   GRU-based encoder

```
embed_dim <- 256
latent_dim <- 1024

source <- layer_input(c(NA), dtype = "int64",
                      name = "english")
encoded_source <- source %>%
  layer_embedding(vocab_size, embed_dim,
                  mask_zero = TRUE) %>%
  bidirectional(layer_gru(units = latent_dim),
                merge_mode = "sum")
```

> **The English source sentence goes here. Specifying the name of the input enables us to fit() the model with a named list of inputs.**

> **Don't forget masking: it's critical in this setup.**

> **Our encoded source sentence is the last output of a bidirectional GRU.**

Next, let's add the decoder—a simple GRU layer that takes as its initial state the encoded source sentence. On top of it, we add a layer_dense() that produces for each output step a probability distribution over the Spanish vocabulary.

Listing 11.29   GRU-based decoder and the end-to-end model

> **The encoded source sentence serves as the initial state of the decoder GRU.**

> **The Spanish target sentence goes here.**

```
decoder_gru <- layer_gru(units = latent_dim, return_sequences = TRUE)

past_target <- layer_input(shape = c(NA), dtype = "int64", name = "spanish")
target_next_step <- past_target %>%
  layer_embedding(vocab_size, embed_dim,
                  mask_zero = TRUE) %>%
  decoder_gru(initial_state = encoded_source) %>%
  layer_dropout(0.5) %>%
  layer_dense(vocab_size, activation = "softmax")

seq2seq_rnn <-
  keras_model(inputs = list(source, past_target),
              outputs = target_next_step)
```

> **Don't forget masking.**

> **Predict the next token.**

> **End-to-end model: map the source sentence and the target sentence to the target sentence one step in the future**

During training, the decoder takes as input the entire target sequence, but thanks to the step-by-step nature of RNNs, it looks only at tokens 1...*N* in the input to predict token *N* in the output (which corresponds to the next token in the sequence, because the output is intended to be offset by one step). This means we only use information from the past to predict the future, as we should; otherwise, we'd be cheating, and our model would not work at inference time.

Let's start training.

Listing 11.30   Training our recurrent sequence-to-sequence model

```
seq2seq_rnn %>% compile(optimizer = "rmsprop",
                        loss = "sparse_categorical_crossentropy",
                        metrics = "accuracy")

seq2seq_rnn %>% fit(train_ds, epochs = 15, validation_data = val_ds)
```

We picked accuracy as a crude way to monitor validation-set performance during training. We get to 64% accuracy: on average, the model predicts the next word in the Spanish sentence correctly 64% of the time. However, in practice, next-token accuracy isn't a great metric for machine translation models, in particular because it makes the assumption that the correct target tokens from 0 to *N* are already known when predicting token *N*+1. In reality, during inference, you're generating the target sentence from scratch, and you can't rely on previously generated tokens being 100% correct. If you work on a real-world machine translation system, you will likely use "BLEU scores" to evaluate your models—a metric that looks at entire generated sequences and that seems to correlate well with human perception of translation quality.

At last, let's use our model for inference. We'll pick a few sentences in the test set and check how our model translates them. We'll start from the seed token, "[start]", and feed it into the decoder model, together with the encoded English source sentence. We'll retrieve a next-token prediction, and we'll reinject it into the decoder repeatedly, sampling one new target token at each iteration, until we get to "[end]" or reach the maximum sentence length.

Listing 11.31   Translating new sentences with our RNN encoder and decoder

```
spa_vocab <- get_vocabulary(target_vectorization)        ◁──┐  Prepare vocabulary to convert
max_decoded_sentence_length <- 20                           │  token index predictions to
                                                            │  string tokens.
decode_sequence <- function(input_sentence) {
  tokenized_input_sentence <-
    source_vectorization(array(input_sentence, dim = c(1, 1)))
  decoded_sentence <- "[start]"                ◁──┐  Seed token
  for (i in seq(max_decoded_sentence_length)) {  │
    tokenized_target_sentence <-
      target_vectorization(array(decoded_sentence, dim = c(1, 1)))
```

```
    next_token_predictions <- seq2seq_rnn %>%
      predict(list(tokenized_input_sentence,      ◁——— Sample the next token.
                   tokenized_target_sentence))
    sampled_token_index <- which.max(next_token_predictions[1, i, ])
    sampled_token <- spa_vocab[sampled_token_index]          ◁——┐
    decoded_sentence <- paste(decoded_sentence, sampled_token)   │
    if (sampled_token == "[end]")     ◁——┐                       │
      break                               │
  }                          Exit condition: either hit
  decoded_sentence           max length or sample a
}                                 stop token.
```

Convert the next token
prediction to a string,
and append it to the
generated sentence.

```
for (i in seq(20)) {
  input_sentence <- sample(test_pairs$english, 1)
  print(input_sentence)
  print(decode_sequence(input_sentence))
  print("-")
}
```

```
[1] "Does this dress look OK on me?"
[1] "[start] este vestido me parece bien [UNK] [end]"
[1] "-"
```

```
...
```

decode_sequence() is working nicely, though perhaps a little slower than we would like. One easy way to speed up eager code like this is to use tf_function(), which we first saw in chapter 7. Let's rewrite decode_sentence() to be compiled by tf_function(). This means that instead of using eager R functions like seq(), predict(), and which.max(), we will use TensorFlow equivalents, like tf$range(), calling model() directly, and tf$argmax().

Because tf$range() and tf$argmax() return a 0-based value, we'll set a function local option: option(tensorflow.extract.style = "python"). This changes the behavior of [for tensors to be 0-based as well.

```
tf_decode_sequence <- tf_function(function(input_sentence) {

  withr::local_options(
    tensorflow.extract.style = "python")     ◁——┐  Now all Tensor subsetting
                                                  with [ will be 0-based until
  tokenized_input_sentence <- input_sentence %>%  this function exits.
    as_tensor(shape = c(1, 1)) %>%
    source_vectorization()

  spa_vocab <- as_tensor(spa_vocab)

  decoded_sentence <- as_tensor("[start]", shape = c(1, 1))

  for (i in tf$range(as.integer(max_decoded_sentence_length))) {

    tokenized_target_sentence <- decoded_sentence %>%
      target_vectorization()
```

```
    next_token_predictions <-
      seq2seq_rnn(list(tokenized_input_sentence,
                       tokenized_target_sentence))

    sampled_token_index <-
      tf$argmax(next_token_predictions[0, i, ])
    sampled_token <- spa_vocab[sampled_token_index]
    decoded_sentence <-
      tf$strings$join(c(decoded_sentence, sampled_token),
                      separator = " ")

    if (sampled_token == "[end]")
      break
  }

  decoded_sentence

})

for (i in seq(20)) {
  input_sentence <- sample(test_pairs$english, 1)
  cat(input_sentence, "\n")
  cat(input_sentence %>% as_tensor() %>%
        tf_decode_sequence() %>% as.character(), "\n")
  cat("-\n")
}
```

i from tf$range() is 0-based.

tf$argmax() returns a 0-based index.

Convert to a tensor before calling tf_decode_sequence(), then convert output back to an R character.

Our `tf_decode_sentence()` is about 10× faster than the eager version. Not bad!

Note that this inference setup, although very simple, is rather inefficient, because we reprocess the entire source sentence and the entire generated target sentence every time we sample a new word. In a practical application, you'd factor the encoder and the decoder as two separate models, and your decoder would run only a single step at each token-sampling iteration, reusing its previous internal state.

Here are our translation results. Our model works decently well for a toy model, though it still makes many basic mistakes.

Listing 11.32   Some sample results from the recurrent translation model

```
Who is in this room?
[start] quién está en esta habitación [end]
-
That doesn't sound too dangerous.
[start] eso no es muy difícil [end]
-
No one will stop me.
[start] nadie me va a hacer [end]
-
Tom is friendly.
[start] tom es un buen [UNK] [end]
```

There are many ways this toy model could be improved: we could use a deep stack of recurrent layers for both the encoder and the decoder (note that for the decoder, this makes state management a bit more involved). We could use an LSTM instead of a GRU. And so on. Beyond such tweaks, however, the RNN approach to sequence-to-sequence learning has a few fundamental limitations:

- The source sequence representation has to be held entirely in the encoder state vector(s), which puts significant limitations on the size and complexity of the sentences you can translate. It's a bit as if a human were translating a sentence entirely from memory, without looking twice at the source sentence while producing the translation.
- RNNs have trouble dealing with very long sequences, because they tend to progressively forget about the past—by the time you've reached the 100th token in either sequence, little information remains about the start of the sequence. That means RNN-based models can't hold onto long-term context, which can be essential for translating long documents.

These limitations are what has led the machine learning community to embrace the Transformer architecture for sequence-to-sequence problems. Let's take a look.

11.5.3 *Sequence-to-sequence learning with Transformer*

Sequence-to-sequence learning is the task where Transformer really shines. Neural attention enables Transformer models to successfully process sequences that are considerably longer and more complex than those RNNs can handle.

As a human translating English to Spanish, you're not going to read the English sentence one word at a time, keep its meaning in memory, and then generate the Spanish sentence one word at a time. That may work for a five-word sentence, but it's unlikely to work for an entire paragraph. Instead, you'll probably want to go back and forth between the source sentence and your translation in progress and pay attention to different words in the source as you're writing down different parts of your translation.

That's exactly what you can achieve with neural attention and Transformers. You're already familiar with the Transformer encoder, which uses self-attention to produce context-aware representations of each token in an input sequence. In a sequence-to-sequence Transformer, the Transformer encoder would naturally play the role of the encoder, which reads the source sequence and produces an encoded representation of it. Unlike our previous RNN encoder, though, the Transformer encoder keeps the encoded representation in a sequence format: it's a sequence of context-aware embedding vectors.

The second half of the model is the *Transformer decoder*. Just like the RNN decoder, it reads tokens 1...N in the target sequence and tries to predict token $N + 1$. Crucially, while doing this, it uses neural attention to identify which tokens in the encoded source sentence are most closely related to the target token it's currently trying to predict—perhaps not unlike what a human translator would do. Recall the query-key-value model: in a Transformer decoder, the target sequence serves as an attention "query" that is used to pay closer attention to different parts of the source sequence (the source sequence plays the roles of both keys and values).

THE TRANSFORMER DECODER

Figure 11.14 shows the full sequence-to-sequence Transformer. Look at the decoder internals: you'll recognize that it looks very similar to the Transformer encoder, except that an extra attention block is inserted between the self-attention block applied to the target sequence and the dense layers of the exit block.

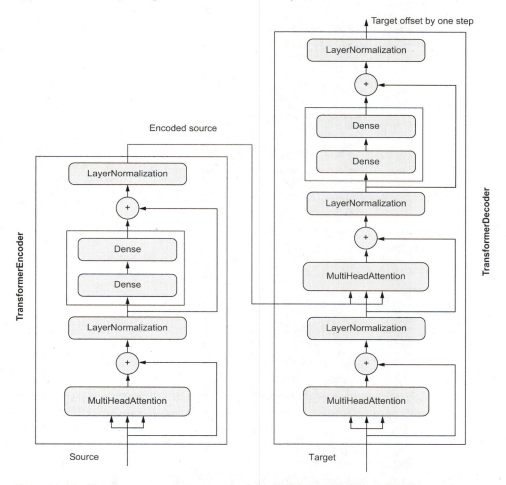

Figure 11.14   The `TransformerDecoder` is similar to the `TransformerEncoder`, except it features an additional attention block where the keys and values are the source sequence encoded by the `TransformerEncoder`. Together, the encoder and the decoder form an end-to-end Transformer.

Let's implement it. Like for the TransformerEncoder, we'll be creating a new layer class. Before we focus on the call(), method, where the action happens, let's start by defining the class constructor, containing the layers we're going to need.

Listing 11.33 **The `TransformerDecoder`**

```
layer_transformer_decoder <- new_layer_class(
  classname = "TransformerDecoder",

  initialize = function(embed_dim, dense_dim, num_heads, ...) {
    super$initialize(...)
    self$embed_dim <- embed_dim
    self$dense_dim <- dense_dim
    self$num_heads <- num_heads
    self$attention_1 <- layer_multi_head_attention(num_heads = num_heads,
                                                   key_dim = embed_dim)
    self$attention_2 <- layer_multi_head_attention(num_heads = num_heads,
                                                   key_dim = embed_dim)
    self$dense_proj <- keras_model_sequential() %>%
      layer_dense(dense_dim, activation = "relu") %>%
      layer_dense(embed_dim)

    self$layernorm_1 <- layer_layer_normalization()
    self$layernorm_2 <- layer_layer_normalization()
    self$layernorm_3 <- layer_layer_normalization()
    self$supports_masking <- TRUE              ◁
  },

  get_config = function() {
    config <- super$get_config()
    for (name in c("embed_dim", "num_heads", "dense_dim"))
      config[[name]] <- self[[name]]
    config
  },
```

This attribute ensures that the layer will propagate its input mask to its outputs; masking in Keras is explicitly opt-in. If you pass a mask to a layer that doesn't implement compute_mask() and that doesn't expose this supports_masking attribute, that's an error.

The `call()` method is almost a straightforward rendering of the connectivity diagram from figure 11.14. But there's an additional detail we need to take into account: *causal padding*. Causal padding is absolutely critical to successfully training a sequence-to-sequence Transformer. Unlike an RNN, which looks at its input one step at a time, and thus will only have access to steps $1 \ldots N$ to generate output step N (which is token $N+1$ in the target sequence), the `TransformerDecoder` is order agnostic: it looks at the entire target sequence at once. If it were allowed to use its entire input, it would simply learn to copy input step $N+1$ to location N in the output. The model would thus achieve perfect training accuracy, but of course, when running inference, it would be completely useless, because input steps beyond N aren't available.

The fix is simple: we'll mask the upper half of the pairwise attention matrix to prevent the model from paying any attention to information from the future—only information from tokens $1 \ldots N$ in the target sequence should be used when generating target token $N+1$. To do this, we'll add a `get_causal_attention_mask(inputs)` method to our `TransformerDecoder` to retrieve an attention mask that we can pass to our `MultiHeadAttention` layers.

Listing 11.34 **TransformerDecoder method that generates a causal mask**

```
get_causal_attention_mask = function(inputs) {
  c(batch_size, sequence_length, .) %<-%
    tf$unstack(tf$shape(inputs))

  x <- tf$range(sequence_length)
  i <- x[, tf$newaxis]
  j <- x[tf$newaxis, ]
  mask <- tf$cast(i >= j, "int32")

  tf$tile(mask[tf$newaxis, , ],
          tf$stack(c(batch_size, 1L, 1L)))

},
```

◁── **The third axis is encoding_length; we do not use it here.**

◁── **Integer sequence [0, 1, 2, … sequence_length-1]**

◁── **Use Tensor broadcasting in our >= operation. Cast dtype bool to int32.**

◁── **Add a batch dimension to mask, then tile (rep()) along the batch dim for batch_size times. The returned tensor has shape (batch_size, sequence_length, sequence_length).**

mask is a square matrix with shape (sequence_length, sequence_length), with 1s in the lower triangle and 0s everywhere else. For example, if sequence_length is 4, mask is:
tf.Tensor([[1 0 0 0]
[1 1 0 0]
[1 1 1 0]
[1 1 1 1]], shape=(4, 4), dtype=int32)

Now we can write down the full `call()` method implementing the forward pass of the decoder.

Listing 11.35 **The forward pass of the TransformerDecoder**

```
call = function(inputs, encoder_outputs, mask = NULL) {

  causal_mask <- self$get_causal_attention_mask(inputs)

  if (is.null(mask))
    mask <- causal_mask
  else
    mask %<>% { tf$minimum(tf$cast(.[, tf$newaxis, ], "int32"),
                           causal_mask) }

  inputs %>%
    { self$attention_1(query = ., value = ., key = .,
                       attention_mask = causal_mask) + . } %>%
    self$layernorm_1() %>%

    { self$attention_2(query = .,
                       value = encoder_outputs,
                       key = encoder_outputs,
                       attention_mask = mask) + . } %>%
```

◁── **Retrieve the causal mask.**

◁── **The mask supplied in the call is the padding mask (it describes padding locations in the target sequence).**

Combine the padding mask with the causal mask.

◁── **Pass the causal mask to the first attention layer, which performs self-attention over the target sequence.**

Use encoder_outputs supplied in the call as the value and key to attention_2().

The output of attention_1() with residual added is passed to layernorm_1().

Pass the combined mask to the second attention layer, which relates the source sequence to the target sequence.

```
self$layernorm_2() %>%
{ self$dense_proj(.) + . } %>%
self$layernorm_3()
```

> The output of attention_2() with residual added is passed to layernorm_2().

> The output of dense_proj() with residual is added and passed to layernorm_3().

```
})
```

PUTTING IT ALL TOGETHER: A TRANSFORMER FOR MACHINE TRANSLATION

The end-to-end Transformer is the model we'll be training. It maps the source sequence and the target sequence to the target sequence one step in the future. It straight-forwardly combines the pieces we've built so far: PositionalEmbedding layers, the TransformerEncoder, and the TransformerDecoder. Note that both the Transformer-Encoder and the TransformerDecoder are shape invariant, so you could be stacking many of them to create a more powerful encoder or decoder. In our example, we'll stick to a single instance of each.

Listing 11.36   End-to-end Transformer

```
embed_dim <- 256
dense_dim <- 2048
num_heads <- 8
```

> Encode the source sentence.

```
encoder_inputs <- layer_input(shape(NA), dtype = "int64", name = "english")
encoder_outputs <- encoder_inputs %>%
  layer_positional_embedding(sequence_length, vocab_size, embed_dim) %>%
  layer_transformer_encoder(embed_dim, dense_dim, num_heads)
```

> Pass NULL for the first argument, so a layer instance is created and returned directly and not composed with anything yet.

```
transformer_decoder <-
    layer_transformer_decoder(NULL, embed_dim, dense_dim, num_heads)

decoder_inputs <-  layer_input(shape(NA), dtype = "int64", name = "spanish")
decoder_outputs <- decoder_inputs %>%
  layer_positional_embedding(sequence_length, vocab_size, embed_dim) %>%
  transformer_decoder(., encoder_outputs) %>%
  layer_dropout(0.5) %>%
  layer_dense(vocab_size, activation = "softmax")

transformer <- keras_model(list(encoder_inputs, decoder_inputs),
                           decoder_outputs)
```

> Predict a word for each output position.

> Encode the target sentence and combine it with the encoded source sentence.

We're now ready to train our model—we get to 67% accuracy, a good deal above the GRU-based model.

Listing 11.37   Training the sequence-to-sequence Transformer

```
transformer %>%
  compile(optimizer = "rmsprop",
          loss = "sparse_categorical_crossentropy",
          metrics = "accuracy")

transformer %>%
  fit(train_ds, epochs = 30, validation_data = val_ds)
```

Finally, let's try using our model to translate never-seen-before English sentences from the test set. The setup is identical to what we used for the sequence-to-sequence RNN model; all that's changed is we're replaced `seq2seq_rnn` with `transformer`, and we drop the extra token that we configured our `target_vectorization()` layer to add.

Listing 11.38 Translating new sentences with our Transformer model

```
tf_decode_sequence <- tf_function(function(input_sentence) {
  withr::local_options(tensorflow.extract.style = "python")

  tokenized_input_sentence <- input_sentence %>%
    as_tensor(shape = c(1, 1)) %>%
    source_vectorization()
  spa_vocab <- as_tensor(spa_vocab)
  decoded_sentence <- as_tensor("[start]", shape = c(1, 1))

  for (i in tf$range(as.integer(max_decoded_sentence_length))) {

    tokenized_target_sentence <-
      target_vectorization(decoded_sentence)[, NA:-1]          ◁─┐  Drop the last token;
                                                                    "python" style is not
                                                                    inclusive of a slice end.
    next_token_predictions <-
      transformer(list(tokenized_input_sentence,
                       tokenized_target_sentence))

    sampled_token_index <- tf$argmax(next_token_predictions[0, i, ])
    sampled_token <- spa_vocab[sampled_token_index]          ◁─┐
    decoded_sentence <-                                          Convert the next token
      tf$strings$join(c(decoded_sentence, sampled_token),        prediction to a string,
                      separator = " ")                           and append it to the
                                                                 generated sentence.
    if (sampled_token == "[end]")
      break

  }

  decoded_sentence

})

for (i in sample.int(nrow(test_pairs), 20)) {
  c(input_sentence, correct_translation) %<-% test_pairs[i, ]
  cat(input_sentence, "\n")
  cat(input_sentence %>% as_tensor() %>%
        tf_decode_sequence() %>% as.character(), "\n")
  cat("-\n")
}
```

Annotations: Sample the next token. / Exit condition

Subjectively, the Transformer seems to perform significantly better than the GRU-based translation model. It's still a toy model, but it's a better toy model.

Listing 11.39   Some sample results from the Transformer translation model

```
This is a song I learned when I was a kid.
[start] esta es una canción que aprendí cuando
➡ era chico [end]                          ◄————————————
-
She can play the piano.
[start] ella puede tocar piano [end]
-
I'm not who you think I am.
[start] no soy la persona que tú creo que soy [end]
-
It may have rained a little last night.
[start] puede que llueve un poco el pasado [end]
```

Although the source sentence wasn't gendered, this translation assumes a male speaker. Keep in mind that translation models will often make unwarranted assumptions about their input data, which leads to algorithmic bias. In the worst cases, a model might hallucinate memorized information that has nothing to do with the data it's currently processing.

That concludes this chapter on natural language processing—you just went from the very basics to a fully fledged Transformer that can translate from English to Spanish. Teaching machines to make sense of language is the latest superpower you can add to your collection.

Summary

- There are two kinds of NLP models: *bag-of-words models* that process sets of words or *N*-grams without taking into account their order, and *sequence models* that process word order. A bag-of-words model is made of `Dense` layers, whereas a sequence model could be an RNN, a 1D convnet, or a Transformer.
- When it comes to text classification, the ratio between the number of samples in your training data and the mean number of words per sample can help you determine whether you should use a bag-of-words model or a sequence model.
- *Word embeddings* are vector spaces where semantic relationships between words are modeled as distance relationships between vectors that represent those words.
- *Sequence-to-sequence learning* is a generic, powerful learning framework that can be applied to solve many NLP problems, including machine translation. A sequence-to-sequence model is made of an encoder, which processes a source sequence, and a decoder, which tries to predict future tokens in target sequence by looking at past tokens, with the help of the encoder-processed source sequence.
- *Neural attention* is a way to create context-aware word representations. It's the basis for the Transformer architecture.
- The *Transformer* architecture, which consists of a `TransformerEncoder` and a `TransformerDecoder`, yields excellent results on sequence-to-sequence tasks. The first half, the `TransformerEncoder`, can also be used for text classification or any sort of single-input NLP task.

12

Generative deep learning

The potential of artificial intelligence to emulate human thought processes goes beyond passive tasks such as object recognition and mostly reactive tasks such as driving a car. It extends well into creative activities. When I first made the claim that in the not-so-distant future, most of the cultural content that we consume will be created with substantial help from AIs, I was met with utter disbelief, even from long-time machine learning practitioners. That was in 2014. Fast-forward a few years, and the disbelief had receded at an incredible speed. In the summer of 2015, we were entertained by Google's DeepDream algorithm turning an image into a psychedelic mess of dog eyes and pareidolic artifacts; in 2016, we started using smartphone applications to turn photos into paintings of various styles. In the summer of 2016, an experimental short movie, *Sunspring*, was directed using a script written by a long short-term memory (LSTM). Maybe you've recently listened to music that was generated by a neural network.

Granted, the artistic productions we've seen from AI so far have been fairly low quality. AI isn't anywhere close to rivaling human screenwriters, painters, and composers. But replacing humans was always beside the point: artificial intelligence isn't about replacing our own intelligence with something else; it's about bringing into our lives and work *more* intelligence—intelligence of a different kind. In many fields, but especially in creative ones, AI will be used by humans as a tool to augment their own capabilities: more *augmented intelligence* than *artificial intelligence*.

A large part of artistic creation consists of simple pattern recognition and technical skill. And that's precisely the part of the process that many find less attractive or even dispensable. That's where AI comes in. Our perceptual modalities, our language, and our artwork all have statistical structure. Learning this structure is what deep learning algorithms excel at. Machine learning models can learn the statistical *latent space* of images, music, and stories, and they can then *sample* from this space, creating new artworks with characteristics similar to those the model has seen in its training data. Naturally, such sampling is hardly an act of artistic creation in itself. It's a mere mathematical operation: the algorithm has no grounding in human life, human emotions, or our experience of the world; instead, it learns from an experience that has little in common with ours. It's only our interpretation, as human spectators, that will give meaning to what the model generates. But in the hands of a skilled artist, algorithmic generation can be steered to become meaningful—and beautiful. Latent space sampling can become a brush that empowers the artist, augments our creative affordances, and expands the space of what we can imagine. What's more, it can make artistic creation more accessible by eliminating the need for technical skill and practice, setting up a new medium of pure expression, factoring art apart from craft.

Iannis Xenakis, a visionary pioneer of electronic and algorithmic music, beautifully expressed this same idea in the 1960s, in the context of the application of automation technology to music composition:[1]

> *Freed from tedious calculations, the composer is able to devote himself to the general problems that the new musical form poses and to explore the nooks and crannies of this form while modifying the values of the input data. For example, he may test all instrumental combinations from soloists, to chamber orchestras, to large orchestras. With the aid of electronic computers the composer becomes a sort of pilot: he presses the buttons, introduces coordinates, and supervises the controls of a cosmic vessel sailing in the space of sound, across sonic constellations and galaxies that he could formerly glimpse only as a distant dream.*

In this chapter, we'll explore from various angles the potential of deep learning to augment artistic creation. We'll review sequence data generation (which can be used to generate text or music), DeepDream, and image generation using both variational autoencoders and generative adversarial networks. We'll get your computer to dream up content never seen before; and maybe we'll get you to dream, too, about the fantastic possibilities that lie at the intersection of technology and art. Let's get started.

---

[1] Iannis Xenakis, "Musiques formelles: nouveaux principes formels de composition musicale," special issue of *La Revue musicale*, nos. 253–254 (1963).

12.1 Text generation

In this section, we'll explore how recurrent neural networks can be used to generate sequence data. We'll use text generation as an example, but the exact same techniques can be generalized to any kind of sequence data: you could apply it to sequences of musical notes to generate new music, to time series of brushstroke data (perhaps recorded while an artist paints on an iPad) to generate paintings stroke by stroke, and so on.

Sequence data generation is in no way limited to artistic content generation. It has been successfully applied to speech synthesis and to dialogue generation for chatbots. The Smart Reply feature that Google released in 2016, capable of automatically generating a selection of quick replies to emails or text messages, is powered by similar techniques.

12.1.1 A brief history of generative deep learning for sequence generation

In late 2014, few people had ever seen the initials LSTM, even in the machine learning community. Successful applications of sequence data generation with recurrent networks began to appear in the mainstream only in 2016. But these techniques have a fairly long history, starting with the development of the LSTM algorithm in 1997 (discussed in chapter 10). This new algorithm was used early on to generate text character by character.

In 2002, Douglas Eck, then at Schmidhuber's lab in Switzerland, applied LSTM to music generation for the first time, with promising results. Eck is now a researcher at Google Brain, and in 2016, he started a new research group there, called Magenta, focused on applying modern deep learning techniques to produce engaging music. Sometimes good ideas take 15 years to get started.

In the late 2000s and early 2010s, Alex Graves did important pioneering work using recurrent networks for sequence data generation. In particular, his 2013 work on applying recurrent mixture density networks to generate human-like handwriting using time series of pen positions is seen by some as a turning point.[2] This specific application of neural networks at that specific moment in time captured for me the notion of *machines that dream* and was a significant inspiration around the time I started developing Keras. Graves left a similar commented-out remark hidden in a 2013 LaTeX file uploaded to the preprint server arXiv: "Generating sequential data is the closest computers get to dreaming." Several years later, we take a lot of these developments for granted, but at the time it was difficult to watch Graves's demonstrations and not walk away awe-inspired by the possibilities. Between 2015 and 2017, recurrent neural networks were successfully used for text and dialogue generation, music generation, and speech synthesis.

---

[2] Alex Graves, "Generating Sequences with Recurrent Neural Networks," arXiv (2013), https://arxiv.org/abs/1308.0850.

Then around 2017–2018, the Transformer architecture started taking over recurrent neural networks, not just for supervised natural language processing tasks but also for generative sequence models—in particular *language modeling* (word-level text generation). The best-known example of a generative Transformer would be GPT-3, a 175 billion parameter text-generation model trained by the startup OpenAI on an astoundingly large text corpus, including most digitally available books, Wikipedia, and a large fraction of a crawl of the entire internet. GPT-3 made headlines in 2020 due to its capability to generate plausible-sounding text paragraphs on virtually any topic, a prowess that has fed a short-lived hype wave worthy of the most torrid AI summer.

12.1.2   *How do you generate sequence data?*

The universal way to generate sequence data in deep learning is to train a model (usually a Transformer or an RNN) to predict the next token or next few tokens in a sequence, using the previous tokens as input. For instance, given the input "the cat is on the," the model is trained to predict the target "mat," the next word. As usual when working with text data, tokens are typically words or characters, and any network that can model the probability of the next token given the previous ones is called a *language model*. A language model captures the *latent space* of language: its statistical structure.

Once you have such a trained language model, you can *sample* from it (generate new sequences): you feed it an initial string of text (called *conditioning data*), ask it to generate the next character or the next word (you can even generate several tokens at once), add the generated output back to the input data, and repeat the process many times (see figure 12.1). This loop allows you to generate sequences of arbitrary length that reflect the structure of the data on which the model was trained: sequences that look *almost* like human-written sentences.

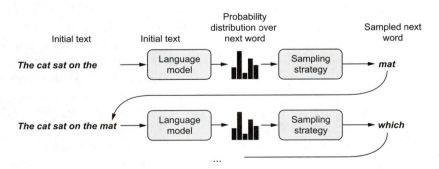

Figure 12.1   The process of word-by-word text generation using a language model

12.1.3   *The importance of the sampling strategy*

When generating text, the way you choose the next token is crucially important. A naive approach is *greedy sampling*, consisting of always choosing the most likely next character. But such an approach results in repetitive, predictable strings that don't look like coherent language. A more interesting approach makes slightly more surprising choices: it introduces randomness in the sampling process by sampling from the probability distribution for the next character. This is called *stochastic sampling* (recall that *stochasticity* is what we call *randomness* in this field). In such a setup, if a word has a 0.3 probability of being next in the sentence according to the model, you'll choose it 30% of the time. Note that greedy sampling can also be cast as sampling from a probability distribution: one where a certain word has probability 1 and all others have probability 0.

Sampling probabilistically from the softmax output of the model is neat: it allows even unlikely words to be sampled some of the time, generating more interesting-looking sentences and sometimes showing creativity by coming up with new, realistic-sounding sentences that didn't occur in the training data. But there's one issue with this strategy: it doesn't offer a way to *control the amount of randomness* in the sampling process.

Why would you want more or less randomness? Consider an extreme case: pure random sampling, where you draw the next word from a uniform probability distribution, and every word is equally likely. This scheme has maximum randomness; in other words, this probability distribution has maximum entropy. Naturally, it won't produce anything interesting. At the other extreme, greedy sampling doesn't produce anything interesting, either, and has no randomness: the corresponding probability distribution has minimum entropy. Sampling from the "real" probability distribution—the distribution that is output by the model's softmax function—constitutes an intermediate point between these two extremes. But there are many other intermediate points of higher or lower entropy that you may want to explore. Less entropy will give the generated sequences a more predictable structure (and, thus, they will potentially be more realistic looking), whereas more entropy will result in more surprising and creative sequences. When sampling from generative models, it's always good to explore different amounts of randomness in the generation process. Because we—humans—are the ultimate judges of how interesting the generated data is, interestingness is highly subjective, and there's no telling in advance where the point of optimal entropy lies.

To control the amount of stochasticity in the sampling process, we'll introduce a parameter called the *softmax temperature*, which characterizes the entropy of the probability distribution used for sampling: it characterizes how surprising or predictable the choice of the next word will be. Given a `temperature` value, a new probability distribution is computed from the original one (the softmax output of the model) by reweighting it in the following way.

Higher temperatures result in sampling distributions of higher entropy that will generate more surprising and unstructured generated data, whereas a lower temperature will result in less randomness and much more predictable generated data (see figure 12.2).

Listing 12.1   Reweighting a probability distribution to a different temperature

```
reweight_distribution <-
  function(original_distribution, temperature = 0.5) {
    original_distribution %>% .
      { exp(log(.) / temperature) } %>%
      { . / sum(.) }
  }
```

original_distribution is a 1D array of probability values that must sum to 1. temperature is a factor quantifying the entropy of the output distribution.

Note that reweight_distribution() will work for both 1D R vectors and 1D Tensorflow tensors, because exp, log, /, and sum are all R generics.

Return a reweighted version of the original distribution. The sum of the distribution may no longer be 1, so you divide it by its sum to obtain the new distribution.

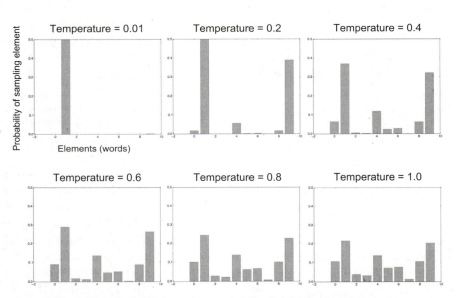

Figure 12.2   Different reweightings of one probability distribution: Low temperature = more deterministic; high temperature = more random

12.1.4   *Implementing text generation with Keras*

Let's put these ideas into practice in a Keras implementation. The first thing you need is a lot of text data that you can use to learn a language model. You can use any sufficiently large text file or set of text files—Wikipedia, *The Lord of the Rings,* and so on.

In this example, we'll keep working with the IMDB movie review dataset from the last chapter, and we'll learn to generate never-read-before movie reviews. As such, our language model will be a model of the style and topics of these movie reviews specifically, rather than a general model of the English language.

PREPARING THE DATA

Just like in the previous chapter, let's download and uncompress the IMDB movie reviews dataset. (This is the same dataset we downloaded in chapter 11.)

Listing 12.2 Downloading and uncompressing the IMDB movie reviews dataset

```
url <- "https://ai.stanford.edu/~amaas/data/sentiment/aclImdb_v1.tar.gz"
filename <- basename(url)
options(timeout = 60 * 10)              <——— 10-minute timeout
download.file(url, destfile = filename)
untar(filename)
```

You're already familiar with the structure of the data: we get a folder named aclImdb containing two subfolders, one for negative-sentiment movie reviews and one for positive-sentiment reviews. There's one text file per review. We'll call text_dataset_ from_directory() with label_mode = NULL to create a TF Dataset that reads from these files and yields the text content of each file.

Listing 12.3 Creating a TF Dataset from text files (one file = one sample)

```
library(tensorflow)
library(tfdatasets)
library(keras)
dataset <- text_dataset_from_directory(      Strip the "<br />" HTML tag that occurs
  directory = "aclImdb",                      in many of the reviews. This did not
  label_mode = NULL,                          matter much for text classification, but
  batch_size = 256)                           we wouldn't want to generate "<br />"
                                              tags in this example!

dataset <- dataset %>%
  dataset_map( ~ tf$strings$regex_replace(.x, "<br />", " "))   <—┘
```

Now let's use a layer_text_vectorization() to compute the vocabulary we'll be working with. We'll use only the first sequence_length words of each review: our layer_ text_vectorization() will cut off anything beyond that when vectorizing a text.

Listing 12.4 Preparing a layer_text_vectorization()

```
                                    We'll consider only the top 15,000 most common words—anything
sequence_length <- 100              else will be treated as the out-of-vocabulary token, "[UNK]".
vocab_size <- 15000      <—┘
text_vectorization <- layer_text_vectorization(
  max_tokens = vocab_size,          | We want to return integer word index sequences.
  output_mode = "int",     <————┘
  output_sequence_length = sequence_length   <—┐
)                                              | We'll work with inputs and targets of
adapt(text_vectorization, dataset)             | length 100 (but because we'll offset the
                                               | targets by 1, the model will actually see
                                               | sequences of length 99).
```

Let's use the layer to create a language-modeling dataset where input samples are vectorized texts and corresponding targets are the same texts offset by one word.

Listing 12.5   Setting up a language-modeling dataset

Convert a batch of texts (strings) to a batch of integer sequences.

```
prepare_lm_dataset <- function(text_batch) {
  vectorized_sequences <- text_vectorization(text_batch)
  x <- vectorized_sequences[, NA:-2]
  y <- vectorized_sequences[, 2:NA]
  list(x, y)
}

lm_dataset <- dataset %>%
  dataset_map(prepare_lm_dataset, num_parallel_calls = 4)
```

Create inputs by cutting off the last word of the sequences (drop last column).

Create targets by offsetting the sequences by 1 (drop first column).

A Transformer-based sequence-to-sequence model

We'll train a model to predict a probability distribution over the next word in a sentence, given a number of initial words. When the model is trained, we'll feed it with a prompt, sample the next word, add that word back to the prompt, and repeat, until we've generated a short paragraph.

Like we did for temperature forecasting in chapter 10, we could train a model that takes as input a sequence of N words and simply predicts word $N+1$. However, several issues exist with this setup in the context of sequence generation.

First, the model would learn to produce predictions only when N words were available, but it would be useful to be able to start predicting with fewer than N words. Otherwise, we'd be constrained to using only relatively long prompts (in our implementation, $N = 100$ words). We didn't have this need in chapter 10.

Second, many of our training sequences will be mostly overlapping. Consider $N = 4$. The text "A complete sentence must have, at minimum, three things: a subject, verb, and an object" would be used to generate the following training sequences:

- "A complete sentence must"
- "complete sentence must have"
- "sentence must have at"
- and so on, until "verb and an object"

A model that treats each such sequence as an independent sample would have to do a lot of redundant work, re-encoding multiple times subsequences that it has largely seen before. In chapter 10, this wasn't much of a problem, because we didn't have that many training samples in the first place, and we needed to benchmark dense and convolutional models, for which redoing the work every time is the only option. We could try to alleviate this redundancy problem by using *strides* to sample our sequences—skipping a few words between two consecutive samples. But that would reduce our number of training samples while providing only a partial solution.

To address these two issues, we'll use a *sequence-to-sequence model*: we'll feed sequences of N words (indexed from *1* to *N*) into our model, and we'll predict the sequence offset by one (from *2* to *N+1*). We'll use causal masking to make sure that, for any *i*, the model will use only words from *1* to *i* to predict the word *i + 1*. This means that we're simultaneously training the model to solve *N* mostly overlapping but different problems: predicting the next words given a sequence of 1 <= i <= N prior words (see figure 12.3). At generation time, even if you prompt the model with only a single word, it will be able to give you a probability distribution for the next possible words.

Next-word prediction
```
the cat sat on the   → mat
```

Sequence-to-sequence
modeling
```
the    → cat sat on the mat
the cat   → sat on the mat
the cat sat   → on the mat
the cat sat on   → the mat
the cat sat on the   → mat
```

Figure 12.3 Compared to plain next-word prediction, sequence-to-sequence modeling simultaneously optimizes for multiple prediction problems.

Note that we could have used a similar sequence-to-sequence setup on our temperature-forecasting problem in chapter 10: given a sequence of 120 hourly data points, learn to generate a sequence of 120 temperatures offset by 24 hours in the future. You'd be solving not only the initial problem but also the 119 related problems of forecasting temperature in 24 hours, given 1 <= i < 120 prior hourly data points. If you try to retrain the RNNs from chapter 10 in a sequence-to-sequence setup, you'll find that you get similar but incrementally worse results, because the constraint of solving these additional 119 related problems with the same model interferes slightly with the task we actually do care about.

In the previous chapter, you learned about the setup you can use for sequence-to-sequence learning in the general case: feed the source sequence into an encoder, and then feed both the encoded sequence and the target sequence into a decoder that tries to predict the same target sequence, offset by one step. When you're doing text generation, there is no source sequence: you're just trying to predict the next tokens in the target sequence given past tokens, which we can do using only the decoder. And thanks to causal padding, the decoder will look at only words *1...N* to predict the word *N+1*.

Let's implement our model—we're going to reuse the building blocks we created in chapter 11: `layer_positional_embedding()` and `layer_transformer_decoder()`.

Listing 12.6 A simple Transformer-based language model

```
embed_dim <- 256
latent_dim <- 2048
num_heads <- 2

transformer_decoder <-
  layer_transformer_decoder(NULL, embed_dim, latent_dim, num_heads)

inputs <- layer_input(shape(NA), dtype = "int64")
outputs <- inputs %>%
```

```
layer_positional_embedding(sequence_length, vocab_size, embed_dim) %>%
transformer_decoder(., .) %>%
layer_dense(vocab_size, activation = "softmax")
```
◁— **Softmax over possible vocabulary words, computed for each output sequence time step.**

```
model <-
  keras_model(inputs, outputs) %>%
  compile(loss = "sparse_categorical_crossentropy",
          optimizer = "rmsprop")
```

12.1.5 *A text-generation callback with variable-temperature sampling*

We'll use a callback to generate text using a range of different temperatures after every epoch. This allows you to see how the generated text evolves as the model begins to converge, as well as the impact of temperature in the sampling strategy. To seed text generation, we'll use the prompt "this movie": all of our generated texts will start with this.

First, let's define some functions to generate sentences. Later, we'll use these functions in a callback.

The vector we will use to convert word indices (integers) back to strings, to be used for text decoding

```
vocab <- get_vocabulary(text_vectorization)

sample_next <- function(predictions, temperature = 1.0) {
  predictions %>%
    reweight_distribution(temperature) %>%
    sample.int(length(.), 1, prob = .)
}
```
The temperature to use for sampling

Implement variable-temperature sampling from a probability distribution.

```
generate_sentence <-
  function(model, prompt, generate_length, temperature) {

    sentence <- prompt
    for (i in seq(generate_length)) {

      model_preds <- sentence %>%
        array(dim = c(1, 1)) %>%
        text_vectorization() %>%
        predict(model, .)

      sampled_word <- model_preds %>%
        .[1, i, ] %>%
        sample_next(temperature) %>%
        vocab[.]

      sentence <- paste(sentence, sampled_word)

    }

    sentence
  }
```

Prompt that we use to seed text generation

Iterate for how many words to generate.

Feed the current sequence into our model.

Retrieve the predictions for the last time step...

...and use them to sample a new token...

...and convert the token integer to a string.

Append the new word to the current sequence and repeat.

sample_next() and generate_sentence() do the work of generating sentences from a model. They work eagerly; they call predict() to produce predictions as R arrays, call sample.int() to pick the next token, and build up the sentence as an R string with paste().

Because we may want to generate many sentences, it makes sense to optimize it a little. We can speed up generate_sentence considerably (~25x) by rewriting it as a tf_function(). To do this, we just need to replace a few R functions with TensorFlow equivalents. Instead of for(i in seq()), we can write for(i in tf$range()). We can also substitute sample.int() with tf$random$categorical(), paste() with tf$strings$join(), and predict(model, .) with model(.). Here is what sample_next() and generate_sentence() look like as tf_function()s:

```
tf_sample_next <- function(predictions, temperature = 1.0) {
  predictions %>%
    reweight_distribution(temperature) %>%        tf$random$catagorical() expects
    { log(.[tf$newaxis, ]) } %>%                  a batch of log probabilities.
    tf$random$categorical(1L) %>%
    tf$reshape(shape())                           tf$random$catagorical() returns a scalar
  }                                               integer with shape (1, 1). Reshape to shape ().


library(tfautograph)     For ag_loop_vars() (more on this soon)

tf_generate_sentence <- tf_function(
  function(model, prompt, generate_length, temperature) {

    withr::local_options(tensorflow.extract.style = "python")

    vocab <- as_tensor(vocab)

    sentence <- prompt %>% as_tensor(shape = c(1, 1))

    ag_loop_vars(sentence)                         Provide a hint to the compiler
    for (i in tf$range(generate_length)) {         that `sentence` is the only
                                                   variable we want after iteration.
      model_preds <- sentence %>%
        text_vectorization() %>%
        model()

      sampled_word <- model_preds %>%
        .[0, i, ] %>%
        tf_sample_next(temperature) %>%
        vocab[.]

      sentence <- sampled_word %>%
        { tf$strings$join(c(sentence, .), " ") }
                                                   Reshape from (1, 1) to (). Note that
    }                                              tf$strings$join() preserves sentence's
                                                   (1, 1) shape throughout iteration.
    sentence %>% tf$reshape(shape())
  }
)
```

On my machine, generating a sentence of 50 words takes approx 2.5 seconds with the eager `generate_sentence()`, and .1 seconds with `tf_generate_sentence()`, a 25× improvement! Remember, it always makes sense to prototype your code first by running it eagerly, and only move to using `tf_function()` once you have it working how you want.

`for` **loops and** `autograph`

One wrinkle with evaluating R functions eagerly before wrapping them with `tf_function(fn, autograph = TRUE)` (the default) is that `autograph = TRUE` gives capabilities that base R doesn't have, like the ability for `for` to iterate over tensors. You can still evaluate expressions like `for(i in tf$range())` or `for(batch in tf$dataset)` eagerly by calling `tfautograph::autograph()` directly, like this:

```
library(tfautograph)
autograph({
  for(i in tf$range(3L))
    print(i)
})
```

```
tf.Tensor(0, shape=(), dtype=int32)
tf.Tensor(1, shape=(), dtype=int32)
tf.Tensor(2, shape=(), dtype=int32)
```

or

```
fn <- function(x) {
  for(i in x) print(i)
}
ag_fn <- autograph(fn)
ag_fn(tf$range(3))
```

```
tf.Tensor(0.0, shape=(), dtype=float32)
tf.Tensor(1.0, shape=(), dtype=float32)
tf.Tensor(2.0, shape=(), dtype=float32)
```

In interactive sessions you can temporarily globally enable `if`, `while`, and `for` to accept tensors by calling `tfautograph:::attach_ag_mask()`.

A `for()` loop that iterates over a tensor in a `tf_function()` builds a `tf$while_loop()`, and it inherits all same restrictions. Every tensor tracked by the loop must have a stable shape and dtype throughout iteration.

The call `ag_loop_vars(sentence)` gives the `tf_function()` compiler a hint that the only variable we're interested in after the `for` loop is `sentence`. This informs the compiler that other tensors, like `sampled_word`, `i`, and `model_preds`, are loop-local variables and can be safely optimized away after the loop.

Note that iterating over a regular R object like `for(i in seq(0, 49))` in a `tf_function()` would not build a `tf$while_loop()`, but would instead evaluate with regular R semantics and would result in the `tf_function()` tracing an unrolled loop (which is sometimes preferable, for short loops with a fixed number of iterations).

Here is the callback where we'll call `tf_generate_sentence()` to generate text during training:

Listing 12.7 The text-generation callback

```
callback_text_generator <- new_callback_class(
  classname = "TextGenerator",

  initialize = function(prompt, generate_length,
                        temperatures = 1,
                        print_freq = 1L) {
    private$prompt <- as_tensor(prompt, "string")
    private$generate_length <- as_tensor(generate_length, "int32")
    private$temperatures <- as.numeric(temperatures)
    private$print_freq <- as.integer(print_freq)
  },

  on_epoch_end = function(epoch, logs = NULL) {
    if ((epoch %% private$print_freq) != 0)
      return()

    for (temperature in private$temperatures) {
      cat("== Generating with temperature", temperature, "\n")

      sentence <- tf_generate_sentence(
        self$model,
        private$prompt,
        private$generate_length,
        as_tensor(temperature, "float32")
      )
      cat(as.character(sentence), "\n")
    }
  }
)
```

> We'll use a diverse range of temperatures to sample text, to demonstrate the effect of temperature on text generation.

> This is a regular R for loop iterating eagerly over an R vector.

> Note we call this function with only tensors and the model, not R numeric or character vectors.

> These were already cast to Tensors in initialize().

```
text_gen_callback <- callback_text_generator(
  prompt = "This movie",
  generate_length = 50,
  temperatures = c(0.2, 0.5, 0.7, 1., 1.5)
)
```

> The set of temperatures we generate text with

Let's `fit()` this thing.

Listing 12.8 Fitting the language model

```
model %>%
  fit(lm_dataset,
      epochs = 200,
      callbacks = list(text_gen_callback))
```

Here are some cherry-picked examples of what we're able to generate after 200 epochs of training. Note that punctuation isn't part of our vocabulary, so none of our generated text has any punctuation:

- With `temperature=0.2`
  - "this movie is a [UNK] of the original movie and the first half hour of the movie is pretty good but it is a very good movie it is a good movie for the time period"
  - "this movie is a [UNK] of the movie it is a movie that is so bad that it is a [UNK] movie it is a movie that is so bad that it makes you laugh and cry at the same time it is not a movie i dont think ive ever seen"
- With `temperature=0.5`
  - "this movie is a [UNK] of the best genre movies of all time and it is not a good movie it is the only good thing about this movie i have seen it for the first time and i still remember it being a [UNK] movie i saw a lot of years"
  - "this movie is a waste of time and money i have to say that this movie was a complete waste of time i was surprised to see that the movie was made up of a good movie and the movie was not very good but it was a waste of time and"
- With `temperature=0.7`
  - "this movie is fun to watch and it is really funny to watch all the characters are extremely hilarious also the cat is a bit like a [UNK] [UNK] and a hat [UNK] the rules of the movie can be told in another scene saves it from being in the back of"
  - "this movie is about [UNK] and a couple of young people up on a small boat in the middle of nowhere one might find themselves being exposed to a [UNK] dentist they are killed by [UNK] i was a huge fan of the book and i havent seen the original so it"
- With `temperature=1.0`
  - "this movie was entertaining i felt the plot line was loud and touching but on a whole watch a stark contrast to the artistic of the original we watched the original version of england however whereas arc was a bit of a little too ordinary the [UNK] were the present parent [UNK]"
  - "this movie was a masterpiece away from the storyline but this movie was simply exciting and frustrating it really entertains friends like this the actors in this movie try to go straight from the sub thats image and they make it a really good tv show"
- With `temperature=1.5`
  - "this movie was possibly the worst film about that 80 women its as weird insightful actors like barker movies but in great buddies yes no decorated shield even [UNK] land dinosaur ralph ian was must make a play happened falls after miscast [UNK] bach not really not wrestlemania seriously sam didnt exist"
  - "this movie could be so unbelievably lucas himself bringing our country wildly funny things has is for the garish serious and strong performances colin writing more detailed dominated but before and that images gears burning the plate patriotism we you expected dyan bosses devotion to must do your own duty and another"

As you can see, a low temperature value results in very boring and repetitive text and can sometimes cause the generation process to get stuck in a loop. With higher temperatures, the generated text becomes more interesting, surprising, and even creative. With a very high temperature, the local structure starts to break down, and the output looks largely random. Here, a good generation temperature would seem to be about 0.7. Always experiment with multiple sampling strategies! A clever balance between learned structure and randomness is what makes generation interesting.

Note that by training a bigger model, longer, on more data, you can achieve generated samples that look far more coherent and realistic than this one—the output of a model like GPT-3 is a good example of what can be done with language models (GPT-3 is effectively the same thing as what we trained in this example, but with a deep stack of Transformer decoders, and a much bigger training corpus). But don't expect to ever generate any meaningful text, other than through random chance and the magic of your own interpretation: all you're doing is sampling data from a statistical model of which words come after which words. Language models are all form and no substance.

Natural language is many things: a communication channel; a way to act on the world; a social lubricant; a way to formulate, store, and retrieve your own thoughts. These uses of languages are where its meaning originates. A deep learning "language model," despite its name, captures effectively none of these fundamental aspects of language. It cannot communicate (it has nothing to communicate about and no one to communicate with), it cannot act on the world (it has no agency and no intent), it cannot be social, and it doesn't have any thoughts to process with the help of words. Language is the operating system of the mind, and so, for language to be meaningful, it needs a mind to leverage it.

What a language model does is capture the statistical structure of the observable artifacts—books, online movie reviews, tweets—that we generate as we use language to live our lives. The fact that these artifacts have a statistical structure at all is a side effect of how humans implement language. Here's a thought experiment: what if our languages did a better job of compressing communications, much like computers do with most digital communications? Language would be no less meaningful and could still fulfill its many purposes, but it would lack any intrinsic statistical structure, thus making it impossible to model as you just did.

12.1.6 *Wrapping up*

- You can generate discrete sequence data by training a model to predict the next token(s), given previous tokens.
- In the case of text, such a model is called a *language model*. It can be based on either words or characters.
- Sampling the next token requires a balance between adhering to what the model judges likely, and introducing randomness.
- One way to handle this is the notion of softmax temperature. Always experiment with different temperatures to find the right one.

12.2 DeepDream

DeepDream is an artistic image-modification technique that uses the representations learned by convolutional neural networks. It was first released by Google in the summer of 2015 as an implementation written using the Caffe deep learning library (this was several months before the first public release of TensorFlow).[3] It quickly became an internet sensation thanks to the trippy pictures it could generate (see, for example, figure 12.4), full of algorithmic pareidolia artifacts, bird feathers, and dog eyes—a byproduct of the fact that the DeepDream convnet was trained on ImageNet, where dog breeds and bird species are vastly overrepresented.

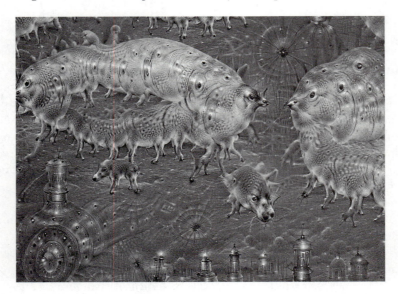

Figure 12.4
Example of a
DeepDream
output image

The DeepDream algorithm is almost identical to the convnet filter-visualization technique introduced in chapter 9, consisting of running a convnet in reverse: doing gradient ascent on the input to the convnet to maximize the activation of a specific filter in an upper layer of the convnet. DeepDream uses this same idea, with a few simple differences:

- With DeepDream, you try to maximize the activation of entire layers rather than that of a specific filter, thus mixing together visualizations of large numbers of features at once.
- You start not from blank, slightly noisy input, but rather from an existing image—thus the resulting effects latch on to preexisting visual patterns, distorting elements of the image in a somewhat artistic fashion.

---

[3] Alexander Mordvintsev, Christopher Olah, and Mike Tyka, "DeepDream: A Code Example for Visualizing Neural Networks," Google Research Blog, July 1, 2015, http://mng.bz/xXlM.

- The input images are processed at different scales (called *octaves*), which improves the quality of the visualizations.

Let's make some DeepDreams.

12.2.1 Implementing DeepDream in Keras

Let's start by retrieving a test image to dream with. We'll use a view of the rugged Northern California coast in the winter (figure 12.5).

Listing 12.9   Fetching the test image

```
base_image_path <- get_file(
  "coast.jpg", origin = "https://img-datasets.s3.amazonaws.com/coast.jpg")

plot(as.raster(jpeg::readJPEG(base_image_path)))
```

Figure 12.5   Our test image

Next, we need a pretrained convnet. In Keras, many such convnets are available—VGG16, VGG19, Xception, ResNet50, and so on—all with weights pretrained on ImageNet. You can implement DeepDream with any of them, but your base model of choice will naturally affect your visualizations, because different architectures result in different learned features. The convnet used in the original DeepDream release was an Inception model, and in practice, Inception is known to produce nice-looking DeepDreams, so we'll use the Inception V3 model that comes with Keras.

Listing 12.10   Instantiating a pretrained `InceptionV3` model

```
model <- application_inception_v3(weights = "imagenet", include_top = FALSE)
```

We'll use our pretrained convnet to create a feature extractor model that returns the activations of the various intermediate layers, listed in the following code. For each layer, we pick a scalar score that weights the contribution of the layer to the loss we will seek to maximize during the gradient-ascent process. If you want a complete list of layer names that you can use to pick new layers to play with, just use `print(model)`.

Listing 12.11   Configuring the contribution of each layer to the DeepDream loss

```
layer_settings <- c(
  mixed4 = 1,
  mixed5 = 1.5,
  mixed6 = 2,
  mixed7 = 2.5
)

outputs <- list()
for(layer_name in names(layer_settings))
  outputs[[layer_name]] <-
    get_layer(model, layer_name)$output

feature_extractor <- keras_model(inputs = model$inputs,
                                 outputs = outputs)
```

Layers for which we try to maximize activation, as well as their weight in the total loss. You can tweak these setting to obtain new visual effects.

Collect in a named list the output symbolic tensor from each layer.

A model that returns the activation values for every target layer (as a named list)

Next, we'll compute the *loss*: the quantity we'll seek to maximize during the gradient-ascent process at each processing scale. In chapter 9, for filter visualization, we tried to maximize the value of a specific filter in a specific layer. Here, we'll simultaneously maximize the activation of all filters in a number of layers. Specifically, we'll maximize a weighted mean of the L2 norm of the activations of a set of high-level layers. The exact set of layers we choose (as well as their contribution to the final loss) has a major influence on the visuals we'll be able to produce, so we want to make these parameters easily configurable. Lower layers result in geometric patterns, whereas higher layers result in visuals in which you can recognize some classes from ImageNet (e.g., birds or dogs). We'll start from a somewhat arbitrary configuration involving four layers, but you'll definitely want to explore many different configurations later.

Listing 12.12   The DeepDream loss

```
compute_loss <- function(input_image) {
  features <- feature_extractor(input_image)

  feature_losses <- names(features) %>%
    lapply(function(name) {
      coeff <- layer_settings[[name]]
      activation <- features[[name]]
      coeff * mean(activation[, 3:-3, 3:-3, ] ^ 2)
    })

  Reduce(`+`, feature_losses)
}
```

Extract activations.

We avoid border artifacts by involving only nonborder pixels in the loss.

feature_losses is a list of scalar tensors. Sum up the loss from each feature.

Now let's set up the gradient-ascent process that we will run at each octave. You'll recognize that it's the same thing as the filter-visualization technique from chapter 9! The DeepDream algorithm is simply a multiscale form of filter visualization.

Listing 12.13   The DeepDream gradient-ascent process

```
gradient_ascent_step <- tf_function(          We make the training step fast
  function(image, learning_rate) {            by compiling it as a tf_function().

    with(tf$GradientTape() %as% tape, {       Compute gradients of DeepDream
      tape$watch(image)                       loss with respect to the current
      loss <- compute_loss(image)             image.
    })

    grads <- tape$gradient(loss, image) %>%    Normalize gradients (the same
      tf$math$l2_normalize()                   trick we used in chapter 9).

    image %<>% `+`(learning_rate * grads)      Repeatedly update the image
                                               in a way that increases the
    list(loss, image)                          DeepDream loss.
  })

                                               This runs gradient ascent for
gradient_ascent_loop <-                        a given image scale (octave).
  function(image, iterations, learning_rate, max_loss = -Inf) {

    learning_rate %<>% as_tensor()

    for(i in seq(iterations)) {    ◁─── This is a regular eager R for loop.

      c(loss, image) %<-% gradient_ascent_step(image, learning_rate)

      loss %<>% as.numeric()
      if(loss > max_loss)          Break out if the loss crosses a certain
        break                      threshold (overoptimizing would create
                                   unwanted image artifacts).
      writeLines(sprintf(
        "... Loss value at step %i: %.2f", i, loss))
    }

    image
  }
```

Finally, the outer loop of the DeepDream algorithm. First, we'll define a list of *scales* (also called *octaves*) at which to process the images. We'll process our image over three different such octaves. For each successive octave, from the smallest to the largest, we'll run 20 gradient ascent steps via `gradient_ascent_loop()` to maximize the loss we previously defined. Between each octave, we'll upscale the image by 40% (1.4×): we'll start by processing a small image and then increasingly scale it up (see figure 12.6).

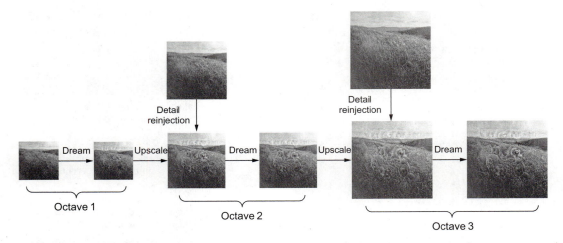

Figure 12.6   The DeepDream process: Successive scales of spatial processing (octaves) and detail reinjection upon upscaling

We define the parameters of this process in the following code. Tweaking these parameters will allow you to achieve new effects!

Gradient ascent step size

Number of scales at which to run gradient ascent

```
step <- 20
num_octaves <- 3
octave_scale <- 1.4
iterations <- 30
max_loss <- 15
```

Size ratio between successive scales

Number of gradient ascent steps per scale

We'll stop the gradient-ascent process for a scale if the loss gets higher than this.

We're also going to need a couple of utility functions to load and save images.

Listing 12.14   Image processing utilities

```
preprocess_image <- tf_function(function(image_path) {
  image_path %>%
    tf$io$read_file() %>%
    tf$io$decode_image() %>%
    tf$expand_dims(axis = 0L) %>%
    tf$cast("float32") %>%
    inception_v3_preprocess_input()
})
```

Util function to load, resize, and format pictures into appropriate arrays

Cast from 'uint8'.

Add batch axis, equivalent to .[tf$newaxis, all_dims()]. axis arg is 0-based.

Util function to convert a tensor array into a valid image and undo preprocessing

```
deprocess_image <- tf_function(function(img) {
  img %>%
    tf$squeeze(axis = 0L) %>%
    { (. * 127.5) + 127.5 } %>%
    tf$saturate_cast("uint8")
})
```

Drop first dim—the batch axis (must be size 1), the inverse of tf$expand_dims().

Rescale so values in [-1, 1] are remapped to [0, 255].

saturate_case() clips values to the dtype range: [0, 255].

```
display_image_tensor <- function(x, ..., max = 255,
                                 plot_margins = c(0, 0, 0, 0)) {

  if (!is.null(plot_margins))
    withr::local_par(mar = plot_margins)
```
Default to no margins when plotting images.

```
  x %>%
    as.array() %>%
    drop() %>%
    as.raster(max = max) %>%
    plot(..., interpolate = FALSE)
}
```
Convert tensors to R arrays.
Convert to R native raster format.

`withr::local_*`

Here we use `withr::local_par()` to set `par()` before calling `plot()`. `local_par()` acts just like `par()`, except that it restores the previous `par()` settings when the function exits. Using funcions like `local_par()` or `local_options()` helps ensure that functions you write don't permanently modify global state, which makes them more predictable and usable in more contexts.

You can replace `local_par()` and do the equivalent with a separate `on.exit()` call like this:

```
display_image_tensor <- function()
  <...>
  opar <- par(mar = plot_margins)
  on.exit(par(opar))
  <...>
}
```

This is the outer loop. To avoid losing a lot of image detail after each successive scale-up (resulting in increasingly blurry or pixelated images), we can use a simple trick: after each scale-up, we'll reinject the lost details back into the image, which is possible because we know what the original image should look like at the larger scale. Given a small image size *S* and a larger image size *L*, we can compute the difference between the original image resized to size *L* and the original resized to size *S*—this difference quantifies the details lost when going from *S* to *L*.

Listing 12.15   Running gradient ascent over multiple successive octaves

```
original_img <- preprocess_image(base_image_path)
original_HxW <- dim(original_img)[2:3]
```
Load and preprocess the test image.

```
calc_octave_HxW <- function(octave) {
  as.integer(round(original_HxW / (octave_scale ^ octave)))
}
```

```
octaves <- seq(num_octaves - 1, 0) %>%                    ◁──────┐  Compute the target shape
  { zip_lists(num = .,                                            │  of the image at different
              HxW = lapply(., calc_octave_HxW)) }                 │  octaves.

str(octaves)
```

```
List of 3
 $ :List of 2
  ..$ num: int 2
  ..$ HxW: int [1:2] 459 612
 $ :List of 2
  ..$ num: int 1
  ..$ HxW: int [1:2] 643 857
 $ :List of 2
  ..$ num: int 0
  ..$ HxW: int [1:2] 900 1200
```

**Save a reference to the original image
(we need to keep the original around).**

```
    shrunk_original_img <- original_img %>% tf$image$resize(octaves[[1]]$HxW)

  img <- original_img              ┌──  Iterate over the different octaves.
  for (octave in octaves) {   ◁────┘
    cat(sprintf("Processing octave %i with shape (%s)\n",
                octave$num, paste(octave$HxW, collapse = ", ")))

    img <- img %>%
      tf$image$resize(octave$HxW) %>%   ◁──┤  Scale up the dream image.
      gradient_ascent_loop(iterations = iterations,
                           learning_rate = step,
                           max_loss = max_loss)            Scale up the smaller version
                                                           of the original image: it will
    upscaled_shrunk_original_img <-              ◁──       be pixelated.
      shrunk_original_img %>% tf$image$resize(octave$HxW)

    same_size_original <-                              Compute the high-quality version
      original_img %>% tf$image$resize(octave$HxW)  ◁─  of the original image at this size.

    lost_detail <-                                    ◁──
      same_size_original - upscaled_shrunk_original_img         The difference between
                                                               the two is the detail
    img %<>% `+`(lost_detail)   ◁──┐  Reinject the lost detail  that was lost when
                                   │  into the dream.           scaling up.
    shrunk_original_img <-
      original_img %>% tf$image$resize(octave$HxW)
  }

  img <- deprocess_image(img)

  img %>% display_image_tensor()

  img %>%
    tf$io$encode_png() %>%
    tf$io$write_file("dream.png", .)   ◁────  Save the final result.
```

Run gradient ascent, altering the dream.

Because the original Inception V3 network was trained to recognize concepts in images of size 299×299, and given that the process involves scaling the images down by a reasonable factor, the DeepDream implementation produces much better results on images that are somewhere between 300×300 and 400×400. Regardless, you can run the same code on images of any size and any ratio.

On a GPU, it takes only a few seconds to run the whole thing. Figure 12.7 shows the result of our dream configuration on the test image.

Figure 12.7   Running the DeepDream code on the test image

I strongly suggest that you explore what you can do by adjusting which layers you use in your loss. Layers that are lower in the network contain more-local, less-abstract representations and lead to dream patterns that look more geometric. Layers that are higher up lead to more-recognizable visual patterns based on the most common objects found in ImageNet, such as dog eyes, bird feathers, and so on. You can use random generation of the parameters in the `layer_settings` vector to quickly explore many different layer combinations. Figure 12.8 shows a range of results obtained on an image of a delicious homemade pastry using different layer configurations.

12.2.2 Wrapping up

- DeepDream consists of running a convnet in reverse to generate inputs based on the representations learned by the network.
- The results produced are fun and somewhat similar to the visual artifacts induced in humans by the disruption of the visual cortex via psychedelics.
- Note that the process isn't specific to image models or even to convnets. It can be done for speech, music, and more.

Figure 12.8   Trying a range of DeepDream configurations on an example image

12.3   *Neural style transfer*

In addition to DeepDream, another major development in deep-learning-driven image modification is *neural style transfer*, introduced by Leon Gatys et al. in the summer of 2015.[4] The neural style transfer algorithm has undergone many refinements and spawned many variations since its original introduction, and it has made its way into many smartphone photo apps. For simplicity, this section focuses on the formulation described in the original paper.

Neural style transfer consists of applying the style of a reference image to a target image while conserving the content of the target image. Figure 12.9 shows an example.

Content target   Style reference   Combination image

Figure 12.9   A style transfer example

[4] Leon A. Gatys, Alexander S. Ecker, and Matthias Bethge, "A Neural Algorithm of Artistic Style," arXiv (2015), https://arxiv.org/abs/1508.06576.

In this context, *style* essentially means textures, colors, and visual patterns in the image, at various spatial scales, and the content is the higher-level macrostructure of the image. For instance, blue-and-yellow circular brushstrokes are considered to be the style in figure 12.9 (using *Starry Night* by Vincent van Gogh), and the buildings in the Tübingen photograph are considered to be the content.

The idea of style transfer, which is tightly related to that of texture generation, has had a long history in the image-processing community prior to the development of neural style transfer in 2015. But as it turns out, the deep-learning-based implementations of style transfer offer results unparalleled by what had been previously achieved with classical computer vision techniques, and they triggered an amazing renaissance in creative applications of computer vision.

The key notion behind implementing style transfer is the same idea that's central to all deep learning algorithms: you define a loss function to specify what you want to achieve, and you minimize this loss. We know what we want to achieve: conserving the content of the original image while adopting the style of the reference image. If we were able to mathematically define *content* and *style*, then an appropriate loss function to minimize would be the following:

```
loss <- distance(style(reference_image) - style(combination_image)) +
        distance(content(original_image) - content(combination_image))
```

Here, `distance()` is a norm function such as the L2 norm, `content()` is a function that takes an image and computes a representation of its content, and `style()` is a function that takes an image and computes a representation of its style. Minimizing this loss causes `style(combination_image)` to be close to `style(reference_image)`, and `content(combination_image)` is close to `content(original_image)`, thus achieving style transfer as we defined it.

A fundamental observation made by Gatys et al. was that deep convolutional neural networks offer a way to mathematically define the `style` and `content` functions. Let's see how.

12.3.1 *The content loss*

As you already know, activations from earlier layers in a network contain *local* information about the image, whereas activations from higher layers contain increasingly global, abstract information. Formulated in a different way, the activations of the different layers of a convnet provide a decomposition of the contents of an image over different spatial scales. Therefore, you'd expect the content of an image, which is more global and abstract, to be captured by the representations of the upper layers in a convnet.

A good candidate for content loss is thus the L2 norm between the activations of an upper layer in a pretrained convnet, computed over the target image, and the activations of the same layer computed over the generated image. This guarantees that, as seen from the upper layer, the generated image will look similar to the original target image. Assuming that what the upper layers of a convnet see is really the content of their input images, this works as a way to preserve image content.

12.3.2 *The style loss*

The content loss uses only a single upper layer, but the style loss as defined by Gatys et al. uses multiple layers of a convnet: you try to capture the appearance of the style-reference image at all spatial scales extracted by the convnet, not just a single scale. For the style loss, Gatys et al. use the *Gram matrix* of a layer's activations: the inner product of the feature maps of a given layer. This inner product can be understood as representing a map of the correlations between the layer's features. These feature correlations capture the statistics of the patterns of a particular spatial scale, which empirically correspond to the appearance of the textures found at this scale.

Hence, the style loss aims to preserve similar internal correlations within the activations of different layers, across the style-reference image and the generated image. In turn, this guarantees that the textures found at different spatial scales look similar across the style-reference image and the generated image.

In short, you can use a pretrained convnet to define a loss that will do the following:

- Preserve content by maintaining similar high-level layer activations between the original image and the generated image. The convnet should "see" both the original image and the generated image as containing the same things.
- Preserve style by maintaining similar *correlations* within activations for both low-level layers and high-level layers. Feature correlations capture *textures*: the generated image and the style-reference image should share the same textures at different spatial scales.

Now let's look at a Keras implementation of the original 2015 neural style transfer algorithm. As you'll see, it shares many similarities with the DeepDream implementation we developed in the previous section.

12.3.3 *Neural style transfer in Keras*

Neural style transfer can be implemented using any pretrained convnet. Here, we'll use the VGG19 network used by Gatys et al. VGG19 is a simple variant of the VGG16 network introduced in chapter 5, with three more convolutional layers. Here's the general process:

- Set up a network that computes VGG19 layer activations for the style-reference image, the base image, and the generated image at the same time.
- Use the layer activations computed over these three images to define the loss function described earlier, which we'll minimize to achieve style transfer.
- Set up a gradient-descent process to minimize this loss function.

Let's start by defining the paths to the style-reference image and the base image. To make sure that the processed images are a similar size (widely different sizes make style transfer more difficult), we'll later resize them all to a shared height of 400 pixels.

Listing 12.16   Getting the style and content images

```
base_image_path <- get_file(          <──── Path to the image we want to transform
  "sf.jpg",  origin = "https://img-datasets.s3.amazonaws.com/sf.jpg")

style_reference_image_path <- get_file(   <──── Path to the style image
  "starry_night.jpg",
  origin = "https://img-datasets.s3.amazonaws.com/starry_night.jpg")

c(original_height, original_width) %<-% {
  base_image_path %>%
    tf$io$read_file() %>%
    tf$io$decode_image() %>%
    dim() %>% .[1:2]
}
img_height <- 400
img_width <- round(img_height * (original_width /
                                 original_height))
```

Dimensions of the generated picture

Our content image is shown in figure 12.10, and figure 12.11 shows our style image.

Figure 12.10   Content image: San Francisco from Nob Hill

Figure 12.11   Style image: *Starry Night* by van Gogh

We also need some auxiliary functions for loading, preprocessing, and postprocessing the images that go in and out of the VGG19 convnet.

Listing 12.17   Auxiliary functions

```
preprocess_image <- function(image_path) {          Util function to open, resize,
  image_path %>%                                     and format pictures into
    tf$io$read_file() %>%                            appropriate arrays
    tf$io$decode_image() %>%
    tf$image$resize(as.integer(c(img_height, img_width))) %>%
    k_expand_dims(axis = 1) %>%
    imagenet_preprocess_input()                      Add a batch dimension.
}

deprocess_image <- tf_function(function(img) {       Util function to convert a
  if (length(dim(img)) == 4)                         tensor into a valid image
    img <- k_squeeze(img, axis = 1)                  Also accept an image with a batch-dim of
                                                     size 1. (This will throw an error if the first
  c(b, g, r) %<-% {                                  axis is not size 1.)
    img %>%
      k_reshape(c(img_height, img_width, 3)) %>%
      k_unstack(axis = 3)                            Unstack along the third axis,
  }                                                  and return a list of length 3.

  r %<>% `+`(123.68)         Zero-center by removing the mean pixel value from ImageNet. This
  g %<>% `+`(103.939)        reverses a transformation done by imagenet_preprocess_input().
  b %<>% `+`(116.779)

  k_stack(c(r, g, b), axis = 3) %>%                  Note that we're reversing the order of the
    k_clip(0, 255) %>%                               channels, BGR to RGB. This is also part of the
    k_cast("uint8")                                  reversal of imagenet_preprocess_input().
})
```

> ### Keras backend functions (`k_*`)
>
> In this version of `preprocess_image()` and `deprocess_image()`, we used Keras backend functions, like `k_expand_dims()` but in earlier versions, we used functions from the `tf` module, like `tf$expand_dims()`. What's the difference?
>
> The Keras package contains an extensive suite of backend functions, all starting with the `k_` prefix. They are a vestige from a time when the Keras library was designed to work with multiple backends. Today it's more common to call directly to functions in `tf` module, where the functions typically expose more features and capabilities. One nicety of the `keras::k_` backend functions, however, is that they all are 1-based and will often do automatic coercion of function arguments to integer as necessary. For example, `k_expand_dims(axis = 1)` is equivalent to `tf$expand_dims(axis = 0L)`.
>
> The backend functions are no longer actively developed, but they are covered by the TensorFlow stability promise, are maintained, and will not be going away anytime soon. You can safely use functions like `k_expand_dims()`, `k_squeeze()`, and `k_stack()` to do common tensor operations, especially when it's easier to reason with consistent 1-based counting conventions. However, when you find the capabilities of the backend functions limiting, don't hesitate to switch over to using the `tf` module functions directly. You can find additional documentation about backend functions at https://keras.rstudio.com/articles/backend.html.

Let's set up the VGG19 network. Like in the DeepDream example, we'll use the pretrained convnet to create a feature exactor model that returns the activations of intermediate layers—all layers in the model this time.

Listing 12.18 Using a pretrained VGG19 model to create a feature extractor

```
model <- application_vgg19(weights = "imagenet",
                           include_top = FALSE)
```
← Build a **VGG19 model** loaded with pretrained **ImageNet** weights.

```
outputs <- list()
for (layer in model$layers)
  outputs[[layer$name]] <- layer$output

feature_extractor <- keras_model(inputs = model$inputs,
                                 outputs = outputs)
```
← A model that returns the activation values for every target layer (as a named list)

Let's define the content loss, which will make sure the top layer of the VGG19 convnet has a similar view of the style image and the combination image.

Listing 12.19 Content loss

```
content_loss <- function(base_img, combination_img)
    sum((combination_img - base_img) ^ 2)
```

Next is the style loss. It uses an auxiliary function to compute the Gram matrix of an input matrix: a map of the correlations found in the original feature matrix.

Listing 12.20   Style loss

```
gram_matrix <- function(x) {            ◁──┐  x has the shape (height, width, features).
  n_features <- tf$shape(x)[3]
  x %>%                                        Flatten the first two spatial axes,
    tf$reshape(c(-1L, n_features)) %>%  ◁──    and preserve the features axis.
    tf$matmul(t(.), .)                  ◁──    The output will have the shape
}                                              (n_features, n_features).

style_loss <- function(style_img, combination_img) {
  S <- gram_matrix(style_img)
  C <- gram_matrix(combination_img)
  channels <- 3
  size <- img_height * img_width
  sum((S - C) ^ 2) /
    (4 * (channels ^ 2) * (size ^ 2))
}
```

To these two loss components, you add a third: the *total variation loss*, which operates on the pixels of the generated combination image. It encourages spatial continuity in the generated image, thus avoiding overly pixelated results. You can interpret it as a regularization loss.

Listing 12.21   Total variation loss

```
total_variation_loss <- function(x) {
  a <- k_square(x[, NA:(img_height-1), NA:(img_width-1), ] -
                x[, 2:NA             , NA:(img_width-1), ])
  b <- k_square(x[, NA:(img_height-1), NA:(img_width-1), ] -
                x[, NA:(img_height-1), 2:NA            , ])
  sum((a + b) ^ 1.25)
}
```

The loss that you minimize is a weighted average of these three losses. To compute the content loss, you use only one upper layer—the `block5_conv2` layer—whereas for the style loss, you use a list of layers that spans both low-level and high-level layers. You add the total variation loss at the end.

Depending on the style-reference image and content image you're using, you'll likely want to tune the `content_weight` coefficient (the contribution of the content loss to the total loss). A higher `content_weight` means the target content will be more recognizable in the generated image.

Listing 12.22   Defining the final loss that you'll minimize

```
style_layer_names <- c(   ◁──┐  The list of layers to
  "block1_conv1",              use for the style loss
  "block2_conv1",
  "block3_conv1",
  "block4_conv1",
  "block5_conv1"
```

```
)
content_layer_name <- "block5_conv2"
total_variation_weight <- 1e-6
content_weight <- 2.5e-8
style_weight <- 1e-6

compute_loss <-
  function(combination_image, base_image, style_reference_image) {

    input_tensor <-
      list(base_image,
           style_reference_image,
           combination_image) %>%
      k_concatenate(axis = 1)

    features <- feature_extractor(input_tensor)
    layer_features <- features[[content_layer_name]]
    base_image_features <- layer_features[1, , , ]
    combination_features <- layer_features[3, , , ]

    loss <- 0
    loss %<>% `+`(
      content_loss(base_image_features, combination_features) *
        content_weight
    )

    for (layer_name in style_layer_names) {
      layer_features <- features[[layer_name]]
      style_reference_features <- layer_features[2, , , ]
      combination_features <- layer_features[3, , , ]

      loss %<>% `+`(
        style_loss(style_reference_features, combination_features) *
          style_weight / length(style_layer_names)
      )
    }

    loss %<>% `+`(
      total_variation_loss(combination_image) *
        total_variation_weight
    )

    loss
  }
```

- **The layer to use for the content loss**
- **The contribution weight of the total variation loss**
- **The contribution weight of the content loss**
- **The contribution weight of the style loss**
- **Initialize the loss to 0.**
- **Add the content loss.**
- **Add the style loss for each style layer.**
- **Add the total variation loss.**
- **Return the sum of content loss, style loss, and total variation loss.**

Finally, let's set up the gradient-descent process. In the original Gatys et al. paper, optimization is performed using the L-BFGS algorithm, but that's not available in Tensor-Flow, so we'll just do mini-batch gradient descent with the SGD optimizer instead. We'll leverage an optimizer feature you haven't seen before: a learning-rate schedule. We'll use it to gradually decrease the learning rate from a very high value (100) to a much smaller final value (about 20). That way, we'll make fast progress in the early stages of training and then proceed more cautiously as we get closer to the loss minimum.

Listing 12.23   Setting up the gradient-descent process

```
compute_loss_and_grads <- tf_function(                          ◁─┐  We make
  function(combination_image, base_image, style_reference_image) {  the training
    with(tf$GradientTape() %as% tape, {                             step fast by
      loss <- compute_loss(combination_image,                       compiling it as
                           base_image,                              a tf_function().
                           style_reference_image)
    })
    grads <- tape$gradient(loss, combination_image)
    list(loss, grads)
  })

optimizer <- optimizer_sgd(                          ┐  We'll start with a learning
  learning_rate_schedule_exponential_decay(          │  rate of 100 and decrease it
    initial_learning_rate = 100, decay_steps = 100,  │  by 4% every 100 steps.
    decay_rate = 0.96))


base_image <- preprocess_image(base_image_path)
style_reference_image <- preprocess_image(style_reference_image_path)
combination_image <-
  tf$Variable(preprocess_image(base_image_path))      ◁─┐  Use a tf$Variable() to
                                                          store the combination
output_dir <- fs::path("style-transfer-generated-images")  image because we'll
iterations <- 4000                                          be updating it during
for (i in seq(iterations)) {                                training.
  c(loss, grads) %<-% compute_loss_and_grads(
    combination_image, base_image, style_reference_image)

  optimizer$apply_gradients(list(      ◁─┐  Update the combination image
    tuple(grads, combination_image)))      in a direction that reduces the
                                           style transfer loss.
  if ((i %% 100) == 0) {
    cat(sprintf("Iteration %i: loss = %.2f\n", i, loss))
    img <- deprocess_image(combination_image)
    display_image_tensor(img)
    fname <- sprintf("combination_image_at_iteration_%04i.png", i)
    tf$io$write_file(filename = output_dir / fname,  ◁─┐  Save the
                     contents = tf$io$encode_png(img))     combination image
  }                                                        at regular intervals.
}
```

Figure 12.12 shows what you get. Keep in mind that what this technique achieves is merely a form of image retexturing, or texture transfer. It works best with style-reference images that are strongly textured and highly self-similar, and with content targets that don't require high levels of detail to be recognizable. It typically can't achieve fairly abstract feats such as transferring the style of one portrait to another. The algorithm is closer to classical signal processing than to AI, so don't expect it to work like magic!

Figure 12.12   Style transfer result

Additionally, note that this style-transfer algorithm is slow to run. But the transformation operated by the setup is simple enough that it can be learned by a small, fast feed-forward convnet as well—as long as you have appropriate training data available. Fast style transfer can thus be achieved by first spending a lot of compute cycles to generate input-output training examples for a fixed style-reference image, using the method outlined here, and then training a simple convnet to learn this style-specific transformation. Once that's done, stylizing a given image is instantaneous: it's just a forward pass of this small convnet.

12.3.4 Wrapping up

- Style transfer consists of creating a new image that preserves the contents of a target image while also capturing the style of a reference image.
- Content can be captured by the high-level activations of a convnet.
- Style can be captured by the internal correlations of the activations of different layers of a convnet.
- Hence, deep learning allows style transfer to be formulated as an optimization process using a loss defined with a pretrained convnet.
- Starting from this basic idea, many variants and refinements are possible.

12.4   Generating images with variational autoencoders

The most popular and successful application of creative AI today is image generation: learning latent visual spaces and sampling from them to create entirely new pictures interpolated from real ones—pictures of imaginary people, imaginary places, imaginary cats and dogs, and so on.

In this section and the next, we'll review some high-level concepts pertaining to image generation, alongside implementation details relative to the two main techniques in this domain: *variational autoencoders* (VAEs) and *generative adversarial networks* (GANs). Note that the techniques I'll present here aren't specific to images—you could develop latent spaces of sound, music, or even text using GANs and VAEs—but in practice, the most interesting results have been obtained with pictures, and that's what we'll focus on here.

12.4.1 *Sampling from latent spaces of images*

The key idea of image generation is to develop a low-dimensional *latent space* of representations (which, like everything else in deep learning, is a vector space), where any point can be mapped to a "valid" image: an image that looks like the real thing. The module capable of realizing this mapping, taking as input a latent point and outputting an image (a grid of pixels), is called a *generator* (in the case of GANs) or a *decoder* (in the case of VAEs). Once such a latent space has been learned, you can sample points from it, and, by mapping them back to image space, generate images that have never been seen before (see figure 12.13). These new images are the in-betweens of the training images.

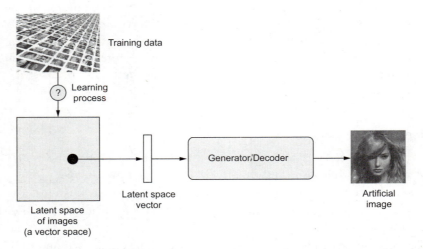

Figure 12.13   Learning a latent vector space of images and using it to sample new images

GANs and VAEs are two different strategies for learning such latent spaces of image representations, each with its own characteristics. VAEs are great for learning latent spaces that are well structured, where specific directions encode a meaningful axis of variation in the data (see figure 12.14). GANs generate images that can potentially be highly realistic, but the latent space they come from may not have as much structure and continuity.

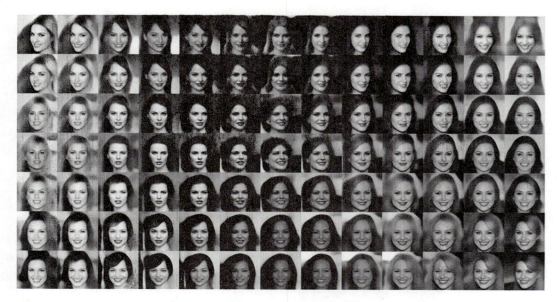

Figure 12.14   A continuous space of faces generated by Tom White using VAEs

12.4.2 *Concept vectors for image editing*

We already hinted at the idea of a *concept vector* when we covered word embeddings in chapter 11. The idea is still the same: given a latent space of representations, or an embedding space, certain directions in the space may encode interesting axes of variation in the original data. In a latent space of images of faces, for instance, there may be a *smile vector*, such that if latent point z is the embedded representation of a certain face, then latent point z + s is the embedded representation of the same face, smiling. Once you've identified such a vector, it then becomes possible to edit images by projecting them into the latent space, moving their representation in a meaningful way, and then decoding them back to image space. Concept vectors exist for essentially any independent dimension of variation in image space—in the case of faces, you may discover vectors for adding sunglasses to a face, removing glasses, turning a male face into a female face, and so on. Figure 12.15 is an example of a smile vector, a concept vector discovered by Tom White, from the Victoria University School of Design in New Zealand, using VAEs trained on a dataset of faces of celebrities (the CelebA dataset).

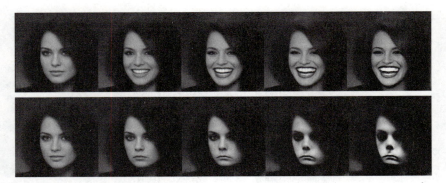

Figure 12.15   The smile vector

12.4.3 *Variational autoencoders*

Variational autoencoders, simultaneously discovered by Kingma and Welling in December 2013[5] and Rezende, Mohamed, and Wierstra in January 2014,[6] are a kind of generative model that's especially appropriate for the task of image editing via concept vectors. They're a modern take on autoencoders (a type of network that aims to encode an input to a low-dimensional latent space and then decode it back) that mixes ideas from deep learning with Bayesian inference.

A classical image autoencoder takes an image, maps it to a latent vector space via an encoder module, and then decodes it back to an output with the same dimensions as the original image, via a decoder module (see figure 12.16). It's then trained by using as target data the *same images* as the input images, meaning the autoencoder learns to reconstruct the original inputs. By imposing various constraints on the code (the output of the encoder), you can get the autoencoder to learn more- or less-interesting latent representations of the data. Most commonly, you'll constrain the code to be low-dimensional and sparse (mostly zeros), in which case the encoder acts as a way to compress the input data into fewer bits of information.

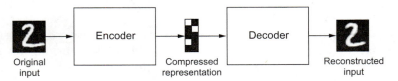

Figure 12.16   An autoencoder mapping an input *x* to a compressed representation and then decoding it back as *x'*

In practice, such classical autoencoders don't lead to particularly useful or nicely structured latent spaces. They're not much good at compression, either. For these reasons,

---

[5] Diederik P. Kingma and Max Welling, "Auto-Encoding Variational Bayes," arXiv (2013), https://arxiv.org/abs/1312.6114.

[6] Danilo Jimenez Rezende, Shakir Mohamed, and Daan Wierstra, "Stochastic Backpropagation and Approximate Inference in Deep Generative Models," arXiv (2014), https://arxiv.org/abs/1401.4082.

they have largely fallen out of fashion. VAEs, however, augment autoencoders with a little bit of statistical magic that forces them to learn continuous, highly structured latent spaces. They have turned out to be a powerful tool for image generation.

Instead of compressing its input image into a fixed code in the latent space, a VAE turns the image into the parameters of a statistical distribution: a mean and a variance. Essentially, this means we're assuming the input image has been generated by a statistical process, and that the randomness of this process should be taken into account during encoding and decoding. The VAE then uses the mean and variance parameters to randomly sample one element of the distribution and decodes that element back to the original input (see figure 12.17). The stochasticity of this process improves robustness and forces the latent space to encode meaningful representations everywhere: every point sampled in the latent space is decoded to a valid output.

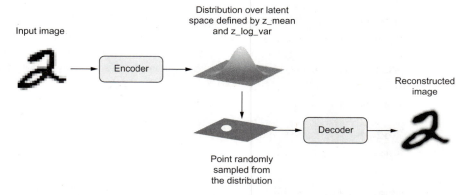

Figure 12.17   A VAE maps an image to two vectors, `z_mean` and `z_log_sigma`, which define a probability distribution over the latent space, used to sample a latent point to decode.

In technical terms, here's how a VAE works:

1 An encoder module turns the input sample, `input_img`, into two parameters in a latent space of representations, `z_mean` and `z_log_variance`.
2 You randomly sample a point `z` from the latent normal distribution that's assumed to generate the input image, via `z = z_mean + exp(z_log_variance) * epsilon`, where `epsilon` is a random tensor of small values.
3 A decoder module maps this point in the latent space back to the original input image.

Because `epsilon` is random, the process ensures that every point that's close to the latent location where you encoded `input_img` (`z-mean`) can be decoded to something similar to `input_img`, thus forcing the latent space to be continuously meaningful.

Any two close points in the latent space will decode to highly similar images. Continuity, combined with the low dimensionality of the latent space, forces every direction in the latent space to encode a meaningful axis of variation of the data, making the latent space very structured and thus highly suitable to manipulation via concept vectors.

The parameters of a VAE are trained via two loss functions: a *reconstruction loss* that forces the decoded samples to match the initial inputs, and a *regularization loss* that helps learn well-rounded latent distributions and reduces overfitting to the training data. Schematically, the process looks like this:

Encode the input into mean and variance parameters.

Draw a latent point using a small random epsilon.

```
c(z_mean, z_log_variance) %<-% encoder(input_img)
z <- z_mean + exp(z_log_variance) * epsilon
reconstructed_img <- decoder(z)
model <- keras_model(input_img, reconstructed_img)
```

Decode z back to an image.

Instantiate the autoencoder model, which maps an input image to its reconstruction.

You can then train the model using the reconstruction loss and the regularization loss. For the regularization loss, we typically use an expression (the Kullback–Leibler divergence) meant to nudge the distribution of the encoder output toward a well-rounded normal distribution centered around 0. This provides the encoder with a sensible assumption about the structure of the latent space it's modeling.

Now let's see what implementing a VAE looks like in practice!

12.4.4 *Implementing a VAE with Keras*

We're going to be implementing a VAE that can generate MNIST digits. It's going to have three parts:

- An encoder network that turns a real image into a mean and a variance in the latent space
- A sampling layer that takes such a mean and variance and uses them to sample a random point from the latent space
- A decoder network that turns points from the latent space back into images

The following listing shows the encoder network we'll use, mapping images to the parameters of a probability distribution over the latent space. It's a simple convnet that maps the input image x to two vectors, z_mean and z_log_var. One important detail is that we use strides for downsampling feature maps instead of max pooling. The last time we did this was in the image segmentation example in chapter 9. Recall that, in general, strides are preferable to max pooling for any model that cares about *information location*—that is to say, *where* stuff is in the image—and this one does, because it will have to produce an image encoding that can be used to reconstruct a valid image.

Listing 12.24   VAE encoder network

```
latent_dim <- 2      ⟵── Dimensionality of the latent space: a 2D plane

encoder_inputs <-  layer_input(shape = c(28, 28, 1))
```

```
x <- encoder_inputs %>%
  layer_conv_2d(32, 3, activation = "relu", strides = 2, padding = "same") %>%
  layer_conv_2d(64, 3, activation = "relu", strides = 2, padding = "same") %>%
  layer_flatten() %>%
  layer_dense(16, activation = "relu")
```

The input image ends up being encoded into these two parameters.

```
z_mean    <- x %>% layer_dense(latent_dim, name = "z_mean")
z_log_var <- x %>% layer_dense(latent_dim, name = "z_log_var")

encoder <- keras_model(encoder_inputs, list(z_mean, z_log_var),
                       name = "encoder")
```

Its summary looks like this:

```
encoder
```

```
Model: "encoder"

_____
 Layer (type)              Output Shape           Param #    Connected to
==================================================================================
 input_1 (InputLayer)      [(None, 28, 28, 1)]    0          []
 conv2d_1 (Conv2D)         (None, 14, 14, 32)     320        ['input_1[0][0]']
 conv2d (Conv2D)           (None, 7, 7, 64)       18496      ['conv2d_1[0][0]']
 flatten (Flatten)         (None, 3136)           0          ['conv2d[0][0]']
 dense (Dense)             (None, 16)             50192      ['flatten[0][0]']
 z_mean (Dense)            (None, 2)              34         ['dense[0][0]']
 z_log_var (Dense)         (None, 2)              34         ['dense[0][0]']
==================================================================================
Total params: 69,076
Trainable params: 69,076
Non-trainable params: 0
_____
```

Next is the code for using z_mean and z_log_var, the parameters of the statistical distribution assumed to have produced input_img, to generate a latent space point z.

Listing 12.25   Latent-space-sampling layer

z_mean and z_log_var here both will have shape (batch_size, latent_dim), for example, (128, 2).

```
layer_sampler <- new_layer_class(
  classname = "Sampler",
  call = function(z_mean, z_log_var) {
    epsilon <- tf$random$normal(shape = tf$shape(z_mean))
    z_mean + exp(0.5 * z_log_var) * epsilon
  }
)
```

Draw a batch of random normal vectors.

Apply the VAE sampling formula.

The following listing shows the decoder implementation. We reshape the vector z to the dimensions of an image and then use a few convolution layers to obtain a final image output that has the same dimensions as the original input_img.

Listing 12.26   VAE decoder network, mapping latent space points to images

Input where we'll feed z

Produce the same number of coefficients that we had at the level of the Flatten layer in the encoder.

```
latent_inputs <- layer_input(shape = c(latent_dim))
decoder_outputs <- latent_inputs %>%
  layer_dense(7 * 7 * 64, activation = "relu") %>%
  layer_reshape(c(7, 7, 64)) %>%
  layer_conv_2d_transpose(64, 3, activation = "relu",
                          strides = 2, padding = "same") %>%
  layer_conv_2d_transpose(32, 3, activation = "relu",
                          strides = 2, padding = "same") %>%
  layer_conv_2d(1, 3, activation = "sigmoid",
                padding = "same")
decoder <- keras_model(latent_inputs, decoder_outputs,
                       name = "decoder")
```

Revert the layer_flatten() of the encoder.

The output ends up with shape (28, 28, 1).

Revert the layer_conv_2d() of the encoder.

Its summary looks like this:

```
decoder
```

```
Model: "decoder"
_____
 Layer (type)                      Output Shape          Param #
================================================================
 input_2 (InputLayer)              [(None, 2)]           0
 dense_1 (Dense)                   (None, 3136)          9408
 reshape (Reshape)                 (None, 7, 7, 64)      0
 conv2d_transpose_1 (Conv2DTranspose) (None, 14, 14, 64) 36928
 conv2d_transpose (Conv2DTranspose) (None, 28, 28, 32)   18464
 conv2d_2 (Conv2D)                 (None, 28, 28, 1)     289
================================================================
Total params: 65,089
Trainable params: 65,089
Non-trainable params: 0
_____
```

Now let's create the VAE model itself. This is your first example of a model that isn't doing supervised learning (an autoencoder is an example of *self-supervised* learning, because it uses its inputs as targets). Whenever you depart from classic supervised learning, it's common to create a new_model_class() and implement a custom train_step() to specify the new training logic, a workflow you learned about in chapter 7. That's what we'll do here.

Listing 12.27   VAE model with custom `train_step()`

```
model_vae <- new_model_class(
  classname = "VAE",

  initialize = function(encoder, decoder, ...) {
    super$initialize(...)
```

```
      self$encoder <- encoder         ◄──  We assign to self instead of private because
      self$decoder <- decoder              we want the layer weights automatically
      self$sampler <- layer_sampler()      tracked by the Keras Model base class.
      self$total_loss_tracker <-
        metric_mean(name = "total_loss")
      self$reconstruction_loss_tracker <-          We use these metrics
        metric_mean(name = "reconstruction_loss")  to keep track of the
      self$kl_loss_tracker <-                      loss averages over
        metric_mean(name = "kl_loss")              each epoch.
    },

  metrics = mark_active(function() {   ◄──
    list(                                    We list the metrics in an active property to
      self$total_loss_tracker,               enable the framework to reset them after
      self$reconstruction_loss_tracker,      each epoch (or between multiple calls to
      self$kl_loss_tracker                   fit()/evaluate()).
    )
  }),

  train_step = function(data) {
    with(tf$GradientTape() %as% tape, {

      c(z_mean, z_log_var) %<-% self$encoder(data)
      z <- self$sampler(z_mean, z_log_var)             We sum the reconstruction loss over
                                                        the spatial dimensions (second and
      reconstruction <- decoder(z)                     third axes) and take its mean over
      reconstruction_loss <-                       ◄── the batch dimension.
        loss_binary_crossentropy(data, reconstruction) %>%
          sum(axis = c(2, 3)) %>%      ◄──
          mean()                            Total loss for each case in the
                                            batch; preserve batch axis.
      kl_loss <- -0.5 * (1 + z_log_var - z_mean^2 - exp(z_log_var))
      total_loss <- reconstruction_loss + mean(kl_loss)     ◄──
    })                                          Add the regularization term
                                                (Kullback–Leibler divergence).
    grads <- tape$gradient(total_loss, self$trainable_weights)
    self$optimizer$apply_gradients(zip_lists(grads, self$trainable_weights))

    self$total_loss_tracker$update_state(total_loss)
    self$reconstruction_loss_tracker$update_state(reconstruction_loss)
    self$kl_loss_tracker$update_state(kl_loss)

    list(total_loss = self$total_loss_tracker$result(),
         reconstruction_loss = self$reconstruction_loss_tracker$result(),
         kl_loss = self$kl_loss_tracker$result())
  }
)
```

Take the mean of loss totals in the batch.

Finally, we're ready to instantiate and train the model on MNIST digits. Because the loss is taken care of in the custom layer, we don't specify an external loss at compile time (loss = NULL), which in turn means we won't pass target data during training (as you can see, we pass only x_train to the model in fit()).

Listing 12.28   Training the VAE

```
library(listarrays)
c(c(x_train, .), c(x_test, .)) %<-% dataset_mnist()

mnist_digits <-
  bind_on_rows(x_train, x_test) %>%
  expand_dims(-1) %>%
  { . / 255 }

str(mnist_digits)

num [1:70000, 1:28, 1:28, 1] 0 0 0 0 0 0 0 0 0 0 ...

vae <- model_vae(encoder, decoder)
vae %>% compile(optimizer = optimizer_adam())
vae %>% fit(mnist_digits, epochs = 30, batch_size = 128)
```

> Provide bind_on_rows() and other functions for manipulating R arrays.

> We train on all MNIST digits, so we combine the training and test samples along the batch dim.

> Note that we don't pass a loss argument in compile(), because the loss is already part of the train_step().

> Note that we don't pass targets in fit(), because train_step() doesn't expect any.

Once the model is trained, we can use the `decoder` network to turn arbitrary latent space vectors into images.

Listing 12.29   Sampling a grid of images from the 2D latent space

```
n <- 30
digit_size <- 28
z_grid <-
  seq(-1, 1, length.out = n) %>%
  expand.grid(., .) %>%
  as.matrix()
decoded <- predict(vae$decoder, z_grid)

z_grid_i <- seq(n) %>% expand.grid(x = ., y = .)
figure <- array(0, c(digit_size * n, digit_size * n))
for (i in 1:nrow(z_grid_i)) {
  c(xi, yi) %<-% z_grid_i[i, ]
  digit <- decoded[i, , , ]
  figure[seq(to = (n + 1 - xi) * digit_size, length.out = digit_size),
         seq(to = yi * digit_size, length.out = digit_size)] <-
    digit
}
par(pty = "s")
lim <- extendrange(r = c(-1, 1),
                   f = 1 - (n / (n+.5)))
plot(NULL, frame.plot = FALSE,
     ylim = lim, xlim = lim,
     xlab = ~z[1], ylab = ~z[2])
rasterImage(as.raster(1 - figure, max = 1),
            lim[1], lim[1], lim[2], lim[2],
            interpolate = FALSE)
```

> Create a 2D grid of linearly spaced samples.

> Get the decoded digits.

> Transform the decoded digits with shape (900, 28, 28, 1) to an R array with shape (28*30, 28*30) for plotting.

> We'll display a grid of 30 × 30 digits (900 digits total).

> Square plot type

> Expand lim so (–1, 1) are at the center of a digit.

> Pass a formula object to xlab for a proper subscript.

> Subtract from 1 to invert the colors.

The grid of sampled digits (see figure 12.18) shows a completely continuous distribution of the different digit classes, with one digit morphing into another as you follow a path through latent space. Specific directions in this space have a meaning: for example, there are directions for "five-ness," "one-ness," and so on.

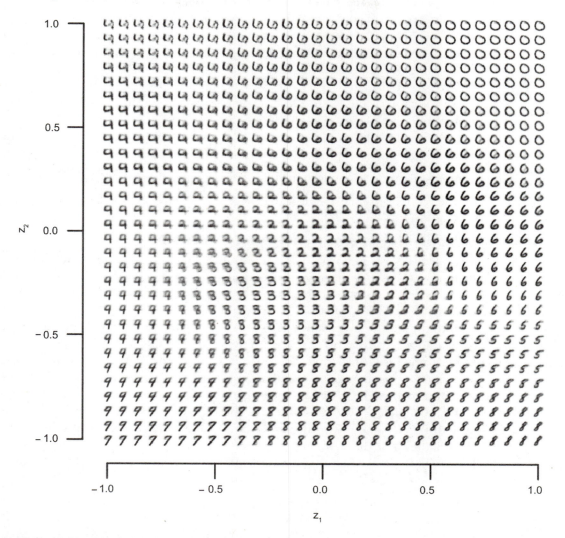

Figure 12.18 Grid of digits decoded from the latent space

In the next section, we'll cover in detail the other major tool for generating artificial images: generative adversarial networks (GANs).

12.4.5 *Wrapping up*

- Image generation with deep learning is done by learning latent spaces that capture statistical information about a dataset of images. By sampling and decoding points from the latent space, you can generate never-before-seen images. There are two major tools to do this: VAEs and GANs.
- VAEs result in highly structured, continuous latent representations. For this reason, they work well for doing all sorts of image editing in latent space: face swapping, turning a frowning face into a smiling face, and so on. They also work nicely for doing latent-space-based animations, such as animating a walk along a cross section of the latent space or showing a starting image slowly morphing into different images in a continuous way.
- GANs enable the generation of realistic single-frame images but may not induce latent spaces with solid structure and high continuity.

Most successful practical applications I have seen with images rely on VAEs, but GANs have enjoyed enduring popularity in the world of academic research. You'll find out how they work and how to implement one in the next section.

12.5 *Introduction to generative adversarial networks*

Generative adversarial networks (GANs), introduced in 2014 by Goodfellow et al.,[7] are an alternative to VAEs for learning latent spaces of images. They enable the generation of fairly realistic synthetic images by forcing the generated images to be statistically almost indistinguishable from real ones.

An intuitive way to understand GANs is to imagine a forger trying to create a fake Picasso painting. At first, the forger is pretty bad at the task. He mixes some of his fakes with authentic Picassos and shows them all to an art dealer. The art dealer makes an authenticity assessment for each painting and gives the forger feedback about what makes a Picasso look like a Picasso. The forger goes back to his studio to prepare some new fakes. As time goes on, the forger becomes increasingly competent at imitating the style of Picasso, and the art dealer becomes increasingly expert at spotting fakes. In the end, they have on their hands some excellent fake Picassos.

That's what a GAN is: a forger network and an expert network, each being trained to best the other. As such, a GAN is made of two parts:

- *Generator network*—Takes as input a random vector (a random point in the latent space), and decodes it into a synthetic image
- *Discriminator network (or adversary)*—Takes as input an image (real or synthetic), and predicts whether the image came from the training set or was created by the generator network

The generator network is trained to be able to fool the discriminator network, and thus it evolves toward generating increasingly realistic images as training goes on: artificial

---

[7] Ian Goodfellow et al., "Generative Adversarial Networks," arXiv (2014), https://arxiv.org/abs/1406.2661.

images that look indistinguishable from real ones, to the extent that it's impossible for the discriminator network to tell the two apart (see figure 12.19). Meanwhile, the discriminator is constantly adapting to the gradually improving capabilities of the generator, setting a high bar of realism for the generated images. Once training is over, the generator is capable of turning any point in its input space into a believable image. Unlike VAEs, this latent space has fewer explicit guarantees of meaningful structure; in particular, it isn't continuous.

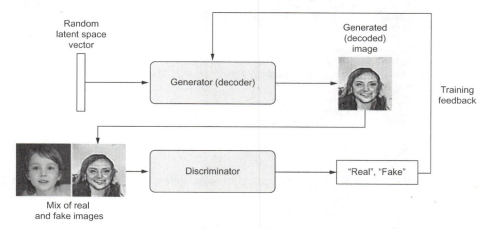

Figure 12.19   A generator transforms random latent vectors into images, and a discriminator seeks to tell real images from generated ones. The generator is trained to fool the discriminator.

Remarkably, a GAN is a system where the optimization minimum isn't fixed, unlike in any other training setup you've encountered in this book. Normally, gradient descent consists of rolling down hills in a static loss landscape. But with a GAN, every step taken down the hill changes the entire landscape a little. It's a dynamic system where the optimization process is seeking not a minimum but an equilibrium between two forces. For this reason, GANs are notoriously difficult to train—getting a GAN to work requires lots of careful tuning of the model architecture and training parameters.

12.5.1 A schematic GAN implementation

In this section, we'll explain how to implement a GAN in Keras in its barest form. GANs are advanced, so diving deeply into the technical details of architectures like that of the StyleGAN2 that generated the images in figure 12.20 would be out of scope for this book. The specific implementation we'll use in this demonstration is a *deep convolutional GAN* (DCGAN): a very basic GAN where the generator and discriminator are deep convnets.

We'll train our GAN on images from the large-scale CelebFaces Attributes dataset (known as CelebA), a dataset of 200,000 faces of celebrities (http://mmlab.ie.cuhk .edu.hk/projects/CelebA.html). To speed up training, we'll resize the images to 64 × 64,

Figure 12.20 Latent space dwellers. Images generated by https://thispersondoesnotexist.com using a StyleGAN2 model. (Image credit: Phillip Wang is the website author. The model used is the StyleGAN2 model from Karras et al., https://arxiv.org/abs/1912.04958.)

so we'll be learning to generate 64×64 images of human faces. Schematically, the GAN looks like this:

- A `generator` network maps vectors of shape (`latent_dim`) to images of shape (`64, 64, 3`).
- A `discriminator` network maps images of shape (`64, 64, 3`) to a binary score estimating the probability that the image is real.
- A `gan` network chains the generator and the discriminator together: `gan(x) = discriminator(generator(x))`. Thus, this `gan` network maps latent space vectors to the discriminator's assessment of the realism of these latent vectors as decoded by the generator.
- We train the discriminator using examples of real and fake images along with "real"/"fake" labels, just as we train any regular image-classification model.
- To train the generator, we use the gradients of the generator's weights with regard to the loss of the `gan` model. This means that at every step, we move the weights of the generator in a direction that makes the discriminator more likely to classify as "real" the images decoded by the generator. In other words, we train the generator to fool the discriminator.

12.5.2 A bag of tricks

The process of training GANs and tuning GAN implementations is notoriously difficult. You should keep in mind a number of known tricks. Like most things in deep learning, it's more alchemy than science: these tricks are heuristics, not theory-backed guidelines.

They're supported by a level of intuitive understanding of the phenomenon at hand, and they're known to work well empirically, although not necessarily in every context.

Here are a few of the tricks used in the implementation of the GAN generator and discriminator in this section. It isn't an exhaustive list of GAN-related tips; you'll find many more across the GAN literature:

- We use strides instead of pooling for downsampling feature maps in the discriminator, just like we did in our VAE encoder.

- We sample points from the latent space using a *normal distribution* (Gaussian distribution), not a uniform distribution.

- Stochasticity is good for inducing robustness. Because GAN training results in a dynamic equilibrium, GANs are likely to get stuck in all sorts of ways. Introducing randomness during training helps prevent this. We introduce randomness by adding random noise to the labels for the discriminator.

- Sparse gradients can hinder GAN training. In deep learning, sparsity is often a desirable property, but not in GANs. Two things can induce gradient sparsity: max-pooling operations and `relu` activations. Instead of max pooling, we recommend using strided convolutions for downsampling, and we recommend using a `layer_activation_leaky_relu()` instead of a `relu` activation. It's similar to `relu`, but it relaxes sparsity constraints by allowing small negative activation values.

- In generated images, it's common to see checkerboard artifacts caused by unequal coverage of the pixel space in the generator (see figure 12.21). To fix this, we use a kernel size that's divisible by the stride size whenever we use a strided `layer_conv_2d_transpose()` or `layer_conv_2d()` in both the generator and the discriminator.

Figure 12.21 Checkerboard artifacts caused by mismatching strides and kernel sizes, resulting in unequal pixel-space coverage: one of the many gotchas of GANs

12.5.3 Getting our hands on the CelebA dataset

You can download the dataset manually from the website: http://mmlab.ie.cuhk.edu.hk/projects/CelebA.html. Because the dataset is hosted on Google Drive, you can also download it using `gdown`:

```
reticulate::py_install("gdown", pip = TRUE)        ◁——— Install gdown.
system("gdown 1O7m1010EJjLE5QxLZiM9Fpjs7Oj6e684")  ◁——
                                                      Download the compressed
                                                      data using gdown.
Downloading...
From: https://drive.google.com/uc?id=1O7m1010EJjLE5QxLZiM9Fpjs7Oj6e684
To: img_align_celeba.zip
 32%|███████████            | 467M/1.44G [00:13<00:23, 41.3MB/s]
```

Once you've downloaded the data, unzip it to a `celeba_gan` folder

Listing 12.30   Getting the CelebA data

```
zip::unzip("img_align_celeba.zip", exdir = "celeba_gan")    ◁—— Uncompress the data.
```

Once you've got the uncompressed images in a directory, you can use `image_dataset_from_directory()` to turn it into a TF Dataset. Because we just need the images—there are no labels—we'll specify `label_mode = NULL`.

Listing 12.31   Creating a TF Dataset from a directory of images

```
dataset <- image_dataset_from_directory(
  "celeba_gan",
  label_mode = NULL,           ◁
  image_size = c(64, 64),
  batch_size = 32,
  crop_to_aspect_ratio = TRUE
)
```

Only the images will be returned—no labels.

We will resize the images to 64 × 64 by using a smart combination of cropping and resizing to preserve aspect ratio. We don't want face proportions to get distorted!

Finally, let's rescale the images to the [0-1] range.

Listing 12.32   Rescaling the images

```
library(tfdatasets)
dataset %<>% dataset_map(~ .x / 255)
```

You can use the following code to display a sample image.

Listing 12.33   Displaying the first image

```
x <- dataset %>% as_iterator() %>% iter_next()
display_image_tensor(x[1, , , ], max = 1)
```

12.5.4 *The discriminator*

First, we'll develop a `discriminator` model that takes as input a candidate image (real or synthetic) and classifies it into one of two classes: "generated image" or "real image that comes from the training set." One of the many issues that commonly arise with GANs is that the generator gets stuck with generated images that look like noise. A possible solution is to use dropout in the discriminator, so that's what we will do here.

Listing 12.34 The GAN discriminator network

```
discriminator <-
  keras_model_sequential(name = "discriminator",
                         input_shape = c(64, 64, 3)) %>%
  layer_conv_2d(64, kernel_size = 4, strides = 2, padding = "same") %>%
  layer_activation_leaky_relu(alpha = 0.2) %>%
  layer_conv_2d(128, kernel_size = 4, strides = 2, padding = "same") %>%
  layer_activation_leaky_relu(alpha = 0.2) %>%
  layer_conv_2d(128, kernel_size = 4, strides = 2, padding = "same") %>%
  layer_activation_leaky_relu(alpha = 0.2) %>%
  layer_flatten() %>%
  layer_dropout(0.2) %>%         ◁──── One dropout layer: an important trick!
  layer_dense(1, activation = "sigmoid")
```

Here's the discriminator model summary:

```
discriminator
```

```
Model: "discriminator"
```

Layer (type)	Output Shape	Param #
conv2d_99 (Conv2D)	(None, 32, 32, 64)	3136
leaky_re_lu_2 (LeakyReLU)	(None, 32, 32, 64)	0
conv2d_98 (Conv2D)	(None, 16, 16, 128)	131200
leaky_re_lu_1 (LeakyReLU)	(None, 16, 16, 128)	0
conv2d_97 (Conv2D)	(None, 8, 8, 128)	262272
leaky_re_lu (LeakyReLU)	(None, 8, 8, 128)	0
flatten_1 (Flatten)	(None, 8192)	0
dropout (Dropout)	(None, 8192)	0
dense_7 (Dense)	(None, 1)	8193

```
Total params: 404,801
Trainable params: 404,801
Non-trainable params: 0
```

12.5.5 *The generator*

Next, let's develop a `generator` model that turns a vector (from the latent space—during training it will be sampled at random) into a candidate image.

Listing 12.35 GAN generator network

Revert the layer_flatten() of the encoder.

```
latent_dim <- 128        The latent space will be made
                         of 128-dimensional vectors.
generator <-
  keras_model_sequential(name = "generator",
                         input_shape = c(latent_dim)) %>%
  layer_dense(8 * 8 * 128) %>%
  layer_reshape(c(8, 8, 128)) %>%
  layer_conv_2d_transpose(128, kernel_size = 4,
                          strides = 2, padding = "same") %>%
  layer_activation_leaky_relu(alpha = 0.2) %>%
  layer_conv_2d_transpose(256, kernel_size = 4,
                          strides = 2, padding = "same") %>%
  layer_activation_leaky_relu(alpha = 0.2) %>%
  layer_conv_2d_transpose(512, kernel_size = 4,
                          strides = 2, padding = "same") %>%
  layer_activation_leaky_relu(alpha = 0.2) %>%
  layer_conv_2d(3, kernel_size = 5, padding = "same",
                activation = "sigmoid")
```

Produce the same number of coefficients we had at the level of the Flatten layer in the encoder.

Revert the layer_conv_2d() of the encoder.

Use Leaky Relu as our activation

This is the generator model summary:

```
generator

Model: "generator"

_____
 Layer (type)                        Output Shape                 Param #
============================================================================
 dense_8 (Dense)                     (None, 8192)                 1056768
 reshape_1 (Reshape)                 (None, 8, 8, 128)            0
 conv2d_transpose_4 (Conv2DTranspose) (None, 16, 16, 128)         262272
 leaky_re_lu_5 (LeakyReLU)           (None, 16, 16, 128)          0
 conv2d_transpose_3 (Conv2DTranspose) (None, 32, 32, 256)         524544
 leaky_re_lu_4 (LeakyReLU)           (None, 32, 32, 256)          0
 conv2d_transpose_2 (Conv2DTranspose) (None, 64, 64, 512)         2097664
 leaky_re_lu_3 (LeakyReLU)           (None, 64, 64, 512)          0
 conv2d_100 (Conv2D)                 (None, 64, 64, 3)            38403
============================================================================
Total params: 3,979,651
Trainable params: 3,979,651
Non-trainable params: 0
_____
```

12.5.6 *The adversarial network*

Finally, we'll set up the GAN, which chains the generator and the discriminator. When trained, this model will move the generator in a direction that improves its ability to fool the discriminator. This model turns latent-space points into a classification decision—"fake" or "real"—and it's meant to be trained with labels that are always "these are real images." So training `gan` will update the weights of `generator` in a way that makes `discriminator` more likely to predict "real" when looking at fake images.

To recapitulate, this is what the training loop looks like schematically. For each epoch, you do the following:

1   Draw random points in the latent space (random noise).
2   Generate images with `generator` using this random noise.
3   Mix the generated images with real ones.
4   Train `discriminator` using these mixed images, with corresponding targets: either "real" (for the real images) or "fake" (for the generated images).
5   Draw new random points in the latent space.
6   Train `generator` using these random vectors, with targets that all say "these are real images." This updates the weights of the generator to move them toward getting the discriminator to predict "these are real images" for generated images: this trains the generator to fool the discriminator.

Let's implement it. Like in our VAE example, we'll use a `new_model_class()` with a custom `train_step()`. Note that we'll use two optimizers (one for the generator and one for the discriminator), so we will also override `compile()` to allow for passing two optimizers.

Listing 12.36   The GAN `Model`

```
GAN <- new_model_class(
  classname = "GAN",

  initialize = function(discriminator, generator, latent_dim) {
    super$initialize()
    self$discriminator  <- discriminator
    self$generator      <- generator
    self$latent_dim     <- as.integer(latent_dim)
    self$d_loss_metric  <- metric_mean(name = "d_loss")
    self$g_loss_metric  <- metric_mean(name = "g_loss")
  },

  compile = function(d_optimizer, g_optimizer, loss_fn) {
    super$compile()
    self$d_optimizer <- d_optimizer
    self$g_optimizer <- g_optimizer
    self$loss_fn <- loss_fn
  },

  metrics = mark_active(function() {
    list(self$d_loss_metric,
         self$g_loss_metric)
  }),

  train_step = function(real_images) {
    batch_size <- tf$shape(real_images)[1]
```

Set up metrics to track the two losses over each training epoch.

train_step is called with a batch of real images.

Sample random points in the latent space.

```
random_latent_vectors <-
  tf$random$normal(shape = c(batch_size, self$latent_dim))
generated_images <-
  self$generator(random_latent_vectors)   <——— Decode them to fake images.

combined_images <-
  tf$concat(list(generated_images,
                 real_images),   <——— Combine them with real images.
            axis = 0L)

labels <-
  tf$concat(list(tf$ones(tuple(batch_size, 1L)),   <┐
                 tf$zeros(tuple(batch_size, 1L))),  │ Assemble labels,
            axis = 0L)                              │ discriminating real
                                                    │ from fake images.

labels %<>% `+`(
  tf$random$uniform(tf$shape(.), maxval = 0.05))   <——┐ Add random noise
                                                      │ to the labels—an
                                                      │ important trick!
with(tf$GradientTape() %as% tape, {
  predictions <- self$discriminator(combined_images)
  d_loss <- self$loss_fn(labels, predictions)
})

grads <- tape$gradient(d_loss, self$discriminator$trainable_weights)
self$d_optimizer$apply_gradients(              <——— Train the discriminator.
  zip_lists(grads, self$discriminator$trainable_weights))

random_latent_vectors <-        <—————| Sample random points in the latent space.
  tf$random$normal(shape = c(batch_size, self$latent_dim))

misleading_labels <- tf$zeros(tuple(batch_size, 1L))  <—┐ Assemble labels that
                                                        │ say "these are all real
                                                        │ images" (it's a lie!).
with(tf$GradientTape() %as% tape, {
  predictions <- random_latent_vectors %>%
    self$generator() %>%
    self$discriminator()
  g_loss <- self$loss_fn(misleading_labels, predictions)
})
grads <- tape$gradient(g_loss, self$generator$trainable_weights)
self$g_optimizer$apply_gradients(              <———┐
  zip_lists(grads, self$generator$trainable_weights))  │ Train the generator.

self$d_loss_metric$update_state(d_loss)
self$g_loss_metric$update_state(g_loss)

list(d_loss = self$d_loss_metric$result(),
     g_loss = self$g_loss_metric$result())
})
```

Before we start training, let's also set up a callback to monitor our results: it will use the generator to create and save a number of fake images at the end of each epoch.

Listing 12.37   A callback that samples generated images during training

```
callback_gan_monitor <- new_callback_class(
  classname = "GANMonitor",

  initialize = function(num_img = 3, latent_dim = 128,
                        dirpath = "gan_generated_images") {
    private$num_img <- as.integer(num_img)
    private$latent_dim <- as.integer(latent_dim)
    private$dirpath <- fs::path(dirpath)
    fs::dir_create(dirpath)
  },

  on_epoch_end = function(epoch, logs = NULL) {
    random_latent_vectors <-
      tf$random$normal(shape = c(private$num_img, private$latent_dim))

    generated_images <- random_latent_vectors %>%
      self$model$generator() %>%
      { tf$saturate_cast(. * 255, "uint8") }      ⟵┐  Scale and clip to uint8 range
                                                   │  of [0, 255], and cast to uint8.
    for (i in seq(private$num_img))
      tf$io$write_file(
        filename = private$dirpath / sprintf("img_%03i_%02i.png", epoch, i),
        contents = tf$io$encode_png(generated_images[i, , , ])
      )
  }
)
```

Finally, we can start training.

Listing 12.38   Compiling and training the GAN

```
epochs <- 100      ⟵——— You'll start getting interesting results after epoch 20.

gan <- GAN(discriminator = discriminator,      ⟵——— Instantiate the GAN model.
           generator = generator,
           latent_dim = latent_dim)

gan %>% compile(
  d_optimizer = optimizer_adam(learning_rate = 0.0001),
  g_optimizer = optimizer_adam(learning_rate = 0.0001),
  loss_fn = loss_binary_crossentropy()
)

gan %>% fit(
  dataset,
  epochs = epochs,
  callbacks = callback_gan_monitor(num_img = 10, latent_dim = latent_dim)
)
```

When training, you may see the adversarial loss begin to increase considerably, whereas the discriminative loss tends to zero—the discriminator may end up dominating the generator. If that's the case, try reducing the discriminator learning rate and increasing the dropout rate of the discriminator. Figure 12.22 shows what our GAN is capable of generating after 30 epochs of training.

Figure 12.22   Some generated images around epoch 30

12.5.7 Wrapping up

- A GAN consists of a generator network coupled with a discriminator network. The discriminator is trained to differentiate between the output of the generator and real images from a training dataset, and the generator is trained to fool the discriminator. Remarkably, the generator never sees images from the training set directly; the information it has about the data comes from the discriminator.
- GANs are difficult to train, because training a GAN is a dynamic process rather than a simple gradient-descent process with a fixed loss landscape. Getting a GAN to train correctly requires using a number of heuristic tricks, as well as extensive tuning.
- GANs can potentially produce highly realistic images. But unlike VAEs, the latent space they learn doesn't have a neat continuous structure and thus may not be suited for certain practical applications, such as image editing via latent-space concept vectors.

These few techniques cover only the basics of this fast-expanding field. There's a lot more to discover out there—generative deep learning is deserving of an entire book of its own.

Summary

- You can use a sequence-to-sequence model to generate sequence data, one step at a time. This is applicable to text generation but also to note-by-note music generation or any other type of time-series data.
- DeepDream works by maximizing the convnet layer activations through gradient ascent in input space.
- In the style-transfer algorithm, a content image and a style image are combined via gradient descent to produce an image with the high-level features of the content image and the local characteristics of the style image.
- VAEs and GANs are models that learn a latent space of images and can then dream up entirely new images by sampling from the latent space. Concept vectors in the latent space can even be used for image editing.

Best practices
for the real world

13

This chapter covers

- Hyperparameter tuning
- Model ensembling
- Mixed-precision training
- Training Keras models on multiple GPUs
  or on a TPU

You've come far since the beginning of this book. You can now train image classification models, image segmentation models, models for classification or regression on vector data, time-series forecasting models, text classification models, sequence-to-sequence models, and even generative models for text and images. You've got all the bases covered.

However, your models so far have all been trained at a small scale—on small datasets, with a single GPU—and they generally haven't reached the best achievable performance on each dataset we looked at. This book is, after all, an introductory book. If you are to go out in the real world and achieve state-of-the-art results on brand-new problems, there's still a bit of a chasm that you'll need to cross.

This penultimate chapter is about bridging that gap and giving you the best practices you'll need as you go from machine learning student to fully fledged machine learning engineer. We'll review essential techniques for systematically improving model performance: hyperparameter tuning and model ensembling. Then we'll look at how you can speed up and scale up model training, with multi-GPU and TPU training, mixed precision, and leveraging remote computing resources in the cloud.

We'll also use this chapter to show how you can access Python packages directly, even when there is no R wrapper conveniently available. This will be an essential skill as you continue in your deep learning journey. You don't need to know Python to use Python packages from R, but if you find yourself ever reading Python documentation and asking questions like, "What are all the underscores?" head over to the appendix, *Python primer for R users*, which will get you up to speed as quickly as possible.

13.1 Getting the most out of your models

Blindly trying out different architecture configurations works well enough if you just need something that works okay. In this section, we'll go beyond "works okay" to "works great and wins machine learning competitions" via a set of must-know techniques for building state-of-the-art deep learning models.

13.1.1 Hyperparameter optimization

When building a deep learning model, you have to make many seemingly arbitrary decisions: How many layers should you stack? How many units or filters should go in each layer? Should you use `relu` as activation, or a different function? Should you use `layer_batch_normalization()` after a given layer? How much dropout should you use? and so on. These architecture-level parameters are called *hyperparameters* to distinguish them from the *parameters* of a model, which are trained via backpropagation.

In practice, experienced machine learning engineers and researchers build intuition over time as to what works and what doesn't when it comes to these choices—they develop hyperparameter-tuning skills. But no formal rules exist. If you want to get to the very limit of what can be achieved on a given task, you can't be content with such arbitrary choices. Your initial decisions are almost always suboptimal, even if you have very good intuition. You can refine your choices by tweaking them by hand and retraining the model repeatedly—that's what machine learning engineers and researchers spend most of their time doing. But it shouldn't be your job as a human to fiddle with hyperparameters all day—that is better left to a machine.

Thus, you need to explore the space of possible decisions automatically, systematically, in a principled way. You need to search the architecture space and find the best-performing architectures empirically. That's what the field of automatic hyperparameter optimization is about: it's an entire field of research—and an important one. The process of optimizing hyperparameters typically looks like this:

1 Choose a set of hyperparameters (automatically).
2 Build the corresponding model.

3 Fit it to your training data, and measure performance on the validation data.
4 Choose the next set of hyperparameters to try (automatically).
5 Repeat.
6 Eventually, measure performance on your test data.

The key to this process is the algorithm that analyzes the relationship between validation performance and various hyperparameter values to choose the next set of hyperparameters to evaluate. Many different techniques are possible: Bayesian optimization, genetic algorithms, simple random search, and so on.

Training the weights of a model is relatively easy: you compute a loss function on a mini-batch of data and then use backpropagation to move the weights in the right direction. Updating hyperparameters, on the other hand, presents unique challenges. Consider these points:

- The hyperparameter space is typically made up of discrete decisions and, thus, isn't continuous or differentiable. Hence, you typically can't do gradient descent in hyperparameter space. Instead, you must rely on gradient-free optimization techniques, which naturally are far less efficient than gradient descent.
- Computing the feedback signal of this optimization process (does this set of hyperparameters lead to a high-performing model on this task?) can be extremely expensive: it requires creating and training a new model from scratch on your dataset.
- The feedback signal may be noisy: if a training run performs 0.2% better, is that because of a better model configuration, or because you got lucky with the initial weight values?

Thankfully, there's a tool that makes hyperparameter tuning simpler: KerasTuner. Let's check it out.

USING KERASTUNER

Let's start by installing the KerasTuner Python package:

```
reticulate::py_install("keras-tuner", pip = TRUE)
```

KerasTuner lets you replace hardcoded hyperparameter values, such as `units = 32`, with a range of possible choices, such as `Int(name = "units", min_value = 16, max_value = 64, step = 16)`. This set of choices in a given model is called the *search space* of the hyperparameter tuning process. To specify a search space, define a model-building function (see the next listing). It takes an `hp` argument, from which you can sample hyperparameter ranges, and it returns a compiled Keras model.

Listing 13.1 **A KerasTuner model-building function**

```
build_model <- function(hp, num_classes = 10) {

  units <- hp$Int(name = "units",
                  min_value = 16L, max_value = 64L, step = 16L)
```

Sample hyperparameter values from the hp object. After sampling, these values (such as the units and optimizer variables here) are just regular R constants.

```
model <- keras_model_sequential() %>%
  layer_dense(units, activation = "relu") %>%
  layer_dense(num_classes, activation = "softmax")

optimizer <- hp$Choice(name = "optimizer",
                       values = c("rmsprop", "adam"))

model %>% compile(optimizer = optimizer,
                  loss = "sparse_categorical_crossentropy",
                  metrics = c("accuracy"))
model
}
```

Different kinds of hyperparameters are available: Int, Float, Boolean, Choice.

The function returns a compiled model.

If you want to adopt a more modular and configurable approach to model-building, you can also subclass the HyperModel class and define a build method, as follows.

Listing 13.2 A KerasTuner `HyperModel`

```
kt <- reticulate::import("kerastuner")

SimpleMLP(kt$HyperModel) %py_class% {

  `__init__` <- function(self, num_classes) {
    self$num_classes <- num_classes
  }

  build <- function(self, hp) {
    build_model(hp, self$num_classes)
  }

}

hypermodel <- SimpleMLP(num_classes = 10)
```

With the object-oriented approach, we can configure model constants like num_classes to be constructor arguments.

The build() method is identical to our prior build_model() standalone function, except now it is invoked by a method of a subclassed kt$HyperModel.

Custom Python classes with `%py_class%`

`%py_class%` can be used to define custom Python classes in R. It mirrors the Python syntax for defining Python classes and allows for an almost mechanical translation of Python to R. It is especially useful when using Python APIs that are designed around subclassing, like kt$HyperModel. The equivalent definition of SimpleMLP in Python, (like you might encounter in the Python documentation for KerasTuner) would look like this:

```
import kerastuner as kt

class SimpleMLP(kt.HyperModel):
    def __init__(self, num_classes):
        self.num_classes = num_classes

    def build(self, hp):
        return build_model(hp, self.num_classes)

hypermodel = SimpleMLP(num_classes=10)
```

See ?'%py_class%' in R for more info and examples.

The next step is to define a "tuner." Schematically, you can think of a tuner as a `for` loop that will repeatedly

- Pick a set of hyperparameter values
- Call the model-building function with these values to create a model
- Train the model and record its metrics

KerasTuner has several built-in tuners available—`RandomSearch`, `BayesianOptimization`, and `Hyperband`. Let's try `BayesianOptimization`, a tuner that attempts to make smart predictions for which new hyperparameter values are likely to perform best given the outcomes of previous choices:

Specify the metric that the tuner will seek to optimize. Always specify validation metrics, because the goal of the search process is to find models that generalize.

Specify the model-building function (or hypermodel instance).

Maximum number of different model configurations ("trials") to try before ending the search.

```
tuner <- kt$BayesianOptimization(
  build_model,
  objective = "val_accuracy",
  max_trials = 100L,
  executions_per_trial = 2L,
  directory = "mnist_kt_test",
  overwrite = TRUE
)
```

To reduce metrics variance, you can train the same model multiple times and average the results. executions_per_trial is how many training rounds (executions) to run for each model configuration (trial).

Whether to overwrite data in directory to start a new search. Set this to TRUE if you've modified the model-building function, or to FALSE to resume a previously started search with the same model-building function.

Where to store search logs

You can display an overview of the search space via `search_space_summary()`:

```
tuner$search_space_summary()
```

```
Search space summary
Default search space size: 2
units (Int)
{"default": None,
 "conditions": [],
 "min_value": 128,
 "max_value": 1024,
 "step": 128,
 "sampling": None}
optimizer (Choice)
{"default": "rmsprop",
 "conditions": [],
 "values": ["rmsprop", "adam"],
 "ordered": False}
```

Objective maximization and minimization

For built-in metrics (like accuracy, in our case), the *direction* of the metric (accuracy should be maximized, but a loss should be minimized) is inferred by KerasTuner. However, for a custom metric, you should specify it yourself, like this:

```
objective <- kt$Objective(        The metric's name, as found in epoch logs
  name = "val_accuracy",   ◁───────
  direction = "max"   ◁──────
)                                  The metric's desired
                                   direction: "min" or "max"
tuner <- kt$BayesianOptimization(
  build_model,
  objective = objective,
  ...
)
```

Finally, let's launch the search. Don't forget to pass validation data, and make sure not to use your test set as validation data—otherwise, you'd quickly start overfitting to your test data, and you wouldn't be able to trust your test metrics anymore:

```
c(c(x_train, y_train), c(x_test, y_test)) %<-% dataset_mnist()
x_train %<>% { array_reshape(., c(-1, 28 * 28)) / 255 }
x_test  %<>% { array_reshape(., c(-1, 28 * 28)) / 255 }
x_train_full <- x_train        Reserve these for later.
y_train_full <- y_train
num_val_samples <- 10000
c(x_train, x_val) %<-%
  list(x_train[seq(num_val_samples), ],
       x_train[-seq(num_val_samples), ])    Set aside a
c(y_train, y_val) %<-%                       validation set.
  list(y_train[seq(num_val_samples)],
       y_train[-seq(num_val_samples)])

callbacks <- c(
    callback_early_stopping(monitor = "val_loss",
                            patience = 5)
)
                              This takes the same arguments as fit() (it simply
tuner$search(   ◁─────────    passes them down to fit() for each new model).
  x_train, y_train,
  batch_size = 128L,
  epochs = 100L,          ◁──────────    Use a large number of epochs (you don't know
  validation_data = list(x_val, y_val),  in advance how many epochs each model will
  callbacks = callbacks,                 need), and use a callback_early_stopping() to
  verbose = 2L                           stop training when you start overfitting.
)
```

Make sure to pass integers where Python functions expect them, not doubles.

The preceding example will run in just a few minutes, because we're looking at only a few possible choices and we're training on MNIST. However, with a typical search space and dataset, you'll often find yourself letting the hyperparameter search run overnight or even over several days. If your search process crashes, you can always restart it—just specify overwrite = FALSE in the tuner so that it can resume from the trial logs stored on disk. Once the search is complete, you can query the best hyperparameter configurations, which you can use to create high-performing models that you can then retrain.

Listing 13.3 | **Querying the best hyperparameter configurations**

```
top_n <- 4L
best_hps <- tuner$get_best_hyperparameters(top_n)
```
**Return a list of HyperParameter objects, which
you can pass to the model-building function.**

Usually, when retraining these models, you may want to include the validation data as part of the training data, because you won't be making any further hyperparameter changes, and thus you will no longer be evaluating performance on the validation data. In our example, we'd train these final models on the totality of the original MNIST training data, without reserving a validation set.

Before we can train on the full training data, though, there's one last parameter we need to settle: the optimal number of epochs to train for. Typically, you'll want to train the new models for longer than you did during the search: using an aggressive `patience` value in the `callback_early_stopping()` saves time during the search, but it may lead to underfitting the models. Just use the validation set to find the best epoch:

```
get_best_epoch <- function(hp) {
  model <- build_model(hp)

  callbacks <- c(
    callback_early_stopping(monitor = "val_loss", mode = "min",
                            patience = 10))        ◁——— Note the very high
  history <- model %>% fit(                              patience value.
    x_train, y_train,
    validation_data = list(x_val, y_val),
    epochs = 100,
    batch_size = 128,
    callbacks = callbacks
  )

  best_epoch <- which.min(history$metrics$val_loss)
  print(glue::glue("Best epoch: {best_epoch}"))
  invisible(best_epoch)
}
```

Finally, train on the full dataset for just a bit longer than this epoch count, because you're training on more data; 20% more in this case:

```
get_best_trained_model <- function(hp) {
  best_epoch <- get_best_epoch(hp)
  model <- build_model(hp)
  model %>% fit(
    x_train_full,
    y_train_full,
    batch_size = 128,
    epochs = round(best_epoch * 1.2)
  )
  model
}
```

```
best_models <- best_hps %>%
  lapply(get_best_trained_model)
```

Note that if you're not worried about slightly underperforming, there's a shortcut you can take: just use the tuner to reload the top-performing models with the best weights saved during the hyperparameter search, without retraining new models from scratch:

```
best_models <- tuner$get_best_models(top_n)
```

One important issue to think about when doing automatic hyperparameter optimization at scale is validation set overfitting. Because you're updating hyperparameters based on a signal that is computed using your validation data, you're effectively training them on the validation data, and thus they will quickly overfit to the validation data. Always keep this in mind.

THE ART OF CRAFTING THE RIGHT SEARCH SPACE

Overall, hyperparameter optimization is a powerful technique that is an absolute requirement for getting to state-of-the-art models on any task or to win machine learning competitions. Think about it: once upon a time, people handcrafted the features that went into shallow machine learning models. That was very much suboptimal. Now, deep learning automates the task of hierarchical feature engineering—features are learned using a feedback signal, not hand-tuned, and that's the way it should be. In the same way, you shouldn't handcraft your model architectures; you should optimize them in a principled way.

However, doing hyperparameter tuning is not a replacement for being familiar with model architecture best practices. Search spaces grow combinatorially with the number of choices, so it would be far too expensive to turn everything into a hyperparameter and let the tuner sort it out. You need to be smart about designing the right search space. Hyperparameter tuning is automation, not magic: you use it to automate experiments that you would otherwise have run by hand, but you still need to handpick experiment configurations that have the potential to yield good metrics.

The good news is that by leveraging hyperparameter tuning, the configuration decisions you have to make graduate from microdecisions (what number of units do I pick for this layer?) to higher-level architecture decisions (should I use residual connections throughout this model?). And although microdecisions are specific to a certain model and a certain dataset, higher-level decisions generalize better across different tasks and datasets. For instance, pretty much every image classification problem can be solved via the same sort of search-space template.

Following this logic, KerasTuner attempts to provide *premade search spaces* that are relevant to broad categories of problems, such as image classification. Just add data, run the search, and get a pretty good model. You can try the hypermodels `kt$applications$HyperXception` and `kt$applications$HyperResNet`, which are effectively tunable versions of Keras Applications models.

THE FUTURE OF HYPERPARAMETER TUNING: AUTOMATED MACHINE LEARNING

Currently, most of your job as a deep learning engineer consists of munging data with R scripts and then tuning the architecture and hyperparameters of a deep network at length to get a working model, or even to get a state-of-the-art model, if you are that ambitious. Needless to say, that isn't an optimal setup. But automation can help, and it won't stop merely at hyperparameter tuning.

Searching over a set of possible learning rates or possible layer sizes is just the first step. We can also be far more ambitious and attempt to generate the *model architecture* itself from scratch, with as few constraints as possible, such as via reinforcement learning or genetic algorithms. In the future, entire end-to-end machine learning pipelines will be automatically generated, rather than handcrafted by engineer-artisans. This is called automated machine learning, or *AutoML*. You can already leverage libraries like AutoKeras (https://github.com/keras-team/autokeras) to solve basic machine learning problems with very little involvement on your part.

Today, AutoML is still in its early days, and it doesn't scale to large problems. But when AutoML becomes mature enough for widespread adoption, the jobs of machine learning engineers won't disappear—rather, engineers will move up the value-creation chain. They will begin to put much more effort into data curation, crafting complex loss functions that truly reflect business goals, as well as understanding how their models impact the digital ecosystems in which they're deployed (such as the users who consume the model's predictions and generate the model's training data). These are problems that only the largest companies can afford to consider at present.

Always look at the big picture, focus on understanding the fundamentals, and keep in mind that the highly specialized tedium will eventually be automated away. See it as a gift—greater productivity for your workflows—and not as a threat to your own relevance. It shouldn't be your job to tune knobs endlessly.

13.1.2 *Model ensembling*

Another powerful technique for obtaining the best possible results on a task is *model ensembling*. Ensembling consists of pooling the predictions of a set of different models to produce better predictions. If you look at machine learning competitions, in particular, on Kaggle, you'll see that the winners use very large ensembles of models that inevitably beat any single model, no matter how good.

Ensembling relies on the assumption that different well-performing models trained independently are likely to be good for *different reasons*: each model looks at slightly different aspects of the data to make its predictions, getting part of the "truth" but not all of it. You may be familiar with the ancient parable of the blind men and the elephant: a group of blind men come across an elephant for the first time and try to understand what the elephant is by touching it. Each man touches a different part of the elephant's body—just one part, such as the trunk or a leg. Then the men describe to each other what an elephant is: "It's like a snake," "Like a pillar or a tree," and so on. The blind men are essentially machine learning models trying to understand the manifold of the training data, each from their own perspective, using their own assumptions (provided by the unique architecture of the model and the unique random weight initialization). Each of them gets part of the truth of the data, but not the whole truth. By pooling their perspectives, you can get a far more accurate description of the data. The elephant is a combination of parts: not any single blind man gets it quite right, but, interviewed together, they can tell a fairly accurate story.

Let's use classification as an example. The easiest way to pool the predictions of a set of classifiers (to *ensemble the classifiers*) is to average their predictions at inference time:

```
preds_a <- model_a %>% predict(x_val)
preds_b <- model_b %>% predict(x_val)
preds_c <- model_c %>% predict(x_val)
preds_d <- model_d %>% predict(x_val)
final_preds <-
  0.25 * (preds_a + preds_b + preds_c + preds_d)
```

Use four different models to compute initial predictions.

This new prediction array should be more accurate than any of the initial ones.

However, this will work only if the classifiers are more or less equally good. If one of them is significantly worse than the others, the final predictions may not be as good as the best classifier of the group.

A smarter way to ensemble classifiers is to do a weighted average, where the weights are learned on the validation data—typically, the better classifiers are given a higher weight, and the worse classifiers are given a lower weight. To search for a good set of ensembling weights, you can use random search or a simple optimization algorithm, such as the Nelder–Mead algorithm:

```
preds_a <- model_a %>% predict(x_val)
preds_b <- model_b %>% predict(x_val)
preds_c <- model_c %>% predict(x_val)
preds_d <- model_d %>% predict(x_val)
final_preds <-
  (0.5 * preds_a) + (0.25 * preds_b) +
  (0.1 * preds_c) + (0.15 * preds_d)
```

These weights (0.5, 0.25, 0.1, 0.15) are assumed to be learned empirically.

Many possible variants exist: you can do an average of an exponential of the predictions, for instance. In general, a simple weighted average with weights optimized on the validation data provides a very strong baseline.

The key to making ensembling work is the *diversity* of the set of classifiers. Diversity is strength. If all the blind men only touched the elephant's trunk, they would agree that elephants are like snakes, and they would forever stay ignorant of the truth of the elephant. Diversity is what makes ensembling work. In machine learning terms, if all of your models are biased in the same way, your ensemble will retain this same bias. If your models are *biased in different ways*, the biases will cancel each other out, and the ensemble will be more robust and more accurate.

For this reason, you should ensemble models that are *as good as possible* while being *as different as possible*. This typically means using very different architectures or even different brands of machine learning approaches. One thing that is largely not worth doing is ensembling the same network trained several times independently, from different random initializations. If the only difference between your models is their random initialization and the order in which they were exposed to the training data, then your ensemble will be low diversity and will provide only a tiny improvement over any single model.

One thing I have found to work well in practice—but that doesn't generalize to every problem domain—is using an ensemble of tree-based methods (such as random forests or gradient-boosted trees) and deep neural networks. In 2014, Andrey Kolev and I took fourth place in the Higgs boson decay detection challenge on Kaggle (http://www.kaggle.com/c/higgs-boson) using an ensemble of various tree models and deep neural networks. Remarkably, one of the models in the ensemble originated from a different method than the others (it was a regularized greedy forest), and it had a significantly worse score than the others. Unsurprisingly, it was assigned a small weight in the ensemble. But to our surprise, it turned out to improve the overall ensemble by a large factor, because it was so different from every other model: it provided information that the other models didn't have access to. That's precisely the point of ensembling. It's not so much about how good your best model is; it's about the diversity of your set of candidate models.

13.2   Scaling-up model training

Recall the "loop of progress" concept we introduced in chapter 7: the quality of your ideas is a function of how many refinement cycles they've been through (see figure 13.1). And the speed at which you can iterate on an idea is a function of how fast you can set up an experiment, how fast you can run that experiment, and, finally, how well you can analyze the resulting data.

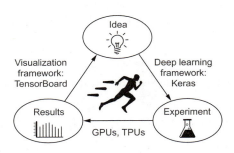

Figure 13.1   The loop of progress

As you develop your expertise with the Keras API, how fast you can code up your deep learning experiments will cease to be the bottleneck of this progress cycle. The next bottleneck will become the speed at which you can train your models. Fast training infrastructure means that you can get your results back in 10–15 minutes, and hence, you can go through dozens of iterations every day. Faster training directly improves the *quality* of your deep learning solutions.

In this section, you'll learn about three ways you can train your models faster:

- Mixed-precision training, which you can use even with a single GPU
- Training on multiple GPUs
- Training on TPUs

Let's go.

13.2.1 Speeding up training on GPU with mixed precision

What if I told you there's a simple technique you can use to speed up the training of almost any model by up to 3×, basically for free? It seems too good to but true, and yet, such a trick does exist—it's *mixed-precision training*. To understand how it works, we first need to take a look at the notion of "precision" in computer science.

UNDERSTANDING FLOATING-POINT PRECISION

Precision is to numbers what resolution is to images. Because computers can process only ones and zeros, any number seen by a computer has to be encoded as a binary string. For instance, you may be familiar with `uint8` integers, which are integers encoded on eight bits: `00000000` represents 0 in `uint8`, and `11111111` represents 255. To represent integers beyond 255, you'd need to add more bits—eight isn't enough. Most integers are stored on 32 bits, with which you can represent signed integers ranging from –2147483648 to 2147483647.

Floating-point numbers are the same. In mathematics, real numbers form a continuous axis: there's an infinite number of points in between any two numbers. You can always zoom in on the axis of reals. In computer science, this isn't true: there's a finite number of intermediate points between 3 and 4, for instance. How many? Well, it depends on the *precision* you're working with—the number of bits you're using to store a number. You can zoom up to only a certain resolution. There are three levels of precision you'd typically use:

- Half precision, or `float16`, where numbers are stored on 16 bits
- Single precision, or `float32`, where numbers are stored on 32 bits
- Double precision, or `float64`, where numbers are stored on 64 bits

The way to think about the resolution of floating-point numbers is in terms of the smallest distance between two arbitrary numbers that you'll be able to safely process. In single precision, that's around 1e-7. In double precision, that's around 1e-16. And in half precision, it's only 1e-3.

Almost every model you've seen in this book so far used single-precision numbers: it stored its state as `float32` weight variables and ran its computations on `float32` inputs. That's enough precision to run the forward and backward pass of a model without losing any information—particularly when it comes to small gradient updates (recall that the typical learning rate is 1e-3, and it's pretty common to see weight updates on the order of 1e-6).

You could also use `float64`, though that would be wasteful—operations like matrix multiplication or addition are much more expensive in double precision, so you'd be doing twice as much work for no clear benefits. But you could not do the same with `float16` weights and computation; the gradient descent process wouldn't run smoothly, because you couldn't represent small gradient updates of around 1e-5 or 1e-6.

You can, however, use a hybrid approach: that's what mixed precision is about. The idea is to leverage 16-bit computations in places where precision isn't an issue and to work with 32-bit values in other places to maintain numerical stability. Modern GPUs

A note on floating-point encoding

A counterintuitive fact about floating-point numbers is that representable numbers are not uniformly distributed. Larger numbers have lower precision: there are the same number of representable values between `2^N` and `2^(N + 1)` as there are between 1 and 2, for any *N*. That's because floating-point numbers are encoded in three parts—the sign, the significant value (called the "mantissa"), and the exponent, in the form

```
<sign> * (2 ^ (<exponent> - 127)) * 1.<mantissa>
```

For example, the following figure shows how you would encode the closest `float32` value approximating Pi.

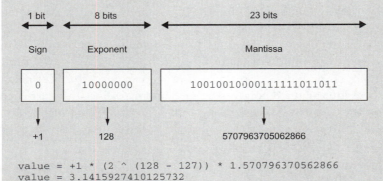

```
value = +1 * (2 ^ (128 - 127)) * 1.570796370562866
value = 3.1415927410125732
```

The number Pi encoded in single precision via a sign bit, an integer exponent, and an integer mantissa

For this reason, the numerical error incurred when converting a number to its floating-point representation can vary wildly depending on the exact value considered, and the error tends to get larger for numbers with a large absolute value.

and TPUs feature specialized hardware that can run 16-bit operations much faster and use less memory than equivalent 32-bits operations. By using these lower-precision operations whenever possible, you can speed up training on those devices by a significant factor. Meanwhile, by maintaining the precision-sensitive parts of the model in single precision, you can get these benefits without meaningfully impacting model quality.

And those benefits are considerable: on modern NVIDIA GPUs, mixed precision can speed up training by up to 3×. It's also beneficial when training on a TPU (a subject we'll get to in a bit), where it can speed up training by up to 60%.

Beware of dtype defaults

Single precision is the default floating-point type throughout Keras and TensorFlow: the tensor or variable you create will be in `float32` unless you specify otherwise. For R arrays, however, the default is `float64`!

Converting an R array to a TensorFlow tensor will result in a `float64` tensor, which may not be what you want:

```
r_array <- base::array(0, dim = c(2, 2))
tf_tensor <- tensorflow::as_tensor(r_array)
tf_tensor$dtype
```

```
tf.float64
```

Remember to be explicit about data types when converting R arrays:

```
r_array <- base::array(0, dim = c(2, 2))
tf_tensor <- tensorflow::as_tensor(r_array, dtype = "float32")
tf_tensor$dtype
```
Specify the dtype explicitly.

```
tf.float32
```

Note that when you call the Keras `fit()` method with R arrays, it will automatically cast them to `k_floatx()`—`float32` by default.

MIXED-PRECISION TRAINING IN PRACTICE

When training on a GPU, you can turn on mixed precision like this:

```
keras::keras$mixed_precision$set_global_policy("mixed_float16")
```

keras::keras is the Python module imported by reticulate.

Typically, most of the forward pass of the model will be done in `float16` (with the exception of numerically unstable operations like softmax), whereas the weights of the model will be stored and updated in `float32`.

Keras layers have a `variable_dtype` and a `compute_dtype` property. By default, both of these are set to `float32`. When you turn on mixed precision, the `compute_dtype` of most layers switches to `float16`, and those layers will cast their inputs to `float16` and will perform their computations in `float16` (using half-precision copies of the weights). However, because their `variable_dtype` is still `float32`, their weights will be able to receive accurate `float32` updates from the optimizer, as opposed to half-precision updates.

Note that some operations may be numerically unstable in `float16` (in particular, softmax and cross-entropy). If you need to opt out of mixed precision for a specific layer, just pass the argument `dtype = "float32"` to the constructor of this layer.

13.2.2 *Multi-GPU training*

Although GPUs are getting more powerful every year, deep learning models are getting increasingly larger, requiring ever more computational resources. Training on a single GPU puts a hard bound on how fast you can move. The solution? You could simply add more GPUs and start doing *multi-GPU distributed training.*

There are two ways to distribute computation across multiple devices: *data parallelism* and *model parallelism.*

With data parallelism, a single model is replicated on multiple devices or multiple machines. Each of the model replicas processes different batches of data, and then they merge their results.

With model parallelism, different parts of a single model run on different devices, processing a single batch of data together at the same time. This works best with models that have a naturally parallel architecture, such as models that feature multiple branches.

In practice, model parallelism is used only for models that are too large to fit on any single device: it isn't used as a way to speed up training of regular models but as a way to train larger models. We won't cover model parallelism in these pages; instead, we'll focus on what you'll be using most of the time: data parallelism. Let's take a look at how it works.

GETTING YOUR HANDS ON TWO OR MORE GPUS

First, you need to get access to several GPUs. You will need to do one of two things:

- Acquire two to four GPUs, mount them on a single machine (it will require a beefy power supply), and install CUDA drivers, cuDNN, and so on. For most people, this isn't the best option.
- Rent a multi-GPU virtual machine (VM) on Google Cloud, Azure, or AWS. You'll be able to use VM images with preinstalled drivers and software, and you'll have very little setup overhead. This is likely the best option for anyone who isn't training models 24/7.

We won't cover the details of how to spin up multi-GPU cloud VMs, because such instructions would be relatively short-lived, and this information is readily available online.

SINGLE-HOST, MULTIDEVICE SYNCHRONOUS TRAINING

Once you're able to call `library(tensorflow)` on a machine with multiple GPUs, you're seconds away from training a distributed model. It works like this:

Everything that creates variables should be under the strategy scope. In general, this is only model construction and compile().

Create a "distribution strategy" object. MirroredStrategy() should be your go-to solution.

```
library(tensorflow)
strategy <- tf$distribute$MirroredStrategy()      <-
cat("Number of devices:", strategy$num_replicas_in_sync, "\n")
with(strategy$scope(), {              <-
  model <- get_compiled_model()         Use it to open a "strategy scope."
})
model %>% fit(      <——  Train the model on all available devices.
  train_dataset,
```

```
    epochs = 100,
    validation_data = val_dataset,
    callbacks = callbacks
)
```

These few lines implement the most common training setup: *single-host, multidevice synchronous training*, also known in TensorFlow as the "mirrored distribution strategy." "Single host" means that the different GPUs considered are all on a single machine (as opposed to a cluster of many machines, each with its own GPU, communicating over a network). "Synchronous training" means that the state of the per-GPU model replicas stays the same at all times—there are variants of distributed training where this isn't the case.

When you open a `MirroredStrategy()` scope and build your model within it, the `MirroredStrategy()` object will create one model copy (replica) on each available GPU. For example, if you have two GPUs, then each step of training unfolds in the following way (see figure 13.2):

1 A batch of data (called the *global batch*) is drawn from the dataset.
2 It gets split into two different sub-batches (called *local batches*). For instance, if the global batch has 256 samples, each of the two local batches will have 128 samples. Because you want local batches to be large enough to keep the GPU busy, the global batch size typically needs to be very large.
3 Each of the two replicas processes one local batch, independently, on its own device: they run a forward pass and then a backward pass. Each replica outputs a "weight delta" describing by how much to update each weight variable in the model, given the gradient of the previous weights with respect to the loss of the model on the local batch.
4 The weight deltas originating from local gradients are efficiently merged across the two replicas to obtain a global delta, which is applied to all replicas. Because this is done at the end of every step, the replicas always stay in sync: their weights are always equal.

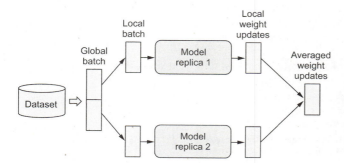

Figure 13.2 One step of `MirroredStrategy` training: Each model replica computes local weight updates, which are then merged and used to update the state of all replicas.

When doing distributed training, always provide your data as a TF Dataset object to guarantee best performance. (Passing your data as R arrays also works, because those are converted to TF Dataset objects by `fit()`. You should also make sure you leverage data prefetching: before passing the dataset to `fit()`, call `dataset_prefetch(buffer_size)`. If you aren't sure what buffer size to pick, try leaving the default value of `tf$data$AUTOTUNE`, which will pick a buffer size for you.

Here's a simple example.

Listing 13.4   Building a model in a `MirroredStrategy` scope

```
build_model <- function(input_size) {
  resnet <- application_resnet50(weights = NULL,
                                 include_top = FALSE,
                                 pooling = "max")

  inputs <- layer_input(c(input_size, 3))

  outputs <- inputs %>%
    resnet_preprocess_input() %>%
    resnet() %>%
    layer_dense(10, activation = "softmax")

  model <- keras_model(inputs, outputs)

  model %>% compile(
    optimizer = "rmsprop",
    loss = "sparse_categorical_crossentropy",
    metrics = "accuracy"
  )

  model
}

strategy <- tf$distribute$MirroredStrategy()
cat("Number of replicas:", strategy$num_replicas_in_sync, "\n")

Number of replicas: 2

with(strategy$scope(), {
  model <- build_model(input_size = c(32, 32))
})
```

In this case, let's train straight from R arrays in memory (which are efficiently converted to a TF Dataset by `fit()`)—the CIFAR10 dataset:

```
c(c(x_train, y_train), c(x_test, y_test)) %<-% dataset_cifar10()
model %>% fit(x_train, y_train, batch_size = 1024)
```

Note that multi-GPU training requires large batch sizes to make sure the device stays well utilized.

In an ideal world, training on *N* GPUs would result in a speedup of factor *N*. In practice, however, distribution introduces some overhead, in particular, merging the weight deltas originating from different devices takes some time. The effective speedup you get is a function of the number of GPUs used:

- With two GPUs, the speedup stays close to 2×.
- With four, the speedup is around 3.8×.
- With eight, it's around 7.3×.

This assumes that you're using a large enough global batch size to keep each GPU used at full capacity. If your batch size is too small, the local batch size won't be enough to keep your GPUs busy.

13.2.3   TPU training

Beyond just GPUs, there is a trend in the deep learning world toward moving workflows to increasingly specialized hardware designed specifically for deep learning workflows (such single-purpose chips are known as ASICs—application-specific integrated circuits). Various companies big and small are working on new chips, but today the most prominent effort along these lines is Google's Tensor Processing Unit (TPU), which is available on Google Cloud and via Google Colab.

Training on a TPU does involve jumping through some hoops, but it can be worth the extra work: TPUs are really, really fast. Training on a TPU V2 will typically be 15× faster than training an NVIDIA P100 GPU.

Here are some tips when using TPUs: when you're using the GPU runtime in the cloud, your models have direct access to the GPU without you needing to do anything special. This isn't true for the TPU runtime; there's an extra step you need to take before you can start building a model: you need to connect to the TPU cluster. It works like this:

```
tpu <- tf$distribute$cluster_resolver$TPUClusterResolver$connect()
cat("Device:", tpu$master(), "\n")
strategy <- tf$distribute$TPUStrategy(tpu)      ⟵  Use TPUStrategy() just like
with(strategy$scope(), { ... })                     tf$distribute$MirroredStrategy().
```

You don't have to worry too much about what this does—it's just a little incantation that connects your runtime to the device. Open sesame.

Much like in the case of multi-GPU training, using the TPU requires you to open a distribution strategy scope—in this case, a TPUStrategy() scope. TPUStrategy() follows the same distribution template as MirroredStrategy()—the model is replicated once per TPU core, and the replicas are kept in sync.

Note there's something else a bit curious about the TPU runtime: it's a two-VM setup, meaning that the VM that hosts your notebook runtime isn't the same VM that the TPU lives in. Because of this, you won't be able to train from files stored on the local disk (that is, on the disk linked to the VM that hosts the instance). The TPU runtime can't read from there. You have two options for data loading:

- Train from data that lives in the memory of the VM (not on disk). If your data is in an R array, this is what you're already doing.
- Store the data in a Google Cloud Storage (GCS) bucket, and create a dataset that reads the data directly from the bucket, without downloading locally. The TPU runtime can read data from GCS. This is your only option for datasets that are too large to live entirely in memory.

You'll also notice that the first epoch takes a while to start. That's because your model is getting compiled to something that the TPU can execute. Once that step is done, the training itself is blazing fast.

Beware of I/O bottlenecks

Because TPUs can process batches of data extremely quickly, the speed at which you can read data from GCS can easily become a bottleneck.

- If your dataset is small enough, you should keep it in the memory of the VM. You can do so by calling `dataset_cache()` on your dataset. That way, the data will be read from GCS only once.
- If your dataset is too large to fit in memory, make sure to store it as TFRecord files—an efficient binary storage format that can be loaded very quickly. On https://keras.rstudio.com, you'll find example code demonstrating how to format your data as TFRecord files.

LEVERAGING STEP FUSING TO IMPROVE TPU UTILIZATION

Because a TPU has a lot of compute power available, you need to train with very large batches to keep the TPU cores busy. For small models, the batch size required can get extraordinarily large—upward of 10,000 samples per batch. When working with enormous batches, you should make sure to increase your optimizer learning rate accordingly; you're going to be making fewer updates to your weights, but each update will be more accurate (because the gradients are computed using more data points), so you should move the weights by a greater magnitude with each update.

You can leverage a simple trick, however, to keep reasonably sized batches while maintaining full TPU utilization: *step fusing*. The idea is to run multiple steps of training during each TPU execution step. Basically, do more work in between two round trips from the VM memory to the TPU. To do this, simply specify the `steps_per_execution` argument in `compile()`—for instance, `steps_per_execution = 8` to run eight steps of training during each TPU execution. For small models that are underutilizing the TPU (or GPU), this can result in a dramatic speed-up.

Summary

- You can leverage hyperparameter tuning and KerasTuner to automate the tedium out of finding the best model configuration. But be mindful of validation-set overfitting!
- An ensemble of diverse models can often significantly improve the quality of your predictions.
- You can speed up model training on GPU by turning on mixed precision—you'll generally get a nice speed boost at virtually no cost.
- To further scale your workflows, you can use the `tf$distribute$Mirrored-Strategy()` API to train models on multiple GPUs.
- You can even train on Google's TPUs by using the `TPUStrategy()` API. If your model is small, make sure to leverage step fusing (via the `compile(…, steps_per_execution = N)` argument) to fully utilize the TPU cores.

Conclusions

This chapter covers

- Important takeaways from this book
- The limitations of deep learning
- Possible future directions for deep learning, machine learning, and AI
- Resources for further learning and applying your skills in practice

You've almost reached the end of this book. This last chapter will summarize and review core concepts while also expanding your horizons beyond what you've learned so far. Becoming an effective AI practitioner is a journey, and finishing this book is merely your first step on it. I want to make sure you realize this and are properly equipped to take the next steps of this journey on your own.

We'll start with a bird's-eye view of what you should take away from this book. This should refresh your memory regarding some of the concepts you've learned. Next, I'll present an overview of some key limitations of deep learning. To use a tool appropriately, you should not only understand what it *can* do but also be aware of what it *can't* do. Finally, I'll offer some speculative thoughts about the future evolution of deep learning, machine learning, and AI. This should be especially interesting to you if you'd like to get into fundamental research. The chapter ends with a short list of resources and strategies for further learning about machine learning and staying up to date with new advances.

14.1 Key concepts in review

This section briefly synthesizes key takeaways from this book. If you ever need a quick refresher to help you recall what you've learned, you can read these few pages.

14.1.1 Various approaches to AI

First of all, deep learning isn't synonymous with AI, or even with machine learning:

- *Artificial intelligence* (AI) is an ancient, broad field that can generally be understood as "all attempts to automate human cognitive processes." This can range from the very basic, such as an Excel spreadsheet, to the very advanced, like a humanoid robot that can walk and talk.
- *Machine learning* is a specific subfield of AI that aims at automatically developing programs (called *models*) purely from exposure to training data. This process of turning data into a program is called *learning*. Although machine learning has been around for a long time, it started to take off only in the 1990s, before becoming the dominant form of AI in the 2000s.
- *Deep learning* is one of many branches of machine learning, where the models are long chains of geometric transformations, applied one after the other. These operations are structured into modules called *layers*: deep learning models are typically stacks of layers—or, more generally, graphs of layers. These layers are parameterized by *weights*, which are the parameters learned during training. The *knowledge* of a model is stored in its weights, and the process of learning consists of finding "good values" for these weights—values that minimize a *loss function*. Because the chain of geometric transformations considered is differentiable, updating the weights to minimize the loss function is done efficiently via *gradient descent*.

Even though deep learning is just one among many approaches to machine learning, it isn't on an equal footing with the others. Deep learning is a breakout success. Here's why.

14.1.2 What makes deep learning special within the field of machine learning

In the span of only a few years, deep learning has achieved tremendous breakthroughs across a wide range of tasks that have been historically perceived as extremely difficult for computers, especially in the area of machine perception: extracting useful information from images, videos, sound, and more. Given sufficient training data (in particular, training data appropriately labeled by humans), deep learning makes it possible to extract from perceptual data almost anything a human could. Hence, it's sometimes said that deep learning has "solved perception"—although that's true only for a fairly narrow definition of perception.

Due to its unprecedented technical successes, deep learning has singlehandedly brought about the third and by far the largest *AI summer*: a period of intense interest, investment, and hype in the field of AI. As this book is being written, we're in the middle of it. Whether this period will end in the near future, and what happens after it ends, are topics of debate. One thing is certain: in stark contrast with previous AI summers, deep learning has provided enormous business value to both large and small technology companies, enabling human-level speech recognition, smart assistants, human-level image classification, vastly improved machine translation, and more. The hype may (and likely will) recede, but the sustained economic and technological impact of deep learning will remain. In that sense, deep learning could be analogous to the internet: it may be overly hyped for a few years, but in the longer term, it will still be a major revolution that will transform our economy and our lives.

I'm particularly optimistic about deep learning, because even if we were to make no further technological progress in the next decade, deploying existing algorithms to every applicable problem would be a game changer for most industries. Deep learning is nothing short of a revolution, and progress is currently happening at an incredibly fast rate, due to an exponential investment in resources and headcount. From where I stand, the future looks bright, although short-term expectations are somewhat overoptimistic; deploying deep learning to the full extent of its potential will likely take multiple decades.

14.1.3   *How to think about deep learning*

The most surprising thing about deep learning is how simple it is. Ten years ago, no one expected that we would achieve such amazing results on machine-perception problems by using simple parametric models trained with gradient descent. Now it turns out that all you need is sufficiently large parametric models trained with gradient descent on sufficiently many examples. As Feynman once said about the universe, "It's not complicated, it's just a lot of it."[1]

In deep learning, everything is a vector—that is to say, everything is a *point* in a *geometric space*. Model inputs (text, images, and so on) and targets are first *vectorized*—turned into an initial input vector space and target vector space. Each layer in a deep learning model operates one simple geometric transformation on the data that goes through it. Together, the chain of layers in the model forms one complex geometric transformation, broken down into a series of simple ones. This complex transformation attempts to map the input space to the target space, one point at a time. This transformation is parameterized by the weights of the layers, which are iteratively updated based on how well the model is currently performing. A key characteristic of this geometric transformation is that it must be *differentiable*, which is required for us to be able to learn its parameters via gradient descent. Intuitively, this means the geometric morphing from inputs to outputs must be smooth and continuous—a significant constraint.

---

[1] Richard Feynman, interview, "The World from Another Point of View," Yorkshire Television, 1972.

The entire process of applying this complex geometric transformation to the input data can be visualized in 3D by imagining a person trying to uncrumple a paper ball: the crumpled paper ball is the manifold of the input data that the model starts with. Each movement operated by the person on the paper ball is similar to a simple geometric transformation operated by one layer. The full uncrumpling gesture sequence is the complex transformation of the entire model. Deep learning models are mathematical machines for uncrumpling complicated manifolds of high-dimensional data.

That's the magic of deep learning: turning meaning into vectors, then into geometric spaces, and then incrementally learning complex geometric transformations that map one space to another. All you need are spaces of sufficiently high dimensionality to capture the full scope of the relationships found in the original data.

The whole process hinges on a single core idea: *that meaning is derived from the pairwise relationship between things* (between words in a language, between pixels in an image, and so on) and that *these relationships can be captured by a distance function*. But note that whether the brain also implements meaning via geometric spaces is an entirely separate question. Vector spaces are efficient to work with from a computational standpoint, but different data structures for intelligence can easily be envisioned—in particular, graphs. Neural networks initially emerged from the idea of using graphs as a way to encode meaning, which is why they're named *neural networks*; the surrounding field of research used to be called *connectionism*. Nowadays the name "neural network" exists purely for historical reasons—it's an extremely misleading name because they're neither neural nor networks. In particular, neural networks have hardly anything to do with the brain. A more appropriate name would have been *layered representations learning* or *hierarchical representations learning*, or maybe even *deep differentiable models* or *chained geometric transforms*, to emphasize the fact that continuous geometric space manipulation is at their core.

14.1.4 *Key enabling technologies*

The technological revolution that's currently unfolding didn't start with any single breakthrough invention. Rather, like any other revolution, it's the product of a vast accumulation of enabling factors—gradual at first, and then sudden. In the case of deep learning, we can point out the following key factors:

- *Incremental algorithmic innovations*—These first began appearing slowly over the span of two decades (starting with backpropagation), and then were developed increasingly faster as more research effort was poured into deep learning after 2012.
- *The availability of large amounts of perceptual data*—This was a requirement in order to realize that sufficiently large models trained on sufficiently large data are all we need. This is, in turn, a byproduct of the rise of the consumer internet and Moore's law applied to storage media.
- *The availability of fast, highly parallel computation hardware at a low price*—Especially the GPUs produced by NVIDIA—first gaming GPUs and then chips designed

from the ground up for deep learning. Early on, NVIDIA CEO Jensen Huang took note of the deep learning boom and decided to bet the company's future on it, which paid off in a big way.

- *A complex stack of software layers that makes this computational power available to humans*—The CUDA language, frameworks like TensorFlow that do automatic differentiation, and Keras, which makes deep learning accessible to most people.

In the future, deep learning will not be used only by specialists—researchers, graduate students, and engineers with an academic profile—it will be a tool in the toolbox of every developer, much like web technology today. Everyone needs to build intelligent apps: just as every business today needs a website, every product will need to intelligently make sense of user-generated data. Bringing about this future will require us to build tools that make deep learning radically easy to use and accessible to anyone with basic coding abilities. Keras has been the first major step in that direction.

14.1.5 *The universal machine learning workflow*

Having access to an extremely powerful tool for creating models that map any input space to any target space is great, but the difficult part of the machine learning workflow is often everything that comes before designing and training such models (and, for production models, what comes after, as well). Understanding the problem domain so as to be able to determine what to attempt to predict, given what data, and how to measure success, is a prerequisite for any successful application of machine learning, and it isn't something that advanced tools like Keras and TensorFlow can help you with. As a reminder, here's a quick summary of the typical machine learning workflow as described in chapter 6:

1. Define the problem. What data is available, and what are you trying to predict? Will you need to collect more data or hire people to manually label a dataset?

2. Identify a way to reliably measure success on your goal. For simple tasks, this may be prediction accuracy, but in many cases, it will require sophisticated, domain-specific metrics.

3. Prepare the validation process that you'll use to evaluate your models. In particular, you should define a training set, a validation set, and a test set. The validation and test set labels shouldn't leak into the training data: for instance, with temporal prediction, the validation and test data should be posterior to the training data.

4. Vectorize the data by turning it into vectors and preprocessing it in a way that makes it more easily approachable by a neural network (normalization and so on).

5. Develop a first model that beats a trivial common-sense baseline, thus demonstrating that machine learning can work on your problem. This may not always be the case!

6 Gradually refine your model architecture by tuning hyperparameters and adding regularization. Make changes based on performance on the validation data only, not the test data or the training data. Remember that you should get your model to overfit (thus identifying a model capacity level that's greater than you need) and only then begin to add regularization or downsize your model. Beware of validation-set overfitting when tuning hyperparameters—your hyperparameters may end up being overspecialized to the validation set. Avoiding this is the purpose of having a separate test set.

7 Deploy your final model in production—as a web API, as part of a JavaScript or C++ application, on an embedded device, and so on. Keep monitoring its performance on real-world data, and use your findings to refine the next iteration of the model!

14.1.6 Key network architectures

The four families of network architectures that you should be familiar with are *densely connected networks, convolutional networks, recurrent networks*, and *Transformers*. Each type of model is meant for a specific input modality. A network architecture encodes *assumptions* about the structure of the data: a *hypothesis space* within which the search for a good model will proceed. Whether a given architecture will work on a given problem depends entirely on the match between the structure of the data and the assumptions of the network architecture.

These different network types can easily be combined to achieve larger multi-modal models, much as you combine LEGO bricks. In a way, deep learning layers are LEGO bricks for information processing. Here's a quick overview of the mapping between input modalities and appropriate network architectures:

- *Vector data*—Densely connected models.
- *Image data*—2D convnets.
- *Sequence data*—RNNs for time series, or Transformers for discrete sequences (such as sequences of words). 1D convnets can also be used for translation-invariant, continuous sequence data, such as birdsong waveforms.
- *Video data*—Either 3D convnets (if you need to capture motion effects), or a combination of a frame-level 2D convnet for feature extraction followed by a sequence-processing model.
- *Volumetric data*—3D convnets.

Now let's quickly review the specificities of each network architecture.

DENSELY CONNECTED NETWORKS

A densely connected network is a stack of `Dense` layers meant to process vector data (where each sample is a vector of numerical or categorical attributes). Such networks assume no specific structure in the input features: they're called *densely connected* because the units of a `Dense` layer are connected to every other unit. The layer attempts to map relationships between any two input features; this is unlike a 2D convolution layer, for instance, which looks only at *local* relationships.

Densely connected networks are most commonly used for categorical data (e.g., where the input features are lists of attributes), such as the Boston housing price dataset used in chapter 4. They're also used as the final classification or regression stage of most networks. For instance, the convnets covered in chapter 8 typically end with one or two Dense layers, and so do the recurrent networks in chapter 10.

Remember, to perform *binary classification*, end your stack of layers with a Dense layer with a single unit and a sigmoid activation, and use binary_crossentropy as the loss. Your targets should be either 0 or 1:

```
inputs <- layer_input(shape = c(num_inputs_features))
outputs <- inputs %>%
  layer_dense(32, activation = "relu") %>%
  layer_dense(32, activation = "relu") %>%
  layer_dense(1, activation = "sigmoid")
model <- keras_model(inputs, outputs)
model %>% compile(optimizer = "rmsprop", loss = "binary_crossentropy")
```

To perform *single-label categorical classification* (where each sample has exactly one class, no more), end your stack of layers with a Dense layer with a number of units equal to the number of classes, and a softmax activation. If your targets are one-hot encoded, use categorical_crossentropy as the loss; if they're integers, use sparse_categorical_crossentropy:

```
inputs <- layer_input(shape = c(num_inputs_features))
outputs <- inputs %>%
  layer_dense(32, activation = "relu") %>%
  layer_dense(32, activation = "relu") %>%
  layer_dense(num_classes, activation = "softmax")
model <- keras_model(inputs, outputs)
model %>% compile(optimizer = "rmsprop", loss = "categorical_crossentropy")
```

To perform *multilabel categorical classification* (where each sample can have several classes), end your stack of layers with a Dense layer with a number of units equal to the number of classes, and a sigmoid activation, and use binary_crossentropy as the loss. Your targets should be multi-hot encoded:

```
inputs <- layer_input(shape = c(num_inputs_features))
outputs <- inputs %>%
  layer_dense(32, activation = "relu") %>%
  layer_dense(32, activation = "relu") %>%
  layer_dense(num_classes, activation = "sigmoid")
model <- keras_model(inputs, outputs)
model %>% compile(optimizer = "rmsprop", loss = "binary_crossentropy")
```

To perform *regression* toward a vector of continuous values, end your stack of layers with a Dense layer with a number of units equal to the number of values you're trying to predict (often a single one, such as the price of a house), and no activation. Various losses can be used for regression—most commonly mean_squared_error (MSE):

```
inputs <- layer_input(shape = c(num_inputs_features))
outputs <- inputs %>%
  layer_dense(32, activation = "relu") %>%
  layer_dense(32, activation = "relu") %>%
  layer_dense(num_values)
model <- keras_model(inputs, outputs)
model %>% compile(optimizer = "rmsprop", loss = "mse")
```

CONVNETS

Convolution layers look at spatially local patterns by applying the same geometric transformation to different spatial locations (*patches*) in an input tensor. This results in representations that are *translation invariant*, making convolution layers highly data efficient and modular. This idea is applicable to spaces of any dimensionality: 1D (continuous sequences), 2D (images), 3D (volumes), and so on. You can use the Conv1D layer to process sequences, the Conv2D layer to process images, and the Conv3D layers to process volumes. As a leaner, more efficient alternative to convolution layers, you can also use *depthwise separable convolution* layers, such as SeparableConv2D.

Convnets, or *convolutional networks*, consist of stacks of convolution and max-pooling layers. The pooling layers let you spatially downsample the data, which is required to keep feature maps to a reasonable size as the number of features grows, and to allow subsequent convolution layers to "see" a greater spatial extent of the inputs. Convnets are often ended with either a Flatten operation or a global-pooling layer, turning spatial feature maps into vectors, followed by Dense layers to achieve classification or regression.

Here's a typical image classification network (categorical classification, in this case), leveraging SeparableConv2D layers:

```
inputs <- layer_input(shape = c(height, width, channels))
outputs <- inputs %>%
  layer_separable_conv_2d(32, 3, activation = "relu") %>%
  layer_separable_conv_2d(64, 3, activation = "relu") %>%
  layer_max_pooling_2d(2) %>%
  layer_separable_conv_2d(64, 3, activation = "relu") %>%
  layer_separable_conv_2d(128, 3, activation = "relu") %>%
  layer_max_pooling_2d(2) %>%
  layer_separable_conv_2d(64, 3, activation = "relu") %>%
  layer_separable_conv_2d(128, 3, activation = "relu") %>%
  layer_global_average_pooling_2d() %>%
  layer_dense(32, activation = "relu") %>%
  layer_dense(num_classes, activation = "softmax")
model <- keras_model(inputs, outputs)
model %>% compile(optimizer = "rmsprop", loss = "categorical_crossentropy")
```

When building a very deep convnet, it's common to add *batch normalization* layers as well as *residual connections*—two architecture patterns that help gradient information flow smoothly through the network.

RNNs

Recurrent neural networks (RNNs) work by processing sequences of inputs one time step at a time, and maintaining a state throughout (a state is typically a vector or set of vectors). They should be used preferentially over 1D convnets in the case of sequences where patterns of interest aren't invariant by temporal translation (e.g., time-series data where the recent past is more important than the distant past).

Three RNN layers are available in Keras: `SimpleRNN`, `GRU`, and `LSTM`. For most practical purposes, you should use either `GRU` or `LSTM`. `LSTM` is the more powerful of the two but is also more expensive; you can think of `GRU` as a simpler, cheaper alternative to it.

To stack multiple RNN layers on top of each other, each layer prior to the last layer in the stack should return the full sequence of its outputs (each input time step will correspond to an output time step). If you aren't stacking any further RNN layers, it's common to return only the last output, which contains information about the entire sequence.

Following is a single RNN layer for binary classification of vector sequences:

```
inputs <- layer_input(shape = c(num_timesteps, num_features))
outputs <- inputs %>%
  layer_lstm(32) %>%
  layer_dense(num_classes, activation = "sigmoid")
model <- keras_model(inputs, outputs)
model %>% compile(optimizer = "rmsprop", loss = "binary_crossentropy")
```

And this is a stacked RNN for binary classification of vector sequences:

```
inputs <- layer_input(shape = c(num_timesteps, num_features))
outputs <- inputs %>%
  layer_lstm(32, return_sequences = TRUE) %>%
  layer_lstm(32, return_sequences = TRUE) %>%
  layer_lstm(32) %>%
  layer_dense(num_classes, activation = "sigmoid")
model <- keras_model(inputs, outputs)
model %>% compile(optimizer = "rmsprop", loss = "binary_crossentropy")
```

TRANSFORMERS

A Transformer looks at a set of vectors (such as word vectors), and leverages *neural attention* to transform each vector into a representation that is aware of the *context* provided by the other vectors in the set. When the set in question is an ordered sequence, you can also leverage *positional encoding* to create Transformers that can take into account both global context and word order, capable of processing long text paragraphs much more effectively than RNNs or 1D convnets.

Transformers can be used for any set-processing or sequence-processing task, including text classification, but they excel especially at *sequence-to-sequence learning*, such as translating paragraphs in a source language into a target language. A sequence-to-sequence Transformer is made up of two parts:

- A `TransformerEncoder` that turns an input vector sequence into a context-aware, order-aware output vector sequence
- A `TransformerDecoder` that takes the output of the `TransformerEncoder`, as well as a target sequence, and predicts what should come next in the target sequence

If you're only processing a single sequence (or set) of vectors, you'd be only using the `TransformerEncoder`.

Following is a sequence-to-sequence Transformer for mapping a source sequence to a target sequence (this setup could be used for machine translation or question answering, for instance):

```
encoder_inputs <- layer_input(shape = c(sequence_length),      Source sequence
                              dtype = "int64")
encoder_outputs <- encoder_inputs %>%
  layer_positional_embedding(sequence_length, vocab_size, embed_dim) %>%
  layer_transformer_encoder(embed_dim, dense_dim, num_heads)

decoder <- layer_transformer_decoder(NULL, embed_dim, dense_dim, num_heads)
decoder_inputs <- layer_input(shape = c(NA),
                              dtype = "int64")         Target sequence so far
decoder_outputs <- decoder_inputs %>%
  layer_positional_embedding(sequence_length, vocab_size, embed_dim) %>%
  decoder(., encoder_outputs) %>%
  layer_dense(vocab_size, activation = "softmax")     Target sequence one
                                                      step in the future
transformer <- keras_model(list(encoder_inputs, decoder_inputs),
                           decoder_outputs)
transformer %>%
  compile(optimizer = "rmsprop", loss = "categorical_crossentropy")
```

And this is a lone `TransformerEncoder` for binary classification of integer sequences:

```
inputs <- layer_input(shape = c(sequence_length), dtype = "int64")
outputs <- inputs %>%
  layer_positional_embedding(sequence_length, vocab_size, embed_dim) %>%
  layer_transformer_encoder(embed_dim, dense_dim, num_heads) %>%
  layer_global_max_pooling_1d() %>%
  layer_dense(1, activation = "sigmoid")
model <- keras_model(inputs, outputs)
model %>% compile(optimizer = "rmsprop", loss = "binary_crossentropy")
```

Full implementations of the `TransformerEncoder`, the `TransformerDecoder`, and the `PositionalEmbedding` layers are provided in chapter 11.

14.1.7 *The space of possibilities*

What will you build with these techniques? Remember, building deep learning models is like playing with LEGO bricks: layers can be plugged together to map essentially anything to anything, given that you have appropriate training data available and that the mapping is achievable via a continuous geometric transformation of reasonable complexity. The space of possibilities is infinite. This section offers a few examples to inspire you to think beyond the basic classification and regression tasks that have traditionally been the bread and butter of machine learning.

I've sorted my suggested applications by input and output modalities in the following list. Note that quite a few of them stretch the limits of what is possible, although a model could be trained on all of these tasks—in some cases, such a model probably wouldn't generalize far from its training data. Sections 14.2 through 14.4 will address how these limitations could be lifted in the future:

- Mapping vector data to vector data:
  - *Predictive health care*—Mapping patient medical records to predictions of patient outcomes
  - *Behavioral targeting*—Mapping a set of website attributes with data on how long a user will spend on the website
  - *Product quality control*—Mapping a set of attributes relative to an instance of a manufactured product with the probability that the product will fail by next year
- Mapping image data to vector data:
  - *Medical assistant*—Mapping slides of medical images to a prediction about the presence of a tumor
  - *Self-driving vehicle*—Mapping car dashcam video frames to steering wheel angle commands and gas and braking commands
  - *Board game AI*—Mapping Go or chess boards to the next player move
  - *Diet helper*—Mapping pictures of a dish to its calorie count
  - *Age prediction*—Mapping selfies to the age of the person
- Mapping time-series data to vector data:
  - *Weather prediction*—Mapping time series of weather data in a grid of locations to the temperature in a specific place one week later
  - *Brain-computer interfaces*—Mapping time series of magnetoencephalogram (MEG) data to computer commands
  - *Behavioral targeting*—Mapping time series of user interactions on a website to the probability that a user will buy something
- Mapping text to text:
  - *Machine translation*—Mapping a paragraph in one language to a translated version in a different language
  - *Smart reply*—Mapping emails to possible one-line replies
  - *Question answering*—Mapping general-knowledge questions to answers
  - *Summarization*—Mapping a long article to a short summary of the article
- Mapping images to text:
  - *Text transcription*—Mapping images that contain a text element to the corresponding text string
  - *Captioning*—Mapping images to short captions describing the contents of the images

- Mapping text to images:
  - *Conditioned image generation*—Mapping a short text description to images matching the description
  - *Logo generation/selection*—Mapping the name and description of a company to a logo suggestion
- Mapping images to images:
  - *Super-resolution*—Mapping downsized images to higher-resolution versions of the same images
  - *Visual depth sensing*—Mapping images of indoor environments to maps of depth predictions
- Mapping images and text to text:
  - *Visual QA*—Mapping images and natural language questions about the contents of images to natural language answers
- Mapping video and text to text:

  - *Video QA*—Mapping short videos and natural language questions about the contents of videos to natural language answers

Almost anything is possible, but not quite *anything*. You'll see in the next section what we *can't* do with deep learning.

14.2   *The limitations of deep learning*

The space of applications that can be implemented with deep learning is infinite. And yet, many applications remain completely out of reach for current deep learning techniques—even given vast amounts of human-annotated data. Say, for instance, that you could assemble a dataset of hundreds of thousands—even millions—of English-language descriptions of the features of a software product, written by a product manager, as well as the corresponding source code developed by a team of engineers to meet these requirements. Even with this data, you could not train a deep learning model to read a product description and generate the appropriate codebase. That's just one example among many. In general, anything that requires reasoning—like programming or applying the scientific method—long-term planning—and algorithmic data manipulation is out of reach for deep learning models, no matter how much data you throw at them. Even learning a simple sorting algorithm with a deep neural network is tremendously difficult.

This is because a deep learning model is just *a chain of simple, continuous geometric transformations* mapping one vector space into another. All it can do is map one data manifold X into another manifold Y, assuming the existence of a learnable continuous transform from X to Y. A deep learning model can be interpreted as a kind of program, but, inversely, *most programs can't be expressed as deep learning models*. For most tasks, either there exists no corresponding neural network of reasonable size that solves the task, or, even if one exists, it may not be *learnable*: the corresponding geometric transform may be far too complex, or there may not be appropriate data available to learn it.

Scaling up current deep learning techniques by stacking more layers and using more training data can only superficially palliate some of these issues. It won't solve the more fundamental problems that deep learning models are limited in what they can represent and that most of the programs you may wish to learn can't be expressed as a continuous geometric morphing of a data manifold.

14.2.1 *The risk of anthropomorphizing machine learning models*

One real risk with contemporary AI is misinterpreting what deep learning models do and overestimating their abilities. A fundamental feature of humans is our *theory of mind*: our tendency to project intentions, beliefs, and knowledge on the things around us. Drawing a smiley face on a rock suddenly makes it "happy" in our minds. Applied to deep learning, this means that, for instance, when we're able to somewhat successfully train a model to generate captions to describe pictures, we're led to believe that the model "understands" the contents of the pictures and the captions it generates. Then we're surprised when any slight departure from the sort of images present in the training data causes the model to generate completely absurd captions (see figure 14.1).

The boy is holding a baseball bat.

Figure 14.1   Failure of an image-captioning system based on deep learning

In particular, this is highlighted by *adversarial examples*, which are samples fed to a deep learning network that are designed to trick the model into misclassifying them. You're already aware that, for instance, it's possible to do gradient ascent in input space to generate inputs that maximize the activation of some convnet filter—this is the basis of the filter-visualization technique introduced in chapter 9, as well as the DeepDream algorithm from chapter 12. Similarly, through gradient ascent, you can slightly modify an image to maximize the class prediction for a given class. By taking a picture of a panda and adding to it a gibbon gradient, we can get a neural network to classify the panda as a gibbon (see figure 14.2). This evidences both the brittleness of these models and the deep difference between their input-to-output mapping and our human perception.

In short, deep learning models don't have any understanding of their input—at least not in a human sense. Our own understanding of images, sounds, and language is grounded in our sensorimotor experience as humans. Machine learning models

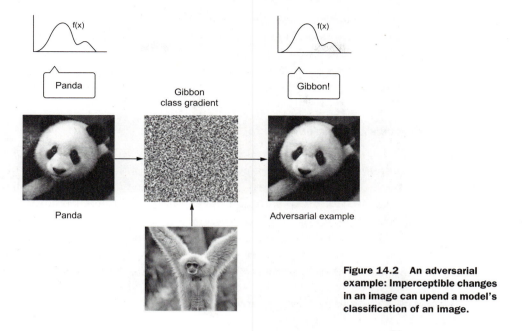

Figure 14.2   An adversarial example: Imperceptible changes in an image can upend a model's classification of an image.

have no access to such experiences and thus can't understand their inputs in a human-relatable way. By annotating large numbers of training examples to feed into our models, we get them to learn a geometric transform that maps data to human concepts on a specific set of examples, but this mapping is a simplistic sketch of the original model in our minds—the one developed from our experience as embodied agents. It's like a dim image in a mirror (see figure 14.3). The models you create will take any shortcut available to fit their training data. For instance, image models tend to rely more on local textures than on a global understanding of the input images—a model trained on a dataset that features both leopards and sofas is likely to classify a leopard-pattern sofa as an actual leopard.

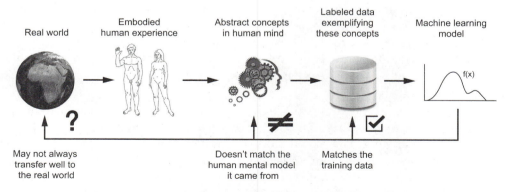

Figure 14.3   Current machine learning models: Like a dim image in a mirror

As a machine learning practitioner, always be mindful of this, and never fall into the trap of believing that neural networks understand the tasks they perform—they don't, at least not in a way that would make sense to us. They were trained on a different, far narrower task than the one we wanted to teach them: that of mapping training inputs to training targets, point by point. Show them anything that deviates from their training data, and they will break in absurd ways.

14.2.2 *Automatons vs. intelligent agents*

Fundamental differences exist between the straightforward geometric morphing from input to output that deep learning models do and the way humans think and learn. It isn't just the fact that humans learn by themselves from embodied experience instead of being presented with explicit training examples. The human brain is an entirely different beast compared to a differentiable parametric function.

Let's zoom out a little bit and ask, "what's the purpose of intelligence?" Why did it arise in the first place? We can only speculate, but we can make fairly informed speculations. We can start by looking at brains—the organ that produces intelligence. Brains are an evolutionary adaption—a mechanism developed incrementally over hundreds of millions of years, via random trial and error, guided by natural selection— that dramatically expanded the ability of organisms to adapt to their environment. Brains originally appeared more than half a billion years ago as a way to *store and execute behavioral programs*. "Behavioral programs" are just sets of instructions that make an organism reactive to its environment: "if this happens, then do that." They link the organism's sensory inputs to its motor controls. In the beginning, brains would have served to hardcode behavioral programs (as neural connectivity patterns), which would allow an organism to react appropriately to its sensory input. This is the way insect brains still work—flies, ants, *C. elegans* (see figure 14.4), and so on. Because the original "source code" of these programs was DNA, which would be decoded as neural connectivity patterns, evolution was suddenly able to *search over behavior space* in a largely unbounded way—a major evolutionary shift.

Evolution was the programmer, and brains were computers carefully executing the code evolution gave them. Because neural connectivity is a very general computing substrate, the sensorimotor space of all brain-enabled species could suddenly start undergoing a dramatic expansion. Eyes, ears, mandibles, four legs, 24 legs—as long as you have a brain, evolution will kindly figure out for you behavioral programs that make good use of these. Brains can handle any modality—or combination of modalities—you throw at them.

Now, mind you, these early brains weren't exactly intelligent per se. They were very much *automatons*: they would merely execute behavioral programs hardcoded in the organism's DNA. They could only be described as intelligent in the same sense that a thermostat is "intelligent." Or a list-sorting program. Or . . . a trained deep neural network (of the artificial kind). This is an important distinction, so let's look at it carefully: what's the difference between automatons and actual intelligent agents?

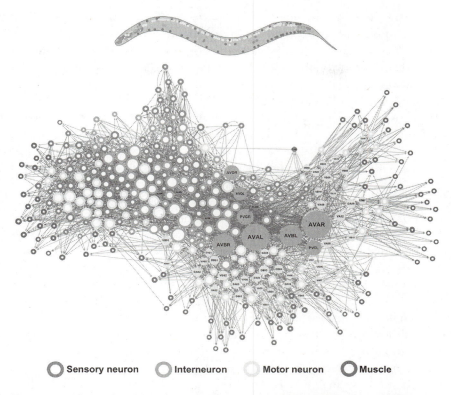

Figure 14.4   The brain network of the *C. elegans* worm: A behavioral automaton "programmed" by natural evolution. Figure created by Emma Towlson (from Yan et al., "Network Control Principles Predict Neuron Function in the *Caenorhabditis elegans* Connectome," *Nature*, Oct. 2017).

14.2.3 *Local generalization vs. extreme generalization*

Seventeenth-century French philosopher and scientist René Descartes wrote in 1637 an illuminating comment that perfectly captures this distinction, long before the rise of AI, and in fact, before the first mechanical computer (which his colleague Pascal would create five years later). Descartes tells us, in reference to automatons,

> *Even though such machines might do some things as well as we do them, or perhaps even better, they would inevitably fail in others, which would reveal they were acting not through understanding, but only from the disposition of their organs.*

René Descartes, *Discourse on the Method* (1637)

There it is. Intelligence is characterized by *understanding*, and understanding is evidenced by *generalization*—the ability to handle whatever novel situation may arise. How do you tell the difference between a student that has memorized the past three years of exam questions but has no understanding of the subject, and a student who actually understands the material? You give them a brand-new problem. An automaton is static, crafted to accomplish specific things in a specific context—"if this, then that"—while an intelligent agent can adapt on the fly to novel, unexpected situations. When an automaton is exposed to something that doesn't match what it is "programmed" to do (whether we're talking about human-written programs, evolution-generated programs, or the implicit programming process of fitting a model on a training dataset), it will fail. Meanwhile, intelligent agents, like humans, will use their understanding to find a way forward.

Humans are capable of far more than mapping immediate stimuli to immediate responses, as a deep net, or an insect, would. We maintain complex, abstract models of our current situation, of ourselves, and of other people, and we can use these models to anticipate different possible futures and perform long-term planning. You can merge together known concepts to represent something you've never experienced before—like imagining what you'd do if you won the lottery, or picturing how your friend would react if you discreetly replaced her keys with exact copies made of elastic rubber. This ability to handle novelty and what-ifs, to expand our mental model space far beyond what we can experience directly—to leverage *abstraction* and *reasoning*—is the defining characteristic of human cognition. I call it *extreme generalization*: an ability to adapt to novel, never-before-experienced situations using little data or even no new data at all. This capability is key to the intelligence displayed by humans and advanced animals.

This stands in sharp contrast with what automaton-like systems do. A very rigid automaton wouldn't feature any generalization at all—it would be incapable of handling anything that it wasn't precisely told about in advance. A hash table or a basic question-answering program implemented as hardcoded if-then-else statements would fall into this category. Deep nets do slightly better: they can successfully process inputs that deviate a bit from what they're familiar with, which is precisely what makes them useful. Our cats vs. dogs model from chapter 8 could classify cat or dog pictures it had not seen before, as long as they were close enough to what it was trained on. However, deep nets are limited to what I call *local generalization* (see figure 14.5): the mapping from inputs to outputs performed by a deep net quickly stops making sense as inputs start deviating from what the net saw at training time. Deep nets can only generalize to *known unknowns*—to factors of variation that were anticipated during model development and that are extensively featured in the training data, such as

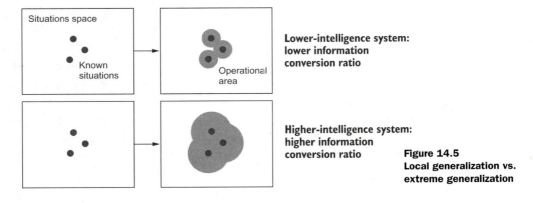

Figure 14.5
Local generalization vs. extreme generalization

different camera angles or lighting conditions for pet pictures. That's because deep nets generalize via interpolation on a manifold (remember chapter 5): any factor of variation in their input space needs to be captured by the manifold they learn. That's why basic data augmentation is so helpful in improving deep net generalization. Unlike humans, these models have no ability to improvise in the face of situations for which little or no data is available (like winning the lottery or being handed rubber keys) that only share abstract commonalities with past situations.

Consider, for instance, the problem of learning the appropriate launch parameters to get a rocket to land on the moon. If you used a deep net for this task and trained it using supervised learning or reinforcement learning, you'd have to feed it tens of thousands or even millions of launch trials: you'd need to expose it to a *dense sampling* of the input space, for it to learn a reliable mapping from input space to output space. In contrast, as humans, we can use our power of abstraction to come up with physical models—rocket science—and derive an exact solution that will land the rocket on the moon in one or a few trials. Similarly, if you developed a deep net controlling a human body, and you wanted it to learn to safely navigate a city without getting hit by cars, the net would have to die many thousands of times in various situations until it could infer that cars are dangerous and develop appropriate avoidance behaviors. Dropped into a new city, the net would have to relearn most of what it knows. On the other hand, humans are able to learn safe behaviors without having to die even once—again, thanks to our power of abstract modeling of novel situations.

14.2.4 *The purpose of intelligence*

This distinction between highly adaptable intelligent agents and rigid automatons leads us back to brain evolution. Why did brains—originally a mere medium for natural evolution to develop behavioral automatons—eventually turn intelligent? Like every significant evolutionary milestone, it happened because natural selection constraints encouraged it to happen.

Brains are responsible for behavior generation. If the set of situations an organism had to face was mostly static and known in advance, behavior generation would be an easy problem: evolution would just figure out the correct behaviors via random trial and error and hardcode them into the organism's DNA. This first stage of brain evolution—brains as automatons—would already be optimal. However, crucially, as organism complexity—and alongside it, environmental complexity—kept increasing, the situations that animals had to deal with became much more dynamic and more unpredictable. A day in your life, if you look closely, is unlike any day you've ever experienced, and unlike any day ever experienced by any of your evolutionary ancestors. You need to be able to face unknown and surprising situations constantly. There is no way for evolution to find and hardcode as DNA the sequence of behaviors you've been executing to successfully navigate your day since you woke up a few hours ago. It has to be generated on the fly, every day.

The brain, as a good behavior-generation engine, simply adapted to fit this need. It optimized for adaptability and generality, rather than merely optimizing for fitness to a fixed set of situations. This shift likely occurred multiple times throughout evolutionary history, resulting in highly intelligent animals in very distant evolutionary branches—apes, octopuses, ravens, and more. Intelligence is an answer to challenges presented by complex, dynamic ecosystems.

That's the nature of intelligence: it is the ability to efficiently leverage the information at your disposal to produce successful behavior in the face of an uncertain, ever-changing future. What Descartes calls "understanding" is the key to this remarkable capability: the power to mine your past experience to develop modular, reusable abstractions that can be quickly repurposed to handle novel situations and achieve extreme generalization.

14.2.5 *Climbing the spectrum of generalization*

As a crude caricature, you could summarize the evolutionary history of biological intelligence as a slow climb up the *spectrum of generalization*. It started with automaton-like brains that could perform only local generalization. Over time, evolution started producing organisms capable of increasingly broader generalization that could thrive in ever-more complex and variable environments. Eventually, in the past few millions of years—an instant in evolutionary terms—certain hominid species started trending toward an implementation of biological intelligence capable of extreme generalization, precipitating the start of the Anthropocene and forever changing the history of life on earth.

The progress of AI over the past 70 years bears striking similarities to this evolution. Early AI systems were pure automatons, like the ELIZA chat program from the 1960s, or SHRDLU,[2] a 1970 AI capable of manipulating simple objects from natural language commands. In the 1990s and 2000s, we saw the rise of machine learning systems capable of local generalization, which could deal with some level of uncertainty and novelty. In the 2010s, deep learning further expanded the local-generalization power of these systems by enabling engineers to leverage much larger datasets and much more expressive models.

Today, we may be on the cusp of the next evolutionary step. There is increasing interest in systems that could achieve *broad generalization*, which I define as the ability to deal with *unknown unknowns* within a single broad domain of tasks (including situations the system was not trained to handle and that its creators could not have anticipated), for instance, a self-driving car capable of safely dealing with any situation you throw at it, or a domestic robot that could pass the "Woz test of intelligence"—entering a random kitchen and making a cup of coffee.[3] By combining deep learning and painstakingly handcrafted abstract models of the world, we're already making visible progress toward these goals.

---

[2] Terry Winograd, "Procedures as a Representation for Data in a Computer Program for Understanding Natural Language" (1971).

[3] Fast Company, "Wozniak: Could a Computer Make a Cup of Coffee?" (March 2010), http://mng.bz/pJMP.

However, for the time being, AI remains limited to *cognitive automation*: the "intelligence" label in "artificial intelligence" is a category error. It would be more accurate to call our field "artificial cognition," with "cognitive automation" and "artificial intelligence" being two nearly independent subfields within it. In this subdivision, "artificial intelligence" would be a greenfield where almost everything remains to be discovered.

Now, I don't mean to diminish the achievements of deep learning. Cognitive automation is incredibly useful, and the way deep learning models are capable of automating tasks from exposure to data alone represents an especially powerful form of cognitive automation, far more practical and versatile than explicit programming. Doing this well is a game-changer for essentially every industry. But it's still a long way from human (or animal) intelligence. Our models, so far, can perform only local generalization: they map space X to space Y via a smooth geometric transform learned from a dense sampling of X-to-Y data points, and any disruption within spaces X or Y invalidates this mapping. They can generalize only to new situations that stay similar to past data, whereas human cognition is capable of extreme generalization, quickly adapting to radically novel situations and planning for long-term future situations.

14.3 Setting the course toward greater generality in AI

To lift some of the limitations we have discussed and create AI that can compete with human brains, we need to move away from straightforward input-to-output mappings and on to *reasoning* and *abstraction*. In the following couple of sections, we'll take a look at what the road ahead may look like.

14.3.1 On the importance of setting the right objective: The shortcut rule

Biological intelligence was the answer to a question asked by nature. Likewise, if we want to develop true artificial intelligence, first, we need to be asking the right questions.

An effect you see constantly in systems design is the *shortcut rule*: if you focus on optimizing one success metric, you will achieve your goal, but at the expense of everything in the system that wasn't covered by your success metric. You end up taking every available shortcut toward the goal. Your creations are shaped by the incentives you give yourself.

You see this often in machine learning competitions. In 2009, Netflix ran a challenge that promised a $1 million prize to the team that achieved the highest score on a movie-recommendation task. It ended up never using the system created by the winning team, because it was way too complex and compute intensive. The winners had optimized for prediction accuracy alone—what they were incentivized to achieve—at the expense of every other desirable characteristic of the system: inference cost, maintainability, and explainability. The shortcut rule holds true in most Kaggle competitions as well: the models produced by Kaggle winners can rarely, if ever, be used in production.

The shortcut rule has been everywhere in AI over the past few decades. In the 1970s, psychologist and computer science pioneer Allen Newell, concerned that his field wasn't making any meaningful progress toward a proper theory of cognition, proposed a new grand goal for AI: chess-playing. The rationale was that playing chess, in humans, seemed to involve—perhaps even require—capabilities such as perception, reasoning and analysis, memory, study from books, and so on. Surely, if we could build a chess-playing machine, it would have to feature these attributes as well. Right?

Over two decades later, the dream came true: in 1997, IBM's Deep Blue beat Gary Kasparov, the best chess player in the world. Researchers had then to contend with the fact that creating a chess-champion AI had taught them little about human intelligence. The Alpha-Beta algorithm at the heart of Deep Blue wasn't a model of the human brain and couldn't generalize to tasks other than similar board games. It turned out it was easier to build an AI that could only play chess than to build an artificial mind—so that's the shortcut researchers took.

So far, the driving success metric of the field of AI has been to solve specific tasks, from chess to Go, from MNIST classification to ImageNet, from Atari arcade games to *StarCraft* and *Dota 2*. Consequently, the history of the field has been defined by a series of "successes" where we figured out how to solve these tasks *without featuring any intelligence.*

If that sounds like a surprising statement, keep in mind that human-like intelligence isn't characterized by skill at any particular task—rather, it is the ability to adapt to novelty, to efficiently acquire new skills and master never-seen-before tasks. By fixing the task, you make it possible to provide an arbitrarily precise description of what needs to be done, either via hardcoding human-provided knowledge or by supplying humongous amounts of data. You make it possible for engineers to "buy" more skill for their AI by just adding data or adding hardcoded knowledge, without increasing the generalization power of the AI (see figure 14.6). If you have near-infinite training data, even a very crude algorithm like nearest-neighbor search can play video games with superhuman skill. Likewise if you have a near-infinite amount of human-written if-then-else statements. That is, until you make a small change to the rules of the game—the kind a human could adapt to instantly—which will require the nonintelligent system to be retrained or rebuilt from scratch.

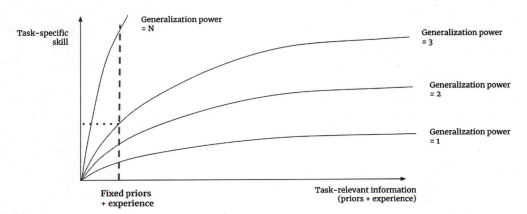

Figure 14.6   A low-generalization system can achieve arbitrary skill at a fixed task given unlimited task-specific information.

In short, by fixing the task, you remove the need to handle uncertainty and novelty, and because the nature of intelligence is the ability to handle uncertainty and novelty, you're effectively removing the need for intelligence. And because it's always easier to find a non-intelligent solution to a specific task than to solve the general problem of intelligence, that's the shortcut you will take 100% of the time. Humans can use their general intelligence to acquire skills at any new task, but in reverse, there is no path from a collection of task-specific skills to general intelligence.

14.3.2   A new target

To make artificial intelligence actually intelligent, and give it the ability to deal with the incredible variability and ever-changing nature of the real world, we first need to move away from seeking to achieve *task-specific skill* and, instead, start targeting generalization power itself. We need new metrics of progress that will help us develop increasingly intelligent systems, metrics that will point in the right direction and that will give us an actionable feedback signal. As long as we set our goal to be "create a model that solves task X," the shortcut rule will apply, and we'll end up with a model that does X, period.

In my view, intelligence can be precisely quantified as an *efficiency ratio*: the conversion ratio between the *amount of relevant information* you have available about the world (which could be either *past experience* or innate *prior knowledge*) and your *future operating area*, the set of novel situations where you will be able to produce appropriate behavior (you can view this as your *skill set*). A more intelligent agent will be able to handle a broader set of future tasks and situations using a smaller amount of past experience. To measure such a ratio, you just need to fix the information available to your system—its experience and its prior knowledge—and measure its performance on a set of reference situations or tasks that are known to be sufficiently different from what the system has had access to. Trying to maximize this ratio should lead you toward intelligence. Crucially, to avoid cheating, you're going to need to make sure you test the system only on tasks it wasn't programmed or trained to handle—in fact, you need tasks that the *creators of the system could not have anticipated.*

In 2018 and 2019, I developed a benchmark dataset called the *Abstraction and Reasoning Corpus* (ARC) [4] that seeks to capture this definition of intelligence. ARC is meant to be approachable by both machines and humans, and it looks very similar to human IQ tests, such as Raven's progressive matrices. At test time, you'll see a series of "tasks." Each task is explained via three or four "examples" that take the form of an input grid and a corresponding output grid (see figure 14.7). You'll then be given a brand-new input grid, and you'll have three tries to produce the correct output grid before moving on to the next task.

Compared to IQ tests, two things are unique about ARC. First, ARC seeks to measure generalization power, by only testing you on tasks you've never seen before. That means that ARC is *a game you can't practice for*, at least in theory: the tasks you will be

---

[4] François Chollet, "On the Measure of Intelligence" (2019), https://arxiv.org/abs/1911.01547.

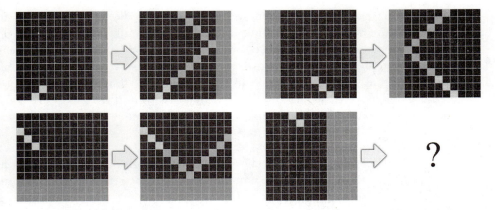

Figure 14.7   An ARC task: The nature of the task is demonstrated by a couple of input-output pair examples. Provided with a new input, you must construct the corresponding output.

tested on will have their own unique logic that you will have to understand on the fly. You can't just memorize specific strategies from past tasks.

In addition, ARC tries to control for the *prior knowledge* that you bring to the test. You never approach a new problem entirely from scratch—you bring to it preexisting skills and information. ARC makes the assumption that all test takers should start from the set of knowledge priors, called "Core Knowledge priors," that represent the "knowledge systems" that humans are born with. Unlike an IQ test, ARC tasks will never involve acquired knowledge, like English sentences, for instance.

Unsurprisingly, deep-learning-based methods (including models trained on extremely large amounts of external data, like GPT-3) have proven entirely unable to solve ARC tasks, because these tasks are non-interpolative and thus are a poor fit for curve-fitting. Meanwhile, average humans have no issue solving these tasks on the first try, without any practice. When you see a situation like this, where humans as young as five are able to naturally perform something that seems to be completely out of reach for modern AI technology, that's a clear signal that something interesting is going on—that we're missing something.

What would it take to solve ARC? Hopefully, this challenge will get you thinking. That's the entire point of ARC: to give you a goal of a different kind that will nudge you in a new direction—hopefully a productive direction. Now let's take a quick look at the key ingredients you're going to need if you want to answer the call.

14.4   *Implementing intelligence: The missing ingredients*

So far, you've learned that there's a lot more to intelligence than the sort of latent manifold interpolation that deep learning does. But what, then, do we need to start building real intelligence? What are the core pieces that are currently eluding us?

14.4.1 Intelligence as sensitivity to abstract analogies

Intelligence is the ability to use your past experience (and innate prior knowledge) to face novel, unexpected future situations. If the future you had to face was *truly novel*—sharing no common ground with anything you've seen before—you'd be unable to react to it, no matter how intelligent you were.

Intelligence works because nothing is ever truly without precedent. When we encounter something new, we're able to make sense of it by drawing analogies to our past experience, by articulating it in terms of the abstract concepts we've collected over time. A person from the 17th century seeing a jet plane for the first time might describe it as a large, loud metal bird that doesn't flap its wings. A car? That's a horseless carriage. If you're trying to teach physics to a grade schooler, you can explain how electricity is like water in a pipe, or how space-time is like a rubber sheet getting distorted by heavy objects.

Besides such clear-cut, explicit analogies, we're constantly making smaller, implicit analogies, every second, with every thought. Analogies are how we navigate life. Going to a new supermarket? You'll find your way by relating it to similar stores you've been to. Talking to someone new? They'll remind you of a few people you've met before. Even seemingly random patterns, like the shape of clouds, instantly evoke in us vivid images—an elephant, a ship, a fish.

These analogies aren't just in our minds, either: physical reality itself is full of isomorphisms. Electromagnetism is analogous to gravity. Animals are all structurally similar to each other, due to shared origins. Silica crystals are similar to ice crystals. And so on.

I call this the *kaleidoscope hypothesis*: our experience of the world seems to feature incredible complexity and never-ending novelty, but everything in this sea of complexity is similar to everything else. The number of *unique atoms of meaning* that you need to describe the universe you live in is relatively small, and everything around you is a recombination of these atoms, a few seeds, endless variation—much like what goes on inside a kaleidoscope, where a few glass beads are reflected by a system of mirrors to produce rich, seemingly ever-changing patterns (see figure 14.8).

Generalization power—intelligence—is the ability to mine your experience to identify these atoms of meaning that can seemingly be reused across many different situations. Once extracted, they're called *abstractions*. Whenever you encounter a new situation, you make sense of it via your accumulated collection of abstractions. How do you identify reusable atoms of meaning? Simply by noticing when two things are similar—by noticing analogies. If something is repeated twice, then both instances must have a single origin, like in a kaleidoscope. Abstraction is the engine of intelligence, and analogy-making is the engine that produces abstraction.

In short, intelligence is literally sensitivity to abstract analogies, and that's in fact all there is to it. If you have a high sensitivity to analogies, you will extract powerful abstractions from little experience, and you will be able to use these abstractions to operate in a maximally large area of future experience space. You will be maximally efficient in converting past experience into the ability to handle future novelty.

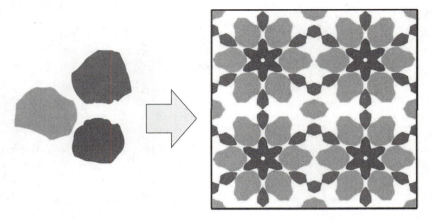

Figure 14.8   A kaleidoscope produces rich (yet repetitive) patterns from just a few beads of colored glass.

14.4.2 *The two poles of abstraction*

If intelligence is sensitivity to analogies, then developing artificial intelligence should start with spelling out a step-by-step algorithm for analogy-making. Analogy-making starts with *comparing things to one another*. Crucially, there are *two distinct ways* to compare things, from which arise two different kinds of abstraction, two modes of thinking, each better suited to a different kind of problem. Together, these two poles of abstraction form the basis for all of our thoughts.

The first way to relate things to each other is *similarity comparison*, which gives rise to *value-centric analogies*. The second way is *exact structural match*, which gives rise to *program-centric analogies* (or structure-centric analogies). In both cases, you start from *instances* of a thing, and you merge together related instances to produce an *abstraction* that captures the common elements of the underlying instances. What varies is how you tell that two instances are related, and how you merge instances into abstractions. Let's take a close look at each type.

VALUE-CENTRIC ANALOGY

Let's say you come across a number of different beetles in your backyard, belonging to multiple species. You'll notice similarities between them. Some will be more similar to one another, and some will be less similar: the notion of similarity is implicitly a smooth, continuous *distance function* that defines a latent manifold where your instances live. Once you've seen enough beetles, you can start clustering more similar instances together and merging them into a set of *prototypes* that captures the shared visual features of each cluster (see figure 14.9). This prototype is abstract: it doesn't look like any specific instance you've seen, though it encodes properties that are common across all of them. When you encounter a new beetle, you won't need to compare it to every single beetle you've seen before to know what to do with it. You can simply compare it to your handful of prototypes, so as to find the closest prototype—

Instances in the wild   Similarity clustering   Abstract prototypes

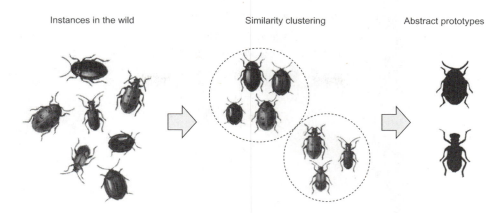

Figure 14.9   Value-centric analogy relates instances via a continuous notion of similarity to obtain abstract prototypes.

the beetle's *category*—and use it to make useful predictions: is the beetle likely to bite you? Will it eat your apples?

Does this sound familiar? It's pretty much a description of what unsupervised machine learning (such as the *K*-means clustering algorithm) does. In general, all of modern machine learning, unsupervised or not, works by learning latent manifolds that describe a space of instances encoded via prototypes. (Remember the convnet features you visualized in chapter 9? They were visual prototypes.) Value-centric analogy is the kind of analogy-making that enables deep learning models to perform local generalization.

It's also what many of your own cognitive abilities run on. As a human, you perform value-centric analogies all the time. It's the type of abstraction that underlies *pattern recognition*, *perception*, and *intuition*. If you can do a task without thinking about it, you're relying heavily on value-centric analogies. If you're watching a movie and you start subconsciously categorizing the different characters into "types," that's value-centric abstraction.

PROGRAM-CENTRIC ANALOGY

Crucially, there's more to cognition than the kind of immediate, approximative, intuitive categorization that value-centric analogy enables. There's another type of abstraction-generation mechanism that's slower, exact, deliberate: program-centric (or structure-centric) analogy.

In software engineering, you often write different functions or classes that seem to have a lot in common. When you notice these redundancies, you start asking, "could there be a more abstract function that performs the same job, that could be reused twice? Could there be an abstract base class that both of my classes could inherit from?" The definition of abstraction you're using here corresponds to program-centric analogy. You're not trying to compare your classes and functions by *how similar* they look, the way you'd compare two human faces, via an implicit distance function. Rather, you're interested in whether there are *parts* of them that have *exactly the same structure*. You're looking for what is called a *subgraph isomorphism* (see figure 14.10): programs can be represented as graphs of operators, and you're trying to find subgraphs (program subsets) that are exactly shared across your different programs.

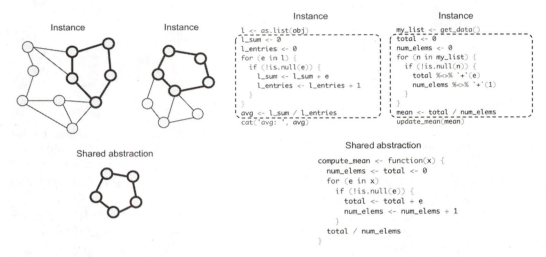

Figure 14.10   Program-centric analogy identifies and isolates isomorphic substructures across different instances.

This kind of analogy-making via exact structural match within different discrete structures isn't at all exclusive to specialized fields like computer science or mathematics—you're constantly using it without noticing. It underlies *reasoning, planning*, and the general concept of *rigor* (as opposed to intuition). Any time you're thinking about objects connected to each other by a discrete network of relationships (rather than a continuous similarity function), you're leveraging program-centric analogies.

COGNITION AS A COMBINATION OF BOTH KINDS OF ABSTRACTION

Let's compare these two poles of abstraction side by side (see table 14.1).

Table 14.1   The two poles of abstraction

Value-centric abstraction	Program-centric abstraction
Relates things by distance	Relates things by exact structural match
Continuous, grounded in geometry	Discrete, grounded in topology
Produces abstractions by "averaging" instances into "prototypes"	Produces abstractions by isolating isomorphic substructures across instances
Underlies perception and intuition	Underlies reasoning and planning

Table 14.1 The two poles of abstraction *(continued)*

Value-centric abstraction	Program-centric abstraction
Immediate, fuzzy, approximative	Slow, exact, rigorous
Requires a lot of experience to produce reliable results	Experience efficient; can operate on as few as two instances

14.4.3 *The two poles of abstraction*

Everything we do, everything we think, is a combination of these two types of abstraction. You'd be hard-pressed to find tasks that involve only one of the two. Even a seemingly "pure perception" task, like recognizing objects in a scene, involves a fair amount of implicit reasoning about the relationships between the objects you're looking at. And even a seemingly "pure reasoning" task, like finding the proof of a mathematical theorem, involves a good amount of intuition. When a mathematician puts their pen to the paper, they've already got a fuzzy vision of the direction in which they're going. The discrete reasoning steps they take to get to the destination are guided by high-level intuition.

These two poles are complementary, and it's their interleaving that enables extreme generalization. No mind could be complete without both of them.

14.4.4 *The missing half of the picture*

By this point, you should start seeing what's missing from modern deep learning: it's very good at encoding value-centric abstraction, but it has basically no ability to generate program-centric abstraction. Human-like intelligence is a tight interleaving of both types, so we're literally missing half of what we need—arguably the most important half.

Now, here's a caveat. So far, I've presented each type of abstraction as entirely separate from the other—opposite, even. In practice, however, they're more of a spectrum: to an extent, you could do reasoning by embedding discrete programs in continuous manifolds, just like you may fit a polynomial function through any set of discrete points, as long as you have enough coefficients. And inversely, you could use discrete programs to emulate continuous distance functions—after all, when you're doing linear algebra on a computer, you're working with continuous spaces, entirely via discrete programs that operate on ones and zeros.

However, there are clearly types of problems that are better suited to one or the other. Try to train a deep learning model to sort a list of five numbers, for instance. With the right architecture, it's not impossible, but it's an exercise in frustration. You'll need a massive amount of training data to make it happen, and even then, the model will still make occasional mistakes when presented with new numbers. And if you want to start sorting lists of 10 numbers instead, you'll need to completely retrain the model on even more data. Meanwhile, writing a sorting algorithm in R takes just a few lines, and the resulting program, once validated on a couple more examples, will work every time on lists of any size. That's pretty strong generalization: going from a couple of demonstration examples and test examples to a program that can successfully process literally any list of numbers.

In reverse, perception problems are a terrible fit for discrete reasoning processes. Try to write a pure-R program to classify MNIST digits without using any machine learning technique: you're in for a ride. You'll find yourself painstakingly coding functions that can detect the number of closed loops in a digit, the coordinates of the center of mass of a digit, and so on. After thousands of lines of code, you might achieve . . . 90% test accuracy. In this case, fitting a parametric model is much simpler; it can better utilize the large amount of data that's available, and it achieves much more robust results. If you have lots of data and you're faced with a problem where the manifold hypothesis applies, go with deep learning.

For this reason, it's unlikely that we'll see the rise of an approach that would reduce reasoning problems to manifold interpolation, or that would reduce perception problems to discrete reasoning. The way forward in AI is to develop a unified framework that incorporates *both* types of abstract analogy-making. Let's examine what that might look like.

14.5 *The future of deep learning*

Given what we know of how deep nets work, their limitations, and what they're currently missing, can we predict where things are headed in the medium term? Following are some purely personal thoughts. Note that I don't have a crystal ball, so a lot of what I anticipate may fail to become reality. I'm sharing these predictions not because I expect them to be proven completely right in the future but because they're interesting and actionable in the present.

At a high level, these are the main directions in which I see promise:

- *Models closer to general-purpose computer programs*, built on top of far richer primitives than the current differentiable layers. This is how we'll get to reasoning and abstraction, the lack of which is the fundamental weakness of current models.
- *A fusion between deep learning and discrete search over program spaces*, with the former providing perception and intuition capabilities, and the latter providing reasoning and planning capabilities.
- *Greater, systematic reuse of previously learned features and architectures*, such as metalearning systems using reusable and modular program subroutines.

Additionally, note that these considerations aren't specific to the sort of supervised learning that has been the bread and butter of deep learning so far—rather, they're applicable to any form of machine learning, including unsupervised, self-supervised, and reinforcement learning. It isn't fundamentally important where your labels come from or what your training loop looks like; these different branches of machine learning are different facets of the same construct. Let's dive in.

14.5.1   *Models as programs*

As noted in the previous section, a necessary transformational development that we can expect in the field of machine learning is a move away from models that perform purely *pattern recognition* and can achieve only *local generalization*, toward models capable of abstraction and reasoning that can achieve *extreme generalization*. Current AI programs that are capable of basic forms of reasoning are all hardcoded by human programmers: for instance, software that relies on search algorithms, graph manipulation, and formal logic.

That may be about to change, thanks to *program synthesis*—a field that is very niche today, but I expect to take off in a big way over the next few decades. Program synthesis consists of automatically generating simple programs by using a search algorithm (possibly genetic search, as in *genetic programming*) to explore a large space of possible programs (see figure 14.11). The search stops when a program is found that matches the required specifications, often provided as a set of input-output pairs. This is highly reminiscent of machine learning: given training data provided as input-output pairs, we find a program that matches inputs to outputs and can generalize to new inputs. The difference is that instead of learning parameter values in a hardcoded program (a neural network), we generate source code via a discrete search process (see table 14.2).

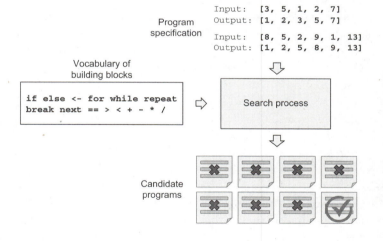

Figure 14.11
A schematic view of program synthesis: Given a program specification and a set of building blocks, a search process assembles the building blocks into candidate programs, which are then tested against the specification. The search continues until a valid program is found.

Table 14.2   Machine learning vs. program synthesis

Machine learning	Program synthesis
Model: differentiable parametric function	Model: graph of operators from a programming language
Engine: gradient descent	Engine: discrete search (such as genetic search)
Requires a lot of data to produce reliable results	Data efficient; can work with a couple of training examples

14.5.2 *Machine learning vs. program synthesis*

Program synthesis is how we're going to add program-centric abstraction capabilities to our AI systems. It's the missing piece of the puzzle. I mentioned earlier that deep learning techniques were entirely unusable on ARC, a reasoning-focused intelligence test. Meanwhile, very crude program-synthesis approaches are already producing very promising results on this benchmark.

14.5.3 *Blending together deep learning and program synthesis*

Of course, deep learning isn't going anywhere. Program synthesis isn't its replacement; it is its complement. It's the hemisphere that has been so far missing from our artificial brains. We're going to be leveraging both, in combination. There are two major ways this will take place:

1 Developing systems that integrate both deep learning modules and discrete algorithmic modules
2 Using deep learning to make the program search process itself more efficient

Let's review each of these possible avenues.

INTEGRATING DEEP LEARNING MODULES AND ALGORITHMIC MODULES INTO HYBRID SYSTEMS

Today, the most powerful AI systems are hybrid: they leverage both deep learning models and handcrafted symbol-manipulation programs. In DeepMind's AlphaGo, for example, most of the intelligence on display is designed and hardcoded by human programmers (such as Monte Carlo Tree Search). Learning from data happens only in specialized submodules (value networks and policy networks). Or consider autonomous vehicles: a self-driving car is able to handle a large variety of situations because it maintains a model of the world around it—a literal 3D model—full of assumptions hardcoded by human engineers. This model is constantly updated via deep learning perception modules that interface it with the surroundings of the car.

For both of these systems—AlphaGo and self-driving vehicles—the combination of human-created discrete programs and learned continuous models is what unlocks a level of performance that would be impossible with either approach in isolation, such as an end-to-end deep net or a piece of software without ML elements. So far, the discrete algorithmic elements of such hybrid systems are painstakingly hardcoded by human engineers. But in the future, such systems may be fully learned, with no human involvement.

What will this look like? Consider a well-known type of network: RNNs. It's important to note that RNNs have slightly fewer limitations than feed-forward networks. That's because RNNs are a bit more than mere geometric transformations: they're geometric transformations *repeatedly applied inside a* for *loop*. The temporal for loop is itself hardcoded by human developers: it's a built-in assumption of the network. Naturally, RNNs are still extremely limited in what they can represent, primarily because each step they perform is a differentiable geometric transformation, and they carry information from step to step via points in a continuous geometric space (state vectors). Now imagine a neural network that's augmented in a similar way with programming primitives, but instead of a single hardcoded `for` loop with hardcoded continuous-space memory, the network includes a large set of programming primitives that the model is free to manipulate to expand its processing function, such as `if` branches, `while` statements, variable creation, disk storage for long-term memory, sorting operators, and advanced data structures (such as lists, graphs, and hash tables). The space of programs that such a network could represent would be far broader than what can be represented with current deep learning models, and some of these programs could achieve superior generalization power. Importantly, such programs will not be differentiable end-to-end, though specific modules will remain differentiable and thus will need to be generated via a combination of discrete program search and gradient descent.

We'll move away from having, on one hand, hardcoded algorithmic intelligence (handcrafted software) and, on the other hand, learned geometric intelligence (deep learning). Instead, we'll have a blend of formal algorithmic modules that provide reasoning and abstraction capabilities, and geometric modules that provide informal intuition and pattern-recognition capabilities (see figure 14.12). The entire system will be learned with little or no human involvement. This should dramatically expand the scope of problems that can be solved with machine learning—the space of programs that we can generate automatically, given appropriate training data. Systems like AlphaGo—or even RNNs—can be seen as a prehistoric ancestor of such hybrid algorithmic-geometric models.

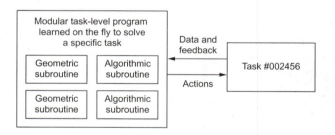

Figure 14.12 A learned program relying on both geometric primitives (pattern recognition, intuition) and algorithmic primitives (reasoning, search, memory)

USING DEEP LEARNING TO GUIDE PROGRAM SEARCH

Today, program synthesis faces a major obstacle: it's tremendously inefficient. To caricature, program synthesis works by trying every possible program in a search space until it finds one that matches the specification provided. As the complexity of the program specification increases, or as the vocabulary of primitives used to write programs expands, the program search process runs into what's known as *combinatorial explosion*, where the set of possible programs to consider grows very fast—in fact, much faster than merely exponentially fast. As a result, today, program synthesis can be used to generate only very short programs. You're not going to be generating a new OS for your computer anytime soon.

To move forward, we're going to need to make program synthesis efficient by bringing it closer to the way humans write software. When you open your editor to code up a script, you're not thinking about every possible program you could potentially write. You have in mind only a handful of possible approaches: you can use your understanding of the problem and your past experience to drastically cut through the space of possible options to consider.

Deep learning can help program synthesis do the same: although each specific program we'd like to generate might be a fundamentally discrete object that performs non-interpolative data manipulation, evidence so far indicates that *the space of all useful programs* may look a lot like a continuous manifold. That means that a deep learning model that has been trained on millions of successful program-generation episodes might start to develop solid *intuition* about the *path through program space* that the search process should take to go from a specification to the corresponding program—just like a software engineer might have immediate intuition about the overall architecture of the script they're about to write, about the intermediate functions and classes they should use as stepping-stones on the way to the goal.

Remember that human reasoning is heavily guided by value-centric abstraction, that is, by pattern recognition and intuition. Program synthesis should be, too. I expect the general approach of guiding program search via learned heuristics to see increasing research interest over the next 10 to 20 years.

14.5.4 *Lifelong learning and modular subroutine reuse*

If models become more complex and are built on top of richer algorithmic primitives, this increased complexity will require higher reuse between tasks, rather than training a new model from scratch every time we have a new task or a new dataset. Many datasets don't contain enough information for us to develop a new, complex model from scratch, and it will be necessary to use information from previously encountered datasets (much as you don't learn English from scratch every time you open a new book—that would be impossible). Training models from scratch on every new task is also inefficient due to the large overlap between the current tasks and previously encountered tasks.

A remarkable observation has been made repeatedly in recent years: training the *same* model to do several loosely connected tasks at the same time results in a model that's *better at each task*. For instance, training the same neural machine-translation model to perform both English-to-German translation and French-to-Italian translation will result in a model that's better at each language pair. Similarly, training an image-classification model jointly with an image-segmentation model, sharing the same convolutional base, results in a model that's better at both tasks. This is fairly intuitive: there's always *some* information overlap between seemingly disconnected tasks, and a joint model has access to a greater amount of information about each individual task than a model trained on that specific task only.

Currently, when it comes to model reuse across tasks, we use pretrained weights for models that perform common functions, such as visual feature extraction. You saw this in action in chapter 9. In the future, I expect a generalized version of this to be commonplace: we'll use not only previously learned features (submodel weights) but also model architectures and training procedures. As models become more like programs, we'll begin to reuse *program subroutines* like the functions and classes found in human programming languages.

Think of the process of software development today: once an engineer solves a specific problem (HTTP queries, for instance), they package it as an abstract, reusable library. Engineers who face a similar problem in the future will be able to search for existing packages, download one, and use it in their own project. In a similar way, in the future, meta-learning systems will be able to assemble new programs by sifting through a global library of high-level reusable blocks. When the system finds itself developing similar program subroutines for several different tasks, it can come up with an *abstract*, reusable version of the subroutine and store it in the global library (see figure 14.13). These subroutines can be either geometric (deep learning modules with pretrained representations) or algorithmic (closer to the libraries that contemporary software engineers manipulate).

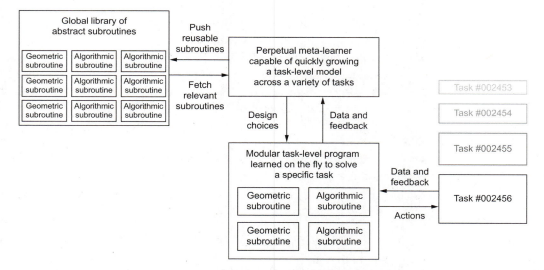

Figure 14.13   A meta-learner capable of quickly developing task-specific models using reusable primitives (both algorithmic and geometric), thus achieving extreme generalization

14.5.5   *The long-term vision*

In short, here's my long-term vision for machine learning:

- Models will be more like programs and will have capabilities that go far beyond the continuous geometric transformations of the input data we currently work with. These programs will arguably be much closer to the abstract mental models that humans maintain about their surroundings and themselves, and they will be capable of stronger generalization due to their rich algorithmic nature.

- In particular, models will blend *algorithmic modules* providing formal reasoning, search, and abstraction capabilities with *geometric modules* providing informal intuition and pattern-recognition capabilities. This will achieve a blend of value-centric and program-centric abstraction. AlphaGo or self-driving cars (systems that require a lot of manual software engineering and human-made design decisions) provide an early example of what such a blend of symbolic and geometric AI could look like.

- Such models will be *grown* automatically rather than hardcoded by human engineers, using modular parts stored in a global library of reusable subroutines—a library evolved by learning high-performing models on thousands of previous tasks and datasets. As frequent problem-solving patterns are identified by the meta-learning system, they will be turned into reusable subroutines—much like functions and classes in software engineering—and added to the global library.

- The process that searches over possible combinations of subroutines to grow new models will be a discrete search process (program synthesis), but it will be heavily guided by a form of *program-space intuition* provided by deep learning.

- This global subroutine library and associated model-growing system will be able to achieve some form of humanlike *extreme generalization*: given a new task or situation, the system will be able to assemble a new working model appropriate for the task using very little data, thanks to rich programlike primitives that generalize well and extensive experience with similar tasks. In the same way, humans can quickly learn to play a complex new video game if they have experience with many previous games, because the models derived from this previous experience are abstract and programlike, rather than a basic mapping between stimuli and action.

- As such, this perpetually learning model-growing system can be interpreted as an *artificial general intelligence* (AGI). But don't expect any singularitarian robot apocalypse to ensue: that's pure fantasy, coming from a long series of profound misunderstandings of both intelligence and technology. Such a critique, however, doesn't belong in this book.

14.6   *Staying up-to-date in a fast-moving field*

As final parting words, I want to give you some pointers about how to keep learning and updating your knowledge and skills after you've turned the last page of this book. The field of modern deep learning, as we know it today, is only a few years old, despite a long, slow prehistory stretching back decades. With an exponential increase in financial resources and research headcount since 2013, the field as a whole is now moving at a frenetic pace. What you've learned in this book won't stay relevant forever, and it isn't all you'll need for the rest of your career.

Fortunately, there are plenty of free online resources that you can use to stay up to date and expand your horizons. Here are a few.

14.6.1   *Practice on real-world problems using Kaggle*

An effective way to acquire real-world experience is to try your hand at machine learning competitions on Kaggle (https://kaggle.com). The only real way to learn is through practice and actual coding—that's the philosophy of this book, and Kaggle competitions are the natural continuation of this. On Kaggle, you'll find an array of constantly renewed data science competitions, many of which involve deep learning, prepared by companies interested in obtaining novel solutions to some of their most challenging machine learning problems. Fairly large monetary prizes are offered to top entrants.

Most competitions are won using either the XGBoost library (for shallow machine learning) or Keras (for deep learning), so you'll fit right in! By participating in a few competitions, maybe as part of a team, you'll become more familiar with the practical side of some of the advanced best practices described in this book, especially hyperparameter tuning, avoiding validation set overfitting, and model ensembling.

14.6.2   *Read about the latest developments on arXiv*

Deep learning research, in contrast with some other scientific fields, takes place completely in the open. Papers are made publicly and freely accessible as soon as they're finalized, and a lot of related software is open source. arXiv (https://arxiv.org)—pronounced "archive" (the X stands for the Greek *chi*)—is an open-access preprint server for physics, mathematics, and computer science research papers. It has become the de facto way to stay up-to-date on the bleeding edge of machine learning and deep learning. The large majority of deep learning researchers upload any paper they write to arXiv shortly after completion. This allows them to plant a flag and claim a specific finding without waiting for a conference acceptance (which takes months), which is necessary given the fast pace of research and the intense competition in the field. It also allows the field to move extremely fast: all new findings are immediately available for all to see and to build on.

An important downside is that the sheer quantity of new papers posted every day on arXiv makes it impossible to even skim them all, and the fact that they aren't peer-reviewed makes it difficult to identify those that are both important and high quality. It's challenging, and becoming increasingly more so, to find the signal in the noise. But some tools can help: in particular, you can use Google Scholar (https://scholar .google.com) to keep track of publications by your favorite authors.

14.6.3   *Explore the Keras ecosystem*

With over one million users as of late 2021 and still growing, Keras has a large ecosystem of tutorials, guides, and related open source projects:

- Your main reference for working with Keras in R is the online documentation at https://keras.rstudio.com and https://tensorflow.rstudio.com. In particular, you'll find extensive developer guides at http://tensorflow.rstudio.com/guides, dozens of high-quality Keras code examples at http://tensorflow.rstudio.com/ examples, and many tutorials at http://tensorflow.rstudio.com/tutorials. Make sure to check them out!

- Don't hesitate to also consult the Python documentation for Keras and Tensor-Flow, available at https://www.tensorflow.org/api_docs/python/tf and https://keras.io/, even if you don't know Python. Almost everything there you can read, understand, and apply to the R interface, all without any knowledge of Python. (If you do encounter some perplexing Python syntax, be sure to consult the appendix.)
- The R source code for Keras and Tensorflow can be found at https://github.com/rstudio/keras and https://github.com/rstudio/tensorflow. The Python and C++ sources are available at https://github.com/keras-team/keras and https://github.com/tensorflow/tensorflow. All are open source.
- You can ask for help and join deep learning discussions in a few places:

  - The Machine Learning section of Rstudio community: https://community.rstudio.com/c/ml/15
  - Stack overflow: https://stackoverflow.com (Be sure to tag your question with both R and Keras.)
  - The (Python) Keras mailing list: keras-users@googlegroups.com.
  - You can follow me (François) on Twitter: @fchollet.

14.7   *Final words*

This is the end of *Deep Learning with R, Second Edition*. I hope you've learned a thing or two about machine learning, deep learning, Keras, and maybe even cognition in general. Learning is a lifelong journey, especially in the field of AI, where we have far more unknowns on our hands than certitudes. So please go on learning, questioning, and researching. Never stop! Because even given the progress made so far, most of the fundamental questions in AI remain unanswered. Many haven't even been properly asked yet.

appendix
Python primer for R users

You may find yourself wanting to read and understand some Python, or even port some Python to R. This guide is designed to enable you to do these tasks as quickly as possible. As you'll see, R and Python are similar enough that this is possible without necessarily learning all of Python. We start with the basics of container types and work up to the mechanics of classes, dunders, the iterator protocol, the context protocol, and more!

A.1   *Whitespace*

Whitespace matters in Python. In R, expressions are grouped into a code block with {}. In Python, that is done by making the expressions share an indentation level. For example, an expression with an R code block might be:

```
if (TRUE) {
  cat("This is one expression. \n")
  cat("This is another expression. \n")
}
```

The equivalent in Python:

```
if True:
  print("This is one expression.")
  print("This is another expression.")
```

Python accepts tabs or spaces as the indentation spacer, but the rules get tricky when they're mixed. Most style guides suggest (and IDEs default to) using spaces only.

A.2   *Container types*

In R, the `list()` is a container you can use to organize R objects. R's `list()` is feature-packed, and there is no single direct equivalent in Python that supports all the same features. Instead there are (at least) four different Python container types you need to be aware of: lists, dictionaries, tuples, and sets.

A.2.1   *Lists*

Python lists are typically created using bare brackets: `[]`. (The Python built-in `list()` function is more of a coercion function, closer in spirit to R's `as.list()`). The most important thing to know about Python lists is that they are modified in place. Note in the example below that `y` reflects the changes made to `x`, because the underlying list object that both symbols point to is modified in place:

```
x = [1, 2, 3]        y and x now refer
y = x                to the same list!
x.append(4)
print("x is", x)
```

```
x is [1, 2, 3, 4]
```

```
print("y is", y)
```

```
y is [1, 2, 3, 4]
```

One Python idiom that might be concerning to R users is that of growing lists through the `append()` method. Growing lists in R is typically slow and best avoided. But because Python's list are modified in place (and a full copy of the list is avoided when appending items), it is efficient to grow Python lists in place.

Some syntactic sugar around Python lists you might encounter is the usage of `+` and `*`. These are concatenation and replication operators, akin to R's `c()` and `rep()`:

```
x = [1]
x
```

```
[1]
```

```
x + x
```

```
[1, 1]
```

```
x * 3
```

```
[1, 1, 1]
```

You can index into lists with integers using trailing `[]`, but note that indexing is 0-based:

```
x = [1, 2, 3]
x[0]
```

```
1
```

```
x[1]
```

```
2
```

```
x[2]
```

```
3
```

```
try:
  x[3]
except Exception as e:
  print(e)
```

```
list index out of range
```

When indexing, negative numbers count from the end of the container:

```
x = [1, 2, 3]
x[-1]
```

```
3
```

```
x[-2]
```

```
2
```

```
x[-3]
```

```
1
```

You can slice ranges of lists using a colon (:) inside brackets. Note that the slice syntax is *not* inclusive of the end of the slice range. You can optionally also specify a stride:

```
x = [1, 2, 3, 4, 5, 6]

x[0:2]
```
Get items at index positions 0 and 1, not 2.

```
[1, 2]
```

```
x[1:]
```
Get items from index position 1 to the end.

```
[2, 3, 4, 5, 6]
```

```
x[:-2]
```
Get items from the beginning up to the second to last.

```
[1, 2, 3, 4]
```

```
x[:]
```
Get all the items (the idiom used to copy the list so as not to modify in place).

```
[1, 2, 3, 4, 5, 6]
```
Get all the items, with a stride of 2.

```
x[::2]
```

```
[1, 3, 5]
```
Get all the items from index 1 to the end, with a stride of 2.

```
x[1::2]
```

```
[2, 4, 6]
```

A.2.2 *Tuples*

Tuples behave like lists, except they are not mutable, and they don't have the same modify-in-place methods like `append()`. They are typically constructed using bare `()`, but parentheses are not strictly required, and you may see an implicit tuple being defined just from a comma-separated series of expressions. Because parentheses can also be used to specify order of operations in expressions like `(x + 3) * 4`, a special syntax is required to define tuples of length 1: a trailing comma. Tuples are most commonly encountered in functions that take a variable number of arguments:

```
x = (1, 2)
type(x)
```
A tuple of length 2

```
<class 'tuple'>
```

```
len(x)
```

```
2
```

```
x
```

```
(1, 2)
```

```
x = (1,)
type(x)
```
A tuple of length 1

```
<class 'tuple'>
```

```
len(x)
```

```
1
```

```
x
```

```
(1,)
```

```
x = ()              ◄——— A tuple of length 0
print(f"{type(x) = }; {len(x) = }; {x = }")    ◄——
```

**Example of an interpolated
string literals. You can do string
interpolation in R using glue::glue().**

```
type(x) = <class 'tuple'>; len(x) = 0; x = ()
```

```
x = 1, 2       ◄——— Also a tuple
type(x)
```

```
<class 'tuple'>
```

```
len(x)
```

```
2
```

```
x = 1,    ◄——┐  Beware a single trailing
type(x)         comma! This is a tuple!
```

```
<class 'tuple'>
```

```
len(x)
```

```
1
```

PACKING AND UNPACKING

Tuples are the container that powers the *packing* and *unpacking* semantics in Python. Python provides the convenience of allowing you to assign multiple symbols in one expression. This is called *unpacking*.

For example:

```
x = (1, 2, 3)
a, b, c = x
a
```

```
1
```

```
b
```

```
2
```

```
c
```

```
3
```

You can access similar unpacking behavior from R using `zeallot::`%<-%`.

Tuple unpacking can occur in a variety of contexts, such as iteration:

```
xx = (("a", 1),
      ("b", 2))
for x1, x2 in xx:
  print("x1 =", x1)
  print("x2 =", x2)
```

```
x1 = a
x2 = 1
x1 = b
x2 = 2
```

If you attempt to unpack a container to the wrong number of symbols, Python raises
an error:

```
x = (1, 2, 3)          Success
a, b, c = x    ⟵┘                Error: x has too many
a, b = x       ⟵────────────    values to unpack.
```

```
Error in py_call_impl(callable, dots$args, dots$keywords):
⟹ ValueError: too many values to unpack (expected 2)
```

```
a, b, c, d = x   ⟵──── Error: x has not enough values to unpack.
```

```
Error in py_call_impl(callable, dots$args, dots$keywords):
⟹ ValueError: not enough values to unpack (expected 4, got 3)
```

It is possible to unpack a variable number of arguments, using * as a prefix to a symbol
(We'll see the * prefix again when we talk about functions.):

```
x = (1, 2, 3)
a, *the_rest = x
a
```

```
1
```

```
the_rest
```

```
[2, 3]
```

You can also unpack nested structures:

```
x = ((1, 2), (3, 4))
(a, b), (c, d) = x
```

A.2.3   *Dictionaries*

Dictionaries are most similar to R environments. They are a container where you can
retrieve items by name, though in Python the name (called a *key* in Python's parlance)
does not need to be a string like in R. It can be any Python object with a hash()
method (meaning, it can be almost any Python object). They can be created using
syntax like {key: value}. Like Python lists, they are modified in place. Note that
reticulate::r_to_py() converts R named lists to dictionaries:

```
d = {"key1": 1,
     "key2": 2}
d2 = d
```

```
d
```

```
{'key1': 1, 'key2': 2}
```

```
d["key1"]
```

```
1
```

```
d["key3"] = 3
d2                     ⟵——— Modified in place!
```

```
{'key1': 1, 'key2': 2, 'key3': 3}
```

Like R environments (and unlike R's named lists), you cannot index into a dictionary with an integer to get an item at a specific index position. Dictionaries are *unordered* containers (however, beginning with Python 3.7, dictionaries do preserve the item insertion order):

```
d = {"key1": 1, "key2": 2}      Error: The integer "I" is not one
d[1]              ⟵————————      of the keys in the dictionary.
```

```
Error in py_call_impl(callable, dots$args, dots$keywords): KeyError: 1
```

A container that closest matches the semantics of R's named list is the `OrderedDict` (http://mng.bz/7y5m), but that's relatively uncommon in Python code, so we don't cover it further.

A.2.4   Sets

Sets are a container that can be used to efficiently track unique items or deduplicate lists. They are constructed using {val1, val2} (like a dictionary, but without :). Think of them as a dictionary where you use only the keys. Sets have many efficient methods for membership operations, like intersection(), issubset(), union(), and so on:

```
s = {1, 2, 3}
type(s)
```

```
<class 'set'>
```

```
s
```

```
{1, 2, 3}
```

```
s.add(1)
s
```

```
{1, 2, 3}
```

A.3   *Iteration with for*

The for statement in Python can be used to iterate over any kind of container:

```
for x in [1, 2, 3]:
  print(x)
```

```
1
2
3
```

R has a relatively limited set of objects that can be passed to for. Python, by comparison, provides an iterator protocol interface, which means that authors can define custom objects, with custom behavior that is invoked by for. (We'll have an example for how to define a custom iterable when we get to classes.) You may want to use a Python iterable from R using reticulate, so it's helpful to peel back the syntactic sugar a little to show what the for statement is doing in Python, and how you can step through it manually.

Two things happen: first, an iterator is constructed from the supplied object. Then, the new iterator object is repeatedly called with next() until it is exhausted:

```
l = [1, 2, 3]
it = iter(l)      ⟵——— Create an iterator object.
it
```

```
<list_iterator object at 0x7f5e30fbd190>
```

Call next() on the iterator until it is exhausted:

```
next(it)
```

```
1
```

```
next(it)
```

```
2
```

```
next(it)
```

```
3
```

```
next(it)
```

```
Error in py_call_impl(callable, dots$args, dots$keywords): StopIteration
```

In R, you can use reticulate to step through an iterator the same way:

```
library(reticulate)
l <- r_to_py(list(1, 2, 3))
it <- as_iterator(l)
```

```
iter_next(it)
```

```
1.0
```

```
iter_next(it)
```

```
2.0
```

```
iter_next(it)
```

```
3.0
```

```
iter_next(it, completed = "StopIteration")
```

```
[1] "StopIteration"
```

Iterating over dictionaries first requires understanding whether you are iterating over the keys, values, or both. Dictionaries have methods that allow you to specify which:

```
d = {"key1": 1, "key2": 2}
for key in d:
  print(key)
```

```
key1
key2
```

```
for value in d.values():
  print(value)
```

```
1
2
```

```
for key, value in d.items():
  print(key, ":", value)
```

```
key1 : 1
key2 : 2
```

A.3.1 Comprehensions

Comprehensions are special syntax that allow you to construct a container like a list or a dict, while also executing a small operation or single expression on each element. You can think of it as special syntax for R's `lapply`. For example:

```
x = [1, 2, 3]
```

```
l = [element + 100 for element in x]     ◁───  A list comprehension built
l                                              from x, where you add 100
                                               to each element
```

```
[101, 102, 103]
```

```
d = {str(element) : element + 100
    for element in x}
d
```

> A dict comprehension built from x, where the key is a string. Python's str() is like R's as.character().

```
{'1': 101, '2': 102, '3': 103}
```

A.4 *Defining functions with def*

Python functions are defined with the `def` statement. The syntax for specifying function arguments and default argument values is very similar to R:

```
def my_function(name = "World"):
  print("Hello", name)

my_function()
```

```
Hello World
```

```
my_function("Friend")
```

```
Hello Friend
```

The equivalent R snippet would be:

```
my_function <- function(name = "World") {
  cat("Hello", name, "\n")
}

my_function()
```

```
Hello World
```

```
my_function("Friend")
```

```
Hello Friend
```

Unlike R functions, the last value in a function is not automatically returned. Python requires an explicit return statement:

```
def fn():
  1
print(fn())
```

```
None
```

```
def fn():
  return 1
print(fn())
```

```
1
```

NOTE   For advanced R users, Python has no equivalent of R's argument "promises." Function argument default values are evaluated once, when the function is constructed. This can be surprising if you define a Python function with a mutable object as a default argument value, like a Python list!

```python
def my_func(x = []):
  x.append("was called")
  print(x)

my_func()
my_func()
my_func()
```

```
['was called']
['was called', 'was called']
['was called', 'was called', 'was called']
```

You can also define Python functions that take a variable number of arguments, similar to ... in R. A notable difference is that R's ... makes no distinction between named and unnamed arguments, but Python does. In Python, prefixing a single * captures unnamed arguments, and two ** signifies that *keyword* arguments are captured:

```python
def my_func(*args, **kwargs):
  print("args =", args)       ◁————————  args is a tuple.
  print("kwargs =", kwargs)   ◁————————
                                           kwargs is a dictionary.
my_func(1, 2, 3, a = 4, b = 5, c = 6)
```

```
args = (1, 2, 3)
kwargs = {'a': 4, 'b': 5, 'c': 6}
```

Whereas the * and ** in a function definition signature *pack* arguments, in a function call, they *unpack* arguments. Unpacking arguments in a function call is equivalent to using do.call() in R:

```python
def my_func(a, b, c):
  print(a, b, c)

args = (1, 2, 3)
my_func(*args)
```

```
1 2 3
```

```python
kwargs = {"a": 1, "b": 2, "c": 3}
my_func(**kwargs)
```

```
1 2 3
```

A.5   *Defining classes with class*

One could argue that in R, the preeminent unit of composition for code is the `function`, and in Python, it's the `class`. You can be a very productive R user and never use R6, reference classes, or similar R equivalents to the object-oriented style of Python classes.

In Python, however, understanding the basics of how `class` objects work is requisite knowledge, because `classes` are how you organize and find methods in Python (in contrast to R's approach, where methods are found by dispatching from a generic). Fortunately, the basics of `classes` are accessible.

Don't be intimidated if this is your first exposure to object-oriented programming. We'll start by building up a simple Python class for demonstration purposes:

```
class MyClass:
    pass        ⟵──── pass means do nothing.

MyClass
```

```
<class '__main__.MyClass'>
```

```
type(MyClass)
```

```
<class 'type'>
```

```
instance = MyClass()
instance
```

```
<__main__.MyClass object at 0x7f5e30fc7790>
```

```
type(instance)
```

```
<class '__main__.MyClass'>
```

Like the `def` statement, the `class` statement binds a new callable symbol, `MyClass`. First note the strong naming convention: classes are typically `CamelCase`, and functions are typically `snake_case`. After defining `MyClass`, you can interact with it, and see that it has type `'type'`. Calling `MyClass()` creates a new object *instance* of the class, which has type `'MyClass'` (ignore the `__main__.` prefix for now). The instance prints with its memory address, which is a strong hint that it's common to be managing many instances of a class, and that the instance is mutable (modified-in-place by default).

In the first example, we defined an empty `class`, but when we inspect it we see that it already comes with a bunch of attributes (`dir()` in Python is equivalent to `names()` in R):

```
dir(MyClass)
```

```
['__class__', '__delattr__', '__dict__', '__dir__', '__doc__', '__eq__',
'__format__', '__ge__', '__getattribute__', '__gt__', '__hash__', '__init__',
'__init_subclass__', '__le__', '__lt__', '__module__', '__ne__', '__new__',
'__reduce__', '__reduce_ex__', '__repr__', '__setattr__', '__sizeof__',
'__str__', '__subclasshook__', '__weakref__']
```

A.5.1 *What are all the underscores?*

Python typically indicates that something is special by wrapping the name in double underscores, and a special double-underscore-wrapped token is commonly called a *dunder*. "Special" is not a technical term; it just means that the token invokes a Python language feature. Some dunder tokens are merely ways that code authors can plug into specific syntactic sugars; others are values provided by the interpreter that would be otherwise hard to acquire; yet others are for extending language interfaces (e.g., the iteration protocol); and, finally, a small handful of dunders are truly complicated to understand. Fortunately, as an R user looking to use some Python features through reticulate, you only need to know about a few easy-to-understand dunders.

The most common dunder method you'll encounter when reading Python code is __init__(). This is a function that is called when the class constructor is called, that is, when a class is *instantiated*. It is meant to initialize the new class instance. (In very sophisticated code bases, you may also encounter classes where __new__() is also defined; this is called before __init__().)

```
class MyClass:

    print("MyClass's definition body is being evaluated")  ◁──┐   Note that this is
                                                                evaluated once, when
    def __init__(self):                                         the class is first defined.
        print(self, "is initializing")
```

```
MyClass's definition body is being evaluated
```
Note the identical memory address between `instance` and what `self` was in the __init__() method.

```
instance = MyClass()
```

```
<__main__.MyClass object at 0x7f5e30fcafd0> is initializing  ◁────┐
```

```
print(instance)
```

```
<__main__.MyClass object at 0x7f5e30fcafd0>  ◁────┘
```

```
instance2 = MyClass()
```

```
<__main__.MyClass object at 0x7f5e30fc7790> is initializing  ◁────┐
```
New instance, new memory address

```
print(instance2)
```

```
<__main__.MyClass object at 0x7f5e30fc7790>  ◁────┘
```

A few things to note:

- The `class` statement takes a code block that is defined by a common indentation level. The code block has the same exact semantics as any other expression that takes a code block, like `if` and `def`. The body of the class is evaluated only *once*—when the class constructor is first being created. Beware that any objects defined here are shared by all instances of the class!
- `__init__()` is just a normal function, defined with `def` like any other function, except it's inside the class body.
- `__init__()` takes an argument: `self`. `self` is the class instance being initialized (note the identical memory address between `self` and `instance`). Also note that we didn't provide `self` when calling `MyClass()` to create the class instance; `self` was spliced into the function call by the language.
- `__init__()` is called each time a new instance is created.

Functions defined inside a `class` code block are called *methods*, and the important thing to know about methods is that each time they are called from a class instance, the instance is spliced into the function call as the first argument. This applies to all functions defined in a class, including dunders. The sole exception is if the function is decorated with something like `@classmethod` or `@staticmethod`:

```
class MyClass:
  def a_method(self):
    print("MyClass.a_method() was called with", self)

instance = MyClass()
instance.a_method()
```

```
MyClass.a_method() was called with <__main__.MyClass object at 0x7f5e30fcadf0>:
```

```
MyClass.a_method()        <———— Error: missing required argument self
```

```
Error in py_call_impl(callable, dots$args, dots$keywords):
  TypeError: a_method() missing 1 required positional argument: 'self'
```

```
MyClass.a_method(instance)      <———— Identical to instance.a_method()
```

```
MyClass.a_method() was called with <__main__.MyClass object at 0x7f5e30fcadf0>
```

Other dunders worth knowing about are:

- `__getitem__`—The function invoked when extracting a slice with `[` (equivalent to defining a `[` S3 method in R).
- `__getattr__`—The function invoked when accessing an attribute with `.` (equivalent to defining a `$` S3 method in R).
- `__iter__` and `__next__`—Functions invoked by `for`.

- __call__—Invoked when a class instance is called like a function (e.g., instance()).
- __bool__—Invoked by if and while (equivalent to as.logical() in R, but returning only a scalar, not a vector).
- __repr__ and __str__—Functions invoked for formatting and pretty printing (akin to format(), dput(), and print() methods in R).
- __enter__ and __exit__—Functions invoked by with.
- Many built-in Python functions are just sugar for invoking the dunder. For example, calling repr(x) is identical to x.__repr__() (see https://docs.python.org/3/library/functions.html). Other built-ins that are just sugar for invoking the dunder include next(), iter(), str(), list(), dict(), bool(), dir(), hash(), and more!

A.5.2 *Iterators, revisited*

Now that we have the basics of class, it's time to revisit iterators. First, some terminology:

- *iterable*—Something that can be iterated over. Concretely, a class that defines an __iter__ method, whose job is to return an *iterator*.
- *iterator*—Something that iterates. Concretely, a class that defines a __next__ method, whose job is to return the next element each time it is called, and then raise a StopIteration exception once it's exhausted. It's common to see classes that are both iterables and iterators, where the __iter__ method is just a stub that returns self. Here is a custom iterable/iterator implementation of Python's range() (similar to seq() in R):

```python
class MyRange:
  def __init__(self, start, end):
    self.start = start
    self.end = end

  def __iter__(self):
    self._index = self.start - 1    ⟵——— Reset our counter.
    return self

  def __next__(self):
    if self._index < self.end:
      self._index += 1    ⟵——— Increment by 1.
      return self._index
    else:
      raise StopIteration

for x in MyRange(1, 3):
  print(x)
```

```
1
2
3
```

Manually doing what `for` does:

```
r = MyRange(1, 3)
it = iter(r)
next(it)
```

```
1
```

```
next(it)
```

```
2
```

```
next(it)
```

```
3
```

```
next(it)
```

```
Error in py_call_impl(callable, dots$args, dots$keywords): StopIteration
```

A.6   *Defining generators with yield*

Generators are special Python functions that contain one or more `yield` statements. As soon as `yield` is included in a code block passed to `def`, the semantics change substantially. You're no longer defining a mere function, but a generator constructor! In turn, calling a generator constructor creates a generator object, which is just another type of iterator. Here is an example:

```
def my_generator_constructor():
  yield 1
  yield 2
  yield 3
```

At first glance, it presents like a regular function:

```
my_generator_constructor
```

```
<function my_generator_constructor at 0x7f5e30fab670>
```

```
type(my_generator_constructor)
```

```
<class 'function'>
```

But calling it returns something special, a *generator object*:

```
my_generator = my_generator_constructor()
my_generator
```

```
<generator object my_generator_constructor at 0x7f5e3ca52820>
```

```
type(my_generator)
```

```
<class 'generator'>
```

The generator object is both an iterable and an iterator. Its __iter__ method is just a stub that returns self:

```
iter(my_generator) == my_generator == my_generator.__iter__()
```

```
True
```

Step through it like any other iterator:

```
next(my_generator)
```

```
1
```

```
my_generator.__next__()         ◁───┐   next(x) is just sugar for calling
                                     │   the dunder x.__next__().
2
```

```
next(my_generator)
```

```
3
```

```
next(my_generator)
```

```
Error in py_call_impl(callable, dots$args, dots$keywords): StopIteration
```

Encountering yield is like hitting the pause button on a functions execution: it preserves the state of everything in the function body and returns control to whatever is iterating over the generator object. Calling next() on the generator object resumes execution of the function body until the next yield is encountered or the function finishes. You can create generators in R with coro::generator().

A.7   *Iteration closing remarks*

Iteration is deeply baked into the Python language, and R users may be surprised by how things in Python are iterable, iterators, or powered by the iterator protocol under the hood. For example, the built-in map() (equivalent to R's lapply()) yields an iterator, not a list. Similarly, a tuple comprehension like (elem for elem in x) produces an iterator. Most features dealing with files are iterators.

Any time you find an iterator inconvenient, you can materialize all the elements into a list using the Python built-in list(), or reticulate::iterate() in R. Also, if you like the readability of for, you can utilize similar semantics to Python's for using coro::loop().

A.8   *import and modules*

In R, authors can bundle their code into shareable extensions called R packages, and R users can access objects from R packages via library() or ::. In Python, authors bundle code into *modules*, and users access modules using import. Consider the line:

```
import numpy
```

This statement has Python go out to the filesystem, find an installed Python module named numpy, load it (commonly meaning: evaluate its __init__.py file and construct a module type object), and bind it to the symbol numpy. The closest equivalent to this in R might be:

```
dplyr <- loadNamespace("dplyr")
```

A.8.1 Where are modules found?

In Python, the filesystem locations where modules are searched can be accessed (and modified) from the list found at sys.path. This is Python's equivalent to R's .lib-Paths(). sys.path will typically contain paths to the current working directory, the Python installation which contains the built-in standard library, administrator-installed modules, user-installed modules, values from environment variables like PYTHONPATH, and any modifications made directly to sys.path by other code in the current Python session (though this is relatively uncommon in practice):

```
import sys
sys.path
```

The current directory is typically on the search path for modules.

```
['',
'/home/tomasz/.pyenv/versions/3.9.6/bin',
'/home/tomasz/.pyenv/versions/3.9.6/lib/python39.zip',
'/home/tomasz/.pyenv/versions/3.9.6/lib/python3.9',
'/home/tomasz/.pyenv/versions/3.9.6/lib/python3.9/lib-dynload',
'/home/tomasz/.virtualenvs/r-reticulate/lib/python3.9/site-packages',
'/home/tomasz/opt/R-4.1.2/lib/R/site-library/reticulate/python',
'/home/tomasz/.virtualenvs/r-reticulate/lib/python39.zip',
'/home/tomasz/.virtualenvs/r-reticulate/lib/python3.9',
'/home/tomasz/.virtualenvs/r-reticulate/lib/python3.9/lib-dynload']
```

Python standard library and built-ins

More standard library and built-ins, this time from the virtualenv

reticulate shims

Additional installed Python packages (e.g., via pip)

You can inspect where a module was loaded from by accessing the dunder __path__ or __file__ (especially useful when troubleshooting installation issues):

```
import os
os.__file__
```

The os module is defined here. It's just a regular text file; take a glance!

```
'/home/tomasz/.pyenv/versions/3.9.6/lib/python3.9/os.py'
```

```
numpy.__path__
```

The numpy module we imported is defined here. It's a directory with lots of stuff; take a glance!

```
['/home/tomasz/.virtualenvs/r-reticulate/lib/python3.9/site-packages/numpy']
```

Once a module is loaded, you can access symbols from the module using . (equivalent to ::, or maybe $.environment, in R):

```
numpy.abs(-1)
```

```
1
```

There is also special syntax for specifying the symbol a module is bound to upon import and for importing only some specific symbols:

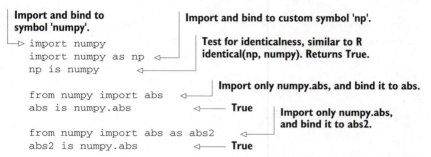

Import and bind to symbol 'numpy'.

Import and bind to custom symbol 'np'.

Test for identicalness, similar to R identical(np, numpy). Returns True.

```
import numpy
import numpy as np
np is numpy
```

Import only numpy.abs, and bind it to abs.

```
from numpy import abs
abs is numpy.abs                    True
```

Import only numpy.abs, and bind it to abs2.

```
from numpy import abs as abs2
abs2 is numpy.abs                   True
```

If you're looking for the Python equivalent of R's library(), which makes all of a package's exported symbols available, it might be using import with a * wildcard, though it's relatively uncommon to do so. The * wildcard will expand to include all the symbols in module, or all the symbols listed in __all__, if it is defined:

```
from numpy import *
```

Python doesn't make a distinction like R does between package exported and internal symbols. In Python, all module symbols are equal, though there is the naming convention that intended-to-be-internal symbols are prefixed with a single leading underscore. (Two leading underscores invoke an advanced language feature called "name mangling," which is outside the scope of this introduction.)

If you're looking for the R equivalent to Python's import syntax, you can use envir::import_from() like this:

```
library(envir)
import_from(keras::keras$applications$efficientnet,
            decode_predictions, preprocess_input,
            new_model = EfficientNetB4)

model <- new_model(include_top = TRUE, weights='imagenet')

predictions <- input_data %>%
  preprocess_input() %>%
  predict(model, .) %>%
  decode_predictions()
```

A.9   *Integers and floats*

R users generally don't need to be aware of the difference between integers and floating-point numbers, but that's not the case in Python. If this is your first exposure to numeric data types, here are the essentials:

- Integer types can represent only whole numbers like 2 or 3, not floating-point numbers like 2.3.
- Floating-point types can represent any number, but with some degree of imprecision.

In R, writing a bare literal number like 3 produces a floating-point type, whereas in Python, it produces an integer. You can produce an integer literal in R by appending an L, as in 3L. Many Python functions expect integers and will signal an error when provided a float. For example, say we have a Python function that expects an integer:

```python
def a_strict_Python_function(x):
  assert isinstance(x, int), "x is not an int"
  print("Yay! x was an int")
```

When calling it from R, you must be sure to call it with an integer:

```r
library(reticulate)
py$a_strict_Python_function(3)
```
← **Error: "AssertionError: x is not an int"**

```r
py$a_strict_Python_function(3L)
py$a_strict_Python_function(as.integer(3))
```
Success

A.10   *What about R vectors?*

R is a language designed for numerical computing first. Numeric vector data types are baked deep into the R language, to the point that the language doesn't even distinguish scalars from vectors. By comparison, numerical computing capabilities in Python are generally provided by third-party packages (*modules*, in Python parlance).

In Python, the numpy module is most commonly used to handle contiguous arrays of data. The closest equivalent to an R numeric vector is a 1D NumPy array, or sometimes, a list of scalar numbers (some Pythonistas might argue for array.array() here, but that's so rarely encountered in actual Python code we don't mention it further).

NumPy arrays are very similar to TensorFlow tensors. For example, they share the same broadcasting semantics and very similar indexing behavior. The NumPy API is extensive, and teaching the full NumPy interface is beyond the scope of this primer. However, it's worth pointing out some potential tripping hazards for users accustomed to R arrays:

- When indexing into multidimensional NumPy arrays, trailing dimensions can be omitted and are implicitly treated as missing. The consequence is that iterating over arrays means iterating over the first dimension. For example, this iterates over the rows of a matrix:

```
import numpy as np
m = np.arange(12).reshape((3,4))
m
```

```
array([[ 0,  1,  2,  3],
       [ 4,  5,  6,  7],
       [ 8,  9, 10, 11]])
```

`m[0, :]` ⟵ **First row**

```
array([0, 1, 2, 3])
```

`m[0]` ⟵ **Also first row**

```
array([0, 1, 2, 3])
```

```
for row in m:
  print(row)
```

```
[0 1 2 3]
[4 5 6 7]
[ 8  9 10 11]
```

- Many NumPy operations modify the array in place! This is surprising to R users (and TensorFlow users), who are used to the convenience and safety of R's (and TensorFlow's) copy-on-modify semantics. Unfortunately, there is no simple scheme or naming convention you can rely on to quickly determine whether a particular method modifies in place or creates a new array copy. The only reliable way is to consult the documentation (see http://mng.bz/mORP), and conduct small experiments at the `reticulate::repl_python()`.

A.11 *Decorators*

Decorators are just functions that take a function as an argument and then typically return another function. Any function can be invoked as a decorator with the @ syntax, which is just sugar for this simple action:

```
def my_decorator(func):
  func.x = "a decorator modified this function by adding an attribute `x`"
  return func

@my_decorator
def my_function(): pass
```

```
def my_function(): pass
my_function = my_decorator(my_function)
```
⟵ **@decorator is just fancy syntax for this line.**

One decorator you might encounter frequently is `@property`, which automatically calls a class method when the attribute is accessed (similar to `makeActiveBinding()` in R):

```
from datetime import datetime
class MyClass:
  @property
  def a_property(self):
    return f"`a_property` was accessed at {datetime.now().strftime('%X')}"

instance = MyClass()
instance.a_property
```

```
'`a_property` was accessed at 10:01:53 AM'
```

You can translate Python's `@property` to R with `%<-active%` (or with `mark_active()`), like this:

```
import_from(glue, glue)
MyClass %py_class% {
  a_property %<-active% function()
    glue("`a_property` was accessed at {format(Sys.time(), '%X')}")
}

instance <- MyClass()
instance$a_property
```

```
[1] "`a_property` was accessed at 10:01:53 AM"
```

```
Sys.sleep(1)
instance$a_property
```

```
[1] "`a_property` was accessed at 10:01:54 AM"
```

A.12 *with and context management*

Any object that defines __enter__ and __exit__ methods implements the "context" protocol and can be passed to `with`. For example, here is a custom implementation of a context manager that temporarily changes the current working directory (equivalent to R's `withr::with_dir()`):

```
from os import getcwd, chdir

class wd_context:
  def __init__(self, wd):
    self.new_wd = wd

  def __enter__(self):
    self.original_wd = getcwd()
    chdir(self.new_wd)

  def __exit__(self, *args):        ◁──┐ __exit__ takes some
    chdir(self.original_wd)              additional argument that
                                         are often ignored.

getcwd()
```

```
'/home/tomasz/deep-learning-w-R-v2/manuscript'
```

```
with wd_context("/tmp"):
    print("in the context, wd is:", getcwd())
```

```
in the context, wd is: /tmp
```

```
getcwd()
```

```
'/home/tomasz/deep-learning-w-R-v2/manuscript'
```

A.13 *Learning more*

Hopefully, this short primer to Python has provided a good foundation for confidently reading Python documentation and code, and using Python modules from R via reticulate. Of course, there is much, much more to learn about Python. Googling questions about Python reliably brings up pages of results, but not always sorted in order of most useful. Blog posts and tutorials targeting beginners can be valuable, but remember that Python's official documentation is generally excellent, and it should be your first destination when you have questions:

- https://docs.Python.org/3/
- https://docs.Python.org/3/library/index.html

To learn Python more fully, the built-in official tutorial is also excellent and comprehensive (but does require a time commitment to get value out of it): https://docs.Python.org/3/tutorial/index.html.

Finally, don't forget to solidify your understanding by conducting small experiments at the reticulate::repl_python().

Thank you for reading!

index